SELECTED PAPERS

STUDIES IN GREEK AND ROMAN HISTORY
AND HISTORIOGRAPHY

This volume contains a selection of the more important and influential of Professor F. W. Walbank's occasional papers. Published over a period of fifty years, they cover a wide range of classical subjects. Three deal with the role of nationality in the Greco-Roman world and with the constitutional character of Greek federal states. Others are concerned with problems of third- and second-century Roman history. Eight papers treat of the antecedents of so-called 'tragic history', of speeches in ancient historians, and of several aspects of Polybius' work. Finally, the selection includes Professor Walbank's detailed discussion of the chronology of Ptolemy IV's death and the accession of Ptolemy Epiphanes. A full bibliography of the author's publications concludes the volume.

Ancient historians should welcome the opportunity to have these papers conveniently collected between one set of covers.

SELECTED PAPERS

STUDIES IN GREEK AND ROMAN HISTORY
AND HISTORIOGRAPHY

FRANK W. WALBANK

Emeritus Professor, University of Liverpool
Honorary Fellow of Peterhouse, Cambridge

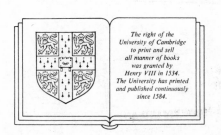

The right of the
University of Cambridge
to print and sell
all manner of books
was granted by
Henry VIII in 1534.
The University has printed
and published continuously
since 1584.

CAMBRIDGE UNIVERSITY PRESS

CAMBRIDGE

LONDON   NEW YORK   NEW ROCHELLE

MELBOURNE   SYDNEY

Published by the Press Syndicate of the University of Cambridge
The Pitt Building, Trumpington Street, Cambridge CB2 IRP
32 East 57th Street, New York, NY 10022, USA
10 Stamford Road, Oakleigh, Melbourne 3166, Australia

First published 1985

Printed in Great Britain by the
University Press, Cambridge

Library of Congress catalogue card number: 85-5905

British Library Cataloguing in Publication Data
Walbank, F. W.
Selected papers: studies in Greek and Roman
history and historiography
1. Classical antiquities – Addresses, essays,
lectures
I. Title
938   DE3

ISBN 0 521 30752 X

UP

CONTENTS

To the memory of
J. F. MOUNTFORD

PREFACE

This book contains some of my articles which various friends and colleagues have assured me that it would be useful to have reprinted. Over the years I have, naturally, changed my mind on some matters and I would not now go along with every statement contained in these pages. But I have resisted the temptation to tinker and improve or to shorten or omit passages which in the context of the volume may seem repetitive, since many of the articles included here have a place in a continuing discussion of the problems with which they deal and it seemed essential to reprint them as they were written. I have added a few notes in square brackets drawing attention to my later views where these are substantially different and giving an occasional bibliographical item where it seemed important (though in general I have not tried to bring bibliography up to date). I have also corrected misprints, false references and the like, where I have spotted them.

The articles fall into three groups – Greek history (including one Ptolemaic paper), Roman history and Greek and Roman historiography. But these categories are not exclusive and I was sometimes in doubt in which to place a particular paper. At the end of the book there is a list of my publications, in which those included here are marked with an asterisk. To help in following up references the original place of publication is given at the beginning of each paper, the original pagination is indicated at the top of each page and the original page divisions are marked by a double line (‖) in the text.

In conclusion I should like to express my warm thanks for the help and courtesy which one expects – and invariably receives – from the staff of the Cambridge University Press and also to my daughter, Dorothy Thompson, for her help in reading the proofs.

F.W.W.

Peterhouse, Cambridge
May 1985

ACKNOWLEDGEMENTS

For permission to republish my thanks are due to: the Council of the Cambridge Philological Society (no. 9), the University of Chicago Press (no. 7), the Journals Board of the Classical Association (nos. 5 and 6), Professor A. E. Samuel on behalf of A. M. Hakkert Ltd (Toronto) (no. 19), Professor O. Reverdin, Président du Conseil, on behalf of the Fondation Hardt (no. 18), the President and Fellows of Harvard College (no. 4), the Council of the Hellenic Society (no. 14), the Editorial Board of *Historia: Zeitschrift für Alte Geschichte* (nos. 13 and 15), the Editorial Board of the *Journal of Egyptian archaeology* (no. 3), Leuven University Press (no. 21), the J. L. Myres Memorial Lecture Committee in the University of Oxford (no. 16), the Editorial Board of *Phoenix*, University of Toronto (no. 1), the Council of the Roman Society (nos. 8, 10, 11, 12 and 17), the Editorial Board of *Scripta classica israelica* (no. 2) and the Editorial Board of *Yale classical studies* (no. 20).

ABBREVIATIONS

AAWB	*Abhandlungen der preussischen Akademie der Wissenschaften, Berlin, Phil.-hist. Klasse*
AAWW	*Anzeiger der österreichischen Akademie der Wissenschaften in Wien, Phil.-hist. Klasse*
ABAW	*Abhandlungen der bayerischen Akademie der Wissenschaften, Phil.-hist. Klasse*
ABSA	*Annual of the British School at Athens*
AHR	*American historical review*
AIPhO	*Annuaire de l'Institut de philologie et d'histoire orientales de l'Université libre de Bruxelles*
AJA	*American journal of archaeology*
AJP	*American journal of philology*
ANRW	*Aufstieg und Niedergang der römischen Welt: Geschichte und Kultur Roms im Spiegel der neueren Forschung*
APF	*Archiv für Papyrusforschung und verwandte Gebiete*
Arch. class.	*Archeologia classica. Rivista della scuola nazionale di archeologia, Roma*
'Αρχ. ἐφ.	'Αρχαιολογικὴ ἐφημερίς
ASAW	*Abhandlungen der sächsischen Akademie der Wissenschaften, Phil.-hist. Klasse*
Atti Acc. Torino	*Atti della Accademia delle scienze di Torino, classe di scienze morali, storiche e filologiche*
BAGB	*Bulletin de l'Association Guillaume Budé*
BCH	*Bulletin de correspondance hellénique*
BICS	*Bulletin of the Institute of classical studies*
Bull. épig.	*Bulletin épigraphique*, ed. J. and L. Robert (in *REG*)
Bursian's Jahresbericht	Bursian's *Jahresbericht über die Fortschritte der klassischen Altertumswissenschaft*
CAF	T. Kock, *Comicorum atticorum fragmenta* (3 vols., Leipzig, 1880–3)
CAH	*Cambridge ancient history*
C et M	*Classica et mediaevalia. Revue danoise de philologie et d'histoire*
CGF	G. Kaibel, *Comicorum graecorum fragmenta* (Berlin, 1899)

CHJ	*Cambridge historical journal*
CIL	*Corpus inscriptionum latinarum*
CP	*Classical philology*
CQ	*Classical quarterly*
CR	*Classical review*
CRAI	*Comptes rendus de l'Académie des inscriptions et belles lettres*
Der Kleine Pauly	*Der Kleine Pauly. Lexikon der Antike* (5 vols., Munich, 1975)
DLZ	*Deutsche Literaturzeitung für Kritik der internationalen Wissenschaft*
EHR	*English historical review*
FGH	*Die Fragmente der griechischen Historiker*, ed. F. Jacoby (3 vols. in 15 parts, Berlin–Leiden, 1923–58)
FHG	*Fragmenta historicorum graecorum*, ed. C. and Th. Müller (5 vols., Paris, 1841–70)
FIRA	*Fontes iuris romani anteiustiniani*², ed. S. Riccobono (Florence, 1941)
G and R	*Greece and Rome*
GDI	*Sammlung der griechischen Dialekt-Inschriften*, ed. H. Collitz and F. Bechtel (Göttingen, 1884–1915)
GHI	M. N. Tod, *A selection of Greek historical inscriptions*, vol. 1²: *To the end of the fifth century B.C.*; vol. 2: *From 403 to 323 B.C.* (Oxford, 1946–8)
GRBS	*Greek, Roman and Byzantine studies*
HRF	H. Peter, *Historicorum romanorum fragmenta* (Leipzig, 1883)
HRR	H. Peter, *Historicorum romanorum reliquiae* (Leipzig, vol. 1² (1914), vol. 2 (1906))
HSPh	*Harvard studies in classical philology*
HZ	*Historische Zeitschrift*
IC	*Inscriptiones creticae*
IG	*Inscriptiones graecae*
IGBulg	*Inscriptiones graecae in Bulgaria repertae*
IGR	*Inscriptiones graecae ad res romanas pertinentes*
ILLRP	*Inscriptiones latinae liberae rei publicae*
ILS	*Inscriptiones latinae selectae*, ed. H. Dessau (3 vols., Berlin, 1892–1916)
Insc. Ital.	*Inscriptiones Italiae*
Insc. Lind.	Ch. Blinkenberg, *Lindos, Fouilles de l'acropole, 1902–14*, vol. 2: *Inscriptions* (2 vols., Berlin–Copenhagen, 1941)
JEA	*Journal of Egyptian archaeology*
JHS	*Journal of Hellenic studies*
JRS	*Journal of Roman studies*

JS	*Journal des savants*
JThS	*Journal of theological studies*
Kl. Schr.	*Kleine Schriften*
LCM	*Liverpool classical monthly*
LEC	*Les études classiques*
LSJ	*Greek–English lexicon*, by H. G. Liddell, R. Scott and H. S. Jones
MH	*Museum Helveticum*
Momigliano, *Terzo contributo*	A. Momigliano, *Terzo contributo alla storia degli studi classici e del mondo classico* (Rome, 1966)
Mon. Germ. Hist., auct. ant.	*Monumenta Germaniae historica, auctores antiqui*
MRR	T. R. S. Broughton, *The magistrates of the Roman Republic* (2 vols., New York, 1951–2; with supplementary volume, 1960)
NAWG	*Nachrichten von der Akademie der Wissenschaften in Göttingen, Phil.-hist. Klasse*
NC	*Numismatic chronicle*
NJbb	*Neue Jahrbücher für Antike und deutsche Bildung*
OCD	*Oxford classical dictionary*
OGIS	*Orientis graeci inscriptiones selectae*
O. Tait	*Greek ostraca in the Bodleian Library at Oxford and various other collections*, ed. J. G. Tait and others (London, vol. 1 (1930), vol. 2 (1955), indexes (1964))
PACA	*Proceedings of the African Classical Association*
P. Berlin	Berlin papyri cited by inventory no.
PBSR	*Papers of the British School at Rome*
PCA	*Proceedings of the Classical Association*
P. Col. Zen.	*Zenon papyri. Business papers of the third century* B.C. *dealing with Palestine and Egypt*, vol. 1, ed. W. L. Westermann and E. S. Hasenoehrl (New York, 1934); vol. 2, ed. W. L. Westermann, C. W. Keyes and H. Liebesny (New York, 1940)
PCPS	*Proceedings of the Cambridge Philological Society*
P. dem. Berl.	W. Spiegelberg, *Demotische Papyrus aus den Königlichen Museen zu Berlin* (Berlin, 1902)
P. dem. Cairo	W. Spiegelberg, *Catalogue général des antiquités égyptiennes du Musée du Caire. Die demotischen Papyrus* (*Die demotischen Denkmäler* 2) (Strasbourg, 1906–8)
P. dem. Hincks	E. Hincks, *Catalogue of the Egyptian manuscripts in the library of Trinity College, Dublin* (Dublin, 1843)
P. dem. Leiden	C. Leemans, *Monumens égyptiens du Musée d'antiquités des Pays-Bas à Leide. Papyrus égyptiens démotiques* (Leiden, 1863)

P. dem. Louvre	Demotic papyri in the Louvre quoted by inventory number
P. dem. Mich.	Demotic papyri in the University of Michigan quoted by inventory number
P. dem. New York Hist. Soc.	H. Abbott, *Catalogue of the museum and gallery of art of the New York Historical Society* (New York, 1868)
P. Giss.	O. Eger, E. Kornemann and P. M. Meyer, *Griechische Papyri im Museum des oberhessischen Geschichtsvereins zu Giessen*, 3 parts (Leipzig–Berlin, 1910–12)
P. Gurob	*Greek papyri from Gurob*, ed. J. G. Smyly (Dublin, 1921)
P. Hib.	*The Hibeh papyri*, vol. 1, ed. B. P. Grenfell and A. S. Hunt (London, 1906)
Phil. Woch.	*Philologische Wochenschrift*
PhQ	*Philological quarterly*
P. Petrie	*The Flinders–Petrie papyri*, ed. J. P. Mahaffy and J. G. Smyly (3 vols., Dublin, 1891, 1893, 1905)
Πρακτικά	Πρακτικά τῆς ἐν 'Αθήναις ἀρχαιολογικῆς ἑταιρείας
Proc. Brit. Ac.	*Proceedings of the British Academy*
P. Tebt.	*The Tebtunis papyri*, ed. B. P. Grenfell and others (4 vols., London, 1902–76)
P. Yale	*Yale papyri in the Beineke Rare Book and Manuscript Library*, ed. J. F. Oates, A. E. Samuel and C. B. Welles (New Haven, 1967)
RAL	*Rendiconti della classe di scienze morali, storiche e filologiche dell'Accademia dei Lincei*
RE	Pauly-Wissowa's *Realencyclopädie der classischen Altertumswissenschaft* (Stuttgart, 1893–1980)
REA	*Revue des études anciennes*
REG	*Revue des études grecques*
RFIC	*Rivista di filologia e di istruzione classica*
RH	*Revue historique*
RhM	*Rheinisches Museum*
RIB	*The Roman inscriptions of Britain*, vol. 1, ed. R. G. Collingwood and R. P. Wright (Oxford, 1965)
RIDA	*Revue internationale des droits de l'antiquité*
RPh	*Revue de philologie*
RSI	*Rivista storica italiana*
Rylands Bulletin	*Bulletin of the John Rylands Library, Manchester*
SAWW	*Sitzungsberichte der philosophisch–historischen Klasse der kaiserlichen Akademie der Wissenschaften in Wien*
SBBerlin	*Sitzungsberichte der preussischen Akademie der Wissenschaften, Phil.-hist. Klasse* (1922–49) or *Klasse für Sprachen, Literatur und Kunst* (1950–69)

SBFrankfurt	*Sitzungsberichte der wissenschaftlichen Gesellschaft an der Johann Wolfgang Goethe-Universität, Frankfurt a/Main*
SCI	*Scripta classica israelica*
SCO	*Studi classici e orientali*
SEG	*Supplementum epigraphicum graecum*
SHA	Scriptores *Historiae Augustae*
SHAW	*Sitzungsberichte der Heidelberger Akademie der Wissenschaften, Phil.-hist. Klasse*
SIFC	*Studi italiani di filologia classica*
SIG	*Sylloge inscriptionum graecarum*³
Spengel, *Rhet.*	L. Spengel, *Rhetores graeci* (Leipzig, 1853–6)
Studi e materiali	*Studi e materiali di storia delle religioni*
SVA	*Die Staatsverträge des Altertums*, vol. 2: *Die Verträge der griechisch-römischen Welt von 700 bis 338 v.Chr.*, ed. H. Bengtson (Munich, 1962); vol. 3: *Die Verträge der griechisch-römischen Welt von 338 bis 200 v.Chr.*, ed. H. H. Schmitt (Munich, 1969)
SVF	*Stoicorum veterum fragmenta*, ed. H. von Arnim (4 vols., Leipzig, 1903–24)
TAPhA	*Transactions and proceedings of the American Philological Association*
TAPhS	*Transactions of the American Philosophical Society*
TGF	*Tragicorum graecorum fragmenta*², ed. A. Nauck (Leipzig, 1889; revised by B. Snell, Hildesheim, 1964)
UPZ	U. Wilcken, *Urkunden der Ptolemäerzeit* (2 vols., Berlin–Leipzig, 1922–57)
Vorsokr.	H. Diels and W. Kranz, *Fragmente der Vorsokratiker* (Berlin, ed. 5 (1934–7), ed. 7 (1954))
Wilcken, *Chrestomathie*	U. Wilcken, *Grundzüge und Chrestomathie der Papyruskunde*, vol. 1: *Historischer Teil* (2 vols., Leipzig–Berlin, 1912)
WS	*Wiener Studien. Zeitschrift für klassische Philologie und Patristik*
WZLeipzig	*Wissenschaftliche Zeitschrift der Karl Marx-Universität, Leipzig*
YClS	*Yale classical studies*
YWCS	*Year's work in classical studies*
ZAeS	*Zeitschrift für ägyptische Sprache und Altertumskunde*
ZPE	*Zeitschrift für Papyrologie und Epigraphik*

In some articles 'Livy(P)' and 'Livy(A)' have been used to indicate the Polybian or annalistic sources used by Livy in the section referred to.

1

THE PROBLEM OF GREEK NATIONALITY*

I

The problem which I propose to discuss in this paper is one which must strike anyone who ponders at all about the history of Greece. Can we speak of a Greek nation? Greece, as we all know, was never united until the Roman conquest within a single state; consequently there can be no history of Greece in the sense that there is a history of Rome. But the concept of a Greek nation trying to realise itself (and failing) has been adopted by many historians as the most fruitful criterion for interpreting the kaleidoscopic relations of the Greek cities. A few quotations will make this clear. 'The story of the Greeks possesses coordination and the true dignity of history only where it strives continuously, and with ever broader results, towards effective political unity, namely in Greece proper.' These words of De Sanctis[1] can be paralleled from Volume 6 of the *Cambridge ancient history*,[2] where Cary writes, '[The Athenian Empire] represented the first resolute attempt to solve the key problem of Greek politics, the assembling of the scattered Greek communities into a United States of Greece', or from a recent work by Pohlenz,[3] 'The League of Corinth brought to fruition that unity of the Hellenes for which the best elements in the people had for so long yearned.'

The authors I have just quoted differ in many ways in their interpretation of Greek history; but all share what may fairly be called the orthodox view of Greek history as the struggle for the unification of the Greek nation. It is perhaps worth observing, even at the risk of covering well-trodden ground, that this interpretation has not always been current. It does not, for instance, occur in the work of the banker and liberal politician who, in the years between 1846 and 1856, was publishing what is still perhaps the most noteworthy English history of classical Greece. For its origins we must turn, not to George Grote, but to the nineteenth-century Germans,[4] and in particular to the *History of*

* [[*Phoenix* 5 (1951) 41–60]]

[1] G. De Sanctis, *Storia dei Greci* 1 (Florence, 1939) 3.
[2] *CAH* 6 (Cambridge, 1933) 26.
[3] M. Pohlenz, *Der hellenische Mensch* (Leipzig, 1947) 137.
[4] See J. R. Knipfing, *AHR* 26 (1920–1) 658ff. As P. Treves, *LEC* 9 (1940) 285 n. 3, points out, it is inexact to attribute the 'unitary' view of Greek history (and particularly of the issue as between Isocrates and Demosthenes) exclusively to the German historians; but historically this view was nurtured mainly on German soil, and against the background of German nineteenth-century political developments.

hellenism of Johann Gustav Droysen.[5] In his first edition of 1833 Droysen set ‖ out to bridge the gap between classical Greece and the coming of Christianity, and he found his link in what he called the Hellenistic Age. Droysen had a passion for progress and the wide horizon. His object was to study Greek history as part of universal history, and his sympathies were always with the *victrix causa*. 'My enthusiasm', he wrote,[6] 'is for Caesar, not Cato, for Alexander, not Demosthenes.' Small wonder that such a man living in the Germany of Bismarck should conceive a devotion to the rising state of Prussia, with its manifest destiny to unite the Fatherland; and Droysen's second edition, published in 1877, under the spell of Prussian success, laid special stress on the forces making for panhellenism and the unity of Greece – above all Isocrates and the kings of Macedon.

It was Droysen who really raised the national issue in Greek history. But it reached its apogee in the twentieth century with Eduard Meyer and Julius Beloch.[7] For many years yet Beloch's *Greek history* will be indispensable. But for all its factual learning it is marred by a curious schematism and tendency towards abstraction. To Beloch the Greeks are one race which at an early stage in its history lost the consciousness of unity, and spent the rest of its span on earth gradually, and never quite successfully, recovering it. 'Particularism', we read,[8] 'was the hereditary curse of the Greek people.' Athens, Sparta, Macedon, and the third-century Confederations, with their 'republican movement', were the successive incarnations of this spirit of national unity striving to be born. Each in turn proved abortive, and finally in the early second century the Symmachy of Antigonus Doson was trampled down beneath the feet of the Roman legions. On this interpretation Greek history shows one highlight – the Persian Wars – when for a short space the cities forgot their quarrels and won deathless glory at Thermopylae, Salamis, and Plataea.

To De Sanctis, a pupil of Beloch, the unity of 481 has become a touchstone for the definition of Greek history. The solidarity then shown in Greece was based, he rightly observes, upon the liberty of the *polis*, and designed for its defence;[9] but this liberty was in reality 'the germ of the greatness of the nation'. Those Greek cities in Crete and western Greece which failed to respond at this historic moment forfeited their place in Greek history, and were henceforth fated to pursue a different path right down to the last days of Greek independence.

The Persian Wars thus occupied an unchallenged place in these histories of Greek unity similar to that which they had long ago enjoyed ‖ in the more

[5] On this see A. Momigliano, *Filippo il Macedone* (Florence, 1934) Introd. xvi (with bibliography); H. E. Stier, *Grundlagen und Sinn der griechischen Geschichte* (Stuttgart, 1945) 25ff.

[6] J. G. Droysen, *Briefwechsel* I (Berlin–Leipzig, 1929) 66ff.; quoted by Stier, *op. cit.* (n. 5) 28. The remark was made in a letter to Friedrich Gottlieb Welcker.

[7] See for example E. Meyer, *Kleine Schriften* I (Halle, 1910) 1–78, 'Zur Theorie und Methodik der Geschichte'; K. J. Beloch, *Griechische Geschichte* 1–4 (Strasbourg–Berlin–Leipzig, 1912–27) *passim*.

[8] *Op. cit.* (n. 7) 3.1.515.   [9] *Problemi di storia antica* (Bari, 1932) 11ff.

expansive prose of the Attic orators. But the other supposedly great moment of Greek unification – the setting up of the League of Corinth by Philip II after Chaeronea – very soon became the centre of polemic. For in proportion as the stock of Philip and Isocrates rose, the reputation of Demosthenes fell, until he began to look like a petty and narrow patriot, blind to the swelling tide of history. Recently, therefore, several historians have brought considerable emotion to the task of rehabilitating Demosthenes, and illuminating the causes for which he fought – the freedom and autonomy of Athens, and (they would argue) ultimately of the other Greek states as well.

The opposing sides in this dispute have tended to mass round the symbolic figures of Demosthenes and Isocrates; but the issue has not been allowed to remain one of Greek unity versus Greek particularism. A careful examination[10] of what Isocrates really advocated led to a toning down of the exaggerations which had made him 'a man of 1848', the ideological forerunner of Philip and Alexander; in the last resort Isocrates, no less than Demosthenes, was shown to have based his aims on the *polis*, and to have fostered unification as the means to a new Athenian hegemony. Simultaneously it was being argued[11] that Demosthenes' whole policy after the Peace of Philocrates in 346, down to Chaeronea, and even down to the Lamian War after Alexander's death, was designed to secure Greek unity in the fullest sense, that is, unity which maintained the liberty and autonomy of the city-state. But in fact this formulation concealed an irreconcilable contrast. For the urge towards the autonomy of the *polis* was a force working against, and not in the direction of, Hellenic unity; and in an acute and pessimistic study Ferrabino demonstrated that this liberty, admitting no restraint, and developing whenever circumstances allowed into domination over others, was the one really potent factor in Greek history. In such domination, taking the form of hegemony, the denial of someone else's liberty was implicit; and not only did this lust for power constantly nullify the quest for liberty, but because any hegemony based on power could only reflect a temporary balance of forces, to be overthrown as soon as that balance changed, there could be no question of national unity.

The impasse seemed complete; Demosthenes and Isocrates were both, it appeared, the spokesmen of the *polis*. Panhellenism and the crusade against Persia, which the latter so sedulously preached, had no more to do with a united Greek nation than had the anti-Macedonian coalition which the former built up in 340 and 339. The conclusion seemed to be that the Greeks had a weak or ineffective national sense; and that conclusion was quickly drawn. 'The concept of the Greek ‖ nation', wrote Berve,[12] 'is best left out of the picture.' But if this was so, what I have called the orthodox account of Greek history was due for revision. What was to take its place?

---

[10] Especially by G. Mathieu, *Les idées politiques d'Isocrate* (Paris, 1925), and U. Wilcken, *SBBerlin* (1929) 313, and *Alexander der Grosse* (Leipzig, 1931).

[11] See W. Jaeger, *Demosthenes* (Berkeley, 1938) 170ff.; P. Treves, *Demostene e la libertà greca* (Bari, 1933) *passim*; *LEC* 9 (1940) 270ff.   [12] *NJbb* (1938) 15.

There have been roughly three answers to this problem. The first is that of Berve, just mentioned; leave nationality out of the picture and concentrate on what really mattered to the Greeks – or those of them who were vocal – the liberty and autonomy of the city, the attempt to establish a real peace, the urge towards hegemony. A second answer draws a distinction, along the lines suggested by several German sociologists, and in particular by Friedrich Meinecke,[13] between the *Kulturnation* and the *Staatsnation*. These expressions are not wholly happy,[14] but they sum up the thesis that a nation need not necessarily be united under a single state to enjoy a consciousness of its own identity; nationhood, on this argument, is something which depends on the possession of several – but not necessarily all – of the following factors: a common habitation, a common language, a common spiritual and intellectual life, and a common state or share in a federation of states.[15] The Greeks possessed sufficient of these in common to rank as, and feel themselves, a nation; but without political unity, they must be regarded as a *Kulturnation* only.

This view has won many adherents; but in the course of the last decade a third answer to the problem has been propounded in two important and very diverse works, Martin's study of the international relations of the Greek city-states, published at Geneva in 1940, and Stier's *Foundations and meaning of Greek history*, published at Stuttgart in 1945.[16] Quite independently, the former implicitly, the latter explicitly, these two scholars have restated the problem of Greek history in national terms; only the nation is now identified, not with Hellas, but ‖ with the individual *polis*. The novelty of this procedure may be obscured by the fact that in practice we have always treated the Greek cities for what they were and claimed to be – independent, autonomous states. Grote,[17] realising this and feeling some difficulty in reconciling it with the idea of a Greek nation, coined the term 'interpolitical' to describe relations between *poleis*, so that 'international' might be reserved for relations with non-Greek states; but the distinction was not made by the Greeks themselves, and it has never been adopted.

[13] See F. Meinecke, *Weltbürgertum und Nationalstaat*[7] (Munich–Berlin, 1928) 3 (and works by A. Kirchhoff and F. J. Neumann there quoted); H. E. Stier, *op. cit.* (n. 5) 108, connects the idea with a remark of Jacob Burckhardt to Arnold von Salis in December 1870 that it is impossible to be at once a culturally important and a politically important people.

[14] But E. Meyer's use of *Volk* and *Nation* (*op. cit.* (n. 7) 1.38ff.) is even less apt.

[15] Meinecke, *op. cit.* (n. 13) 1, who adds 'a common origin'; but this is manifestly lacking in the population of most nations throughout history and seems therefore somewhat irrelevant. *Cf.* F. Schulz, *Principles of Roman law* (Oxford, 1936) 109–39, but one may question his view that there was ever a single 'Roman' nation covering the whole Empire. J. Stalin, *Marxism and the national and colonial question* (New York, 1936) 8 (reprinting an essay of 1913), defines a nation as 'a historically evolved, stable community of language, territory, economic life, and psychological make-up, manifested in a community of culture', and treats each factor as essential. But this somewhat rigid definition would exclude Switzerland with its three (or four) tongues, and contemporary Germany with its economic division along the frontier between the eastern and western zones of occupation.

[16] V. Martin, *La vie internationale dans la Grèce des cités* (*VI–IVe siècle av. J.-C.*) (Geneva, 1940); Stier, *op. cit.* (n. 5).   [17] Grote, *History of Greece* 2 (1846) 340ff.

However, if we are to understand the foundations of Greek political thought and action, Stier's thesis will require some consideration, for (as Meinecke rightly insists) the identification of State and Nation is by no means an automatic occurrence. A state like Switzerland (or Great Britain) can contain several distinct cultural units, and conversely a single cultural unit like the German people may, as in the centuries before Bismarck and again at the present time, be divided amongst several states.

II

A full examination of the thesis that the Greeks regarded the *polis* and not the whole Greek people as the nation would require a comprehensive survey of the whole of Greek history, and this is clearly beyond the scope of a paper. We must therefore content ourselves with considering the general case, and the more convincing of the evidence with which Stier supports his thesis, accompanying it with such qualifications as seem necessary. First, then, the arguments for identifying the *polis* with the nation.

It has been widely assumed in the past that the word *Hellene* began by having a 'national' sense and later, especially in Hellenistic times, came to mean 'possessing Greek culture'. For instance, in Ptolemaic and Roman Egypt the Hellenes were also known as οἱ ἀπὸ τοῦ γυμνασίου, 'those from the gymnasium', and frequently had non-Greek names. From Tebtunis we have a list of five Ἑλλήνων γεωργ[ῶν], 'Greek farmers', of whom only one has a Greek name.[18] And it has been thought that the beginning of this extension in the meaning of the word can be traced to the fourth century, when Isocrates wrote,[19] 'Athens has become the teacher of the other cities, and has made the name of Greek (τὸ τῶν Ἑλλήνων ὄνομα) no longer a mark of race (γένος) but of intellect (διάνοια), so that it is those who share our upbringing (τῆς παιδεύσεως) rather than our common nature (τῆς κοινῆς φύσεως) who are called Hellenes.' This passage has attracted great attention, Jaeger going so far as to claim it as[20] 'a higher ‖ justification for the new national imperialism, in that it identifies what is specifically Greek with what is universally human'. 'Without the idea which [Isocrates] here expresses for the first time', he continues, '...there would have been no Macedonian Greek world-empire, and the universal culture which we call Hellenistic would never have existed.' Unfortunately for this claim, it has been shown[21] that in this passage Isocrates is not extending the term Hellene to non-Greeks, but restricting its application; he is in effect saying, 'Hellenes are no longer all who share in the γένος and common φύσις of the Greek people, as hitherto, but only those who have gone to school to

---

[18] See F. Zucker, *Das neue Bild der Antike* 1 (Leipzig, 1942) 380; W. Otto, *Kulturgeschichte des Altertums* (Munich, 1925) 117. [*P. Tebt.* 1.247 = 4.1107.]

[19] *Paneg.* 50.   [20] *Paideia* 3 (Oxford, 1945) 79–80.

[21] By Wilcken, *SBBerlin* (1922) 114 n. 3; *cf.* J. Jüthner, *Hellenen und Barbaren* (Leipzig, 1923) 34ff.; *WS* 47 (1929) 26ff.

Athens; henceforth "Greece" is equivalent to Athens and her cultural following.' Thus Isocrates gives the term a cultural value; but he cannot be regarded as initiating a wider concept of Hellas.

So far Stier's argument seems well based; what follows is more controversial. There is, he claims, evidence for the view that from the earliest times (and not merely from the fourth or third century) the word 'Hellene' was a cultural, not a national term.[22] It is now generally agreed that the original Ἕλληνες were a small tribe in south Thessaly, and that this name was extended in a way which can easily be paralleled – consider for example the names *Graeci* or *Allemands* – to cover the Greeks in a wider sense. Both Hesiod and Archilochus know the form Πανέλληνες;[23] and Hesiod was evidently acquainted with the shorter form Ἕλληνες since it is to him we owe our first reference to Hellen, the eponymous hero of the Hellenes. The extension of the name first in the longer, and then in the abbreviated form can, therefore, perhaps be attributed to the eighth century. Stier, however, now argues that since the Macedonians were excluded from the Ἕλληνες, yet appear to have been a Greek-speaking people, the criterion for inclusion was evidently not race or tongue, but cultural level; and in support of this he quotes the fact that not until Roman times[24] are the Hellenes spoken of as an ἔθνος, the ‖ term normally applied to such Greek people as the Boeotians or Arcadians, and even the bigger divisions like the Ionians and the Dorians. When in the *Laws* (iii.692d–693a) Plato refers to the services rendered by Athens and Sparta to Hellas in resisting Xerxes, he reckons among the worst of the consequences of defeat the racial confusion which must have ensued. 'Virtually all the Greek stocks (τὰ τῶν Ἑλλήνων γένη)', he writes, 'would have been mixed up one with another, and barbarians with Greeks and Greeks with barbarians.' Clearly the Hellenes are not here being treated as a single racial and national stock, but rather as a cultural group comprising several nations.

This is not very convincing. The special case of Macedon, a somewhat remote

[22] This summary is restricted to what seem the stronger of Stier's arguments. He brings forth many which are merely perverse; e.g. that ἑλληνίζειν meant primarily 'to speak correctly', and that there was no Greek language (as opposed to dialects). The absence of a standard literary Greek is irrelevant to the question of nationality; there are signs of German national consciousness as early as Walther von der Vogelweide, but no standard German till Luther created it in the fifteenth century.

[23] *Cf.* Hes. *Op.* 528; Archil. 52 (*cf.* Strabo viii.6.6, c370); the date of both poets is uncertain; on Archilochus see A. A. Blakeway in *Greek poetry and life* (Oxford, 1936) 34–55; F. Jacoby in *CQ* 35 (1941) 97–109; H. Gundert in *Das neue Bild der Antike* i (1942) 130–52. A date *c.* 700 B.C. seems most probable. The word Πανέλληνες occurs in *Iliad* ii.530 (the Catalogue) but this line is usually taken to be an interpolation; on the possible change in accentuation Ἑλλῆνες—Πανέλληνες—Ἕλληνες see W. Schulze, *SBBerlin* (1910) 806.

[24] An interesting passage in this connection is Polyb. xi.19.4; Hannibal kept together many men who were not only not ὁμοέθνεσιν but not even ὁμοφύλοις. These included Libyans, Iberians, Ligurians, Celts, Phoenicians, Italians, and Hellenes. Stier, *op. cit.* (n. 5) 388 n. 113, dismisses this as Roman: but Polybius was Greek enough to get this sort of thing right. In fact, the passage does not contradict Stier's view; for Polybius distinguishes two types of grouping, ἔθνη and φυλαί, of which the latter are wider (οὐδ' ὁμοφύλοις); the Hellenes may here be included as a distinct φυλή or race (containing various ἔθνη).

and certainly mixed people containing Thracian and Illyrian as well as Greek-speaking elements, is not sufficient to destroy the general impression that in classical times the Ἕλληνες regarded themselves as a body of kin. An ἔθνος they may not be; a γένος they certainly are,[25] and γένος suggests kinship, not culture. This is supported by the early appearance in Hesiod of the eponymous Hellen,[26] the invented ancestor of the race; and when the Argead kings of Macedon were admitted to parity among the Greeks and to the Olympic games as a symbol of this, it was on genealogical grounds, *i.e.* those of kinship and race, not on grounds of culture, that their claims were made and accepted. It is to genealogy that Stier would attribute the many references to Hellenes as kinsmen and blood-relatives, συγγένεις and ὅμαιμοι.[27] But to minimise their importance on that account is to neglect the idea behind the invention of Hellen;[28] and those who argue that the Ἕλληνες form a cultural group over against the βάρβαροι would perhaps win more support for their thesis if they could point to an eponymous Barbar as ancestor to the βαρβαρόφωνοι. In view of these difficulties Stier cannot be said to have made out a case for thinking that 'Hellas' was originally a cultural rather than a racial or national concept; in this respect the orthodox view must continue to stand. ‖

III

Let us pass to a further point. How, it may be asked, is the thesis of a Greek nation and a national consciousness in the minds of the Greeks to be reconciled with the geographically dispersed character of the Hellenic settlements? The expression 'Hellas' normally (though not invariably)[29] comprised all Greek cities, no matter where they lay – on the shores of the Euxine, on the coastal plateau of Cyrenaica, or on the seaboard of Spain. Clearly there was never any question of uniting all these within a single nation – a geographical absurdity, unless one envisaged a vast empire like the Roman, embracing not merely the Greeks, but the whole of the provinces which their cities fringed. It was therefore virtually impossible for all the Greek cities to follow a common destiny. But for all that, there is something artificial[30] in seizing upon one group of cities on the Greek peninsula, and upon one great epoch in their common

---

[25] *Cf.* Stier, *op. cit.* (n. 5) 99: 'stets begegnet...der viel weitere Begriff γένος'.

[26] Tzetz. *ad Lycophron.* 284, fr. 7 Rzach. Hellen's three sons were Dorus, Xuthus, and Aeolus, *i.e.* the Dorians, Ionians, and Aeolians. 'This is not mythology, but early ethnological theory cast in the traditional mythological form of a genealogy' (H. J. Rose, *OCD s.v.* 'Hellen').

[27] See the passages from Isocrates, Aristophanes, Lysias, and Herodotus quoted by Stier, *op. cit.* (n. 5) 385 n. 78.

[28] Similarly the acceptance of the Dorians as part of the general stock of the Greeks is reflected in the story of the return of the Heracleidae.

[29] Hellas is used in a limited sense too, as for instance when Theopompus (*FGH* 15 F 193) excludes Sicily, and Demosthenes limits it to central Greece: τίς ὁ συσκευάζεσθαι τὴν Ἑλλάδα καὶ Πελοπόννησον Φίλιππον βοῶν, ὑμᾶς δὲ καθεύδειν; (19.303); *cf.* Ephorus, *FGH* 70 F 20. But a certain fluctuation is to be expected when the concept in question did not form a political unit.

[30] See above, n. 1.

history, the Persian Wars, in order to establish a criterion of 'Greek' history that excludes western Greece and the scattered cities of the rest of the Mediterranean. For Sicily, no less than continental Greece, had its problem of unity against outside aggression, whether from barbarians like the Carthaginians or from the Athenians who were Greeks. In the speech advocating a general peace in Sicily in 424 B.C., which Thucydides (IV.64.3) puts in the mouth of Hermocrates of Syracuse, there is a vigour and capacity for thinking beyond the *polis* (if still ultimately in its interests) which is uncommon in Greece of the classical period. 'There is no disgrace', he asserts, 'in kinsmen (οἰκείους) giving way to one another, a Dorian to a Dorian, or a Chalcidian to his brethren; above and beyond this we are neighbours, live in the same country, are girt by the same sea, and go by the same name of Sicilians.' Here surely – it might be said – is a theme of Sicilian unity around which a history of the Sicilian Greeks might be written; it could tell of the Sicilian–Greek nation striving to achieve birth. But in fact, as Freeman saw,[31] there clearly was never any such thing. As far as nationality goes (and ruling out such sentiment as attached to the name of Ionian and Dorian) there was no essential difference between the attitude of the average Syracusan towards a Theban or a Corinthian, and his attitude towards a man of Messana or Leontini.

Despite such alliances of convenience as marked the Persian Wars in Greece proper, or the burst of pan-Sicilian self-interest in the face of Athenian ambitions which led to the Peace of Gela, the Greek cities ‖ everywhere remained separate and divided, each with its own laws, without rights of intermarriage, with different calendars and currencies, and (until some co-ordination was achieved about 400 B.C.) with different scripts and alphabets. The vigour with which the member of the *polis* maintained his own political identity may be illustrated from the story of Plataea.[32] In 427, after a long siege, Plataea was obliged to surrender to the Spartans, its remaining inhabitants were massacred or enslaved, and a year later the city was razed to the ground by the Thebans.[33] Those Plataeans who had already escaped and so avoided this catastrophe were, as a very exceptional measure, granted Athenian naturalization. Nevertheless, twenty years later Aristophanes (*Frogs* 694) still refers to them as Plataeans; and during the early decades of the fourth century they keep making their appearance as a separate group. From the time of the King's Peace in 386 they once more resettle the ancestral site,[34] only to be expelled yet again in 373 by Thebes, the old enemy.[35] Finally in 338 after the battle of Chaeronea the remnants of the people came back to Plataea, this time to stay.[36]

Everything, as Martin points out, favoured the success of the amalgamation

---

[31] E. A. Freeman, *History of Sicily* I (Oxford, 1891) introduction: 'Sicily never was the home of any nation, but rather the meeting place of many.'
[32] *Cf.* Martin, *op. cit.* (n. 16) 322–4.
[33] Thuc. III.52, 68.   [34] Paus. IX.1.4.
[35] Diod. xv.46.5.   [36] Paus. IX.1.8.

with Athens – the destruction of the old city, the lustre of the new, the solid advantages offered by the change; 'but national sentiment', he comments, 'resisted injuries and enticements alike, and survived all fortune's wreckage. The history of Plataea attests yet again the unparalleled tenacity with which that sentiment maintained its grip upon the Greek cities.' Faced with such an example one is tempted to doubt whether the Greeks were ever moved by ideals other than those of autonomy and freedom in their political life, by αὐτονομία and ἐλευθερία, the slogans of resistance to all bids for hegemony which might upset the balance of power in which their security rested.

IV

At this conclusion, however, one is brought up short. Granted that one may not treat Isocrates as the theorist of the League of Corinth, surely one may not dismiss entirely the current of panhellenism which runs through Aristophanes' *Lysistrata*, the Olympic orations of Gorgias and Lysias, to the long series of speeches or pamphlets in which Isocrates himself repeatedly flogged the theme of Greek concord. And what on the other hand of the many forms in which in practice Greeks joined together in leagues and alliances, to say nothing of the amphictyonies and the international festivals? All this, we are now assured, may be neglected. First the propaganda: analyse it, says Stier, and where do you ‖ find Greek national unity put forward as an ideal? Aristophanes' object is peace, an end of war, and amity between the cities, a policy which he claims to be in the common interest of all Greeks. But this is a very different matter from a national Greek state. Similarly Gorgias' Olympian speech of 392 and that of Lysias of 388 do not in essentials go beyond an anti-Persian crusade under Athenian or Spartan hegemony;[37] and though Isocrates turned to Athens, Thessaly, Syracuse, Sparta, and Macedon in succession in his search for the ideal leader, he too could not get beyond the same unreal context. How unreal it was became clear when finally he chose Philip II of Macedon to lead a pacified and single-minded Hellas against Persia; for if there is any practical trace of unity in fourth-century Greece, it was realised in the coalition which Demosthenes raised against Philip. For the next hundred and fifty years the one constant basis of common action in Greece is hostility towards Macedon. At the same time, we are not to imagine that Demosthenes was out to build a national state. He more than any man was anchored in the *polis*, and his alliance was always an instrument of Athenian freedom and hegemony, however idealistically conceived.

Isocrates remained a theorist. With Demosthenes we bridge the gap between theory and action. But if Demosthenes' league was in reality partial and particularist, so were all the other movements which various scholars have

---

[37] Gorgias: Aristotle, *Rhet.* III.14, 1414b30ff. Lysias: Dion. Hal. *Lys.* 28.9; cf. Lysias 33. The date of Gorgias' speech is controversial; I follow A. Momigliano, *op. cit.* (n. 5) 184.

acclaimed as steps towards the realisation of the nation; and this not least because of the very character of a Greek συμμαχία,[38] which weighted it heavily against playing a role in the creation of a national state. A συμμαχία is primarily an alliance for the purpose of war. It is normally made for a limited period of time, and reflects a particular situation and a definite and essentially temporary balance of forces between its members. Frequently the problem of leading the combined forces is solved by formally conferring the hegemony on one state; thus Sparta was *hegemon* in the Peloponnesian League, and after Chaeronea the League of Corinth took the novel step of making an individual, Philip II, *hegemon* – though many Greeks regarded this as a serious diminution of the rights of the *poleis* and something very like monarchy. The difficulty involved in transforming such a war-alliance into an instrument of political unification in time of peace has been acutely analysed by Martin, who points out that any attempt by the *hegemon* – the war-leader – to centralise political power was always felt by the rest to be an encroachment and an abuse. In the classic example of the fifth-century Delian League this feeling was behind a series of revolts, until finally it was only the Athenian navy which held the cities || together, and Thucydides (II.63.2) makes Pericles candidly admit that the free association of cities had become an Athenian tyranny. Isocrates also proposed to work through a συμμαχία and therefore, quite logically, he felt the need for an enemy – Persia – to serve as a *raison d'être*. But there was nothing in his programme which offered any hope that if Greece could have been allied under one of his prospective *hegemones*, and if the war against Persia could have been carried to a successful conclusion as a Greek (and not a Macedonian) enterprise, the coalition would have developed into a national state any more than the Athenian Confederacy after Salamis and Plataea.

Thus the Symmachies fell between two stools. Either they were based on a shared leadership, like the league against Sparta of 395, between Athens, Corinth, Argos, and Boeotia, in which case the balance was always delicate and usually shortlived; or one state enjoyed an acknowledged hegemony, and by the adoption of long-term aims tended to transform its military ascendancy into politial superiority, and the alliance into an empire, which in turn caused the revulsion and stimulated the revolt of the subjects at the first opportunity. In these circumstances alliances could not develop into an instrument of panhellenic unity.

Finally, the Greeks themselves never felt such alliances to be more than combinations of sovereign states. War between Greek states was not normally thought of or spoken of as 'civil war'; nor was any political distinction drawn between Greeks from another city and any other foreigners. Both, for instance, were included equally in the Spartan expulsions of aliens. Such common feeling as existed between the Greeks as Greeks was of a cultural or religious character. The common religious centres and festivals were comparable with

---

[38] On this topic see especially the excellent analysis of Martin, *op. cit.* (n. 16) 124ff.

the international shrines and sports gatherings of the modern world; and such bodies as the Delphic Amphictyony were of the same character – religious, not political, and certainly not capable of developing into instruments of national unification.

V

I have given the thesis in outline only. Much of it is obviously exaggerated, though a good deal is true; and its adherents support it with a great many detailed arguments for which there is no room here. Many of the more dubious or paradoxical points – for instance, the assertion that there was no Greek language, but only a collection of Greek dialects, which are virtually separate languages – I have omitted, as I have the elaborate *tour de force* in which Stier marshals a set of impressive arguments for a possible thesis that Europe constitutes a single nation, a thesis which would of course be quite misleading. But I have not, I think, misrepresented the case, nor ignored any vital part of it. In criticism it will be useful first to consider a number of specific points. ‖

First of all, as we have seen, the idea that Hellas is a purely cultural concept cannot be accepted, in view of the Greek stress on common ancestry and kinship. Consequently we ought not to neglect any evidence, scattered and scanty though it may be, which treats Hellas as something more than an international society of autonomous city-states. There are, for instance, several passages in which war between Hellenes is described as civil war. Granted, this is exceptional; granted, too, the term may be used in an extended sense. But for all that, these passages do presuppose in their readers a certain response, and for that reason they cannot be simply dismissed. Two writers use the word στάσις to describe quarrels between Greek cities at the time of the Persian Wars. Theognis speaks of στάσις Ἑλλήνων λαοφθόρος, and Herodotus tells[39] how the Athenians refused to press their claim to hegemony at Salamis lest Greece should thereby perish; for, he adds, 'civil war (στάσις ἔμφυλος) is as much worse than a war waged in concord as war is worse than peace'. Again Plato in the *Republic* (v.470) distinguishes between war and civil war, πόλεμος and στάσις, reserving the second title for wars within the Hellenic γένος, which is of the same kin and family, οἰκεῖον καὶ σύγγενες.

This was certainly not the common politician's view. But it meant something, an idea in some men's minds, which was to find an echo increasingly in the next century. When for example in his *Panegyricus*[40] of 380 Isocrates wrote that the Athenians of old had regarded the cities of Greece as mere dwelling places, and Hellas as a common fatherland (κοινὴν πατρίδα τὴν Ἑλλάδα) he is undoubtedly rounding off a highly elaborate period with a striking formulation. Such a formulation may be concerned with propaganda rather than factual

---

[39] Theognis 781; Hdt. viii.3; *cf.* H. Bengtson, *Einführung in die alte Geschichte* (Munich, 1949) 55.

[40] *Paneg.* 81. *Cf.* H. Berve, *Gnomon* 9 (1933) 302; Stier, *op. cit.* (n. 5) 118.

accuracy; but it must not be too far removed from the mental climate of the times and from the ideas current in the minds of the ordinary listeners. The fortunes of this particular formulation can, it so happens, be traced further. In the *Philippus* (127), written in 346, Isocrates, with the verbal economy of a publicist, used it again – with a difference; for now he admitted that the other potential leaders of Greece were too bound up in their own laws and constitutions; Philip alone could treat all Hellas as his πατρίς. Once again, it may be objected, a metaphor and a fine phrase. But when, after the death of Alexander, the Athenians tried to stir up a last rally for freedom in the so-called Lamian War – the Hellenic War, as the ancient sources term it – they tacitly reverted to Isocrates' original use of the phrase by summoning the Greeks to resistance against Macedon with a reminder of how during their own former efforts against the Persians they had regarded Hellas as the 'common fatherland'.[41] ‖

The point is not whether such expressions were sincere or even true: it is that they would not have been uttered had they not been calculated to have some effect; and the same is true of the panhellenic themes of the orators and the various references to common Greek action, such as Pericles' invitation to the Greek cities to send representatives to Athens to deliberate on peace and common action among the Hellenes, ἐπ' εἰρήνῃ καὶ κοινοπραγίᾳ τῶν Ἑλλήνων.[42] In this case, as Larsen argues,[43] it is no doubt true that Pericles was hoping to persuade the other cities to submit to the Athenian hegemony. What is significant is the panhellenic note which he thought it worth while to sound. Slight though this evidence may be when taken separately, or even when put into the balance against the tremendous weight of testimony for the attitude which made the separate *polis* the final criterion in all political decisions, it nevertheless points to the recognition of a concept of Hellas which was not simply a cultural union.

When on the report that Xerxes was at Sardes the Greek states resolved to appeal to Crete, Corcyra, and the Western cities, to come to the aid of Hellas,[44] their plea was made to cities with whom they felt themselves to be bound by ties of kinship. Within this group of states political relations were of a different character from those between Greeks and non-Greeks. For instance the conventions of warfare, which persisted from early times throughout the whole of Greek history, and which Berve,[45] who is in general sceptical about any idea of Greek nationality, counts among 'the few factors making for unity', laid down a standard of conduct in inter-Greek wars which was not observed or even expected to be observed in wars against barbarians.

The oath sworn by members of the Amphictyonic League[46] included an

[41] Diod. xviii.10.3.
[42] Plut. *Per.* 17; *cf.* V. Ehrenberg, *JHS* 70 (1950) 101.
[43] *CP* 39 (1944) 158.   [44] Hdt. vii.145.   [45] *NJbb* (1938) 13.
[46] Aeschines 2.115, 3.109–11; for discussion of this controversial topic see F. Hampl, *Die griechischen Staatsverträge des 4. Jahrhunderts v. Chr. Geb.* (Leipzig, 1938) 4–6; Busolt-Swoboda, *Griechische Staatskunde* 2 (Munich, 1926) 1262, 1294; L. Robert, *Études épigraphiques et philologiques*

undertaking not to destroy any city belonging to a fellow member, not to reduce it to starvation, and not to cut off the supply of running water. Its date is uncertain, but it goes back to at least 590, at the end of the First Sacred War, and probably earlier. Historically the convention may well have arisen out of the perennial frontier raids between neighbouring cities, for the acquisition of land and booty, raids which the Greeks always distinguished from a major conflict offering a real threat to existence.[47] But by extension it served to humanise any wars ‖ between Greek cities, and tended towards the formulation of a whole series of νόμιμα πάσης ῾Ελλάδος.[48] Since these conventions between Greeks go back to an early date, we may dismiss the idea that they rest on a recognition of merely cultural equality: they are a symbol of a consciousness of ties of real or pretended kinship.

This kinship is expressed more clearly than anywhere else in Herodotus who, in a famous passage,[49] records the reply of the Athenians after Salamis, when the Spartans were afraid lest they might make a separate peace with Xerxes. Such a course, they say, is unthinkable, and that for many reasons. First there was the burning of the Athenian temples. 'Then', they continue, 'there is our common brotherhood with the Greeks: our common language, the altars and the sacrifices of which we all partake, the common character which we bear – did the Athenians betray all these, of a truth it would not be well.' These are clear, unambiguous words – common blood, common tongue, common religion, and a common way of life; they can scarcely be reconciled with the picture which we have just examined of an international community of completely independent national states.

VI

We must therefore frankly admit that the evidence is contradictory – so long as we insist on considering Greek history exclusively in terms of the *polis*. The field of reference must clearly be extended in order to discover some more flexible criterion. The root of the trouble in most discussion of nationality in Greece lies in too static an interpretation of the concept of a nation and in the

(Paris, 1938) 293–316; D. W. Prakken, *AJP* 51 (1940) 62; G. Daux, *RA* (1941) 176; J. A. O. Larsen, *CP* 39 (1944) 145–7.

[47] *Cf.* Martin, *op. cit.* (n. 16) 332–40, quoting the wars between Tegea and Mantinea over the draining of the area, and the curious treaty of Thuc. v.46.2, by which Argos and Sparta agreed to make peace for fifty years, save any war waged for the possession of Cynuria: and for such a war the convention was carefully laid down.

[48] Eur. *Supplices* 311; *cf.* von Scala, *Studien des Polybios* I (Leipzig, 1890) 299–324, who collects a number of examples from Euripides (especially), Thucydides, Plato, Xenophon, Aristotle, and later writers. He shows that though the Peripatos in some cases transcended the limitation to Hellenes in applying these ideas, and though the Stoa ignored any criterion beyond the individual, in practice the conventions, as applied by the Greek states, continued to operate for Greeks only. There was a deterioration in practice after the third century, and especially after the coming of the Romans.

[49] Hdt. viii.144; *cf.* Stier, *op. cit.* (n. 5) 87ff., 100.

attempt to establish too rigid a parallel with the modern world. In fact, as Eduard Meyer pointed out,[50] nations are a very advanced and complicated product of historical development, not something beyond history, as Stier suggests. 'Nations arise and nations decay', writes Bengtson,[51] 'and this very process is the object of historical study.' In Greece, as elsewhere, all the political units were in a constant state of evolution which is liable to be obscured by the apparent rigidity of the *polis* itself. It is often said – not without justice – that Aristotle's political thought was rooted in the *polis*. But Aristotle recognised in the ἔθνος organised in villages, κατὰ κώμας, a traditional political unit alongside the city-state, self-sufficient as regards the bare ‖ necessities (αὐτάρκης ἐν τοῖς ἀναγκαίοις), though not adapted to pursue the good life.[52] Down to a late period peoples such as the Acarnanians, Aetolians and Arcadians were distributed among clans and cantons; in Arcadia, for instance, several such cantons were fused to form the cities of Tegea, Mantinea and Orchomenus during the sixth and fifth centuries, whereas Megalopolis was set up out of forty original communities as a deliberate act of Theban policy after Leuctra. Hence it is possible to trace the dissolution of the old tribal units, the crystallisation into cities often harbouring the bitterest hostility towards each other, and finally the uneasy union of such cities in a new confederacy which restores the original ethnic unity on a higher plane.

The two stages of this process we know as synoecism and federalism; and where the first was carried through completely, as in Attica, the second never became necessary. But Attica was unique in the Greek world. The usual picture elsewhere is one of *ethne* and *poleis* at various stages of development, which often became involved in keen rivalries. Thus in Boeotia there was a constant tension between the unity of the *ethnos*, as expressed through the Boeotian League, and the typical claims to hegemony pressed by the most vigorous *polis*, Thebes. It is clear that the concept of 'nation' is of as little help in the comprehension of such rivalries and tensions as it would have been as a means of solving them.

Both synoecism and federalism continued to play an important role in Greece down to the latest days. As the areas where the *polis* predominated became tangled in the problems raised by the urge towards unlimited expansion and the resistance which it evoked – the problem of the Peloponnesian War, and the subsequent wars against Sparta and Thebes – the loose federations of the more backward or politically weaker areas came to play an increasingly important role.[53] It was from such districts as these, from Achaea, from Arcadia and from Aetolia, that the federal movement took its rise in the fourth and third centuries.

[50] *Op. cit.* (n. 7) 1.38ff.

[51] *Op. cit.* (n. 39) 46; cf. F. Schulz, *op. cit.* (n. 15) 109–39.

[52] Aristotle, *Politics* III.14, 1285b; IV (VII).4, 1326b. *Cf.* M. Gelzer, 'Das Problem des Klassischen und die Antike', *Acht Naumburger Vorträge*, published by W. Jaeger (Leipzig, 1931) 101 = *Kleine Schriften* 3 (Wiesbaden, 1962) 3–12; cf. Stier, *op. cit.* (n. 5) 392 n. 155. See especially Martin, *op. cit.* (n. 16) 32ff.

[53] On this see Momigliano, *op. cit.* (n. 5) 65ff.

It may well be argued that federalism, like synoecism, has little to do with national unity. On the other hand, the federal state incorporates a principle of unification by consent, which enables it to grow larger without necessarily meeting the nemesis of the expanding hegemonic state. The Macedonian-controlled Leagues from 338 down to 224 were debarred from fostering unity in Greece precisely because they were Macedonian. Their political structure was often admirable. Both the League of Philip II and the League of Antigonus Doson have been praised as being among the most statesmanlike achievements of their ‖ kind in world history;[54] but both stood for outside domination, and though they may have had the support of one faction within the cities for reasons of party rivalry, they outraged the Greek feeling for freedom and autonomy. The Achaean Confederation on the contrary came within a very little of uniting the whole Peloponnese in a single state, and, what is more, of building up a genuine allegiance and feeling of being Achaean. One need only turn to the enthusiastic account of Polybius (II.37.7ff.) – an Arcadian – to realise this; under its control, he writes, 'the whole Peloponnese only falls short of being a single city in the fact of its inhabitants not being enclosed by one wall, all other things being, both as regards the whole and as regards each separate town, very nearly identical'. The architect of this remarkable structure was Aratus, a Dorian from Sicyon, who had advanced to a broader allegiance.

But the Achaean Confederation foundered; and the fault was not entirely with Aetolia or with Sparta, unable to forget its past and sink its identity. Quite apart from the social and economic unrest which played into the hands of Spartan kings advancing a revolutionary programme, one cannot ignore the fact that the bigger *poleis* of the Peloponnese were never wholly absorbed. A tendency to independent action in times of crisis and even outright differences of policy in such cities as Argos and Corinth set definite limits on the possibility of expansion. Whether there was ever an 'Achaean nation' is arguable: that the Confederacy was incapable of developing into a 'Greek nation' is certain.

VII

Thus the story of federalism reveals the same fission and contrasts as the story of the fifth- and fourth-century *poleis*; and though it may demonstrate the inadequacy of the concept of the *polis* as nation for an understanding of Greek political development, it leaves enough of Stier's case intact to show how tenuous and feeble was the movement towards unity at all periods. The Greeks possessed enough of the components of a nation to conceive a national idea; but except in times of crisis, when this idea inspired them to common action and even to self-sacrifice, their violent political and patriotic feelings were expressed through the medium of smaller political units.

[54] For the League of Corinth see J. A. O. Larsen, *CP* 39 (1944) 160; for the Symmachy of Doson see A. Ferrabino, *La dissoluzione della libertà nella Grecia antica* (Padua–Milan, 1929) 84.

This formulation underlies certain general difficulties in the interpretation of Greek history. The view that Greek history is the struggle for the national state must be rejected. As Stier and Martin have shown, anything built around a concept so weakly felt and so ineffective in action must be quite false to the ideas and aims of the Greeks themselves, and for that reason stands condemned. ‖ Furthermore, the story of Greece as the conflict of completely independent national states striving for freedom and autonomy is also to be rejected, not because it would be a pointless story of failure, as Ferrabino argues, but because such a formulation ignores various positive values and achievements in the political field, including the concept of a Greek nation, which must be given their full value. Starting out from the second position, Jaeger has attempted to interpret Greek history as *paideia*,[55] the unfolding record of Greek thought directed towards the training of the human spirit. Jaeger has given us a stimulating concept and a remarkable book; and though it has been argued[56] that the interpretation of Greek history is not to be built on the exposition of a culture which grew up primarily in opposition to the main assumptions of Greek politics, this paradoxical criticism is not convincing. Many of the great names in the history of Greek thought, it is true, were bitterly opposed to the idea of liberty fundamental in Greek politics. But all accepted the framework of the *polis*. Socrates, for example, died rather than challenge its claims by the flight that was open to him. Moreover there was never a healthy intellectual development which did not involve a strong element of friction against established society and its ideals. In illustration of this one need look no further than the sequence which ran from Sallust to Tacitus, and the attitude of protest to be found in almost every writer under the early Roman Empire.

But if *paideia* withstands this criticism, it fails as a full interpretation of Greek history simply because it concentrates almost entirely on what was thought and said to the exclusion of what was done and experienced; and consequently it does not help us with our problem, which is really one of a vital idea which appears to be at constant variance with practical politics – the idea of the Greek nation. Droysen, Beloch, Meyer, Stier – all in turn have brought different criteria to the task of resolving this contradiction, and all have reached different conclusions. It is therefore worth while considering if the problem has been properly formulated. When a historian defines the history of Greece in terms of a struggle for unity, or describes the building of the ‘United States of Greece’ as ‘the key problem of Greek politics’, what exactly does he mean?

VIII

I want to suggest that there is a permanent danger of over-simplifying the process of historical thinking, and that in approaching any period, or people,

---

[55] W. Jaeger, *Paideia* 1–3 (Oxford, 1939–45). A second edition of vol. 1 with notes was published in 1946.
[56] Ferrabino, *op. cit.* (n. 54) 107ff.

or problems, it is important that we should make certain conscious distinctions, and organise our ideas at several different levels.[57] Suppose, for example, we are concerned with Greek history between the ‖ battle of Mantinea and the Lamian War. First of all – and let us, for convenience of analysis and without prejudice call this the lowest level – we should investigate the various policies and aims of Greek and non-Greek statesmen, the interests likely to influence them, the actions of the various states, and their outcome, in terms of the concepts and ideals and knowledge actually available to the people concerned. That is to say, we should try to read ourselves, for example, into Demosthenes' mind, and understand how it looked to him, and what he was hoping to do. We shall be preoccupied with particular incidents inside a general framework of ideals which are not our own: we shall be concerned with εἰρήνη, αὐτονομία, ἐλευθερία, ἡγεμονία – preferably kept in their Greek forms to connote Greek ideas. We shall try to assess just what a phrase like κοινὴ πατρίς used of Hellas means to different people in this general context.

This or something like it, I take it, is what Collingwood meant by re-enacting past thoughts; it is an activity which lies at the very heart of historical study, and in it there is no room for moral judgements, but only for estimates of success and failure in the carrying out of various divergent aims. If we consider the period I have mentioned in these terms, we must I think agree that it is a record, very largely, of political failure. Freedom, autonomy, peace, hegemony – not one of these often contradictory aims was achieved for long at a time. If we stop here, the history of the fourth century in Greece must appear anything but satisfying.

However, it is essential that we should not stop here. In so far as the historian seeks to relive the past he deliberately restricts himself to the knowledge available at the time of which he writes. But he is also living in his own age, with all the advantages of knowing how the play ended; and he can see each act in relation to the whole. Now because of what De Sanctis has called the 'creativity of history'[58] its process is not a mere series of permutations and combinations similar to that of shuffling cards or shaking dice. Out of the clash of deeds and policies, the genius or the malice of outstanding individuals, the unthinking obedience or the revulsion of the mass, the victories, defeats, migrations, conquests, and settlements, the social struggles, the shifting currents of trade, and all the infinite variety of a thousand and one other factors, something new is constantly coming to birth; and what is born in this way is neither a haphazard nor an arbitrary creation, but stands in a logical sequence to all that has preceded it. From the impasse of fourth-century politics, with the crisis of inter-state relations after Mantinea, the revival and impact of Macedon, and the social and economic problems of the Greek mainland, sprang Macedonian hegemony, the plan to ‖ conquer Persia, and

[57] Indirectly the following section owes a good deal to Momigliano's *Filippo, op. cit.* (n. 5) *passim.*

[58] *Op. cit.* (n. 1) 1.8: 'La storia infatti e eminentemente creatrice, vale a dire consiste nel perenne superamento di quel che in qualsiasi istante e dato.'

the Hellenistic Age with its new values. The unravelling of this pattern is also the task of the historian.

At this stage he is no longer concerned with reliving the past. When Glotz brought the third-century temple accounts from Delos into relation with the fourth-century wage rates from Eleusis, he was able to tell a story about the standard of living among labourers in the Aegean area in the early Hellenistic period which had never existed before in anyone's mind:[59] it had been there objectively in the social relations of ordinary men, no doubt experienced by each one as domestic hardship and distress, but never reduced to the form and context in which Glotz now presented it. This kind of history is concerned with trends and currents; and because it must necessarily pass from the specific to the general, it is a perpetual invitation to discover schemes and patterns which transfer the motivation of events and the responsibility for their occurrence from the control of men to some mystical power or realm existing outside the process of events. Here, if he is not constantly on the alert, the historian will find logical and verbal abstractions, puffed up into metaphysical entities, waiting around every corner. But it is a risk he must run: for the full understanding of the past requires its interpretation not merely in the light of the past, but also in the light of the future – our past and present.

This distinction can help us, I think, in approaching the problem of Greek nationality. The idea of a Greek nation is alien to the thought of most Greeks at most periods throughout Greek history. Consequently when one tries to pin it down, it seems to dissolve, or reveals itself only in the sentiments of the exceptional person now and then; and its influence on action is negligible. Yet, when we analyse the course of Greek history in the light of after-knowledge, we can clearly trace a movement towards integration in larger units, arising out of the circumstances existing from time to time, taking various forms including synoecism and federalism, and possible because ultimately the Greeks felt themselves to be a single people, ὅμαιμόν τε καὶ ὁμόγλωσσον. In that sense Greek unity and even the Greek nation are concepts which can be studied and discussed without patent absurdity.

This trend towards integration was diverted into various channels and failed to complete itself – for reasons which have been emphasised repeatedly. From this failure what lesson is the historian to draw? Is he indeed to draw any lesson at all? 'Past events', wrote Polybius (XII.25e.6), 'make us pay particular attention to the future, if we really make thorough enquiry in each case into the past.' 'If my history be judged useful by those enquirers who desire an exact knowledge of the past as an aid to the interpretation of the future', wrote Thucydides (1.22.4), '...I shall be content.' To draw such lessons implies the ‖ passing of judgements on the past, and those judgements must be made *ex eventu*. To many historians this involves an illegitimate step, which they condemn as rank intellectual snobbery towards the past, with its assumption

---

[59] *JS* 11 (1913) 16, 206, 251; *cf.* W. W. Tarn in *The Hellenistic age* (Cambridge, 1923) 108ff.

of 'We know better!' For example, in his inaugural lecture at Rome on the essence and characteristics of Greek history,[60] De Sanctis claimed that 'we ought not to do the actors in the drama of Greek history the injustice of closing with a *fabula docet*, and so pointing out to them what they ought to have done in place of what they actually did'. But is there really any injustice towards the past – which indeed lies beyond justice and injustice – in trying to judge its achievements in the light of knowledge which it never possessed – provided always that we keep this activity quite distinct from that of analysing the past in its own terms? In the days before we adopted sociology and psychology as our guides to action, men learnt their sociology and psychology from the salutary lessons of history. Some may feel that we should still be prepared to study those lessons and that a historian ought not to shrink from pointing them.

For after all, though the historian is apt to believe that the subject he has chosen for study is one which he came to by chance, or because it seemed to have been neglected, or because it arose out of some earlier work, or for some other wholly personal reason, fifty years hence it will be quite obvious that the themes chosen by historians today, and the treatment accorded to them, were directly related to contemporary problems, or, to use De Sanctis' words,[61] to the spiritual needs of men and women living in the middle of the twentieth century. 'La vita è maestra della storia', he writes: life is the master of history – but conversely history is the master of life. Between the two there is a Heracleitean flux; and if it is the needs of our own time which determine our selection of historical themes, are we not then entitled to receive from our studies in exchange, not merely the enrichment of experience which comes from an added understanding of the integration of all that is past in the present – for this integrated essence is often subtle and remote – but also that wisdom which is the fruit of watching men partly like and partly unlike ourselves meeting, and either solving or failing to solve, problems that are partly like and partly unlike those which we ourselves have to face? If this is also one of the legitimate tasks of history, we can still turn with profit to the problem of Greek national unity.[62]

[60] *Op. cit.* (n. 9) 27.

[61] *Op. cit.* (n. 1) 1.9–10; *cf.* Bengtson, *op. cit.* (n. 39) 2.

[62] This paper was read before the General Meeting of the Classical Association at Liverpool on 3 April 1951.

2

WERE THERE GREEK FEDERAL STATES?*

It appears to be very difficult to get an acceptable definition of a federal state. The one thing that most authorities seem agreed on is that it represents some sort of a compromise. Freeman, in his unfinished *History of federal government*, of which the first and only volume appeared in 1863,[1] saw the federal state as a compromise between a system of large states and a system of small states, and also from another aspect as a compromise between absolute independence and absolute subjection. More recently, Sir Kenneth Wheare[2] has defined a federal government as one in which there is a co-ordinate division of powers between the central government and the member states, so that both operate in their respective spheres directly and independently upon the individual citizen. A state of this sort – and Wheare admits that his definition is formulated primarily with the example of the United States in mind[3] – is a compromise between a unitary state like Great Britain or France and a confederation like the original American Confederation of 1777 (in which the central government was subordinate to those of the regions).

Wheare's definition seems to rule out nearly all federal experiments before 1787 – which may be why his book on *Federal government* ignores the ancient world almost completely: the word 'Achaea' does not figure in the index, and he accuses Freeman of using the term 'federal government' too loosely 'even for a historian'.[4] Yet states like Achaea and Aetolia contained both central and city governments and have generally been held to fall within a history of federalism. The bulk of Freeman's work, even in the expanded edition which Bury brought out in 1893,[5] is concerned with the ancient world; and in recent years ‖ the subject has received an impetus from J. A. O. Larsen's comprehensive study of *Greek federal states*[6] which demonstrates a growing knowledge of the working of those states and of the cities comprising them since the time of Freeman. There are still serious gaps; and we must always bear in mind a point stressed by Wheare, that a federal constitution and a federal

* [*SCI* 3 (1976/7) 27–51]

[1] E. A. Freeman, *History of federal government from the foundation of the Achaian League to the disruption of the United States* 1 (London, 1863).

[2] K. C. Wheare, *Federal government* (London, 1946); I have used ed. 3 (London, 1953).

[3] *Op. cit.* (n. 2) 1.   [4] *Op. cit.* (n. 2) 16 n. 2.

[5] *History of federal government in Greece and Italy*, ed. J. B. Bury (London, 1893).

[6] J. A. O. Larsen, *Greek federal states* (Oxford, 1968).

government are not necessarily the same thing. What one wants to know is how things worked in practice; and for that our evidence is not always adequate. Discussion, therefore, still goes on about whether the Achaean federation, for example, embodied anything like Wheare's co-ordinate division of power, and to what extent the cities were subordinate to the centre. In this paper I am raising this question afresh, because a striking new work has recently appeared, in which it is argued that the Greek federal states (so-called) were neither federal states nor confederacies – neither *Bundesstaat* nor *Staatenbund* – but quite simply unitary states.

The book in which Dr Adalberto Giovannini argues this case[7] is, I believe, important. It contains a clear and plausible statement of a paradoxical and heretical point of view. It is most readable, indeed exciting; and it underlines several undoubted truths that have gone either unnoticed or at least without clear formulation. It is to Giovannini's arguments that I propose to direct this paper, and I hope that, though I shall end up disagreeing with him, I shall not be unfair to his argument, and to a work from which I have learnt a great deal. One difficulty in such a discussion is verbal. What are we to call states like Aetolia and Achaea while actually arguing about their definition? Giovannini uses the Greek term *sympoliteia*, though in fact he subsequently concludes that this is an improper use of the word.[8] I propose to call them simply 'federal states', but since I hope to show that that is what they were, the difficulty is perhaps less serious for me than it was for him. ‖

I

Giovannini begins his argument by discussing terminology.[9] There is, he says, no Greek word for 'a federal state'. It is of course true that Greek has no word meaning 'a federal state' and nothing else. But words can, and do, change their meaning, and it is rare in any language to find a complete correspondence between any name and one particular institution. The city-state itself had not the exclusive use of the word *polis*, for this also means a citadel or fortress or even the rights of citizenship. Several words – including *politeuma*, which is used in the treaty sworn between Rome and Aetolia in autumn 211[10] – appear to be used to mean 'a federal state'; but the three commonest are *koinon* (literally meaning 'common thing'), *ethnos* (literally 'people') and *sympoliteia* (literally 'shared citizenship *or* constitution'). Giovannini argues that in all the passages where these words appear to be so used, the meaning is in fact a different one; I shall consider his arguments one by one. First, *koinon*; and here he makes

---

[7] A. Giovannini, *Untersuchungen über die Natur und die Anfänge der bundesstaatlichen Sympolitie in Griechenland* (Hypomnemata, Heft 33, Göttingen, 1971). Giovannini is here reviving a view advanced eighty years ago by E. Szanto, *Das griechische Bürgerrecht* (Freiburg/Breisgau, 1892).

[8] *Op. cit.* (n. 7) 24.   [9] *Op. cit.* (n. 7) 14–24.

[10] H. H. Schmitt, *Staatsverträge des Altertums (SVA)* 3 (Munich, 1969) no. 536 l. 20, τοῖς Αἰτωλοῖς [εἰς τὸ αὐτῶν] πολίτευμα ποτιλαμβάνειν [ἐξέστω...].

an important point. *Koinon* is never used in Greek (as it almost always is by modern historians of Greece) to mean 'federal states' in the plural. In the singular it means the central authority as distinct from the member-cities. But since the central authority of a *polis* was more commonly referred to as the *demos*, the people, the word *koinon* tended to be associated more specifically with federal states or such political organisations as alliances or religious amphictyonies. The word, therefore, acquired a close connection with composite bodies, and when the *koinon* of the Achaeans makes a dedication to the statesman Aristaenus,[11] it seems likely that to those reading it the phrase meant 'the federal authority of the Achaeans'; clearly the difference between this and 'the Achaean Federation' is little more than a nuance. Next comes *ethnos*, which Larsen translates 'nation' (he renders *koinon* 'commonwealth').[12] *Ethnos* ‖ is frequently used both of tribal communities, like the Molossians or the Macedonians, and of developed federal states, like the Achaeans or the Aetolians; and it is frequently contrasted with *poleis* – 'cities' – indeed the phrase πόλεις καὶ ἔθνη, cities and *ethne*, is often employed to mean 'states of every kind' (in the Hellenistic period the word δυνάσται, 'princes', is sometimes added).[13] The people in an *ethnos*, it is widely believed, were conscious of a shared origin and held cults and customs in common; and the use of this word to describe a federal state has been taken to indicate that such a state had evolved out of a tribal community and still kept its 'ethnic' character. Giovannini, however, rejects this view.[14] The word *ethnos*, he argues, originally meant nothing more than 'a group'. He points out, quite correctly, that in Homer the phrase ἔθνος Ἀχαιῶν does not mean 'the Achaean people', it means 'a band of Achaeans';[15] and in later authors we meet an *ethnos* of workers, peasants or serfs, of priests, money-changers and merchants, of thieves, rhapsodes, heralds and catamites, while the male and female sexes can constitute an *ethnos*.[16] *Ethnos*, he argues, is a vague word; and in the phrase 'cities and *ethne*', the second word is purely negative – what is left in the 'political spectrum' when you have taken away the cities.

I find this hypothesis unacceptable. It is true that in the Hellenistic age *ethnos* is used to describe states that are not cities, *poleis*.[17] But nearly all *ethne* are

---

[11] *SIG* 702 note; here τὸ κοινὸν τῶν Ἀχαιῶν honours Aristaenus for his goodwill εἰς τὸ ἔθνος καὶ τοὺς συμμάχους καὶ τοὺς ἄλλους Ἕλλανας.

[12] *CP* 57 (1962) 250–1 (quoted also by Giovannini, *op. cit.* (n. 7) 19 n. 41); Larsen, *op. cit.* (n. 6) xiv.

[13] See Walbank, *Historical commentary on Polybius* 2 (Oxford, 1967) 117, on Polyb. IX.1.4; R. Weil, *Aristote et l'histoire: essai sur la 'Politique'* (Paris, 1960) 376ff.

[14] For the view of an *ethnos* as a community conscious of its common origin, cults and customs see Weil, *op. cit.* (n. 13) 380ff.; for the rejection of this see Giovannini, *op. cit.* (n. 7) 15.

[15] *Cf.* Hom. *Il.* XVII.552.

[16] Plato, *Gorg.* 455b (workers); Dem. 23.146 (peasants); Plato, *Leg.* VII.776d (serfs); Arist. *Metaph.* I, 981b25 (priests); Dem. 23.146 (merchants and money-changers); Plato, *Resp.* I.351c (thieves); Xen. *Symp.* 3.6 (rhapsodes); Plato, *Pol.* 290b (heralds); Dem. 61.4 (catamites); Xen. *Oecon.* 7.26 (the sexes). I take these references from Giovannini, *op. cit.* (n. 7) 15.

[17] See above, n. 13; *cf.* Larsen, *CP* 57 (1962) 250.

'peoples' with a tribal or kinship basis, and if *ethnos* originally signified simply 'a group', then it is an odd word for the Greeks to have adopted to describe a people which felt itself to be something like what we mean by a 'nation'. Since the groups themselves go back to ancient times, it would seem more likely that it is the other ‖ uses of *ethnos* that are derivative. In English we use the word 'tribe' in the same way. Giovannini argues that an *ethnos* need not have 'ethnic' origins (in the modern sense) and quotes the example of the Epirotes[18] – whose name means 'the people of the mainland (*epirus*)'. But the Epirote federation is exceptional in having developed out of the Molossian tribal state (as Giovannini himself emphasises a few pages earlier)[19] and consequently cannot be used in support of the view that an *ethnos* is simply a group. But in any case I doubt if the origins of a particular name are very important; in Italy the Latins certainly felt themselves to be a *gens* or *natio*, although the word *Latini* means simply 'men of the flat country'.[20] In fact, Aristotle, who has a good deal to say about *ethne*, clearly gave the word a positive content and meaning. In a passage in the *Politics*[21] he remarks that a city with too big a population becomes more like an *ethnos*. Here, clearly, *ethnos* cannot just mean 'not a city', for this would make the remark repetitious. It must mean a political body with its own characteristics, which differ from those of a *polis* in a positive way. So even if the 'group' meaning came first (which I find highly improbable), it is clear that the 'ethnic' meaning was firmly established by the time of Aristotle and before the hey-day of the federal states. This seems to me to be an important point. The argument that federal states like Achaea were called *ethne* merely because they were not cities, neglects what was clearly the predominant meaning of the word *ethnos* in classical times. Whether military or religious factors played the greater role in the origins of federal states is a question which cannot yet be answered;[22] but it seems clear that the political organisation of the *ethnos* took place within a context of kinship and tribal cohesion – as indeed one would expect in early society.

There is a further point. Not only does Aristotle show that he has a positive concept of an *ethnos*; he also distinguishes an *ethnos* that is still purely tribal from one organised on federal lines. In a passage in the *Politics* (II.2, 1261 a 27), where he is concerned with defining the city, he remarks that a *polis* differs from an alliance, because whereas a *polis* ‖ needs the greatest amount of variety and differentiation, an alliance benefits from a mere extension in the number of its members, since its usefulness depends upon *quantity*. He then remarks, almost incidentally, that a *polis* also differs from an *ethnos*, where the people are not scattered in villages, but are like the Arcadians. The passage has been much discussed;[23] but clearly it differentiates between two kinds of *ethne* – those in

---

[18] *Op. cit.* (n. 7) 16 n. 25.

[19] *Op. cit.* (n. 7) 11 n. 7.

[20] *Cf.* Walbank, *HSPh* 76 (1972) 149.

[21] *Pol.* VII.4, 1326 b 2f.

[22] *Cf.* Giovannini, *op. cit.* (n. 7) 13.

[23] See Newman, *The Politics of Aristotle* 2 (Oxford, 1887) 231–3, commenting on the passage; Weil, *op. cit.* (n. 13) 269–72.

which the people live in villages and those in which they live like the
Arcadians – and this appears to mean that (like the fourth-century Arcadians)
they are organised in cities within a federal state. Such a federal state, then,
differs from a city because, like an alliance, it can benefit simply from territorial
expansion.

Now if Aristotle draws this clear and positive distinction between cities and
ethne, and if in discussing *ethne* he distinguishes between those organised like
the Arcadians (*i.e.* federally) and those not so organised, then it becomes rather
difficult to accept the view that *ethne* are so called in the Hellenistic age solely
because they are not cities.

The third word frequently used of federal states in Hellenistic times is
sympoliteia.[24] It crops up on inscriptions and in Polybius, and can refer to several
complex political structures, in which cities were incorporated in one or other
of a variety of ways, for example unions of two or more cities, such as that
between Plarasa and Aphrodisias in Caria,[25] cities which have *absorbed* other
cities, as Miletus absorbed Pidasa or Myus,[26] and of course federal states.[27] It
is also used to describe the relationship of two states linked by *isopoliteia*
(literally 'equality of citizenship'),[28] ‖ that is the mutual grant of the potential
rights of citizenship, which became actual only if and when the citizen of one
city took up residence in the other – a relationship which existed for example
between Cydonia and Apollonia in Crete,[29] or between Cius and Lysimacheia
and the Aetolian federation.[30] In fact Aetolia made substantial use of
isopoliteia,[31] under that name, both within the federation and with outside
states; among the latter known to us are Messene and Phigaleia in the
Peloponnese, Ceos (which was linked to Naupactus), Tricca in Thessaly,
Heraclea (probably Heraclea-by-Latmos), Vaxos in Crete, Acarnania and
perhaps such states as Phocis and Boeotia and (for a time) the cities of eastern
Arcadia. Polybius generally chose to neglect *isopoliteia* and to include examples
of it under the more general term *sympoliteia*.[32]

---

[24] See Giovannini, *op. cit.* (n. 7) 20–4.

[25] *Cf. OGIS* 453, lines 5ff.; for a full discussion of this kind of *sympoliteia* with examples taken
especially from Asia Minor see L. Robert, *Villes d'Asie mineure: études de géographie ancienne*[2] (Paris,
1962) 54ff. For evidence for such a *sympoliteia* between Oricus and Corcyra see H. W. Parke, *Oracles
of Zeus: Dodona, Olympia, Ammon* (Oxford, 1967) 261 n. 6 (*cf.* Robert, *Bull. épig.* (1971) no. 382).

[26] Strabo xiv.1.10, C 636 (Myus); G. Kawerau and A. Rehm, *Das Delphinion in Milet* (Berlin,
1914; vol. 1.3 of Th. Weigand, *Milet: Ergebnisse der Ausgrabungen und Untersuchungen seit dem Jahre
1899*) 149 (Pidasa).

[27] *E.g.* Polyb. ii.41.12 (of the Achaean Federation); see below, nn. 33–40.

[28] *Cf. SIG* 472, for a Messenian decree establishing ἰσοπολιτεία between Messene and Phigaleia.

[29] *Cf.* Polyb. xxviii.14.3; Polybius uses the word συμπολιτεία, but if this is Apollonia πρὸς
Κνωσῷ, the relationship will be ἰσοπολιτεία (*cf.* Guarducci, *IC* 1, p. 3). In other respects too
Polybius' phraseology here recalls that found in other ἰσοπολιτεία agreements from Crete (*cf.* van
Effenterre, *La Crète et le monde grec de Platon à Polybe* (Paris, 1948) 288–9).

[30] *Cf.* Polyb. xviii.3.12; here too Polybius says συμπολιτευομένους, but ἰσοπολιτεία is probably
meant. See Busolt-Swoboda, *Griechische Staatskunde* 2 (Munich, 1926) 1511 n. 3.

[31] On this see Larsen, *op. cit.* (n. 6) 202–7.

[32] *SIG* 472 (Messene and Phigaleia); *SVA* 3.508 (*isopoliteia* decree of Naupactus for Ceos and
of Ceos for the Aetolian Federation); *IG* 9[2].1.178; *SIG* 622; *IC* 2, p. 64 no. 18, p. 65 no. 19 (Vaxos);

Clearly then a great variety of political patterns can be covered by
'*sympoliteia*', which is a word by no means restricted to any one meaning, nor
indeed very sharply defined. But among its various meanings, so it has usually
been assumed, are 'an act of union' in one of the compound political
organisations I have mentioned, and 'the union itself' which results from that
act. 'To share in the *sympoliteia*' of the Achaeans, μετέχειν τῆς τῶν Ἀχαιῶν
συμπολιτείας, was taken to mean 'to join the federation'; 'to withdraw from
the *sympoliteia* of the Achaeans', ἀφίστασθαι τῆς τῶν Ἀχαιῶν συμπολιτείας,
was 'to leave the Achaean Federation'.[33] Giovannini denies this.[34] *Sympoliteia*,
he insists, is an activity, not an institution; it means 'a sharing of political ‖
life'. It is a sort of symbiosis, something that is happening within a state that
is a going concern. You do not create *a sympoliteia*, you share in (or cease to
share in) *the sympoliteia* of an existing state.

Giovannini deduces this meaning from the verb *sympoliteuein*, 'to have a share
in political life', and he may well be right in regarding it as the original one.
But – as in his discussion of the word *ethnos* – he does not seem to me to make
sufficient allowance for the natural development in word-usage. In 280/79 the
four Achaean cities of Dyme, Patrae, Tritaea and Pharae came together;[35] five
years later (Polybius tells us) the people of Aegium expelled its tyrant and
'began to share in their *sympoliteia*'.[36] After the death of Demetrius of Macedon,
many Peloponnesian tyrants yielded to Aratus' threats, laid down their power
and 'shared in the Achaean *sympoliteia*'.[37] In 182, after their revolt, the
Messenians were restored to their original position in the *sympoliteia*; and
various cities were separated from Messenia and, having set up inscriptions (to
mark their adherence), began to share in 'the common *sympoliteia*'.[38] About
the same time the Achaean general announced at an assembly that the Spartan
leaders were anxious 'to share in the *sympoliteia*'.[39] I need not quote further
examples. My point is that in all these passages the phrase which I translate
'to share in the *sympoliteia*' clearly implies 'to join the federation'; and I believe
that to Polybius' readers the word *sympoliteia* conveyed the sense of 'federation'.
This view is confirmed by a passage in Book II,[40] in which Polybius remarks
that Lydiades, the tyrant of Megalopolis, with greater foresight than his
fellow-tyrants, without waiting for the death of Demetrius of Macedon had laid
down his tyranny and 'had shared in the ethnic *sympoliteia*', *i.e.* he had joined
the Achaean federation. The use of the pluperfect tense 'had shared' underlines
what is implicit in the other passages I have quoted, namely that Polybius is

---

IG 9².1.3 A (Acarnania); Plut. *Arat.* 16.1 (with Porter's note); Polyb. xx.4–5 (Boeotia); for Phocis
see Larsen, *op. cit.* (n. 6) 206–7; for the Arcadian cities *cf.* Polyb. ii.46.2, with Larsen, *The classical
tradition: literary and historical studies in honor of H. Caplan* (Ithaca, 1966) 52–3.

[33] *E.g.* Polyb. ii.44.5, xxiii.9.14.   [34] *Op. cit.* (n. 7) 22–4.
[35] Polyb. ii.41.11.   [36] *Ibid.* ii.41.13.
[37] *Ibid.* ii.44.4.   [38] *Ibid.* xxiii.17.2.
[39] *Ibid.* xxiii.17.8.
[40] *Ibid.* ii.44.3; Polybius here uses the phrase τῆς ἐθνικῆς συμπολιτείας, perhaps because
Megalopolis was not part of the Achaean *ethnos*.

thinking far more of the *act* of union ‖ than of the shared political life that ensued from it; and what one joins is an organisation, not the communal activity that characterises it.

So, to sum up my argument so far, I can find no evidence in the vocabulary used in relation to federal states for the view that the Greeks did not distinguish them from unitary states. My reasons are: first that that view does not distinguish between the original meanings of *koinon, ethnos* and *sympoliteia* and the developed meanings which those words acquired when used in reference to federal states; secondly, that the negative definition of an *ethnos* as simply what is not a *polis* takes no account of the normal later meaning of the word, nor of Aristotle's distinction between *ethne* that are federally organised and those that are not, nor of the social conditions of early Greece when the later *ethne* first arose; and thirdly, that it is wrong to assume that because the Greeks had no word which they used exclusively to denote a federal state, they had therefore no concept of that institution.

Thus, the first argument against the existence of federal states in Greece, that from terminology, does not seem to be made out. We may now consider the arguments drawn from the supposed political behaviour of the federal states and their component cities, and the way the Greeks regarded both of these.

II

I will begin with a paradoxical aspect of Giovannini's argument, which becomes clear if we consider the situation in the United States of America. It usually comes as a surprise to anyone visiting the United States for the first time from a country like England or France to discover that this great power, which presents a single diplomatic front to the outside world, proves at closer quarters to be made up of a large number of separate and in many respects independent sovereign states, each exceedingly jealous of its own rights, but with no existence at all at the international level. No ambassadors travel abroad from Pennsylvania, Wyoming signs no treaties; yet there is a whole range of political and judicial activities in which the states are sovereign and in which no appeal lies from state decisions.

Now if Giovannini is right, the situation in a Greek federal state like Achaea is the exact opposite of this. There, he argues, we have a state ‖ made up of a large number of cities, which can be seen, from literary texts and inscriptions alike, engaging in a constant exchange of envoys, sacred missions, arbitrations, delegates to games, with cities and states outside Achaea, granting freedom from plunder, passing honorary decrees for foreigners, in short indulging in a full round of intensive interstate activity; and yet, he tells us, these same cities lack all political identity, and from that point of view constitute mere bricks in a unitary structure.[41] If this were true, it would be very remarkable, and

---

[41] Giovannini, *op. cit.* (n. 7) 93, 'Die Ethne...sind Einheitsstaaten wie Athen oder Sparta gewesen.'

would certainly show that in calling bodies like the Achaean Federation 'federal states' we should be using the word 'federal' in a very different sense from any that we might give that word today.

Giovannini's account of the status of the constituent cities in the Greek federal states is basic to his argument. If Achaea and Aetolia, to mention two examples, are to merit the name of 'federal states', then it must be possible to show that the cities no less than the central government exercised some autonomous powers within their own sphere. It is both interesting and relevant to consider whether – and to what extent – the cities within the various federal states had to ratify federal decisions, how far they shared, as cities, in the taking of such decisions, and what was the character of the manifold relations which the cities enjoyed with the outside world. But the answer to the question whether Achaea was or was not a federal state does not depend upon these questions or the answers they receive – though naturally activity by the cities of the kind I have mentioned underlines their importance in the state as a whole. The essential thing, if one is to disprove the allegation that Achaea was a unitary state, is to demonstrate that there existed an area of autonomous city activity.

Before coming to that, however, I must make one more point. I have already mentioned the distinction which Sir Kenneth Wheare has drawn between constitutions and governments. In the same way we should be careful not to confuse the *theoretical* relationship of *polis* and federal centre with the kaleidoscopic relationships which can be seen existing in real historical situations. To take one example, a second-century ‖ inscription, discovered in 1946, tells how Araxa in Caria,[42] a small city belonging to the Lycian Federation, fought wars against nearby Bubon and Cibyra, sent a prominent citizen Orthagoras on embassies to Cibyra, and only in the last resort appealed for help to the central government (the *koinon* of the Lycians). Or again, according to Polybius, the western Achaean cities of Dyme, Pharae, Tritaea and Patrae, which were somewhat isolated geographically from the rest of the federation, possessed some kind of separate organisation, since we hear, at the time of the Social War of 220–217, of a sub-division (*synteleia*) of Patrae under the command of a sub-general (*hypostrategos*).[43] This body acts, in practice, with some independence – the cities even withholding federal taxes to pay for regional forces – and its existence is not easily reconciled with the concept of Achaea as a unitary state. Similar district sub-divisions are also to be found in Aetolia, and though less is known about them, their existence points in the same direction.[44] In fact, one may say, the bonds between the separate parts – cities and groups of cities – and the federal centre seem to tighten and slacken with

---

[42] *Cf.* Bean, *JHS* 68 (1948) 46–56, no. 3; *cf.* Moretti, *RFIC* 78 (1950) 326–50; Larsen, *CP* 51 (1956) 151–68.

[43] Polyb. v.94.1, reading Πατρικῆς for πατρικῆς; on the *synteleia* of the western cities see Larsen, *CP* 66 (1971) 84–6.

[44] For Aetolian *tele* see Walbank, *op. cit.* (n. 6) 1.623–4 on v.92.7; Larsen, *op. cit.* (n. 13) 197ff.

the increase or decrease in outside pressures; and this *real* relationship between them is one of the factors that must be taken into account in any assessment of the role of the cities, no less than their 'constitutional position'.

We can now turn to Giovannini's main argument, which is designed to minimise the political aspect of the cities. The federal states, he declares, were, with the exception of Arcadia, ancient unified political structures, and not created at some late date by a union of the cities composing them. It is, he adds, the fallacy of this second view that has landed scholars in the embarrassing position of having to keep moving the supposed date of the foundation of the Aetolian Federation further and further back, to keep up with the discovery of new evidence for its ‖ earlier existence.[45] Achaea too, he argues, is not represented by Polybius as a late creation. On the contrary, his account of its early history goes back to legendary times and the rule of the kings. It was after the despotical rule of Ogygus' sons that the Achaeans changed their government to a democracy, and after that, right down to the time of Philip and Alexander, they kept their common state, τὸ κοινὸν πολίτευμα – which consisted of twelve cities – a democracy.[46] He makes a further point. Such federations, *ethne*, with cities embedded in their structure, are not, he says, unique in the Greek world. They find a close parallel in Hellenistic Macedonia, which was also an *ethnos* with cities – the only difference being that Macedonia was a monarchy.[47] But in both the monarchy and the federal state the central power completely predominates. How then are we to define the relationship of the cities to the central government? It is comparable, we are told, with the relationship of demes (virtually parishes) to the city which they compose, demes such as we find at Athens, Rhodes, Cos and many other cities.[48] Evidence apparently to the contrary is discarded. For example, we possess the text of a treaty from about 216 B.C. between Anactorium and the federal Acarnanian state of which it was a member, on the subject of the control of the shrine and festival of Actian Apollo. This treaty has been interpreted by Habicht, who first published the inscription, and by Schmitt, who reprinted it in *Staatsverträge des Altertums*, as an indication of the degree of independence enjoyed by a federal city relative to its central body.[49] Giovannini rejects this interpretation since, he says, the situation depicted in the treaty can be paralleled at Cos, where the city borrowed money from one of its demes ‖ and paid it back by

---

[45] *Cf.* Giovannini, *op. cit.* (n. 7) 74–5; the decisive evidence which caused the date for the 'founding' of the federal state to be pushed back was the discovery of the Athenian inscription of 367 (Schweigert, *Hesperia* 8 (1939) 5ff. = *GHI* 2.137), which contained a reference to the *koinon* of the Aetolians.

[46] Polyb. II.41.3–8; but Polybius' account of a continuous democracy from the time that Ogygus' sons were expelled is certainly untrue, for not only do we know that Achaea was oligarchic throughout most of the fourth century, but a direct adoption of democracy, following upon monarchy, is contrary to all political experience (see my *Commentary, op. cit.* (n. 13) 1.229–30 *ad loc.*).

[47] Giovannini, *op. cit.* (n. 7) 76–80.

[48] *Ibid.* 81–2.

[49] Ch. Habicht, *Hermes* 85 (1957) 87–9 = *SVA* 3.523.

instalments.[50] The comparison between federal cities and demes is pressed further. If a double citizenship – that of the city and that of the federation – is characteristic of a federal state, that too, it is argued, can be paralleled in the normal *polis*, where every citizen is a member both of the city and of his own deme, which he names on formal occasions, just as an Achaean citizen calls himself an Achaean from such-and-such a city.[51] The only difference is that the federal cities, unlike demes and unlike the member states of a modern federation, have an international role to play. But this, we are told, is not of a political character. It is something that happens because the only form of real community which a Greek could envisage was the *polis*, the city. Only a *polis* could be a living community, a *Lebensgemeinschaft* – certainly not an *ethnos* such as the Aetolians or the Macedonians.[52] A state of that kind was adapted to the relationships established by international law, but not to the cultural and social relationships essential to the lives of free men in the Greek world. For social relationships the only vehicle was the *polis*, and that is why a Greek living in a federal state called himself 'an Achaean from Aegium' or whatever it might be. In short, for Giovannini the 'international' aspect of the cities which form part of federal bodies is simply an aspect of their function as Greek living communities and has nothing to do with political powers: these are wholly reserved to the central government, which in consequence is as much a unitary state as a city like Athens or Rhodes.[53]

III

That is the argument: and now I want to examine it a little more closely. We can start, I think, by allowing Giovannini his point[54] that many of the *ethne*, states like Achaea and Aetolia, go back to early ‖ times – though indeed their political organisation before the growth of the cities must remain conjectural. But not all *ethne* had an uninterrupted political development from early times. Whatever the early history of Arcadia, the federal Arcadian state was a fourth-century creation.[55] Moreover, the antiquity of the *ethnos* does not in itself tell us anything about the role of the cities which in later times at any rate compose it; and this is crucial to the argument. Whether voting in federal assemblies was by cities or by individuals is a matter about which we are uncertain. Giovannini denies that voting was by cities, and also that the cities had any share in the ratification of federal decisions.[56] But there is sufficient evidence to render that hypothesis at any rate doubtful. Take, for example the

[50] W. R. Paton and E. L. Hicks, *The inscriptions of Cos* (Oxford, 1891) no. 383, ll. 7ff.; this arrangement is not however a treaty.

[51] *E.g. SIG* 380, Αἰτωλὸς ἐκ Ναυπάκτου; *SIG* 492, ᾿Αχαιὸς ἐξ Αἰγίρας; *SIG* 60, Βοιότιος ἐχς ᾿Ερχυμενῦ.   [52] *Cf.* Giovannini, *op. cit.* (n. 7) 86–7.

[53] *Ibid.* 92; Giovannini quotes E. Szanto, *op. cit.* (n. 7) 119, for this view.

[54] *Op. cit.* (n. 7) 74ff.

[55] On the founding of the fourth-century federations see Larsen, *op. cit.* (n. 6) 183ff. It is clear that in Arcadia federal union was a conscious political movement, strongly supported and contested.   [56] *Op. cit.* (n. 7) 28f.; 37f.

Acarnanian inscription[57] which records a federal decree recognising the festival of Artemis Leucophryene at Magnesia, granting freedom from plunder to the temple and requiring the federal cities to provide *theorodokoi* – hosts for the sacred delegates who came to announce the festival;[58] there follow the names of a number of Acarnanian cities which 'voted in the same terms'. Giovannini declares that their vote was merely in relation to the provision of *theorodokoi*; but that is not a natural interpretation of the wording, which certainly implies that the federal vote was ratified (or echoed) by the cities named.[59] If that is so, such ratification was clearly possible, in Acarnania at any rate (though of course it does not follow that all such decrees needed to be or were so ratified). Similarly in the matter of federal voting. Several passages of Livy, for which the source is Polybius, and especially several referring to an Achaean federal assembly of 198, speak of the participation, and some specifically of the voting, of *populi*, 'peoples'. The speech delivered in 198 by the Achaean ‖ leader Aristaenus in favour of abandoning the Macedonian alliance for an alliance with Rome, aroused no murmur of opposition, Livy tells us, *ex tot populis*, 'from so many peoples'.[60] When it was over, not merely individuals but *universi populi* began to argue about it.[61] Eventually, those from the cities of Dyme, Megalopolis and Argos left the meeting, whereupon the alliance with Rome was confirmed by 'the remaining peoples of Achaea', *ceteri populi Achaeorum*.[62] Similarly in 189 war was declared on Sparta 'by the agreement of all the states, *omnium civitatum*', which were attending the Achaean meeting.[63] In Boeotia, in 197, a motion to join Rome was approved by the votes of all the Boeotian states, *omnium Boeotiae civitatum*;[64] and in the same year, though not all the *populi* of Acarnania were present or agreed with the proposal, the magistrates of that federation put through a motion to join Rome.[65] The evidence comes from Livy, and it is easy to argue, with Giovannini,[66] that voting by cities is a cumbersome method, alien to the practice of Greek democracies, and one which does not leave its mark elsewhere in our records of federal constitutional practice, and consequently that in each of the above passages Livy must somehow have misunderstood or misrepresented what Polybius said.[66a] Well,

[57] *IG* 9².1.582.

[58] Giovannini, *op. cit.* (n. 7) 28 n. 23, erroneously states that the names of the towns 'beziehen sich auf den Beschluss dieser Städte, sich an den Festspielen *durch eigene Theorie* vertreten zu lassen'. There is no reference in the decree to sending *theoroi*, but only to the appointing of *theorodokoi*.

[59] The Greek words are κατὰ τὰ αὐτὰ δὲ ἐψηφίσαντο Θυρρεῖα κτλ.

[60] Livy xxxii.20.7. Giovannini, *op. cit.* (n. 7), discusses this and the following passages on pp. 37–8 n. 31. Both the Achaean meeting of 198 and that of 189 were in fact *synkletoi*, and it is possible that in Achaea voting by cities (perhaps with some sort of proportional representation) was restricted to these meetings, where there was only one item on the agenda, and that *synodoi* employed voting by individuals (a point made by J. L. O'Neil in an unpublished Cambridge thesis). What word *populi* will have translated is not clear; perhaps πόλεις or even δῆμοι (cf. xxx.32.9, though the emended ὑμετέροις makes this parallel a little dubious).

[61] Livy xxxii.22.8. [62] *Ibid.* xxxii.23.1.
[63] *Ibid.* xxxviii.32.1. [64] *Ibid.* xxxiii.2.6.
[65] *Ibid.* xxxiii.16.3. [66] *Op. cit.* (n. 7) 38 n. 31.

[66a] It could be argued that voting units were a Roman concept; but Rome offers no parallel for a body in which voting is by cities or peoples.

if he did, he did it pretty consistently and in a wide variety of passages. The evidence may be indecisive, but it suggests that voting in federal bodies – or in some federal bodies – was by cities; and many scholars in fact ‖ believe that this was the method used.[66b] However, as I have said, this is not an issue that is decisive one way or the other for the constitutional position of the cities.

It is far more important to ascertain the powers of the cities to manage their own affairs independently of the government. In 1912 Swoboda published a long article analysing the powers of the Achaean cities,[67] and since then inscriptions[68] have made more evidence available – not all of which Giovannini has used. Swoboda's material will not always support the conclusions he drew from it, but it provides a clear indication that the cities of Achaea enjoyed considerable independence in spheres which may not necessarily in each instance be definable as 'political', but which were of vital importance to the Greeks living in them. Thus in the third century we find Dyme[69] granting its citizenship to groups of foreigners; and in the early second century Stymphalus grants its citizenship to refugees from Elatea and sends embassies to the Achaean Confederation (to which it belonged) on their behalf.[69a] The federal government may have given its approval,[70] but there is no evidence of that. The cities had their own laws, and their own judicial sanctions, involving fines, imprisonment, banishment or execution; there is some evidence that the federal government interested itself in sentences of banishment, but none of a general right of appeal from the city courts.[71] Furthermore the cities retained a substantial degree of ‖ variety in their constitutions.[71a] Megara, for example,[72] continued to have a 'king' (*basileus*) as eponymous magistrate, whereas Argos had a general (*strategos*),[73] along with an assembly called the ἁλιαία,[74] found also at Epidaurus.[75] The existence of 'law-writers',

---

[66b] It is the usual view; cf. A. Aymard, *Les assemblées de la confédération achaienne* (Bordeaux, 1938) 377ff.; Larsen, *op. cit.* (n. 6) 230; and other authorities quoted by Giovannini, *op. cit.* (n. 7) 37 n. 31. For a possible compromise, which would deal with Giovannini's objection that voting by cities was a long and clumsy procedure see above, n. 60.

[67] *Klio* 12 (1912) 17–50.   [68] See for instance Larsen, *CP* 66 (1971) 81–6.

[69] *SIG* 531.   [69a] *SEG* 11.1107.

[70] As was the case when Naupactus in Aetolia granted citizenship to Ceos (*SIG* 522). Giovannini, *op. cit.* (n. 7) 40, argues that in many instances what looks like an action taken on the independent responsibility of a city may have had the backing of the central government or may even have been instigated by it.

[71] Cf. Swoboda, *Klio* 12 (1912) 28–9, quoting Polyb. iv.17.6ff., for Achaean intervention in a matter concerning exiles at Cynaetha; however, there is no evidence in this passage that the Achaean authorities had any *right* to intervene.

[71a] This is true also of Aetolia. The chief magistrates in the Aetolian cities were usually *archontes*, but Naupactus had a board of *theoroi*; for references see J. Touloumakos, *Der Einfluss Roms auf die Staatsform der griechischen Stadtstaaten des Festlandes und der Inseln im ersten und zweiten Jhdt.v.Chr.* (Göttingen, 1967) 34 n. 4, 35 nn. 1–2.

[72] See the inscription republished by L. Robert, *RPh* 13 (1939) 107–8 with commentary; the article is reprinted in *Opera minora selecta* (Amsterdam, 1969–) 2.1250–75.

[73] For the Argive *strategia* see Plut. *Arat.* 44; *SEG* 14.255; *IG* 4.357, l. 9.

[74] For the ἁλιαία in Argos cf. *IG* 4.557, l. 1; also *IG* 4.479, l. 1 (from Nemea), and 497, l. 2 (from Mycenae = *SIG* 594); cf. Swoboda, *Klio* 12 (1912) 37 n. 6.

[75] *IG* 4² 1.60.

nomographoi,[76] in many cities also underlines their powers to make their own laws.

A long treaty between two Achaean cities, Aegeira and Stymphalus,[77] dating to the late third century, makes no reference to the federal body to which both belonged. The two cities negotiate details for the management of law-suits involving citizens of both, virtually as if they were independent states. The same document also throws light on the question of citizenship, since it lays down that certain citizens of Ceryneia, another Achaean city, who are for some unmentioned reason resident in Stymphalus, shall be treated for the purpose of the arrangements made with Aegeira as if they were citizens of Stymphalus. This, as Larsen has pointed out,[78] confirms the picture given by an inscription of Epidaurus,[79] a casualty list of 146, which shows more than half of the fallen to be non-Epidaurians. These casualties are apparently Achaeans from other cities permanently resident in Epidaurus, yet not citizens of that city – and this fact, like the treaty between Stymphalus and Aegeira, shows that in Achaea, far from citizenship being universal or interchangeable between city and city, there was not even the kind of reciprocal arrangement implied by *isopoliteia*, which we find enjoyed in cities in and connected with Aetolia.[80] ‖

Taken together this evidence suggests that the cities of Achaea had a considerable sphere of activity in which they exercised both theoretical and practical independence. Similarly, the vast network of inter-city intercourse, to which I have already drawn attention, implies the possession of real powers by the cities. Quite apart from the voting of honorific titles and similar gestures of slight import, we find cities settling frontier disputes – such as that between the Acarnanian town of Stratus and the Aetolian town of Agrinium,[81] or arbitrating on differences like those between the Achaean town of Pagae and the Boeotian town of Aegosthena.[82] Cities negotiate with outside powers for loans and subventions: Cytenium, a Doric city of the Aetolian federation, for instance, collects from various other cities and rulers to finance the rebuilding of its walls, going as far abroad as Xanthus in Lycia, with which it claims distant relations of kinship.[83] True, a letter from the Aetolians went in support; but Cytenium was acting like any Greek city in sending out such an embassy. So too was Megalopolis when, with Achaean approval, she dispatched envoys to Antigonus Doson, the king of Macedon, to sound him about the possibility of his helping the federation against Cleomenes of Sparta, a mission of great delicacy;[84] and we have already seen Lycian Araxa sending an embassy to the

---

[76] See Swoboda, *Klio* 12 (1912) 27 n. 2, for evidence from Sicyon, Troezen, Hermione, Megalopolis, Tegea.

[77] *SVA* 3.567 (not mentioned by Giovannini); on this see Larsen, *CP* 66 (1971) 81–4.

[78] *Ibid.* 83–4.

[79] *IG* 4².1.28.   [80] See above, nn. 28–30.

[81] *IG* 9².1.3A.

[82] See the inscription quoted in n. 72 above.

[83] For the unpublished inscription see M. J. Mellink, *AJA* 70 (1966) 155.

[84] Polyb. II.48.6–8.

town of Cibyra.[85] A treaty made in 196 between the cities of Miletus and Magnesia contains the names of several ambassadors who were involved in the settlement.[86] They included Damoxenus from the *koinon* of the Achaeans, and others from Megalopolis, Patrae and another Achaean city, the name of which can no longer be read. It is interesting to find the *koinon* and the separate cities acting alongside each other in a matter which, since it involved a treaty, was clearly of some political substance. Of course, the federal body usually exercised ‖ overriding control over the cities, or tried to.[87] But this does not alter the fact that the cities of a Greek federation give every appearance of enjoying, on the international stage, a far greater degree of independence, and of exercising a much higher degree of political and even military autonomy than the units making up a modern federal state; it is a situation which is not at all easily reconciled with the definition of the central body as a unitary state.

IV

We may now turn to the suggested resemblance between federal states and a monarchy such as Macedonia, with its Greek cities, some of which were originally colonies and others royal foundations. There is of course a difference between the two categories, but in practice both, like many Hellenistic foundations, were alike controlled by the king through his officials. It is this fact that seems to me to invalidate the comparison, for there is surely all the difference in the world in reality between a city dominated (or founded and dominated) by a king, and a free city which has voluntarily joined a federal state, as Megalopolis or Argos joined Achaea. What Macedon and the federal *ethne* have in common is perhaps an origin in tribal conditions. In the *Politics*, Aristotle remarked[88] that an *ethnos* can have a king, and Epirus down to 232 furnishes an example of an organisation with a king at its head, which should probably be described as an alliance, yet clearly possesses many of the characteristics of a federation.[89] But the comparison carries no implications for the federal cities, and it ignores the capacity of a federation to absorb cities more or less with their consent and without the implications of conquest or injury to the identity of the new member. ‖ Megara could leave Achaea (in special circumstances) to join Boeotia and several years later return to Achaea; throughout these manoeuvres it remained undoubtedly, in its own consciousness, Megara, a free Greek city.

[85] See above, n. 42.   [86] *SIG* 588.

[87] See Giovannini, *op. cit.* (n. 7) 76ff. On the control of the cities of Macedonia by the king see Bengtson, *Historia* 4 (1955) 462–3. Here Bengtson seeks, on the basis of the phraseology used, to divide the cities granting asylia to the Asclepieum at Cos in 242 into two groups, one containing Cassandreia and Philippi, the other Amphipolis and Pella; but his argument is invalidated by the fact that Amphipolis (line 31) uses the phrase καθάπερ καὶ ὁ βασιλεὺς ᾿Αντίγονος προαιρεῖται, just like Philippi.

[88] *Pol.* iii.14, 1285 b 31 f.

[89] See N. G. L. Hammond, *Epirus* (Oxford, 1967) 557ff., and P. R. Franke, *Alt-Epirus und das Königtum der Molosser* (Kallmünz-Opf., 1954) 30f.

The further suggestion that federal cities are simply comparable to demes in an ordinary *polis* is ingenious but cannot, I think, be taken very seriously. It is true that an Achaean calls himself 'an Achaean from Aegium' or whatever city he hails from, and that an Athenian mentions his deme on official occasions within the city. But if the Achaean mentions Aegium because it is only the city that constitutes a real vehicle of Greek culture – I do not myself believe that, but it is Giovannini's view[90] – that is certainly not why the Athenian mentions his deme. Moreover, cities in federal states also possessed demes. Each of the twelve cities of Achaea consisted of seven or eight demes, out of which they were originally constituted (though at what date the synoecism took place we do not know).[91] In this they are precisely like cities without federal connections; and that fact militates against a facile comparison of demes to cities, since if demes provide Athens with a two-tier structure, demes and cities must provide Achaea (and doubtless other federal states) with a three-tier structure. Demes in fact are a normal feature of Greek cities and must be regarded as irrelevant to the question of whether federal cities are real *poleis* or not. In view of this it seems to me that the fact that Cos makes financial arrangements with one of its demes provides no real parallel to the treaty between Acarnania and its constituent city of Anactorium.[92] Equally unconvincing, I suggest, is the argument that the vast network of activity between cities, much of it – though by no means all – non-political, exists only because the cities are the sole and essential instruments of Greek social life.[93] For this is simply not so, and I will quote one or two examples to prove it. An inscription from Aegium,[94] dating to the 220s, contains an ‖ Achaean decree honouring Phocian and Boeotian hostages, who had been lodged in Achaea, awarding them *proxenia* – an honorary position as foreign representative of Achaea – freedom from taxation, freedom from plunder and several other honours normally included in such grants. The recipients' cities are mentioned, but it is the Achaean federal body that confers the honour. Elsewhere the reverse situation can be found. In 276, to celebrate the preservation of Delphi from the Galatians, the city of Chios passed a decree[95] praising the Aetolian *koinon* and crowning it with a golden crown for its services to the gods and its successful efforts against the barbarians; the same decree approves the recognition of the Aetolian festival of the *Soteria*, commemorating those events, and the appointment of sacred delegates (*theoroi*) to it. There is no question here of a *koinon* not being a 'living community' for purposes of Greek intercourse! From 197 onwards we have a list of Delphic *proxenoi*, representatives abroad, a document of importance for Delphic chronology.[96] These *proxenoi* are usually given the names of their cities; but under the year 194/3 we find several Acarnanians not further

---

[90] *Op. cit.* (n. 7) 87.

[91] *Cf.* Strabo, VIII.3.1, C 337, for the demes of Patrae and for seven or eight demes in each of the other Achaean cities; see Freeman, *op. cit.* (n. 5) 192–3; Ernst Meyer, *RE*, 18.4 (1949) 'Patrai', cols. 2203–4.

[92] See above, nn. 49–50.

[93] See above, n. 52.

[94] *SIG* 519.

[95] *Ibid.* 402.

[96] *Ibid.* 585.

distinguished: clearly it was not essential to name a man's city any more than it was a hundred years earlier when Delphic *proxenia*[97] was accorded to several Aetolians (not further qualified). This list of examples could easily be extended; and indeed Giovannini is himself elsewhere[98] perfectly aware that the *koinon* of a federal state can give and receive honours. Since so much of Greek life within a federal state (as elsewhere) was lived within the confines of a city, it is natural that much of the social and political intercourse was at the city level. But the examples I have quoted show that the distinction between cities as 'living Greek communities' and federal states, *ethne*, as a kind of political machinery, is quite artificial and not borne out in real life. Equally untrue is the hypothesis that the units making up a federal state had to be cities because only cities could act as vehicles of social and cultural exchange. It is contradicted by the situation in the ‖ Molossian *ethnos*, the lineal precursor of the Epirote federal state, which developed out of the Epirote alliance; which in turn arose as the Molossians absorbed other tribes, the Thesprotians and later the Chaonians, towards the end of the fourth century.[99] Now the units of the Molossian *ethnos*, like those of the Epirote Federation (which was formed in 232),[100] were not cities but tribal sub-divisions; and it is by means of these tribal sub-divisions that Molossians and Epirotes describe themselves or are described on extant inscriptions. Yet no one has questioned the Greekness of Epirus (whatever the ultimate racial origins of its people, which may well have contained Illyrian elements). Towards the end of the third century Epirus was one of the federations included in Antigonus Doson's Hellenic Alliance.[101] Yet an Epirote usually mentioned not his city (if he had one) but his tribe or sub-tribe; and others referred to him in the same way. A third-century inscription from Epidaurus records fines of 1,000 staters imposed upon unruly athletes for brawling at the festival of Asclepius. Two of these are Philistus the son of Callisthenes, an Argive from Achaea,[102] a contestant in the pentathlon, and Simacus the son of Phalacrion, an Epirote from the Thesproti, a pancratiast. In this context of games at a panhellenic festival both men are unquestionably Greeks; yet the Epirote is described by tribe, not by city. There

[97] *Ibid.* 383; Giovannini, *op. cit.* (n. 7) 36 n. 21, admits that the name of the city was often omitted – which is odd if it is only through the city that one's Greekness is made evident.

[98] *Op. cit.* (n. 7) 19.

[99] Giovannini, *op. cit.* (n. 7) 11 n. 7, 'der epeirotische Bund [ist] der direkte Nachfolger des vom Stamm der Molosser gebildeten Staates'.

[100] See Giovannini, *op. cit.* (n. 7) 94–8, and independently Hammond, *op. cit.* (n. 89) 528ff. The same is true of the Epirote Federation; *cf. GDI* 1339, a resolution of the Epirotes, in which everyone mentioned appends his tribal ethnic (Hammond, *op. cit.* (n. 89) 653 quoting further evidence). For the same practice among the Chaonians and Thesprotians see Habicht, *Arch. class.* 25–6 (1973–4) 316 and n. 20.   [101] *Cf.* Polyb. IV.9.4.

[102] *Cf. SIG* 1076. The phrase Φίλιστος Καλλισθένους Ἀργεῖος ἀπ' Ἀχαίας, instead of the usual Ἀχαιὸς ἀπ' (or ἐξ) Ἄργους. Hiller von Gaertringen in *SIG* 1076 suggests that Achaea is 'oppidulum...ignotum agri Argivi'; but no such *oppidulum* is known, nor is it clear why the authorities at Epidaurus should have chosen to specify from what hamlet in Argive territory Philistus came. Perhaps the meaning is 'an Argive, *i.e.* from Achaean (rather than Amphilochian) Argos'. But one's impression is that the unusual order is not a matter of any consequence.

could hardly be a clearer indication that one need not belong to a *polis* to be a Greek.

To sum up my argument, it seems to me that the theory that a Greek federal state was really a unitary state, in which the cities are merely ‖ vehicles of social intercourse and the *ethnos* is the sole political body,[103] arrogating complete political power to itself, breaks down, and for these reasons:

1. The cities, as I have shown, were by no means powerless, but were substantially concerned in a wide range of activities, some clearly political, in which the city exercised real sovereignty.

2. The position of cities within a federal body was not substantially different from that of cities elsewhere, for they too were exposed to the erosion or loss of their independence, and that not through voluntary action, but more often by force; but despite subjection these cities maintained a consciousness of their identity as separate bodies. Similarly, it is *prima facie* absurd to suppose that cities like Argos, Corinth, Sicyon and Megara surrendered their political identity and felt themselves to be diminished because they had joined the Achaean Federation.

3. The supposed parallel between cities in a federal state and demes in an independent city is superficial and unconvincing. In fact federal cities themselves possess demes, and in this as in other respects are comparable to Greek cities elsewhere. Nor is the suggested parallel between federal cities and cities inside a Hellenistic monarchy a significant one.

4. The definition of federal cities as 'cultural units', indispensable for Greek life but without political power, breaks down because on the one hand cities and *ethne* are found engaging, side by side, in identical cultural and political activities, and on the other hand it is quite possible to be a Greek within the Molossian or Epirote *ethnos* without, apparently, belonging to a city at all.

V

We must therefore reject this new theory, which involves drawing an artificial distinction between one kind of *polis* and another, which a ‖ Greek would have found it hard to comprehend. On the other hand, perhaps we ought not to try to force Greek federal states into a category defined in the light of institutions which originated two thousand years later. As we saw, the absence of words meaning 'federal state' and nothing else need not imply that the institution itself did not exist. Aristotle's political thought was deeply rooted in the experience of the *polis*. Yet in his late collection of constitutions,[104] he included Arcadia, Thessaly, and probably Lycia, Achaea and Epirus. Such states were not *poleis* – though, as Larsen has pointed out,[105] there was a short

---

[103] A point worth noting is that Polybius (II.37.11) remarks that under the Achaean Federation the Peloponnese 'falls short of being a single city in the fact that its inhabitants do not possess a single fortified refuge (περίβολος), all other things both as regards the whole and as regards each city being very nearly similar'. Here Polybius is stressing the concord existing in Achaea and making a rhetorical point rather than delivering a juridical statement. Even so, his remark concedes that Achaea merely *resembles* a unitary state.

[104] See Weil, *op. cit.* (n. 13) 309, 383, for the evidence.　　　　[105] *Op. cit.* (n. 6) 280 n. 3.

period in the fourth century when it looked as if the word *polis* was about to be extended to cover federal bodies; and indeed the word *politai* was commonly used to refer to their citizens.[106] Neither were such states identical with primitive *ethne* where the people lived in villages (though villages will have continued to exist, no doubt, just as the tribal divisions persisted in Epirus). There was in fact development, and that is why one has to discuss Greek federal states historically as well as analytically.

It is true that we are not always able in every case to declare how far city rights were held autonomously, how far they were conceded by the central power, and how far they were exercised *de facto* either by tradition or to meet the current situation without any real definition of the constitutional issue. The situation may have varied from one federal body to another. Swoboda assumed[107] that federations had a written constitution. Polybius does indeed refer to 'the oaths, laws and inscribed pillars which hold together our common federation *(sympoliteia)*';[108] but we do not know how far these defined the points that interest us. We hear of the 'agreement', *homologia*, when a new state entered the federation;[109] but the treaty between Orchomenus and the Achaean Federation which mentions this is mainly concerned with the regulation of immediate problems and not with general constitutional principles.[110] In fact, we are not in a position to define the juridical basis of the rights ‖ of *koinon* and *polis* in each case; but those rights were none the less real and none the less independently exercised from time to time, as I hope to have shown. It is not the first nor the only example of a political institution which is fully operative for a considerable time before political theorists get round to telling us what it is.

The federal states made a valuable contribution to the political life of the Greek world, especially in the Hellenistic period. They developed out of the older *ethne* in a way which we cannot always trace in detail, and were based primarily on peoples conscious of a tribal or ethnic unity; but by incorporating other cities of different ethnic origins, they came to represent something quite new. At a time when large territorial kingdoms were dominating the political scene, they enabled small and weak states to play a significant role. For that reason they merit the place which Freeman and Larsen assigned to them in the history of federalism, and their exclusion would be an unnecessary impoverishment of that history.

---

[106] *Ibid.* 85 n. 4.   [107] *Klio* 12 (1912) 23.
[108] Polyb. xxiv.8.4.   [109] *SIG* 490, line 9.
[110] So correctly Giovannini, *op. cit.* (n. 7) 33.

3

THE ACCESSION OF PTOLEMY EPIPHANES: A PROBLEM IN CHRONOLOGY*

Writing in 1930,[1] Holleaux had to admit that 'the true date of Philopator's death remains a mystery'; one reason why this is still true today is that hitherto no historian has taken into account the evidence of the demotic papyri in considering this problem. Since, in his *Archons of Athens in the Hellenistic age* (Cambridge, Mass., 1931),[2] Dinsmoor has now furnished new calculations, it seems worth while to reconsider the whole of the evidence, both demotic[3] and Greek, and to attempt a solution of this ancient crux.

Such evidence as we have is not consistent. According to the Canon of the Kings, contained in Ptolemaeus' *Almagest*, Philopator died in the year 544 of the era of Nabonassar of Babylon (reckoned from 27 February 747). Making the necessary adjustment to the Julian calendar, we find that this is the year 13 October 205–12 October 204. Actually the Canon gives this as the first year of Epiphanes' reign. But it is the custom of the compiler to ignore fractions of a year at the end of a reign; thus a king's first year was that in which he came to the throne, his last was his last full year.[4] If, then, the Canon is reliable, Epiphanes ascended the throne some time during the year 13 October 205–12 October 204; and this date is confirmed by the evidence of the Rosetta Stone,[5] a decree dated Xandikos 4 (Macedonian) = Mecheir 18 (Egyptian) of Epiphanes' ninth year, a date which has universally been equated with 27 March (Julian).[6] This decree was enacted to commemorate the Anacleteria, or Coming of Age ceremony, of Epiphanes, which had taken place most probably[7] on the previous Phaophi 17, which was the anniversary of the date ἐν ἧι παρέλαβεν τὴν βασιλείαν παρὰ τοῦ πατρός (l. 47), and is to be equated

* [*JEA* 22 (1936) 20–34]

[1] In *CAH* 8 (1930) 149 n. 1.

[2] Appendix G, 471ff.

[3] I would take this opportunity of expressing my very warmest thanks to Mr T. C. Skeat, of the British Museum, who has given me invaluable help in the collecting of this evidence.

[4] See K. J. Beloch, *Griechische Geschichte* 4.2 (Berlin–Leipzig, 1927) 166; W. Kubitschek, *Grundriss der antiken Zeitrechnung* (Munich, 1928) 61.

[5] *OGIS* 90; translated by E. Bevan, *History of Egypt under the Ptolemaic dynasty* (London, 1927) 263ff.

[6] Except by M. Holleaux, *CAH* 8 (1930) 188, who makes it 28 March.

[7] This is the generally accepted view (*cf.* Holleaux, *loc. cit*); it is based on the position of the description of the Anacleteria in Polybius (xviii.55; see below, p. 39), and also on the fact that the Rosetta inscription refers to the crowning of Epiphanes as an event occurring some time previously.

with 26 November for the year of the Anacleteria, whether this was in fact in 197 or 196.[8] Actually this date is not legible upon ‖ the Rosetta Stone, but is confirmed by a hieroglyphic inscription of fourteen years later, the Damanhûr Stele, set up to celebrate a *sed*-festival, or repetition of the Anacleteria ceremony, in Epiphanes' twenty-third year.[9] The year in which the Anacleteria took place, and that in which the Rosetta Decree was enacted have been much disputed, but this problem now appears to have been solved by Dinsmoor, who shows (*Archons* 492) that at the end of the third and beginning of the second centuries the Macedonian calendar in Egypt still approximated closely to the Attic lunar calendar. In 196 there was a new moon on 22 March and if the Rosetta Decree was enacted in that year, Xandikos 1 fell upon 24 March. In neither 197 nor 195 does a new moon occur at anything approaching this date. It can therefore be taken as certain that the Anacleteria of Epiphanes was towards the end of 197, probably on 26 November and that it was commemorated by the Rosetta inscription of 27 March 196. True, this deduction appears to ignore an important piece of evidence from the Tebtunis papyri,[10] a synchronism from Year 4 of Epiphanes, in which the Macedonian and Egyptian calendars already seem to be equated on the basis of Thoth 1 = Dystros 1. But the only safe deduction from this papyrus is[11] that for the years 4 to 9 of Epiphanes, both a revised and a normal Macedonian calendar were in existence. Where, as in the Rosetta inscription the latter is employed, there seems no reason to doubt that it was still running true to the moon. Dinsmoor's claim thus appears to be justified; and it is clear that an Anacleteria in 197, early in Epiphanes' ninth year,[12] implies that his first year was reckoned as 205/4. Indeed, if one is prepared to follow the majority of historians in regarding Phaophi 17 as the date of Epiphanes'

[8] See W. B. Dinsmoor, *Archons*, 479; G. De Sanctis, *Storia dei Romani* 4.1 (Turin, 1923) 128, puts it on 28 November, forgetting that the Egyptian calendar gained one day on the Julian in every four years. Ernst Meyer, *Untersuchungen zur Chronologie der ersten Ptolemäer auf Grund der Papyri* (2. Beiheft zum *APF*, Leipzig, 1925) 39ff., has a theory that the anniversary of Epiphanes' accession (for like most scholars he refers Phaophi 17 to this event) was celebrated in both the Egyptian and Macedonian calendars, in the former by the priests, in the latter nationally. According to him, Epiphanes ascended the throne on Phaophi 17, 203, which was the end of Dystros by the Macedonian calendar; owing to the divergence between the two calendars, the end of Dystros had, by 197 or 196, become equivalent to the second week in Mecheir. Therefore the national anniversary, with the Anacleteria, was a few days before Mecheir 18 = Xandikos 4, when the actual decree was enacted; the priests would celebrate it as usual on Phaophi 17. But Dinsmoor, *Archons*, 488, demonstrates that Epiphanes, and probably Philopator, both reckoned their accession by the Egyptian date, and this is the natural inference from the mention of Phaophi 17, without any Macedonian equivalent, on the Damanhûr stele. Furthermore, the Rosetta Decree itself suggests a greater period of time between the Anacleteria and the enactment of the decree than Meyer allows. This theory is therefore to be rejected. (*Cf.* Beloch, *op. cit.* (n. 4) 4.2.176.)

[9] *Cf.* Bevan, *op. cit.* (n. 5) 267 n. 2.

[10] *P. Tebt.* 3.1, no. 820. μηνὸς Αὐδναίου Αἰγυπτίων δὲ Ἐπεὶφ [πε]ντεκαιδεκάτηι.

[11] *Cf.* Grenfell and Hunt, *P. Hib.* p. 348.

[12] The text of the Rosetta Decree refers to a remission of taxes up to and including the eighth year (ἕως τοῦ ὀγδόου ἔτους—l. 29), made in connection with the Anacleteria ceremony at Memphis.

accession, this event can be narrowed down to 28 November 205; how far this identification is justified will be considered later.

In favour of this dating is the fact that the Anacleteria is described in Book xviii of Polybius,[13] a book which gives the events of Olympiad 145.4, *i.e.* 197/6. De Sanctis,[14] and Holleaux,[15] who oppose the dating to suit their own theories of the accession, place the Anacleteria in November 196, and the enactment of the Rosetta Decree in March 195, and consequently have to assume that Polybius extended this book to include events as late as the November following the summer in which the Olympiad year actually finished. Admittedly, Polybius' Olympiad year was not rigid; De Sanctis has rightly shown[16] that it normally ended with the campaigning season, and could be extended to include events even later than that when they were closely connected with other events inside the Olympiad. But the Anacleteria is related in Polybius in connection with the revolt of Scopas, which is itself in September or October,[17] and so is outside those limits. And in any case the evidence of the full moon is against this view.

Additional support for 205 as the date of Epiphanes' accession comes from the evidence ‖ relating to his birth. From the Rosetta Decree it is known that Epiphanes was born on Mesore 30, but no indication of the year is given. There is, however, evidence from a papyrus[18] that Philopator, following the custom of earlier Ptolemies, had elevated his infant son to a share in the throne by Pharmouthi 25 of 'the year thirteen'. Unfortunately it is not known what kind of year is referred to, but in view of the fact that an Egyptian month is mentioned, it is probably safe to rule out the Macedonian calendar. Now the three possibilities[19] on the basis of the Egyptian year are:

(a)   13th fiscal year, beginning Mecheir 1, *i.e.* 14 March 210.
(b)   13th Egyptian year, beginning Thoth 1, *i.e.* 15 October 210.
(c)   13th regnal year, beginning unknown; perhaps September 210.[20]

In relation to these three datings Pharmouthi 25 would give us (a) 6 June 210,

---

[13]   Polyb. xviii.55.

[14]   *Op. cit.* (n. 8) 4.1.128 n. 41.

[15]   *REA* 15 (1913) 9 n. 3; *CAH* 8.149 n. 2, 188.

[16]   *Op. cit.* (n. 8) 3.1.219ff. *Cronologia polibiana.*

[17]   Holleaux, *REA* 15 (1913) 9 n. 3. Holleaux's assumption, however, that the rumour of Epiphanes' death, which broke up the conference of Lysimacheia in 196 (Livy xxxiii.41.1), is to be connected with the revolt of Scopas, is quite arbitrary and unsupported by any evidence; Scullard, *History of the Roman world from 753 to 146* (London, 1935) 271, adopts the same view.

[18]   *P. Gurob* 12; *cf.* Wilcken, *APF* 7 (1924) 71. It may be observed that there is no evidence for H. Gauthier's improbable suggestion (*Le livre des rois d'Égypte* (5 vols., Cairo, 1907–17) 4.267) that Philopator actually abdicated his authority in favour of his infant son, and that this abdication led to the revolt in Upper Egypt.

[19]   I have taken these calculations from Dinsmoor, *Archons*, 479.

[20]   *Ibid.* 488; for our present purpose it is sufficient to observe that the regnal year is unlikely to have begun *more* than twelve months after the fiscal year. In any case the Egyptian year is probably indicated: certainly by the third year of Epiphanes the Egyptian year, beginning with Thoth 1, was being employed even by Greek officials; *cf. P. Petrie* 3. 57b, where Thoth of Year 4 comes almost immediately after Epeiph of Year 3.

(b) 6 June 209, (c) probably 6 June 209; the year *may* be 210, but not, in view of the date when the fiscal year begins, 208. Thus we may assume that Epiphanes was born before June 209; the 30th of Mesore previous to this works out as 9 October 210,[21] and we may provisionally accept this as the date of Epiphanes' birth.

Now Justinus has a statement[22] that Philopator died leaving a son five years old; according to Hieronymus[23] the son was only four. From Epiphanes' birth on 9 October 210 to a (provisionally accepted) accession on 28 November 205 is nearly five years two months, a figure which fits Justinus, but is hard to reconcile with Hieronymus; however, Hieronymus is notoriously unreliable, and this very passage contains further chronological inconsistencies. For Hieronymus states that Antiochus 'filiam suam Cleopatram per Euclen Rhodium septimo anno regni adulescentis despondit Ptolomaeo, et tertio-decimo anno tradidit'. O. Leuze[24] has pointed out that from Livy,[25] who is here following Polybius, we know that this marriage did in fact take place in the winter of 194/3,[26] which is only the eleventh year of Epiphanes' reign, reckoning from autumn 205, the outside limit. Similarly the evidence is against the statement that the betrothal to Cleopatra was in the seventh year.[27] Polybius,[28] and Livy following him,[29] both give the reply of Antiochus to the Roman envoys at Lysimacheia in 196; in this reply τὰ δὲ πρὸς Πτολεμαῖον αὐτὸς ἔφη διεξάξειν εὐδοκουμένως ἐκείνῳ· κρίνειν γὰρ οὐ φιλίαν μόνον, ἀλλὰ καὶ μετὰ τῆς φιλίας ἀναγκαιότητα συντίθεσθαι πρὸς αὐτόν. This suggestion of a betrothal in autumn–winter 196 receives apparent support in the statement in the *Chronicon ‖ Paschale* that it took place during the consulship of Purpurio and Marcellus, *i.e.* 196;[30] but this support is in fact illusory, for, as Leuze demonstrates,[31] the *Chronicon* is based on a series of faulty synchronisms between Egyptian royal years, Olympiads and Roman consul-years, and is thus quite worthless. Hieronymus must therefore stand alone; and at first sight his *septimo anno*, with its implication of an accession in 203, appears to be an obvious error. However, in view of the fact that there is other strong evidence pointing to 203, it may be observed that Bevan regards this particular passage as trustworthy[32] because of the reference to Eucles of Rhodes: 'Jerome seems to

---

[21] This is contrary to the views of Bevan, *op. cit.* (n. 5) 236, and Letronne, *OGIS* 90, who make the year 209, and the day 8 and 9 October respectively.

[22] Just. xxx.2.6.   [23] Hieron. *In Daniel.* xi.13–14.

[24] *Hermes* 58 (1923), 221–9.   [25] Livy xxxv.13.4.

[26] Incorrectly given as 193–192 by B. Niese, *Geschichte der griechischen und makedonischen Staaten* (3 vols., Gotha, 1893–1903) 2.674.

[27] This date is a source of great confusion in both Bevan and Niese. Bevan places it in 196/5 (*op. cit.*, (n. 5) 269), which implies an accession in 202; whereas earlier he gives this as 203 (*ibid.* 250). Niese (*op. cit.* (n. 26) 2.639) puts the betrothal in 199/8, which means an accession in 205; but he, too, gives this elsewhere (*ibid.* 573) as taking place in 203.

[28] Polyb. xviii.51.10.

[29] Livy xxxiii.40. Livy's translation is 'id agere ut brevi etiam adfinitas iungatur'. The word *brevi* is merely inserted for rhetorical effect in Livy's usual manner, and is not to be pressed too closely. See K. Witte, *RhM* 65 (1910) 276ff.   [30] Livy xxxiii.24.

[31] *Op. cit.* (n. 24) 222 n. 1.   [32] *Op. cit.* (n. 5) 269 n. 3.

have some substantial source behind him, since he states that the Seleucid envoy was a certain Eucles of Rhodes.' The statement is certainly consistent with the well-known Seleucid habit of employing Rhodians,[33] and it may go back to a Rhodian source, such as Zeno or Antisthenes;[34] on the other hand Leuze makes out a good case[35] for believing that Hieronymus took his dates from Eusebius, and if this is so they merit scarcely any confidence whatever.

Of equal importance with the evidence relating to Epiphanes' birth is that which deals with his death. A number of documents have now been discovered which are dated to the twenty-fifth year of Epiphanes;[36] and since it is known that Epiphanes died in the year 181/80[37] – probably in or shortly after May 180 – it is easily calculated that by this date Epiphanes was regarded as having come to the throne before Thoth 1 (= 13 October) 204.[38] A series of documents with synchronisms between the years of the sacred bull Apis and the years of Epiphanes and Philometor[39] serves further to show that the same dating existed in the fourteenth year of Epiphanes; and, as we saw, it was confirmed for the ninth year by the Rosetta Stone. Demotic papyri, with protocols giving the full details of the eponymous priests, exist for the years 2, 3, 5, 7, and 8 of Epiphanes,[40] and the fourth year is covered by || two Greek papyri already

---

[33] For example, the Hagesandros referred to in certain Cretan inscriptions as working on behalf of Teos as Antiochus' agent; *cf.* Holleaux, *Klio* 13 (1913) 148 n. 3, who also quotes the case of the Rhodian Menelaus, son of Menecrates, referred to as a φίλος τοῦ βασιλέως 'Αντιόχου in an inscription of Calymna (*OGIS* 243).

[34] *Cf.* Polyb. xvi.14ff.

[35] *Op. cit.*, (n. 24) 224ff.

[36] *E.g.* O. Tait 96, dated Pharmouthi 16 = 20 May; R. Mond and O. H. Myers, *The Bucheum* 2. Inscriptions (London, 1934) no. 8, dated Pharmouthi 8 = 12 May.

[37] Polyb. xxiv.6; Diod. xxix.29; *cf.* Niese, *op. cit.* (n. 26) 3.91; Bevan, *CAH* 8.496.

[38] It is certain that by 181 all documents, Greek and demotic, were dated by the Egyptian calendar, according to which a king's first year was reckoned from his accession to the fifth epagomenal day following it, and his second and succeeding years from Thoth 1. The Macedonian months were now equated with the Egyptian (see above, n. 10).

[39] See H. Brugsch, *ZAeS* 22 (1884) 126ff.; H. Gauthier, *op. cit.* (n. 18) 4.278ff. Apis 'born of the cow Ta-Amon' was in its twentieth year in Year 14/15 of Epiphanes; it died in its twenty-fourth year, and was followed by Apis 'born of the cow Ta-Ranen', the first year of which = Epiphanes 19/20. Epiphanes' last year 24/5 thus corresponds to Year 6 of Apis (born of Ta-Ranen), and Philometor 1 = Apis (born of Ta-Ranen) 6/7; this is confirmed by the synchronism Philometor 8 = Year 13 of the same Apis.

[40] Year 2: *P. dem. Leiden* 373 b+c (Hathur), *P. dem. Cairo* 30753 (Hathur), *P. dem. Cairo* 30700 (Phamenoth). *P. dem. Cairo* 30697+30780 (Pauni).

Year 3: *P. dem. Cairo* 30689+30781+30782 (Hathur), *P. Berlin* (Greek) 11768 ('Αρτεμίσιος), *P. dem. Cairo* 30659 (Mecheir).

Year 5: *P. dem. New York Hist. Soc.* 373 a+b (Phaophi).

Year 7: *P. dem Louvre* 2435 (Hathur), *P. dem. Hincks* 2 a+b. (Tubi).

Year 8: *P. dem. Louvre* 2408 (Pharmouthi).

This evidence will be found in G. Plaumann, *RE* 8.2 (1913) 'Hiereis', cols. 1443–4; H. Gauthier, *op. cit.* (n. 18) 4.275ff.; H. Thompson's supplement to Plaumann's list in *Studies presented to F.Ll. Griffith* (London, 1922) 16–37; K. Sethe and J. Partsch, *Demotische Urkunden zum ägyptischen Bürgschaftsrecht* (*ASAW* 32 [1920]); W. Spiegelberg, *Die demotischen Papyrus* (Strasbourg, 1906–8). [Reference should now be made to P. W. Pestman, *Chronologie égyptienne d'après textes démotiques* (*P.L.Bat.15*) (Leiden, 1967); W. Clarysse and G. van der Veken, *The eponymous priests of Ptolemaic Egypt* (*P.L.Bat.24*) (Leiden, 1983).]

referred to;[41] further, it is highly probable that certain mutilated documents in the Cairo collection referred to Year 1 of Epiphanes, though none actually survives with that date legible.[42] Thus a series of documents covering the whole reign of Epiphanes, with the exception of Year 6, appears to support the theory of an accession in the course of the year 205/4.

There is, however, one significant exception. A demotic inscription in Berlin, published by Stern in 1884,[43] gives the details of the life of a priest named Khaᶜḥap, who was born in Year 11, Phamenoth 14 of one Ptolemy, and died in Year 2, Tybi 4 of another, aged 69 years, 9 months, 20 days. Stern shows that the Ptolemies in question can only be Philadelphus and Epiphanes respectively; but his calculations may no longer be considered valid, since he regarded Philadelphus as dying in his thirty-eighth year, whereas in fact he lived until Choiak of his thirty-ninth.[44] Now it is known from a Bucheum inscription[45] that as late as Philadelphus' thirteenth year his reign was being reckoned from Soter's death, though later it was ante-dated to his association on the throne with Soter. Hence Thoth 1 of Year 12 is probably 30 October 272 (not 274); and sixty-nine complete years from this brings us to Thoth 1, 203 (13 October), which should therefore be the first day of Epiphanes' *second* year. If the inscription is reckoning Philadelphus' years from his co-regency, one obtains the impossible result that Epiphanes' second year began on 13 October 205; the date from Soter's death is thus plainly preferable. But even so, it does violence to the tradition of an accession in 205/4, which is apparently supported by the rest of the archaeological evidence.

It may be convenient at this point to deal with the evidence of Eusebius' Chronicle; for an oversight of this co-regency of Soter and Philadelphus has caused a permanent error in his dates.[46] According to Eusebius, Epiphanes' accession was in 203/2 (translation of Hieronymus) or 202/1 (Armenian version). The Armenian version is normally the less reliable,[47] but neither is evidence fit to base an argument upon. For our present purpose Eusebius is better ignored.

The main obstacle to placing Epiphanes' accession in November 205 is Polybius xv.25ff. This passage, consisting largely of a fragment found in the Escorial, but also supported by other fragments from the Excerptae Valesianae and the Codex Urbinas, gives a detailed account of the accession of Epiphanes, and of the regency and downfall of Agathocles. Its position in Book xv has

[41] *P. Petrie* 3.57b and *P. Tebt.* 3.1, no. 820; *cf.* also *P. Tebt.* 1.8.

[42] Sethe and Partsch, *op. cit.* (n. 40). The Rosetta inscription (*OGIS* 90) also points to the existence of a normal Year 1; see l. 16 μηθὲν πλεῖον διδῶσιν εἰς τὸ τελεστικὸν οὗ ἐτάσσοντο ἕως τοῦ πρώτου ἔτους ἐπὶ τοῦ πατρὸς αὐτοῦ, where the reference is almost certainly to the first year of Epiphanes.

[43] In *ZAeS* 22 (1884), 101ff.

[44] Beloch, *op. cit.* (n. 4) 4.2.171.

[45] Mond and Myres, *op. cit.* (n. 36) 2. Inscriptions no. 3, pp. 3, 28–9.

[46] Dinsmoor, *Archons*, 471; on the unreliability of Eusebius see Leuze, *op. cit.* (n. 24) 225–7.

[47] See R. Helm, *AAWB* 1923, vol. 4; Kubitschek, *op. cit.* (n. 4) 54.

never been seriously challenged,[48] and since the book retails the events of Olympiad 144.2, it would follow that the accession is to be dated 203/2. It should be observed that in the previous book Polybius had given an account of Egyptian events stretching over a long period (ἐκ πλείονος χρόνου πεποιήμεθα τὴν ἐξήγησιν),[49] the conclusion of which was a 'unified study of the character of Ptolemy Philopator' (σωματοειδῆ ποιήσας τὴν τοῦ βασιλέως προαίρεσιν);[50] whereas the other events contained in Book xiv belong to Olympiad 144.1, *i.e.* 204/3.[51] ‖

The assumption that Epiphanes' accession was in 203 is strikingly confirmed by the events following the agreement made by Philip V of Macedon and Antiochus III of Syria to plunder the possessions of the young king.[52] This agreement followed immediately upon the two kings' learning of Philopator's death.[53] Now it is a fact that Antiochus' invasion of Coele-Syria did not begin until 202,[54] and no hostile act against Egypt is recorded of Philip until his capture of Samos in spring 201.[55] Philip appears to have played a double game; and connected with this is the visit of Ptolemy, son of Sosibius, who was sent to Macedon by Agathocles soon after Epiphanes' succession,[56] and did not return to Egypt until after Agathocles' overthrow.[57] These facts are all consistent with an agreement between Philip and Antiochus in the winter of 203/2, and the accession of Epiphanes in 203. But they offer insuperable difficulties to the view that the accession was in 205; for in this case one has to assume either that Philip and Antiochus held their hands for three and two years respectively, or that (notwithstanding Polybius) the agreement was not made until two years after Philopator's death.

Further, there is the evidence relating to Scopas the Aetolian. The withdrawal of the Aetolians from the First Macedonian War by a separate peace in 206 had been followed by economic distress in Aetolia, and Scopas and Dorimachus were therefore appointed νομογράφοι to carry through legislation for the cancelling of debts, etc.[58] Using this as a handle, Scopas then tried to secure

[48] Holleaux, *REG* 13 (1900) 190, considered the possibility that the Escorial fragment came from Polyb. xiv. but rejected it in his later consideration of the passage.

[49] Polyb. xiv.12.

[50] Notable as an exception to Polybius' usual practice: *cf.* I. Bruns, *Die Persönlichkeit in de Geschichtsschreibung* (Berlin, 1898) 1–11, 84–100.

[51] *Cf.* Polyb. xiv.1a.5: οὐ τὰς ἐκ τῶν δυεῖν ἐτῶν πράξεις κατατετάχαμεν εἰς μίαν βύβλον.

[52] Polyb. iii.2.8, xv.20, xvi.1.9; App. *Mac.* 4; Just. xxx.2.8; Hieron. *In Daniel.* xi.13.

[53] According to Polyb. xv.20.1, they had previously offered him help – probably in the internal troubles referred to in Polyb. xiv.12.4.

[54] Polyb. xvi.22a; Just. xxxi.1; Hieron. *In Daniel.* xi.11ff.; Holleaux, *CAH* 8.151–2.

[55] See Holleaux, *REA* 22 (1920) 237ff., *CAH* 8.151; Bickermann, *RPh* 61 (1935) 162ff. Passerini, *Athenaeum* 9 (1931) 260, would put back the capture of Samos into 202, in accordance with his theory of an open break between Egypt and Macedon in winter 203/2; but he scarcely meets Holleaux's arguments in favour of 201, and in particular the evidence of Polyb. xvi.2.9: τὰς γὰρ ἐν τῇ Σάμῳ ναῦς οὐκ ἠδυνήθη καταρτίσαι πάσας. [56] Polyb. xv.25.13.

[57] Polyb. xvi.22.3. From Polyb. xv.24a and 25.19 it is clear that the account of the reception of this Ptolemy by Philip was contained in Book xv of Polybius, and therefore that it occurred during, or within the month or two following, the Olympiad year 203/2.

[58] Polyb. xiii.1–1a.

election to the generalship of Aetolia for the year 205/4, but failing in this went off to Alexandria;[59] he would thus reach Egypt in the autumn or winter of 205, and had at any rate time to obtain the king's favour, command over a considerable force of men, and a daily income of ten minae. This is not absolutely incompatible with the death of Philopator in 205, but it goes far more easily with a later date.

Finally, Justinus has the otherwise unrecorded tradition that the death of Philopator was *diu occultata* by the palace clique.[60]

Thus the evidence points three different ways. The mass of the demotic documents, the Rosetta and Damanhūr inscriptions, and Justinus' statement concerning Epiphanes' age ‖ when Philopator died, suggest that the death of Philopator and accession of Epiphanes occurred during the Egyptian year 205/4, possibly on 28 November 205; the Khaᶜḥap inscription, edited by Stern, supports an accession in 204/3 – on 28 November 204, if one accepts the usual equation with Phaophi 17; and finally the evidence of Polybius, with some support from the details relating to Scopas and the agreement between Philip and Antiochus, is in favour of an accession in the year 203/2 – 28 November 203, on the basis of the same equation. Hieronymus, Eusebius, and the *Chronicon Paschale* have been discarded as too unreliable. And finally we have Justinus' assumption of a gap between the death of Philopator and the accession of his son.

The attempts to solve the problem fall into four groups; in none has the demotic evidence been taken into account.

(a) *Philopator died and Epiphanes succeeded in November 203.* This view, which involves the rejection of the Canon, and is contradicted by Justinus and the Rosetta evidence, is that adopted by Ernst Meyer,[61] Bevan,[62] Wilhelm,[63] Welles,[64] Jouguet,[65] and Ferguson.[66] Of these Bevan is by no means consistent, for he places the Anacleteria in 197 and the Rosetta Decree in March 196, yet translates 'in the ninth year' without comment, though by his own reckoning it would be only the seventh.[67] Holleaux, in a series of comments on this

---

[59] Polyb. XIII.2.1: ὅτι Σκόπας Αἰτωλῶν στρατηγὸς ἀποτυχὼν τῆς ἀρχῆς, ἧς χάριν ἐτόλμα γράφειν τοὺς νόμους, μετέωρος ἦν εἰς τὴν Ἀλεξανδρείαν. This passage is translated by W. R. Paton in the Loeb edition 'when he fell from the office, by power of which he ventured to draft these laws'; I doubt, however, if χάριν can bear this sense, and prefer to take ἀρχή as the office of στρατηγός. There is support for this in an inscription (*SIG* 597B), which refers to a Λύκωπον Πολεμάρχου Καλυδώνιον as general of the Aetolians about 205–201. Pomtow (commenting on *SIG* 546A) puts Lycopus' office in 205/4, and this fits in remarkably well with the opposition Scopas received from Alexander of Calydon (Polyb. XIII.1a). Apparently Alexander was successful in getting his own candidate from Calydon elected against Scopas, who then went to try his fortunes in Egypt; *cf.* Lenschau, Bursian's *Jahresbericht* 54 (1928) 148; Holleaux, *CAH* 8.147; Passerini, *Athenaeum* 11 (1933) 319. [See also Walbank, *Historical commentary on Polybius* 2 (Oxford, 1967) 413–14 ad loc.]

[60] Just. XXX.2.6.

[61] *Op. cit.* (n. 8) 39ff.
[62] *Op. cit.* (n. 5) 250.
[63] *AAWW* 57 (1920) 40–57.
[64] *Royal correspondence of the Hellenistic age* (Newhaven, Conn., 1934) 167.
[65] *L'impérialisme macédonien et l'hellénisation de l'orient* (Paris, 1926) 257.
[66] *Hellenistic Athens* (London, 1911) 267.
[67] *Op. cit.* (n. 5) 263.

problem[68] also adopts this view, but he makes an attempt to face the difficulty of the Rosetta evidence; first of all he reduces the discrepancy of two years to one by putting the Anacleteria in 196 instead of 197,[69] and then deals with the remaining year by saying that 'for some reason hitherto unexplained' Epiphanes' first year was counted as his second.[70] This explanation is plainly inadequate.

(b) *Philopator died and Epiphanes succeeded in November 205.* This view involves the rejection of the evidence of Justinus and Polybius, and the ignoring of the historical situation during the years in question. Dinsmoor, who adopts this theory,[71] falls back upon the suggestion of Holleaux that the fragment Polyb. xv.25 may be from Book xiv; the other objections he ignores. This date is also more or less the one adopted by Wałek-Czernecki,[72] who considers that the death of Philopator was early enough to influence Philip at the Peace of Phoenice; but I know of no detailed defence of this bold theory.

(c) *Philopator died and Epiphanes succeeded in November 204.* This theory, which seeks to solve the problem by a compromise, is that adopted by De Sanctis,[73] if I have understood him correctly; for his account is decidedly ambiguous. He begins by pointing out, like Holleaux,[74] that the proclamation of the accession of Epiphanes is described in Polyb. xv, which gives the events of Ol. 144.2 = 203/2. Philopator's death cannot, therefore, he claims, be earlier than 204/3; and in fact, as he justly points out, the summary of that Ptolemy's character in Polyb. xiv.11–12, was probably inserted in connection with his death ‖ in the year 204/3. This seems to assume a gap of at any rate part of a year between Philopator's death and the proclamation of Epiphanes' succession; but De Sanctis makes no reference to such a gap. Instead he speaks of Philopator's death being '*circa* quella ol.', i.e. Ol. 144.1 = 204/3. This is the first difficulty in his account. The second is that, quoting from the Rosetta inscription, he speaks of the day 'in cui l'Epifane salì al trono' (the Greek being ἐν ἧι παρέλαβεν τὴν βασιλείαν παρὰ τοῦ πατρός), i.e. Phaophi 17, without making clear whether he refers this to the death of Philopator (in which case the accession is of a purely theoretical kind), or to the actual proclamation to the soldiers described in Polyb. xv. For this ambiguous date 'there is the choice between 28 November 204 and 28 November 203'; either is possible, 'tenuto conto della elasticità della cronologia polibiana'. But the former is preferable.

If by 'the day on which Epiphanes received the kingdom from his father' De Sanctis means the day on which Agathocles proclaimed him king before

[68] *REG* 12 (1899) 35 n. 1, 13 (1900) 190 n. 2; *BCH* 30 (1906) 473 n. 2; *Klio* 8 (1908) 268 n. 6; *REA* 15 (1913) 9 n. 3; *Rome, la Grèce et les monarchies hellénistiques* (Paris, 1921) 71 n. 1; *RPh* 50 (1926) 215–16; *CAH* 8.148–9.

[69] See above, p. 40.   [70] *CAH* 8, *loc. cit.*

[71] *Archons*, 493, note continued from 492.

[72] *RPh* 49 (1925) 45ff., 52 (1928) 24 note. See the criticism by Holleaux, *RPh* 50 (1926) *loc. cit.*

[73] *Op. cit.* (n. 8) 4.1.1 n. 2; *cf.* also 127 n. 39, 128 n. 41.

[74] *BCH* 30 (1906) 473 n. 2.

the Macedonians, then his theory is open to an overwhelming objection. De Sanctis has himself already admitted that this incident is contained in Polyb. xv, and that this book gives the events of Ol. 144.2 = 203/2; here, then, is a discrepancy which 'the elasticity of Polybian chronology' will not bridge. For although De Sanctis has shown elsewhere[75] that Polybius occasionally includes events which are later than the actual Olympiad year with which a particular book is concerned, the only examples he can find for events being taken from a preceding Olympiad year are certain details which Polybius puts under Ol. 140.1, because they are strictly relevant to, though in point of time they precede, the period at which his history proper begins. Plainly these events, at the opening of his work, occupy a unique position and constitute no precedent for the economy of the later books.

On the other hand De Sanctis may mean to imply that the quotation from the Rosetta inscription refers to the date of Philopator's death, and that this was later taken as the official accession date of Epiphanes, without any regard for the actual date (in 203/2) when Agathocles proclaimed him king. In this case his omission of all reference to the gap of about eight months between the two events is inexplicable; nor is it clear how and when the actual date of Philopator's death was later discovered, after the interval during which it had, presumably, been concealed.

In either case, reckoning from November 204[76] to his postponed Anacleteria in November 196 and the Rosetta inscription in 195, De Sanctis obtains the requisite eight years between the accession and the coming of age. But apart from its ambiguity, his solution has the disadvantages of fitting neither the Canon and archaeological evidence nor Polybius, of ignoring the historical situation as revealed in the bargain between Philip and Antiochus, and of misinterpreting the date of the Rosetta inscription. It may therefore be safely rejected.

(d) *Epiphanes succeeded in November 203, Philopator having died some time previously.* This view, which is that of Niese,[77] Bouché-Leclercq[78] and Niccolini,[79] and more recently of Cary,[80] Paola Zancan[81] and Granier,[82] rests on the statement of Justinus, already mentioned, that the death of Philopator was *diu occultata.* The main weakness of this view is that it fails ‖ to take full account of the Rosetta inscription; thus Niese,[83] for example, puts the Anacleteria in March 196, and calls this Epiphanes' ninth year; whereas by his own reckoning it is only his seventh. And in any case the full weight of the demotic evidence is against it.

---

[75] *Op. cit.* (n. 8) 3.1.219ff.

[76] Dinsmoor, (n. 8) *loc. cit.*, is mistaken in placing De Sanctis among those scholars who accept November 203 as the date of Epiphanes' accession.   [77] *Op. cit.* (n. 26) 2.573 n. 2.

[78] *Histoire des Lagides* (4 vols., Paris, 1903–7) 1.335–7.

[79] *La confederazione achea* (Pavia, 1914) 110 n. 2.

[80] *History of the Greek world from 323 to 146* (London, 1932) 93.

[81] *Il monarcato ellenistico nei suoi elementi federativi* (Padua, 1934) 44–5.

[82] *Die makedonische Heeresversammlung* (Munich, 1931) 140–4.

[83] *Op. cit.* (n. 26) 2.673.

This general *impasse* has two causes: first a false assumption, and secondly a failure to see that there are two distinct, and in their own way correct, versions of the date of accession; these are the official date of 205/4, as given in the Canon, the Rosetta inscription and the mass of the demotic evidence, and the actual date, as given in Polybius. The clue which eventually reconciles these two versions is Justinus' statement that the death of Philopator was *diu occultata*. In fact, difficult though it may at first sight appear, the only solution compatible with all the evidence is that the death was concealed for about a year. As De Sanctis saw,[84] Polybius relates the death in Book xiv (204/3), and takes this opportunity to survey the Egyptian events covering a number of years and to give a short character-sketch of the dead king.[85] To fit the Canon this death must have been before 12 October 204, and to fit Polybius, later than midsummer 204; it may be provisionally placed in September of that year. The two men in highest authority at that time were Sosibius and Agathocles, and the decision to conceal the death must have come from them. We can only guess at their motives. Mutual jealousy may have influenced them, both realising that without the nominal authority of Philopator, their joint control must soon develop into an open struggle for power. There is, however, a much more probable explanation in the international situation. The year 204 marked a crisis in the eastern Mediterranean. In 205 Philip V of Macedon had made the Peace of Phoenice[86] with Rome, and was henceforward free to turn his attention east; the summer of 204 was distinguished by his unscrupulous manoeuvres to stir up war between Rhodes and his allies in Crete,[87] and by the freebooting expedition of Dicaearchus,[88] an Aetolian in Philip's pay, whom he sent plundering in the Cyclades. As yet Philip had shown no hostility towards Egypt, but he was at least dangerous.

Antiochus constituted a more immediate threat. He had returned from his eastern Anabasis in the previous winter of 205/4, when Philip was winding up his affairs in the West, and at once he turned his eye towards Egypt.[89] Years of internal revolt[90] and the weak rule of an effeminate king had rendered Egypt easy prey to a determined aggressor; and in spite of his feebleness, it was a major disaster that at this very moment Philopator should die, leaving a five-year-old

[84] See above, p. 46.

[85] Polyb. xiv.12.3: Πτολεμαῖος ὁ βασιλεύς, περὶ οὖ νῦν ὁ λόγος, *i.e.* it is something directly connected with the king which occasions these Egyptian details in Polybius. As it is distinctly stated that the war which occupied Ptolemy's last years contained nothing μνήμης ἄξιον, his death is the only event to which Polybius can be referring.

[86] Livy xxix.12.13.

[87] *Cf.* Herzog, *Klio* 2 (1902) 316ff.; Holleaux, *Klio* 13 (1913) 145ff.; *REG* 30 (1917) 89ff.; M. Segre, *RFIC* 61 (1933) 365. This is the so-called Κρητικὸς πόλεμος.

[88] Polyb. xviii.54.8, Diod. xxviii.1; *cf.* Holleaux, 33 (1920) 223.

[89] A letter from Antiochus to the people of Amyzon is preserved, dating from spring 203, which shows the king already expanding at Egypt's expense; Amyzon had been a Ptolemaic possession, but in spring 203 it entered the dominions of Syria. (*Cf.* Ernst Meyer, *op. cit.* (n. 8) 41; Wilhelm, *AAWW* 57 (1920) 57; Welles, *op. cit.* (n. 64) 165ff.) For the fear of Antiochus felt even before his agreement with Philip *cf.* Polyb. xv.25.13, 25.17.

[90] Bevan, *op. cit.* (n. 5) 236ff.

boy to succeed him. Sosibius and Agathocles realised the danger, if not from a combination of Syria and Macedon, at any rate from Syria. They saw (and events proved them right) that the moment the news of Philopator's death was published, it would be the signal for attack; and not unreasonably they resolved to postpone making it public as long as possible, in the hopes that in the meantime something might happen to ‖ ease the situation. For there was at least a chance of a clash between Antiochus and Philip, both young and ambitious, both recently free from entanglements elsewhere, and Philip, moreover, of a hasty temperament and jealous of his more successful rival. Under these circumstances, any expedient was justified which might postpone the crisis.

The main obstacle to the concealment would have been Arsinoe, had she still been living with Philopator as his queen. A women of spirit,[91] it is highly improbable that she would have submitted to a scheme which, with her on the throne, would have been quite unnecessary; for Hellenistic queens had repeatedly shown themselves able to deal with political crises.[92] There is, however, reason to believe that Arsinoe was no longer queen, but that for some years she had been divorced or at least separated from Philopator; though for reasons of policy (Arsinoe was popular with the people of Alexandria)[93] it is improbable that there was an open breach, and she seems to have continued living in the royal palace. An inscription[94] from the last years of Philopator's reign is inscribed 'On behalf of Ptolemy the great Father-loving God, Saviour and Victor, and of Ptolemy the Son', omitting any reference to Arsinoe; whereas a slightly earlier inscription[95] has the dedication 'On behalf of King Ptolemy and Queen Arsinoe and Ptolemy the Son, Father-loving Gods, etc.' Bevan's comment[96] on the omission in the later inscription is that 'in a private dedication, the dedicator might choose which members of the royal family to pray for'. But, in normal conditions, the omission of Arsinoe would have been, to say the least, invidious and impolitic; and it is easier to assume that she was by this time in definite disfavour. This view is supported by a fragment from Joannes Antiochenus,[87] which reads: ὅτι Πτολεμαίου (᾿Αγαθοκλείαν) τὴν ἑαυτοῦ γυναῖκα ἐκβαλόντος καὶ μιᾷ τινί τῶν ἑταιρίδων συναφθέντος, εἶτα τελευτήσαντος Πτολεμαίου, ἡ ᾿Αγαθοκλεία ᾿Αρσινόην διαφθείρει δόλῳ· καὶ ταύτης σὺν τοῖς βασιλείοις διαφθαρείσης πολλῆς τε ταραχῆς ἐντεῦθεν Αἰγυπτίοις ἀναφθείσης, ὅ τε τῆς Συρίας βασιλεὺς Σέλευκος, καὶ τῆς Μακεδονίας Φίλιππος, ἐλπιδι τοῦ κρατήσειν τῆς χώρας σὺν προθυμίᾳ στρατεύουσιν κτλ.

In spite of the obvious errors of *Agathokleia* for *Arsinoe* and *Seleukos* for *Antiochos*, the fragment is in accordance with the rest of our evidence; and Müller seems to be right in his suggestion[98] that σὺν τοῖς βασιλείοις

[91] See the story of her in Athen. vii.276a; *cf.* Bevan, *op. cit.* (n. 5) 236.
[92] See G. Macurdy, *Hellenistic queens* (Baltimore, 1932).
[93] *Cf.* Polyb. xv.25.9.   [94] *OGIS* 89.
[95] *OGIS* 86, the 'elephant-hunters' inscription'.   [96] *Op. cit.* (n. 5) 243.
[97] Joann. Antioch. fr. 54 (*FHG* 4.558).
[98] Commenting in *FHG ad loc.*

διαφθαρείσης means that Arsinoe was burnt to death in a deliberately started fire, which burnt down part of the palace.[99] But the problem arises: when did Arsinoe's death take place? Now it appears very probable that in this fire we have an explanation of the μετὰ δ' ἡμέρας τρεῖς ἢ τέτταρας with which the Escorial fragment of Polybius[100] opens, namely that the burning of the palace was used by Sosibius[101] and Agathocles as a pretended explanation of the deaths of Philopator and Arsinoe at one and the same time. Some days after it was over they summoned the army, announced the accession of Epiphanes, and produced two urns, one actually containing the ashes of Ptolemy, the other purporting to hold those of Arsinoe (who had perished in the fire), but really full of spices.[102] ‖

It is in the dating of these events at Alexandria that most scholars seem to have taken an unjustifiable step: they have assumed that the expression ἐν ἧι παρέλαβεν τὴν βασιλείαν παρὰ τοῦ πατρός, in the Rosetta inscription (l. 47), necessarily refers to the crowning of Epiphanes by Agathocles on this occasion, and accordingly they have dated the events of Polyb. xv.25.3. to 28 November (= Phaophi 17) of whatever year their particular theory requires. A little consideration will show that this identification is not merely unwarranted, but highly improbable. The date Phaophi 17, along with Mesore 30, Epiphanes' birthday, is singled out on the Rosetta Stone as a special festival and day of good omen (αἳ δὴ πολλῶν ἀγαθῶν ἀρχηγοὶ πᾶσίν εἰσιν); but there were for Epiphanes, as for most of the later Ptolemies, not one, but two days on which in some sense he became king, the first when he was inaugurated by his father as co-regent, shortly after his birth, and certainly before 6 June 209,[103] the second the occasion described in Polybius. There was a precedent, in the reign of Philadelphus, for actually reckoning one's accession from the date of co-regency; and though admittedly the phrase παρέλαβεν τὴν βασιλείαν παρὰ τοῦ πατρός is used in the Canopus decree[104] in reference to Euergetes' independent accession,[105] this is no reason for assuming that it always bore this

---

[99] Müller's other suggestion is that τοῖς βασιλείοις here means 'the royal treasury'; but why should Arsinoe perish 'with the treasury'? In any case a fire is indicated.

[100] Polyb. xv.25.3.

[101] Sosibius slips out of the story soon after the accession of Epiphanes, so that it appears probable that he died about now. The sketch in Polyb. xv.25.1–2 was most likely inserted in connection with his death; cf. Holleaux, *REA* 14 (1912) 370ff.

[102] Polyb. xv.25.6–7; Just. xxx.1.1, 2.6. Justinus suggests that Arsinoe was murdered before Philopator's death; this is, from its lack of motive, improbable. Arsinoe was never a serious rival to Agathocleia, and her murder could only serve to enrage the people of Alexandria. Joannes' version, on the contrary, is in accordance with the account given by Polybius.

[103] See above, pp. 40–1.

[104] *OGIS* 56, l. 7.

[105] Dinsmoor, *Archons*, 486. Tarn, *Antigonos Gonatas* (Oxford, 1913) 433, would make a rigid distinction between διαδέξασθαι and παραλαβεῖν, which are, he claims, the official terms used for 'to accede' in the case of kings who began their reign as co-regents and those who followed a dead predecessor respectively. But this distinction cannot be upheld, since the term παραλαβεῖν is employed in reference to Epiphanes, about whose co-regency there is no question. Nor is there evidence to support a view that where a king was for a time co-regent, the term διαδέξασθαι was restricted to his assumption of co-regency and παραλαβεῖν to his independent accession.

meaning. As a festival of good omen and celebration there could be little hesitation in Epiphanes' particular case in a choice between the date of co-regency, no doubt marked by full pomp and religious rites, and that of the ceremony performed by Agathocles, when the urns of Philopator and the murdered Arsinoe were so shamelessly displayed to the people. Thus there is *prima facie* a good case for the assumption that Phaophi 17 was the anniversary not of Epiphanes' accession, but of his co-regency.[106] This is supported by the dates we know; if the king was born on 9 October 210, the following Phaophi 17 (= 30 November) would be a reasonable time to elevate him to a share in the throne, allowing the appropriate interval for preparations to be made.

However, for the present it is sufficient if we merely admit the possibility that the Rosetta Decree does not serve to date with certainty the events of Polyb. xv.25.3. What, then, does the position in Polybius tell us of their date? Simply that they occurred during the Olympiad 144.2 = 203/2; which in effect means within the limits August 203 and the end of the campaigning season 202. Now we have already seen from the Berlin demotic inscription of Khaᶜhap that Epiphanes' second Egyptian year was regarded as beginning on Thoth 1, 203 = 13 October; on this basis, his first Egyptian year, which was reckoned from his accession until this date, began some time between 13 October 204, and 12 October 203. By a combination of this evidence and what can be deduced from Polybius, the accession can be narrowed down to the period August–12 October 203. The only objection to this dating is the false identification with Phaophi 17, already discussed: it allows for a period of something between ten and fourteen months (August–October 204 to August–October 203) during which Philopator's death was concealed.

The problem now arises: why, after a year's successful concealment, did Agathocles and ‖ Sosibius decide during the late summer or early autumn of 203 to murder Arsinoe and have Epiphanes declared king? Here, of course, one is driven back on conjecture, but the most likely answer appears to be that the secret of Philopator's death had leaked out and perhaps reached Arsinoe. Once the facts began to be whispered abroad in Alexandria (and sooner or later this was inevitable) Agathocles' best course was to admit Philopator's death boldly; and whether Arsinoe knew the truth or not, as a popular figure for the discontented people of Alexandria to rally round, and an obstacle to complete control of the boy Epiphanes, she was safer out of the way. The burning of the palace was a clever device for the creation of an official legend of the simultaneous and accidental deaths of the king and queen; and this legend, whether believed or not, would, like all such official legends, compel general acceptance as long as Agathocles remained in power.

We may, then, assume Arsinoe's ignorance of the actual death of the king, and the outside world probably never saw Philopator now; towards the end

---

[106] This is the view taken by Smyly, *P. Gurob*, introduction, and Gauthier, *op. cit.* (n. 18) 4.275; but it is illogical to assume with the latter that Phaophi 17 is the date both of the co-regency and of the separate accession.

of his reign he seems to have given himself up increasingly to the pleasures provided for him by the small palace clique.[107] The oriental court, to which that of Ptolemy approximated more and more, was fashioned on a policy of secrecy, and there were analogies for concealments and impersonations; thus in the sixth-century Persian court the Magus was able to hold the throne as Great King for some time after the death of Cambyses, 'never leaving the acropolis, and never calling any of the prominent Persians into his presence' until the imposture was detected by one of his wives.[108] And an analogy nearer home was the concealment of the death of Berenice by Euergetes in 246, at the time of the Third Syrian War; by the help of this, Euergetes seems to have advanced through Seleucid territory as far as Seleuceia-on-the-Tigris, and obtained the allegiance of the governors of the upper provinces.[109]

Just how many people were a party to the plot cannot be ascertained with any certainty. Scopas the Aetolian, who held an important position in the army,[110] must undoubtedly have been involved; this may in fact be in Polybius' mind when he writes[111] οὐκ ἠρκεῖτο τούτοις, ὃς τὸ πρότερον προσκαρτερῶν τῷ πλείονι διετέλεσε, μέχρι διὰ τὴν ἀπληστίαν καὶ παρ' αὐτοῖς τοῖς διδοῦσι φθονηθεὶς τὸ πνεῦμα προσέθηκε τῷ χρυσίῳ. But whether he was the sole confederate of Agathocles and Sosibius is not easy to determine. The population of Alexandria would be no obstacle, for, as we saw, Philopator had long ago ceased to be a public figure. But the hoodwinking of the court circle was more difficult. The pretence that the king was seriously ill or a permanent invalid, though from many points of view the easiest way out, would in fact have defeated the very ends of the concealment, if our hypothesis as to Agathocles' reasons is correct. An invalid king, too ill to see any one, would afford as easy a prey to an unholy alliance between Philip and Antiochus as would an infant on the throne. And so the probability is that the concealment was effected by bribery in some cases and exclusion in others; and where any one promised to be particularly difficult to manage, there is nothing in the records of Agathocles and Sosibius to suggest that they would stop short of murder.[112]

So far our theory appears to fit the facts; but there is still a mass of evidence unexplained, including the Rosetta Stone, according to which Epiphanes' second year began on 13 October, not of 203, but of 204; and, as we saw, this was the version given by the Canon. Evidently, then, at some time between Epiphanes' second year, when the gravestone to Khaʿḥap ‖ was set up, and his ninth year, when the Macedonian calendar-equation proves that the accession date was regarded as 205/4, a year must have been omitted; or alternatively a break occurred part of the way through one Egyptian year, and the period from then to the next Thoth 1 was regarded as a new year, with

---

[107] Polyb. xiv.11.   [108] Hdt. iii.68.
[109] Cary, *op. cit.* (n. 80) 88 and 398; authorities quoted, 399.
[110] Polyb. xiii.2.3.
[111] Polyb. xiii.2.4–5. The words τοῖς διδοῦσι refer, however, not merely to Agathocles and Sosibius, but to Tlepolemus and Aristomenes as well.
[112] *Cf.* Polyb. xv.25.1–2, 26a, giving their respective crime-sheets.

a fresh set of eponymous priests. The latter possibility cannot be entirely ruled out, for there is a certain case from the reign of Philopator of a priest and priestess holding office for less than a year.[113] However, the first suggestion is in itself preferable, if it can be reconciled with the evidence.

Fortunately this not only allows for such a suppression of a year, but even points to a reason why it should have occurred at one particular time. From the details given above[114] it will be seen that we have no records at all dated to the sixth year of Epiphanes. Admittedly this would in itself prove little, since there are no records for the reign of Philopator later than Year 15 (Hathur (?) = December (?) 208).[115] But it is significant that from the records dated to Epiphanes' seventh year and onwards there has been a double change in the protocol; not only is Epiphanes now for the first time included as a god in the cult of Alexander and his own ancestors, but a new priestess-ship to Arsinoe Philopator now appears.[116] Evidently at some time just previous to the seventh year this double change had been carried through with the appropriate religious rites; and it has been plausibly suggested[117] that the institution of a priestess-ship to his mother by Epiphanes was an act of expiation for her murder by Agathocles.

A glance at the international situation at the end of Epiphanes' fifth year (reckoning his second year from October 203) may suggest a reason for such an act of expiation, and also for the year's change in the calendar. Epiphanes' sixth year would normally have begun on Thoth 1 (= 12 October) 199. Now the summer of 199 had been marked by a series of military disasters for Egypt;[118] after his victory at Panium in spring or summer 200, Antiochus had successfully shut Scopas up in Sidon, and throughout the winter of 200 and the first half of 199 three Egyptian armies had tried in vain to relieve it.[119] It is not unreasonable to deduce a deterioration of Egyptian morale in the face of disasters like these; and what more natural than an attempt by the government to restore this morale by religious means! Just as the Anacleteria of Epiphanes was held in late autumn 197 to offset the bad effects of the conspiracy of Scopas;[120] and just as, from time to time, it was customary to hold a *sed*-festival[121] to 'recharge' the king with *mana*; so now the popular morale was restored by the deification of Epiphanes, and the institution of a priestess to Arsinoe. The latter innovation suggests that the events surrounding the death of Philopator had made a deep impression in Alexandria; and so

---

[113] Thompson, *op. cit.* (n. 40) 19, nos. 30a, 30b, 31.

[114] See above, n. 40. [This hypothesis of an omitted year, based precariously on an *argumentum ex silentio*, was rendered invalid by the discovery of evidence covering year 6 of Epiphanes (200/199), viz. *P. dem. Mich.* 4526A. See below, p. 55 n. 125.]

[115] Thompson, *op. cit.* (n. 40) no. 38 of the Alexandrian dates.

[116] *Cf. P. dem. Louvre* 2435, in Plaumann, *RE* 8.2 '*Hiereis*', no. 58; *cf.* Gauthier, *op. cit.* (n. 18) 4.276.   [117] Bouché-Leclercq, *op. cit.* (n. 78) 1.349, n. 2.

[118] See Holleaux, *Klio* 8 (1908) 267–81, for the chronology of the Fifth Syrian War.

[119] Hieron. *In Daniel.* xi.15–16.

[120] Polyb. xviii.55: νομίζοντες δὲ λήψεσθαί τινα τὰ πράγματα κατάστασιν καὶ πάλιν ἀρχὴν τῆς ἐπὶ τὸ βέλτιον προκοπῆς.   [121] Bevan, *op. cit.* (n. 5) 262.

makes it probable that the concealment of Philopator's death for about a year was by this time widely known. With the knowledge arose a question: who had been king between the death of Philopator and the accession of Epiphanes? Plainly, Epiphanes himself, who had been co-regent since 30 November 210; and if so, the current dating, which made his reign begin in autumn 203, was incorrect, and must be altered. There were two alternatives: either Epiphanes could follow the precedent of Philadelphus and begin to date his reign from his co-regency, or he could move his date ‖ of accession back to the time of his father's death, and call his sixth year his seventh. Apparently he, or his government, chose the latter; and so the seventh year of Epiphanes was made to begin on Thoth 1 (12 October) 199.[122] His ninth year, in which the Rosetta Stone was set up, therefore began in 197, as Dinsmoor calculated; and similarly all the remaining demotic evidence falls into place.

Thus two distinct traditions were established for the accession of Epiphanes, an official one which survives in the Canon, the Rosetta and Damanhūr inscriptions, and the documentary evidence, and a historical one which, as in Polybius, gives the actual events of early autumn 203, and which is also preserved in the inscription of Khaʿḥap. These two traditions, and the general mystery with which the events of the interregnum were shrouded, account for the two different dates presented by our sources, and for the omission of all details of the concealment in the surviving authorities. This omission, however, presents only an apparent obstacle to the explanation I have suggested. If we had Polybius complete, there can be no doubt that we should find there a full account of the whole matter; for Polybius, it must be remembered, dealt with Philopator's death in Book xiv, and postponed the account of its announcement by Agathocles to Book xv, that is, until the next Olympiad year. This in itself presents a difficulty which can hardly be solved except on the assumption of a passage of time between the two events; and when this gap is confirmed by a definite statement of Justinus, there seems no justification for further doubt. With the text of Polybius in its present fragmentary state, it might well have happened that no hint whatever of the concealment had survived; but in fact there are two such hints, the one certain, the other possible. First, the use of the word ἀνθομολογεῖσθαι[123] in connection with Agathocles' announcement of Philopator's death is inexplicable unless it is assumed that that death had previously been concealed; and secondly it is a possibility, if nothing more, that the details of the court circle, which appear in Polyb. xiv.11,[124] were inserted as part of an explanation of how a close cabal was able to conceal Philopator's death for about a year. On the other hand,

---

[122] Such a change in the calendar for little more than superstitious reasons would be by no means unprecedented in the Hellenistic world; for a much more flagrant example *cf.* Plut. *Alex.* 16, according to whom Alexander, to satisfy the religious scruples of his soldiers against fighting in Daisios, inserted a second Artemisios.

[123] Polyb. xv.25.4: τὸν τοῦ βασιλέως καὶ τὸν τῆς βασιλίσσης θάνατον ἀνθωμολογήσαντο. The word ἀνθομολογεῖσθαι, when it does not signify 'to agree with', has always the meaning 'to admit to, to confess' in Polybius; *cf.* v.56.4, x.38.3, xii.28.7, xxix.6.11; xxx.8.7.

[124] Fragments from Athenaeus, vi.251c and xiii.756c.

they would be equally in place in a mere discussion of Philopator's character. In conclusion, it should be noticed that Justinus' statement that Epiphanes was five years old at his father's death is in accordance with the explanation here offered; for if Philopator died August–September 204, Epiphanes would be five years, ten months old at that time.[125]

I append a table of relevant dates:

9 October	210	Birth of Epiphanes
30 November	210	Epiphanes elevated to the throne as co-regent
6 June	209	First documentary evidence of this
Autumn	206	Aetolia makes a separate peace with Philip V
Summer	205	Peace of Phoenice between Philip and Rome
Autumn	205	Scopas fails to be elected general in Aetolia and comes to Egypt
13 October	205	Beginning of Philopator's last year, according to the Canon
Winter	205/4	Return of Antiochus from the upper provinces
Summer	204	Philip active in promoting war between Rhodes and certain cities in Crete
		Plundering expedition of Dicaearchus in the Cyclades
August–Sept. (*circa*)	204	Death of Philopator: concealment of this ‖
Spring	203	Antiochus' letter to the people of Amyzon
August–Sept. (*circa*)	203	Burning of part of the palace at Alexandria: murder of Arsinoe
(Five days later)		Accession of Epiphanes. Deaths of Philopator and Arsinoe revealed. First Egyptian year of Epiphanes begins
Autumn	203	Agathocles sends Philammon, the murderer of Arsinoe, to Cyrene, Pelops to Antiochus, Ptolemy, son of Sosibius, to Philip, Scopas to Aetolia, and Ptolemy, son of Agesarchus, *via* Greece to Rome
		Death of the elder Sosibius about this time
13 October	203	Beginning of Epiphanes' second Egyptian year
Winter	203/2	Philip and Antiochus make an agreement for the partition of the Ptolemaic possessions
13 February	202	Death of the priest Khaᶜhap
Summer	202	Antiochus moves against Coele-Syria (details uncertain)

[125] On the problem of the date of Epiphanes' accession see now E. Bikerman, *Chronique d'Égypte* 15 (1940) 128–9; T. C. Skeat, *Reigns of the Ptolemies* (Munich, 1954) 32; A. Samuel, *Ptolemaic chronology* (Munich, 1962) 108–14; F. W. Walbank, *Historical commentary on Polybius* 2 (Oxford, 1967) 435–7, where it is argued that Philopator died in summer 204 and that Epiphanes acceded after a short concealment of his father's death. Polybius recorded the latter in Book xiv but delayed the account of the proclamation of Epiphanes until Ol. 144.2 = 203/2 for compositional reasons. The day 'on which he took over the kingdom from his father' (Phaophi 17) will be, not that of Epiphanes' co-regency with Philopator, but (as Bikerman shows) that of a ceremony held at Memphis on 28 November 204 after the events in Alexandria described in Polyb. xv.25.5. The Khaᶜhap inscription no longer constitutes a problem. John Ray, who kindly re-examined the text at my request, tells me that it had been misread. Khaᶜhap was born in Year 12 (not 11), i.e. in 274/3 (actually 11 May 273), which puts his death on 13 February 203, in Epiphanes' second year.⟧

Autumn	202	Ptolemy returns from Philip to Alexandria, where he finds Agathocles displaced by Tlepolemus
April	201	Philip initiates his aggressive policy against Egypt with the capture of Samos
Spring–summer	200	Antiochus' victory at Panium
Autumn 200–spring	199	Siege of Sidon
12 October	199	Beginning of Epiphanes' seventh (= sixth) year: Epiphanes now elevated to the Alexander-cult: institution of a priestess to Arsinoe Philopator
Summer–autumn	197	Conspiracy of Scopas
26 November	197	Anacleteria of Ptolemy Epiphanes
27 March	196	Rosetta Decree enacted
October (*circa*)	196	Conference of Lysimacheia between Antiochus and the Roman commissioners
Autumn	196	Bethrothal of Epiphanes to Antiochus' daughter Cleopatra
Winter	194/3	Marriage of Epiphanes and Cleopatra

4

NATIONALITY AS A FACTOR IN
ROMAN HISTORY*

I

In the *De Officiis*[1] Cicero has some interesting remarks on the various levels at which men can associate. First there is the very general bond which joins all human beings; then, coming a little closer, we have the sharing of the same *gens*, *natio*, or *lingua*, a very strong form of human association. Still more intimate is the link between those who enjoy the same *civitas*: for *cives* have many things in common between them, the forum, shrines, porticoes, streets, laws, legal rights, courts, the vote, and in addition social intercourse and friendships and the business contacts which link large numbers of men together. Closer still is the bond between kinsmen. With the last I am not concerned; but what is the difference between *gens*, *natio*, *lingua*, and on the other hand *civitas*? *Civitas* here seems to have its narrow sense – not the legal rights of a Roman citizen living, for example, in Narbonne, but the intimate association of those who walk the same streets and forum, vote in the same booths, worship at the same temples, and contract friendships and business ties with each other. *Gens*, *natio* and *lingua* signify the wider community, the Latins, Sabines, Volscians, Samnites and Etruscans, referred to by Cicero elsewhere, in a fragmentary passage of the *De Republica*[2] – 'Italiae Latium aut eiusdem Sabinam aut Volscam gentem...Samnium...Etruriam'; and he goes on to mention Magna Graecia, the Assyrians, the Persians and the Carthaginians. It is these groupings that come as near as we shall get to the modern concept of a 'nation'. But it is worth noting that for the passage cited from the *De Officiis* Cicero's source was Panaetius.[3] Perhaps, then, the original referred to a Greek context, and the *civitas* with its streets and forum, its laws, rights and law courts, was a Greek πόλις; in which case the wider grouping, the *gens* or *natio*, will have been the γένος or ἔθνος, ‖ the Hellenic race or one of the various stocks that composed it – what Plato[4] calls τὰ τῶν Ἑλλήνων γένη.

The Greeks of course had a clear concept of being united by common kinship and ancestry and of being in some sense separate from the non-Greek world of barbarians. One need hardly list the factors which contributed to this notion, or those elements in Greek history which bear witness to its persistence.[5] The important and perhaps somewhat disheartening fact is that this concept of

* [*HSPh* 76 (1972) 145–68]

[1] Cic. *Off.* 1.53.   [2] Cic. *Rep.* III.7.
[3] *Cf.* Cic. *Att.* XVI.11.4.   [4] Plato, *Leg.* III.693a.
[5] *Cf.* Walbank, *Phoenix* 5 (1951) 41–60 [above, pp. 1–19].

Hellas as a nation never found expression in the political organisation of the Greek world, which remained fragmented into a variety of individual sovereign states. Before looking at the form which those states took, we may perhaps pause for a moment at this concept of the 'nation'. In the middle of the twentieth century the idea of a nation, with its inherent right to political independence, is among the most potent political forces at work. Yet to define a nation is not easy. Political theorists have tried to isolate its essentials. Meinecke, who made one of the more outstanding contributions to this discussion, argued that nationhood depends on sharing some – not necessarily all – of the following: a common habitation, a common language, a common spiritual and intellectual life, and a common state or share in a federation of states; and he devised two German terms, *Staatsnation* and *Kulturnation*, to describe the nation existing as it were *in esse* and that existing only *in posse*.[6]

Much of this is valid. But it does not perhaps bring out sufficiently one fundamental point – that ultimately men constitute a nation because and when they believe they constitute one; and the real distinction is not so much that between a *Kulturnation* and a *Staatsnation*, but that between a group of men who have succeeded in asserting their right to be treated as a nation and a similar group who have yet to do so. Incidentally, it is often the very struggle to win independence that itself creates the consciousness of being a nation. A few years ago a German scholar wrote a book[7] to prove, among other things, that in Greece the separate πόλεις were so highly differentiated that we ought to regard them as constituting separate nations. On this hypothesis, Hellas as a whole was the ancient equivalent, not of modern Germany or Italy or Great Britain, but of modern Europe. The argument is not convincing. ‖ Many of the concepts and the loyalties which go to make up the reality of a modern nation are certainly present in the Greek πόλις: but the Greek πόλις is not a nation, not because it is small – today Albania and the United States both rank as nations – but because there existed a sufficient number of powerful ideas which meant something real to Greeks everywhere, common blood (it was believed), a common tongue (despite the dialects), a common religion (despite the local cults), and a common way of life, which cannot be reconciled with the notion of Athens, Thebes and Sparta as separate nations.

There is a further point. Not only was the πόλις not an independent nation; it was by no means the only form of Greek political organisation. There is a formula which is very common on Hellenistic inscriptions – peoples, cities and princes, ἔθνη, πόλεις καὶ δυνάσται.[8] Polybius uses it[9] almost as a synonym for the content of political history, 'the doings of peoples, cities and princes'. In

---

[6] F. Meinecke, *Weltbürgertum und Nationalstaat*[7] (Munich–Berlin, 1928) 3.

[7] H. E. Stier, *Grundlagen und Sinn der griechischen Geschichte* (Stuttgart, 1945).

[8] *Cf.* Diod. xix.57.3; *OGIS* 229, l. 11; *ibid.* 441, l. 132; *SIG* 590, ll. 12–14; *ibid.* 760; Rostovtzeff, *Social and economic history of the Hellenistic world* (Oxford, 1941) 502–3, 1347, 1439–40; Sall. *Epist. Mithr.*: 'namque Romanis cum nationibus, populis, regibus cunctis una et ea vetus causa bellandi est: cupido profunda imperi et divitiarum'.

[9] Polyb. ix.1.4, with my commentary.

classical Greece it appears in a shorter form, ἔθνη καὶ πόλεις (without the δυνάσται), as a comprehensive phrase to cover states of every kind; it occurs in the Amphictyonic oath recorded by Aeschines[10] and in the document setting up the Hellenic League of Philip II;[11] and it continues right down into the Roman Empire. Aelius Aristides, for example, in his famous speech on Rome applies it[12] to the cities and provinces of the Empire of the second century A.D. In both classical and Hellenistic times much of Greece proper fell under the category of ἔθνη, peoples, rather than of πόλεις, cities. The peoples were there before the cities. Indeed, it was only with the breaking up of the unity of the peoples that the cities arose; and it is significant, as Larsen has pointed out,[13] that ἔθνος can be used to describe a federal state like Achaea just as well as a more primitive tribal community like the Thesprotians, the Agraeans, or the fifth-century Aetolians. Transition to a federal state was often easier for a community organised in villages with a strong tribal sense than it was ‖ for more highly differentiated cities, and if, for example, we study the development of the Boeotian Federation, we find that it was the particularism and ambition of the powerful *polis* of Thebes that constituted the greatest obstacle to lasting union. Whereas in an area like Achaea, where the cities were small and unambitious, the consciousness of belonging to the ἔθνος seems to have assisted federal union at an early date, and led to a development free from strong feelings of particularism; it is noteworthy that Achaea could absorb Naupactus and Calydon, cities lying across the Corinthian Gulf,[14] as members of the confederacy in the early fourth century just as easily as the revitalised confederacy of the third century was to absorb Sicyon, Argos, Corinth and Megalopolis.[15]

In its early days the πόλις too seems to have had potentialities for growth. The synoecism of Attica created a small territorial state with a single citizenship – that of Athens – within its boundaries. But Athens was not typical, and this flexibility was not a characteristic of the later πόλις, which seems to have conceived expansion only in terms of hegemony and empire. I have digressed a little to discuss these points because they show that whereas in Greek history the concept of a Greek nation remained almost an abstract idea to which one paid lip service in crisis or on ceremonial occasions, the growing points towards greater unity lay in the ἔθνη, whether tribal areas or federal states; it is hardly necessary to add that federalism is one important way to the birth of a nation.

---

[10] Aeschin. *Ctes.* 110.   [11] *IG* 4².1.68, l. 78.

[12] Ael. Arist. *ad Romam* 31; J. H. Oliver, 'The ruling power', *TAPhS* 43.4 [1953] 918, for epigraphical evidence.

[13] J. A. O. Larsen, *CP* 40 (1945) 78 n. 72; *Representative government in Greek and Roman history* (Berkeley, 1955) 22–3.

[14] *Cf.* Xen. *Hell.* iv.6.1–14; W. M. Oldfather, 'Naupaktos', *RE* 16.2 (1935), cols. 1989–90; von Geisau, 'Kalydon', *RE* 10.2 (1919) col. 1763.

[15] Sicyon, 251 (Plut. *Arat.* 9.4); Corinth, 243 (Plut. *Arat.* 18–23); Argos, 229 (Plut. *Arat.* 35); Megalopolis, 235 (Plut. *Arat.* 30).

The failure of the Greeks to realise their potentiality as a nation was due to several causes of which the particularism of the πόλις was only one (though an important one). Philip II's victory at Chaeronea led to an attempt to impose Greek unity from without, and not unnaturally union on those terms was resisted and rejected. Shortly afterwards Alexander's campaigns in Asia, the overthrow of the Persian empire, and the setting-up of Greco-Macedonian monarchies over the Middle East opened up new perspectives, which made the question of a Greek national state even more academic than it had been in the fifth and fourth centuries. The geographical element had always been a serious obstacle to Greek unity. Obviously contiguity must be an important factor in the creation of a national state – consider the problem of Pakistan – and the wide scatter of Greeks over the length and breadth ‖ of the Mediterranean during the eighth, seventh and sixth centuries had produced a configuration incapable of being drawn together within a single political unity. The new *diaspora* after Alexander was accompanied by the rise, not now of independent *poleis*, but of multiracial monarchies in Egypt, Asia Minor and the Middle East, which created a new world and added the new element to the old formula, which now became 'peoples, cities and *princes*'.

II

Faced with the particularism of the *polis* and later with the reality of the wide territorial monarchy, the idea of the Greek nation remained ghost-like; and I have prefaced my discussion of nationality as a factor in Roman history with these remarks on Greece because the history of Rome, even more than that of Greece, seems to evolve inside a field enclosed within the two poles of the city-state and the multiracial empire. In the *gens* or *natio* of Cicero's terminology we find a unit which is not at first sight very significant for the growth of Rome, except as an obstacle which stood in her way. Rome could develop into a nation only by some form of expansion; and the first area which appears to invite such expansion is of course Latium. Despite their name, drawn as were those of the Volsci and the Hernici from the area where they lived, the flat country, the Latins, like those peoples, constituted and felt themselves to be what the Greeks would have called an ἔθνος, a tribal or ethnic unit. At a later date the Romans used to speak of them as the *nomen Latinum*, and Mommsen argued[16] that *nomen* in this phrase meant *Stamm* or tribe, a view in which he has been widely followed.[17] This is perhaps not very likely.[18] Latin has two perfectly good words, *gens* and *natio*, to describe a tribal community; and the Romans used the word *nomen* in non-tribal contexts, as when they spoke of the *nomen Albanum* in relation to Alba Longa.[19] But there is, after all, no need to tie up the question of Latin

[16] T. Mommsen, *Römisches Staatsrecht*[3] 3 (Leipzig, 1871–88) 608 n. 1.
[17] *Cf.*, for example, Ernst Meyer, *Römischer Staat und Staatsgedanke* (Zurich, 1948) 15.
[18] See on this P. Catalano, *Linee del sistema sovranazionale romano* 1 (Turin, 1965) 216ff.
[19] Livy 1.23.4.

ethnic unity with the phrase *nomen Latinum*, which despite Livy's use of it in connection with events of 495 B.C.[20] could well be a term adopted after 338 to describe the new sort of ‖ Latins whose Latinity had a juridical rather than an ethnic basis; and even if it was used earlier, it may have indicated the more political aspects of Latin organisation. Latin ethnic unity is clear enough without it; already in Hesiod[21] one encounters Latinus, personifying the tribe.

Whether Latium and Rome together could ever have evolved into a nation is, however, a question not easily answered, especially in view of the uncertainty which surrounds the early relations of Rome with the Latins. Recently, De Visscher[22] has argued that an original close relationship is to be deduced from the phrase *ius Quiritium*, which was used – our evidence comes from the early Empire – to describe the rights which, when given to a Junian Latin, made him the equivalent of an ordinary Roman freedman. De Visscher suggests[23] that this usage derives from archaic times, when the phrase was used to designate the rights of the community of the Quirites *vis-à-vis* other Latins, while in relation to the outside, non-Latin world the Roman 'maintained the solidarity of the *nomen Latinum*'. I confess I find it difficult to imagine exactly how these archaic Romans 'maintained the solidarity of the Latin name'. They may have avoided describing Roman rights as *ius Quiritium* when dealing with non-Latins, but presumably they called themselves Romans; and it is because there is nothing anywhere in our tradition to suggest that a Roman faced with a query about his *origo* would ever have answered it by replying 'Latinus sum' that De Visscher's argument seems to me unsatisfactory.

It is true that our tradition is Roman and therefore puts Rome in the forefront of the picture. But despite this, it is clear that Rome was not simply a typical Latin city. Tradition and archaeology are agreed in tracing several distinct elements, whether cultural, tribal or racial, in her foundation; and her striking position on the northern marches of Latium singled her out from other peoples within the Latin community. The earliest growth of Rome is recorded under the first kings. The details are probably as legendary as the kings themselves; but the location of the places named suggests a logical pattern of expansion in the lower valley of the Tiber and the foothills beyond the Anio, and the important point for the present discussion is that it was an expansion similar to that of Athens inside Attica – that is, expansion by means of synoecism. The towns or communities in question were incorporated in the Roman state and their inhabitants simply became Romans. ‖

This development seems to have been checked by the time of the Etruscan domination, or at least of its later phase. For the process of synoecism practised by Rome found a counterpart in the other cities of Latium and the number of separate communities had already diminished by this same process of political cannibalism. By the reign of Superbus one has the impression that

[20] Livy II.22.7.   [21] Hes. *Theog.* 1013.
[22] *Études de droit romain public et privé*[3] (Milan, 1966) 101–16 (= *Studi in onore di Ugo Paoli* (Florence, 1955) 239–51).   [23] *Ibid.* 103ff.

Latium consisted of differentiated cities which resisted further Roman expansion along the earlier lines. Out of the various religious leagues existing in
early Latium had developed political associations, probably facilitated by the
sense of kinship; the most important such association seems to have been that
connected with the council of the Lucus Ferentinae.[24] According to Livy and
Dionysius, the younger Tarquin gained some control of this federal body.[25]
Judging from the evidence contained in the treaty between Rome and
Carthage,[26] which dates to the first year of the Republic, direct Roman – which
probably means previous direct Etruscan – domination of Latium was confined
to a group of coastal towns stretching down to Tarracina; but this treaty also
recognises another group of Latin people, not subject to Rome, and these may
represent the League of the Lucus Ferentinae with which Rome enjoyed
relations of a different kind, perhaps even membership of the League amounting
to virtual hegemony.

The details, however, are speculative and not to be pressed. Nor are they
important for the present discussion; here the point is rather that at an early
date Roman expansion into Latium in the form of straightforward synoecism
seems to have been checked and a relationship based on specific *foedera* to have
taken its place. After the expulsion of the Tarquins there is a period when Rome
is fighting the Latin League, and this ends after the battle of Lake Regillus
with the famous Latin Treaty of 493 associated with the name of Spurius
Cassius.[27] Although it is true that we later find special conditions in the
relationship of Rome with the Latins, including interchangeability of citizenship (which may link with the *isopolity* referred to by Dionysius),[28] and though
the connection with the Latins always remained something distinct from the
relations with the other Italian peoples, nevertheless the Latin Treaty put the
seal on a new development already foreshadowed in the treaty with Gabii[29]
and perhaps, if we had the evidence, in treaties with other ‖ states. I need not
go into the question of whether the Latin Treaty was made with the League
as a whole or with all the members of it separately; for in either case, this
instrument, which was to govern the relations between Rome and Latium
down to 338, directed them on bilateral lines – Rome was one party, the Latins
another. Rome, a developed city under the Tarquins, gradually came to
dominate federal Latium not from within, like Thebes inside the Boeotian
Confederacy, but from without, on the basis of the treaty. It was this
relationship that ensured that Latium, including Rome, was never to evolve
into a nation.

However, Rome was to have a second opportunity to create a nation, and
this time apparently with more success. The Romans were a people of political
ingenuity and did not remain constricted within the system set up by the treaty

[24] Dion. Hal. III.45–8.
[25] Livy I.50–1; Dion. Hal. III.45–8.   [26] Polyb. III.22.4–13.
[27] Livy II.33.9; Dion. Hal. VI.95; Cic. *Balb.* 53.   [28] Dion. Hal. IV.58.4.
[29] *Ibid.*

of 493. Repeatedly, for one reason or another, they reverted to the older method of synoecism, the expansion of Roman territory and with it the expansion of the *civitas Romana*. As I have indicated, this process was not novel; it had operated effectively in early Attica. But the new feature about it in the case of Rome was that it continued to be used in a world of developed cities, and that it recognised no territorial limitations. This expansion of the principle of the city-state gradually made headway against the system of alliances and opened up new political vistas in Italy. 'Rome had to reach out,' writes Haarhoff,[30] 'adapting, rather than adopting, what was new, and bringing a new nation to birth.' The unification of Italy was a Roman achievement carried out despite the immense racial confusion of a peninsula which contained Gauls, Etruscans, Greeks, Illyrians, Sabellians and Latins – and Phoenicians, if one counts in Sicily. Already something of the significance of what was happening was evident to the peoples of the East, Greeks and Levantines, who used the words *Italici* and 'Ρωμαῖοι indiscriminately for any inhabitants of Italy and Sicily whom they happened to run against; and the Italians themselves used the name *Italici* on eastern inscriptions from the early second century onward.[31] The Social War, it is true, may seem to suggest that the first evidence of anything like the concept of an Italian nation was inspired not by Rome, but by the opposition movement culminating in armed rebellion. Certainly Corfinium was renamed 'Italia', and Samnite coins depict the Italian bull, the symbol of Italy, 'Viteliu', the cattle-country, goring the Roman wolf. Marsic coins show eight ‖ warriors representing the peoples who had joined the *coniuratio* swearing an oath together against Rome.[32] But appearances are deceptive. All this, as Brunt has shown,[33] was only a second best. The real aim of the allies was to attain Roman citizenship, to be absorbed in the Roman state; and once this was conceded, they seized it with alacrity. The Samnites may be the exception. They are shown in our sources as the irreconcilables.[34] But even this intransigence may be the invention of Sulla, seeking to justify the massacre of the supporters of an opposing faction.[35] The truth is that, by the beginning of the first century B.C., Rome had created Italy, an Italy which stretched technically to the Rubicon, but in effect to the Alps;[36] and the Italian struggle was really designed to force the Romans to bring the Italian nation to birth. After 88 Italy enjoyed a common status symbolised by a common dress – 'Romanos rerum dominos gentemque togatam';[37] the use

---

[30] T. J. Haarhoff, *The stranger at the gate* (Oxford, 1948) 123.

[31] *Cf.* Brunt, *JRS* 55 (1965) 100 n. 72, quoting Hatzfeld, *Les trafiquants italiens dans l'orient hellénique* (Paris, 1919) 238ff.

[32] For the Italian coins, see H. A. Grueber, *Coins of the Roman Republic in the British Museum* (London, 1910) 2.317ff.   [33] *JRS* 55 (1965) 90–109.

[34] See Vell. Pat. II.27 for Pontius Telesinus' remark that Rome must be utterly destroyed, and the wolves rooted out from their lair. [See now E.T. Salmon, *Samnium and the Samnites* (Cambridge, 1967).]

[35] So Brunt, *op. cit.* (n. 31) 97.

[36] See the note in my commentary on Polyb. III.61.11 for the shift from the Aesis to the Rubicon frontier, probably by 133.   [37] Virg. *Aen.* 1.282.

of Latin was expanding everywhere, even outside the solid Latin areas of central Italy; and one can trace a revealing imitation of Roman ways and institutions throughout the peninsula. Italy stood out for close on three centuries as distinct from the overseas possessions of Rome; and the special juridical concept of *ius Italicum* underlined its unity and this contrast.[38]

The unity was not achieved all at once. Italy possessed many *populi*, both cities and tribes, and full assimilation was hardly completed in some areas before the end of the Republic. But gradually, in the century following the Social War, the peninsula was transformed into a chess-board of *municipia*, each with its *territorium*. The problem of loyalties seemed solved. In the *De Legibus* Cicero enunciated the new doctrine that each *municeps* possesses two *patriae*, 'unam naturae, alteram civitatis';[39] and Virgil, a man from Cisalpine Gaul, uses 'Roman' and 'Italian' as virtually interchangeable terms. Nevertheless, one must make qualifications. The citizenship remained that of a city, not of a country; for Cato it was Tusculum and Rome, not Tusculum and ‖ Italy. Although the idea was envisaged,[40] nothing was done to allow citizens to exercise their voting rights within their municipalities; it was as Romans they voted, not Italians, and so appropriately they must continue to vote in Rome. Moreover, one of the features for which the Roman citizenship is commonly and justly applauded, its capacity for extension, meant that by the time of Augustus – indeed from the end of the third century B.C. – there were already *cives Romani*, some settled in *coloniae*, overseas. This geographical extension of Roman and Latin rights to individuals, cities, and eventually whole provinces, and even grants of *ius Italicum* to selected areas abroad,[41] were to render it increasingly hard to say wherein the special character and national identity of Italy consisted. In fact, *civitas Romana* was not merely an inadequate basis as a definition of the Italian nation; it was in the long run destined to destroy that very concept.

During the last hundred years the modern world has witnessed the break-up of several large units like the Austro-Hungarian and Turkish empires and the liquidation of vast colonial areas like the British and French empires, and the substitution of national states. The history of Rome presents this picture in reverse – the breaking down of national groups and the substitution of one vast supranational state. The element of growth within that state was the Roman citizenship: but the modern practice of equating citizenship with nationality can only lead to confusion if we apply it in the Roman world. And if modern experience merely hinders the understanding of the Roman problem, the experience of Greece helps us even less, for in Greece, as I have indicated, the question of nationality was bound up with the problem of combining, of sinking particularism in the larger unit; and because this was never a real possibility, was never indeed wholeheartedly tried, the concept of the Greek nation

[38] On *ius Italicum* see Mommsen, *op. cit.* (n. 16) III.631 n. 2, 684 n. 1 (later grants outside Italy).
[39] Cic. *Leg.* II.2.5.   [40] Suet. *Aug.* 46.
[41] See above, n. 38.

remains something ghost-like on the fringe of real political experience. In the developed Roman Empire, on the other hand, the concept of nationality and nationalism is something to be outgrown (as in the case of Italy) or overwhelmed, when it finds expression in separatism and resistance to the imperial state. Greek political activity, one might say, takes place below the national level, Roman above it; but in either case nationality and nationalism are condemned to impotence.

III

By the time the Romans had been driven to grant *civitas* to all the peoples of Italy, they had already won a footing in many parts of the ‖ Mediterranean world. Here, in the provinces, Romans came into contact with a wide variety of peoples of different race and language, who naturally formed their own impressions of the ruling power; and insofar as the problem of nationality arises in imperial times, it is in this context that it has to be looked for. Recently there has been a great growth of interest in the attitudes of the non-Roman peoples, contrasted with the main tradition of Roman history, which was of course pro-Roman and generally concerned with the views and achievements of the Roman governing class. As examples of this trend one thinks of the work of Fuchs[42] on the ideological opposition to Rome; of Haarhoff's study[43] of exclusiveness and co-operation in the classical world; of Frend's history of the Donatist movement[44] in North Africa; and of Lambrechts' work[45] on the persistence of the local religions of north Gaul and Germany; and it is not without significance that two of these scholars themselves come from countries in which problems of race relations and what Toynbee has called 'linguistic nationalism' are especially troublesome. However, it is easier to identify elements in provincial culture as being of local origin and resistant to Romanisation than it is to assess how far such survivals indicate conscious opposition to Rome and genuine nationalist feeling. Much depended on the attitude of the Romans themselves toward native culture, and in general this tended to be tolerant. Native, non-Roman cults and language were something to be left alone, not (with a few exceptions) eradicated or ironed into uniformity. True, the Romans were less willing to absorb as citizens peoples whom they felt to be foreign than they were those who were more easily assimilated and Romanised.[46] In general they preferred to extend citizenship,

[42] H. Fuchs, *Der geistige Widerstand gegen Rom in der antiken Welt* (Berlin, 1938).
[43] See above, n. 30.
[44] W. H. C. Frend, *The Donatist church* (Oxford, 1952); see the criticism of Peter Brown, 'Christianity and local culture in Late Roman Africa', *JRS* 58 (1968) 85–95.
[45] P. Lambrechts, *De geestelijke Weerstand van de westelijke provincies tegen Rome* (Brussels, 1966).
[46] A. N. Sherwin-White, *The Roman citizenship* (Oxford, 1939) 116–17, argues that the cities of north Etruria provide an example of this reluctance; but against the view that the Romans had only one *foedus* with an Etruscan city – Falerii – see now W. V. Harris, *Rome in Etruria and Umbria* (Oxford, 1971) 85–113.

followed in due course by the full *de facto* equality which consisted of access to high office, to peoples who were able and willing to Romanise themselves. In practice these were the peoples of the West, who were less civilised and for that reason offered less resistance to the higher culture of Rome. ‖

The Romans of course had the normal share of suspicion of foreign peoples; but it is rarely based on a sense of their racial inferiority. When they speak contemptuously of the peoples of northern Europe and the western Mediterranean lands, it is their cultural backwardness rather than anything specifically racial which they are decrying. This lower cultural level makes them ready to endure what would be intolerable for a Roman. ‘Omnes nationes’, declares Cicero,[47] ‘servitutem ferre possunt: nostra civitas non potest’ – slavery is something tolerable to all *nationes*, but not to our state. The Gauls, he observes in the *Pro Fonteio*,[48] have no respect for oaths; they make war on all religions, they once set out to sack Delphi and they besieged the Capitol; even to this day they maintain the foul practice of human sacrifice. They are *immanes et barbarae nationes*, he tells Quintus,[49] like the Africans and the Spaniards. Their savagery is partly the result of the harsh surroundings in which they live; as Livy remarks[50] of the Raeti, whom he believes to be sprung from Etruscan origins, ‘the very region has rendered them savage so that they retain nothing of their ancient manners except the sound of their language – and even that is corrupt’.

This kind of criticism has mixed origins and is not all to be taken at its face value. There was a tradition going back to the Greeks for describing foreign and barbarous peoples.[51] In particular the notion that national characteristics are shaped by the kind of country and climate in which one lives is an old Greek theory[52] which first appears in Hippocrates’ famous work, *On climates, waters, and places*, which attributed variations in national character and temperament to differences in climate. This doctrine, which was to exercise a widespread influence right down to modern times (when both Buckle in England and Montesquieu in France expound doctrines closely allied to it), found an important champion in Aristotle, who in the seventh book of the *Politics* distinguished three groups:[53] the peoples who live in cold ‖ regions and in Europe and are in consequence extremely courageous but lacking in intelligence and artistic skill – which results in their being free but without the *polis*, and incapable of ruling others; secondly the Asians, who are artistic and intelligent, but cowardly, and therefore slaves; and thirdly the nation of the Greeks, τὸ

---

[47] Cic. *Phil.* x.20.   [48] Cic. *Font.* 30.

[49] Cic. *QFr.* I.1.28–9.   [50] Livy v.33.

[51] See K. Trüdinger, *Studien zur Geschichte der griechisch-römischen Ethnographie* (Basel, 1918) 126ff.; A. Dihle, ‘Zur hellenistischen Ethnographie’, in *Grecs et barbares* (Entretiens sur l’antiquité classique 8, Geneva, 1962) 207–39.

[52] See F. W. Walbank, *C et M* 9 (1948) 179ff.; R. Pöhlmann, *Hellenische Anschauungen über den Zusammenhang zwischen Natur und Geschichte* (Leipzig, 1889) 12ff. There is a good example in Poseidonius fr. 76 van Straaten, dealing with Athens.

[53] Arist. *Pol.* VII.7.2–3, 1327b19; *cf.* Gelzer, *Kleine Schriften* 3 (Wiesbaden, 1964) 4–5.

τῶν Ἑλλήνων γένος, which lies between and therefore shares the good characteristics of both, uniting courage with intelligence, mostly living in *poleis*, and capable of ruling over everyone – if only, he adds, they could unite under a single constitution, μιᾶς τυγχάνον πολιτείας! This climatic notion clearly influenced the popular view of the eastern peoples as well as the northern; the unfortunate *publicani* of Asia, exclaims Cicero[54] with indignation, have been handed over by Gabinius 'in servitutem Iudaeis et Syris, nationibus natis servituti', peoples born to be slaves. And very much later we find Socrates in his *Historia Ecclesiastica*[55] explaining that the austerity of the Phrygians and Paphlagonians (members of the Novatian church) is the result of the climate; they live in the zone between the Scythians and the Thracians, who are inclined to violent passions, and the peoples of the East who are the victims of their own appetites, and that is why they have no interest in horse-racing and the theatre, and regard fornication with horror.[56]

These traditional modes of thought are obviously not without their influence at Rome. On the other hand, one should not attribute too much to any formal theory. There is clearly a popular element in this stigmatising of national characteristics which is to be found in all peoples at all times: a national image of one's neighbour and enemy – often identical – is created, and belief in it becomes something like an article of faith. And where peoples live in close conjunction, as the Romans increasingly did as they administered or emigrated to their empire, prejudice and irritation play their part in heightening the colours. The same thing had happened earlier. From Ptolemaic Egypt we have evidence of racial friction; in the Zenon papyri an Arab complains of victimisation because he cannot play the Greek – Ἑλληνίζειν; and another document records the complaint of a priest that the cleruch billeted on him despises him because he is an Egyptian.[57] At this time the Greeks are the dominant people in Egypt. But a hundred years later the situation is reversed, for now a *katochos* of the Sarapeum at Memphis complains that he is persecuted by the Egyptians ‖ because he is a Greek.[58] Such instances of racial prejudice arise naturally where two peoples share a single country and[59] can easily be paralleled in many places today; they are quite understandable without any pseudo-scientific theory of national characteristics.

Frequently, too, the Roman picture was coloured by long years of bitter fighting. The phrase *Gallicus tumultus* could still produce a shudder in the Roman hearer centuries after the Gauls had ceased to threaten anyone in Italy, and a reference to the suspension of army leave on the occasion of a *tumultus Italicus Gallicusve* appears in the charter of the Caesarian *colonia Genetiva*

---

[54] Cic. *Prov. Cons.* 10.   [55] Socrates, *Hist. Eccl.* iv.28.

[56] On this, see A. H. M. Jones, *JThS* 10 (1959) 297–8.

[57] *P. Col. Zen.* 2.66; *P. Yale* 46 col. i, l. 13.

[58] See W. Peremans, 'Egyptiens et étrangers dans l'Egypte', in *Grecs et barbares* (Entretiens sur l'antiquité classique 8, Geneva, 1962) 121–66.

[59] On Greeks and Orientals in the Seleucid kingdom see D. Musti, *SCO* 15 (1966) 136–7.

Julia in Spain.[60] But there is another aspect of the evidence which deserves attention, the influence of rhetoric. Many of the examples I have quoted have been from Cicero; and one may recall Quintilian's remark about him:[61] 'Where *nationes* are concerned, Cicero employs a flexible procedure: when he is about to deny any credibility to Greek witnesses, he concedes them their science and literature, and claims to be a lover of their race, while damning the Sardinians and inveighing against the Allobroges as if they were avowed enemies.' Clearly Cicero could not get away with saying anything that would sound completely paradoxical; but his testimony (and much of a similar character) is to be taken *cum grano salis*, because it is subordinated to the rhetorical exigencies of the moment.

There is one thing common to these Roman references to people of foreign nationalities, they never make that rigid differentiation which the Greeks of the classical period made between themselves and the barbarians. Indeed, this distinction meant so little to the Romans originally that they were even prepared to accept the Greek valuation and count themselves barbarians. In Plautus' *Captivi*[62] the cities and laws of Italy are 'barbarae urbes, barbarica lex'; in the *Miles*[63] Naevius is a 'barbarus poeta'; and in the *Mostellaria*[64] there is talk of a 'porridge-eating barbarian workman', ('pultiphagus opifex...barbarus'). But as Hellenic customs and values became more widespread with the growth of Hellenisation in Italy, the Romans came to resent this appellation: ‖ Cato somewhat dyspeptically complained[65] that 'nos quoque dictitant barbaros', and Lucilius[66] reserved the unseemly name for the enemies of Rome: 'bello vinci a barbaro Viriato Annibale'. The problem of how the Romans fitted into the old categories of Greeks and barbarians continued, however, to be troublesome.[67] *Barbarus*, which had begun as a purely onomatopoeic word to describe the incomprehensible noises made by the foreigner, had acquired, especially since the days of the Persian Wars, when Greek national feeling perhaps came nearest to meaning something real, a tone of contempt; and Greek emotion was whipped up in the panhellenic rhetoric of Gorgias, Lysias, and Isocrates. Clearly the Romans were not barbarians (though Greeks might so describe them either thoughtlessly or with intent to hurt);[68] when Ovid at Tomi laments[69] that he is now literally the barbarian, this is meant as an outrageous paradox:

> barbarus hic ego sum qui non intelligor ulli
> et rident stolidi verba Latina Geti.

---

[60] *ILS* 6087, ch. lxii, l. 31.   [61] Quint. *Inst.* xi.1.89.

[62] Plaut. *Capt.* 884 and 492.   [63] Plaut. *Miles* 211.

[64] Plaut. *Mostell.* 828.   [65] Pliny, *NH* xxix.7.14.

[66] Lucil. *Sat.* 615 Marx.

[67] *Cf.* K. Christ, 'Römer und Barbaren in der hohen Kaiserzeit', *Saeculum* (1959) 273–88; A. J. Toynbee, *Hannibal's legacy* (London, 1965) 2.435ff.

[68] *Cf.* Polyb. xviii.22.5; see H. H. Schmitt, *Hellenen, Römer und Barbaren* (Progr. Aschaffenburg 1957/8).

[69] Ovid, *Trist.* v.10.37–8.

But they were not Greeks either – for when Heracleides Ponticus,[70] in describing the sack of Rome by the Gauls in 390, had used the term πόλις Ἑλληνίς of Rome, this was merely evidence of that writer's ignorance or irresponsibility. Indeed, the Romans would not have thanked anyone for such a description. From the time of their earliest contacts with Greeks, they had had an ambivalent attitude toward them. On the one hand, the achievements of classical and Hellenistic Greece from Homer onwards entitled her to genuine respect; and it was of course to Greece that the Romans turned for their earliest lessons in all branches of art and literature. Moreover, cultured Romans like Flamininus and Scipio appreciated recognition on equal terms by the Greeks whom they had 'liberated'. But at the same time the undisciplined political life of cities like Tarentum or Corinth,[71] and the slippery character of individual Greeks who had gained nothing from deracination and perhaps a spell of slavery thrown in, led old-fashioned ‖ Romans from Cato to Juvenal to despise the *Graeculus esuriens*.[72] Cato saw corruption as the first fruit of Greek learning and even alleged that Greek doctors were in league to poison their honest Roman patients:[73] when Carneades shocked the Romans by his amoral defence of self-interest in politics, Cato was the first to urge that he be sent quickly about his business.[74] And so, eventually, the Romans had to reconcile themselves to being neither the one thing nor the other; and when in the *De Finibus*[75] Cicero wants to say that Epicurean influence has been widely felt throughout the whole known world, the terms he employs to make that point are *Graecia, Italia* and *barbaria* – a formula which, incidentally, illustrates very clearly the incorporation of Italy in Rome from the Social War onward.

IV

This assimilation of Italy is in fact the pattern for what later happens all over the empire. Usually the granting of *civitas* and Latin rights is the recognition of Romanisation already achieved; and this goes steadily ahead, eroding national distinctions. Everywhere the number of *cives Romani* grows, despite caution on the part of conservative emperors like Augustus himself, and despite Roman prejudice against barbarous Gauls or decadent Greeks and Syrians. The double process, the extension of Roman power and Romanisation and the rewarding of its attainment by grants of citizenship, did not, however, go unopposed by subject peoples, who could not always appreciate the value of a *pax Romana* which took away their freedom. The extent and depth of this resistance is not always easily assessed, nor how far it is national in inspiration. Imperial expansion always meets resistance. Melos rejected the demands of

---

[70] Plut. *Cam.* 22.2.
[71] *Cf.* Dion. Hal. xix.5, *cf.* vi.3; Livy, *Epit.* 12; Val. Max. ii.2.5; App. *Sam.* 7.2 (Tarentum); Paus. vii.14.1–3, *cf.* Polyb. xxxviii.9.1 and 6 (Corinth).
[72] Juv. 3.60–80.   [73] Pliny, *NH* xxix.14.
[74] Plut. *Cat. Mai.* 22.5.
[75] Cic. *Fin.* ii.49; *cf.* Christ, *op. cit.* (n. 67).

Athens and was destroyed; Rhodes successfully resisted Demetrius Poliorcetes. But this did not make either Rhodes or Melos a nation. Perhaps resistance can fairly be called national when it is inspired by conscious opposition to values and customs because they are Roman and tries deliberately to revive those of a native culture. Such resistance need not be military: it can be a cultural movement with a national base, like Welsh or Scottish nationalism today. Fuchs has assembled[76] sufficient evidence from the eastern parts of the Roman ‖ empire over a period lasting from the early second century B.C. down to the later Empire to show that there were always Greeks, Syrians and Egyptians ready to inveigh against Roman ways. An outstanding example is Lucian's *Nigrinus*, which contrasts the delights of Athens, absorbed in Platonic philosophy, with the absurdities and Philistinism of contemporary life at Rome;[77] and in the previous century wandering philosophers like Dio Chrysostom[78] and Apollonius of Tyana[79] preached the values of Greek culture and warned their listeners against too much Romanisation. In the fourth century we find Libanius voicing his alarm when Greek youths go off to Berytus to learn Latin and study Roman law.[80] But, above all, Egypt – the province which Seneca describes as *in contumelias praefectorum ingeniosa*[81] – 'with a genius for insulting its governors', provides examples in the acts of the Alexandrine martyrs of a whole series of no doubt largely imaginary insults hurled at Roman magistrates and emperors by Alexandrian envoys.[82] Quite recently, Lambrechts[83] has tried to show that there was similar resistance to Rome in the West, pointing to the survival of the native Celtic tongue down to the fourth century and even beyond, and more particularly analysing the evidence for the continued practice of native religions – of the *Matres*, or *Matronae*, in Roman Germany, and of *Epona* and the Celtic versions of Mars, Mercury and Hercules in Celtic areas – and the appearance in the last centuries of the western empire of Celto-Roman temples, for instance, at Autun and Périgueux and at many places in Britain on sites important in pre-Roman times such as Maiden Castle.[84]

Now this evidence – it is set out in full in Lambrechts' and Fuchs' essays – is certainly proof of the persistence of native cultures. But to take the western area first, Lambrechts himself shows that what he has described is a cultural resistance to Rome without any corresponding political hostility. The fact, underlined by him, that many of the dedications to native gods are made by Roman officials, that in Britain the worship of Mars Ocelus, dea Brigantia,

[76] *Op. cit.* (n. 42).   [77] Lucian, *Nigr.* 12ff.
[78] Dio Chrys. *Or.* 32.69, 95, 34.38ff., 38.36ff. *Cf.* Fuchs, *op. cit.* (n. 42) 50.
[79] Apoll. *Epist.* 63, 70; *cf.* Philostr. IV.27; Ed. Meyer, *Kleine Schriften* 2 (Halle, 1924) 133ff., 148ff., 159ff., 171ff.; Fuchs, *op. cit.* (n. 42) 50.
[80] Libanius, *Or.* 1.214, 234; 2.43f.; 43.3ff.; 48.22ff.; *Epist.* 951, 1011; Fuchs, *op. cit.* (n. 42) 51.
[81] Sen. *Helv.* 69.6.
[82] Ed. Meyer, *op. cit.* (n. 79) 2.175ff.
[83] *Op. cit.* (n. 45).   [84] *Ibid.* 11–15, 21.

and deus Antenociticus is ‖ linked with imperial cult[85] – for example, the altar set up in Cumberland to *dea nympha Brigantia* by M. Cocceius Nigrinus, a *procurator Augusti*, 'pro salute et incolumitate domini nostri invicti imperatoris M. Aureli Severi Antonini Pii Felicis Augusti totiusque domus divinae'[86] – that even emperors worship the local gods, for example, Diocletian and Maximian making a dedication on an inscription from Aquileia to Belenus,[87] a Celtic form of Apollo – all this goes to show that the movement had the full support of Roman authority and was indeed a development of traditional practice, which encouraged diversity and the survival of what was rooted in the native soil.

In the East it is different. One can hardly disguise the anti-Roman character of much of the evidence. But here too one must be chary of reading too much into some of it. Whether, as has been suggested,[88] Lucian drew on Juvenal for his *Nigrinus*, is not clear; certainly his account of the horrors of life in Rome is bound to recall the famous third satire. But it would of course be as wrong to regard Juvenal as unpatriotic for what he writes there as it would be to take Johnson's *London* as evidence that its author was anything other than a good loyal Tory. Rome could be attacked as well on moral as on nationalist grounds – and was so attacked by Tacitus,[89] Lucan,[90] and the author of the *Commentariolum Petitionis*.[91] Verbal battles were one way of keeping up one's morale in a world where Rome was undisputed mistress and her government autocratic. The Christians are of course another matter. When Hippolytus, bishop of Rome under Elagabalus (or Commodus),[92] prophesies in his *Commentary on Daniel*[93] that Rome will fall with the rise of democracies among the nations, κατὰ ἔθνη, and that ten kings will partition the Roman empire according to them, he is drawing on ancient traditions, some of them going back to the Sibylline oracles, which flourished from the second century B.C. onwards. But his purpose is religious, not nationalist; he attacks the Roman empire because he believes it to be a Satanic counterfeit of true ‖ Christian unity. Since the Christians generally preached the early coming of the end of the world and so of the Roman Empire, it is natural that their prophecies should have taken on an anti-Roman shape and utilised many old rhetorical clichés to underline their lesson; and that when the Roman state showed its hostility, the Christians should have retaliated by drawing on the vast anti-Roman literature of the Near East. But the Christians' victory under Constantine, which was to change the nature of the Empire, was not of course a victory for nationalism; it was a victory for a religion which refused to compromise and gained strength from its martyrdoms. No purely nationalist movement under the Roman Empire showed a similar vitality.

[85] *Ibid.* 15; *cf.* Collingwood-Wright, *RIB* 1327, 1328 (deus Antenociticus) 623, 627, 2066 (dea Brigantia).   [86] *CIL* 7.875 = *RIB* 2066.   [87] *ILS* 625.
[88] So Mesk, *WS* 34 (1912) 373ff.; 35 (1913) 1ff.; criticised by Fuchs, *op. cit.* (n. 42) 52 n. 64.
[89] Tac. *Ann.* xv.44.   [90] Lucan vii.405.
[91] Auct. *Comm. Pet.* 54; *cf.* Fuchs, *op. cit.* (n. 42) 54 n. 66.
[92] See S. Mazzarino, *End of the ancient world* (London, 1966) 39–40, 113.
[93] Hippolytus, *In Daniel.* 2.7, 12; 4.13; *cf.* Mazzarino, *op. cit.* (n. 92) 48.

V

The success of Rome in imposing acceptance of her rule over so vast an area and in assimilating so many different peoples and cultures was achieved partly by crude violence, *debellare superbos*, partly through understanding once the issue was decided, *parcere subiectis*, and partly through the ingenious use of her elastic citizenship to unify and win over the ambitious to Roman ways. Although the *pax Romana* rarely meant a world at peace, and indeed after the second century became little more than an empty aspiration, there are very few wars throughout the history of the Empire which even superficially look like nationalist risings. I can only touch quite cursorily on this subject here; it is perhaps worth looking briefly at the Roman experience in three areas – Gaul, the Near East and North Africa.

The Gauls had been put down by force of arms and terrorism under Julius Caesar, but already by 12 B.C. a generation had passed since the fighting ceased and the great altar at Lugdunum and the *concilium Galliarum* were evidence of effective pacification and the adherence of the upper classes.[94] The revolts under Tiberius were small, short-lived, and insignificant, and sprang mainly from the personal difficulties of their leaders, Florus and Sacrovir, who were weighed down by debt; sixty out of sixty-four tribes ignored the movement.[95] That there was still some residual national feeling among the Aedui seems probable, however, from the fact that when in A.D. 69 the Boian Mariccus raised a ‖ revolt as *adsertor Galliarum et deus*,[96] a divine liberator of Gaul, he carried several Aeduan cantons with him. But the more serious revolt the same year, based mainly among the Treviri and the Lingones, was a mixed affair.[97] Inter-tribal jealousies kept most of Gaul loyal; indeed the fact that the tribes in revolt had earlier supported Verginius Rufus[98] against Vindex deterred the rest of the Gauls from having anything to do with them now. And though we hear of the Druids prophesying *vana superstitione*,[99] Julius Sabinus claimed descent from Caesar and took his name – hardly, one would have thought, an advantage in a strongly nationalist movement.

After this, Gaul seems settled and there is nothing like a nationalist rising until the *Galliarum imperium* in the mid third century. This name for Postumus' empire appears only in Eutropius;[100] the *Historia Augusta*[101] calls the Gallic emperors *adsertores Romani nominis*, a name significant in its contrast to the title given to Mariccus, *adsertor Galliarum*. Sherwin-White has shown, decisively, I

---

[94] *Dio Cass.* LIV.32.1; Livy, *Epit.* 139. For the year 12 B.C. see Hirschfeld on *CIL* 13.1.227; Larsen, *op. cit.* (n. 13) 224 n. 6; Suet. *Claud.* 2 makes it 10 B.C. On the peaceful character of Gaul see the emperor Claudius in *ILS* 212, ll. 34–6.

[95] *Cf.* Sherwin-White, *op. cit.* (n. 46) 251–2.

[96] Tac. *Hist.* II.61.

[97] For a coin of this year personifying Gallia see T. G. E. Powell, *The Celts* (London, 1958) pl. 47d.

[98] Tac. *Hist.* IV.69.

[99] *Ibid.* IV.54.

[100] Eutrop. IX.9.3.

[101] SHA. *Tyr. Trig.* 5.5 (vita Lolliani).

think, that there is no sound evidence that Postumus and his successors were playing on nationalist feelings. Their coin-types[102] all echo traditional legends such as *Aequitas Augusta, Aeternitas Augusta, Roma Aeterna, Fides* or *Concordia Militum*, and *Pax Augusta*; and of the series featuring Hercules, only two of the sixteen titles which the hero is given are local, and of these *Deusoniensis* is Germanic and refers to Köln-Deutz across the Rhine, while *Magusanus* is said by Camille Jullian[103] to be a Greco-Roman form of cult. Even granted that Hercules had special associations with Gaul, Postumus' use of his name on coins cannot then be construed as a mark of Gallic nationalist feeling; and indeed this Gallic empire seems better regarded as a local piece of self-help, intended to preserve the power and traditions of Rome in the West at a time when the central government was temporarily too weak to shoulder this burden.

When one turns to the East, some special features emerge. We have already examined briefly some of the anti-Roman ideas and traditions which circulated there, to be drawn upon in due course by the Christian ‖ Church. But Palestine provides an example of a movement perhaps unique in the history of the Empire. The excavations at Masada[104] and the discovery of the Dead Sea Scrolls[105] have recently aroused popular interest in the Jewish movement, in which the combination of social struggle and national resistance was charged with the powerful currents that are generated by fanaticism. The combination is not unique: to some extent, Druidism lent force to the resistance in Gaul and Britain. But I can recall no example in Roman history where Roman methods proved in the long run so unavailing as they did in the case of the Jews; and this seems to reflect the peculiar union of elements in the Jewish movement.

A similar combination of religion and nationalism has been identified by some scholars in the Donatist movement in North Africa, which made use of the native languages, Punic and Libyan, and has been accused of supporting native pretenders and even the Goths against the Roman government. Like the Jews, too, the Donatists had their fanatical wing in the wandering bands of *circumcelliones*. But here the likeness ends. A. H. M. Jones[106] has shown convincingly that there is no evidence for a North African national consciousness actuating the supporters of Donatist Christianity. His analysis is decisive for the view that the professors of the Donatist belief, both the more orthodox and the more fanatical, were moved almost solely by religious motives; and even if Frend[107] were right in suggesting that the form their religious beliefs took, in their fearful and gloomy character, their superstition

---

[102] *Cf.* Sherwin-White, *op. cit.* (n. 46) 277–8.
[103] C. Jullian in *CRAI* (1896) 298ff.; Sherwin-White, *op. cit.* (n. 46).
[104] *Cf.* Y. Yadin, *Masada: Herod's fortress and the Zealots' last stand* (London, 1966); S. Applebaum, 'The Zealots: the case for revaluation', *JRS* 61 (1971) 155–70.
[105] See, for example, R. de Vaux, *L'archéologie et les manuscrits de la Mer Morte* (London, 1961); but the literature is vast.
[106] *JThS* 10 (1959) 240–98.
[107] *Op. cit.* (n. 44) 75ff.

and their obsession with martyrdom, owed much to the widespread worship of the Punic Baal Hamon, under the Roman name of Saturn, from which they were converted, this would not make the Donatist creed in any sense a nationalist movement.

VI

There is a passage in Aelius Aristides' famous panegyric on Rome,[108] however, which suggests that something like a nation had grown up – difficult though such an idea appears – in the empire as a whole. In ‖ one of his more memorable sections he remarks that the population of the empire is divided into two parts, 'the better part of the world's talent, courage and leadership, whom the Romans have admitted to citizenship and even kinship, and the rest who form the subject element, ὑπήκοόν τε καὶ ἀρχόμενον'. 'The word Roman', he continues,[109] 'you have caused to be the label not of membership in a city, but of some common nationality, γένους ὄνομα κοινοῦ τινος, and this not just one among all, but one balancing all the rest.' Instead of the old division of the world into Hellenes and Barbarians, the Romans have set up a new division into Romans and non-Romans.

This statement is at first striking. But it is almost certainly mere rhetoric. Aristides is echoing a famous passage of Isocrates' *Panegyricus*[110] in which he said that the Athenians had made the name of Hellene synonymous with that of their own city; this was to restrict a nation to a city, and so the Romans in contrast must be shown to have expanded their city so as to convert it into a nation. There is no more to it than that; elsewhere Aelius Aristides normally uses the word *Romani* for all the inhabitants of the empire, citizens and *peregrini* alike. This is perhaps a sign of the success which the Romans had had in forging a supranational state. I have already suggested that the extension of Roman *civitas*, a force acting against nationalism, attracted first the upper classes and then ultimately (and less effectively) the rest of the population to Rome. The building of a supranational loyalty was an aim consciously pursued. Already in the first century, the Elder Pliny[111] spoke of substituting Latin for the wild and dissonant tongues of the various peoples, uniting the empires and imposing *humanitas* on all. It was perhaps recognition of some degree of success in achieving this end, among other reasons (many of them more important and more mundane), that led Caracalla to promulgate the *Constitutio Antoniniana*[112] granting Roman citizenship to all but an insignificant number of the inhabitants of the empire. By this action, of course, he substantially reduced the importance of *civitas*; and he also encouraged the revival of an old distinction. The fiction that the Roman empire was to be identified with the whole world, the *orbis terrarum* – perhaps always something of an affectation – was rather easier when *civitas* was not coterminous everywhere with the

---

[108] *Ad Romam* 59.   [109] *Ibid.* 63.
[110] Isoc. *Paneg.* 56.   [111] Pliny, *NH* III.39.
[112] *Cf.* Dio Cass. LXXVIII.9–10; *P. Giss.* 40 no. 1 = *FIRA* 1.88.

frontiers. The pattern under the early Empire had been one much more of shades and gradations, with ‖ intermediate zones;[113] there were still barbarians to subdue within the frontiers and areas of Roman influence without. But now in the late Empire the contrast between Romans and barbarians once again becomes more rigid: we hear more of *barbari* – partly no doubt because there were far more *barbari* around to hear of – but if they are to be found within the frontiers it is because they have been brought in or forced their way in. The old distinction, which, Aelius Aristides boasted, had been superseded by Rome, was now back in a new form and was to grow more important down to the end of the western Empire. It created new loyalties; and how far the poorer citizens of the provinces shared these is a matter of guess-work. In a full discussion of the available evidence Jones[114] discounts the more sensational tales of collaboration put out by Orosius and Salvian, but concludes that in general the peasantry was apathetic and docile. 'The Roman Empire', he adds, 'seems never to have evoked any active patriotism from the vast majority of its citizens.'[115] This apathy may also help to explain why nationalism failed to develop into a movement of consequence within the Roman empire. Differences of race, language, religion and custom all counted then as they have always counted; and innate conservatism defended them in many areas, often with the willing consent of the ruling power. But these differences usually fell short of inspiring militant nationalism, and for this I see two main reasons. First, the well-tried Roman device, originally used to good effect on the plebeians within the Roman state, of rewarding conformism and right thinking with political recognition and ultimate equality – equality, that is, in the holding of office and even the imperial throne; this accounted for the upper classes and the more ambitious sections within the peoples the Romans had to deal with. Secondly, the great care taken never to allow anything like Greek or modern democracy to flourish meant that the poor saw nothing in their national differences important enough to be worth fighting about. Toynbee has observed that it is the combination of nationalism with democracy that has made it such a formidable force in the nineteenth and twentieth centuries. Because Rome offered the upper classes too much and the rest too little, nationalism remained undeveloped as a political force. In some places like Gaul it withered and died; and once any people had been conquered, it was rare for their resentment to flower into revolt. Judaea, as we saw, was the exception, ‖ and there nationalism became a dynamic force only through the inspiration of religion.

Nationalism, then, was to play only a small role in Roman history. There was a moment when the unification of Italy seemed likely to create an Italian nation. But because the *civitas* remained Rome, not Italy, Rome advanced from the city-state to the world-empire. To share the same *gens, natio, lingua* – this,

---

[113] Christ, *op. cit.* (n. 67) 283–4.
[114] *The later Roman Empire* (Oxford, 1964) 3.1059ff.
[115] *Ibid.* 1062.

Cicero saw, was a close bond: but the bond of *civitas* was closer. *Civitas* in his context meant the community of the city-state, where fellow-citizens shared the same social life. It was the achievement of the Romans to develop and extend the political aspect of that *civitas* and the binding-forces and emotions inherent in it, until eventually it coincided with the length and breadth of the empire. In the modern world we are disposed to restrict *civitas* and subordinate it to the concept of nationality with which it is so closely linked. One is not called upon to say which is the better way; but certainly to recognise the difference is to be made aware of one of the great gulfs that lie between the modern world and that of Rome.[116]

[116] A James Loeb lecture given at Harvard University on 12 November 1970.

5

POLYBIUS, PHILINUS, AND THE FIRST PUNIC WAR*

Polybius' sources for his account of the First Punic War are not in question. It is agreed that Fabius Pictor and Philinus of Agrigentum, whom he criticises didactically in 1.14–15, were his sole authorities. But, as Gelzer has most recently pointed out,[1] difficulties soon appear when one begins to assign the various sections of the narrative to one or other of Polybius' predecessors. This task has frequently been attempted, and a good deal of common ground has been won. It is not my purpose in this paper to go over that ground again. What I propose to do is, first, to discuss the most recent article on Philinus of Agrigentum, which is in my opinion based on false principles and comes to novel, but wrong, conclusions; this done I shall try to relate what can be discovered with certainty about the character of Philinus' work to the general body of Hellenistic historical writing and historical theory. I hope that such a study may help to throw light on one part of Polybius' direct literary inheritance.

I

It is no longer necessary today to emphasise the importance of Gelzer's work[2] on Fabius Pictor and the beginnings of historical writing at Rome. In general Gelzer's theory[3] was too extreme to be accepted in its entirety; but he showed conclusively that Fabius' history was composed with the definite purpose of publicising the Senate's political programme, its προαίρεσις, in the civilised world of Greece, which was now coming into contact with Roman policy and Roman methods.[4]

* [CQ 39 (1945) 1–18]

Note. This paper was read on 26 May 1944 at a Joint Meeting of the Oxford Philological Society and the Oxford Branch of the Classical Association. I take this opportunity of thanking those who there or elsewhere have made critical suggestions, and in particular Drs F. Jacoby, A. Momigliano, and P. Treves.

[1] On Polybius' sources for the First Punic War (1.6–64) see J. Luterbacher, *Philologus* 66 (1907) 396–426; F. Reuss, *Philologus* 60 (1901) 102–48; *Philologus* 68 (1909) 410–27; De Sanctis, *Storia dei Romani* 3.1 (Turin, 1916) 224–47 (with references to earlier literature); L. Sisto, *Atene e Roma* 12 (1931) 176ff.; and M. Gelzer, *Hermes* 68 (1933) 133–42.

[2] M. Gelzer, *Hermes* 68 (1933) 129–66: 'Römische Politik bei Fabius Pictor'; *Hermes*, 69 (1934) 46–55: 'Der Anfang römischer Geschichtsschreibung'. Gelzer's picture of Fabius was to some extent anticipated in F. Leo, *Geschichte der römischen Literatur* 1 (Berlin, 1913) 85ff.

[3] See below, Addendum, pp. 94–8, for a general criticism of Gelzer's theory.

[4] The older view of Fabius as an annalist pure and simple had been supported by T. Mommsen's view (*Römische Forschungen* 2 (Berlin, 1864–79) 272ff.) that he was the source of Diodorus' annalistic

In his earlier article (1933) Gelzer applied his conception of Fabius' purpose and method to isolate those passages in Polybius' version of the First Punic War which could be attributed to the Roman senator. His work demonstrated the necessity of revising the view that Polybius' account was a mechanically constructed patchwork of easily separable material from Philinus and Fabius.[5] For one thing, Fabius himself probably employed Philinus as a source;[6] and in any case Polybius' narrative often contains Punic and Roman traditions in close relation within a single chapter.

I stress this interweaving of the two strands in our tradition not because it is in any sense a new point but because it is implicitly contradicted by the latest study on Philinus, Professor Richard Laqueur's article in *RE*,[7] published in 1938. Laqueur has ‖ made Gelzer's work the foundation of a study which contains much that is acute and justly said, but is spoilt by the fondness for paradox which is an unfortunate characteristic of Laqueur's work. In particular, Laqueur has attributed an excessive and perverse importance to the different indications of time in Polybius' narrative, and has attempted to employ these mechanically as a criterion of source analysis. It is well known that for the fourteen years 263 to 250 Polybius mentions all the Roman consuls with the exception of those for 259 and 252, and one of those for 257.[8] For the rest of the war his references are much more scanty, only three consuls being mentioned in eight years.[9] On the old view of Fabius Pictor the explanation of this divergence seemed simple. Consul names indicated the use of Fabius; their absence that of Philinus. Characteristically, Laqueur switches this doctrine upside down. Not only was Fabius no annalist, he argues, but, like Cato[10] – for whom the fact is expressly testified – he never mentioned consuls at all. Thus Polybius' account of the Gallic Wars in II.18ff., which is certainly derived from Fabius,[11] does not date by consul-years, but by such expressions as 'not long afterwards', 'twelve years later', and the like. This 'suppression of the individual' Laqueur regards as typical of the early Republic, and in contrast to the ethos of the Hellenistic world, with its insistence upon individual personality. Hence it is likely to be Philinus, the Sicilian historian, who feels it necessary to give the unfamiliar Roman names to balance the Carthaginian.

notices (most conveniently consulted in *Diodors römische Annalen bis 302 a. Chr. samt dem Ineditum Vaticanum*, herausgegeben von A. B. Drachmann (Kleine Texte, Bonn, 1912)). But this theory has frequently been exploded. *Cf.* A. Klotz, *RhM* 86 (1937) 206–24, developing a view previously expressed by Ed. Meyer.

[5] *Cf.* Jacoby in *FGH*, Commentary on 174, p. 598; *contra* Beloch, *Griechische Geschichte* 4.2 (Berlin–Leipzig, 1927) 11.

[6] This is generally accepted; see authorities quoted by Gelzer, *Hermes* (1933) 133 n. 5.

[7] R. Laqueur, *RE* 19.2 (1938) 'Philinos (8)', cols. 2180–93.

[8] 1.16.1 (263), 17.6 (262), 20.4 (261), 21.4 and 22.1 (260), 24.9 (258), 25.1 (257: one omitted), 26.11 (256), 36.10 (255), 38.6 (254), 39.1 (253), 39.8 (251), 39.15 (250).

[9] 1.49.3 (249): P. Claudius Pulcher, 52.5 (249: L. Iunius Pullus, attributed to 248), 59.8 (242: C. Lutatius Catulus).

[10] *Cf.* Nepos, *Cato* 3; Pliny *NH* VIII.11: listed by Peter, *HRF* 'M. Porcius Cato', T.2 and F.88.

[11] *Cf.* Beloch, *Römische Geschichte* (Berlin–Leipzig, 1926) 132ff.

In this way Laqueur sets up a new criterion: for analysing Polybius' account of the First Punic War any reference to a consul is *ipso facto* a mark of Philinus, whereas dates by intervals or by years of the war[12] reveal the use of Fabius Pictor.

This theory is undoubtedly wrong. In the first place, the only evidence that might confirm Laqueur's view that Fabius did not mention consuls by name is a passage from Livy (x.37.14)[13] which reads: 'Fabius writes that both consuls (for 294) were active in Samnium and near Luceria, that the army was marched into Etruria (but by which consul he does not add), and that many men were slain on both sides in a battle near Luceria, etc.' Clearly, however, this passage indicates nothing beyond the fact that on a particular occasion Fabius did not say which of the two consuls carried out a certain operation;[14] indeed, that Livy thought fit to comment on the omission is, if anything, evidence that it was unusual. Further, against Laqueur there is the fact (which he ignores) that in the very section which deals with the Gallic Wars, and is by general consent admitted to be derived from Fabius, Polybius mentions by name five consuls, as well as C. Flaminius, the tribune of 232.[15] Laqueur, moreover, draws no distinction between 'interval dating' and dating 'by years of the ‖ war'. The two are in fact quite separate. In surveying the history of a long period like that of the Gallic Wars, as Polybius does in Book II, it is natural to indicate time intervals; indeed without a system like A.U.C. or A.D. this is the only comprehensible method, consul years being meaningless without a table for conversion into some scheme dating from a fixed year. Hence in selecting his material from Fabius Polybius would naturally indicate the number of years intervening between the events he records, whether in fact such interval-dates were already in Fabius or not. The fact that he nevertheless mentions five consuls seems clear proof that not only these but others too were in Fabius' narrative, had Polybius but cared to record them, especially as there is good reason to think that Polybius' account of the Gallic Wars considerably abridged that of Fabius.[16] In short, 'interval dating' and the mention of consuls by name are in no sense alternative systems.[17]

[12] *E.g.* 1.41.4 (fourteenth year), 56.2 (eighteenth year); 56.11 (σχεδὸν ἐπὶ τρεῖς ἐνιαυτούς), 58.6 (δύ' ἔτη πάλιν), 59.1 (ἔτη σχεδὸν ἤδη πέντε), 63.4 (ἔτη...εἴκοσι καὶ τέτταρα).

[13] Peter, *HRF* F.19.

[14] So correctly Klotz, *RhM* 86 (1937) 215. This fragment had already previously been associated with Cato's practice by Schwartz, *RE* 5.1 (1903) 'Diodoros (38)', col. 693.

[15] II.19.8 (Lucius Caecilius and Manius Curius; Polybius calls Lucius 'consul', but he was in fact praetor for 283; *cf.* Beloch, *op. cit.* (n. 11) 133), 21.7 (232: M. Aemilius Lepidus), 23.6 (225: L. Aemilius and C. Atilius). C. Flaminius is given as tribune in 232 (21.8); on the date see Mommsen, *op. cit.* (n. 4) 2.401 n. 23. Peter, *HRF* F.23 (Oros. IV.13.5 = Eutrop. III.5) also mentions consuls by name, and goes on to quote Fabius as a source. But it is safer to draw no conclusions from this, as the reference will have come *via* Livy. One may ignore the suggestion of E. Pais, *Storia di Roma dalle origini all' inizio delle guerre puniche* 5 (Rome, 1928) 66 n. 2, that Polybius' account of the Gallic Wars is derived from Timaeus or Philinus.

[16] *Cf.* Beloch, *op. cit.* (n. 11) 100.

[17] It is worth while examining exactly *how* Polybius uses consul names. Admittedly they serve to define the year (*cf.* Beloch, *op. cit.* (n. 5) 4.2.11: 'bis zum Jahre 250 ist die Anordnung annalistisch'), but not in the rigid annalistic way to be seen in Diodorus or Livy. Polybius

We now come to the other allegedly alternative form of dating, that by 'years of the war', which Laqueur believes to be characteristic of Fabius Pictor. It has always been held, and reasonably, that this dating is most likely to be used in a monograph on the war rather than in a long history like that of Fabius.[18] It is not indeed very probable (though not impossible) that Fabius dated events of the First Punic War by years of that war. However, before we can assume that such references come on the contrary from Philinus, it must be asked whether he, in contrast to Fabius, wrote a war-monograph; if he did, it is highly probable that Polybius' two references to 'years of the war' are taken, as scholars have thought, from him.

The view that Philinus wrote only on the First Punic War is based on the fact that Diodorus, after using him for this, goes over to Polybius for his account of the Mercenary War in Africa.[19] Laqueur, it is true,[20] reverts to the view that for the later war Diodorus is still using Philinus direct; but he quotes nothing out of Diodorus which was not already in Polybius, and has no answer to the arguments put forward by Mommsen over fifty years ago. On the other hand, it should be noted as a ‖ possibility that Diodorus may have had access to Philinus only through an intermediate source (as Beloch argued),[21] in which case this source *may* have omitted the Mercenary War; Polybius, using Philinus direct, would get his account of that war from him, whereas Diodorus would be thrown back on Polybius.[22] However, this is pure hypothesis; there is no

invariably introduces them in connection with some historical action; and if, as in 259 (*cf.* 24.8), there was nothing worth recording, the consuls are omitted. (The omission of the names of the consuls at the beginning of 250 (41.2) is due to their having been mentioned already in 39.15.) For the second half of the war the principle is the same; names occur in connection with important events. Hence because the years between Hamilcar's arrival in Sicily in 247 and the last battle in 242 are passed over in a rapid, schematic fashion, no consul's name is given for that period. Polybius mentions P. Claudius Pulcher (249), his colleague, L. Iunius Pullus, whom he wrongly believed to be one of the pair for 248, and finally C. Lutatius (but not his colleague) in 242. The point is this: the omission or inclusion of consul names follows upon the character of the events described, and cannot be magnified into a major criterion for distinguishing Fabius from Philinus. *Prima facie* any reference to a consul may have come from either source; and the serious result of putting too high an importance upon such references is to be seen in Laqueur's discussion of those passages in Polybius I (22.1, 26.11, and 36.10) where consul names occur in the middle of sections which he admits to be derived from Fabius Pictor. No one will be ready to believe that in each of these cases Polybius made a cross-reference from Philinus.

[18] Fabius' history, like those of Cincius Alimentus and Cato (*cf.* Gelzer, *Hermes* 68 (1933) 129 n. 2), was fairly detailed in discussing the *origines*, sketchy for the intermediate years, and fuller again from the time of the Punic Wars onward; *cf.* Dionys. Hal. 1.6.2; Corn. Nep. *Cato* 3.3. See further, below, p. 97 n. 105.

[19] *Cf.* Jacoby, *FGH* 2D, p. 598.

[20] *Op. cit.* (n. 7) col. 2190 following Unger, *RhM* 34 (1879) 90ff. E. Täubler, *Die Vorgeschichte des II. punischen Krieges* (Berlin, 1921) 118–19, supports the same thesis, transposing Diod. xxv.5.3 and 9, and referring fr. 9 to Matho's last fight (Polyb. 1.87, 8–10); but it clearly refers to Spain. See in general Schwartz, *op. cit.* (n.14) col. 689; De Sanctis, *op. cit.* (n. 1) 3.1.385 n. 10; and especially Mommsen, *op. cit.* (n. 4) 2.266 n. 60.

[21] Beloch, *op. cit.* (n. 5) 4.2.12; Wendling, *Hermes* 28 (1893) 335ff., also assumes an intermediate source, later than Poseidonius, between Philinus and Diodorus; *contra* Jacoby, *FGH* 2D, p. 598, line 40.

[22] On the whole, Polybius' source for the Mercenary War seems to be rather more hostile towards Hanno, and more uncritically pro-Barcine than Philinus. Contrast the picture of Hanno

strong argument for the view that Diodorus used an intermediary, and I raise the point merely to show the impossibility of certainty in the matter.

Various scholars have suggested that our tradition for the early years and rise to power of Hiero II of Syracuse owes something to Philinus. These years are sketched by Polybius in 1.8.2–9.8, and also by Diodorus in xxii.13, two passages which diverge considerably from each other, but without containing any actual contradictions. The usual (and most probable) view, as expressed for instance by Meltzer and Beloch,²³ is that both accounts are derived from Timaeus. It has, however, been argued that the differences between them are so great as to postulate different sources; accordingly Reuss suggested that Philinus is the source of the version in Diodorus, and Laqueur that he is the source of that in Polybius.²⁴ The problem is not one into which we can enter here. Both views imply that Philinus wrote something more than a monograph on the First Punic War; but both assume and do not prove this point.²⁵

Again, in a Zürich dissertation of 1935²⁶ Margrit Kunz has suggested that Philinus is the authority for a short passage in Diodorus, xiii.90, dealing with the fate of the famous bull of Phalaris. This passage is of some interest and I hope to deal with it elsewhere;²⁶ᵃ but Frl. Kunz was unfortunate in linking it with the name of Philinus, for it contains a reference to historical details subsequent to the fall of Carthage in 146, a century after the First Punic War, with which Philinus is generally assumed to be contemporary.²⁷

The only safe conclusion is, therefore, that Philinus *probably* wrote a monograph on the First Punic War, since we know of him as an authority on that war, whereas ‖ he cannot actually be shown to have written on anything

in Polyb. 1.72.3 with the favourable account of his humane treatment of Hecatompylus in Diod. xxiv.10.1–2 (*cf.* the vagueness of Polyb. 1.73.1).

²³ O. Meltzer, *Geschichte der Karthager* (2 vols., Berlin, 1879–96) 2.550–1; Beloch, *op. cit.* (n. 5) 4.2.10–11; *cf.* De Sanctis, *op. cit.* (n. 1) 3.1.95, n. 11; A. S. von Stauffenberg, *König Hieron II. von Syrakus* (Stuttgart, 1933) 19, 93. Beloch points out that Philinus would hardly have been so favourably disposed towards Hiero, who had deserted the Carthaginians; and also that Polybius' account corresponds very closely with that in Justinus, who summarised Trogus, who in turn used Timaeus. Schwartz, *op. cit.* (n. 14) col. 688 claims that it is impossible to determine Diodorus' source in Book xxii.

²⁴ F. Reuss, *Philologus* 68 (1909) 412; Laqueur, *op. cit.* (n. 7) cols. 2181–2. Laqueur makes Timaeus the source of Diodorus xxii.13, whereas in 1936 (*cf. RE* 6a.1 (1936) 'Timaios (3)', col. 108) he was doubtful whether Timaeus went beyond 272, and did not carry his analysis of Diodorus past Book xx.

²⁵ Laqueur shows that Polybius' use of βάρβαροι to describe the Mamertini in 1.9 may not be used (as De Sanctis claims, *op. cit.* (n. 1) 3.1.225) to prove that Timaeus was here the source, since the word occurs too in 11.7, which cannot derive from Timaeus. Equally, however, this use cannot be taken as proof that Philinus was the source of 1.9, since more than one Greek historian may have called the Mamertini barbarians, or indeed Polybius may have repeated the word in 1.11 after using it twice (following Timaeus) in 1.9. Only a very rigid view of Polybius' relation to his sources would deny the possibility of his having used a word which was not in his immediate source, but which he had himself employed two chapters earlier. Hence the verdict must be *non liquet*.

²⁶ Margrit Kunz, *Zur Beurteilung der Prooemien in Diodors historischer Bibliothek* (Diss. Zürich, 1935) 13–14.   〚²⁶ᵃ *Cf. CR* 59 (1945) 39–42.〛

²⁷ *Cf.* De Sanctis, *op. cit.* (n. 1) 3.1.224. This view is based on the character of Diodorus' description of the siege of Agrigentum (xxiii.8) and of the expedition of Regulus (xxiii.17), and on the general character of the tradition: it seems likely.

else. This conclusion, tentative as it is (and must be, since it rests on an *argumentum ex silentio*), on the whole supports the view that references in Polybius to 'years of the war' will be derived from Philinus rather than Fabius. There are in fact only two such references and their context is such as not to contradict this general conclusion.

In 41.4 Polybius describes the setting out of the consuls for Sicily in 250, and adds: 'This was in the fourteenth year of the war.' In 56.2 the ravaging of the Italian coast by Hamilcar Barca (his first active measure against the enemy after arriving in Sicily in 247) is dated parenthetically to the eighteenth year of the war. It is of course evident that the outset of Hamilcar's campaign had a significance for his admirer, Philinus, which it did not possess for Fabius. On the other hand, the date of the resumption of the Roman naval policy (not, by the way, the start of the siege of Lilybaeum, to which De Sanctis and Beloch both refer the dating)[28] is in itself an event which must have interested either the Roman or the Sicilian historian, or indeed anyone writing an intelligent history of this largely naval war. Thus references to 'years of the war' *may* be from Philinus; but there can be no automatic certainty in the matter. Indeed the main result of a close analysis must be to show the very tenuous basis of the criteria – 'consul-years' and 'years of the war' – which Laqueur has tried to set up mechanically as a short cut in the process of separating the two strands in Polybius' narrative. The only safe method is the painstaking assessment of each passage from the point of view of the known methods, style and purpose of the sources in question – in short, the method adopted by De Sanctis, and by Gelzer in his study of Fabius Pictor. In the second half of this paper I propose to discuss some of the facts which can be elicited upon the method, style and purpose of Philinus.

II

The famous story of Regulus appears in its earliest form[29] in Polybius I, where it serves as the text for a chapter (35) of sententious reflections. Regulus had not yet become – to Polybius at least – the later paragon of Roman *fides* and patriotism, dying a horrible death at Carthage rather than dishonour himself and his country. On the contrary, he was still an outstanding example of ὕβρις. 'He who so short a time previously', writes Polybius, 'refused either pity or mercy to those in distress was now, almost immediately, led captive himself and forced to implore pity for his own life.' On the subject of Regulus Polybius makes three points. First, Regulus' fate teaches us to distrust Fortune, especially when we are prospering. Secondly, the arrival and success of

---

[28] De Sanctis, *op. cit.* (n. 1) 3.1.252; Beloch, *op. cit.* (n. 5) 4.2.285–6.

[29] On the Regulus saga and its growth see the excellent article by Klebs in *RE* 2.2 (1896) 'Atilius (51)', cols. 2088–92; De Sanctis, *op. cit.* (n. 1) 3.1.154–6. I am not convinced by the attempt of T. Frank, *CP* 30 (1926) 311ff., to defend the authenticity of Regulus' peace-mission; the legend seems to stand or fall as a whole. E. Pais's attempt to defend the whole legend in *Ricerche sulla storia e sul diritto pubblico di Roma* 4 (Rome 1921) 411–37, is uncritical.

Xanthippus, the Spartan mercenary captain, who reorganised the Punic forces and turned the scales against Regulus, confirms the old adage, found in Euripides that 'one wise counsel conquers many hands'.[30] Finally, taken together these two facts contribute to that instruction and improvement which comes through the reading of history, and is a less hurtful if less spectacular method of acquiring knowledge than personal experience; in short, serious history (πραγματική ἱστορία) is the best discipline for life. ‖

Each of these ideas can be paralleled from many parts of Polybius' work. The first – the need to distrust Fortune – implies a philosophy similar to that commonly found in Herodotus and the tragedians, and treats Tyche as a force which brings a sudden reversal of one's lot at the moment of excessive good fortune (1.35.2: καὶ μάλιστα κατὰ τὰς εὐπραγίας) as a result of folly and pride. Here Tyche is not wholly capricious, as it is, for instance, in Livy, *Epit.* 18, which, in discussing Regulus' downfall, says merely: 'quaerente deinde fortuna, *ut magnum utriusque casus exemplum in Regulo proderetur*, etc.'; on the contrary Polybius stresses Regulus' refusal to show pity or mercy at the time of his success. Hence his downfall was the result of his own ὕβρις and a fitting moral spectacle to contemplate. The best parallel in Polybius to this conception of Tyche occurs in connection with the last years of Philip V of Macedon, the crimes of whose youth find their retribution in a personal tragedy – the fatal quarrel between Demetrius and Perseus, his two sons, ending in the former's death – and the downfall of the whole realm of Macedon, the agent in both cases being Tyche.[31]

It is, however, well known that Polybius' conception of Tyche is far from consistent. Even in those passages where the word seems to designate a conscious, personal force, the character of this force varies considerably. Sometimes,[32] as here, Tyche bestows the fitting penalty on crime; but on occasion she is capricious and hands out an unfair reward,[33] damaging the innocent and giving glory to scoundrels; sometimes she takes a delight in mere change for its own sake, as when, after the crucifixion of Spendius, the leader of the Carthaginian mercenaries, his opponent Hannibal is taken and crucified on the same cross, 'as if it were the design of Fortune to compare them, and give both belligerents in turn cause and opportunity for inflicting on each other

[30] Polyb. 1.35.4: ἓν σοφὸν βούλευμα τὰς πολλὰς χέρας νικᾷ (Eurip. *Antiope* fr. 31 Dindorf = Nauck, *TGF* 200). Euripides was in fact referring to the strength of autocracy as against ochlocracy, but Polybius may well be quoting from some collection of proverbs; Themistius, *Or.* 16, p. 207 D, refers to the line as famous, and it is quoted by Plutarch, Sextus Empiricus, Galen, Eustathius and others; cf. C. Wunderer, *Polybios-Forschungen* 2 (Leipzig, 1901) 57–8, 87.

[31] See *JHS* 58 (1938) 55–68 [below, pp. 210–23], for a full discussion of this tragic treatment of Philip's last years; see especially Polyb. xv.20.5.

[32] *E.g.* iv.81.5 (Cheilon's assassination of the ephors, τῆς τύχης τὴν ἁρμόζουσαν αὐτοῖς ἐπιθείσης δίκην); xx.7.2 (the downfall of the Boeotians, ὥσπερ ἐπίτηδες ἀνταπόδοσιν ἡ τύχη ποιουμένη βαρέως ἔδοξεν αὐτοῖς ἐπεμβαίνειν); cf. 1.84.10 where the agent is τὸ δαιμόνιον.

[33] *E.g.* xv.20.5 (a person εἰκότως τῇ τύχῃ μεμψάμενος ἐπὶ τῶν ἀνθρωπείων πραγμάτων); xvi.32.5 (one is justified in blaming Fortune for not saving Abydus); xxxii.4.3 (Fortune sometimes grants a fine death to the worst men, a blameworthy procedure).

the cruellest punishments'.[34] Thus justice and caprice shade off into each other; and similarly, besides the conception of Fortune operating as the instrument of just retribution, to which Polybius' moral purpose leads him, wherever possible, to incline, there are other passages in which the pure jealousy of Tyche is to the fore,[35] as in the famous prayer with which Polybius ends his work.

The reflections on Regulus as an example of the power of Tyche are thus typically Polybian. Yet the very vagueness of Polybius' own usage indicates that the concept of Tyche is one common to many writers of the Hellenistic period. One example is Diodorus' account (whether derived from Duris or Timaeus)[36] of Agathocles' extraordinary changes of fortune, which show a typical mixture of caprice and retribution. ‖ After losing the greater part of his army in a defeat in Sicily, Agathocles managed to vanquish his conquerors with a tiny band of men in Africa (Tyche capricious). Subsequently he killed his friend Ophellas, and on the anniversary of the day on which he did this he lost his two sons and all his forces (Tyche retributive). The god, like a good lawgiver, thus took double vengeance on him, Ophellas' friends being the very ones to lay hands on Agathocles' sons. ταῦτα μὲν οὖν ἡμῖν εἰρήσθω πρὸς τοὺς καταφρονοῦντας τῶν τοιούτων.

Here is Polybius' just, avenging force in a non-Polybian passage, clear proof that it was common form in the third and second centuries. It is therefore interesting to find that Diodorus[37] makes the same point as Polybius about Regulus, whose pride was such ὥστε τὸ μὲν δαιμόνιον νεμεσῆσαι. It is generally agreed that in this passage Diodorus is using Philinus, and that he did not take up Polybius as his source until Book xxv, with its account of the Mercenary War; and this view is supported by another passage in Diodorus, xxiv.9, in which a Roman commander Fundanius treats with contempt Hamilcar's request for a truce to bury the dead, only to find himself shortly afterwards obliged to come with a similar request himself: by replying that he made war on the living and not on the dead, Hamilcar was thus able to reveal his nobility

---

[34] Polyb. 1.86.7. This was the aspect of Tyche stressed by Demetrius of Phalerum; *cf.* Polyb. xxix.21.3–6.

[35] Polyb. xxxix.8.2 (τὴν τύχην ὡς ἔστιν ἀγαθὴ φθονῆσαι τοῖς ἀνθρώποις – particularly when we think that our life has been most blessed and most successful); *cf.* too Diod. xxvii.6.2 (νέμεσίς τις θεοῦ), xxvii.15.2, xxxi.11.3 – all passages derived from Polybius.

[36] Diod. xx.70; for the latest discussion see B. L. Ullman, *TAPhA* 73 (1942) 39. Ullman makes the source Duris, with Schwartz, *RE* 5.2 (1905) 'Duris (3)', cols. 1853–6; but he admits that R. Schubert, *Geschichte des Agathokles* (Breslau, 1887) 181, and Laqueur, *RE* 6A.1 (1936) 'Timaios', col. 1174 (*cf.* G. Pasquali, *SIFC* 16 (1939) 76–7), have good arguments for deriving it from Timaeus, who is known to have been very fond of synchronisms and curious coincidences of time, such as play so large a part in the history of Agathocles (*cf.* especially Diod. xx.43.7). For an example of such a coincidence, specifically attributed to Timaeus, see the story of the statue of Apollo and Alexander's capture of Tyre in Diod. xiii.108.4–5.

[37] Diod. xxiii.15.2–6. On Diodorus' use of Philinus in his account of the First Punic War see Meltzer, *op. cit.* (n. 23) 2.557. His narrative in Books xxiii and xxiv contains many details not in Polybius, *e.g.* Hanno's victories in Libya at Hecatompylus, xxiv.10.1–2. In addition he also used a Roman annalist (*cf.* E. Meyer, *Kleine Schriften* 2 (Halle, 1924) 227 n. 4), but this can scarcely have been the source of these reflections on Regulus. See also above, n. 21.

of character. This anecdote is not in Polybius; yet it is so very clearly parallel to the story of Regulus, that it seems likely that Diodorus had both from the same source,[38] and that source will have been Philinus.

The conclusion is confirmed when we examine the two other points which Polybius makes in connection with Regulus; for both are also in Diodorus. He, like Polybius, stresses the amazing change wrought by 'one man, and one man alone': παράδοξον γὰρ ἐφαίνετο πᾶσιν εἰ προσγενομένου τοῖς Καρχηδονίοις ἑνὸς μόνου ἀνδρός, τηλικαύτη τῶν ὅλων ἐγένετο μεταβολή κτλ. (xxiii.15.5). Again we have a concept which is normally regarded as typically Polybian; for Polybius has similar reflections about Hannibal (ix.22.1, 6), Lyciscus of Aetolia (xxxii.4.2), and Archimedes of Syracuse.[39] Finally, Polybius' sententious observation on the advantage that accrues from the study of such events is also in Diodorus, who remarks (xxiii.15.4) that τοῖς δὲ ἰδίοις συμπτώμασι τοὺς ἄλλους ἐδίδαξε μέτρια φρονεῖν ἐν ταῖς ἐξουσίαις – by his own misfortunes Regulus taught others not to be carried away by insolence in time of prosperity; and a little farther down Diodorus observes (15.6) that those who purpose similar folly are frequently deflected by the historian's condemnation of others' faults, while the honest praise of good characters diverts men's minds towards virtue.

Thus Polybius seems to have taken over the whole substance of this chapter from his predecessor, a conclusion which Laqueur draws,[40] without, however, seeing its full ‖ implications for a study of Philinus. Laqueur observes, perfectly correctly, that this chapter establishes Philinus as the writer of a 'lehrhaft-pragmatische', *i.e.* a didactic and moralising, form of history. This is not perhaps surprising, for plainly the idea of learning vicariously from the misfortunes of others was a commonplace of Greek historical writing. It is the keynote of Polybius' general introduction (1.1f.), and it can be paralleled in Thucydides and Isocrates:[41] from Polybius' time onwards it becomes the

---

[38] I am not convinced by Münzer's argument (*RE* 7.1 (1910) 'Fundanius (5)', col. 292) that the Fundanius story is probably 'von der römischen aristokratischen Geschichtsschreibung in tendenziöser Weise ausgebeutet', as an attack on a member of a plebeian house. The story seems to me to betray a pro-Barcine rather than an anti-plebeian source.

[39] *Cf.* Polyb. viii.3.3: μία ψυχὴ τῆς ἁπάσης ἐστὶ πολυχειρίας ἐν ἐνίοις καιροῖς ἀνυστικωτέρα; 7.7: οὕτως εἷς ἀνήρ καὶ μία ψυχὴ δεόντως ἡρμοσμένη πρὸς ἕνια τῶν πραγμάτων μέγα τι χρῆμα φαίνεται γίνεσθαι καὶ θαυμάσιον (echoed by Livy xxiv.34.1: 'unus homo'). The doctrine is linked up, not very convincingly, by von Scala, *Die Studien des Polybios* (Stuttgart, 1890) 94, with Heracleitus, *Vorsokr.*⁵ (ed. Diels–Kranz) fr. 49; εἷς ἐμοὶ μύριοι ἐὰν ἄριστος ᾖ. It seems to be a general commonplace of the Hellenistic age, and finds an echo in Ennius' famous line on Fabius: 'unus homo nobis cunctando restituit rem'.

[40] *RE* 19.2 (1938) 'Philinos (8)', col. 2187; *cf.* L. Sisto, *Atene e Roma* 12 (1931) 181; C. Davin, *Beiträge zur Kritik der Quellen des I. Punischen Kriegs* (Progr. Schwerin, 1889), who discusses the relationship between Polybius', Diodorus', and Dio's accounts of the First Punic War (especially Polyb. 1.29.3–36.4), and concludes (p. 16): 'die ethische und die pragmatische Beurteilung der Vorgänge ist bei den drei Autoren die gleiche: die Uebereinstimmung aber lässt sich nur aus einer gemeinsamen Quelle erklären, und diese kann...nur Philinos sein'. But Davin's method and purpose are different from those of the present essay, and it would be irrelevant to discuss his arguments in detail.

[41] *Cf.* Thuc. 1.22, ii.48.3; Isoc. 2.35, 6.59.

normal mode. The prologue to Diodorus, probably derived from Poseidonius,[42] develops at some length the theme of the two ways of learning, by personal experience and vicariously. Cicero calls history the *magistra vitae*; and similar sentiments are echoed by Dionysius of Halicarnassus, Sallust, Strabo, Pliny, Lucian, and others.[43] Hence it is no wonder if Philinus takes his place in this company of moralising historians. It is perhaps more interesting that his work can clearly be associated with that of the writers of 'tragical history', that Hellenistic school which Polybius criticises no less strongly because he occasionally follows it.

In a first-class article in the *TAPhA* for 1942, Professor B. L. Ullman[44] has discussed the character of the Hellenistic school of 'tragic' historians who, from the time of Isocrates, confounded the two separate literary categories, which Aristotle had kept sharply distinct, of tragedy and history. Polybius' criticisms of this school are well known;[45] in various passages he attacks the historians Theopompus, Timaeus and Phylarchus, and certain unnamed historians writing on Hannibal's crossing of the Alps, and others writing on Hieronymus' downfall at Syracuse, etc., for a style of presentation that is inaccurate, sensational, and full of wonders (παράδοξον), but pays no regard to cause and effect. However, as Ullman points out, this tragic approach is also to be found in Polybius' own work, especially in his account of the downfall of the royal house of Macedon; and I believe that it plays a greater part in his general historical philosophy than has been generally admitted. For sensationalism pure and simple he had no time; but when by adducing the περιπέτειαι which have befallen others he could help the reader himself to endure the vicissitudes of fortune, τύχης μεταβολάς (1.1.2–2.1), as a moralist Polybius could not resist including such events in his work. The extent to which he gives way to this temptation may be judged from the fact that the word παράδοξος occurs fifty-one times in Books I–III, apart from such synonyms as παράλογος, ἀνέλπιστος, ἀπροσδόκητος, etc.[46] The responsibility for this, Polybius would have argued, lay not in himself but in Tyche. She it was who caused history to develop on tragic lines – witness the supreme drama, the rise of Rome to world-wide domination in fifty-three years. 'For though Fortune is ever producing something new (καινοποιοῦσα) and ever playing a part (ἐναγω-

[42] Diod. I.1; this passage is derived from Ephorus by K. Lorenz, *Untersuchungen zum Geschichtswerk des Polybius* (Stuttgart, 1931) 10; G. L. Barber, *The historian Ephorus* (Cambridge, 1935) 103; and Ullman, *TAPhA* 73 (1942) 30 n. 31; but the general tone of the passage is hard to reconcile with a fourth-century source. It is almost certainly Stoic and post-Polybian.

[43] Cic. *De Or.* II.9.36; Dion. Hal. 1.2.1; Sall. *Jug.* 4.1–2; Strabo 1.1.22ff. C 13; *cf.* Joseph. *AJ* 1.3, 4; Pliny, *Ep.* v.8.11; Lucian, *Hist. conscr.* 39 fin., 42, and 43; Herodian 1.1.3. See Lorenz, *op. cit.* (n. 42) 10.

[44] B. L. Ullman, *TAPhA* 73 (1942) 25–53: 'History and Tragedy'.

[45] *Cf. JHS* 58 (1938) 55–68 [below, pp. 210–23]. See Polyb. II.56, III.47.6–48.12, 58.9, VII.7.1–2.6, x.2.5–6, XII.24.5, 26b.4ff., xv.34.1–36.11 (probably criticising Ptolemy of Megalopolis), xvi.12.7–9, 14.1, 17.9, 18.2, xxix.12.1–3.8.

[46] Lorenz, *op. cit.* (n. 42) 11–12. This feature cannot of course be divorced from the question of the historical method pursued by Polybius' sources, and in particular Fabius; see below.

νιʒομένη) ‖ in the lives of men, she has not in a single instance ever put on such a showpiece (οὔτ᾽ ἠγωνίσατ᾽ ἀγώνισμα) as in our own times' (1.4.5).[47] To Polybius Tyche is a stage-manager and play-producer. The tragic scheme with its novelties and *peripeteiai* is there objectively in the fabric of events; the conscientious moral historian cannot do less than record these.[48] This train of ideas is very clearly expressed in the early chapters of the first book of Polybius, where the historian specifically links up the fact that Fortune has brought all the affairs of the world together into a composite whole (σωματοειδής) with the obligation of the historian to relate this process under a 'synoptical view' and in a single world history that shall bear the same character as the events themselves.[49]

On the other hand, Polybius was very ready to criticise his fellow-historians for sensationalism, by showing *either* that the wonders they recorded were not rooted in fact (and therefore not the work of Tyche, objectively true) *or* that they were related to no scheme of cause and effect (and were therefore not harnessed to a moral purpose). In practice, as one might expect, Polybius himself did not always find the line easy to draw. It is not difficult to persuade oneself that a good story with a good moral is there 'objectively' and not the

[47] The phrase οὔτ᾽ ἠγωνίσατ᾽ ἀγώνισμα has been generally misunderstood; *e.g.* 'neque certamen ullum, quale nostra memoria, certaverat' (Schweighaeuser; *cf.* von Scala, *op. cit.* (n. 39) 172); 'or act such a drama' (Shuckburgh); 'ever achieved such a triumph' (Paton). None gets the exact force. An Amorgos inscription of *c.* 225–175 B.C. (*IG* 12.7.226, lines 4–6) speaks of a κωμῳδός (playwright? or actor? perhaps an actor-manager, owning a troupe of players?) and uses the phrase δράματα ἀγωνίʒεσθαι, *i.e.* 'to put on plays for competition' at a local festival. The meaning is the same here, with the substitution for δρᾶμα of ἀγώνισμα 'a show-piece' (*cf.* Thuc. 1.22: ἀγώνισμα ἐς τὸ παραχρῆμα; used of plays by Aristotle, *Poet.* IX.10, 1451 b 37). Polybius uses the same metaphor of Tyche as a play-producer elsewhere, *e.g.* XI.5.8: τῆς τύχης ὥσπερ ἐπίτηδες ἐπὶ τὴν ἐξώστραν ἀναβιβαʒούσης τὴν ὑμετέραν ἄγνοιαν; *cf.* XXIII.10.16; XXIX.19.2 (with σκήνην for ἐξώστραν). [*Cf.* fr. 212 B-W.] In XXIII.10.12 he (or his excerptor: *cf.* *JHS* 58 (1938) 64) has the expression τρίτον δ᾽ ἡ τύχη δρᾶμα...ἐπεισήγαγεν. So too Diodorus XXXII.10.5, in a passage the source of which is doubtful, but is certainly either Polybius or later: τῆς τύχης ὥσπερ ἐν δράμασι τὸ παράδοξον τῆς περιπετείας ἀγούσης εἰς ἔγκλημα.

[48] Sometimes it is men's own excessive conduct which brings its περιπέτεια, with results the very opposite of what is contemplated; in such cases they may be said 'to put themselves, or their folly, on the stage', *i.e.* make an Aristotelian tragedy of their lives; *cf.* V.15.2: Apelles and the Macedonian counsellors, inspired by drink, attacked Aratus and so ἐξεθεάτρισαν αὑτούς. Their own downfall was the reverse of their intentions. In more general terms (XI.8.7), those who try to imitate τῶν εὐτυχούντων (Paton: 'favoured by fortune') in unessentials ἐκθεατρίʒουσι τὴν ἑαυτῶν ἀκρισίαν – they make a 'tragic' display of their own lack of judgement, to their own detriment (μετὰ βλάβης). In all such cases, Polybius would have said, Tyche was really fulfilling her function as stage-manager.

[49] *Cf.* 1.3.3–6, 4.1–11. For σωματοειδής as a quality of historical events see 1.3.4; in XIV.12.5 it is applied to the description of the end of Ptolemy IV's reign in a single account οἱονεὶ σωματοειδῆ 'as a unified whole' (not, as Paton, 'a life-like picture'). See, for the same idea, Cic. *Fam.* V.12.4: 'a principio enim coniurationis usque ad reditum nostrum videtur mihi modicum quoddam *corpus* confici posse.' The idea of the corpus or σῶμα in literature seems to go back to the Platonic-Aristotelian conception of the unity of a literary work; *cf.* Plato, *Phaedrus* 264c (every λόγος must be like a ʒῷον); Arist. *Poet.* 23.1–2, 1459a 17ff. (who, however, specifically excepts history from its application!). See Lorenz, *op. cit.* (n. 42) 87 n. 92, 99 n. 227. The novelty in Polybius is that, assisted by his conception of Tyche as 'producer', he projects the idea of the unity of an historical work on to the objective course of historical events.

result of the historian's selection of material, or a shaky tradition; and in one case at least this tendency to excuse sensationalism, if it conduced to virtue, is applied by Polybius to events in real life, and the moral criterion turned into a justification of obscurantism. Polybius' view of religion as an instrument for controlling the lower orders has been frequently noticed.[50] It is religion, in Polybius' opinion, that maintains the cohesion of the Roman state. ‖ 'These matters', he writes, 'are clothed in tragic garb (ἐκτετραγῴδηται) and introduced (παρεισῆκται)[51] to such an extent into their public and private life, that nothing could exceed it, a fact which will surprise many.... The multitude must be held in by invisible terrors and suchlike pageantry (τοῖς ἀδήλοις φόβοις καὶ τῇ τοιαύτῃ τραγῳδίᾳ). Therefore, I think, not that the ancients acted rashly and at haphazard in introducing among the common people (παρεισαγαγεῖν εἰς τὰ πλήθη) notions concerning the gods and beliefs in the terrors of Hades, but that the moderns are most rash and foolish in banishing such beliefs.' It has not, I think, been observed that Polybius is here interpreting (and justifying) the Roman state religion in terms similar to those in which he condones the writing of 'tragic' history. The analogy is, however, directly drawn by Diodorus in a prologue which is very reminiscent of Polybius, and derives probably from Poseidonius and certainly from post-Polybian material.[52] 'If', writes Diodorus (I.2.2), 'myths about Hades, containing fictional material, conduce greatly to inspiring men to piety and justice, how much more must we suppose history...capable of shaping men's characters in ways of honour?'[53] The connection is revealing; it shows how very much moral aims governed Polybius both as a citizen and as a historian, and how very far he was from applying in practice the criterion of objective, unvarnished truth.[54]

Now the criticism of Regulus retailed by both Polybius and Diodorus suggests that Philinus adopted the same approach towards history. The works of Tyche, the stress on the accomplishments of one man, the *peripeteia* which befell Regulus through a fault in his character, are all marks of the tragic school, and their exploitation in the interests of morality puts Philinus in a line of

[50] Polyb. vi.56.6ff. *Cf.* B. Farrington, *Science and politics in the ancient world* (London, 1939) 166–8; 'Examiner', *Greece and Rome* 12 (1943) 59.

[51] παρεισάγω is used elsewhere by Polybius in the sense of introducing a character or material into a narrative; *cf.* iii.20.3 on the sensational (θαυμάσιον) picture of the solemn sitting of the Senate drawn by Sosylus and Chaereas; iii.47.7 on the kind of Hannibal the 'tragic' historians introduce into their works; v.2.6 on the sons of Aeacus introduced into a poem by Hesiod.

[52] See above, n. 42.

[53] For the myths of Hades as an ingredient of tragedy *cf.* Arist. *Poet.* 14.2–3, 1453 b 7; 18.3, 1456 a 3; *cf.* Ullman, *op. cit.* (n. 44) 31 n. 33. For the function of such myths as an ingredient of 'political' religion *cf.* Arist. *Metaph.* xii.8.13, 1074 b. This idea seems to have been first expressed by Critias in his *Sisyphus* (*cf.* *Vorsokr.*[5] 2.386, fr. 25). See further B. Farrington, *op. cit.* (n. 50) 87ff.

[54] For instance, in several places (ii.56.10, xii.25 b, xxxvi.1.7) Polybius stresses the duty of the historian to record what was actually said (τοὺς κατ᾿ ἀλήθειαν εἰρημένους (λόγους)); but another very revealing passage (xii.25 i.4ff.; on which see C. Wunderer, *op. cit.* (n. 30) 2.11) shows plainly that he drew no clear distinction between the actual words spoken and τοὺς ἁρμόζοντας καὶ καιρίους (λόγους), which we shall record εἰ μέλλομεν μὴ βλάπτειν, ἀλλ᾿ ὠφελεῖν τοὺς ἀναγινώσκοντας. ⟦On xii.25 i see, however, my *Commentary* 2.397–9, and below, p. 152.⟧

development which Ullman has traced from Ephorus[55] down to Polybius and beyond; the essence of this school may be summed up in the phrase 'sensationalism harnessed to a didactic purpose'. Its tenets are clearly revealed in a passage in which Polybius pays homage to the service done to their country by the historians of the Persian invasion or the Gallic attack on Delphi. 'For there is no one', he goes on (II.35.8),[56] 'whom hosts of men or abundance of arms or vast resources could frighten into abandoning his last hope, that is to fight to the end for his native land, if he kept before his eyes what part the unexpected (τὸ παράδοξον) played in those events, and bore in mind how many myriads of men, what determined courage, and what armaments were brought to naught by the resolve and power of those who faced the danger with intelligence and coolness (σὺν νῷ καὶ μετὰ λογισμοῦ).' In this curious partnership between Tyche and ‖ the rational faculties of man,[57] which is to serve as a lesson and a spur to others, we have a typical example of this particular Hellenistic approach to history. For historians of this school morality is the cloak under which sensationalism steals in; but as in the case of our own Sunday press, the cloak is often a little threadbare, and we find the 'tragic' criterion operating in its own right.

An interesting example, for instance, of the way in which Philinus adopted this tragic style with its stress on the pattern wrought by Tyche, and the changes she occasions in men's fortunes, is probably to be seen in Polybius' treatment of the two battles of Drepana in 249 B.C. and the Aegates Islands in 242 B.C. Polybius' accounts of these two battles are of a somewhat stylised nature. Both contain an elaborate description of the relative advantages of the two sides, beginning with the Carthaginians at Drepana and the Romans at the Aegates Islands: in each case the description is punctuated with the remark that the other side found things exactly the opposite – τοῖς γε μὴν Ῥωμαίοις τἀναντία τούτων συνέβαινε (1.51.8) and περὶ δὲ τοὺς Καρχηδονίους τἀναντία τούτοις ὑπῆρχεν (61.4). Each battle too is preceded by a speech from the ultimate victor, Adherbal (49.10) and Lutatius Catulus (60.5). Now this parallelism is quite conscious. Polybius remarks specifically (61.2) that 'as the condition of each force (*i.e.* at the Aegates Islands) was just the reverse of what it had been at the battle of Drepana, the result also was naturally the reverse for each'.

Clearly, Polybius has used the same source for both battles; and this is almost

---

[55] Ullman, *op. cit.* (n. 44) 30–1. Ephorus wrote Παράδοξα and was clearly not hostile to the sensational in itself; but according to Strabo, VII.3.9, C302, he criticised writers who told only of the savagery of the Sauromatae εἰδότες τὸ δεινόν τε καὶ τὸ θαυμαστὸν ἐκπληκτικὸν ὄν· δεῖν δὲ τἀναντία καὶ λέγειν καὶ παραδείγματα ποιεῖσθαι. (παραδείγματα are 'lessons' as in Thuc. III.40.) Ullman's case is weakened by his assumption that the preface to Diodorus comes from Ephorus (see above, n. 42).   [56] *Cf.* Ullman, *op. cit.* (n. 44) 41 n. 81.

[57] On this combination of foresight and courage, and its relation to the factor of Tyche, as developed in Polybius, see Lorenz, *op. cit.* (n. 42) 43ff. (who, however, seems to me to overstress the Stoic influence in the notion of ὁρμή and λόγος; his parallels from Thucydides for the τόλμα of the Athenians appear to invalidate this part of his argument); E. Täubler, *Tyche: historische Studien* (Leipzig, 1926) 89.

unanimously admitted to have been Philinus.[58] This alone would not prove that Polybius' schematic treatment was also in his source. But it is scarcely mere chance that Diodorus (following Philinus) stresses the figure 117 as being that of the Roman sinkages at Drepana and the Punic losses at the Aegates Islands (XXIV.1.5, 11.1), though in the latter battle it includes both sunk and captured. Whether this numerical coincidence inspired the schematisation or is to be regarded as part of it is not clear. But it certainly suggests that Polybius' treatment of the battles goes back to Philinus. It is consistent with what we have learnt to recognise as his historical method in the incidents of Regulus and Fundanius; it suits the concept of a Tyche which casts events into a balanced pattern, requiting good fortune with ill, and ill with good.

III

It is time to sum up. Of Philinus of Agrigentum we know from Polybius[59] that he was pro-Carthaginian and anti-Roman, and it has been conjectured with great plausibility that this attitude was reinforced by the harsh treatment of his native town by the Romans, after its capture in 261.[60] Philinus' particular interest in Greeks in Carthaginian employ, such as Alexon the Achaean mercenary, who had once saved Agrigentum (Polyb. 1.43.2ff.), or the Spartan Xanthippus, who saved Carthage, has been taken to indicate that he may himself have held a similar position. To these conjectures we are now in a position to add that his work, which was most probably a monograph on the First Punic War, was written in the manner of the Hellenistic ‖ 'tragic' school, with special stress on παράδοξα, sensations, unexpected reversals of fortune, and the prominent part played in human affairs by Tyche. These characteristics, which break through in Polybius himself, were by his testimony[61] particularly likely to appear in the works of οἱ τὰς ἐπὶ μέρους γράφοντες πράξεις, writers of particular studies in contrast to authors of universal history (like himself), because 'dealing with a subject which is circumscribed and narrow, they are compelled for lack of facts to make small things great and to devote much space to matters not really worthy of record'. On the other hand, Polybius never makes against Philinus the charges he so freely flings against Theopompus, Timaeus and Phylarchus – perhaps because, like Polybius himself, Philinus was inclined to harness his sensationalism to a didactic conception of history.[62]

[58] For Philinus as the source for Drepana and the Aegates Islands see De Sanctis, *op. cit.* (n. 1) 3.1.228–9; Gelzer, *Hermes* 68 (1933) 141; Laqueur, *RE* 19.2 (1938) 'Philinos (8)', cols. 2188–9, who all agree on this point. Reuss, however, *Philologus* 60 (1901) 137, makes Polybius' source for Drepana Fabius Pictor.   [59] Polyb. 1.14ff.

[60] Polyb. 1.19.15; *cf.* Diod. XXIII.9.1; Oros. IV.6.6, who both state that the population was enslaved. This statement is questioned by Beloch, *op. cit.* (n. 5) 4.1.653 n. 1, but it was the Roman custom to enslave the population of conquered towns and there is no valid reason to reject the tradition.

[61] *Cf.* VII.7.6; XXIX.12; and see the other passages quoted by Ullman, *op. cit.* (n. 44) 42–3.

[62] It may also be assumed that Philinus followed the traditional custom of writing and including

Unfortunately – for this warning must be uttered – these literary characteristics are not of a kind to make it easier to isolate those passages in Polybius' narrative of the First Punic War which go back to Philinus, for there seems good reason to think that a similar element was present in the history of Fabius Pictor. This is, I think, evident from what can be recovered of Fabius' account of the beginnings of Rome from Dionysius and Plutarch's *Life of Romulus*.[63] The version associated with Fabius and Diocles of Peparethus is described in Plutarch[64] as δραματικὸν καὶ πλασματῶδες, dramatic and fabulous; but, adds Plutarch, one ought not to disbelieve it when one observes what kind of deeds are the handiwork of Tyche, and considers that the Roman state would never have reached the heights it has, without some divine start (μὴ θείαν τινὰ ἀρχὴν λαβόντα) which had in it elements of the great and the extraordinary (μηδὲν μέγα μηδὲ παράδοξον ἔχουσαν).[65] Whether Fabius followed Diocles or *vice versa*,[66] it is generally admitted that his account of Romulus' birth and upbringing is a pure drama in prose. As De Sanctis observes,[67] the use of the cradle for the ἀναγνώρισις was taken directly from Sophocles' play of *Tyro*, the daughter of Salmoneus, a work which obviously played an important role in the shaping of the Romulus legend.[68] Whether this tragic element reached Fabius from Diocles cannot perhaps be determined with certainty. The important thing for our purpose is that it ranges Fabius alongside of Philinus, as an historian whose work showed the influence of the 'tragic' school, a point which Dr Tarn came near making forty years ago, in his article on the fleets of the First Punic War, when he spoke of 'the deliberate introduction by Fabius of an element of wonder into this war'.[69] For it seems improbable that Fabius treated the early events of Roman history after a fashion markedly different from his treatment of the later; indeed the well-known story of the *corvus* ‖ and the *peripeteia* accomplished by it (a story not in Philinus)[70] is an excellent

speeches in his narrative; this may be the explanation of such passages in Polyb. 1 as 27.1 (where the observations of the Punic commanders repeat the arguments of 26.1), and 32.8, 44.1, 45.3, 49.10, 60.5, where phrases like παρακαλέσας τῷ καιρῷ τὰ πρέποντα may represent a full-dress speech in an original source. However, the phrase occurs elsewhere in Polybius (*e.g.* II.64.1, III.71.8, 108.2, 111.11, IV.80.15, v.53.6, 60.3, VIII.13.5, XI.11.2), and is perhaps merely Polybius' substitute for the rhetorical commonplaces which a Timaeus would have introduced at such points (*cf.* P. La-Roche, *Charakteristik des Polybius* (Leipzig, 1857) 64).

[63] Dion. Hal. 1.79ff.; Plut. *Rom.* 3ff.

[64] Plut. *Rom.* 8.

[65] Dion. Hal. 1.84.1 also gives a version which he says is Fabian, and after criticising it for being τῶν μυθωδεστέρων and δραματικῆς μεστὸν ἀτοπίας, he explains it away in euhemerising terms.

[66] On this particular crux see most recently A. Momigliano, *JRS* 33 (1943) 102, whom I believe to be right in accepting the traditional account. To the authorities he quotes add Rosenberg, *RE* I A. 1 (1914) 'Romulus', col. 1085, and De Sanctis, *op. cit.* (n. 1) 1.214ff.

[67] *Op. cit.* (n.1) 1.214ff.

[68] *Cf.* H. Last, *CAH* 7 (1928) 366; E. Täubler, *op. cit.* (n. 57) 70, 71; the influence of Sophocles' *Tyro* is rejected by M. Cary, *History of Rome* (London, 1935) 40.

[69] W. W. Tarn, *JHS* 27 (1907) 51 n. 19. Another example may be the stress on the womanly character of Teuta in Polyb. II.4.8, 8.12.

[70] On the *corvus* (κόραξ), alleged to have been used at Mylae (Polyb. 1.22), see Tarn, *Hellenistic military and naval developments* (Cambridge, 1930) 111–12, 149–50. It is generally agreed that the

example of the kind of thing that was typical of the sensational historian, and incidentally prompted Tarn's observation.

Fabius wrote for a Greek audience and, especially where he could draw on Greek sources, he wrote 'tragic history' after the Hellenistic school.[71] This means, however, that it is impossible to use literary criteria to separate the Fabian parts of Polybius from those where Philinus is the source. On the other hand, our closer definition of the character of Philinus' work, and the knowledge that Polybius' account of the First Punic War is part of the introduction to his history proper, should make us much more suspicious about Polybius' independence of his sources in Book I, even for comments of a type which seem essentially Polybian in character: the chapter on Regulus makes that clear. It is therefore not improbable that other passages in Book I containing criticism and comments go back directly to either Fabius or Philinus.

Let us take a single example, Polybius' criticism of the Roman consuls for the disaster off Camarina in 255 B.C., on their way back from Africa (37.1–6), and the general reflections which follow on Roman naval policy (37.7–10). Gelzer seems to allot this chapter to Fabius;[72] and the specific charge against the consuls, M. Aemilius Paullus and Ser. Fulvius Paestinus Nobilior, that they sailed along the south coast of Sicily, can indeed have come into the tradition only at a later date, when it was no longer apparent that while the Carthaginians held the western tip of Sicily there was no alternative route for a Roman fleet sailing to and from Africa.[73] On the other hand, the general observations which follow on the subject of Roman naval disasters, caused by a headstrong policy in the face of nature, were no longer pertinent at any time after the First Punic War, and certainly point to the hand of a contemporary.[74] This is confirmed by the similarity between these reflections and those on Regulus two chapters before. Lorenz has already pointed to the use of words such as βία (§§ 7 and 10), ὁρμή (§ 7), τόλμα (§ 10), and βιαιομαχεῖν (§ 9);[75] and the reference to the Roman tendency to try to fight not merely men and

Carthaginian defeat recorded by Polyb. 1.21.9–11 is in fact Philinus' version of the battle of Mylae, which Polybius failed to recognise because the *corvus* was omitted (*cf.* Beloch, *op. cit.* (n. 5) 4.1.654 n. 1; Lenschau, *RE* 7.2 (1912) 'Hannibal (3)', cols. 2321–2; Tarn, *JHS* 27 (1907) 51 n. 19; De Sanctis, *op. cit.* (n. 1) 3.1.128–9 n. 73, 226). [See now my *Commentary* I, 76–7.]

[71] *Cf.* Pasquali, *Enciclopedia italiana* (1936) *s.v.* 'Roma', 909. 'La storia di Fabbio Pittore...era, almeno nelle intenzioni, arte, quale la teoria ellenistica esigeva che fosse la storiografia.' This is true, but it is only half the story; much of Fabius must have reflected his exiguous Roman sources. See below, Addendum, pp. 94–8.

[72] *Hermes* 68 (1933) 140: 'Die hier vorgebrachten Einzeltatsachen wird er nicht erfunden haben.' The implication seems to be that he had them from Fabius.

[73] Meltzer, *op. cit.* (n. 23) 2.308; De Sanctis, *op. cit.* (n. 1) 3.1.158.

[74] So Laqueur, *RE* 19.2 (1938) 'Philinos (8)', col. 2187; the argument that the reference to Rome's invariable success on land was contradicted by the Hannibalic War is less cogent, since if the reflections were those of Polybius himself, it might well be argued that the victories in the East had dimmed the memory of the years 218–216 B.C.

[75] On this question of terminology see Lorenz, *op. cit.* (n. 42) 45, who, however, again claims Stoic influence (see above, n. 57).

the works of men, but the very sea and atmosphere, *i.e.* Nature herself,[76] is also the mark of ὕβρις similar to that which led to the fall of Regulus. Equally there is the didactic element here as well: the Romans are to learn from their disaster (§ 10: διορθώσονται; *cf.* 35.6: διορθώσεως). Thus internal evidence confirms Laqueur's assumption that Polybius' criticism at this point has been taken more or less as it stands from Philinus.[77] ‖

A final point. What were Philinus' politics? Laqueur argues[78] that he was an aristocrat, on the grounds that Polybius (1.14.2) refers to his (and Fabius') βίος καὶ αἵρεσις – which appears to mean his 'way of life and conduct', his 'character and principles', as Paton translates it.[79] On the basis of this assumption Laqueur then goes on to build up a fantastic version of Philinus' political development. The aristocracy of Agrigentum,[80] he supposes, joined Rome, among them Philinus, who having thus transformed his partisan attitude (which Polybius comments on), became interested in giving an objective, didactic account of the war. Later he found his way to Rome, where he investigated Roman institutions: he recognised in his one-time foes a people who could do the world a real service (particularly in a certain firmness in dealing with barbarian mercenaries), and they in turn saw in him a historian who could write an objective account of the war. Thus he became exactly the kind of man from whom Polybius could learn a lesson! In short, were it not for his unfortunately having failed to survive, Philinus would by this time undoubtedly have been dissected into layers and rearranged in successive editions; as it is,[81] having no original text to work on, Laqueur has lent him a shadowy and spurious personality borrowed from Polybius. I think, however, that this particular structure can be very simply demolished. Diodorus (XXIII.1.2) states that on his arrival in Agrigentum in 264 the Carthaginian Hanno fortified the citadel πείσας τὸν δῆμον φίλον ὄντα συμμαχῆσαι Καρχηδονίων. Thus it was the popular party at Agrigentum which

---

[76] The accusation recalls Xerxes flogging the Hellespont to avenge the destruction of his bridge: Hdt. VII.35–6; Aesch. *Pers.* 745ff.

[77] It may be argued that the didactic attitude towards Rome is inconsistent with Philinus' anti-Roman policy; but lecturing one's enemy has always been a popular enough device of rhetoric. In any case, if the reflections are Polybius' own, it is hard to explain their *irrelevance*; other Polybian criticisms of Roman conduct are concerned with specific incidents (*e.g.* 1.83.11, 88.8ff., III.28.1 (seizure of Sardinia); III.26.6 (help given to Mamertines)), and not as here with Roman character.

[78] *Op. cit.* (n. 7) col. 2192.

[79] On the various meanings of αἵρεσις in Polybius see J. L. Strachan-Davidson, *Selections from Polybius* (Oxford, 1888) 7.

[80] I keep Laqueur's terminology, though in fact 'aristocracy' is an unsuitable word to describe the ruling class in the Greek states of the third and second centuries, with its stress on wealth rather than blood. The real situation comes out in the Achaean formula πλουτίνδα καὶ ἀριστίνδα (*IG* 7.188, line 8), where πλουτίνδα expresses the reality, ἀριστίνδα the propaganda phrase in which the reality is muffled. See further A. Aymard, *Les assemblées de la confédération achaïenne* (Bordeaux, 1938) 56 n. 4, 137 n. 4, 335ff.

[81] Successive editions are the only way of reconciling the anti-Roman tendency on which Polybius comments with the *objective*, didactic work which Laqueur's theory postulates (and for which there is no evidence).

favoured Carthage. Therefore, if we are to draw any conclusions at all on the political views of Philinus, the pro-Carthaginian, it must surely be that he was a democrat. If, on the other hand, this deduction seems too tenuous, then at least it must be granted that even less can be concluded from a phrase like βίος καὶ αἵρεσις. We may therefore dismiss the whole of Laqueur's fantastic and wholly unfounded picture of Philinus' later development. Whether he visited Carthage or Rome is a subject on which, in the absence of any evidence, there can be no profitable speculation.[82]

However, Laqueur's article, for all its exaggerations, contains something of value; and that is the point, which I believe he has made successfully, that Philinus was a didactic historian, not dissimilar in temperament to the greater figure who chose to use him as a source for the First Punic War. On the basis of Laqueur's work it is possible to advance to a slightly clearer picture of a third-century historian, who ‖ occupies a mere four lines in Susemihl, but may have played a considerable part in the development of Polybius' ideas and sense of history.[83]

ADDENDUM:

M. Gelzer's theory of the origins of Roman historiography

In two articles, published in *Hermes* of 1933 and 1934,[84] Gelzer argued that Fabius, Cincius, Acilius and Postumius Albinus, the earliest Roman historians, are to be sharply differentiated from the later school of 'annalists'. They were fully fledged political historians, putting the senatorial case in Greek to a Greek public, while the later Latin annalists composed jejune records in the sacerdotal tradition, for a Roman aristocracy of politicians and priests with a professional taste for antiquarian knowledge; Cato's innovation was to write genuine political history in Latin. Already in 1936 J. Vogt[85] made some valid points against this theory. Apart from the inherent improbability of the Romans' providing a propagandist history for Greek consumption before undertaking their own evaluation of the Roman past, Gelzer's theory implied too rigid a definition of the character of *annales*; if the second-century *Latin* annalists like Piso could give a combination of senatorial and pontifical material, why not also their Greek-writing predecessors? Finally, there was Cicero's famous comment (*De Or.* II.52) on the early annalists (specifically including Fabius), who, following the same manner of writing

---

[82] One should note the change in Laqueur's picture of Polybius' development. In his book *Polybios* (Leipzig, 1913) 261–77, he banished the view of Tyche as subject to law, and therefore a proper study for the historian, the concept of world-history, Stoicism, and the didactic-utilitarian approach, to the fifth edition of the *Histories*; whereas the influence of Philinus came in in editions 2 and 3. Now that Philinus has been shown (rightly, I believe) to have been a didactic-utilitarian writer, Laqueur's famous scheme seems ripe for revision. How its author intends to resolve this contradiction is not yet apparent; but it will be difficult to find a way out which does not offer violence to the original system.

[83] F. Susemihl, *Geschichte der griechischen Litteratur in der Alexandrinerzeit* (Leipzig, 1891–2) 634.

[84] See above, n. 2. Gelzer is followed in essentials and amplified by F. Altheim, *Epochen der römischen Geschichte* 2 (Frankfurt, 1935) 305ff. For the usual view of the development of annalistic writing at Rome, which Gelzer attacked, see for example, the discussion of Cichorius, *RE* 1.2 (1894) 'Annales', cols. 2255–6; E. Pais, *op. cit.* (n. 29) 4.177–224.

[85] J. Vogt, *Gnomon* 12 (1936) 524–6, in a review of Altheim's *Epochen der römischen Geschichte* 2; see, too, De Sanctis, *RFIC* 61 (1933) 548.

as that in the *annales maximi*, 'sine ullis ornamentis monumenta solum temporum, hominum, locorum gestarumque rerum reliquerunt'; this statement could not fairly be dismissed as referring to nothing beyond style and language.

Telling as these points are, Gelzer's argument deserves closer attention. A fundamental point for his thesis is Sempronius Asellio's distinction[86] between *res gestae* and *annales*: 'Verum inter eos qui annales relinquere voluissent, et eos qui res gestas a Romanis perscribere conati essent, omnium rerum hoc interfuit. annales libri tantummodo quod factum quoque anno gestum sit, ea demonstrabant, id est quasi qui diarium scribunt, quam Graeci ἐφημερίδα vocant. nobis non modo satis esse video, quod factum esset, id pronuntiare, sed etiam, quo consilio quaque ratione gesta essent, demonstrare.' Fabius, Gelzer argues, wrote *res gestae* by Asellio's definition. The opening words of the extract show that Asellio envisages a number of predecessors of this type; and one of Fabius' successors, A. Postumius Albinus, was clearly designated by Polybius (xxxix.1.4) as a writer of πραγματικὴ ἱστορία. The implication is that πραγματικὴ ἱστορία – such as Polybius himself writes – is to be identified with the *res gestae* of Asellio, who, it is agreed, wrote under the strong influence of Polybius.[87]

There is a fallacy here. In defining *res gestae* Asellio undoubtedly had in mind Polybius, whose insistence on the importance of causality needs no illustration. The only point is really whether the authors of *res gestas a Romanis* included anyone besides Polybius – and Asellio himself, Polybius' first true follower in Latin. Certainly there is nothing in what Asellio says to indicate that these authors were Fabius and his successors.[88] Throughout our Roman records Fabius figures as the writer of ‖ *annales*,[89] whether in their original Greek form or in the later Latin translation.[90] We have no reason to believe that to Sempronius Asellio he was anything different.

What then of the πραγματικὴ ἱστορία of Postumius Albinus? Here two points need making. First, Polybius only says that Postumius *tried* to write πραγματικὴ ἱστορία (ποίημα γράφειν καὶ πρ. ἱστ. ἐνεχείρησεν). Secondly, it is doubtful if πραγματικὴ ἱστορία here means anything more than 'serious history'. Certainly it does not mean 'history which investigates causes' or 'history with a didactic purpose', as generations of scholars, despite Schweighaeuser's clear explanation,[91] have continued to take it. Often Polybius uses the phrase πραγματικὴ ἱστορία as nothing more than a synonym for ἱστορία. Where he defines it more closely (ix.1–2), it distinguishes a political and military narrative based on sober fact from the more mythical types of composition dealing with genealogies, or with the foundations of cities, colonisation, and relation-

---

[86] *HRF* 1 and 2 (Peter) = Gell. v.18.8.

[87] *Cf.* Kornemann, *Klio* 11 (1911) 256; Peter ad F 2 (*HRR* 1². 179), comparing Polyb. iii.20.5.

[88] The reference to the Greek translation of *diarium* shows that Asellio was not limiting himself to Roman theory or practice.

[89] F 3: *in Fabi Pictoris Graecis annalibus* (Cic. *Div.* 1.21.43); F 24 (Pliny, *NH* x.71); F 27 (Pliny, *NH* xiv.89); Cic. *De Or.* ii.12.52 (*annalium confectio*).

[90] The Latin version (*cf.* Peter, *HRR* 1² 112–13) was probably a translation, not the work of the later jurist; *cf.* Schanz-Hosius, *Geschichte der römischen Literatur* 1 (Munich, 1927) 172; Beloch, *op. cit.* (n. 11) 98, against Münzer, *RE* 6.2 (1909) 'Fabius (128)', col. 1843.

[91] In his commentary on i.2.8 (vol. 5 (1792) 125–30): *cf.* especially: 'Ubi Postumium Albinum ait graece πρ. ἱστ. scripsisse, non cogitavit de peculiari quadam ratione, qua scripta erat illa historia; nihil quidquam amplius significat nisi quod Cicero in Bruto (21.81 = T2) ait, *Albinus qui Graece scripsit historiam*, aut quod Gellius (xi.8.2 = F 1) *Albinus res Romanas oratione graeca scriptitavit* aut Plutarchus in Catone mai. (12 = T 4) 'Ἀλβῖνος ἱστορίαν ἑλληνιστὶ γράψας.' Schweighaeuser's analysis of the meaning of πραγματικὴ ἱστορία will be found repeated in Strachan-Davidson, *op. cit.* (n. 79) 3–5.

ships. For the analysis of cause and effect implied in Asellio's *res gestae* Polybius had a separate expression – ἀποδεικτικὴ ἱστορία.[92] In his account of the geology of the Black Sea (IV.40.1) he contrasts his own ἀποδεικτικὴ διήγησις with the account of others ἐν αὐτῇ τῇ φάσει κείμενον. Elsewhere (X.21.8) he opposes the encomium, which is written κεφαλαιώδης καὶ μετ᾽ αὐξήσεως τῶν πράξεων to history which, κοινὸς ὢν ἐπαίνου καὶ ψόγου, ζητεῖ τὸν ἀληθῆ καὶ τὸν μετ᾽ ἀποδείξεως καὶ τῶν ἑκάστοις παρεπομένων συλλογισμῶν (*sc.* ἀπολογισμόν).[93] A similar contrast exists between his own introductory books, written ἐπικεφαλαιούμενοι (II.40.4; *cf.* I.13.7, II.1.4, 14.1), and the main body of his work, ἡ ἀποδεικτικὴ ἱστορία (II.37.3; *cf.* III.1.3).

In Polybius, then, ἀποδεικτική – Asellio's *res gestae* – and πραγματική clearly represent two separate ideas, the former being concerned with method, the latter with content; and in one passage (X.21.3) Polybius admits the possibility that authors who describe the foundation of cities – a type of history which is specifically contrasted in IX.1–2 with πραγματική – τὰς διαθέσεις καὶ περιστάσεις μετ᾽ ἀποδείξεως ἐξαγγέλλειν. Thus if the meaning of πραγματική in Polybius' criticism of Postumius is to be pressed (which I question), it implies 'a history dealing with political and military events', and not 'a history based on the principle of causality'.[94] Hence it is not identical with Asellio's *res gestae*, and does not in any way contradict the traditional picture of Postumius as an 'annalist'.[95]

In any case, Gelzer made far too much of this passage from Asellio, which is ‖ merely one man's definition, at variance both with that of Gellius himself[96] and with the view (which Gellius also quotes) of the learned Verrius Flaccus, who understood by *annales* an account of the past and by *historia* a record of one's own time.[97] In fact both Flaccus' and Asellio's definitions are developed out of the primary meaning of *annales*, an account written *per annos*, like the 'annales pontificum maximorum, quibus nil potest esse ieiunius' (Cic. *Leg.* I.2.6), or the various Latin successors of Cato, who are known to have composed bare chronicles containing such political and sacerdotal details as those with which Livy concludes each consular year. Gelzer claims that this element was absent from Fabius' work. On the other hand, the fourth book of Cato's *Origines* contained the famous passage:[98] 'Non lubet scribere, quod in tabula apud pontificem maximum est, quotiens annona cara, quotiens lunae aut solis lumine caligo aut quid obstiterit.' This assertion is hard to understand as a mere definition of Cato's position

[92] See Schweighaeuser, *loc. cit.*, and Strachan-Davidson, *op. cit.* (n. 79) 5–6.

[93] There is the same distinction in Plut. *Galba* 2.3: τὰ μὲν οὖν καθ᾽ ἕκαστα τῶν γενομένων ἀπαγγέλλειν ἀκριβῶς τῆς πραγματικῆς ἱστορίας ἐστίν (as opposed to biography). It is noteworthy that the same meaning is expressed elsewhere (*Alex.* 1), by the word ἱστορία alone: οὐ γὰρ ἱστορίας γράφομεν, ἀλλὰ βίους.

[94] That Postumius' history, like Fabius', went back to the *origines* of Rome (*cf.* F 3 (Peter)), which will scarcely be from a separate work: *HRR*, pp. cxxv–cxxvi), and so will have ranked technically among the accounts of the κτίσεις of a town (as Gelzer and Altheim admit: *cf.* too Cato's title, *Origines*), is another reason for not pressing the meaning of πραγματική, which excludes this branch of history.

[95] Macrobius III.20.5, referring to Postumius' work, speaks of *annali primo* (F 2 (Peter)).

[96] Gell. v.18.7 contrasts *res gestae* which *per annos scribuntur* (*annales*) with those written *per dies* (*diarium* or ἐφημερίς). Asellio of course distinguishes *annales*, written after the manner of those, *qui diarium scribunt*, from *res gestas a Romanis*, which show 'quo consilio quaque ratione gesta essent'.

[97] Verrius Flaccus' view won a certain following; it is also recorded by Servius, *ad Aen.* 1.373: 'inter historiam et annales hoc interest: historia est eorum temporum quae vel vidimus vel videre potuimus, dicta ἀπὸ τοῦ ἱστορεῖν i. q. videre. annales vero sunt eorum temporum, quae aetas nostra non novit.'   [98] F 77 = Gell. II.28.6.

(as the first *Latin* historian) relative to the pontifical *tabula*. It surely implies predecessors whose works *had* included pontifical material, and would seem to be directed at Fabius.[99] How far Cato really broke away from the annalistic tradition is another matter. One innovation, which has been interpreted as an anti-aristocratic gesture,[100] was his omission of the names of consuls.[101] But in the ancient manner he probably exaggerated the novelty of his own practice.

If the later Roman tradition made Fabius the author of *annales*, this probably means that he wrote with a year-by-year chronological system. But this, as Mommsen long ago observed,[102] does not imply that the 'annalistic' (year-by-year) scheme was never abandoned. It is quite likely that Fabius treated such topics as the Gallic Wars *en bloc*, and there were no doubt several similar instances. Polybius too wrote normally by Olympiad years, but on occasion allows himself the liberty of combining related events from a series of years within a single passage.[103] Gelzer is not therefore justified in setting up a rigid *either... or* on this question, as if the fact that Fabius occasionally treated events outside the year-by-year chronology rules out any annalistic scheme at all. Similarly it is a false antithesis to insist that because Fabius wrote with a political purpose, in order to present the Roman case to a Greek audience, therefore he cannot have given the jejune details of the corn supply, expiation of prodigies, etc., which are so familiar to us from Livy. To argue in this way is to ignore Fabius' literary ancestry, Roman and Greek. The Greek side has been discussed above.[104] It appears in the 'tragic' scheme borrowed (probably) from Diocles, and from writers such as Timaeus and Philinus, and shows itself in a fondness for παράδοξα and sensationalism. A part of this inheritance appears too in Fabius' general scheme – full for the origins of Rome, summary for the early 'historical' period, and fuller again for ‖ contemporary events – a scheme found not only in Cincius, Cato, and Ennius,[105] but also in the Περσικά of Ctesias, and the 'Ατθίδες of, for example, Hellanicus and many of the Atthidographers.[106] But for much of Fabius' history there can have been no Greek sources, but only the raw, indigenous material, the Fasti, pontifical records, lists of magistrates, and family traditions, *tituli*, *elogia*, *laudationes*[107] written in crabbed and halting Latin, formal in expression, repetitive and entirely lacking in literary pretensions. It is surely going too far to suggest that Fabius showed no trace of all this, no reflection of his Roman sources or the traditional

[99] *Cf.* Momigliano, *JRS* 33 (1943) 102.

[100] Scullard, *History of the Roman world from 753 to 146 B.C.* (London, 1935), 417.

[101] See above, n. 10.

[102] *Op. cit.* (n. 4) 2.363 n. 113; *cf.* Schanz-Hosius, *op. cit.* (n. 96) 1.171.

[103] *Cf.* Polyb. XIV.12.1ff., giving the reasons why Polybius made the reign of Ptolemy Philopator an exception to his normal practice of writing κατ' ἐνιαυτόν: XXXII.11.3ff. His method was thus a practical compromise between the Thucydidean διαίρεσις κατ' ἐνιαυτούς (in fact κατὰ θέρη καὶ χειμῶνας) and the arrangement κατὰ γένος, which Ephorus adopted in polemical opposition to his predecessor. On this see H. Bloch, *Athenian studies presented to W. S. Ferguson* (Cambridge, Mass., 1940) 308–16.

[104] See too Zimmerman, *Klio* 26 (1933) 257ff.; Kornemann, *HZ* 165 (1932) 287.

[105] *Cf.* J. Vahlen, *Ennianae Poesis Reliquiae*² (Leipzig, 1903) praef. clxxiv. Ennius devoted the first three of his eighteen books to the kings, and by the sixth book had reached Pyrrhus.

[106] *Cf.* Peter, *HRR*, lxxiv. See further F. Jacoby, *RE* 8.1 (1912) 'Hellanikos (7)', cols. 138–42; L. Pearson, *The local historians of Attica* (Philadelphia, 1942) 8; Jacoby, *RE* 11.2 (1922) 'Ktesias (1)', cols. 2040ff.; R. Laqueur, *RE* 13.1 (1922) 'Lokalchronik', especially cols. 1092ff., who stresses the emphasis given to epic and myth in the Atthides. Androtion and Philochorus (whom Peter mentions) are in this respect hardly typical; they pay much less attention to the earlier period, especially Androtion. See also H. Bloch, *op. cit.* (n. 103) 344–6.

[107] *Cf.* Beloch, *op. cit.* (n. 11) 96–8.

background of his own senatorial circle, that on the contrary he sprang up all armed *à la grecque*, like Pallas from the head of Zeus.

The political purpose of Fabius and his immediate successors is established: that is Gelzer's achievement. But annalists they remained, *exiles* in style, 'non exornatores rerum sed tantummodo narratores' (Cic. *De Or.* II.54), writing usually *per annos* (like Thucydides, as well as Valerius Antias), but occasionally modifying their scheme (like Polybius), probably rounding off the account of each year with the jejune details of elections, prodigies, and priesthoods (like Livy), sometimes following their Hellenistic models into the realm of 'tragic' history, but more often recording the simple details of campaigns culled from their Roman sources – in short, the legitimate and recognisable offspring of third- and second-century Rome.

6

NAVAL *TRIARII* (Polyb. 1.26.6)*

The Roman fleet which defeated the Carthaginians off Cape Ecnomus in 256 B.C. had a dual function: it was a naval force, prepared to meet the enemy at sea, and also an army of picked troops intended for landing on the coast of Africa. Its four squadrons were manned each by a legion, and both aspects were reflected in the terminology. τὸ δὲ μέρος ἕκαστον διττὰς εἶχε προσηγορίας· πρῶτον μὲν γὰρ ἐκαλεῖτο στρατόπεδον καὶ πρῶτος στόλος καὶ τὰ λοιπὰ κατὰ λόγον (Polyb. 1.26.6). In addition, however, the fourth squadron (or legion) καὶ τρίτην ἐπωνυμίαν ἔτι προσειλήφει· τριάριοι γὰρ ὠνομάζοντο κατὰ τὴν ἐν τοῖς πεζικοῖς στρατοπέδοις συνήθειαν. It is odd that our earliest reference to *triarii* should be in a naval context; and the significance of Polybius' statement appears to have been overlooked.

The first two Roman squadrons, we are told (Polyb. 1.26.11ff.), advanced in diverging lines, led by two ἑξήρεις side by side, and opening out behind to a wide base line, along which were deployed the third and fourth squadrons, so that the whole formed a hollow triangle. How far this account is trustworthy need not concern us here.[1] The point is that someone saw a resemblance between the fourth squadron and the *triarii* of the manipular army.[2]

Now in this army the *velites* were taken from the youngest and poorest (νεωτάτους καὶ πενιχροτάτους: Polyb. VI.21.7); those next to them (τοὺς δ' ἑξῆς – presumably in age) were made *hastati*; those in the prime of life became *principes*; and the oldest of all (τοὺς πρεσβυτάτους) *triarii*. Clearly this distinction, based on age (and in the case of the *velites* on income too), did not apply to the squadrons at Ecnomus, where all four legions were chosen from picked troops (τὰς ἀρίστας χεῖρας: 1.26.5). Moreover, we do not hear of similar titles – *velites*, *hastati*, or *principes* – for the troops of the other three squadrons; they would in any case have been both superfluous and confusing.

The real explanation must be that the name *triarii* was simply a popular

* [[CR 64 (1950) 10–11]]

---

[1] Tarn, *Hellenistic military and naval developments* (Cambridge, 1930) 149–51, thinks it came from a Carthaginian observer who misunderstood the movements of the first two squadrons; cf. De Sanctis, *Storia dei Romani* 3.1 (Turin, 1916) 141. It is accepted as reliable by J. Kromayer in J. Kromayer and G. Veith, *Schlachtenatlas zur antiken Kriegsgeschichte: Römische Abteilung* 1 (Gotha, 1922) col. 5, and T. Frank, *CAH* 7 (1925) 681.

[2] *Cf.* Gelzer, *Hermes* 70 (1935) 274: 'Nach ihrer taktischen Bedeutung wird die vierte Abteilung auch mit der Beziehung *triarii* belegt.' F. Cornelius, *Cannae* (*Klio*, Beiheft 26, 1932) 33 n.1.

nickname given by troops[3] to whom the sea ‖ and its ways were still novel. But whether the fourth squadron was dubbed 'the old men' by the rest, or themselves adopted a title indicating 'tried veterans', is less clear. (προσειλήφει is no help, for it commonly means either 'received' or 'took'.) As the oldest of the legionaries the *triarii* may have had certain privileges and prestige. To the centurion of their first maniple fell the duty of sounding the bugle at the beginning of each night watch (Polyb. vi.35.12, 36.5). But, if the *triarii* were excused from attendance on the military tribune in camp (vi.33.8–10), so too were the youthful *velites* (*ibid.*); and such duties as guarding the horse-squadron (vi.33.10) were not obviously more honourable or responsible than those of the other troops. The proverb *res ad triarios rediit*[4] signified that an issue was desperate, *i.e.* the defences were down to the last line; but it tells us nothing about the quality or repute of the *triarii* themselves. All this then is inconclusive. Yet in general it is commoner for nicknames to be given by others than to be voluntarily assumed; and the likelihood is that the rest of the forces dubbed the fourth squadron *triarii*.[5]

The humorous nickname has always been typical of camp-life. One recalls the nicknames of Caligula (Tac. *Ann.* 1.41.3) and Caracalla (Dio lxviii.3.3), the centurion Lucilius ominously known as *cedo alteram* (Tac. *Ann.* 1.23.4) and his later counterpart *manu ad ferrum* (Vopisc. *Aurel.* 6.2), the *muli Mariani*, carrying their own *vasa* and *cibaria* on a forked stick (Plut. *Mar.* 13), and the *senatus caligatus* (βουλὴ καλιγᾶτα) – the two veteran legions who tried to mediate between Caesar and L. Antonius (Dio xlviii.12.3). An eye for incongruous analogy can be seen in the *sambucae* at Syracuse (Polyb. viii.4.2,11)[6] and the famous *corvus* or κόραξ of this very battle of Ecnomus (Polyb. 1.22);[7] and how any confusion between the functions of the different services appealed to the soldiers' sense of humour is clear from the joke about using men of the tenth legion as cavalry, which Caesar thought worth recording (*BGall.* 1.42). It is a form of humour which changes little. The recent war gave us 'ducks' and 'snowdrops',[8] to quote two examples out of many; and the author of a tall story is still exhorted to tell it to the horse marines. It is among such phrases that Polybius' naval *triarii* belong; they form part of the history, not of Roman naval organisation, but of military slang.

---

[3] L. J. D. Richardson, *CQ* 39 (1945) 59–62, argues that the word τερθρεία was first used to describe the office of the τερθρηδών or πρωρεύς, and was then applied to a military office. 'The analogy between the military and naval careers may well have reflected itself in a...transference of terminology, perhaps at first playfully applied' (p. 61). This is very much what I suggest happened with the word *triarii* in 256 B.C. Polybius may not have fully appreciated the point of the joke.

[4] Livy viii.8.11; *cf.* Seneca, *Tranq.* 4.5; Varro, *Ling.* v.89.

[5] Polybius' source will of course be Fabius Pictor.

[6] *Cf.* C. Wunderer, *Polybios-Forschungen* 3 (Leipzig, 1909) 48: 'jedenfalls ein Soldatenwitz mit Beziehungen, die wir nicht mehr recht verstehen'. For further examples of instruments of war with metaphorical names taken from soldiers' slang see pp. 74ff. of this pamphlet.

[7] On the *corvus* see now J. H. Thiel, *Studies in the history of roman sea-power in Republican times* (Amsterdam, 1946) 432–47; E. de Saint-Denis, *Latomus* 5 (1946) 359–67.

[[8] 'Ducks' were amphibious vehicles, 'snowdrops' were U.S. military police.]]

7

ROMAN DECLARATION OF WAR IN THE THIRD AND SECOND CENTURIES*

The Roman machinery for declaring war in accordance with the traditional rites of the *ius fetiale* is not without its importance for an analysis of the exact course of events in such critical years as 218 or 200 B.C. Elsewhere[1] I have shown that by the end of the third century, as a result of changes in the fetial procedure of the early Republic, the senatorial *legati*, who by this time took the place of the priestly *fetiales*, now went out armed with a conditional declaration of war, authorised beforehand by the Senate and the people, so that, if the reply to their *rerum repetitio* was unfavourable, they could immediately convey the Roman decision of war. Whether the casting of a bloodstained spear into enemy territory was still carried out – either on the frontier or by a legal fiction in Rome[2] – is not always clear and is in any case unimportant. In effect, from the moment the *legati* had spoken their last words (which in the older procedure constituted the *testatio* or *denuntiatio belli*) the two peoples were at war. Put schematically, the earlier formula was: 'res repetuntur, bellum denuntiatur, senatus censet, populus iubet, bellum indicitur.' By the time of the Second Punic War it had changed to: 'senatus censet, populus iubet, res repetuntur, bellum denuntiatur, bellum indicitur.'

When did this change take place? The conditional nature of the vote in the *comitia* is specifically recorded for the war with Perseus,[3] and it is clearly implied in both the Polybian and annalistic accounts of the events leading up to the Second Punic and Second Macedonian wars. The purpose of the present note is to emphasise that there is evidence for a conditional war-motion in 238/7 B.C. and that recognition of this fact clarifies the picture of the events which preceded the Roman annexation of Sardinia.

I

Shortly after the end of the First Punic War, in 238 or 237 B.C., the Romans occupied Sardinia; the exact date is controversial and does not concern us

* [CP 44 (1949) 15–19]

---

[1] *JRS* 27 (1937) 180–207 (esp. 192–7), written in conjunction with A. H. McDonald; 31 (1941) 82–93 [below, pp. 181–92].

[2] *Cf.* G. Wissowa, *Religion und Kultus der Römer*[2] (Munich, 1912) 553–4.

[3] Livy (A) XLII.31.1: 'nisi populo Romano satisfecissent'.

here.[4] Learning of the Roman intentions, the Carthaginians, now free of their difficulties in Africa, resisted these claims on the grounds that Sardinia was theirs[5] and prepared an expedition against the island.[6] Thereupon the Romans, interpreting ‖ these preparations as levelled against themselves, πόλεμον ἐψηφίσαντο πρὸς τοὺς Καρχηδονίους.[7] The latter, yielding to circumstances (εἴξαντες τοῖς καιροῖς), gave up their claim to Sardinia and paid a further indemnity (προσέθηκαν) of 1,200 talents to the Romans ἐφ᾽ ᾧ μὴ κατὰ τὸ παρὸν ἀναδέξασθαι τὸν πόλεμον.

Elsewhere[8] the clause by which the Carthaginians agreed to pay this sum is described by Polybius as ἐπισυνθῆκαι, and other sources are agreed in regarding it as a supplement to the treaty of 241.[9] This would suggest that, despite the war-motion, a state of war did not actually ensue; and this is implied by Polybius when he writes (III.27.7): Ῥωμαῖοι Καρχηδονίοις πόλεμον ἐξενέγκαντες ἕως δόγματος,[10] although a few lines farther down he describes the Sardinian affair as ὁ δεύτερος πόλεμος (III.28.1)[11] The course of the negotiations emerges most clearly from Polybius III.10.1–3, and the parallel with the interviews with the Roman *legati* at Carthage in 218 and at Abydus in 200 is instructive.[12] The close analogy provided by these two parallel interviews leaves little doubt that in 238/7, too, a Roman embassy was sent to Carthage after the passing of the war-motion. ἀπαγγειλάντων αὐτοῖς πόλεμον, writes Polybius; but the purpose of these *legati* in terms of the *ius fetiale* must have been *ad res repetendas*. In reply, the Carthaginians πρῶτον εἰς πᾶν συγκατέβαινον – they were ready to negotiate on all points, to argue the rights

[4] One tradition, represented by Dio Cassius (Zonar. VIII.18, p. 400A) and Sinnius Capito (*ap.* Fest., p. 322M, *s.v.* 'Sardi venales'), attributed it to Ti. Gracchus, the consul of A.U.C. 516 (238 B.C.). But there may be some confusion between this Gracchus and his grandson who operated in Sardinia in 177 (*cf.* E. Täubler, *Die Vorgeschichte des zweiten punischen Kriegs* (Berlin, 1921) 20, 32ff.; Ed. Meyer, *Kleine Schriften* 2 (Halle, 1924) 385–6); and the Livian tradition (Eutrop. III.2) puts the annexation under the consuls for 237. Polybius (III.10.1) dates the affair after the conclusion of the Mercenary War, which lasted three years and four months (I.88.9); but whether this should be calculated from autumn 241 to the end of 238 (G. De Sanctis, *Storia dei Romani* 3.1 (Turin, 1916) 396 n. 30) or from the beginning of 240 to the early summer of 237 (Ed. Meyer, *op. cit.*, 2.383 n. 2) is uncertain. Polybius may therefore have dated the Sardinian incident late in 238 (O. Meltzer, *Geschichte der Karthager* (Berlin, 1879–96) 2.387) or early in 237.

[5] Polyb. 1.88.9.

[6] *Ibid.*: παρασκευαζομένων μεταπορεύεσθαι τοὺς ἀποστήσαντας αὐτῶν τὴν νῆσον. This must imply an expedition.   [7] Polyb. 1.88.10.

[8] Polyb. III.27.7.

[9] *Cf.* App. *Pun.* 5: καὶ τόδε ταῖς προτέραις συνθήκαις ἐνεγράφη. E. Täubler, *Imperium Romanum* 1 (Berlin, 1913) 94ff.; *op. cit.* (n. 4) 22 n. 35.

[10] *Cf.* Täubler, *op. cit.* (n. 4) 22: 'man muss den Krieg als beschlossen, aber noch nicht als verkündet denken'.

[11] This contradiction is a sign that Polybius had not fully mastered the fetial procedure involved and the distinction between the popular resolution and the actual *belli denuntiatio*.

[12] Polyb. III.20.7–21.8, 33.1–4; Livy (A) XXI.18.3–14 (Carthage); Polyb. XVI.34.3–7; Livy (P) XXXI.18. 1–4 (Abydus). In *JRS* 27 (1937) 197, the parallelism of these two interviews is set out; *cf.* Täubler, *op. cit.* (n. 4) 23: 'Für den Fall, dass eine römische Gesandtschaft nach Karthago ging [*i.e.*, in 238 or 237], ist also nach dem Beispiel von 218 zu denken, dass sie nicht die blosse Kriegserklärung, sondern eine Alternative mit sich trug.' But Täubler has not seen that this now became the regular practice.

and wrongs of it;[13] but the Romans insisted on a plain 'yes' or 'no' (οὐκ ἐντρεπομένων), whereupon the Carthaginians accepted the terms – ἐφ' ᾧ μὴ κατὰ τὸ παρὸν ἀναδέξασθαι τὸν πόλεμον, as Polybius says in another passage (1.88.12); but in the changed circumstances of 218 (Polyb. III.33.4) ἀν-εφώνησαν...δέχεσθαι φάσκοντες. The terms accepted were then added as an ἐπισυνθήκη to the treaty of 241.

Clearly this narrative implies that, as in 218 (*cf.* Polyb. III.20.7: δύο προτείνοντες αὐτοῖς), the Roman *legati* were armed with a conditional war-motion; and a refusal to accept the terms of the ultimatum would have led to an immediate state of war. Thus we can trace the operation of the modified fetial procedure outlined above on four separate occasions, in 238/7, in 218, in 200, and in 172/1. It is clear and well defined, an excellent example of the Roman capacity to adapt traditional institutions to suit changed circumstances. In the second half of this paper I shall discuss a recent article in which it is argued, on the contrary, that by the year 200 fetial practice was virtually moribund. ‖

II

In the course of a valuable discussion of the Greek and Roman traditions of the origins of the *Bellum Philippicum*,[14] E. J. Bickerman has argued that by the end of the third century fetial procedure had decayed to such a degree that hostilities with Macedon began without any formal declaration of war on the part of the Romans (*denuntiatio belli*) other than the conveying of the *indictio belli* to a Macedonian outpost in Illyria on the arrival of the Roman army there in September 200. Since this view both implicitly and explicitly rejects that put forward by A. H. McDonald and me in 1937 and developed in the earlier part of this paper, it will be necessary to examine some of the arguments adduced in its support.

In a well-known passage (XIII.3.7) Polybius asserts that in the second century

---

[13] So Paton (Loeb ed.), correctly. Schweighaeuser translates 'omnes consentiebant condiciones'; and in Polyb. XXI.15.11, Scipio's advice to Antiochus εἰς πᾶν συγκαταβαίνειν was obviously 'to submit to everything', not 'to negotiate on all points'. Liddell–Scott–Jones, like Schweighaeuser, takes that to be the meaning here; but Polybius continues: ὑπολαμβάνοντες αὐτοὺς νικήσειν τοῖς δικαίοις, and it is difficult to see (a) how submitting to everything would enable the Carthaginians to conquer by the justice of their cause; (b) in that case, what the difference would be between εἰς πᾶν συγκατέβαινον here and εἴξαντες τῇ περιστάσει in §3. Shuckburgh's rendering ('the latter was at first inclined to resist at all hazards, because the goodness of her cause gave her hopes of victory') is certainly wrong; Polybius knew and said (1.88.11) that military resistance was never contemplated.

[14] *CP* 40 (1945) 137–48 (referred to below under its author's name alone). Formerly (*RPh* 61 (1935) 173), Bickerman had argued that the famous interview between M. Aemilius Lepidus and Philip V at Abydus in 200 B.C. was not a declaration of war but an example of the traditional *denuntiatio belli*, which had to be followed by a *senatus consultum* and a war-vote of the centuries. The chronological difficulties implicit in this view (*cf.* *JRS* 27 (1937) 194 n. 92) have led to its modification, though Bickerman still has 'some doubts' (p. 139 n. 25), and suggests that κατὰ τοὺς καιροὺς τούτους in Polyb. XVI.34.1 is merely a transitional phrase, and that, in fact, Lepidus' interview with Philip took place shortly after the beginning of the siege of Abydus rather than about the time of its fall. See further below, n. 26.

B.C. 'some slight traces of the ancient principles of warfare survive among the Romans; for they make declarations of war, they very seldom use ambuscades, and they fight hand-to hand at close quarters'. This statement, it is suggested, is evidence that at the date when Polybius wrote 'from the ancient system of formal war-making there remained only the solemn declaration of hostilities'.[15] Closer examination shows this view to rest upon a misunderstanding of Polybius' argument. In this chapter, starting out from an example of Philip V's treachery, Polybius goes on to discuss the practice of οἱ ἀρχαῖοι – obviously Greeks – who entered into a convention not to use secret missiles or those discharged from a distance,[16] and who preceded both wars and battles by formal declarations (τοὺς πολέμους...προύλεγον καὶ τὰς μάχας...καὶ τοὺς τόπους). Nowadays, he continues, this is considered poor generalship; but of this ἀρχαῖα αἵρεσις περὶ τὰ πολεμικά the Romans alone still maintain traces, for they declare war, seldom use ambuscades, and fight at close quarters.

Clearly there is no reference here to the *details* of fetial procedure. The words τοὺς πολέμους προύλεγον are of general application and do not connote the *indictio belli* to the exclusion of the *rerum repetitio* and the *denuntiatio*.[17] Nor do they indicate the use of *fetiales* rather than senatorial *legati*:[18] Polybius was not concerned with such niceties. The fact that προλέγειν governs μάχας and τόπους as well as πολέμους shows that Polybius is not using it as a *technicus terminus* (= *indicere*) at all; and the ἀρχαῖα αἵρεσις περὶ τὰ πολεμικά is Greek, not Roman. We may not, therefore, quote this passage for any detailed discussion of the fetial procedure of the second century.

Further arguments are also adduced for assuming an excessive decrepitude in the *ius fetiale* at this time. The *rerum repetitio*, ‖ it is argued, had by 200 B.C. 'evolved into an exchange of embassies with proposals and counterproposals; accordingly the Senate could dispense with a final *denuntiatio belli*'.[19] There is,

---

[15] Bickerman, pp. 138–9.

[16] Strabo X.1.12. C448 refers to this convention made by the cities of Euboea at the time of the Lelantine War.

[17] As Bickerman implies, when he continues (p. 139): '*Accordingly* [italics mine], the annalistic narrative [in Livy]...duly notes the *indictio belli* at its chronological place but does not mention any solemn *denuntiatio belli*.' No conclusions are to be drawn from this *argumentum ex silentio*.

[18] *Cf.* Wissowa, *op. cit.* (n. 2) 554: '...länger hielt sich die Tätigkeit der Fetialen beim Abschluss des *foedus*, am längsten bei der formalen Kriegserklärung'. As evidence for the last point Wissowa quotes this passage of Polybius; he, too, is taking ἀρχαῖα αἵρεσις περὶ τὰ πολεμικά as a reference to the Roman *ius fetiale*.

[19] In support of this view Bickerman mentions (p. 138 n. 16) the 'final mission sent to Perseus of Macedon' early in 172 'ad res repetendas...renuntiandamque amicitiam' (Livy (A) XLII.25.1–12). The envoys subsequently reported that owing to Perseus' refusal to accept the Roman demands, 'se amicitiam et societatem renuntiasse' (25.12). But (a) this passage has been recognised to be an annalistic fabrication since the time of Nissen, *Kritische Untersuchungen über die Quellen der vierten und fünften Dekade des Livius* (Berlin, 1863) 246–7; *cf.* A. Heuss, *Die völkerrechtlichen Grundlagen der römischen Aussenpolitik in republikanischer Zeit* (Leipzig, 1933) 50–1; Walbank, *JRS* 31 (1941) 90 n. 60; (b) without entering here into the vexed question of *amicitia*, one may note that *amicitiae renuntiatio* is quite distinct from both *denuntiatio belli* and *indictio belli*, for in Livy (A) XXXVI.3.8 the *fetiales* are asked whether 'prius societas et amicitia eis (= Aetolis) renuntianda esset quam bellum indicendum'.

in fact, no reason whatever to assume that the exchanges of embassies which preceded, for example, the war with Antiochus were a substitute for the formal *rerum repetitio*; and it is only necessary to read the account of the interview at Carthage in 218 or that at Abydus in 200[20] to see that on both occasions the senatorial *legati* presented specific demands for satisfaction, failing which war would ensue. This can hardly be anything other than the *rerum repetitio*; and, as I have shown elsewhere,[21] the rejection of this *rerum repetitio* is followed immediately by a *denuntiatio belli*, which has the full force of a declaration of war because the conditional authorisation of the Senate and people has already been obtained.[22]

Dr Bickerman, however, insists that the meeting at Abydus was inconclusive. 'Lepidus' protest was simply an enlarged renewal[23] of the note transmitted in Athens, and the war was voted in Rome about the time of the colloquy in Abydus and independently of its outcome.…An ultimatum was thought unnecessary.'[24] This view is contradicted by Polybius xvi.35. After (but clearly not very long after) the fall of Abydus, an Achaean embassy reached Rhodes and begged the people to come to terms with Philip. (Rhodes had, of course, been at war with Macedon since the campaigns of 201.) However, the Roman *legati* promptly ‖ came forward (ἐπελθόντων) and urged the Rhodians μὴ ποιεῖσθαι διαλύσεις πρὸς Φίλιππον ἄνευ ῾Ρωμαίων, whereupon the Rhodians

---

[20] See above, n. 12.

[21] *JRS* 27 (1937) 194, 31 (1941) 87ff.

[22] In effect the *denuntiatio belli* is now the declaration of war, though the term *indictio belli* was still officially reserved for the traditional ceremony of throwing the bloodstained spear. But there is little doubt that the term *indictio belli* often came to be used to denote the new type of *denuntiatio* (as I suspect it is in Livy (A) xxxi.8.4; see the next note). Certainly Livy uses it inaccurately in two places to describe the older type of *denuntiatio*, which had still to be followed by the decision of senate and people (1.32.5, 9, vii.32.1–2). Bickerman attributes to Holleaux and me the view that the ultimatum delivered to Nicanor at Athens (Polyb. xvi.27.1–3) was the *denuntiatio* and that delivered at Abydus the *indictio* (p. 139). This was Holleaux's view (*CAH* 8 (1930) 164), but it is not mine. In *JRS* 27 (1937) 195 (*cf. Philip V of Macedon* (Cambridge, 1940) 131), I have shown that the interview with Nicanor was an irregular and unauthorised *démarche* – unauthorised because, owing to an unfortunate hitch in the *comitia*, it had been delivered before the carrying of the war-motion by the centuries.

[23] The Abydus ultimatum contained new clauses in favour of Ptolemy, Athens and Rhodes, who were not mentioned in that delivered to Nicanor; therefore, Bickerman argues (*cf. RPh* 61 (1935) 173), the later interview cannot be a declaration of war, since 'the subsequent stages of a declaration of war (*testatio, denuntiatio, indictio belli*)) should have the same scope as the *rerum repetitio* and refer to it'. In fact, the *testatio* and the *denuntiatio belli* are identical (*cf.* Livy 1.32.9 (*testatio*); x.12; Cic. *Rep.* ii.17 (*denuntiatio belli*)); and the *indictio* was traditionally the ceremonial throwing of a spear (*cf.* Livy x.45.7), though later it became confused with the *denuntiatio belli*. Hence, it is difficult to see how they can have the same scope, except in so far as all three terms are used of the same action. Moreover, Bickerman is here ignoring the change in procedure by which the *denuntiatio* had become the effective declaration of war; and though he argues (p. 139) that 'as a matter of fact, the *indictio belli* was conveyed to a Macedonian post in Illyria when a Roman army had crossed the Adriatic about mid-September 200', this is pure surmise; according to Livy (A) xxxi.8.4 (which he quotes), the Senate instructed the consul to send whomsoever he thought fit 'ex eis qui extra senatum essent…ad bellum indicendum'; but this will refer to the sending of Lepidus to Abydus, for, as we saw in the last note, Livy is liable to confuse the *denuntiatio* and the *indictio belli* (with which it had now virtually coalesced), and in 200 Lepidus was not yet a Senator (*JRS* 27 (1937) 195–6).   [24] Bickerman, p. 139.

resolved to stand by Rome. It is difficult to see how the Rhodians could make peace ἄνευ ʻΡωμαίων unless the Romans were themselves already at war with Philip; and indeed, Lepidus had stated to Philip at Abydus that μὴ βουλομένῳ πειθαρχεῖν ἑτοίμως ὑπάρξειν τὸν πρὸς ʻΡωμαίους πόλεμον. Finally, the complete parallelism in the course of the interviews at Carthage in 238/7 and 218 and at Abydus in 200[25] confirms the view that, from the time of Lepidus' last words to Philip, Rome and Macedon were at war.[26]

We must therefore conclude that the meeting at Abydus ended with a *denuntiatio belli* initiating a state of war between Rome and Macedon. The modified procedure was carried out in full, and it is incorrect to say that 'an ultimatum was thought unnecessary because Philip did not answer the note handed over in Athens but continued his aggressions, by his conduct breaking peace and friendship with Rome'.[27] This interpretation of events is unacceptable because it does not take account of the conditional nature of the war-vote of the centuries, as a result of which, from the middle of the third century, the *denuntiatio belli* had become the effective declaration of war.

[25] See above, n. 12.

[26] Bickerman (p. 139) sees yet a further objection in the fact that the *fetiales* were consulted as to whether the *indictio belli* should be delivered to Philip in person or not (Livy (A) xxxi.8.3): 'this would have been superfluous if Lepidus had been sent to make the declaration to the king himself'. But this difficulty is caused by Bickerman's chronology, which makes the war-vote and Lepidus' visit to Abydus coincide. If the war-measure was passed by the centuries late in July, Lepidus could have heard of the instructions of the *fetiales* a month later, in time to sail north to Abydus and deliver the declaration of war at the beginning of September (*cf. Philip V* (n. 22) 315–16). It is only by rejecting Polybius' dating of Lepidus' visit to Abydus (see above, n. 14) that it can be made to coincide with the war-motion. Naturally, no conclusions are to be drawn from Dio in Zonar. ix.15.2: ἐπεὶ μηδὲν ὧν ἐπετάττετο ἔπραττε, τὸν πόλεμον ἐψηφίσαντο.

[27] Bickerman, p. 139.

8

SOME REFLECTIONS ON HANNIBAL'S PASS*

Few historical problems have produced more unprofitable discussion than that of Hannibal's pass over the Alps. But if there is still no clear answer, some headway had at least been made in defining the question – which is half the battle. Kahrstedt put the matter as succinctly as anyone. 'Mit Topographie ist nicht zum Ziele zu kommen, weisse Felsen und tiefe Schluchten, Flusstäler und steile Abhänge gibt es überall. Das Problem ist literarhistorisch, nicht topographisch.'[1] Hence a feeling of dismay at finding the question reopened without, apparently, any realisation of what sort of question it is. For in fact Sir Gavin de Beer's forthright and attractive little book,[2] despite its ingenious attempt to introduce new kinds of evidence, never comes to grips with the fundamental issue – the relationship between Polybius' account and Livy's. This central question is dismissed with a fatal facility: 'each account complements and supplies what was missing from the other' (p. 33). If one is to get anywhere with this problem one must treat it more seriously than that; and it may therefore perhaps be worth while, yet again, to reconsider the evidence and to indicate the limits within which the answer is to be sought (without any guarantee that it will necessarily be found). Such a survey can offer none of the 'certainties' or the excitement to be found in *Alps and elephants*; it will propose no novelties; and if it is not to become unreadable, it had better avoid all but the most obvious and necessary references to a fantastically inflated modern literature.

I

Livy's account of Hannibal's crossing of the Alps is to be found in XXI.31.1ff. If one omits the passage 31.9–12, and the first words of 32.6, his version corresponds to that in Polybius III.49.5–56.4, sufficiently closely to suggest that both go back ultimately to the same source. But after bringing Hannibal to the so-called 'Island' between the Rhône and a tributary (the name of which

* [*JRS* 46 (1956) 37–45]

[1] U. Kahrstedt, *Geschichte der Karthager von 218–146* (Berlin, 1913) 181.
[2] G. de Beer, *Alps and elephants* (London, 1955) pp. xv + 123, with 14 figs. and a map. His theory has received wide publicity in various broadcasts, including a television programme on 12 June 1956 which included a film of much of Hannibal's supposed route over the Col de Grimone and the Col de la Traversette.

is uncertain), and after letting him there settle a dispute between two brothers, whom he specifically calls Allobroges (xxi.31.5ff.), Livy continues:

(9) sedatis Hannibal certaminibus Allobrogum cum iam Alpes peteret, non recta regione iter instituit, sed ad laevam in Tricastinos flexit; inde per extremam oram Vocontiorum agri tendit in Trigorios, haud usquam impedita via, priusquam ad Druentiam flumen pervenit...(10–12, description of the Druentia, 'amnis Galliae fluminum difficillimus transitu'; 32.1–5, account of Scipio's action = Polyb. iii.49.1–4.) (32.6) Hannibal ab Druentia campestri maxime itinere ad Alpes cum bona pace incolentium ea loca Gallorum pervenit.

This passage in Livy corresponds to nothing in Polybius. As to its origins there seem to be two possibilities. Either it goes back to the same primary source, and represents fuller detail, which Polybius has omitted; or it comes from a separate source (or sources), which either Livy or the account on which he draws has introduced to supplement the other. The first alternative runs up against a serious difficulty. If the Druentia is the Durance, a march thither from the 'Island' (wherever precisely on the Rhône this is to be located) clearly involves the crossing of a considerable pass. But it is manifestly Polybius' belief that right up to the moment when ἤρξατο τῆς πρὸς τὰς Ἄλπεις ἀναβολῆς Hannibal was marching παρὰ τὸν ποταμόν (iii.50.1). Whether this was in fact the Rhône or a tributary such as the Isère need not concern us here. The point is that his narrative does not allow for a march over high ground from the Rhône to the Durance. De Beer, it is true, claims to have found evidence for this part of Hannibal's march in Polybius. In Polyb. iii.50.5, Hannibal camps πρὸς ταῖς ὑπερβολαῖς, and de Beer is 'almost certain that the battle on this site was at the Col de Grimone' (p. 60). The Col de Grimone lies between the Drôme and the Buech, well to the west of Gap, and de Beer believes it to be the ‖ *Cremonis iugum*, which Coelius gave as Hannibal's pass (Livy xxi.38.6). But, unfortunately for this hypothesis, the battle at this pass is identical with that in Livy xxi.32.9ff., and de Beer knows very well (p. 75) that this took place *after* the crossing of the Druentia (31.12, 32.6). He dismisses the discrepancy as unimportant, but it surely invalidates his identification of Polybius' ὑπερβολαί with the Col de Grimone, or any other pass between the Rhône and the Durance.[3]

The plain fact is that Polybius' account cannot be reconciled with a march from the Rhône to the Durance. According to him[4] Hannibal, after leaving

---

[3] For his account of the fight with the Gauls and the capture of the citadel de Beer (p. 54) quotes both Polyb. iii.51.11, and Livy xxi.33.11; he then continues: 'on the following day Hannibal led his army in comparative safety [Livy: marching in open country, campestri maxime itinere]', and his footnote gives a reference to Livy xxi.32.6. Only a reader who is following the argument with great attention will note that this second passage of Livy precedes the account of the seizure of the fortress, and refers to the section of the march 'ab Druentia...ad Alpes'. In placing it without comment after the seizure of the fortress, de Beer is being perhaps less candid with his reader than his sharp criticism of his predecessors might lead one to expect.

[4] Polyb. iii.50.1.

the 'Island', marches for ten days along a river, and then begins the 'ascent of the Alps'. In Livy the insertion of the passage XXI.31.9–12, 32.6, has the effect of transferring the whole narrative of the Alpine crossing to a locality across the Druentia; but the corresponding events in Polybius occur in a district approached directly from 'the river', which must be either the Rhône or its tributary. Since it is incredible that this détour was described in Polybius' source, and that he simply omitted it and conflated the river at the 'Island' with the Druentia, it seems an inescapable conclusion that the passage XXI.31.9–12, 32.6, must come from a separate version of Hannibal's march,[5] of which we possess neither the beginning nor the end.

Now de Beer has argued that this interpolated section in Livy provides a convincing account of a route leading up the Rhône from the Aygues, up the Drôme, over the Col de Grimone to Gap, and across the Durance at a point immediately below its conjunction with the Guil, to continue in due course over the Col de la Traversette. The particular combination of Aygues, Col de Grimone, and Col de la Traversette is new. But a proposed crossing of the upper stream of the Durance is not, and against it the objection has often been raised that the raging stream of Livy XXI.31.10–12 is hard to reconcile with the upper reaches of that river. In order to discount this criticism de Beer has assembled (pp. 43–8) some interesting material on the flow of the rivers of south-eastern France. In those fed from glaciers and icefields the maximum flow is in May–June; whereas those fed from springs outside the glacial area 'have a minimum flow in summer, rise in level and in volume of water carried with the onset of autumn rains, and are at their highest and wildest in winter' (p. 46). The Durance is of the former type in its 'upper reaches...above the confluence with the Guil'; but 'below its junction with the Guil and the Ubaye the Durance shows not only its summer peak but also an autumnal rise towards a winter peak' (pp. 46–7). This point is made on two graphs representing the Durance 'in its middle reaches' and 'in its lower reaches'; the latter presumably refers to the reaches 'below the junction with the Guil and the Ubaye', and shows a high flow in April–May and an even higher peak in October–November. But in fact the relevance of these data to de Beer's own hypothesis is not very apparent. Both the Guil and the Ubaye are themselves rivers rising in the Alps and so presumably subject to summer peak flow. De Beer's second graph applies to the stretch 'below the junction with the Ubaye'; but how far below is not clear. In any case he makes Hannibal cross the Durance just below the confluence with the Guil (and so well above that with the Ubaye) at a point which can by no stretch of meaning be called the 'lower reaches' of the river. Thus the difficulty of applying Livy's account of the crossing of the Druentia to the upper waters of the Durance remains.[6] ‖

---

[5] The point has often been made; see, for example, Ed. Meyer, *Kleine Schriften* 2 (Halle, 1924) 413–14.

[6] The problem of 'peak flow' is of course affected by one's view of the date Hannibal can be assumed to have been in this part of Gaul. Both Polyb. II.54.1 and Livy XXI.35.6 make the date

What then of the three tribes? Can they help in determining the original context of Livy XXI.31.9–12, 32.6, and discovering into what view of the pass they then fitted? Here again de Beer has new evidence to adduce. He quotes the work of Etienne Clouzot[7] (which follows that of Auguste Longnon) to demonstrate that there was an unbroken continuity between the boundaries of the Celtic tribes prior to the Roman conquest of Gaul, the Gallic *civitates* of Roman Gaul, and the dioceses of the Christian church. Hence 'the map of the ecclesiastical subdivisions of south-eastern France reproduces the territories of the Celtic tribes of pre-Roman Gaul' (p. 35). This argument jumps several steps. First, our knowledge of the Gallic *civitates* rests in the main on the *Notitia Galliarum*, which hardly goes back beyond A.D. 400, and in any case merely lists the *civitates* without defining their boundaries; and secondly, even if, for the sake of argument, one accepts the thesis of complete continuity, there remains a gap of a hundred years between Hannibal's passage and the Roman conquest of Provence, during which many of the tribes may have changed their areas.[8] But in fact the boundaries of the ecclesiastical dioceses do not tally in all cases with our classical evidence for the areas in question. We know of two names for towns of the Tricastini, Noeomagus (Ptolemy II.10.7) and Augusta Tricastinorum(Pliny, *NH* III.36). It has been argued that Noeomagus is the modern St Paul-Trois-Châteaux; but if this is so, it becomes less easy to identify it with Augusta Tricastinorum,[9] for the likelihood is that this town is identical

---

when he was on the pass as 'close on the setting of the Pleiades'; and the 'morning setting' of the Pleiades was about 7–9 November, as de Beer correctly states (pp. 100–3). But from the time of Hesiod (*Op.* 383ff.) the setting of the Pleiades was an indication of the approach of winter; and it is possible in view of the reference in our sources to snow already gathering that this astronomical reference is not to be given too much weight. The first snow on the high passes can be expected towards the end of September, or indeed earlier. In 1947 the first snow was reported from Switzerland (2 ft on the Furka Pass, 7,990 ft) on 24 September; and D. Freshfield, *Hannibal once more* (London, 1914) 43ff., describes how in 1881 on the Col du Bonhomme the first snow fell on 15 August and the second a fortnight later (though this was probably exceptional). In our sources the astronomical reference is associated with the reference to the fall of snow, and *may* be derived erroneously from it: *cf.* C. Jullian, *Histoire de la Gaule* I (Paris, 1908) 487 n. 3; De Sanctis, *Storia dei Romani* 3.2 (Turin, 1917) 79. The journey from New Carthage to the Po Valley took five months (Polyb. III.56.3; Livy XXI.38.1); and though we are handicapped by having no clear indication of the date at which Hannibal set out, a start as late as early June (implied if he was on the pass early in November) would need some explanation. but if Hannibal was in Gaul in mid-September rather than the end of October, the rate of flow of the Durance 'in its lower reaches' would not, according to de Beer's graph, reach more than 350 cubic metres per second, compared with 750 at the end of October. The sceptic can of course argue that no graph necessarily covers the conditions of a particular year for which no independent records are available; and this is true for all arguments about the climatic conditions of 218 B.C.

[7] E. Clouzot, *Recueil des historiens de la France: Pouillés des provinces d'Aix, d'Arles et d'Embrun* (Paris, 1923); *Pouillés des provinces de Besançon, de Tarentaise et de Vienne* (Paris, 1940).

[8] De Beer (p. 37) acknowledges the existence of this century's gap in his argument, but dismisses it as unimportant, since 'there is no record of any disturbance of the settled inhabitants of south-eastern Gaul in the second century B.C., and it may be safely concluded that the territories occupied by these tribes remained substantially the same'. But where would such a record survive? Clearly this is an *argumentum ex silentio*, and not a very secure one.

[9] Augusta Tricastinorum is identified with St Paul-Trois-Châteaux by E. Desjardins, *Géographie historique et administrative de la Gaule romaine* (Paris, 1876–93) 2.226, and by other scholars listed in

with the Augusta of the Antonine Itineraries (*Itin. Ant.* 358; *Itin. Hieros.* 554), which the Peutinger Map calls Augustum, and which lay 22 *m.p.* from Valentia (Valence) and 23 *m.p.* from Dea Vocontiorum (Die), on the site of modern Aouste-en-Diois. This identification is supported by Ptolemy's account (II.10.7–8) of the position of the tribes of this area, which certainly points to Tricastinian territory on the right bank of the Drôme, well outside the area of the medieval diocese. This account de Beer summarises correctly (p. 37): 'The Tricastini were...living east of the Segallauni, north of the Vocontii, and south of the Allobroges.' It is not reconcilable with the diocesan boundaries marked on de Beer's sketch-map, which limits the Tricastini to the area around St Paul-Trois-Châteaux, due west of the Vocontii. Further, Strabo (IV.I.II, C 185) assigns the lower ground towards the Rhône between the Durance and the Isère to the Cavari: τῶν δὲ Καουάρων ὑπέρκεινται Οὐοκόντιοί τε καὶ Τρικόριοι καὶ Ἰκόνιοι καὶ Μέδυλλοι. This may mean that one passed through the territories of these tribes in succession as one moved eastward away from the Rhône and the Cavari;[10] or equally it may mean that one passed through their territories in succession as one moved from north to south (or, more probably, from south to north) along a line east of the territory ‖ of the Cavari, whose successive neighbours they would be. This seems to leave no room for the Tricastini; but, although Ptolemy distinguishes them, they may in Strabo's time have formed part of the Cavari.[11] Nevertheless, on the present evidence one cannot exclude the possibility that at the time of Augustus some at least of their territory lay north of the Drôme. But if this uncertainty exists in relation to the Tricastini, the situation of the Trigorii and Vocontii may also have changed between 218 and the period for which definite evidence is available; and in view of this it would seem hazardous to build very much on the evidence of the dioceses.

An old difficulty in Livy xxi.31.9 is that on leaving the 'Island' Hannibal is made to turn *ad laevam*. This expression may be either an insertion of Livy to link together his two sources; or it may have stood in the original source to which he turned for his interpolation. Against the former explanation is the fact that, far from smoothing over the transition, the phrase creates an almost insuperable difficulty. To turn left from the 'Island' (which must, it is agreed, lie on the Rhône) would have taken Hannibal west or north-west; in fact, to get to the Alps he had to go east (or north-east, or south-east). In order to

---

Scherling, *RE* 7A.1 (1939) 'Tricastini.' col. 81. For the view that Noeomagus and Augusta Tricastinorum are both to be identified with Aouste-en-Diois see A. Berthelot, *REA* 37 (1935) 203.

[10] De Beer (p. 37) states that 'Strabo said that the Vocontii were "above" the Cavari, and the Tricorii "above" the Vocontii'. This is a possible interpretation of what Strabo *meant*, but it is misleading as an account of what he said.

[11] For this theory see F. Vallentin, *Bulletin épigraphique de la Gaule* 2 (1882) 210ff. It gains support from the new fragments of the Arausio land register, which show that part of the territory of the *colonia* had been taken from (and restored to) the Tricastini; *cf.* A. Piganiol, *CRAI* (1950) 62–3. This implies that Tricastinian land stretched south of the later diocese of St Paul-Trois-Châteaux.

resolve this difficulty de Beer argues (p. 38) that Hannibal, having marched north from his Rhône crossing to the 'Island' (which he locates between the Rhône and the Aygues), did not take 'the direct route to Italy' but 'turned left' and continued northwards, *i.e.* he 'turned left' relative to a route which he might have taken – but did not, in so far as he continued to go north, as before! De Beer's map makes a poor attempt at disguising the fact with a swerve away from the Rhône just north of the Aygues, so that there can be a comparable swerve back – 'to the left'. There is nothing of this in either Livy or Polybius.

It has been plausibly argued that in Livy's source '*ad laevam*' referred to Hannibal's change of direction immediately after he crossed the Rhône, when he quite obviously turned left in order to follow it upstream.[12] In that case the march through the territory of the tribes mentioned in Livy might originally have been a march from south to north, or indeed a march beginning from south to north and continuing north-east or east (for it does not follow that the 'second source' which gave these names also had the details about the 'Island'). It has also been argued that the account of the crossing of the Druentia in Livy XXI.31.10–12 originally (in Livy's source) referred to a crossing in the lower reaches of the river;[13] and as de Beer's graph demonstrates, this would fit the lower part of the stream much better than would a crossing near the Guil. Against this there are, however, two objections. First, it is not very probable that Hannibal's crossing of the Rhône was south of the confluence with the Durance,[14] and if it was north of that river, the hypothesis would not apply. Secondly, following Desjardins (*Géographie de la Gaule* 1.164ff.), de Beer argues (pp. 30–1) that in Hannibal's time the Durance flowed into the Rhône in four separate channels. This is a technical matter on which it is hard for the layman to form a judgement; but if it is true it provides a further argument against this hypothesis.[15]

It has also been suggested that Livy's *Druentia* was perhaps after all not the Durance.[16] There can, of course, be no question of altering Livy's text; the correctness of *Druentia* is confirmed by Silius (III.468) and Ammianus (XV.10.11),[17] both of whom go back ‖ ultimately to Livy or his source. It should

[12] For the view that the change of direction '*ad laevam*' was immediately after the crossing of the Rhône in the original on which Livy drew see Kahrstedt, *op. cit.* (n. 1) 149–50; De Sanctis *op. cit.* (n. 6) 3.2.72.

[13] For this hypothesis see O. Viedebantt, *Hermes* 54 (1919) 355–8; R. L. Dunbabin, *CR* 45 (1931) 52ff.

[14] This would in any case involve the use by Livy of a third source, distinct from that which mentioned the names of the tribes, to explain how he came to get his reference to the Durance crossing *after* Hannibal had passed through their territory – a point not considered by Spenser Wilkinson, *Hannibal's march* (Oxford, 1911) 21, who believes that the fording of the Durance described by Livy in reality took place near its junction with the Rhône.

[15] See below, p. 113.

[16] W. Osiander, *Der Hannibalweg* (Berlin, 1900) 74ff., thought it was the Drac; and others would make it the Drôme (Druna).

[17] Silius followed Livy; Ammianus' immediate source is less clear. W. Sontheimer (*Klio* 20 (1926) 19–53) argued for Claudius Quadrigarius; but the verbal echoes suggest a direct use of Livy,

perhaps be noted that Ammianus makes the Druentia a river on the Italian side of the Alps; and river names are of course among those most commonly duplicated. But the likelihood is that Ammianus is simply being careless; and this transposition is not to be used as an argument that the Druentia was some other river. It is of course not impossible that the Drac or the Drôme was at some stage known as the *Druentia* (just as we have many Avons and Dees); but no one could call this a very convincing hypothesis, and the reference to the Durance must, I think, be left as a feature of Livy's second source. But in this case it is not easy to identify the route there indicated with that suggested by Polybius. Attempts have been made (for example by Sontheimer) to reconcile the two routes (in favour of the Mt Genèvre); but they always run up against the difficulty that Polybius has no knowledge of a march over high land from the 'Island' to the Durance. And after all, by Livy's time (*cf.* xxi.38.6), there was already hot controversy as to the pass actually crossed. It is certainly not to be ruled out *a priori* that a contradiction existed between the routes described in Livy's two sources.

<h2 style="text-align:center">II</h2>

At this point it may be worth while to revert to Polybius and to try to locate the 'Island'. Its position depends partly on the statistics of the march and partly on the identification of the tributary of the Rhône which bounded its eastern side. The 'Island' was four days' march from the Rhône crossing (Polyb. III.49.5); but unfortunately the site of this crossing is also undefined. Polybius (III.42.1) places it 'four days' march from the sea', at a point where the stream is single. Now it is true that there is nothing in Polybius to indicate that Hannibal chose an unusual crossing; and the regular point for crossing the Rhône in classical times was Beaucaire–Tarascon.[18] On the other hand, he was aiming at a northerly route,[19] and so is likely to have made for a point north of the Durance. South of the Durance he would be more open to observation from tribes close to the coast on the left bank of the Rhône and within easy reach of possible Roman interference.[20] From Polyb. III.50.1, where Hannibal is said to have covered 800 stades in ten days, de Beer deduces that his average speed was 80 stades a day, which is equivalent to 14 km. On this basis four

and certainly exclude a Greek source like Timagenes. Ammianus (xv.9.2) mentions Timagenes as his source for the Gallic migrations: but this does not mean that he also followed him on Hannibal's Alpine crossing (as de Beer assumes, p. 34 n. 36).

[18] Strabo iv 1.3, C 178–9; *cf. Peut. Tab.* and *Anon. Rav.* On the other hand, as de Beer observes (p. 26), the Antonine Itinerary and the Jerusalem Itinerary put the crossing at Fourques–Arles. This, for Hannibal, was open to the same objection as Tarascon–Beaucaire, but more so. It is the crossing adopted by de Beer (pp. 25–8), and by several of his predecessors; it is pertinently criticised by Freshfield, *op. cit.* (n. 6) 62ff.

[19] Neither Polybius nor Livy contains any suggestion that Hannibal changed his original route; indeed Polyb. III.47–8, implies that the journey was well planned and reconnoitred. Nor will the provisioning of Hannibal's army in the 'Island' (Polyb. III.49.10–12; *cf.* Viedebantt, *Hermes* 54 (1919) 362) have been improvised overnight.

[20] For this point see Jullian, *op. cit.* (n. 6) 1.464 n. 4; De Sanctis, *op. cit.* (n. 6) 3.2.70.

days' march would be 56 km and this, measured up the west branch of the Rhône from Aigues-Mortes, brings one to Fourques near Arles. These calculations are, however, based on two fallacies. First, it is highly unlikely that Hannibal kept to the coast as far as Aigues-Mortes before turning upstream; Polyb. III.41.7, δεξιὸν ἔχων τὸ Σαρδόνιον πέλαγος, does not imply a march close to the sea, but merely indicates a general direction. It seems obvious that Hannibal must have known where he was to cross and have made for that point by the shortest practicable route; in which case the 'four days' is a general indication of distance calculated to the nearest point, and not necessarily related to Hannibal's own march at all. More important, however, de Beer seems to have gone wrong over Polybius' measurements. Polybius reckons the distance from the ἀναβολή τῶν ῎Αλπεων to the Po valley as 1,200 stades (III.39.10), and according to III.56.3, it took fifteen days, an average of 80 stades a day. But the march 'along the river' from the 'Island' to ἡ πρὸς ῎Αλπεις ἀναβολή is given as 800 stades and took ten days, also an average of 80 stades a day. It is clearly absurd to assume the same speed in the Alps as in a river valley, and the likeliest explanation of this discrepancy appears to be that from the 'Island' onwards the distance has been averaged out on the rough basis of a march of 80 stades a day, to make a total of 2,000 stades covered in twenty-five days. ‖

This does not, however, affect a simple calculation which de Beer seems to have overlooked. According to Polyb. III.39.9, the distance from the Rhône crossing to the 'ascent of the Alps' was 1,400 stades; and according to III.50.1, that from the 'Island' to the 'ascent towards the Alps' was 800 stades. Now it may be true, as just suggested, that the figures from the 'Island' onwards were based on an average; but if so, that applies to both the 1,400 and the 800, and clearly does not affect the distance from the Rhône crossing to the 'Island', which simple subtraction shows to be 600 stades.[21] This, reckoned at 8⅓ stades to the *mille passus*, works out at about 106 km[22] or 26.5 km a day, which is by no means impossible, since Hannibal was in a hurry to leave Scipio behind. This figure of 600 stades seems decisive against de Beer's identification of the 'Island' with the area between the Rhône and the Aygues, even if one puts the Rhône crossing as far south as Arles.[23] But in fact 'four days from the sea' suggests a point much farther north, and, as has already been argued on other grounds, a point above the junction with the Durance. The natural interpretation, without pressing the words too closely, would be that the Rhône crossing lay roughly halfway between the 'Island' and the sea;[24] at any rate,

[21] This takes the natural view that the ἀναβολή τῶν ῎Αλπεων of Polyb. III.39.9, is identical with ἡ πρὸς τὰς ῎Αλπεις ἀναβολή of Polyb. III.50.1. Not all critics have accepted this: see for its defence Freshfield, *op. cit.* (n. 6) 9–10.

[22] At 8⅓ stades to the Roman mile, Polybius' stade measured 177·5 metres: de Beer, pp. 25–6.

[23] From the confluence of the Aygues with the Rhône to Arles, where de Beer locates Hannibal's crossing, is only 62 km.

[24] For our present purpose nothing is gained by listing the various locations of this crossing, ranging from Arles to as far north as St Etienne-des-Sorts, Pont-St Esprit or Bourg-St Andéol.

these data are easily reconcilable with the view that the 'Island' lay at the junction of the Rhône and the Isère.

The name of the tributary of the Rhône at the 'Island' is, as de Beer correctly observes,[25] differently given in the MSS of both Polybius and Livy. Polybius (III.49.6) reads ἡ δὲ σκαρας (σκωρας C), Livy (XXI.31.4) *ibi (s)arar*. Proper names are of course especially liable to manuscript corruption; and in arguing that the forms *Skaras* and *Arar* should be retained as identifiable alternatives for the river now called the Aygues,[26] de Beer is perhaps at his least convincing. In the first place the relevant passages in Livy and Polybius are almost certainly derived from the same ultimate source; hence it seems reasonable to suppose that the forms which appear in our MSS represent two corruptions of the same name, and not the correct forms of two alternative names.[27] De Beer's argument implies two wholly independent but similar sources. He has not argued this case because he has virtually ignored the source-problem; but in any event it is a case which would not be easy to sustain.

In favour of *Arar* in Livy he adduces its appearance in Silius III.452. But in fact Silius is not here describing Hannibal's march to the 'Island', but is giving a general account of the Rhône; and since he took his geographical embroideries from separate sources,[28] and a reference to its main tributary, the Arar (Saône), was part of the regular description of the Rhône (*cf.* Silius XV.501), Silius may be left out of the picture. The emendations to ἡ δ' 'Ισάρας and *ibi Isara* are not certain,[29] but they are fairly close to the MSS readings, they are consonant with the assumption of a common ultimate source, and they give us the name of a river which fits the rest of our data. There seems about a 90 per cent chance that they are right: whereas de Beer's attempt to identify the river in question as the Aygues, and to saddle it with two separate names, is manifestly wrong. ‖

De Beer himself thinks it is 'a certainty' (p. 75). What is the evidence? Joanne's *Dictionnaire géographique de la France* lists a series of references to the Aygues dating from A.D. 825, when the form is *Egrum*, through *Araus*, *Icarus*, *Equer*, *Aigarus*, *Equeris* (1218), *Ecaris* (1272), *Ycaris* (1321), *Aqua Yquarum* (1393), *Egue* (1393), *Yguaris* (1414), *Yquaris* (1492), *Iquarius* and *Ica* (sixteenth century).

---

[25] But the observation is not as novel as a hasty reading of de Beer's polemic might suggest. The readings of both sources are fully discussed by Spenser Wilkinson, *op. cit.* (n. 14) 18–19, and by C. Torr, *Hannibal crosses the Alps*[2] (Cambridge, 1925) 7–10; the Oxford Livy, as de Beer himself admits, gives a perfectly clear account of the readings; and if Büttner-Wobst prints ἡ δ' 'Ισάρας (de Beer transliterates *he d'Isaras*, neglecting the iota subscript), it is only fair to take into account the first sentence of his introduction, which states that he regards this part of his work as 'nihil aliud... nisi supplementa editionis Hultschianae'. Hultsch (to whose edition de Beer makes no reference) gives a fair account of the readings of the MSS of Polybius at the point in question.

[26] The Aygues was also the choice of Fortia d'Urban (1821).

[27] Logically the possibility exists that the same original source gave both names, and that one was followed by Polybius and the other by the line of descent which ended in Livy; but this seems too improbable to be worth mentioning except in a footnote.

[28] See J. Nicol, *The historical and geographical sources used by Silius Italicus* (Oxford, 1930) 129ff.

[29] See the comments of Ed. Meyer, *op. cit.* (n. 5) 2.413 n. 1.

In many of these forms de Beer sees the equivalent of Polybius' *Skaras*. 'The
"s"', he tells us, 'dropped out at a...date which in the south of France is found
to have been about the thirteenth century' (p. 21). Further, as G. M. Young
has pointed out to him, the modern form Aygues 'suggests an old form *aqua*,
and the transition to the modern Aygues is explained by the form *Aqua Yquarum*
found in 1393'. I do not understand how this isolated form *Aqua Yquarum*
'explains' the modern form. Surely *Aygues* is the same word as the sixteenth-
century *Iquarius*, *Equeris* in 1218, and *Icarus*, *Equer*, and *Aigarus* of an unspecified
earlier date. The suggestion that the underlying root is *aqua*, meaning 'water'
or 'river' (*Aiga*, *aigua* in old Provençal and *aigo* or *aigue* in modern Provençal),
seems extremely plausible. But if so, it has been the basis of the name from
the outset, not since 1393; and the attempt to find a link with *Skaras* breaks
down – especially as the Aygues was the *Egrum* in 825, yet according to de
Beer's own argument the 's' should not have disappeared until the thirteenth
century.

Against the identification with the Aygues there is also the reference to the
Allobroges. According to Livy XXI.31.5, here following his main source, they
lived 'hard by' the 'Island', and the brothers whose dispute Hannibal settled
belonged to that tribe. De Beer would discredit this statement of Livy ('he was
surely mistaken' (p. 32)) on the grounds that he contradicts himself: he 'stated
that the inhabitants of the "Island" were Allobroges (XXI.31.9)', but had 'just
said that the Allobroges lived near the "Island", not in it'. In fact Livy does
not say anywhere that the Allobroges inhabited the 'Island'; but this attempt
to distinguish between living 'in the "Island"' and 'hard by' is something of
a quibble, for we do not know how large Livy took the 'Island' to be (Polybius'
comparison with the Nile Delta, though Jullian[30] thought it went back to his
source, may well be his own contribution). Nor is Livy's identification of the
brothers as Allobroges to be rejected simply because Polybius says that
Hannibal was later attacked by οἱ κατὰ μέρος ἡγεμόνες τῶν Ἀλλοβρίγων
(III.50.2); the latter may well have been dissident chieftains of a people in a
state of στάσις. That Livy calls the attackers *Galli* (XXI.32.6ff.) may be
connected with his insertion of the passage 31.9–12, which has brought
Hannibal east of the Durance, where Allobroges would be quite out of
place – though not indeed more out of place than they are in de Beer's account,
since on the evidence of the medieval dioceses he has to locate their territory
north of the Isère (pp. 36–7), and so at least thirty miles[31] away from
Hannibal's supposed route up the Drôme and over the Col de Grimone, which
according to his map is in the country of the Vocontii and the Trigorii.
Granted, the town taken by Hannibal (Polyb. III.51.11; Livy XXI.33.11) is not
unambiguously Allobrogian, since the remnants of the Allobroges were forced
to fly εἰς τὴν οἰκείαν, and the town was subsequently empty because the

[30] *Op. cit.* (n. 6) 1.474 n. 3.
[31] Probably rather more, since Vienne was their capital.

inhabitants were abroad in search of plunder;[32] but our sources are not inconsistent with its being Allobrogian, for Hannibal recovered from it the animals and prisoners which the Allobroges had taken, and it is clear that they were at least using it as a base. In any case it is not easy to see why Allobroges should have gone so far outside their own territory as de Beer's theory postulates, in order to attack a formidable enemy who was obviously marching away as fast as he could.

These arguments seem decisive against the view that the 'Island' lay at the confluence of the Aygues and Rhône, and so against de Beer's interpretation of Hannibal's route. His attempt to identify the Col de Grimone with the *Cremonis iugum* is in any case far-fetched. Livy (xxi.38.6) criticised Coelius Antipater for the view that Hannibal crossed the Alps *per Cremonis iugum*, because this pass and the *Poeninum* 'eum non in Taurinos sed per Salassos montanos ad Libuos Gallos deduxerint'. The location of these tribes can, of course, ‖ be fixed only for a date much later than the third century; the difficulty in this respect is the same as for the Tricastini, Vocontii and Trigorii. But according to Strabo (iv.6.11, C 208), the Salassi occupied the upper valley of Aosta, and stretched over the Alps as far as the Isère; similarly Ptolemy (iii.1.30, 32) makes Augusta Praetoria and Eporedia cities of the Salassi, and Vercellae and Laumellum cities of the Libici, who appear to be identical with Livy's *Libui*.[33] Unless there had been very violent changes in the location of these tribes since the time of Hannibal, it seems all but certain that the *Cremonis iugum* was the Little St Bernard, or at least that Livy believed it to be so; and it is surely risky to assume that Livy has misunderstood Coelius (whom he read, but we cannot), and that the *Cremonis iugum* was in reality the Col de Grimone ('clearly the same word', de Beer, p. 41). For apart from the inherent improbability of the argument, it assumes that Coelius regarded this, and not the pass over the Alps, as Hannibal's main pass.

III

Nevertheless, the *Cremonis iugum* may well contain the clue to Livy's odd contamination of two sources. He is quite certain, *cum inter omnes constet* (xxi.38.6), that Hannibal came down among the Taurini. If, having brought Hannibal to the 'Island', following his main source, which derives ultimately from that followed by Polybius, he discovered that it was bringing Hannibal over what he took to be the wrong pass, he may well have turned (at xxi.31.9) to a fresh source which, either as it stood or with some adaptation, brought Hannibal into the upper Durance valley, and so to a pass which would let him descend among the Taurini. This done, he could revert to his main source for

[32] The point is emphasised by de Beer, p. 60.
[33] See also Pliny, *NH* iii.124.

the lively account of the details of the march over the summit, now applied to what he believed to be the real route over the Mt Genèvre.[34]

This main source was probably Coelius, who, as Livy tells us, took Hannibal over the Little St Bernard.[35] Now the likelihood is that both Coelius and Polybius used Silenus;[36] hence we are brought back to the problem of Polybius' version, and what pass is represented by it. In Book III Polybius mentions by name only the Allobroges and the Insubres (56.3),[37] both of whom, however, would fit the theory of an advance up the Isère to Bourg-Saint-Maurice and a march over the Little St Bernard to the Val d'Aosta. On the other hand, Strabo tells us (IV.6.12, C 209 = Polyb. XXXIV.10.18) that Polybius made Hannibal cross a pass διὰ Ταυρίνων; and though the words ἦν 'Αννίβας διῆλθεν are not in all MSS of Strabo, and have been impugned as a misrepresentation of Polybius' views, there seems no good reason to reject them.[38] It is quite possible that in III.56.3, Polybius is merely indicating a general direction; if Hannibal had already contacts with the Insubres, their territory may well have been his first important goal. Moreover, Coelius' pass was not *necessarily* that of Silenus; he may have supplemented Silenus from other sources.[39] However, the reference to the Insubres in Polybius, taken together with Coelius' known support for the Little St Bernard, and Livy's switch from a source of Polybian colour in order to bring Hannibal over the Mt Genèvre into the Taurini, creates a strong case for anyone who cares to interpret Polybius' account as one of a march through the Little St Bernard. Summarising, one may say that Polybius' narrative can be reconciled with either the Little St Bernard or one of the group debouching on the valley of Susa and Turin, but that Livy has contaminated two traditions, giving two separate passes, which are ultimately irreconcilable.[40] ‖

Any final decision must depend on the weight assigned to the separate items of evidence. Despite the reference to the Insubres in Polyb. III.56.3, Hannibal's first action in the Po valley was apparently the seizure of the chief town of the

---

[34] This suggestion is that of Kahrstedt, *op. cit.* (n. 1) 150, and it still seems the most plausible.

[35] Livy XXI.38.5.

[36] For the use of Silenus by Polybius and (*via* Coelius) by Livy see Kahrstedt, *op. cit.* (n. 1) 148ff.

[37] His words are κατῆρε τολμηρῶς εἰς τὰ περὶ τὸν Πάδον πεδία καὶ τὸ τῶν 'Ινσόμβρων ἔθνος (56.3). The Insubres had their capital at Mediolanum, and perhaps controlled several other peoples such as the Laevi and the Anares – which might explain why Ptolemy (III.1.29) reckons Ticinum, the capital of the Laevi, as an Insubrian town; see Philipp, *RE* 9.2 (1916) 'Insubres,' col. 1590.

[38] See De Sanctis, *op. cit.* (n. 6) 3.2.65.

[39] A. Klotz, *Livius und seine Vorgänger* (Berlin–Leipzig, 1940–1) 102, thinks Coelius conflated Silenus and Fabius.

[40] The evidence from Servius (*ad Aen.* x.13) must be mentioned. If he has quoted Varro aright, Varro placed Hannibal's pass between the Corniche route and 'the pass by which Pompey went to Spain', which is no doubt the Mt Genèvre. But the same passage distinguishes Hannibal's pass from Hasdrubal's, though Livy (XXVII.39.7) and Appian (*Hann.* VII.52) both agree that Hasdrubal crossed by the same pass as his brother. Altogether, this passage – which may not necessarily be enumerating the passes in geographical order from south to north – is too obscure to help very much, especially as we do not know on what source Varro was drawing. See De Sanctis, *op. cit.* (n. 6) 3.2.65–6.

Taurini (Polyb. III.60.9), which Appian (*Hann.* 5) calls Taurasia, and which probably stood on the site of Turin. Ed. Meyer has shown[41] how unlikely it is that, having come down the Dora Baltea, he should then have lost time marching west to Turin, with Scipio at Placentia. Indeed, it seems altogether more likely (though it cannot be proved) that Hannibal reached the Po valley by way of the Valle di Susa, and hence that he crossed by either the Mt Genèvre (or one of the passes from the Durance valley lying south of the Mt Genèvre) or the Mt Cenis (Great or Little, or the subsidiary Col du Clapier).

Those who accept the evidence of Livy's secondary source, with its reference to the Druentia, must choose the former alternative. But if one hesitates to accept a version which reaches us in a contaminated form and runs counter to Polybius, then the details of Hannibal's march to the 'Island', and subsequently through the territory of the Allobroges (*i.e.* up the Isère valley), make it probable that his pass lay in the Mt Cenis group, approached by way of the Isère and the Maurienne. The Mt Genèvre can be reached from the junction of the Rhône and the Isère only by passing over an intermediate col; and the only reason for making Hannibal take so difficult a route is the reference to the Druentia in Livy's subsidiary source. The argument that the Mt Cenis passes were not used in antiquity has been adequately refuted, most recently by Knoflach (*Klio* 25 (1932) 405–6), who emphasises the effects of a built road over the Mt Genèvre in concentrating traffic through the western Alps. Thus, on balance, the evidence seems to the writer to favour one of this group of passes.

Greater certainty is, on the present evidence, likely to prove illusory. It seems on the whole improbable that the analysis of the sources can be unravelled much further. The identification of particular hills and valleys was a form of self-deception from the start. And though it would clearly be rash to reject the possibility of some completely new approach, the evidence from ecclesiastical records and the findings of natural science has so far merely raised false hopes. Perhaps in this matter of Hannibal's pass we have reached a stage at which we should ponder an observation of Marc Bloch: 'there are times when the sternest duty of the savant, who has first tried every means, is to resign himself to his ignorance and to admit it honestly'.[42]

[41] *Op. cit.* (n. 5) 2.411 n. 1.
[42] *The historian's craft* (Manchester, 1954) 60.

9

THE SCIPIONIC LEGEND*

A man must probably be in some way exceptional to acquire a legend. Scipio Africanus was clearly exceptional and his legend follows a common pattern. In its fully developed form it has obvious parallels with that of Alexander; and its most sensational feature, the divine snake which visits the hero's mother, is shared with several other heroic or would-be heroic figures in Greek and Roman history, Aristomenes, Aratus, Augustus and Galerius.[1] Such legends rarely spring from deliberate policy, though policy can play a part in fostering them. They seem partly to arise from some popular need, and Professor Lily Ross Taylor has gone so far as to suggest[2] that Scipio's night-visits to the temple of Jupiter were the invention of 'a soul-weary populace looking for a saviour'. Perhaps; but they could equally well be the invention of a Greek historian – or indeed they may have been genuine. The trouble is that once the legend has got going, it grows like a religion, fed by fresh facts, suitably distorted, along with purely fictional features.

The best discussion of the Scipionic legend which I know is Professor Scullard's in his monograph on Scipio;[3] but since 1930 there have been several other accounts, including a book by R. M. Haywood[4] (with an important review by De Sanctis[5]), A. Klotz's work on Livy's sources and a special article by him in *Hermes* (1952),[6] and some relevant pages by A. J. Toynbee.[7] In view of the lack of unanimity which these show still to exist about the growth and character of the legend, it is perhaps worth while examining the problem yet again, especially as one or two pieces of evidence have not always been given their full weight.

I

The story was fully developed by the Augustan age when, according to Gellius,[8] C. Oppius, who wrote a life of Africanus, and Hyginus both recorded

* [PCPS 13 (1967) 54–69]

1 Suet. *Aug.* 94 (Augustus); Paus. II.10.3 (Aratus); *id.* IV.14.7 (Aristomenes); Aur. Vict. *Epit.* 40.17 (Galerius); *cf.* E. Meyer, *Kleine Schriften* 2 (Halle, 1924) 436 n. 5.
2 *The divinity of the Roman emperor* (Middletown, Conn., 1931) 55.
3 *Scipio Africanus in the Second Punic War* (Cambridge, 1930) 70ff.
4 *Studies on Scipio Africanus* (Baltimore, 1933).　　　　5 *RFIC* 64 (1936) 189–203.
6 *Livius und seine Vorgänger* (Leipzig–Berlin, 1940–1) 178ff.; *Hermes* 80 (1952) 334–43 (reprinted from *Festschrift Zucker*).
7 *Hannibal's legacy* (Oxford, 1965) 2.500–8.　　　　8 Gell. VI.1.

the story of the snake, and Livy described,[9] not without scepticism, how from his youth upwards *arte quadam* Scipio used to underline his *virtutes* by giving out that he had received divine visions and admonitions in dreams ('aut per nocturnas visa species aut velut divinitus mente monita agens'), and how he used to go daily to the Capitol and commune there in silence before any important action, public or private. Hence he gained credence for the popular belief ('seu consulto seu temere volgatae') that he ‖ was a man of divine origin, and for the story – already, Livy adds, attributed to Alexander – of his conception as a result of his mother's intercourse with a snake. Scipio showed considerable skill in neither affirming nor denying these stories; and there were many others of the same kind, *alia vera alia adsimulata*, which had in the case of this young man carried admiration beyond human bounds. It was because of these that Scipio was appointed to the Spanish command.

The account in Dio[10] is so close that it must go back to Livy or his source; and Valerius Maximus has a similar version[11] headed 'De simulata religione'. The *De Viris Illustribus* adds[12] that a snake crawled over Scipio as an infant, that he was reckoned to be the son of Jupiter, and that when he went late at night to the Capitol, the dogs never barked. The parallel with Hercules, another son of Jupiter (or Zeus) who had to cope with snakes in his cradle, is not coincidental. We find Scipio compared to Hercules by Cicero in the *De Republica*[13] and Silius Italicus developed the parallel fully by making Pomponia describe Scipio's conception along the familiar lines of the Alcmena story and gave Scipio, like Hercules, a choice between pleasure and virtue.[14] This aspect of the legend may perhaps have arisen in reply to Punic propaganda which, *via* Greek historians, associated Hannibal's journey with that of Hercules; Livy mentions a sacrifice to Hercules before Hannibal left Spain,[15] and N. J. de Witt has argued plausibly[16] that the hero who, according to some versions, guided him across the Alps was Hercules himself, who appeared as a *deus ex machina* in the worked-over version of the march. In that case, the legend would appear to go back well beyond the Augustan age; and other evidence confirms this. In 110 Cn. Blasio struck a coin portraying Scipio and on the reverse three figures representing the Capitoline triad;[17] and at some period Scipio's *imago* had been placed in the *cella* of Jupiter Optimus Maximus from whence it was brought out on the occasion of Cornelian funerals.[18] Unfortunately we cannot be sure when this dedication took place. Ed. Meyer speaks[19] of a recognition by the family and the state of Scipio's divine origin, but both Haywood[20] and

---

[9] Livy xxvi.19.   [10] Dio xvi, fr. 57.39.

[11] Val. Max. i.2.1.   [12] *De Vir. Ill.* 49.

[13] Cic. *Rep.* fr. 3 = Lactantius, *Div. Inst.* 1.18.

[14] Sil. xiii.628ff., xv.69ff.; see on this A. R. Anderson, *TAPhA* 54 (1928) 31–7.

[15] Livy xxi.21.9.   [16] N. J. de Witt, *TAPhA* 67 (1941) 60–1.

[17] H. Mattingly, *Roman coins* (London, 1928) 74. [M. H. Crawford, *Roman republican coinage* (Cambridge, 1974) 1.309–10, denies that this coin portrays Scipio.]

[18] Val. Max. viii.15.1; App. *Hisp.* 23.

[19] *Op. cit.* (n. 1) 2.434.   [20] Haywood, *op. cit.* (n. 4) 28.

De Sanctis[21] have observed that this would be difficult soon after Scipio's death, in view of the hostility of the nobles towards him, and De Sanctis rightly adds that a mask deposited before 83 B.C. would probably have been destroyed in the fire that burnt down the Capitoline temple in that year. His own, not implausible, suggestion that Sulla put it there after his reconstruction of the temple in order to glorify the great Cornelian and perhaps to link his own *felicitas*[22] with that of Scipio, fits in with his belief that the legend received a considerable increment in Sullan times at the hands of Sullan annalists. It is also to the age of Sulla that he attributes the speech which Livy puts into the mouth of Ti. Gracchus in 187,[23] in which Gracchus contrasts ‖ Scipio's arrogance with his earlier moderation, when he had prevented the people from making him perpetual consul and dictator and had vetoed the setting up of various statues to him and prevented a decree being passed to bring his *imago* in triumphal garb from the temple of Jupiter. Haywood is inclined to regard Gracchus' speech as genuine[24] or based on genuine material. But even Livy himself has doubts;[25] and Cicero seems not to know of any extant speech of Gracchus.[26] The contents, moreover, seem quite anachronistic for the early second century, and whether De Sanctis[27] is right in making it Sullan, or Mommsen[28] and Meyer[29] in assuming it to be based on an anti-Caesarian forgery, I think it has to be regarded as irrelevant to the early development of the legend.

So too another item adduced by Haywood.[30] In a letter recorded by Nepos,[31] Cornelia, the mother of the Gracchi, writing to Gaius, urges him to postpone his political activities until she is dead. 'Ubi mortua ero,' she continues, 'parentabis mihi et invocabis deum parentem. in eo tempore non pudet te eorum deum preces expetere, quos vivos atque praesentes relictos atque desertos habueris?' Inexplicably Haywood refers the words *deum parentem* to Africanus; but there can be no doubt that Cornelia is referring to her own dead self – 'you will invoke me as *deus parens*'. The masculine form *deus* need cause us no embarrassment since by a fortunate chance Festus[32] has recorded the information that 'masculino genere parentem appellabant antiqui etiam matrem'; and a passage of Charisius[33] records clearly that Gracchus said that 'suos parentes amat' speaking of his mother and adds that someone (there is a gap in our text, but it may be Cornelia[34]) 'in alia epistola "tuus parens sum" ait, cum de se loqueretur'. The plural *eorum deum* in the second sentence of

[21] *RFIC* 64 (1936) 190.
[22] On *felicitas* cf. Cic. *Leg. Man.* 47; Plut. *Sulla* 34.2; Haywood, *op. cit.* (n. 4) 13.
[23] Livy xxxviii.56.12–13.   [24] Haywood, *op. cit.* (n. 4) 16–18.
[25] Livy xxxviii.56.5, 'orationes quoque, si modo ipsorum sunt quae feruntur, P. Scipionis et Ti. Gracchi abhorrent inter se'.
[26] Cicero, *Brutus* 79.   [27] *RFIC* 64 (1936) 189ff.
[28] Mommsen, *Römische Forschungen* 2 (Berlin, 1879) 502.
[29] Ed. Meyer, *Caesars Monarchie und das Principat des Pompeius*³ (Stuttgart–Berlin, 1922) 531–2.
[30] *Op. cit.* (n. 4) 22.   [31] Nepos, fr. 2 Winstedt.
[32] Festus, p. 151 Müller.   [33] Charisius, p. 79 P.
[34] *Contra* Nipperdey.

Cornelia's letter will be a rhetorical turn reflecting her emotion;[35] certainly Africanus had never been *vivus et praesens* for C. Gracchus. So this item proves to be a red herring.

That more or less exhausts the testimony for the development of the legend until we reach Polybius. But before assessing his contribution, we may perhaps consider what part Ennius played in the matter, since according to Horace[36] Scipio owed much of his fame to *Calabrae Pierides*, the Muses of Calabria. Ennius' contribution has been elaborately discussed by A. Elter,[37] whose interpretation of Horace, *Carm.* iv.8 ‖ (a poem whose authenticity has been sometimes questioned) is full of ingenuity, but highly speculative. Not many, perhaps, would go with him the whole way in his theory that Ennius' *Scipio*[38] contained the formulation of a canon of heroes – Liber, Aeacus, the Dioscuri, Hercules and Romulus – which was to be accepted by later Roman writers and play its part not only in the deification of Roman emperors but even in the concept of Christian saints. But, whatever the truth about this canon of heroes, Elter's theory that Ennius attempted also to heroise Scipio Africanus, a view developed further by A. R. Anderson in *TAPhA* (1928),[39] deserves serious consideration.

In addition to the *Scipio* Ennius also wrote three couplets which are not irrelevant to this question. They are

(a) Lactantius, *Div. Inst.* 1.18.[40]

> si fas endo plagas caelestum ascendere cuiquam est
> mi soli caeli maxima porta patet

– words quoted in Cicero's *De Republica*[41] with the comment 'est vero Africane; nam et Herculi eadem ista porta patuit'.

(b) Seneca, *Ep.* 108.32 and Cicero, *Leg.* ii.57.

> hic est ille situs cui nemo civis neque hostis
> quivit pro factis reddere opis pretium.

(c) Cicero, *Tusc.* v.49.

> a sole exoriente supra Maeotis paludes
> nemo est qui factis aequiperare queat.

These three couplets certainly imply some kind of attempt to heroise Scipio, as Cicero's comparison with Hercules recognises. True, heroisation may not be a Roman concept; but Ennius was not a Roman.[42]

---

[35] So Nipperdey, *ad loc.*   [36] Hor. *Carm.* iv.8.15–20.

[37] A. Elter, *Donarem pateras* (Bonn, 1907); I owe the loan of a copy of this work to the kindness of Dr C. Ligotz of the Warburg Institute. Elter argues that Ennius heroised Romulus in the *Annales* and set out the full canon, with the attempted addition of Scipio, in the *Scipio*. For the canon he quotes Hor. *Carm.* i.12.25ff., iii.3.9ff., iv.5.1, *Epist.* ii.1.5ff.; Cic. *Tusc.* 1.27, and many other passages. *Carm.* iv.8, he believes to be largely echoing Ennius' *Scipio*, often verbally.

[38] *Cf.* J. Vahlen, *Ennianae Poesis Reliquiae*³ (Leipzig, 1928) ccxvff. and *Varia* ii.1–14.

[39] *TAPhA* 54 (1928) 7–58, especially 31–7 on Scipio.

[40] *Cf.* Seneca, *Ep.* 108.34.   [41] Cicero, *Rep.* fr. 3.

[42] Elter, *op. cit.* (n. 37) 40; Taylor, *op. cit.* (n. 2) 45–6; Haywood, *op. cit.* (n. 4) 20.

Scaliger suggested joining (c) and (a) together; but there are no solid grounds for this. However, the third couplet is certainly unsatisfactory as it stands. The Maeotic Sea is later used as an indication of the boundary of the Roman empire by Aelius Aristides[43] and by Dexippus copying him.[44] But, as Professor Skutsch has remarked to me in a letter, this couplet sounds incomplete, for if one means 'everybody throughout the whole world' – as in the previous couplet where *nemo civis neque hostis* conveys this sense – one does not normally say 'from the extreme east', but 'from the extreme east to the extreme west';[45] and this difficulty was felt, to his credit, by Mamertinus, who quoted the passage in his panegyric celebrating Maximian's birthday ‖ in A.D. 291[46] and there displayed a good sense of rhetoric (if a somewhat inadequate mastery of metre and geography) by quoting it in the form 'a sole exoriente ad usque meotis paludes', from the rising sun as far as the marshes of Maeotis – which does not get one very far. Professor Skutsch tells me that he is inclined to assume a lacuna with the loss of one pentameter and one hexameter, in which the missing compass bearing (or bearings, if north and south were also given) were described.[47] It is just possible that the text is complete as it stands, and the sense 'there is no one coming from the east who can vie with my achievements'; such a sentiment would fit the context of the early second century and the war with Antiochus.[48] But the reference to the Maeotis, which must be the boundary of the *oecumene* rather than the east in general, is rather against this interpretation, and I think Skutsch's view is to be accepted. In view of Cicero's slightly cavalier attitude towards quotation,[49] the omission may well be his rather than that of a scribe.

Before leaving Ennius I may perhaps also mention a suggestion which Professor Skutsch has made in an article shortly to appear in *Harvard Studies*,[50]

[43] Ael. Arist. *ad Rom.* 28.   [44] Dexippus, *FGH* 100F12.

[45] Or, to round off the circle, from the extreme north to the extreme south; *cf.* E. Norden, *RhM* 54 (1899) 469–82; W. Hartke, *Römische Kinderkaiser* (Berlin, 1951) 355–88, especially 360; J. H. Oliver, *The ruling power* (*TAPhS* 43 (1953)) 937–8. The Maeotis or the Phasis often represents the north rather than the east (as in Ael. Arist. *ad Rom.* 82; *Hdt.* IV.45.1); but hardly here.

[46] *Pan. Lat.* XI.16.3 (p. 114, 9 Baehrens).

[47] He would restore, *exempli gratia*:

> A sole exoriente supra Maeotis paludes
> ⟨ad mare quo fessos ille remittit equos
> nostra virum volitant quae fortia facta per ora⟩
> nemo est qui factis aequiperare queat.

[48] See on this the material assembled by H. Fuchs, *Der geistige Widerstand gegen Rom in der antiken Welt* (Berlin, 1938), and in particular the story in Phlegon of Tralles (*FGH* 257F36 (III), p. 1175, lines 29ff.) on the authority of one Antisthenes the Peripatetic, which seems to include stories going back to the period immediately after the Romano-Syrian War (Fuchs, *op. cit.*, 29 n. 16), amongst them the prophecy by a Roman consul of an army that shall cross the Hellespont led by an eastern king. But the dating of these Sibylline prophecies is uncertain, and this may well be later than Scipio's time. For the antithesis between Asia and Europe, East and West, in the propaganda of the Romano-Syrian War see Walbank, *CQ* 36 (1942) 142–3, especially 142 n. 7.

[49] On Cicero's loose way of quoting see Vahlen, *op. cit.* (n. 38) xxxix ff. and especially liii, '(Cicero) quem toties vidimus non totos versus sed indicii causa pauca verba afferre'.

[50] *HSPh* 70 (1966) 125ff.

of which he has kindly shown me a proof, and which he has allowed me to mention here. In the prologue to Plautus' *Amphitruo* Mercury declares that he has heard other gods including Neptune speak of benefits they have bestowed.[51] Skutsch suggests that Plautus is here referring to Neptune's appearance in the prologue of Ennius' *Andromache*, which Wilamowitz showed to have been based on Euripides' *Troades*,[52] where Poseidon speaks the prologue. What, he asks, were the benefits which Neptune could claim to have bestowed on the Roman people? If the *Andromache* appeared shortly before the *Amphitruo* round about 190 B.C. clearly the most recent outstanding example of such a benefaction was the help which, so the story went, had been given by Neptune to Scipio in his taking of New Carthage. It would be tempting to carry this hypothesis still further by observing that, in view of the comparisons which we find between Scipio and Hercules – of which I have already spoken – and of the divine birth of both these heroes after events which were later assimilated to each other,[53] an indirect reference to a compliment to Scipio was perhaps specially appropriate in the ‖ prologue to the *Amphitruo*. But remembering what sort of play the *Amphitruo* is, I think we must reject this possibility – especially as it is doubtful whether the comparison with Hercules was already part of the tradition so early.

In fact, when all this is added up, it seems that Ennius plays only a slight part in the creation of the Scipionic legend as it existed when Polybius wrote; and it is to Polybius that I now turn.

II

Polybius' account of Scipio's character occurs in Book x at the point in his narrative[54] where he harangues his troops before crossing the Ebro in spring 209, prior to his capture of New Carthage.[55] Towards the end of his description of New Carthage in x.11.4 Polybius mentions that he is giving the length of the walls from his own personal observation, οὐκ. . .ἐξ ἀκοῆς. . .ἀλλ' αὐτόπται; and the journey to Spain in the course of which he visited New Carthage probably took place in 151/50,[56] when the younger Scipio went there. It will have been on his return from Spain on this occasion that Polybius crossed the Alps in Hannibal's wake.[57] His accounts both of Hannibal's Alpine crossing and of Scipio's capture of New Carthage show signs, however, of being derived primarily from literary sources, and it is significant that the reference to autopsy is in both cases introduced marginally, as it were, and I would suggest primarily to add authority to what Polybius says. His account of the taking

[51] Plaut. *Amph.* 41ff.
[52] Wilamowitz, *Kleine Schriften* 4 (Berlin, 1962) 374 n. 2.
[53] See above, n. 12.   [54] Polyb. x.2.1ff.
[55] Described in Polyb. x.7–15.
[56] See my *Historical commentary on Polybius* 1 (Oxford, 1957) 4; Polyb. xxxv.4–8; Livy, *Epit.* 48; Oros. iv.21.1; Val. Max. iii.2.6.
[57] Polyb. iii.48.12, with my note *ad loc.*

of New Carthage and of Scipio's character can probably be dated to the 150s, with slight additions later.

Scipio, Polybius tells us, was represented by all other writers as a man favoured by Fortune, and owing most of his successes to chance, whereas in reality he was, like the Spartan Lycurgus, extremely calculating. It was not true that Lycurgus drew up the Spartan constitution on the advice of the Pythia, and Scipio likewise did not win an empire for his country by following dreams and omens (ἐξ ἐνυπνίων ὁρμώμενον καὶ κληδόνων). Both however realised that a pretence to divine inspiration would assist their various purposes: hence Lycurgus' invocation of oracles and Scipio's pretence that his projects were divinely inspired (μετά τινος θείας ἐπιπνοίας ποιούμενος τὰς ἐπιβολάς). Polybius then goes on to claim as the authority for his interpretation of Scipio C. Laelius,[58] Scipio's lifelong friend, and he retails two stories in support of this. The first of these is specifically attributed to Laelius. It tells how Scipio won a reputation for bravery by saving his father's life at the Ticinus and so, on the basis of this reputation, was subsequently able to act with the prudence proper to a general without any risk of having his courage impugned.[59] The second tells how he was elected to the aedileship along with his brother and how he managed to associate a carefully planned operation with an alleged prophetic dream; and this, Polybius implies, but does not actually say, was also derived from Laelius.[60] ‖

Eduard Meyer believed[61] that Laelius was Polybius' source not only for these incidents and for much of his account of the taking of New Carthage, but also for his cynical interpretation of Scipio's actions and attitudes; Laelius, he argued, was a Stoic rationalist. I mention this view merely to observe that it has been adequately refuted by Laqueur,[62] who pointed out that 'Stoic rationalism' means nothing before the time of Panaetius, the first Stoic to reject the belief in prophetic dreams, and noted correctly that there is in any case no evidence at all that Laelius was a Stoic. In fairness, however, one should add that we do not know that Laelius was *not* a rationalist. But Polybius' rationalism is so clearly in keeping with his own views as expressed elsewhere that it is to be regarded as his own contribution; and in him too it had nothing to do with Stoicism (though Laqueur thought it had).[63] Just as in Book VI he interprets the Roman state religion as designed, and admirably so, to keep the lower orders disciplined[64] – his own view, he specifically adds, ἐμοί γε μὴν δοκοῦσι τοῦ πλήθους χάριν τοῦτο πεποιηκέναι – and as in Book XVI he is prepared to acquiesce in false stories of miracles if they contribute to the instilling of popular piety,[65] so here he approves of what he takes to be Scipio's policy of attributing his achievements to the gods in order to impress and

---

[58] Polyb. x.3.2, ἀπὸ νέου...μέχρι τελευτῆς.
[59] Polyb. x.3.3–7.　　　　　　　　　　[60] Polyb. x.4.1–5.8.
[61] *Op. cit.* (n. 1) 2.423–57.
[62] *Hermes* 56 (1921) 151ff.; *cf.* De Sanctis, *RFIC* 64 (1936) 191.
[63] *Hermes* 56 (1921) 152.　　　　　　　[64] Polyb. vi.56.6–15.
[65] Polyb. xvi.12.9.

encourage the soldiers.[66] (Incidentally, it would be interesting to know if his account of Numa in Book VI followed the same pattern; for it is the interpretation of his transactions as a pious fraud which we find in Livy.[67]) Polybius' picture of Scipio is his reply to that of the divinely favoured leader which he found in his sources, and he supports it with the three incidents of the rescue at the Ticinus, the election to the aedileship and the taking of New Carthage. Of these three the first may well have happened; but the story of the election to the aedileship is ridiculous since in the first place it makes P. Scipio aedile in 217, whereas he really held this post in 213, and secondly it makes his colleague his brother Lucius, whereas it was in fact M. Cornelius Cethegus; L. Scipio was not aedile until 195. Thirdly, it makes L. Scipio his elder brother though in fact he was younger. If C. Laelius recounted a story so implausible, one can only charitably suppose that in his dotage he let himself be imposed on by a popular fiction – a hypothesis clearly not impossible, but one that one would accept only reluctantly. True, in the interviews between Polybius and Laelius the young Greek and the elderly Roman may well have talked at cross-purposes on several matters; how good was Polybius' Latin or Laelius' Greek? And apart from this they may have taken very different things for granted.[68] But this could hardly explain the retailing of a story full of factual inaccuracies, and I am therefore tempted to think that the aedileship incident, which Polybius is careful not to attribute specifically to Laelius, does not derive from him. ‖

III

This brings us to New Carthage, the other incident for which, it is implied, Laelius was a source. Besides Polybius' account we have several others including especially that in Livy. The relationship between Livy and Polybius at this point is a subject of controversy. Kahrstedt[69] and De Sanctis[70] both argue that Livy, whose account bears a strong similarity to that of Polybius, draws on Coelius, who in turn used both Polybius and at least one further source, possibly Silenus of Caleacte.[71] On this hypothesis the Roman point of view from which both Polybius and Livy recount the episode derives from Polybius' use of Laelius' personal comments and the account of the enterprise which Scipio himself wrote in the form of a letter to Philip V of Macedon,[72] in which he confirmed that his operations were based on the calculations expounded by Polybius, including information about the lagoon. On the other hand Klotz has argued[73] that the additional information in Livy forms an integral part

---

[66] Polyb. x.2.12–13.
[67] Livy 1.24.3–4 (= Val. Antias?; *cf.* Ogilvie, *Commentary on Livy 1–5* (Oxford, 1965) *ad loc.*).
[68] *Cf.* De Sanctis, *RFIC* 64 (1936) 192.
[69] U. Kahrstedt, *Geschichte der Karthager* 3 (Berlin, 1913) 279ff.
[70] De Sanctis, *Storia dei Romani* 3.2 (Turin, 1917) 372.
[71] See also Meyer, *op. cit.* (n. 1) 2.449–51 n. 2.
[72] Polyb. x.9.3.   [73] *Locc. citt.* (n. 6).

of the narrative and can only be explained as coming from a source common
to both Polybius and Livy (who again probably got it *via* Coelius). On this
view the Roman colouring must derive from the common original source,
which Klotz identifies as Fabius Pictor.

As between these two views one must, I think, opt for the former. To me
it is decisive that in several places Livy echoes Polybius' interpretation of
Scipio's exploitation of the divine element. To take one instance, in his account
of Scipio's speech before the crossing of the lagoon,[74] Livy remarks 'hoc cura
ac ratione compertum in prodigium ac deos vertens Scipio'; despite the
absence of any directly corresponding passage, this scepticism must ultimately
go back to Polybius. Further a contradiction in the account of Scipio's camp
in two passages of Polybius (x.9.7 and 11.1–3), which probably derives from
the combination of two sources, is faithfully reproduced in Livy (xxvi.42.6,
42.9). I think then we must assume that Polybius derived his account from
several sources, one of which may, as I hope to show in a moment, have been
Silenus; in addition there was Scipio's letter to Philip and perhaps also Fabius
Pictor, for a Roman source like Fabius could have obtained information about
Mago's dispositions[75] from Mago himself when a prisoner at Rome[76] perhaps
more easily than Silenus in the camp of Hannibal. Livy will go back ultimately
to Polybius, probably *via* Coelius; but he incorporates information not in
Polybius which has sometimes the appearance of not being due to elaboration
(*e.g.* on the part played by the fleet)[77] and this Coelius may have added from
elsewhere.

Now Polybius tells us that he had before him sources in which Scipio was
represented as a man enjoying divine favour; the word used is θεῖος[78] and
Scipio's achievements ‖ are said to have been attributed εἰς θεοὺς καὶ τύχας.[79]
Ed. Meyer goes further and argues[80] that the legend as we know it from the
Augustan tradition is a product of Hellenistic historiography; and though I
find it difficult to be certain just how far the legend had gone in the sources
available to Polybius, Meyer's contention can be sustained in general by a
comparison of Polybius' comments on those who have written on Scipio with
what he has to say about historians of Hannibal's Alpine crossing.[81] He does
not name these historians – as in the case of Scipio they are spoken of in the
plural – and for their identity scholars have hesitated between Chaereas and
Sosylus, whom he criticises earlier in Book III, and Silenus, who was, we know,
a source for Coelius, and related the story of Hannibal's dream after the capture
of Saguntum,[82] or (as Livy relates it)[83] before the crossing of the Ebro, and
also, most likely, the story of another dream which Hannibal had later in the

[74] Livy xxvi.45.9.
[75] Polyb. x.12.2–3.   [76] Polyb. x.19.8.
[77] Livy xxvi.42.5, 43.1, 44.10.   [78] Polyb. x.2.6–7.
[79] Polyb. x.5.8, 9.2.   [80] *Op. cit.* (n. 1) 2.435–8.
[81] Polyb. III.47.6–48.12.   [82] Cic. *Div.* I.49.
[83] Livy xxi.22.6ff.; *cf.* Val. Max. 1.7 ext. 1; Sil. III.163ff.; Zon. VIII.23.

temple of Juno Lacinia.[84] We cannot be sure, but Silenus would undoubtedly fit the subject of Polybius' criticism; for this writer (or writers, though I doubt if in fact we ought to take the plural too seriously) claimed that Hannibal had depended on the help of gods and heroes to get him through the desolate mountains. Polybius retorts that on the contrary his journey was based on prudent calculations and enquiries from the natives whom he used as guides; writers who neglect the facts and turn the crossing into a subject of sensational narrative are like tragedians who require a *deus ex machina* to extricate them from their difficulties.[85] Polybius, on the contrary, can speak with authority since he has talked with those who were present and has been over the land himself. The criticism of the historians of Scipio's attack on New Carthage is remarkably similar. Scipio, like Hannibal, did not have to depend on fortune and divine intervention, but worked out his plans with foresight. Like Hannibal, he enquired from the natives, the local fishermen (Livy says they were from Tarraco), who told him about the daily ebb in the lagoon. Polybius knows because he has questioned an eyewitness, C. Laelius, and has visited the site for himself. If there is any *deus ex machina* in this case, it is Neptune whom Scipio himself produces as a trick to inspire his men.

The correspondence is so close that it certainly looks as though Polybius was dealing with a similar or identical source in both cases; and I would suggest that this is Silenus, whom we know to have been a historian of the Hannibalic War, and to have given a version of the taking of New Carthage.[86] Against this it may be urged that a writer who accompanied Hannibal in camp and, like Sosylus, remained with him *quamdiu Fortuna passa est*,[87] will hardly have produced an account so laudatory of Scipio; and Meyer has argued[88] that when Polybius twice speaks of authors who refer Scipio's success εἰς θεοὺς καὶ τύχας it is Silenus who referred them εἰς...τύχας and some other unspecified historians, more favourable to Scipio, who referred them εἰς θεούς. I find this distinction ingenious, but unconvincing. The phrase 'to refer to the gods and fortune' occurs four times in all in the surviving parts of Polybius, twice ‖ here[89] and twice placed in the mouth of Hasdrubal[90] at the siege of Carthage in 146; and in all four cases it is associated with a contemptuous attitude on Polybius' part. I suspect therefore that it is a general phrase used in a context of unworthy superstition. Meyer's own analysis[91] of the story of Hannibal's dream shows that Silenus must have written it after Hannibal's failure was apparent; like Orpheus, he looked back, and so lost his chance to destroy Rome. This will have been written after Hannibal left Italy; and the reference in Cicero to the dream in the temple of Juno supports this, for it was towards the end of the war that Hannibal found himself at the Lacinian promontory. Silenus

---

[84] Cic. *Div.* 1.48; cf. Meyer, *op. cit.* (n. 1) 2.368–70.
[85] Polyb. iii.47.6–48.12.
[86] Livy xxvi.49.3.
[87] Nepos, *Hann.* 13.3.
[88] *Op. cit.* (n. 1) 2.447–8.
[89] Polyb. x.5.8, 9.2.
[90] Polyb. xxxviii.7.11, 8.8.
[91] *Op. cit.* (n. 1) 2.368–71.

then can have concentrated on sensational aspects of the story on either side, once he had parted from Hannibal; and indeed, even if he still sympathised with the Punic cause, this was not damaged by the suggestion that Mago owed his defeat to the action of the gods rather than to his own negligence.

Whether then it was Silenus or someone else whom Polybius was criticising, it is clear that a substantial element in the Scipionic legend was in existence before the middle of the second century. How much it is not easy to say. Schur,[92] without bothering very much about the evidence, asserted that the full legend was already developed. Haywood, however, argues[93] that the stories of divine birth and temple-visits did not arise before the Augustan age. Now the tradition clearly links the temple-visits with Scipio's communing with the gods, with the abnormal silence of the guardian dogs on the Capitol and with his divine birth; and there is a distinct possibility that these are implied in a passage in Polybius x[94] where, at the end of the story of Scipio's election to the aedileship, Polybius adds that people who had heard of the dreams (that is the dreams foretelling his election) now believed that Publius μὴ μόνον κατὰ τὸν ὕπνον, ἔτι δὲ μᾶλλον ὕπαρ καὶ μεθ' ἡμέραν διαλέγεσθαι τοῖς θεοῖς, 'that he communed with the gods not only in his sleep, but still more in reality and by day'. This is a very odd way of saying that people were now convinced that Scipio enjoyed divine favour in reality and did not merely dream of success; and though Polybius has no reference to temple-visits, it is indeed a remarkable coincidence if at the time he wrote this he knew nothing of the tradition, incorporating the temple-visits and communing with Jupiter, which we know appeared in the Augustan writers.[95] Indeed, if we consider this passage in conjunction with the earlier one, which I have already quoted,[96] in which Polybius says that Scipio, like Lycurgus, did not really act ἐξ ἐνυπνίων...καὶ κληδόνων, and compare the passage (also quoted) from Livy's fully developed form of the legend,[97] in which Scipio *arte quadam* represented his actions to the multitude as due to visions and admonitions in dreams, it is hard to resist the conclusion that they all reflect a similar context in a developed form of the legend. I conclude, then, that a substantial part, though obviously not every detail, of the Scipionic legend was in existence by the 50s of the second century, and was recorded in the Greek writer ‖ or writers (including Silenus) whom Polybius criticised, but whom he also probably used as one of his sources.[98]

One noteworthy feature of the legend was Scipio's alleged visits to the temple of Jupiter and one would like to know whether these really took place. Haywood,[99] who regards the main aspects of the tradition as Augustan, argues that Scipio would not have gone to the temple for prayer and meditation; 'it was not', he writes, 'the old Roman conception of what one did in a temple'.

---

[92] W. Schur, *Scipio Africanus und die Begründung der römischen Weltherrschaft* (Leipzig, 1927) 96.
[93] *Op. cit.* (n. 4) 26.   [94] Polyb. x.5.5.
[95] Above, pp. 120–1.   [96] Polyb. x.2.9; above, p. 126.
[97] Livy xxvi.19.3–4; above, p. 121.
[98] As he used Fabius and Philinus as sources for the First Punic War, despite his criticisms.
[99] *Op. cit.* (n. 4) 25.

One might reply that it does not seem to have caused any difficulty to Livy; but Livy of course lived two centuries after Scipio. Nevertheless can one say with certainty that for a man like Scipio the anthropomorphising and Hellenising of the old Roman gods had not already proceeded far enough to make such behaviour explicable?[100] On the other hand, visits to the Capitol were only possible while Scipio was in Rome, and, as Meyer remarks,[101] before his Spanish command Scipio was a young man with connections and promise but no achievements, for whom therefore much publicised temple-frequenting would have been more than a little absurd. Consequently, despite Livy's version,[102] which makes the sedulous cultivation of the full legend and popular belief in it the cause of Scipio's election to the Spanish command, one may reasonably suppose that the visiting of temples, if genuine, can have occurred to any significant extent only after his return to Rome. It may then be felt that this weighs somewhat against the genuineness of this tradition; on the other hand, it obviously does not rule it out. However, it is true that a legend normally reflects a man's greatness and is not its precursor, and it is therefore hard to believe that the Scipionic legend can have existed at all before the Spanish campaigns; and since it is first of all in connection with the capture of New Carthage – leaving aside the silly story of the aedileship – that features of it appear, it is to New Carthage that we must now return.

IV

It is not easy to discover what really happened there, for although Polybius had access to at least three and probably more versions, including Scipio's own narrative and discussions with Laelius, and is therefore clearly our best source, he is so patently concerned to make a case about Scipio's rationalist exploitation of religion that scholars have tended to distrust any part of his account which involves this theme. According to Polybius,[103] Scipio, while still in winter quarters, learnt of the existence of a shallow lagoon on the inside of the city, connected by a channel with the sea, through which there was a fall in its water level each evening.[104] On arriving at New Carthage, the day before the attack began, he harangued his troops and promised ‖ them among other things that there would be a manifest intervention of Neptune (Polybius of course calls him Poseidon) on the Roman side,[105] in accordance with a promise the god had made to him in a dream. When on the next day at the expected time the level of the water fell and the wading party was sent across the lagoon, the

---

[100] Despite Warde Fowler's argument (*Religious experience of the Roman people* (London, 1911) 364–5; *cf.* Haywood, *op. cit.* (n. 4) 26 n. 1) that ‘the idea of conforming his life to the will of any of these *numina* would of course be absolutely strange to him – the expression would have no meaning whatever for him’.

[101] *Op. cit.* (n. 1) 2.438.   [102] Livy XXVI.19.

[103] Polyb. x.6ff.

[104] Polyb. x.8.7; the lagoon is now dry land (*cf.* Scullard, *op. cit.* (n. 3) 289–99).

[105] Polyb. x.11.7–8.

army was struck with the thought that this was happening μετά τινος θεοῦ προνοίας, 'by some divine providence'.[106] The incident thus serves to illustrate Polybius' thesis that Scipio did not owe his success 'to the gods and fortune',[107] but to his own foresight;[108] like Lycurgus,[109] however, he deliberately represented the fruit of calculation as the beneficent intervention of divine power.[110]

The first difficulty raised by this account is that of the ebb. Although slight tides do occur at some points, especially in the western reaches and the Adriatic, the Mediterranean is of course in general tideless; moreover, if the drop in the level of the lagoon at New Carthage was a tidal phenomenon (Polybius does not say it was), he must be wrong in stating that it happened daily ἐπὶ δείλην ὀψίαν. He could of course be generalising on the basis of what was true for the day for which Scipio planned the attack, but this is not what he says. Alternatively, the fall in the water had some other cause such as wind action. Haywood quotes the American *Mediterranean pilot* for the regular blowing of south-westerly *virazones* from 10 a.m. to sunset during the summer, and these could have caused a build-up of water in the lagoon which dropped when the wind dropped. Alternatively there could have been an evening land breeze. Livy mentions[111] a north wind which combined with a tide to make the water fall; and Scullard[112] quotes several examples of similar phenomena due to wind from the Red Sea, the Crimea, the Suez Canal and Geneva. It is also attested that at the present time north or north-east winds can lower the level of the water by one to one and a half feet in the neighbourhood of Cartagena.[113] On the whole therefore the incident sounds more like a wind phenomenon than a tide, despite Polybius' use in x.14.2 and 7 of the word ἄμπωτις. Scullard, incidentally, also considers[114] the possibility of volcanic phenomena, but rightly dismisses this as unlikely. Tide or wind, either explanation presents certain difficulties. If it was tidal (and so its time predictable for the day of the attack) why, it has been said, did Scipio launch a violent assault in the morning instead of waiting for the drop in the water later in the day? Having promised his men Neptune's help,[115] why did he embark on a dangerous operation which, had it succeeded, would have rendered the god's help superfluous? And why did Mago do nothing to guard against an obvious risk? If on the other hand the ebb was caused by wind action, clearly Scipio could not count with certainty on its taking place; how then in that case could he on the previous day promise with any confidence that his men would witness the intervention of the god? ‖

These difficulties would of course disappear if the whole story of the ebb were an invention. But the character of Polybius' sources excludes this hypothesis.

---

[106] Polyb. x.14.11.   [107] Polyb. x.9.2.
[108] Polyb. x.2.13.   [109] Polyb. x.2.8–11.
[110] Polyb. x.2.12.   [111] Livy xxvi.45.8.
[112] *Op. cit.* (n. 3) 76–91; see too Polyb. 1.75.5–10, for an example at the R. Bagradas, near Carthage.
[113] *Mediterranean pilot*[6] 1 (London, 1926) 69; *cf.* Scullard, *op. cit.* (n. 3) 78–9 n. 3.
[114] Scullard, *ibid.* 79.   [115] Polyb. x.8.7.

As we saw, they included Scipio's own account of the operation as well as Laelius' remarks. Hence Polybius cannot have described a purely imaginary ebb. On the other hand, the difficulties I have mentioned are perhaps less serious than they seem. If one assumes that the cause of the ebb was wind, the risk of its non-occurrence will have been much reduced if Scipio had his local informants with him and they had assured him that the weather conditions made it reasonably certain that it would take place as usual. They are not mentioned, but a good general of Scipio's calibre would hardly fail to ensure their presence. Further, the morning attack may well have been intended to exhaust the enemy rather than to capture the city by direct assault across the isthmus. Polybius emphasises this aspect[116] and De Sanctis is right to draw attention to it.[117] Scipio purposely posted his men near his camp in order to draw out the Carthaginians, 'well knowing that if he destroyed those who were so to speak the steel edge of the population of the town he would cause universal dejection'. As the attacker Scipio controlled the time-table. There was perhaps a slight risk that if events went too well he might prematurely force an entrance before the ebb was due. But this would not be very serious, since, as Scullard pertinently observes,[118] the lagoon was fordable even without the ebb: καθόλου μέν ἐστι τεναγώδης ἡ λίμνη καὶ βατὴ κατὰ τὸ πλεῖστον, says Polybius.[119] It was therefore possible to send the wading party across at any time, without waiting for the ebb, and this is no doubt what Scipio would have done, had his frontal attack led to a break-through. Thus the extension of the front which was to overwhelm the Punic resistance was not entirely tied to the moment of the ebb (as De Sanctis argues) but naturally Scipio planned to exploit this, as Polybius says, since with subsequent fighting to be done it was better for his men to remain as dry as possible.

Such seems to have been Scipio's strategy, and it fits Polybius' account. But some questions still remain. In particular, did Scipio really refer to Neptune and if so, when? Ed. Meyer regarded the whole story of Scipio's prior knowledge of the ebb and of his reference to Neptune as unhistorical, the product of popular historiography;[120] he believed that the attack across the lagoon was improvised when Scipio noticed a drop in the surface level at a time when his land attack was faltering. This view is unacceptable, first because unless the lagoon virtually emptied (which is improbable, since our sources, which would be likely to exaggerate the phenomenon, nowhere say so) a fall in its level could give Scipio no certainty that it was now fordable, if he had made no previous enquiries; and secondly because it is incredible that, having consulted Scipio's own account of the operation, Polybius could have made the crossing of the lagoon a manoeuvre planned in advance, if it was in fact an improvisation – unless indeed we are to assume that what Scipio wrote to Philip was pure fiction.

---

[116] Polyb. x.12.7.
[118] *Op. cit.* (n. 3) 80–1.
[120] *Op. cit.* (n. 1) 2.438ff.

[117] *RFIC* 64 (1936) 192.
[119] Polyb. x.8.7.

However, accepting the view that the fording of the lagoon was an integral part of ‖ Scipio's strategy, we are still confronted with contradictory versions of the reference to Neptune. According to Polybius,[121] Scipio delivered a speech the day before the attack outlining his purpose and adding that Neptune had appeared to him in his sleep to suggest this enterprise – that is the attack on New Carthage – and to promise that he would render conspicuous aid to the whole army. Livy however has Scipio withhold all reference to Neptune until the short speech which he delivered at the very moment the troops were about to plunge into the waters of the lagoon.[122] It has been said that Polybius' account is only credible if the conspicuous help was something of which Scipio could be absolutely certain. But I have already argued that the risk that the ebb would not occur was very slight; and in any case the difficulty is more apparent than real. For if the men had to be sent across before the ebb, it would not be too difficult to explain this manoeuvre as involving the collaboration of Neptune. At the worst, the victorious army was not going to challenge Scipio on the fulfilment of his promise or worry much about it. One could always invent an epiphany in some other part of the field. It is, after all, the prophecies that come off that are remembered: the others tend to be forgotten.

For this reason Livy's position for the speech seems less plausible than Polybius'; and though Kahrstedt suggested[123] that Livy's position is the correct one, and that Polybius has transposed the reference to the previous day so as to give credence to what he considers to be Polybius' unscrupulous rationalising of the event, turning spontaneous words of encouragement into a prophetic claim to supernatural help, I think we must rather assume with Meyer[124] and Klotz[125] that it is Livy – or perhaps his source – who has shifted the speech for rhetorical reasons. Indeed the other view would carry serious implications for Polybius' integrity as a historian; for he repeatedly insists that the speeches recorded by a historian should correspond to what was actually said.[126] *Prima facie*, then, Polybius' account of Scipio's words is to be accepted. Its rejection has generally been due to unwillingness to accept his picture of Scipio as a man who cynically exploited religion to get his way with the troops or the people – a picture which seems to be his answer to the Scipionic legend. Perhaps, however, one should distinguish here between the main elements of the legend, all incidentally linked with the name of Jupiter – the temple-visits and the divine birth – and the speech at New Carthage, which preceded and probably gave rise to the existence of the legend, and involved Neptune, with whom, strangely, Scipio's name is not subsequently linked at all. Admittedly, the reference to a dream by Scipio recalls the legend, and I do not exclude the

[121] Polyb. x.11.5.

[122] Livy xxvi.45.6–9; the wording here seems to exclude the possibility of a previous reference in the lacuna at 43.8–44.1.

[123] *Op. cit.* (n. 69) 3.291.   [124] *Op. cit.* (n. 1) 2.450 n.

[125] A. Klotz, *Appians Darstellung des zweiten punischen Krieges* (Paderborn, 1936) 74.

[126] See my lecture *Speeches in Greek historians* (Oxford, 1965) 7ff. [below, pp. 248ff.].

possibility that subsequent working-over may have brought in some colouring, probably *via* Silenus. But I think it is very likely that it was Scipio's reference to a dream on this occasion that set off the legend of the 'dreamer'. Certainly I can see no reason to question Polybius' statement that Scipio ‖ delivered a speech the day before the attack, in the course of which he promised Neptune's help, intending that this pseudo-prophecy would be fulfilled when his wading party crossed the lagoon to attack the north side of the city.

V

It seems likely, then, that the beginnings of the legend are to be seen in the events at New Carthage. They were of course very much the stuff of which legend is made, for we know of more than one historical occasion when the unexpected crossing of water was interpreted as a mark of divine favour – Cyrus, for instance, crossing the Euphrates,[127] Lucullus crossing the Euphrates,[128] the waves doing *proskynesis* to Alexander at Mt Climax,[129] and of course the Israelites crossing the Red Sea – not to mention a contemporary θεῖος ἀνήρ, Chairman Mao swimming the Yangtse. The capture of New Carthage was an outstanding military achievement, the first in the train of events leading to the expulsion of the Carthaginians from Spain. From its capture onwards Scipio's fame must have become almost legendary among his own men and probably among the enemy too. When Silenus and the other Hannibal-historians produced their histories – in Silenus' case at least after the war was over – they probably had the legend in a fairly developed form – though we cannot say precisely what was already there. Shortly afterwards Ennius made his contribution with the attempted heroisation of Scipio. But soon Scipio fell under a cloud and died not long afterwards in retirement, almost exile, at Liternum.

What was Scipio's own attitude towards the legend? We might be able to answer this more confidently if, like Polybius, we could read his letter to Philip. Polybius probably had access to this through Aemilianus, since had it been published Cicero would hardly have written[130] 'nulla...eius ingenii monumenta mandata litteris, nullum opus otii, nullum solitudinis munus exstat'. Pédech[131] has recently suggested that this letter was written in 190 to impress Philip and lead him to grant the Romans passage through Macedonia;[132] but it seems more likely that Scipio sent it later when the two men were already friends,[133] and it may have dealt with the Spanish campaigns as a whole, though indeed the attack on New Carthage involved elements of speed and surprise which were bound to have especially interested Philip.

[127] Xen. *Anab.* 1.4.18.   [128] Plut. *Luc.* 24.5.
[129] Callisthenes, *FGH* 124F31; *cf.* Arr. *Anab.* 1.26.2.
[130] Cic. *Off.* III.4.
[131] P. Pédech, *La méthode historique de Polybe* (Paris, 1964) 381.
[132] *Cf.* Livy XXXVII.7.8–10.
[133] *Cf.* Walbank, *Philip V of Macedon* (Cambridge, 1940) 211.

I think it is fair to assume that this letter contained nothing to contradict what Polybius tells us of Scipio's plans and tactics,[134] and of his use of the ebb and of the fighting around the isthmus. But we do not of course know the exact circumstances in which Scipio sent it, whether in response to a request from Philip, and if so what form it took. Whether it mentioned the pseudo-prophecy we cannot tell, but it is unlikely to have said much of the more developed aspects of the legend; they were not ‖ relevant, and one can hardly picture Scipio writing about supernatural help to Philip V! But this is speculation and tells us nothing about Scipio's attitude towards the legend or indeed towards Roman religion. De Sanctis seems to believe[135] that the very existence of the legend implies Scipio's belief in it, and he criticises Haywood for what he calls 'the middle way', which implies that Scipio made no claim to divine inspiration. We have to choose, he says, between the Polybian assumption of a cynical, calculating Scipio, and a man convinced, like Oliver Cromwell, of his own mission and divine inspiration; he means of course that we have to choose the second. This conclusion, like Haywood's, I question because I doubt whether we have enough evidence to confirm the view that Scipio was a mystic. Warde Fowler, it is true, called him 'that strange soldier-mystic';[136] but then Warde Fowler believed that it was Africanus who was chosen to receive the Magna Mater at Rome.[137] The only occasion when we know that Scipio claimed that he was to receive divine aid was at the taking of New Carthage, when I think we have to regard his speech as a morale-booster – or trick, call it which you will. Even so, human beings are too complicated for us to assume that Scipio could not say what Polybius represents him as saying in his speech there and at the same time believe genuinely in the gods and even think that he was in some way specially regarded by them. Perhaps he really did believe the ebb was some kind of manifestation of Neptune's benevolence.[138] Unfortunately by the time Polybius wrote the legend was already in existence and the main lines laid down. By then the truth was past recall: the temple-visits, made at dead of night when there were few about, and unnoticed apparently by the temple dogs, are too vague for us to base much upon them.

Reluctantly therefore we reach the conclusion that although we may accept Polybius' account of what happened at New Carthage, the picture he constructs on the strength of it is too 'rationalised', too unsubtle and altogether too Polybian to be convincing. But we have nothing to put in its place. Of Scipio's competence as a commander we know a great deal. Of his arrogance and lack of success as a politician we know something too (though here legend of another kind, reflecting the hostility of the nobles, has been busy). But of

---

[134] Polyb. x.9.3.

[135] *RFIC* 64 (1936) 192–3.   [136] *Op. cit.* (n. 100) 330.

[137] This Scipio however was Cnaei f. (Livy xxix.10).

[138] One might even believe in the dream as the product of elation – if it were not quoted by Scipio to explain the whole campaign and so necessarily dated to the period before he crossed the Ebro (Polyb. x.11.7).

his attitude towards the gods and his own destiny, and of his real personality, we know very little; and it is perhaps safer to accept a *non liquet* as the answer . to this problem. Of his greatness and of his importance in the development of the Roman empire there is however no doubt. If there were no other evidence, we could guess this from the existence of the Scipionic legend.[139]

[139] A paper read to the History Faculty of the University of London on 23 February and to the Cambridge Philological Society on 2 March 1967; it owes something to helpful discussion on both occasions.

10

POLYBIUS AND ROME'S EASTERN POLICY*†

I

Any discussion of the policy of the Roman Senate towards the Hellenistic world at the end of the third century B.C. must inevitably take account of the work of two men who wrote their most important books around this topic. One is, of course, Polybius, the other Maurice Holleaux. Holleaux's book on Rome, Greece and the Hellenistic monarchies appeared in 1921;[1] but it came as the culmination of several studies on this subject, which had been exercising his attention particularly since 1913.[2] Today, then, we stand virtually at the fiftieth anniversary of Holleaux's thesis, and we can appropriately consider how far it has stood the test of time. However, that is not my main purpose in this paper, which will be concerned much more with what Polybius has to say on the subject. As everyone knows, it is the evidence of Polybius that stands behind Holleaux's remarkable reconstruction of Roman policy; and Holleaux's problem is quite central to Polybius' interests – indeed it is very close to, though not identical with, his main theme. 'Who', he asks,[3] 'is so worthless and so indolent as not to want to know by what means and under what constitutional system the Romans in less than fifty-three years have succeeded in subjecting nearly the whole inhabited world to their sole government – a thing unique in history?' It is perhaps not unfair to judge a historian by the degree of success he attains in tackling his main theme. If that seems a reasonable proposition, we may ask ourselves: Does Polybius in fact offer a satisfactory answer to the question he has raised?

From one point of view it is, of course, quite obvious that if he had given an answer that was entirely satisfactory to everybody, generations of later historians from the Roman annalists onwards would not have occupied their time furnishing alternative explanations. But the difficulty about Polybius' account of Roman imperialism in the eastern Mediterranean is not simply one of deciding whether or not one regards it as convincing; it is also that of explaining why his work contains a curious – and I may add curiously

* [JRS 53 (1963) 1–13]

† A presidential paper read to the Annual General Meeting of the Roman Society in London on 18 June 1963.

[1] M. Holleaux, *Rome, la Grèce et les monarchies hellénistiques* (Paris, 1921).
[2] An article on the negotiations between Antiochus III and the Romans appears in that year; cf. *REA* 23 (1913) 1–24 = *Études d'épigraphie et d'histoire grecques*, ed. L. Robert (6 vols., Paris, 1939–68) 5.156–79. [3] 1.1.5.

neglected – paradox, which at once becomes apparent if one compares Polybius' own account of Roman expansion with the picture of Roman actions and motives which Holleaux constructed on the basis of Polybius' narrative. Put briefly, Holleaux's thesis is that down to 200 B.C. the Romans, as a result of long indifference to the Greek world, had no eastern policy; they intervened in Greece in the two Illyrian Wars and the First Macedonian War through a succession of accidents, and disengaged themselves on each occasion as quickly as possible. 'For many years,' Holleaux remarks in his preface,[4] 'we have been told complacently of the invincible attraction exercised by the power of Hellenism at all times upon the Romans, of the instinctive force driving them towards it, of the historical and psychological laws which required them to become the masters of the Greek states, and of their firm and long-standing resolve to subjugate them. Once again people are beginning to talk, every day a little more' – we are of course in 1920 – 'of the passionate ambitions of the Roman Senate, of its need to dominate, of its spirit of "imperialism" and "militarism". We are practically back again in the position of Bossuet, declaring that "when the Romans had tasted the sweets of victory, they were eager that all should yield to them and asserted nothing less than the right to bring first their neighbours and subsequently the whole universe under their laws". People are even beginning to believe... in the vast "plan of expansion" methodically worked out by the Senate. But in the authentic history that a vigilant critic must distinguish from what is apocryphal I have found nothing to justify such views; rather I have discovered there the very opposite and I have ventured to say so.' ‖

There is passion here as well as rhetoric. And Holleaux's thesis had a remarkable success. Through the chapters which he wrote for the *Cambridge ancient history* on the first two Macedonian Wars and the Syrian War,[5] it fairly soon became the orthodox view of Roman imperialism in England as well as in France, and indeed in the world of scholarship generally. Naturally it did not go without criticism, and over the years some valid points seem to me to have been made against it. Indeed it would be very odd if no progress at all had been made in this field in the course of fifty years. But since I shall be arguing in the course of this paper that in the main Holleaux's explanation of Roman expansion across the Adriatic is still the most satisfactory, it will perhaps be as well if I indicate at once what these points seem to me to be, and to what extent they shake Holleaux's main theory.

(1) First, and largely as a result of the work of Professor Alfred Heuss of Göttingen,[6] we now have a clearer picture of the juridical principles underlying Roman relations with foreign states; in particular, Heuss's discussion of such

[4] *Op. cit.* (n. 1) iii–iv.
[5] *CAH* 7 (1928) 822–57; 8 (1930) 116–240 = *Études d'épigraphie* 4.76–114; 5.295–432 (French text with supplementary bibliography).
[6] A. Heuss, *Die völkerrechtlichen Grundlagen der römischen Aussenpolitik in republikanischer Zeit*, Klio Beiheft 31 (Leipzig, 1933). On *deditio* see also A. Piganiol, *RIDA* 5 (1950) 339–47, '*Venire in fidem*'.

concepts as *amicitia* and *deditio* has demonstrated that *amicitia* can arise as the result of any friendly contact and does not have to be based on a *foedus*. Consequently, Roman relations with Greek states can be envisaged in a more flexible form and one may assume looser but still valid connections without the formal bond of a treaty. To take one example, one need no longer be so sceptical about the *amicitia* established with Ptolemy II after the Pyrrhic War, an event widely recorded in the annalistic tradition[7] and recently defended by a Canadian scholar, Dr Neatby, who alleges[8] parallels between the third-century Roman coinage and that of the Ptolemies at the same period. But this does not affect Holleaux's theory substantially, though it may facilitate changes of emphasis here and there, for example on the role of Athens.

(2) Secondly, there is a growing body of evidence that there were more contacts between Rome and the Greek world from the sixth century onwards than Holleaux knew of or was willing to admit. It is only fair to add that this evidence is of a very mixed kind, and it is not at all certain what it really adds up to. I can mention only a selection.[8a] We note for example that Greek vases were to be found in sixth-century Rome,[9] and that by the fifth century Greek loan words such as *triumpus* and *poena* had already established themselves in Latin.[10] Clearly regal and early Republican Rome was not isolated from the Greek world. Furthermore, we now have epigraphic evidence of the cult of the Dioscuri at Lavinium in the fifth century,[11] at a date when Hellanicus of Lesbos was already recording a version of Rome's foundation by Aeneas.[12] By the fourth century Theopompus,[13] Aristotle,[14] Heracleides Ponticus[15] and Theophrastus[16] all knew of Rome's existence; and Strabo's account[17] of protests to Rome by Alexander and Demetrius Poliorcetes about Italian piracy may be authentic even if the Roman embassy to Alexander at Babylon is safer dismissed as apocryphal.[18] In the third century Xenagoras wrote[19] of Odysseus' three sons named Antias, Ardeas and Rhomaios, while Callimachus also retailed a legend[20] about a Roman Caius. By this time, too, as one might expect,

---

[7] Eutrop. II.15, 'legati Alexandrini a Ptolomaeo missi Romam venere et a Romanis amicitiam quam petierant obtinuerunt'; *cf.* App. *Sic.* 1; Dion. Hal. xx.14; Dio, fr. 41; Zon. VIII.6.11; Val. Max. IV.3.9; Justin. XVIII.2.9; Livy, *Epit.* 14; *cf.* XXVII.4.10. See Holleaux, *op. cit.* (n. 1) 64ff.

[8] L. H. Neatby, *TAPhA* 81 (1950) 89–98.

[8a] For the archaeological evidence A. Blakeway, *JRS* 25 (1935) 129–49, remains valuable.

[9] *Cf.* E. Gjerstad, *The Etruscans and Rome in ancient times* (Malmö, 1962) 149–50.

[10] *Cf. XII tabulae* 8.4 (Riccobono, *FIRA* 1.54) for *poena*; *carmen arvale* (*CIL* 1.2².2 = E. H. Warmington, *Remains of Old Latin* 4 (London, 1940) 251) for *triumpus*; *cf.* Momigliano, *JRS* 53 (1963) 121.

[11] *Cf.* F. Castagnoli, *Studi e materiali* 30 (1959) 109ff.; S. Weinstock, *JRS* 50 (1960) 112–18 (with bibliography).

[12] *FGH* 4F84 = Dion. Hal. 1.72.2.

[13] *FGH* 115F317 = Pliny, *NH* III.57.

[14] Plut. *Cam.* 22.2.   [15] *Ibid.* 22.3.

[16] Pliny, *NH* III.57. On these fourth-century writers see W. Hoffmann, *Rom und die griechische Welt im 4. Jahrhundert* (Leipzig, 1934) 105f.

[17] v.3.5. C 232.

[18] *Cf.* Cleitarchus, *FGH* 137F31 = Pliny, *NH* III.57.

[19] *FGH* 240F29 = Dion. Hal. 1.72.5.   [20] Fr. 106–7 Pfeiffer.

Italians were frequenting the Aegean. From the first half of the third century we possess a bilingual Latin–Greek dedication from Lindos on Rhodes,[21] concerning a L. Mr. f. Ol(ius), probably an oil-merchant. But as far as the ‖ unpublished inscription from Chios,[22] which mentions *Rhomaioi* on that island, records a dedication to *Rhome* and refers to the celebration of the birthday of Romulus and Remus, is concerned, I shall be very much surprised if it turns out to be earlier than the second century.[23]

It has also been pointed out[24] that Rhodian vase handles are found in South Italy in 300 B.C. A Roman appears on an Aetolian proxeny list of 263.[25] It was also a Roman ship that picked up Aratus of Sicyon in 252.[26] Then there are the controversial lines in Lycophron[27] and that vexed passage in Polybius,[28] which seems to record nearly 140 years sharing of ἐπιφανέστατα καὶ κάλλιστα ἔργα by the Rhodians and Romans, interpreted by Schmitt[29] as common action by the two powers against pirates. These two passages I am inclined to leave aside because I think the date of the lines in Lycophron is still *sub judice*[30] (though in any case they are not incomprehensible in the context of the Pyrrhic War), and because I believe that in Polybius xxx.5.6, however one explains the intrusion, the words πρὸς τοῖς ἕκατον have to go, leaving us with the years from 200 to 164 for a convincing 'nearly forty years' of collaboration in glorious enterprises between Rhodes and Rome.

But in any case I find some difficulty in growing very excited about all this evidence. It is not all new, and much of it is trivial. No doubt occasional Romans, or Italians using the Roman name, were active in eastern waters from the fourth and third centuries; and one would expect early Rome to share the Etruscan contacts with Greece. Naturally too the Hellenistic world had heard of Rome: Italy was not *ultima Thule*. And Rome, like Etruria, had its Greek contacts (including perhaps the embassy reputedly sent to Greece at the time of the Decemvirate).[31] But it is a very big jump indeed from these fragments of evidence of economic or cultural associations to an assumption that the Roman Senate was keenly interested in mainland Greece and allowed Greek affairs to play an important part in the shaping of Roman policy in the third

[21] *Insc. Lind.* 92 = Degrassi, *ILLRP* 1.245 ⟦reading [L]u(cius) M⟨a⟩r(ae) Foli[os]⟧.

[22] *Cf.* N. M. Kontoleon, Πρακτικά (1953) 270f. ⟦Now published; see P. S. Derow and W. G. Forrest, *ABSA* 77 (1982) 79–92; they leave the date undecided.⟧

[23] In the course of a recent discussion in Paris M. Louis Robert expressed his firm belief in a second-century date for this inscription.

[24] *Cf.* H. H. Schmitt, *Rom und Rhodos* (Munich, 1957) 36 n. 2, quoting information communicated by Miss V. Grace that several vase handles published in *IG* 14 date to 300 or earlier.

[25] *IG* 9.7a51.   [26] Plut. *Arat.* 12.

[27] 1226ff., 1444ff.

[28] xxx.5.6. ⟦On this passage see now my *Historical commentary on Polybius* 3 (Oxford, 1979) 423–6.⟧

[29] *Op. cit.* (n. 24) 1–49.

[30] See especially A. Momigliano, *CQ* 44 (1945) 44–53 = *Secondo contributo alla storia degli studi classici* (Rome, 1960) 446–53. The argument for a second-century date is stated in detail by K. Ziegler in *RE* 13.2 (1927) 'Lykophron (8)', cols. 2316–81.

[31] Livy iii.31; Dion. Hal. x.52.54; but this is probably apocryphal. See now E. Ruschenbusch, *Historia* 12 (1963) 250ff.

century, and one for which I should want to see more convincing evidence than has yet been put forward.

(3) Thirdly, it is true that the annalistic tradition is not to be dismissed quite so readily as Holleaux dismissed it.[32] Annalistic is certainly not synonymous with worthless. But here, it seems to me, with the swing of the pendulum we have reached a point at which the danger lies rather in giving the annalists too much credence than too little. Let me take a concrete and familiar example. Livy, following an annalistic source, records (xxx.26.1–4) that in 203 *legati sociarum urbium ex Graecia*, representatives of allied cities in Greece, came to Rome to complain that *regia praesidia*, Macedonian garrisons, had ravaged their land and that Philip had refused to listen to their complaints; and they also reported help sent by Philip to Hannibal at Zama under a general Sopater. Holleaux dismissed[33] the whole of this as part of the annalistic case which sought to saddle Philip with the responsibility for the Second Macedonian War, in my opinion rightly. But recently attempts have been made to resuscitate this story as a genuine record on the grounds that there is definite evidence, which Holleaux misconceived, for Macedonian encroachment in Illyria between the First and Second Macedonian Wars. At the conference held in Locris between Philip and his enemies in 198 Flamininus demanded[34] that the king should hand over τοὺς κατὰ τὴν Ἰλλυρίδα τόπους...ὧν γέγονε κύριος μετὰ τὰς ἐν Ἠπείρῳ διαλύσεις, a passage translated in an exemplary manner by Livy as 'ea Illyrici loca quae post pacem in Epiro factam occupasset'. Holleaux argued[35] that Livy had misunderstood Polybius and he succeeded in convincing some of his readers (including myself)[36] that μετὰ τὰς ἐν Ἠπείρῳ διαλύσεις ‖ meant 'in virtue of and as a result of' the peace in Epirus. This is a possible meaning of the Greek words; but Mr Balsdon[37] and Dr Badian[38] have independently and rightly pointed out that in the same sentence Polybius goes on to say that Philip is required to restore to Ptolemy all the cities which he has taken μετὰ τὸν Πτολεμαίου τοῦ Φιλοπάτορος θάνατον – which quite obviously cannot mean 'by virtue of and as a result of Philopator's death'. μετὰ must have the same meaning in both halves of the sentence; and so Holleaux was wrong.

But to have shown this is, I suggest, not at all the same as proving that the annalistic story of Philip's attack on *sociae urbes* deserves any credence.[39] Illyria is not Greece; nor are towns in Illyria *sociae urbes in Graecia*. Moreover, why is Livy so reticent about where these *sociae urbes* are to be found and indeed

---

[32] For a defence of the annalistic tradition see J. P. V. D. Balsdon, *CQ* 52 (1953) 158–64; *JRS* 44 (1954) 30–42.

[33] *Op. cit.* (n. 1) 278 n. 1; *CAH* 8.156 n. 1 = *Études d'épigraphie* 5.340 n. 1.

[34] Polyb. XVIII.1.14.   [35] *Op. cit.* (n. 1) 278 n. 1.

[36] *Philip V of Macedon* (Cambridge, 1940) 103 n. 4.

[37] *CQ* 52 (1953) 163ff.

[38] *PBSR* 20 (1952) 91 n. 102.

[39] See A. H. McDonald, *JRS* 53 (1963) 187–91, reviewing B. Ferro, *Le origini della II guerra macedonica* (Palermo, 1960).

how they came to be *sociae urbes* at all? The vagueness of the passage seems to me to bear the marks of annalistic fabrication and to render it quite worthless.

(4) The fourth ground on which Holleaux's argument can be properly criticised is for his picture of the Roman Senate. As Professor Carcopino was quick to remark,[40] this was a less monolithic body than Holleaux allowed it to be. It is well known that political decisions in any but a completely autocratic state usually represent a compromise between divergent aims and interests, and different men may well support the same policy for quite different reasons. Within the Roman ruling class there was an intense political life, with keen rivalries which could concern policies as well as personalities. Since the work of Münzer[41] and Scullard[42] we cannot neglect the groupings within the circle of the Senate, and we must allow for the possibility that political rivalry between the *gentes* played a part in the shaping of policy and the taking of decisions. Indeed Holleaux himself later grew more receptive to this point of view. When in 1921 he sought to explain[43] the delay in the ratification of the Roman–Aetolian treaty during the First Macedonian War, he attributed it to the supine and inactive character of the Senate, which was not really interested in the Greek front; but in his subsequent discussion in *CAH* 8.125 he has come round to Kahrstedt's[44] theory that certain senators were positively opposed to the alliance. In this case, as it happens, both explanations are probably wrong. Mr Balsdon has argued[45] that the Romans had to have substantial tokens of ultimate victory before they could persuade the Aetolians to come in on their side, and his view is confirmed by a Polybian passage in Livy (xxv.23.9), overlooked by Holleaux, which shows that as early as winter 213/12 the Romans were interested in winning Aetolian support. After all, the Romans had fought enough wars to recognise the importance of allies. As regards the delay in the ratification of the treaty once it was made, Dr Badian has, I think, very satisfactorily explained this[46] as due first to the Senate's decision to wait for Laevinus' return from Greece, and subsequently to a series of purely fortuitous events recorded in Livy which will have prevented Laevinus giving any attention to the matter during 210, so that ratification was ultimately left to the consuls of 209.

However, this is a detail in Holleaux's interpretation. Because the Romans, involved in Greece, can be shown to have displayed a realistic attitude in acquiring Greek allies, it does not follow that Holleaux was wrong in his general picture of the Senate's fundamental indifference to Greek affairs. And this view

---

[40] *JS* 21 (1923) 112–21, 173–81; 22 (1924) 16–30 = *Points de vue sur l'impérialisme romain* (Paris, 1934) 21–69.

[41] F. Münzer, *Römische Adelsparteien und Adelsfamilien* (Stuttgart, 1920); see also his many articles on the Roman *gentes* in *RE*.

[42] H. H. Scullard, *Roman politics, 220–150 B.C.* (Oxford, 1951).

[43] *Op. cit.* (n. 1) 211–12.

[44] *Geschichte der Karthager von 218 bis 146* (Berlin, 1913) 485.

[45] *JRS* 44 (1954) 31.

[46] *Latomus* 17 (1958) 197–211.

is not, I suggest, shaken by anything that has been written on the grouping of the *gentes*. Indeed, the identifying of the policies of the various senatorial groupings[47] – and even of the groupings themselves in some cases – is still largely hypothetical, and it has yet to be shown that they substantially affected the Senate's decision at the end of the third century, or indeed that Roman factions were insufficiently ‖ patriotic to close the ranks behind a unanimous policy when real danger threatened or seemed to threaten. The sequence of events recorded in Polybius and the Polybian parts of Livy confirms Holleaux's thesis that the Romans left Greece after Phoenice without any intention of returning and that the Second Macedonian War represents a remarkable *volte-face* in their eastern policy. Individual senators may have made reservations and seen further: but there is no evidence that they counted for much in the decisions taken. Carcopino himself was obliged to admit that the texts did not support his thesis. 'I hesitate', he writes,[48] 'to sacrifice to the texts the probabilities, in my opinion of greater weight, which, going beyond the texts, though not contradicting them, arise throughout the whole of this tragic period, out of the Punic invasion, the opposition of Senate and People, the divisions among the senators themselves, and the growing predominance among the *patres* of a militarist spirit.'

This, as Carcopino recognises, is an *a priori* theory, and in fact it finds no support in Polybius; it should not shake our confidence that by and large Holleaux's thesis, despite the criticisms I have mentioned, remains the most satisfactory account of what was happening at the end of the third century.

Now it is precisely for this reason that I find myself in difficulties. Holleaux based his theory on Polybius' narrative, so much so that he and his supporters have sometimes been charged with 'polybiolatry'. Yet it is in direct contradiction to Polybius' own interpretation, as distinct from his narrative of events. Polybius lived for eighteen years at Rome in contact with the leading Roman statesmen of the Scipionic circle; he was at that time preoccupied with this very problem of Roman imperialism; he had every opportunity to question Greeks and Romans alike. Yet his analysis of the rise of Rome bears no resemblance to that put forward by Maurice Holleaux on the basis of his own narrative. This is a contradiction which has only rarely been noted, and even then it has been skirted round. Yet surely it demands some explanation in any assessment of Roman imperialist policy. I should like therefore to consider next some of the passages in which Polybius explains how he envisages the process of Roman expansion.

II

The Hannibalic War played a fundamental part in the development of Roman imperial policy, as Polybius emphasises. But it is perhaps not wholly without

---

[47] For an alleged 'Greek lobby' see W. G. Forrest, *JRS* 46 (1956) 170–1; and for a 'Claudian faction' with special interests in Greece and Macedonia see T. Dorey, *AJP* 80 (1959) 288–95.

[48] *Points de vue* (n. 40 above), 58.

significance that he is not entirely consistent about what he believed that part to be. In 1.3.6 the victory in that war is stated to be the first step in a plan of universal aggression, by virtue of which the Romans stretched out their hands to grasp the rest and crossed into Greece and Asia with their armies; but in III.2.6 it is only as a result of this victory over Hannibal that they came to conceive this project of world dominion. The inconsistency is real; but other passages, which I discuss below, make it quite clear that it was the former view that Polybius really held – namely, that the Second Punic War was part of the process of advance to world dominion and did not merely lead the Romans to initiate the project.[49] For instance, when he describes the two ranks at Zama as preparing to fight in order to decide who shall be masters not only of Europe and Africa, but of the other parts of the *oecumene*, ὅσα νῦν πέπτωκεν ὑπὸ τὴν ἱστορίαν (which must mean 'that are now known'),[50] he clearly assumes that the Romans already have this ambition, a view also to be found in the words attributed to Scipio before the same battle (xv.10.2), which I shall say something more about shortly. Polybius envisages a process of expansion, in which one stage inevitably leads to the next. In 1.6 the conquest of Italy is traced from the truce made with the Gauls in 387 B.C. which becomes οἷον ἀρχὴν τῆς συναυξήσεως, and is followed by the fall of the Latins, Etruscans, Celts and Samnites, whereupon '(the Romans) now for the first time attacked the rest of Italy not as if it were a foreign country, but as if it rightfully belonged to them'. It is noteworthy that Polybius offers no discussion of the causes of each of these conflicts, which, it is true, lie outside the period of his main history: they simply form part of the process of expansion, and when in due course the clash takes place between Rome and Carthage these ‖ two states are described as τὰ περὶ τῆς τῶν ὅλων ἀρχῆς ἀμφισβητήσαντα (1.3.7), 'the two states which disputed for world empire'. To understand that process means understanding two things: what were the policies and what were the material resources on which the Romans relied (ποίοις διαβουλίοις ἢ ποίαις δυνάμεσι καὶ χορηγίαις χρησάμενοι: 1.3.9). The Romans first went into Sicily because they were afraid to see the Carthaginians masters of that island, with Messana as a base for attacking Italy (1.10.5–9); but once Agrigentum had fallen, they conceived the ambition to possess the whole of Sicily themselves (1.20.1–2). It was the experience of the First Punic War that gave the Romans the courage to aim at universal dominion and to achieve it (1.63.9); their progress was not τύχη nor αὐτομάτως, due to chance, as some of the Greeks said. Here then in 241 we have Polybius' considered date for the beginning of the Roman policy of world domination.

The Gallic Wars had given the Romans the psychological and physical training essential for such an enterprise (II.20.8–10); henceforward they could be neither daunted by horrors nor worn down by hardships. When Flaminius

---

[49] As is assumed by E. J. Bickerman, *CP* 40 (1945) 148 n. 120.
[50] [Polyb. xv.9.5]; *cf.* II.14.7; IV.2.2; K. E. Petzold, *Historia* 9 (1960) 251–2.

initiated his policy of dividing up the *ager Gallicus* in 232, this led the Gauls to believe that the Romans were no longer concerned merely with hegemony and sovereignty over them, but were proposing to expel and exterminate them completely (ii.21.9); and indeed after the Gallic defeat at Telamon this became Roman policy, τοὺς Κελτοὺς ἐκ τῶν τόπων τῶν περὶ τὸν Πάδον ὁλοσχερῶς ἐκβαλεῖν (ii.31.8). Now this stepping up of aggressive policy is psychologically credible; but as Heuss has pointed out,[51] in Polybius' scheme it recalls the similar change of objective in Sicily after the capture of Agrigentum, and may well be part of a rationalised interpretation of Roman expansion in terms of psychological probability. After all, what evidence did Polybius command for what either Gauls or Romans *thought*, as distinct from what they did, fifty or even twenty years before he was born?

Certainly such a rationalised interpretation might well see each episode as growing out of the one before, with all contributing to a single overall pattern of expansion – which is in fact the thesis specifically formulated in iii.32.7: 'I regard the war with Antiochus as deriving its origin from that with Philip, the latter as resulting from that with Hannibal, and the Hannibalic War as a consequence of that about Sicily, the intermediate events, however many and various their character, all tending to the same purpose.' Behind it all is the pattern of world dominion. This was a conscious aim. For example, when he discusses the treatment of Syracuse after its revolt during the Hannibalic War had been suppressed, Polybius justifies the seizure of the gold and silver by the Romans because 'it was impossible for them to aim at world empire (τῶν καθόλου πραγμάτων ἀντιποιήσασθαι) without weakening the resources of other peoples and strengthening their own'.[52] Here, the Romans have clearly already embarked on their path towards world dominion.

Something else however must be said about Polybius' theory. In 1.3, as I have indicated, Roman imperialism is explained rationally as the result of natural and conscious ambition (ἐθάρσησαν... τὰς χεῖρας ἐκτείνειν). But in the next chapter (1.4) the whole process is seen on a different level in terms of a plan superimposed by Tyche. It is Tyche who, in the period covered by Polybius' work, has caused the history of the whole Mediterranean to grow together into a single whole. When Polybius saw the overthrow of the Macedonian monarchy after Perseus' defeat at Pydna in 168, he recalled the words of Demetrius of Phalerum, who had prophesied that just as Persia had in times gone by fallen at the hands of the Macedonians, so too Macedonia in her turn would fall (xxix.21). 'Nearly a hundred and fifty years ago', remarks Polybius in wonder, 'he uttered the truth about what was to happen afterwards.' If something can be foretold, clearly it is pre-ordained. Thus the rise of Rome – the counterpart of the fall of Macedon – is seen as part of a transcendental plan, engineered by Tyche.

---

[51] *HZ* 169 (1949–50) 487–8.
[52] Polyb. ix.10.11.

III

The passages I have just been discussing show that Polybius' view of Roman expansion is quite consistent, and that it bears no resemblance at all to the careful analysis of Roman policy which Holleaux based on the facts recorded by Polybius himself. This is partly the ‖ result of a difference in procedure. Holleaux is careful to link up the question of motivation at each stage with his analysis of detailed events. But in Polybius the general theory of Roman expansion and the narrative of particular incidents make little direct contact, except on such occasions as I have mentioned, viz. the growth of ambition in Sicily after the fall of Agrigentum, or the growth of ambition in the Po Valley after Telamon – where, as I suggested, there is reason to think that he is being schematic. Indeed, Heuss has made a strong case[53] for thinking that the initiating of a naval policy in Sicily was inspired by Roman alarm at the Carthaginian reinforcement of troops in Sardinia and the ravaging of the Italian coast, and so came well before the capture of Agrigentum and the supposed change in Roman policy at that time; in which case defence played a bigger part in Roman policy than Polybius' narrative would suggest. In the case of the Gauls, too, the Romans will hardly have been blind to the danger of warlike Celts settled in the Po Valley; so perhaps the expedition of T. Manlius Torquatus and Q. Fulvius Flaccus in 224[54] need not be interpreted as aggressive imperialism.

Perhaps here I may say a word too about an argument of Professor Bickerman, who suggests[55] that a motivation to be found in many of our sources which draw on annalistic material, namely that a Machiavellian Rome used the pretext of defending her allies as a cover for what was really aggression, goes back to Polybius – and perhaps, he adds, to Philip V of Macedon, who, according to Polyb. xvi.24.3, was afraid of Roman intervention against him in 201, 'since the war in Africa was over'. This, I think, misinterprets Polybius. What Philip feared was that his enemies in Greece, in particular Rhodes and Pergamum, might win the Senate over to a policy of war against him, a thing they could hope to accomplish now that the Romans were free of the war with Carthage. But this is a very different matter from saying that the Romans were merely waiting for the end of the Hannibalic War to be free to attack Philip, using the defence of their allies as a pretext. Similarly, when Aristaenus, speaking to the Achaeans in 198, argues[56] that now, in contrast to the First Macedonian War, the Romans *defuncti bello Punico* have brought substantial forces over to Greece under their own command, this does not imply, as Bickerman thinks,[57] that the Senate had been *waiting* for the end of the Hannibalic War to do this. We need not then accept Bickerman's ingenious theory that this idea of Roman duplicity was transmitted by Philip to Polybius

[53] *HZ* 169 (1949–50) 488ff.
[55] *CP* 40 (1945) 147ff.
[57] *CP* 40 (1945) 148 n. 121.

[54] Polyb. ii.31.8.
[56] Livy (P) xxxii.21.18.

through such Macedonian historians as Heracleitus of Lesbos or Strato. Admittedly, the view that Rome used her allies' wrongs as an excuse for aggression was attributed by Polybius to contemporaries of the Hannibalic War, and I shall shortly be considering the text of Rhodian and Macedonian speeches containing this allegation.[58] But there is no reason to think that Polybius himself believed it, nor are there grounds for Bickerman's further suggestion[59] that Polybius had 'perhaps already explained the Peace of Phoenice as a Roman stratagem to gain time to invade Africa' – a thesis that can be sustained only if one attributes to him views found only in Justinus, Appian and Dio.[60]

It is safer, then, to restrict ourselves to what goes back unambiguously to Polybius. And concerning this an immediate question is: Where did he get his theory from? To answer this we need not look very far. As Professor Stier points out in an extremely interesting, if somewhat emotionally charged, study of Rome's rise to world power, Polybius assumed on the basis of experience that it was the nature of a sovereign state to expand.[61] This he certainly believed of Philip V, that he coveted universal empire, τῆς τῶν ὅλων ἐλπίδος ἐφίεται (v.102.1),[62] following a tradition of the Antigonid house. Similarly, Polybius may be behind the statement in Plutarch's *Flamininus* (9.6) that Antiochus III, after his eastern anabasis, was πρὸς τὴν ἁπάντων ἡγεμονίαν ἀποβλέποντα. That such ambitions were seriously entertained by Philip, I see no reason to believe; but they are part of Polybius' picture of him, perhaps too of his picture of Antiochus and of Hellenistic kings generally. The same attitude, applied more generally, is to be found in Thucydides' ‖ observation in the Melian dialogue[63] that 'of the gods we believe and of men we know that they rule wherever they can' or in Alcibiades' remark that we cannot by careful husbandry limit an empire as we would like.[64] Later writers echo it with critical overtones. For instance in the letter of Mithridates to the king of Parthia in Sallust's *Histories*[65] it is asserted that the Romans have but a single reason for all their wars, 'cupido profunda imperi et divitiarum'. But to Polybius this affords no grounds for criticism. Imperial ambition is a thing he accepts and on the whole approves, or is at least realistic enough not to condemn.

In the case of Rome his approval has something to do with the transcendental interpretation which he superimposes on Roman motives in order to make the rise of Rome take its place in the grand scheme of world unity planned by Tyche. I have already spoken of the inspiration he derived from the supposed prophecy of Demetrius of Phalerum, which put the Romans directly in line after the Persians and Macedonians. It was perhaps this that convinced him in the first place that the rise of Rome was part and parcel of, one might almost

---

[58] Below, pp. 150–1.   [59] *CP* 40 (1945) 148.
[60] Justin, xxix.4.11; App. *Mac.* 3.4; Zon. ix.15.1.
[61] H. E. Stier, *Roms Aufstieg zur Weltmacht und die griechische Welt* (Cologne–Opladen, 1957) 38ff.
[62] *Cf.* xv.24.6.   [63] Thuc. v.105.2.
[64] Thuc. vi.18.3.   [65] *Hist.* iv.69.5, Maur.

say, a divine plan. But it is also just possible that he was reinforced in this belief by ideas which he would find prevalent at Rome on his arrival there after Pydna.

IV

Sometime between 189 and 171 B.C. a virtually unknown Roman chronologist called Aemilius Sura composed a book in which he listed the succession of world empires – Assyria, Media, Persia, Macedonia and, finally, 'duobus regibus Philippo et Antiocho, qui a Macedonibus oriundi erant, haud multo post Carthaginem subactam devictis, summa imperii ad populum Romanum pervenit.'[66] An American scholar, J. W. Swain,[67] has shown that this concept of four successive world-dominating monarchies, to be superseded by a fifth empire, that of Rome, is an adaptation of an old oriental idea, and that it must have reached Rome from Asia Minor, evidently after the war with Antiochus. There is independent evidence for the prevalence of these ideas. Justinus (xxx.4.4) reports that the earthquake which damaged Rhodes and other cities of Asia in 198 was interpreted by *vates* to mean that the Roman empire would devour that of the Greeks and Macedonians ('oriens Romanorum imperium vetus Graecorum ac Macedonum voraturum'). Plutarch knows of the same tradition.[68] Just where the Romans became acquainted with this belief in the succession of world empires is not certain. Swain thinks they had it from the Persian priests of the Temple of Persian Artemis at Hiera Kome, about 20 miles from Magnesia, and this is certainly an interesting theory, if hypothetical. The important point is, however, that Polybius must have encountered the theory at Rome, in which case it may have reinforced the mystical idea which he had derived from Demetrius' supposed prophecy of the fated rise of Rome to world dominion. However, this cannot be proved; and when (in 1.2) Polybius is discussing earlier empires, he mentions Sparta as well as Persia and Macedonia, and is in fact more interested in comparing them than with tracing their sequence.

In any case, I have said enough about the origin of Polybius' ideas on Roman world-dominion. It is time to turn to our earlier problem. How much credence do they merit? Not only Polybius' ideas, moreover: for, if we are to accept his word, this belief in an aggressive Roman imperialism was also shared by contemporaries of the events themselves. Before discussing Polybius' own views, it would seem important to come to some decision as to whether we are dealing with the genuine opinions of Greeks who lived through the Macedonian Wars, or whether Polybius has put his own opinion into their mouths.

[66] Vell. Pat. 1.6.6.   [67] *CP* 35 (1940) 1–21.
[68] *De Pyth. or.* 11.399c.

V

Altogether I have five passages in mind, all of them in reported speeches. They are as follows.

(1) IX.37.7. Speaking at Sparta in the late spring of 210 against the proposal that Sparta should join the Roman–Aetolian alliance directed against Macedonia and her ‖ friends, Lyciscus of Acarnania asserts that Greece is threatened with a war against men of another race (πρὸς ἀλλοφύλους ἀνθρώπους) who intend to enslave her (περὶ δουλείας); and that the Aetolians have allied themselves with barbarians.

(2) XI.5.1ff. An ambassador to Aetolia, who according to the superscription to the fragment is Thrasycrates of Rhodes, states in 207 that in fighting alongside the Romans the Aetolians are making war ἐπ’ ἐξανδραποδισμῷ καὶ καταφθορᾷ τῆς Ἑλλάδος; and that the reference is not merely to the harsh terms of the treaty which gave the territory to the Aetolians but the moveables to the Romans (I pass over the distinctions now disclosed in the text from Thyrreum),[69] but applies in a general way to Roman ultimate policy, is clear from the next chapter, where Thrasycrates continues (6.1) with the words: ‘It is only too evident that the Romans, if they get the war in Italy off their hands, will next throw themselves with their whole strength on Greek lands on the pretext that they are helping the Aetolians against Philip, but in reality with the intention of conquering the whole country.’ The speech ends with an appeal to the Aetolians to help in the securing τῆς ἐλευθερίας καὶ τῆς σωτηρίας.

(3) XV.10.2. In his speech to the troops at Zama in 202 Scipio assures them that victory will not only bring them the possession of Africa, but they will gain for themselves and their country undisputed command and sovereignty over the rest of the world, τῆς ἄλλης οἰκουμένης τὴν ἡγεμονίαν καὶ δυναστείαν ἀδήριτον αὐτοῖς τε καὶ τῇ πατρίδι περιποιήσουσιν.

(4) In a passage in Livy (XXXI.29.6), derived from Polybius, Macedonian envoys to the Aetolian council in spring 199 repeat Thrasycrates’ allegation that the Romans use the supposed wrongs of their allies in order to further their imperial ambitions. ‘Messanae ut auxilio essent, primo in Siciliam transcenderunt; iterum, ut Syracusas oppressas ab Carthaginiensibus in libertatem eximerent; et Messanam et Syracusas et totam Siciliam ipsi habent vectigalemque provinciam securibus et fascibus subiecerunt.’

(5) Finally, as early as 217, at a conference held at Naupactus as a preliminary to the conclusion of the Social War between the Achaean and Aetolian Confederations, the Aetolian Agelaus made a great impression by his warning (Polyb. V.104) that whichever side proved victorious in the Second Punic War would not rest content with Sicily and Italy, but would come to

Greece 'and extend their ambitions and their power beyond the bounds of justice', ἥξειν δὲ καὶ διατενεῖν τὰς ἐπιβολὰς καὶ δυναμεῖς αὐτῶν πέρα τοῦ δέοντος; and he concluded with the famous metaphor of the cloud in the west, which Lyciscus was to echo in his speech of 210 (IX.37.10), accusing the Aetolians of invoking τηλικοῦτο νέφος ἀπὸ τῆς ἑσπέρας.

As I have suggested, these five passages admit of two possible explanations. Either from the early years of the Hannibalic War, or even before that, there was a widespread belief among the Greeks (which may or may not have been well founded) that the Romans were an aggressively imperialistic people; or else Polybius has attributed his own (later) interpretation to historical characters, and the speeches he records are to be regarded as nothing more than rhetorical compositions. Any decision on this point must in fairness take account of Polybius' own views on the role of speeches in a historical composition – a subject on which he expressed his opinion in several places. In XXXVI.1.7 he gives it as his considered view that whereas it is the business of statesmen to speak relevantly and to the point, according to the needs of the situation, the historian on his side should restrict himself to recounting ⟨τὰ⟩ κατ' ἀλήθειαν ῥηθέντα...καὶ τούτων τὰ καιριώτατα καὶ πραγματικώτατα, what was actually said...and of this the most vital and effective parts. This obviously does not exclude reshaping and rewording the material; for in XXIX.12.10, though the exact text is uncertain,[70] the meaning is plainly that Polybius asks his readers' ‖ pardon if in the course of his long work they catch him out using the same style, disposition and treatment, and even the same words as on a former occasion; and this, he says, applies to descriptions of battles, reports of speeches (ἡ...περὶ...δημηγοριῶν ἀπόφασις) and other parts of his history. But the substance of the speeches must be accurately recorded; and Timaeus is condemned (XII.25 a 5) for not setting down the words spoken nor the sense of what was really said, οὐ...τὰ ῥηθέντα γέγραφεν, οὐδ' ὡς ἐρρήθη κατ' ἀλήθειαν. Elsewhere Phylarchus[71] and Chaereas and Sosylus[72] are criticised on the same grounds, the two latter historians for recording speeches which they alleged to have been delivered in the Senate after the fall of Saguntum, when on their own admission they could have had no authentic information.

There is one passage, it is true, where Polybius has expressed himself so confusedly as to lead no less a scholar than A. W. Gomme to assert[73] that

---

[70] Ziegler, RE 21.2 (1952) 'Polybios', col. 1524, following Heyse, reads εἰ μὴ ἐπίπαν φανείημεν ἢ λήμμασι χρώμενοι τοῖς αὐτοῖς and interprets this to mean that Polybius 'bittet...um Entschuldigung, wenn die Reden in der Gestaltung des Stoffes und in der Form nicht vollkommen wahrheitsgetreu ausfielen'. But if ἐπίπαν is right, μή is unacceptable here on account of hiatus, and there is no trace of it in what can be read of the text. Further, the words τοῖς αὐτοῖς...τοῖς τῆς λέξεως ῥήμασι refer to descriptions of battles as well as speeches and therefore must mean 'the same words as I have used elsewhere' and not 'the words that were actually pronounced'.

[71] II.56.10.　　　　　　　　[72] III.20.1.

[73] A historical commentary on Thucydides 2 (Oxford, 1956) 11; cf. C. Wunderer, Polybios-Forschungen 2 (Leipzig, 1901) 11.

Polybius 'implies, in the manner of Dionysius, that it is the historian's duty
to *choose* arguments suitable to the speaker and the occasion'. The passage in
question is XII.25 i. 3–9; I have dealt with it elsewhere[74] and cannot analyse it
in detail here. I will simply say that in my view the difficulties in it spring from
the fact that Polybius speaks now (§6) as a historian and now (§8) as the
statesman reading and profiting from the study of history – a double role which
he of course combined in his own person.[75] It is the statesman, in real life, who
has to choose between different arguments, and in making his choice he can
learn from the study of speeches in history; but the historian's duty is quite
unambiguous, as Polybius' last words show. 'If,' he says, 'after indicating the
situation and the motives and inclinations of the people who are discussing it,
writers report in the next place what was actually said (τοὺς κατ' ἀλήθειαν
ῥηθέντας λόγους) and then make clear why the speakers either succeeded or
failed, we' – *i.e.* the statesmen who are reading the history – 'shall be able to
apply the lesson to different circumstances, and treat any situation that arises
with hopes of success.'[76]

If I am right in my interpretation of a culpably obscure chapter, it contains
no contradiction of the views which Polybius has expressed elsewhere on the
nature and function of speeches in historical writing. His claim then is quite
clear. The speeches he has recorded are an accurate version, in substance, of
what was actually said; and it is in the light of this claim that the passages
I have just quoted must be considered. Now it must, I think, be noted that
to some extent, for all these, Polybius is at the mercy of his sources. He did
not himself hear any of these speeches; and I must confess that La-Roche[77]
seems to me quite justified in describing Scipio's speech before Zama as a mass
of commonplaces. I feel no confidence that this speech represents what Scipio
actually said – despite the fact that on such occasions commonplaces are what
one can reasonably expect. But this does not mean that Polybius improvised.
In view of the principles which he enunciates so consistently and with such
vigour, it seems to me more likely that he took his account of Scipio's speech
in good faith from whatever source he used for the battle of Zama. If this is
so, it is not, I admit, very much to his credit as a critical historian. And anyone who chooses to regard this speech as Polybian improvisation can certainly
point out that Scipio's remark about fighting to win undisputed sovereignty
over the rest of the world corresponds closely with Polybius' own expressed
estimate (XV.9.2) for the significance of the battle. So perhaps this is a case
where it is better to suspend judgement.

I have deliberately mentioned this rather dubious passage first. But for the
rest, I can see no reason why the remarks which Polybius records were not

---

[74] See *Miscellanea di studi alessandrini in memoria di Augusto Rostagni* (Turin, 1963) 203–13.
[75] *Cf.* M. Gelzer, *Gnomon* 29 (1957) 402, recalling his discussion in *Festschrift für C. Weickert*
(Berlin, 1955) 88.
[76] XII.25 i. 8.
[77] P. La-Roche, *Charakteristik des Polybios* (Leipzig, 1857) 67.

actually made. An enemy of Rome such as Lyciscus of Acarnania, or a neutral from Rhodes trying to bring the First Macedonian War to an end may well have represented the Romans as barbarians who had come to enslave Greece; and the same arguments would come quite naturally to a Macedonian speaker in 199. Moreover, Dr Hatto Schmitt has pointed out[78] that Polybius ‖ never, in his own person, refers to the Romans as barbarians. If Lyciscus uses the word, then it seems reasonable to assume that it represents the speaker's view and not the historian's. The fifth passage I mentioned was from Agelaus' speech in 217; and this seems to be a genuine record of a point of view which obviously convinced his listeners, who proceeded to make peace. The vivid metaphor of the cloud in the West was remembered and I regard it as evidence for the genuineness of the speech. Indeed there were many good reasons why the Greeks in general should assume that the Romans were there to conquer and subjugate them. As we saw, it was an accepted view among realistic Greeks that if a power could expand, it would. In Herodotus' account of the Persian debate before 480[79] – its authenticity is irrelevant – Xerxes is made to assert the principle that military empires must by their very nature expand until they meet with some check; and I have already quoted the reply which, according to Thucydides, the Athenians gave the Melians on this point.[80] As Professor Larsen has recently pointed out in a discussion of freedom and the obstacles to it in the ancient world[81] (and both Madame de Romilly[82] and Professor Aymard[83] have made the same point), love of liberty and the desire to dominate others are twin impulses deeply implanted in Greek hearts. This holds good for the Hellenistic age as well, for, as Stier has observed,[84] if there was a Hellenistic balance of power, it was an uneasy equilibrium between contending forces and not an accepted principle to which states subscribed out of conviction. Naturally, then, the Greeks assumed that the Romans were fighting to conquer and annex; and even after the crowds assembled at the Isthmus in 196 had heard Flamininus' famous proclamation and every Roman soldier had left Greece, the Aetolians were still sufficiently dominated by this idea to call in Antiochus as 'liberator'. Moreover, men are always wont to attribute a greater consistency of purpose and more Machiavellian aims to their adversary than he necessarily possesses. We simplify through ignorance; and it is significant that even as early as 264 (if we can believe Diodorus)[85] Hiero of Syracuse brought up against Ap. Claudius what was later to become the standard accusation that the Romans were concealing imperialist ambitions under the pretence of bringing help to those in trouble.

In the case of Rome this prejudice was reinforced by a general hostility

[78] *Hellenen, Römer und Barbaren* (Progr. Aschaffenburg, 1957–8).
[79] Hdt. vii.8–11.   [80] Above, n. 63.
[81] *CP* 57 (1962) 231.
[82] *Thucydide et l'impérialisme romain* (Paris, 1947) 73 and *passim*.
[83] *L'Orient et la Grèce* (Paris, 1953) 292f.; *cf.* Walbank, *Historical commentary on Polybius* 1 (Oxford, 1957), on Polyb. v.106.5.
[84] *Op. cit.* (n. 61) 36ff.   [85] Diod. xxiii.1.4.

towards the dominant power perhaps comparable to the anti-American feeling found in many European countries today. I have just mentioned the Aetolians, who let this feeling swamp all sense of self-preservation. But there is evidence for its widespread existence elsewhere in the Sibylline oracles.[86] It does not therefore seem odd to me that the Greeks should feel and say such things about the Romans, and that they did so is not in itself a strong argument that the Romans had in fact such imperialist ambitions.

But Polybius himself is a more serious problem, since as a historian specifically concerned with Roman world-power he should have been applying stricter criteria. There are, however, several reasons why Polybius has committed himself to an interpretation of Roman policy which is inconsistent with the detailed narrative which his honesty and sincerity have led him to write. In the first place, Polybius was also a Greek and he therefore began with the assumptions a Greek would naturally make about the normal tendency of imperial states to expand. There is a parallel to this in his comments on Roman religion, which he interpreted entirely from the standpoint of the sceptical, rationalist Greek.[87]

Secondly, Polybius' decision to write the history of the rise of Rome to world power was taken only after 168 and his arrival at Rome. In retrospect what had happened may have appeared inevitable and this can have brought about some interpretation of Rome's rise in the light of later events. But I would not lay too much stress on this suggestion; for when he is analysing the *detailed* causes of the wars in which the Romans were involved, he makes it clear that the Second Punic War was the responsibility of the Carthaginians and the Third Macedonian War that of Philip (not Perseus: xxII.18.10). Here he cannot ‖ avoid some degree of inconsistency with the view which I have already outlined, that from the Hannibalic War onward Roman policy formed part of a vast plan of universal expansion. It is because this inconsistency is inherent in the *Histories* that I do not feel compelled to assume with Professor Bickerman[88] that had a passage of Polybius survived explicitly assigning the responsibility for the Second Macedonian War, it would necessarily have laid it at the door of the Romans.

This contradiction between the detailed account and the overall picture cannot be explained away, and for it, I suspect, the main responsibility must rest with the intrusive concept of Tyche. Polybius' theory of Tyche is at variance with the rational analysis of motives and causes to which he attributed so much importance. It superimposes a general pattern on events, and it creates the presumption that a process in which the Romans played the leading role was one which they themselves planned. Thus Polybius is led to postulate a development with a certain logical inevitability, which ignores the detailed analysis of the actual events and the specific motives of those who took part

---

[86] *Cf.* J. W. Swain, *CP* 35 (1940) 1-21.
[87] Polyb. VI.56.6-12 with my commentary.
[88] *CP* 40 (1945) 148.

in them. How Polybius envisaged Tyche is a problem which need not exercise us here.[89] Concerning Tyche his views fluctuate. Sometimes it is a mere circumlocution for 'it happened that...'; sometimes it is the incalculable element in human affairs which occasions sudden reversals of fortune, often for the sake of producing some ironical contrast. But when he speaks of Tyche in relation to the rise of Rome, Polybius seems to be envisaging a power akin to Providence, which comes in to upset and indeed contradict the reasoned analysis of the 'pragmatic' historian.

In view of this we are, I suggest, justified in neglecting both the interpretation of Roman motives put forward by enemies of Rome or by Greeks with an axe to grind, and equally the interpretation implicit in Polybius' grand scheme dominated by Tyche, in favour of the detailed account of events which he provides and on which Holleaux drew for his remarkable and still dominating analysis of Roman imperial policy. This conclusion involves some criticism of Polybius' merits. If I am right, the direct answer which he gives to the problem raised by the rise of Rome is one which we cannot accept. Rome did *not* become mistress of the *oecumene* in fifty-three years as a result of imperial ambitions fostered by the directing hand of Providence. That is an over-simplification. Similarly, though their constitution was undoubtedly an important factor in the success of the Romans in their imperial undertakings, its merits were somewhat different from those postulated in Book VI of the *Histories*. Here too the facts have been pressed into a schematic pattern, and the 'mixed constitution' is too mechanical and too artificial a construction to define the realities of optimate government in the second century.[90]

And so, with this point I return to the question which I raised at the beginning of this paper, one's judgement of Polybius as a historian of the rise of Rome. I have not attempted to disguise his shortcomings. On the one hand, a disposition to arrange events in a schematic form – and here one may recall the somewhat jejune and one-sided concept of cause which he produces in explanation of the outbreak of various wars[91] – on the other his conviction that the rise of Rome was a transcendental affair. But a history is not necessarily the worse because it is sustained by a conviction that it reveals a purpose; and perhaps without Demetrius of Phalerum and Polybius' belief that he had witnessed the unfolding of a superhuman plan there would have been no *Histories* – certainly no *Histories* in the form we have them in today. At least we can congratulate ourselves that the dichotomy in his thought and writing is so clear to detect and that the detailed events can tell their own story independently of the author's views about the purpose of Providence.

The Roman historians from the time of Fabius Pictor onward had their own

---

[89] See my *Commentary* (n. 83) 1.16ff.
[90] *Cf.* C. O. Brink and F. W. Walbank, *CQ* 4 (1954) 97–122; K. von Fritz, *The theory of the mixed constitution in antiquity* (New York, 1954) 155ff.
[91] *Cf.* especially III.6.10–14 (Alexander's war against Persia), 7.1–3 (Antiochus' war against Rome), 9.6–10.6 (the Hannibalic War).

purposes in writing history and made their own reconstruction of motives and events to suit them. That they had access to information which is not to be found in Polybius is certain; and their different interests, often as Roman senators, led them to stress different aspects – for ‖ example, the formal procedure of the *fetiales*, which did not, as far as we can see, interest Polybius at all. Critically analysed, this material can fill in gaps in the Polybian account. But the more one studies it in both bulk and detail, the clearer it becomes that propaganda motives and the justification of Roman behaviour and policies have played a major part in the shaping of the annalistic tradition. And so, despite the contradictions in his thought, which I have tried to bring into relief in this paper, we are left with the truism that Polybius' narrative still remains the essential basis for any reconstruction of Roman policy during these critical years; and that should mean that in essentials Maurice Holleaux's thesis still stands.[92]

[92] [On the problem of Roman republican imperialism see now W. V. Harris, *War and imperialism in republican Rome 327 – 70 B.C.* (Oxford, 1979), with the critique of J. A. North, *JRS* 71 (1981) 1–9.]

11

POLITICAL MORALITY AND THE FRIENDS
OF SCIPIO*

I

The dramatic date is the Feriae Latinae of 129 B.C., the consulship of
Tuditanus and Aquilius, the scene the gardens of Scipio Aemilianus, the theme
for discussion the Roman state. Who could expound the subject better than
Aemilianus himself for, says Laelius,[1] 'not only is it proper that an eminent
statesman rather than anyone else should discuss the state, but also I recollect
that you used to converse very frequently with Panaetius on this subject in
company with Polybius – two Greeks who were perhaps the best versed of them
all in politics – and that you assembled many arguments to prove that the form
of government handed down to us by our ancestors is by far the best of all'.
Here is Cicero's assurance that sometime before 129 Panaetius, Scipio and
Polybius used to discuss the Roman state together – though he does not tell
us when or where. According to Velleius,[2] Scipio kept Polybius and Panaetius,
praecellentis ingenio viros, beside him *domi militiaeque*, so many opportunities for
such conversations offered themselves. Was Panaetius perhaps present, like
Polybius, at the siege of Carthage? Possibly, though there is no proof.[3] For it
is now generally agreed that Panaetius' voyage with Telephus' fleet[4] and the
two years devoted to general education (πρὸς φιλομάθησιν) – or was it
research? – before he went to Athens (which we learn of from a fragmentary
passage in the *Index Stoicorum* discovered at Herculaneum)[5] have nothing to do
with any ships the Rhodians may have sent to help Rome during the siege of
Carthage (as Cichorius thought), but belong to Panaetius' early years.[6]

In fact we have no idea when Panaetius first made Scipio's acquaintance
nor where; but they must have been in contact for some time before the eastern
embassy of 140[7] when Scipio invited the Greek to accompany him on his visit
to Cyprus, Syria, Pergamum and Athens.[8] There is good evidence for their

* [*JRS* 55 (1965) 1–16]

[1] Cic. *Rep.* 1.34. [2] Vell. Pat. 1.13.3.
[3] *Cf.* Cichorius, *RhM* 63 (1908) 220.
[4] Perhaps the Rhodian mentioned in xxix.10.4 (where no author is named, the references are
to Polybius). *Cf.* Pohlenz, *RE* 18.3 (1949) 'Panaitios', col. 440; von Gaertringen, *RE*, Suppl. 5
(1931) 'Rhodos', col. 800.
[5] *Stoicorum Index Herculanensis*, cols. 55–77, conveniently consulted in M. van Straaten, *Panaetii
Rhodii Fragmenta* (Leiden, 1952) fr. 1. See for this incident § 56.
[6] *Cf.* Pohlenz, *Antikes Führertum* (Berlin, 1934) 130–1 n. 3; Tatakis, *Panétius de Rhodes* (Paris,
1931) 26 (against Cichorius, *loc. cit.*).
[7] On the date of this see Astin, *CP* 54 (1959) 221ff.; Scullard, *JRS* 50 (1960) 69 n. 43.
[8] Plut. *Mor.* 777A = *FGH* 87 F 30; *cf.* 87 F 6 with *app. crit.*

presence together at Rome, where Panaetius enjoyed the friendship of many members of Scipio's circle – C. Laelius,[9] who had studied under him at Athens, Q. Mucius Scaevola,[10] who was later to become Cicero's mentor, C. Fannius,[11] who, like Scaevola, was Laelius' son-in-law, and Q. Aelius Tubero,[12] the son of Scipio's sister, and the man to whom Panaetius dedicated several works. Since Panaetius ventured in a published letter to Tubero to express an opinion on the merits of a poem by Appius Claudius the censor,[13] it seems only reasonable to assume that he had an adequate knowledge of Latin; and this too probably implies residence at Rome. Finally, according to the Herculaneum papyrus,[14] he lived alternately at Rome and Athens, probably during the decade following the eastern journey of 140; but evidently Cicero did not believe him to be at Rome in 129,[15] the dramatic date of the *De Republica*, and after Scipio's death the same year, if not before, he appears to have settled permanently at Athens, where he became head of the Stoa, and there published his book on *Duty* (Περὶ τοῦ καθήκοντος), on which Cicero drew for so much of the *De Officiis*.[16]

So much is clear; but it is not known when Panaetius first came to Rome, nor whether he was there before 140 (though on the whole it seems likely). And unfortunately we are equally in the dark about Polybius' later movements. If Panaetius and Polybius were ‖ present with Scipio *militiae*, as Velleius says, this must have been either in Spain in 151 (which seems very early for Panaetius), at Carthage in 148–146 (when Polybius was certainly present) or at Numantia in 133 (when Scipio was at great pains to call up his friends and clients as a counter-blast against the obstruction of the Senate, and when Polybius may for that reason have been present – though his *Bellum Numantinum* is the only piece of evidence that this old man of nearly seventy made the journey from Greece to Spain on this occasion). Carthage or Numantia – either is possible, or even both; and there, I think, one has to leave it. Somewhere, at some unspecified date or dates, Scipio and the Greeks used to hold political discussions.[17]

II

There is no direct account of the form these discussions took; but it is possible to draw some conclusions from what the two Greeks wrote about the Roman state and about the Roman empire. As Greeks they were bound to be especially concerned with the relationship between Rome and their own world, for both

---

[9] Cic. *Fin.* 11.23 and 24.

[10] Cic. *De Or.* 1.75.   [11] Cic. *Brut.* 101.

[12] Cic. *Fin.* iv.23; *cf. Rep.* 1.14.

[13] Cic. *Tusc.* iv.4; *cf.* Pohlenz, *op. cit.* (n. 4) col. 423.

[14] § 63.   [15] Cic. *Rep.* 1.15.

[16] See especially Pohlenz, *op. cit.* (n. 6) 125–6, who argues convincingly that it was published after Scipio's death.

[17] For various views concerning the date of Panaetius' arrival in Rome see Brink and Walbank, *CQ* 4 (1954) 103 n. 3.

Achaea and Rhodes had learnt from experience the price of Roman displeasure. Polybius' central theme is the growth of the Roman empire and in particular the qualities of the Roman state which had enabled the rulers of Rome to make themselves masters of the known world between Cannae and Pydna. Imperial achievement is never far away from his mind. Discussing the Spartan constitution, for instance, he observes that 'for the purpose of maintaining security and freedom the legislation of Lycurgus is amply sufficient, and to those who admit this to be the object of political constitutions we must grant that there is not and never was any system or constitution superior to that of Lycurgus'. 'But,' he continues, 'if anyone aims at greater things and regards it as finer and more glorious to be the leader of many men and to rule and lord it over many and have the eyes of all the world turned to him, then it must be conceded that from this point of view the Laconian constitution is defective, while that of Rome is superior and better framed for the attainment of power.'[18] Does this second point of view represent that of Polybius himself? Although in one passage,[19] where he perhaps speaks primarily as an Achaean, he gives the impression that it would have been better had Lycurgus made the Spartans contented and moderate (αὔταρκες ... καὶ σῶφρον) in their foreign policy instead of ambitious, domineering and aggressive, clearly his real complaint against Lycurgus was that he neither rendered his people contented and willing to forgo expansion nor on the other hand provided them with adequate means to implement an aggressive policy.[20] That the Romans successfully conquered the world is a mark in favour of their constitution, which facilitated this operation; Polybius in fact admires and approves of imperial ambition, and it is the story of Rome's successful career in that field that forms the central theme of his work.

For his account of Roman history down to Pydna Polybius had a single purpose – to explain how and thanks to what kind of constitution Rome had achieved her imperial success.[21] But what happened after Pydna was another story. In Book III, therefore, Polybius explains why he proposes to extend his *History* to cover the next two decades, down to the fall of Carthage and Corinth and their immediate aftermath. 'If from their success or failure alone', he writes,[22] 'we could form an adequate judgement of how far states and individuals are worthy of praise or blame, I could here lay down my pen, bringing my narrative to a close with the last-mentioned events' – that is the Third Macedonian War and Antiochus Epiphanes' attack on Egypt – 'in accordance with the plan originally set out. ... But since judgements regarding either victors or vanquished based purely on the actual struggle (αὐτῶν τῶν ἀγωνισμάτων) are by no means final ... I must append ... an account of

---

[18] VI. 50. 2–5. B. Shimron, *Historia* 13 (1964) 147–55, argues that in reality the Lycurgan regime, as applied by Cleomenes III, was adapted to expansion; hence Polybius' refusal to discuss Cleomenes' reforms and his treatment of the king as a tyrant.

[19] VI.48.7–8.   [20] VI.49.8.

[21] *Cf.* I.1.5.   [22] III.4.1f.

the subsequent policy of the conquerors and their method of universal rule, as well as of the various opinions and appreciations of their rulers entertained by the rest, and ‖ finally I must describe what were the prevailing and dominant tendencies and ambitions of the various peoples in their public and private lives. ... Contemporaries will thus be able to see clearly whether Roman rule is acceptable or the reverse and future generations whether their government should be considered to have been worthy of praise and admiration or rather of blame.'

I have quoted this passage at length because of its importance for an understanding of the later books of Polybius. The rise of Rome to world empire reflected a transcendental plan, the work of Tyche. But that did not absolve the Romans from submitting their subsequent rule to the judgement of present and future generations. How does Polybius intend that judgement to go? Is he in fact for or against Rome in the final decision? The answer is not easy; but one thing is clear. In defining his object in these later books Polybius is replying to expressed criticism of Rome. From the time of the Hannibalic War onwards there had been plenty of people in Greece ready to accuse the Romans not only of having aggressive intentions towards other states, and the desire to subjugate them, but also of exploiting the supposed grievances of their allies in the interest of their imperial ambitions. A Rhodian ambassador to Aetolia in 207 is reported to have alleged that 'if the Romans get the war in Italy off their hands, they will next throw themselves with their whole strength on Greek lands on the pretext that they are helping the Aetolians against Philip, but in reality with the intention of conquering the whole country'.[23] In 199 Macedonian envoys to the Aetolian council make the same charge and quote past incidents to support it: 'it was to help Messana that they first crossed into Sicily; the second time was in order to liberate Syracuse oppressed by the Carthaginians. Both Messana and Syracuse together with the whole of Sicily are now in their hands and they have reduced it to a tax-paying province subject to their rods and axes.'[24] The words are Livy's, the source is Polybius.

A yet clearer case arises at the time of the Third Punic War. In accordance with his undertaking to recount 'the opinions and appreciations of their rulers entertained by the rest', Polybius records four points of view prevalent in Greece concerning the rights and wrongs of Roman policy towards Carthage. This passage is discussed in more detail below. For the present we may note that the hostile views given there are those accusing the Romans on the one hand of sharp practice, of using ἀπάτη καὶ δόλος, deceit and fraud, to break down the defences of Carthage step by step, and on the other hand of pursuing a new policy of terrorism – of not being content merely to subjugate their enemies, but of setting out rather to annihilate them; and this policy, it was alleged, had been initiated with the Roman treatment of Perseus of Macedon,

[23] XI.6.1f.   [24] Livy XXXI.29.6.

and had now been completely revealed in the decision concerning Carthage.[25] Polybius attributes these criticisms to the Greeks; but according to a passage in Livy which is almost certainly Polybian[26] the sharp practice directed against Perseus by Q. Marcius Philippus and by A. Atilius Serranus on the eve of the Third Macedonian War encountered similar criticism among some of the senators at Rome. 'It was not by ambushes and night affrays,' they are reported to have said, 'by pretended flight followed by sudden attacks upon an enemy who was off his guard, nor with a pride in trickery rather than true glory that our ancestors had waged war.' These phrases are almost a direct translation of the arguments which Polybius attributes to the hostile Greeks in 146. And these senators conclude disapprovingly that this is a new sort of cleverness, *nova sapientia*.

III

Polybius reports these views faithfully, even if, as the repetition may lead us to suspect, a little schematically.[27] But where, in this dispute, does he stand personally? Before an attempt can be made to answer this, we must examine his general attitude towards the Romans throughout the later books covering the period after 168/7. 'The final end achieved by my history', he tells us, 'will be to gain knowledge of what was the condition of each ‖ people after the struggle for supremacy was over and all had fallen under the dominion of Rome, down to the disturbed and troubled time that afterwards ensued, ἕως τῆς μετὰ ταῦτα πάλιν ἐπιγενομένης ταραχῆς καὶ κινήσεως. About this latter ... I was induced to write as if starting on a new work.'[28] Now there are two reasons why he treats this period of ταραχή καὶ κίνησις as a new work, first because of the magnitude of the actions and the unexpected character (τὸ παράδοξον) of the events contained in it, and secondly because he himself not only witnessed most of these, but also took part and was even the main agent in some. Thus the fresh start applies, not to the period after 168/7, as some scholars have thought,[29] but only to these later years of 'confusion and disturbance'. Just where Polybius regarded these years as beginning is not made quite clear. In the chapter following the phrases I have quoted[30] he claims to summarise the events of the disturbed years; but he includes the expulsion of Ariarathes from Cappadocia which occurred as early as 158. In fact, it is hard to distinguish any rigid line of demarcation, and it looks as if Polybius regarded the period from 168 onwards, which is the aftermath of the fifty-three

[25] XXXVI.9.5–8, 9–11.

[26] Livy XLII.47; see Kahrstedt, *Klio* 11 (1911) 415–30; Walbank, *JRS* 31 (1941) 82–93; J. Briscoe, *JRS* 54 (1964) 66–77.

[27] On the repetition of words and phrases in his work see XXIX.12.10.

[28] III.4.12–13.

[29] *Cf.* R. Thommen, *Hermes* 20 (1885) 199; F. Susemihl, *Geschichte der griechischen Literatur in der Alexandrinerzeit* (2 vols., Leipzig, 1891–2) 2.108 n. 104.

[30] III.5.

years of Rome's rise to power, as gradually shading off into one of confusion and disturbance as the year 150 approached and as warfare culminated in the disasters which enveloped Carthage, Macedonia and Greece. If one can draw a line, it probably was envisaged as falling about 152/1. For after then, as Polybius says, events became παράδοξον. No longer, in his view, did policy now obey the rules of reason. In Macedon, for example,[31] the story of the false Philip appeared at first sight to be quite inadmissible (οὐδ' ἀνεκτός). This Philip fallen from heaven into Macedonia (ἀεροπετὴς Φίλιππος) had no good reason for his campaign, yet quite unbelievably he won victory after victory; and the Macedonians, after being well treated at the hands of Rome, which had brought them, as all confessed, freedom instead of slavery and put an end to internal struggles, rushed to fight for this impostor who exiled, tortured and murdered them in large numbers. In such a situation one can speak only of a heaven-sent infatuation (δαιμονοβλάβεια).[32]

The same is true of the disaster that befell the Greeks. For this was a catastrophe which was both universal and discreditable and without any of those redeeming features which in earlier misfortunes of Greece had given grounds for feelings of consolation and pride; such unmitigated disaster was almost unprecedented, and indeed 'the whole country was visited by an uparalleled attack of mental disturbance, people throwing themselves into wells and down precipices'.[33] Behaviour at that time was of such a kind, and everyone was so much the victim of madness and demoralisation – ἄνοια καὶ ἀκρισία – such as it would be hard to discover even among barbarians, that one can only attribute the fact that Greece did ultimately emerge to the success of some kind of resourceful and ingenious good fortune (τύχη τις ... πανοῦργος καὶ τεχνική) in countering the ἄνοια and μανία of the statesmen in charge.

That is how Polybius saw it; and it is not far to the conclusion that in these cases δαιμονοβλάβεια and μανία describe policies which he could neither accept nor understand; for he was, as he has said, an active and interested party in the politics of those times. The years 150 to 146, it is true, do not reveal the complete and abrupt change in Roman policy which, from the first century B.C. onwards, has frequently been attributed to them.[34] But they do represent the climax of a new trend, and they also represent a significant and welcome change in Polybius' personal situation. From 167 to 151 he had been an exile at Rome, comfortably off no doubt, mixing in agreeable and influential company, but none the less deprived of full freedom of movement and personal initiative. He was the victim of Roman policy, unfair but beyond challenge. It was during those years that he planned and wrote a good many books of his *Histories*. At Rome he had every chance to meet people, to discuss, to assess. But he was essentially the onlooker, considering Roman policy objectively and,

---

[31] XXXVI.10.   [32] XXXVI.17.12–15.   [33] XXXVIII.16.7.
[34] See the just comments of W. Hoffmann, *Historia* 9 (1960) 309–44.

we might well expect, critically. Indeed, Books III to XXXIII furnish an almost unbroken run of remarks hostile to Rome. I will mention briefly some of the more striking. ‖

A number of eminent but unnamed Romans attempted to incite Attalus to acts of treachery against King Eumenes, his brother, while at Rome;[35] when they were thwarted in this, thanks to the advice of the physician Stratius, the Senate broke its promise to hand over Aenus and Maronea to Pergamum and instead liberated the two Thracian towns. Prusias II of Bithynia came to Rome and behaved in an utterly contemptible manner;[36] for this very reason he received a kindly answer – ἔλαβε δι' αὐτὸ τοῦτο φιλάνθρωπον, thus demonstrating that servility towards Rome paid dividends. When shortly afterwards Eumenes arrived in Italy, the Senate, feeling embarrassed, passed a decree forbidding the city to all kings, thereby humiliating him and ensuring that the Galatians, learning of his humiliation, would attack him.[37] Polybius may be wrong in detecting such far-sighted cunning in the Senate's decision; but he evidently retails a belief current at Rome, and he does so without comment. The Athenians sent an embassy to ask for the possession of Delos, Lemnos and Haliartus. Polybius goes out of his way to expose the injustice of the claim to Haliartus as being quite unworthy of Athens; he records the Senate's decision to accede to their request, merely remarking that the whole transaction proved less profitable to Athens than the Athenians had anticipated.[38] Obviously Polybius disapproves of the Roman decision; but as he does not mention the motives of the Senate, we cannot tell in this case whether he believed them to have some Machiavellian purpose or merely regarded them as the victims of Athenian persuasiveness.

There are several other passages similar to this. Thus, the enemies of Ariarathes of Cappadocia, Diogenes and Miltiades, made great headway against him when his affairs came before the Senate – since falsehood had no difficulty in gaining the day.[39] Here the suggestion is that the Senate were hoodwinked, just as on another occasion they were hoodwinked by Heracleides, who persuaded them to pass a *senatus consultum* favourable to Laodice and Alexander, seduced by his charlatanry (ταῖς γοητείαις),[40] and as Ti. Sempronius Gracchus and his colleagues were deceived when they were sent to investigate the situation in the Seleucid kingdom.[41] But sometimes the Senate just do not care about what is right, as when the Prienians appealed to Rome about the demand of Ariarathes that they hand over to him the money deposited with them by Orophernes, and the Romans οὐ προσεῖχον τοῖς λεγομένοις,[42] or of course as on the numerous occasions when they refused to allow the Achaean and other exiles to return,[43] persuaded by men like Charops

[35] XXX.1–3.
[37] XXX.19.12–13.
[39] XXXII.10.
[41] XXX.27, 30.7–8.
[43] *E.g.* XXX.32.

[36] XXX.18.7.
[38] XXX.20.
[40] XXXIII.18.10.
[42] XXXIII.6.8.

and Callicrates. In these instances a combination of blindness and negligence leads to bad decisions: frequently, however, as in the expulsion of Eumenes, Machiavellian motives are explicitly attributed to the Senate.

IV

When the Senate rejected Demetrius' appeal to be restored to the Seleucid throne – this was the Demetrius whom Polybius himself later helped to escape from Rome – they acted thus, ὡς ἐμοὶ δοκεῖν, says Polybius, because they were suspicious of a young man of twenty-three and thought that they would be better served by the youth and incapacity of Antiochus IV's son.[44] When the younger of the two Ptolemy brothers came to Rome asking for the agreement between himself and his elder brother to be revised, the Senate acceded to his request, which coincided with their interests. Here, exceptionally, Polybius adds a general observation: 'Very many Roman decisions are of this kind: profiting by others' mistakes they effectively (πραγματικῶς) increase and build up their own power, simultaneously doing a favour and appearing to confer a benefit on the party at fault.' And in this case they sent *legati* to ensure that their decision was implemented and that Egypt remained weak and divided.[45] Self-interest was now usual in Roman decisions. In the many appeals which reached the Senate from Carthage and Masinissa, the Carthaginians always came off second best, 'not because they had not right on their side, but because the judges were convinced that it was in their own interest to decide against them'.[46] ‖

Sometimes, as in the case of Eumenes' expulsion, one may feel that Polybius goes too far in attributing a sinister purpose to the Senate. For instance, when Leptines, the murderer of Cn. Octavius, was sent by Demetrius to Rome and admitted his crime quite openly, attempting to justify it, the Senate almost ignored the embassy, and kept the grievance open because, ὡς ἐμοὶ δοκεῖν, they took the view that once the guilty party was punished, the Roman people would regard the incident as closed, and they preferred to keep the grievance open for future exploitation.[47]

The same Machiavellian attitude, the *nova sapientia*, as some senators had styled it,[48] appears in Roman declarations of war at this time. In the case of the Dalmatians, in 157/6, they had, it is true, good grounds. A series of outrageous actions had led to protests, but the Dalmatians had contested the right of Rome to interest itself in the matter, and had treated the envoys with discourtesy and even violence. But the real motive behind the Senate's decision to declare war on them, according to Polybius, was that they judged it a suitable time for making war on Dalmatia, suitable both because the army was growing slack after twelve years peace since the Third Macedonian War, and

[44] XXXI.2.   [45] XXXI.10.
[46] XXXI.21.   [47] XXXII.3.11–13.
[48] Livy XLII.47.9.

also because they thought it high time for them to resume activity in Illyria. And so by fighting the Dalmatians they hoped to inspire terror in them (καταπληξάμενοι) and cause them to obey.[49] 'But to the world at large they said it was because of the insult to their ambassadors.'

The case of Carthage is not dissimilar. There the Romans, we are told,[50] had long ago decided upon their policy – our text says merely τούτου κεκυρωμένου, but there can be little doubt that war is meant; however, they were looking for a suitable occasion and a pretext that would appeal to foreign nations (καιρὸν ... ἐπιτήδειον καὶ πρόφασιν εὐσχήμονα πρὸς τοὺς ἐκτός). 'For the Romans', Polybius adds, 'paid great attention to this matter, καλῶς φρονοῦντες – and rightly'; and he quotes a saying of Demetrius of Phalerum, that 'when a war seems to be just (δικαῖα ... εἶναι δοκοῦσα) it increases the profits of victory and reduces the bad results of failure, while if it is thought to be unjust, this has the opposite effect'. So strongly were the Romans convinced of this that their disputes with each other about the effect on foreign opinion very nearly made them desist from going to war.

The only debates Polybius here mentions on the eve of the Third Punic War concern the question whether the pretext to hand was sufficiently convincing to make a reasonable impression on foreign peoples. However, his account is only fragmentary and can be reasonably supplemented from Appian, Plutarch and Diodorus,[51] who are agreed that Scipio Nasica opposed the policy of annihilating Carthage with the argument that fear of an outside enemy was a salutary check on internal disputes and the growth of elements hostile to the continued domination of the Senate. It has recently been argued by Hoffmann[52] that these debates are apocryphal and irrelevant to the real issues raised at Rome in the years immediately before 150. His two strongest arguments are, first, that according to Polybius the Senate had long ago made up its mind and was merely awaiting a convenient pretext to declare war on Carthage, and secondly that the theme of a *metus hostilis* as a salutary curb on civil strife was a well-worn rhetorical cliché.

To take the last point first, it is certainly true that the theme that a threat from abroad cements unity and concord at home appears frequently in both Greek and Latin literature, and that on many occasions when it was almost certainly not employed. For example, Hoffmann has shown convincingly that it was never used as an argument by the elder Scipio after Zama, and that Cato never said it was.[53] But in 202 such an argument is clearly stamped as anachronistic. This is not true of the situation around 150. As Professor Lily Ross Taylor has shown in her paper on some 'forerunners of the Gracchi',[54]

---

[49] XXXII.13.   [50] XXXVI.2.

[51] Plut. *Cato Mai.* 27.3; App. *Pun.* 69; Diod. XXXIV.33.4–6 (based on Poseidonius). See Gelzer, *Philologus* 86 (1931) 284–5 = *Kleine Schriften* (Wiesbaden, 1963) 2.39–72; Strasburger, *JRS* 55 (1965) 42 n. 23.

[52] *Historia* 9 (1960) 340.   [53] *Ibid.* 319–22.

[54] L. Ross Taylor, *JRS* 52 (1962) 19–27, especially 21ff.

the Third Punic War was preceded in 151 by tribunician activity concerning the military draft, which carried revolutionary implications, and (if the Lex Aelia and Lex Fufia belong to 150, as she has plausibly argued) by attempts to counter tribunician legislation by arming magistrates with new powers of obstruction. Against this background of political unrest Scipio Nasica's appeal to the salutary bond of an external threat makes reasonably good sense. ‖

As regards the argument that the Romans had, according to Polybius, already made up their minds, this does not seem to exclude the other discussion and indeed Appian gives both. The Senate, he says,[55] had decided to make war, but delayed for the moment the actual resolution for war through lack of a *prophasis* – which is of course precisely Polybius' argument. This gave a breathing space during which the rival arguments of Cato and Nasica could be thrashed out; and it is specifically with the question of keeping a salutary threat, and not with the question of having a plausible excuse for war, that Scipio Nasica's name is linked. In fact, however, both Polybius and Appian may well be exaggerating the firmness of the Senate's decision in the late 150s to make war, for there is an earlier occasion in the history of Rome and Carthage where Polybius oversimplifies the Senate's position. I refer to the outbreak of the war with Hannibal. 'The Romans,' says Polybius,[56] 'when the news of the fall of Saguntum reached them, most certainly did not hold a debate on the question of war, as some authors allege.... For how could the Romans, who a year ago had announced to the Carthaginians that their entering the territory of Saguntum would be regarded as a *casus belli*, now when the city itself had been taken by assault, assemble to debate whether they should go to war or not?' On this occasion the annalistic tradition (less jealous than Polybius for the reputation of Rome) records considerable opposition to the war before and after the fall of Saguntum;[57] and Hoffmann has indeed demonstrated[58] that the embassy to Carthage will not have left Rome before 15 March 218, though Saguntum fell in late autumn or early winter 219. But such delay did not fit Polybius' picture of Roman policy at the time (probably derived from Fabius), hence he discounted it. Similarly, his picture of Roman motivation in 150 – clearly a much-debated and controversial question, as his outline of the Greek views about Roman policy makes clear – may well have been tailored to fit a general theory of Roman action at this time. Nasica's views were almost certainly not those of Aemilianus, nor were they those of his friend Polybius. Nasica had argued that Carthage must be maintained so as to ensure internal harmony at Rome. Polybius, on the contrary, in the course of his discussion of the Roman constitution, which was probably published about the same time, asserted that 'when the Romans are freed from fears from abroad (τῶν ἐκτὸς φόβων) and reap the consequent prosperity, any tendency

---

[55] App. *Pun.* 69.   [56] III.20.1ff.
[57] Livy XXI.6.7, 16.2; Dio, fr. 55; Zon. VIII.22; Otto, *HZ* 145 (1932) 513.
[58] Hoffmann, *RhM* 94 (1951) 77ff.: *contra* Gelzer, *Gnomon* 29 (1957) 409 (= *Kl. Schr.* (n. 51) 3 (1964) 211), who argues that the names of the legates are invented.

to excess and disproportion is countered by the checks of the mixed constitution, which automatically restores the equilibrium'.[59] Thus, in his opinion, the Roman mixed constitution itself contained sufficient built-in guarantees to preserve internal harmony so long as it was maintained intact. And so he let his account of the outbreak of the Third Punic War follow the pattern already outlined for the Dalmatian War – a united Senate clear on the desirability of fighting and concerned primarily to find a pretext that would look most convincing to foreigners who might judge Roman policy. Whether, like Appian, he also mentioned Nasica's arguments, we cannot tell;[59a] but he is unlikely to have given them much prominence, for the reason I have just suggested.

V

Concerning the attitude he attributed to the Senate, Polybius carefully refrains from expressing his own approval or disapproval; for even if we assume the words *nova et nimis callida sapientia* in Livy to be adapted from Polybius – and this seems reasonably certain – they are given only as the view of the older *patres, veteres et moris antiqui memores*, who hark back with regret to those days of high principle, when the Senate would turn over a potential poisoner to Pyrrhus, and always declared war before waging it;[60] they do not necessarily represent the view of Polybius. Clearly he believed that Roman practice had changed; this is admitted both by the more conservative section of the Senate and by the Greeks who criticise Roman actions in the Third Punic War; and it is at first sight tempting to link this change with the moral loosening which Polybius also detects in Rome after she has begun to fight and win her overseas wars in Greece.

This moral change had of course been detected earlier: Polybius did not need lynx-eyes to reveal it. As early as 184 Cato's censorship had been celebrated by the erection of ‖ a statue in the temple of Salus with an inscription stating that 'when the Roman state was tottering to its fall, he was made censor and by helpful guidance, wise restraints and sound teachings restored it again'.[61] Restored it, yes, but not permanently. Nearly twenty years later, when Aemilianus was a young man, his virtue was already exceptional. Most youths, Polybius tells us,[62] no doubt with some exaggeration in the interest of Scipio, had at this time abandoned themselves to love affairs with boys or taken to frequenting the company of prostitutes; they spent their time at concerts and dinner-parties and generally led extravagant lives, paying a talent for a boy-favourite and 300 drachmas for a jar of caviare. At this point Polybius sententiously quotes a saying of Cato deducing the likely ruin of the Republic

---

[59] VI.18.5–8.
[59a] XXXVI.1.1 is perhaps against it.   [60] Livy XLII.47.9ff.
[61] Plut. *Cato Mai.* 19.3.; *cf.* Walbank, *Commentary on Polybius* I (Oxford, 1957) 647–8.
[62] XXXI.25.3ff.

from such goings-on. Obviously these were all danger-signals, and Polybius with his strong moral purpose is quick to point out and to contrast them with the kind of behaviour he admires: in the individual this means the qualities possessed by Aemilianus – moderation (σωφροσύνη), generosity and integrity in money matters (περὶ τὰ χρήματα μεγαλοψυχία καὶ καθαρότης) and courage (ἀνδρεία);[63] and in a nation political stability[64] in the face of inside or outside threats, and a capacity for building an empire.[65] Naturally these qualities in the state derive from the right qualities in its citizens; indeed Polybius is disposed to assess these personal qualities on a utilitarian standard, just as for example the possession by Rome of a well-established state-religion is judged on the basis of its social usefulness.[66] A man who is open to bribes (as most Greeks were[67]) is an unreliable guardian of his country's interests; and without a strong religion, the people get out of hand and no one displays any financial integrity.[68] These things were important τοῦ πλήθους χάριν, for the sake of the people. There is no evidence that Polybius regarded their absence from an individual or a state as laying them open to condemnation on purely ethical grounds, or was indeed in the least interested in that aspect.

In fact, in judging any action of a government, the criterion Polybius adopts is generally utilitarian: was it conducive to the stability or power to expand of the state in question? And since that is so, there is no reason to suppose that he regarded what may look to us, and certainly looked to some contemporaries, as Machiavellian decisions on the part of Rome, as indicative of moral decline. With this in mind, let us now examine in more detail the arguments which he quotes as having been brought forward by the Greeks in their assessment of Roman policy towards Carthage.[69]

VI

Four arguments are reported. The first view is sympathetic to the Roman action in destroying Carthage. The Romans, it was urged, had acted in a wise and statesmanlike manner in defence of their empire (φρονίμως καὶ πραγμα-τικῶς βουλεύσασθαι περὶ τῆς δυναστείας). Carthage had frequently disputed the supremacy with them (ἠμφισβητηκυῖαν ... ὑπὲρ τῆς ἡγεμονίας) and might do so again. To secure the dominion of their own country (τὴν ἀρχήν) was the act of far-sighted men. This is not a question of *security*: it is not the safety of Rome that is at stake – that is nowhere the view to which Polybius subscribes – but her empire. The reply to this, which Polybius quotes next, is that the destruction of Carthage is a departure from the principles (προαίρεσις) which had previously governed Roman policy. Hitherto they had been satisfied

---

[63] XXXI.25.2, 25.9, 29.1.
[64] *Cf.* Book VI *passim*, and especially 56.1–5.
[65] VI.50.3–6. [66] VI.56.6ff.
[67] XVIII.34.7. [68] VI.56.11–15.
[69] XXXVI.9.

to fight only until their opponents had submitted and agreed to obey (συγχωρῆσαι ... ὅτι δεῖ πείθεσθαι σφίσι). The new policy, first adumbrated in their elimination of the kingdom of Macedonia, was to annihilate their opponents – in this case despite the fact that Carthage had accepted all the conditions put to them. In adopting these methods Rome was giving herself up to a lust for domination like Athens and Sparta and would end like them – presumably, Polybius means, as a tyrannical city, for I do not think, with Hoffmann,[70] that Polybius is here attributing to his spokesmen a forecast of the ultimate fall of Rome. ‖

The policy which the second group advocate is one which the Romans themselves had in the past claimed to follow. In the conference following Cynoscephalae it was specifically advocated by Flamininus, who remarked[71] that the Romans never exterminated their adversaries after a single war, and that brave men ought to be hard on their enemies in battle, if conquered they should be γενναῖοι καὶ μεγαλόφρονες and if victorious moderate, gentle and humane, μέτριοι καὶ πραεῖς καὶ φιλάνθρωποι. At first sight this might appear to be Polybius' view too. For in a passage criticising the behaviour of the Carthaginians in Spain after the death of the two Scipios[72] he remarks that they made the mistake of treating the natives in an overbearing manner – 'for they imagined that there is one method by which power should be acquired and another by which it should be maintained; they had not learnt that those who preserve their supremacy best are those who adhere to the same principles by which they originally established it'. The reason of course is that 'with a change of character in the rulers the disposition of their subjects changes likewise', and from being allies and friends they turn to enemies. This clearly commits Polybius to approval of a policy of mild rule – on utilitarian grounds: and it is because of these utilitarian grounds that one may not conclude that he was therefore opposed to Roman policy against Carthage in the Third Punic War. For obviously if you propose after defeating a people to make them your subjects and go on ruling them – as the Romans had done in Italy – a generous policy of *parcere subiectis* may yield the best results. But if instead of governing your defeated enemy you decide, on general grounds of policy, to exterminate him, as the Athenians had exterminated the Melians, that is quite another matter, and from a utilitarian point of view may prove equally effective and so praiseworthy. The reply of the second group of Greeks is in fact based ultimately on ethical grounds – exterminating your defeated enemy is to behave like a tyrant, and to behave like a tyrant is a bad thing. It does not begin to meet the arguments of the first group, which are based on self-interest, but attempts to shift the basis of the discussion. It is hard to believe that it represents Polybius' view.

The third argument put forward by the Greeks is again one critical of Rome,

---

[70] *Historia* 9 (1960) 311; it is of course true that neither Athens nor Sparta maintained her dominant position for long; that of Sparta lasted only twelve years (1.2.3).

[71] XVIII.37.2–3, 7.   [72] X.36.2–3.

and is really only a variant on the second. It is almost word for word the criticism levelled by the older Roman senators against Q. Marcius Philippus on the eve of the Third Macedonian War – namely that the Romans had hitherto prided themselves on certain principles in the declaring and waging of war, excluding night attacks and ambushes and all kinds of deceit and sharp practice. But against Carthage they had used both, at once offering and concealing things simultaneously until they had forced their enemy into a false and disadvantageous position. 'This savoured more of the procedure of a tyrant than of a civilised state, and could only be described as impiety and treachery (ἀσέβημα καὶ παρασπόνδημα).' This accusation is an attempt to judge Rome in the light of her own professions and against the background of the *iustum bellum* and integrity of policy which had counted for so much in the Roman προαίρεσις and had enabled the Senate to make great capital of their charges of *perfidia Punica*. In Polybius' text it is developed at some length and takes up sixteen lines. The fact that the fourth group, who reply to it, are allowed just over thirty lines for their answer is an indication of its seriousness and perhaps even more of where Polybius' own sympathies lay.

The reply once more takes the well-known form of shifting the ground of the accusation. This was based fundamentally on moral issues – on a moral code and whether or not it had been kept. The answer of the supporters of Roman policy reduces the question to one of legality. The Carthaginians, it is pointed out, had handed themselves over *in fidem populi Romani* and in so doing had of course given away all their right to challenge the Roman orders; hence there was no question of impiety (ἀσέβημα) or treachery (παρασπόνδημα). Indeed some people argued that there was not even a question of injustice. The text then goes on to analyse the nature of ἀσέβημα – a sin against the gods, against the parents or against the dead, of παρασπόνδημα – a violation of sworn or written agreements, and ἀδίκημα – what is done contrary to law and custom. It was an easy matter to show that the Romans had not sinned against the gods, against their parents or against the dead (which ruled out impiety) and that they had not violated any sworn agreement or treaty (which ruled out treachery). Indeed it was the Carthaginians themselves who had broken the treaty when they attacked Masinissa! Nor, finally, did the Romans break any laws or ‖ customs or their word: they simply received an act of *deditio* and when the Carthaginians refused to obey their orders, they resorted to force. The whole weight of the moral issue is thus neatly thrust aside by an apparent resort to sweet reason and logical definition. The intangibles – the long series of unjust decisions, the Numidian provocation, the atmosphere in which Carthage was led into a false step and then buoyed up with the illusory hope of generous treatment – all these are left out. The Romans were in a morally impregnable position, so long as one kept to strict definitions, which seem almost designed to facilitate the dismissal of the charges made.

It must have been along these lines that the supporters of a 'firm' policy towards Carthage attempted to counter the charges made by those opponents who argued, not like Nasica that the destruction of Carthage was contrary to Roman interest, but that the way it was being engineered was discreditable to Rome's reputation as a state founded on moral principles. The supporters of that policy included Scipio Aemilianus, who was the agent of its implementation, and Polybius, who followed the whole operation through from Scipio's headquarters, will certainly have sympathised with it. We saw earlier that in analysing the period following Pydna Polybius drew a distinction between the immediate aftermath and the period of ταραχὴ καὶ κίνησις about which he wrote 'as if starting on a new work'; and we saw that this later period coincided with his own release from his restrictions as a detainee in Italy and the opportunity which this brought to play a more active part in world politics at Carthage and in Greece. In his account of the first period his attitude towards Rome is cynical and detached; in the second, when he is emotionally committed, he sees the policy of Rome's opponents as irrational and insane. This has already been illustrated from what he has to say about the Macedonians and the Greeks. The Carthaginians come out of it hardly any better. Hasdrubal, their leader, is described as an empty-headed braggart lacking in statesmanlike or military capacity.[73] His lack of realism in facing the certainty that Carthage was doomed strikes no chord of sympathy in Polybius, who thinks he is simply a fool, and goes out of his way to describe his unlovely personal appearance – pot-bellied and red in the face because he had continued his feasting amid his people's distress. The Greeks and Carthaginians were alike in their leaders at this time of crisis.

There can, therefore, be little doubt that Polybius accepts the Roman case over Carthage; and this creates a strong presumption that in general he accepted the 'new diplomacy' as the legitimate instrument of an imperially-minded state, including the elimination of dangerous or intransigent opponents. Flamininus had outlined the older policy of *parcere subiectis* in his defence of Roman policy in Macedonia against Aetolian criticism. To Polybius its practicability was dubious, as another passage makes plain. At a difficult moment in the Third Macedonian War Perseus sent envoys offering terms. 'It was unanimously decided', Polybius records,[74] 'to give as severe a reply as possible, it being in all cases the traditional custom of the Romans to show themselves most imperious and severe in times of defeat and most lenient after success. That this is noble conduct (καλόν)', he adds, 'everyone would admit, but perhaps it is open to doubt if it is possible under certain circumstances.' It is not quite clear whether it is the feasibility of toughness in time of trouble or of lenience in time of success – *parcere subiectis* – that Polybius finds dubious; perhaps both. For, besides the arguments I have already quoted, there is evidence which points to his having believed that in some circumstances an imperial state was justified in adopting a policy not of mildness but of frightfulness or terrorism.

---

[73] XXXVIII.7.1; see further on Hasdrubal XXXVIII.20.   [74] XXVII.8.8.

In chapters 2 and 4 of Book XXXII, Diodorus has some interesting remarks on Roman policy, for which Gelzer has convincingly argued[75] that Polybius was the original source. According to this passage, which probably belongs to the introduction to the book, Diodorus states that 'those whose object is to gain hegemony over others use courage and intelligence (ἀνδρείᾳ καὶ συνέσει) to acquire it, moderation and consideration for others (ἐπιεικείᾳ καὶ φιλανθρωπίᾳ) to extend it widely, and paralysing terror (φόβος καὶ κατάπληξις) to secure it against attack'. Two chapters further on Diodorus gives as examples in support of this ‖ doctrine the careers of Philip II and Alexander of Macedon, and the Romans; and though it is clear from the instances quoted from Philip and Alexander that the three stages – acquisition, extension and securing of empire – are not necessarily envisaged as always following that chronological order, in the case of Rome the use of paralysing terror coincides with the third stage when they razed Corinth to the ground, rooted out the Macedonians (Perseus is meant), destroyed Carthage and the Celtiberian city of Numantia, and cowed many by terror.

Book XXXII of Diodorus covers the Third Punic, Fourth Macedonian and Achaean Wars, for which Polybius is his source; it seems virtually certain that these general remarks are also from him. As Adcock plausibly observes,[76] 'Polybius probably yielded to the temptation to defend Roman frightfulness by treating it as though it followed some kind of natural law.' He had a strong incentive to do so. The elimination of Perseus was the direct result of the victory of Aemilius Paulus, who subsequently carried out a more direct programme of terrorism in Epirus; Carthage and Numantia were destroyed by Polybius' friend and pupil Scipio Aemilianus, the latter on his own initiative without waiting for the decision of the Senate; and if the fall of Corinth had no direct connection with Polybius' friends, it was the outcome of a policy in Achaea for which he expresses his unmitigated condemnation, and the prelude to a period of reconstruction in which he was to play a most effective and flattering role.

I think, then, we may take it as established that Polybius saw Roman policy from the time of the Third Punic War onwards as intelligently organised to maintain the empire which a happy combination of Tyche and Roman merit had successfully acquired; very properly it did not pay too much regard to sentiment where political interests were concerned, and took account of such traditional concepts as the *bellum iustum* and proper fetial procedure in the declaration of wars only in so far as these had their practical repercussions on public opinion. It is a pretty ruthless approach; but Polybius was ruthless, and success was apt to be his main criterion. This can be seen from his lack of sympathy for failure in peoples or individuals. Politics is a risky game and if,

---

[75] Diod. XXXII.2 and 4; *cf.* Gelzer, *Philologus* 86 (1931) 290ff. = *Kleine Schriften* (n. 51) 2.64ff.; Adcock, *CHJ* 8 (1946) 127–8; Bilz, *Die Politik des P. Cornelius Scipio Aemilianus* (Würzburg, 1935) 31; Astin, *Latomus* 15 (1956) 180; Strasburger, *JRS* 55 (1965) 46 n. 58. [Against the attribution to Polybius see below, pp. 289–90.]   [76] *Loc. cit.* (n. 75).

like those Greeks who had made the mistake of backing Perseus of Macedon
and carrying their cities with them, you lost, then the right course was to face
the situation and perish bravely;[77] no one, he says, could approve men like
the brothers Hippocritus and Diomedon at Cos, or Deinon and Polyaratus at
Rhodes, who were known to have done all they could to further Perseus' cause,
yet could not bring themselves to commit suicide. They did not leave to
posterity the slightest ground for pitying or pardoning them. Similarly
generals who have staked all on success and failed and then cannot resolve to
perish on the field add disgrace and shame to their disaster: Hasdrubal earns
praise for avoiding this fate at the Metaurus.[78] The same ruthlessness in
demanding consistency of action can be illustrated from Polybius' account of
what happened when Philip was attacking Abydus and the citizens had sworn
that if fortune went against them they would slaughter all the women and
children and die fighting; after the most horrible scenes of carnage in battle
Glaucides and Theognetus called together a few of the elder citizens and,
Polybius says, 'sacrificed in the hopes of personal advantage all that was
splendid and admirable in the resolution of the citizens by deciding to save
the women and children alive and to send out ... the priests and priestesses
to Philip to beg for mercy and surrender the city to him'.[79] It is interesting
to observe that when he tells this story from Polybius Livy cuts out all praise
of the Abydene resolve; to his Augustan sensibility the whole affair was one
of unrelieved horror.[80]

VII

So much for Polybius' moral criteria. We can now return to his programme.
As we saw, he had appended his account of Roman policy after Pydna with
the express purpose of enabling readers, both now and in the future, to judge
Roman rule, and to estimate not merely how successful it was from the point
of view of Roman security and the preservation of empire but, to repeat his
own words, so that 'contemporaries will be able to see clearly ‖ whether Roman
rule is acceptable or the reverse and future generations whether their
government should be considered worthy of praise and admiration or rather
of blame'. Acceptable or the reverse, φευκτὴν ἢ τοὐναντίον αἱρετήν: acceptable
to whom? The implication of these words is that the Roman empire is to be
judged from the point of view of the subject peoples – to which Polybius himself
belongs; and his somewhat cynical and detached attitude towards the evidence
for Roman policy which he quotes for the years between 168 (or earlier) and
about 151 might seem to give some basis for such a judgement. From the point
of view of the vanquished this would hardly have been favourable to Rome,
for throughout these years, as we saw, Rome pursued her own ends by the most
Machiavellian means, wars were entered into (as in Dalmatia) at the time

---

[77] xxx.7.2–4.   [78] xi.2.1–11.
[79] xvi.31–3.   [80] Livy xxxi.17.

Rome chose and to further Roman ends; and Roman decisions were given to suit her own private interests rather than the course of justice. But with the time of ταραχή καὶ κίνησις there is a subtle but unmistakable change in Polybius' judgement. From this point onwards he becomes more and more identified with Roman policy of the most ruthless kind. All discussions concerning the rights and wrongs of this policy, for example the Greek views on the Third Punic War, approach the question from the point of view of Rome. Despite Polybius' concern with whether the Roman empire was φευκτή ἤ ... αἱρετή, the presentation remains obstinately centred on the ruling power, and one is nowhere given the grounds on which one can draw a conclusion concerning the acceptability of the Roman empire to the people living under it. 'Neither rulers themselves', says Polybius,[81] 'nor their critics should regard the end of action as being merely conquest and the subjection of all to their rule; since no man with any intelligence goes to war with his neighbours simply for the sake of crushing an adversary.' What then in Polybius' opinion *is* the end of imperial action? What is the further criterion other than the subjection of other states and the maintenance of one's empire in safety? The question is posed: but nowhere in the *Histories* will you find the answer. For that the Romans had to wait for Panaetius.

But before considering Panaetius' contribution it is legitimate first to enquire what view the Romans themselves had taken of this problem. Strictly speaking, they had taken no view of it at all, since the idea of justifying their growing empire was not one that had at first occurred to them. Why should it? Certain things were understood. The aristocratic tradition of the early Republic assumed that Rome never went to war without good reason; all Roman wars conformed to the definition of the 'just war', provoked by offences committed against either Rome or her allies, whose defence was an obligation due to *fides*, and aggravated by refusal to make due reparation; such a war was declared with due formalities by the *fetiales* and the Romans entered it sustained by a useful conviction of self-righteousness. This was an ancient conception, as simple and Roman in its way as Polybius' picture of almost automatic expansion from one position of strength to another was simple and Greek; and Gelzer has demonstrated[82] that it was part and parcel of the Roman propaganda presented in the pages of Fabius Pictor and the other early senatorial historians. But the rather different issues involved in the possession of an empire hardly reached the consciousness of the Romans until the middle of the second century.

It was in 156–5, more than a decade after Polybius had established himself in the family circle of Scipio Aemilianus, that a famous trio of Greek philosophers arrived in Rome to plead on behalf of Athens for the remission of a fine of 500 talents imposed by a court of arbitration for the plunder of Oropus. They were Carneades, the leader of the Academy, the Stoic Diogenes

---

[81] III.4.9–10.
[82] Gelzer, *Hermes* 68 (1933) 129–66 = *Kleine Schriften* (n. 51) 3.51–92.

and Critolaus the Peripatetic; and they took the opportunity provided by their stay in Rome to lecture on philosophical topics.[83] Carneades was a great master of eloquence – Lucilius in one of his poems made Neptune remark of a very knotty problem that it could not be solved even if Orcus were to send Carneades up again![84] – and the Roman intelligentsia, the φιλολογώτατοι τῶν νεανίσκων, as Plutarch calls them,[85] had never heard anything like his two lectures on Justice and its application to international affairs, ‖ delivered on two successive days, on the second of which the speaker refuted all the theories which he had put up as an Aunt Sally on the previous day.

Carneades' devastating attack on justice is known to us from L. Furius' reproduction of its arguments in Cicero's *De Republica* III[86] and from the sketch given in Lactantius' *Divinae Institutiones* v, entitled *de iustitia*;[87] Cicero made C. Laelius answer Carneades, but Lactantius exposes some of the weaknesses in Laelius' case. The demolition of justice as a guide to follow in international affairs was accomplished fairly straightforwardly by an appeal to the concept of self-interest, τὸ σύμφερον, as developed by the sophists and by Thrasymachus in Plato's *Republic* I. It was not therefore really new. But expounded in the brilliant rhetoric of Carneades, which was *violenta et rapida*,[89] his arguments seemed devastating; and the cautious Cato, taking the view that speeches of this kind made it impossible to sift falsehood from truth,[89] urged the Senate to settle the matter of the Athenians' fine with all speed 'so that these men may return to their schools and lecture to the sons of Greece, while the youth of Rome give ear to their laws and magistrates, as in the past'.[90]

Polybius was in the audience at these lectures;[91] but there is nothing in the *Histories* to suggest that he was shaken or worried by what Carneades had to say. To a Greek already preoccupied with the question of empire the idea of τὸ σύμφερον as a criterion of conduct was of course familiar, and Polybius will have regarded much of Carneades' thesis as consisting of truisms. But for the Romans it was different. Cato's alarm was genuine and is likely to have been widely felt. Rome now possessed an empire. Was it indeed based on injustice, as Carneades said? Suddenly the Romans found themselves desperately in need of a philosophy of empire. Polybius caught a glimpse of the problem but that was all. As we saw, he raised the question of judging the Roman achievement; and although he nowhere says that the interest of the subject peoples is to be part of the criterion in assessing Roman rule, on the other hand he does not say that he is merely concerned with the interest of Rome. And indeed, if it is only the interest of Rome that matters, why bother to consider the condition

---

[83] Plut. *Cato Mai.* 22; Cic. *Acad.* II.137, *De Or.* II.155, *Tusc.* IV.5, *Att.* XII.23; Gell. VI.14.8f., XVII.21.48; Pliny, *NH* VII.30.112.

[84] Lucilius I.31 Marx, 'non Carneades si ipsum … Orcus remittat'.

[85] Plut. *Cato Mai.* 22.	[86] Cic. *Rep.* III.6ff.

[87] Lact. *Div. Inst.* v.14f., especially 17 *ad fin.*

[88] Gell. VI.14.8–10 (quoting Polybius and Rutilius Rufus); *cf.* Macrob. I.5.

[89] Pliny, *NH* VII.30.	[90] Plut. *Cato Mai.* 22.5.

[91] Gell. VI.14.10.

of the conquered peoples at all? So Polybius did in fact come within measuring distance of formulating the problem; but he failed to do so because, when he did move beyond the somewhat cynical and objective position of the 60s and 50s, it was to identify himself closely with Roman policy in its most ruthless phase; consequently both Roman frightfulness and Roman *mansuetudo* are judged by Polybius solely in terms of Roman self-interest.

As Capelle showed many years ago,[92] Panaetius gave the Romans what they were looking for; and what immediately follows draws widely on his arguments. As a philosopher and especially as a Stoic Panaetius felt the need not merely to take account of the Roman world-empire, but also to explain it in moral terms. Both the *Index Stoicorum*[93] and Cicero in the *De Legibus*[94] inform us that Panaetius published a work on politics; and Cicero contrasts it with earlier Stoic writings on the subject as being designed *ad usum popularem et civilem*. It was probably this work which contained Panaetius' view on the Roman empire; and it is generally agreed that it was Panaetius' argument that Cicero attributed to C. Laelius in the *De Republica*,[95] as a reply to Carneades' views (for which L. Furius had served as mouthpiece), and that St Augustine discussed in the *De civitate Dei*.[96] Empire, he claims, is just and in accordance with nature because for certain sorts of men servitude is useful and to their own advantage, in as much as it deprives the wicked of the power to do wrong, and makes them better by subduing them. The rule of an imperial power over its conquered subjects is comparable to the rule of god over man, of the mind over the body, and of reason over passion: it follows what is virtually a universal law – *veluti a natura sumptum nobile exemplum*. Although he had raised the question of how the Roman empire was to be judged, Polybius had failed to lay down any other criterion than the self-interest of the imperial power; consequently he left the matter where Carneades left it. But Panaetius' answer ‖ rests, ostensibly, on justice, if we accept that definition of justice which is common to Plato and the Stoics,[97] viz. the assigning to each party of what is appropriate to it and in accordance with its deserts.

This theory, as Capelle showed, goes back in essentials to the doctrines of Plato and Aristotle on slavery.[98] Both these philosophers found a justification for slavery in the belief that some men are designed by nature to be slaves (φύσει δοῦλοι), while others are naturally fitted to be their masters. Stoicism had refused to recognise such distinctions as real; and therefore it represents a

---

[92] W. Capelle, *Klio* 25 (1932) 86–113.
[93] § 62.   [94] Cic. *Leg.* III.14.
[95] Cic. *Rep.* III.33–41, especially 36; *cf.* A. Schmekel, *Die Philosophie der mittleren Stoa* (Berlin, 1892) 55ff. For a dissenting view [which I now find convincing; *cf.* my *Polybius* (Berkeley–Los Angeles–London, 1972) 182] see Strasburger, *op. cit.* (n. 75) 45 n. 50.
[96] August. *De civ. D.* XIX.21.
[97] Plato, *Resp.* I.331f.; *SVF* 3, fr. 262; it is also known to Aristotle, *Eth. Nic.* V.5, 1130b 31, VI, 1131a24 (but he regards it as only one form of justice). *Cf.* Walbank (*op. cit.* n. 61), commenting on VI.6.11.
[98] For Plato slavery is not a problem: *cf. Resp.* V.469B–C; *Leg.* 766B, 778A. For a defence of the institution see Arist. *Pol.* I, especially 3–7.

modification of Stoic doctrine when Panaetius employs this Aristotelean ethic governing the relations between men as individuals as the basis of a theory justifying the domination of whole peoples by others. One need not necessarily accept Pohlenz's view[99] that Panaetius was acting as the mouthpiece of the Scipionic circle; but we may be sure that his views were welcome to the aristocratic Roman group in which he moved. His philosophical exposition coincided conveniently with the traditional pattern of caste distinctions and the mutual relations of patrons and clients which coloured so large an area of Roman thought and custom, and which, as Badian has shown,[100] had already made its impression upon one field of foreign policy, that in which the *amicitia* which bound several small powers to Rome was conceived as the relationship of clients towards their patrons.

There are such obvious flaws both in Panaetius' theory of empire and in the theory of slavery on which it was based that we experience some difficulty in regarding either as wholly sincere. But these should not blind us to the importance of his formulation. This gave the Roman aristocracy a justification of the Roman empire which satisfied their consciences and flattered their feelings of self-esteem, and it provided a doctrine which can be traced in later years. The precise relationship of Poseidonius' views to those of his teacher Panaetius is a well-known crux;[101] but Capelle seems to have established the fact that Poseidonius approved both Panaetius' general theory and its application to the Roman empire. In the first place he was able to support it with a concrete and relevant example of a people not only designed by nature to be subjected but – what is more unusual – itself aware of the fact.[102] For the Mariandyni, Poseidonius related in the eleventh book of his *Histories*, recognising their innate weakness of intellect (διὰ τὸ τῆς διανοίας ἀσθενές), delivered themselves up voluntarily into servitude to more intelligent men and became the serfs of the people of Heraclea Pontica, on condition that their needs should be satisfied and they should not be sold outside the territory of the city. What the Heracleotes were able to do peaceably, thanks to the co-operation of the inferior people, the Romans had done in many parts of the world more violently, but equally to the mutual advantage of both parties – as Poseidonius was able to show in the case of several Spanish peoples now profiting from the *pax Romana*.[103]

In support of this interpretation of Poseidonius' thought Capelle also quotes one of Seneca's letters (90) in which Poseidonius is specifically quoted for the view that in the golden age power was in the hands of *sapientes* who protected the weak and rendered it unnecessary to have those laws which were instituted

---

[99] Pohlenz, *op. cit.* (n. 4) cols. 437–8.
[100] *Foreign clientelae* (Oxford, 1958) 11f., 55ff.
[101] *Cf.* Seel, *Römisches Denken und römischer Staat* (Berlin, 1937) 96; see, however, Strasburger, *op. cit.* (n. 75) 44ff.
[102] Athen. VI.263c = *FGH* 87 F 8; *cf.* Capelle, *op. cit.* (n. 92) 99–100.
[103] *Cf.* Strabo III.2.6, C 144; 3.5, C 154; 3.8, C 156 (*cf.* 3.15, C 163); Capelle, *loc. cit.*

once corruption had set in and kingship had changed into tyranny. In this letter Seneca asserts that 'naturae ... est, potioribus deteriora submittere', and illustrates the point both from the world of nature where the tallest elephant leads the herd, and from the world of men where 'pro summo est optimum' and where early man entrusted himself to the best, *commissi melioris arbitrio.* There can, I think, be little doubt that Poseidonius is the source of all this and not only for the remark about the golden age.[104] It is true that there is a difference between the rule of the stronger and the rule of the better, but it is a difference which can be bridged by such an evolutionary || concept as we find in Polybius' account of political development in his sixth book.[105] There the primitive *monarchos* shifts the basis of his power from sheer might to moral pre-eminence and thereby becomes a *basileus*: and the reference in this letter of Seneca to the perversion of *regnum* into *tyrannis* shows that Poseidonius was dealing with a similar range of ideas.

Seel has argued, in criticism of Capelle's view, first that only the reference to the golden age in this letter of Seneca belongs to Poseidonius, and secondly that Poseidonius saw the identity of might and right, which lies behind Panaetius' theory of imperialism, as a characteristic only of the golden age.[106] Neither argument is, I think, cogent. I am not impressed by Seel's attempt to distinguish in Letter 90 Seneca's own views from those of Poseidonius. And the fact that Poseidonius saw this rule *potioribus deteriora submittere* exemplified in a particularly refined and Platonic form in the *saeculum aureum* need not exclude its existence in other forms at other times, for instance in the cases of the Spaniards and the Mariandyni.[106a] Seel is I think right when he argues that if pushed to its logical extreme Panaetius' theory could become an argument against the legitimacy of Roman predominance. For the Greeks, whose culture and humanity were at least equal to if not greater than that of the Romans, would by that token be justified in claiming independence from Roman subjection;[107] and if indeed, as Capelle argued, Panaetius saw the ultimate end of the imperial relationship as one in which the subject peoples were raised to the moral level of their rulers, then it had within it the seeds of its own destruction.

This is ultimately true, as modern experience has shown. For where imperialism has been interpreted in this Panaetian sense, it has undoubtedly assisted the movement of colonial peoples to independence. It was also ultimately true for Rome, for, as I hope to indicate below, the Panaetian theory of empire was to be a factor in the changing relationship between Rome and the provinces which is so striking a characteristic of the Principate. But this is

---

[104] *Cf.* T. Cole, *Historia* 13 (1964) 451, who, however, draws a distinction between Poseidonius' view and that of Polybius.

[105] VI.5.9–7.3.   [106] *Cf.* Seel, *op. cit.* (n. 101) 64ff.

[106a] Naturally it need not represent Poseidonius' total judgement on the role of Rome (see Strasburger, *op. cit.* (n. 75) 40ff.).

[107] So Seel, *op. cit.* (n. 101) 64ff.

not an argument against the view that Panaetius' theory was welcomed by the Romans, for it fulfilled an immediate need and gave the answer to an instant and pressing problem. In such circumstances it is not in human nature to work out the ultimate implications of what one is accepting; and it is only, it seems, by a pure paradox that Panaetius' theory can be regarded as a threat to the security of the empire in the second century B.C. It was certainly widely accepted. Livy[108] describes how the loyalty of the Roman allies in Italy in the face of war and devastation at the hands of Hannibal was to be explained 'because they were ruled by a just and moderate *imperium* and, what constitutes the one bond of loyalty (*fides*), they did not refuse to obey their betters (*melioribus parere*)'.

Panaetius' doctrine of imperialism as a beneficial symbiosis of victors and vanquished carried far-reaching implications. It helped the Romans gradually to assume the obligations that empire imposes. The Roman principles enunciated by Flamininus to the Aetolians and recorded with personal reservations as to their practicability by Polybius – namely that you treated your enemy mildly once he was beaten – could now be developed with all the support of a formal philosophical doctrine; and if this was slow to find practical application under the Republic, the setting up of the Principate brought its full expression as an imperial ideal, especially when the original notion of the mutual advantage of rulers and ruled was transmuted and vitalised by the specifically Roman notion of progressive Romanisation, leading step by step to a proportionately greater share in privilege.

When Petillius Cerialis harangues the Gauls in A.D. 70 after their revolt, these are the arguments Tacitus puts into his mouth:[109] 'All is common between us. You often command our legions. You govern these and other provinces. There is no privilege, no exclusion. ... Therefore love and cherish peace and the city in which we enjoy an equal right, conquered and conquerors alike.' This is a long way from the Mariandyni surrendering themselves as serfs to the Heracleotes, or even from the Gauls' own experience of Caesar's wars. But common both to Poseidonius' story and to Cerialis' imperial programme is the concept of a relationship of mutual advantage, such as could never have developed out of the unilateral view of empire, which Carneades expounded and Polybius found himself unable ‖ to transcend. From Panaetius, more directly, these ideas of empire and the moral duty of the ruler towards the ruled were passed down to Lactantius and Augustine and through them, as Capelle has observed, they exercised a by no means negligible influence on medieval thought; and, as I have suggested, it is perhaps not wholly naïve to detect them lurking behind the theory of trusteeship towards less developed peoples, which has helped to transform imperialism and has played a part in its eradication in many parts of Africa.

[108] Livy XXII.13.11; *cf.* Capelle, *op. cit.* (n. 92) 97.   [109] Tac. *Hist.* IV.74.

VIII

Our conclusion, then, is somewhat ironical. Polybius, the student of practical politics and the observer of what men think and do, interpreted the Roman empire as an expression of men's natural behaviour, self-seeking and utilitarian; he tried on that basis to extract some sort of lesson from the years after Pydna. His attempt to find a criterion for judgement which went beyond mere conquest and domination proved sterile, because he was increasingly tied to the point of view of the imperial power, and it is symbolic that his history should end, like Xenophon's, in years of ταραχὴ καὶ κίνησις. Panaetius, on the other hand, produced a picture of the imperial relationship which was manifestly a piece of special pleading and was being openly disproved before men's eyes as evidence of Roman misgovernment multipled and even the Senate was driven to set up a permanent *quaestio de repetundis*. Yet, because what men believe to be their motives may ultimately prove the decisive factor in shaping their conduct, the myth of Panaetius eventually became something like a blueprint for generations of trustworthy Roman civil servants, who lived laborious and strenuous lives in distant provinces, and whose achievements are preserved to posterity only by the chance survival of an inscription here and there. It was largely to them that the Roman empire owed its greatness; and pondering on what they did, one is made aware in a salutary way of the limitations of political realism.[110]

[110] A paper read at the Fourth International Congress of Classical Studies, Philadelphia, on 28 August 1964.

12

A NOTE ON THE EMBASSY OF Q. MARCIUS PHILIPPUS, 172 B.C.*

Fifty years separated the Declaration of Corinth in 196 and the destruction of Corinth in 146, two milestones in the history of Greco-Roman relations. Exactly midway between these two events comes the embassy of Q. Marcius Philippus, notorious for a piece of sharp practice which aroused the compunction of a section of the Roman Senate itself,[1] and as the prelude to a war regarded by many in Greece as the first step in a policy which was to end in the ruin of two of the greatest cities of the Mediterranean world.[2] The object of the following note is to examine in some detail the date and purpose of this embassy.

I

The first Roman forces to cross the Adriatic in the war with Perseus consisted of a detachment under Cn. Sicinius, the praetor for 172, which was marshalled at Brundisium, with orders to proceed at once to Epirus on the Ides of February, A.U.C. 583.[3] The annalistic details of the size of Sicinius' forces are suspect, but there is no reason to question this date, which corresponds to November 172 (Julian).[4] Now Sicinius' general instructions are described in Livy XLII.18.2, a passage which Nissen claims to be Polybian;[5] in XLII.27. 3–6 details of his forces are given after an annalist;[6] and in XLII.36.8–9 he is said to be in Epirus before the end of his year of office, with 5,000 infantry and 300 cavalry – this passage being also derived by Nissen from Polybius.[7]

[1] *Cf.* Livy (P) XLII.47.4–9; Diod. XXX.7.1.

[2] Polyb. XXXVI.9.7: νῦν δὲ προοίμιον μὲν ἐκτεθεῖσθαι τῆς ἰδίας προαιρέσεως τὰ κατὰ Περσέα, βαστάσαντας ἐκ ῥιζῶν τὴν Μακεδόνων βασιλείαν, τετελειωκέναι δὲ κατὰ τὸ παρὸν διὰ τῆς περὶ Καρχηδονίων διαλήψεως.

[3] Livy (A) XLII.27.5: 'Cn. Sicinius praetor ut exercitum paratum ad traiciendum haberet, C. Popilio consuli ex auctoritate senatus C. Licinius praetor scribit, ut et legionem secundam ... et ⟨ex⟩ sociis Latini nominis quattuor milia peditum, ducentos equites idibus Februariis Brundisi adesse iuberet.'

[4] Kahrstedt, *Klio* 11 (1911) 428; De Sanctis, *Storia dei Romani* 4.1 (Turin, 1923) 398.

[5] H. Nissen, *Kritische Untersuchungen über die Quellen der vierten und fünften Dekade des Livius* (Berlin, 1863) 246. According to his scheme, the Polybian section ends at the close of §5, and 18.6–28.13, is annalistic.

[6] I omit all consideration of such annalistic passages as 19.6 and 22.5–7, where entirely contradictory accounts of Sicinius' movements are given.

[7] *Op. cit.* (n. 5) 249. Nissen makes the preceding annalistic section end at 36.8 – *consulibus*. One may neglect W. Soltau's attribution of all ch. 36 to Polybius (*Livius' Geschichtswerk seine Komposition und seine Quellen* (Leipzig, 1897) 45).

Immediately upon the last indication come the words (Livy (P) XLII.37.1):
'Paucis post diebus Q. Marcius ⟨et⟩ A. Atilius et P. et Ser. Cornelii Lentuli
et L. Decimius, legati in Graeciam missi, Corcyram peditum mille secum
advexerunt.' Hence the ‖ orthodox view is that Marcius' embassy crossed over
to Corcyra shortly after Cn. Sicinius reached Apollonia, *i.e.* in November 172;
and since it returned to Rome after activity κατὰ χειμῶνα,⁸ or, according to
Livy, *principio hiemis*,⁹ that is perhaps in January,¹⁰ its stay in Greece will have
been a little over a month.

This view has long ago been challenged by Kahrstedt in an important
article, the general neglect of which is my excuse for briefly recapitulating his
arguments.¹¹ Fundamentally the problem turns on whether the account of
Marcius' departure in the Livian passage beginning 'paucis post diebus' can
be linked chronologically with the preceding description of Sicinius' arrival
in Apollonia, in short whether the latter detail is also of Polybian origin.
Kahrstedt points out that the Polybian narrative in Livy of the progress of
Marcius' embassy contradicts the idea that there were already any Roman
troops on the eastern shores of the Adriatic. Thus at the time of Marcius'
interview with Perseus on the Peneus in Thessaly,¹² which is subsequent to
the commissioners' visit to Epirus and Aetolia, and the holding of a conference
at Larisa,¹³ it is stated that the Romans had 'nihil satis paratum ad bellum,
non exercitum, non ducem'¹⁴ – which would be untrue if Sicinius were already
in Epirus with some 5,000 men. Further, it is expressly stated that without the
advantages of the armistice which Perseus was willing and indeed eager to
accept, the Romans might have been forestalled by his seizing 'omnia
opportuna loca ... ante ... quam exercitus in Graeciam traiceretur'.¹⁵
Finally, Marcius opens the interview near Tempe with a reference to complaints
from Perseus which had reached him in a letter upon his arrival at Corcyra:
this letter had enquired 'quid ita legati cum militibus venerimus et praesidia
in singulas urbes dimittamus'.¹⁶ The reference here is clearly to the 1,000 men
brought by the embassy, and afterwards divided up among the various envoys,

---

⁸ Polyb. XXVII.2.12: οὖτοι μὲν ταῦτα διαπράξαντες ἐν τοῖς Ἕλλησι κατὰ χειμῶνα. ... ἀπέπλεον
εἰς τὴν Ῥώμην.

⁹ Livy (P) XLII.44.8: 'Marcius et Atilius ... principio hiemis Romam redierunt.'

¹⁰ See De Sanctis, *op. cit.* (n. 4) 398, who thinks that the crossing of Sicinius and Marcius will
have been 'a un dipresso contemporaneo'.

¹¹ Kahrstedt, *Klio* 11 (1911) 415–30, 'Zum Ausbruch des 3ten makedonischen Krieges'. This
essay is ignored by De Sanctis and omitted from the bibliography to Benecke's chapter on Perseus
in *CAH* 8 (1930) 758–9. Kahrstedt's findings are accepted by Münzer, *RE* 2A.2 (1923) 'Cn.
Sicinius (8)', cols. 2197–8, and rejected by implication by Geyer, *RE* 19.1 (1937) 'Perseus',
col. 1011. All reference to Sicinius and his force is omitted in E. Pais–J. Bayet, *Histoire romaine*
(Paris, 1926). Owing to war conditions I have been unable to consult P. Heiland's Jena dissertation
(1913): *Untersuchungen zur Geschichte des Königs Perseus von Makedonien (179–68)*. [Heiland criticises
Kahrstedt on pp. 40–50 of this work.]

¹² Livy (P) XLII.38.8f.   ¹³ *Ibid.* 38.1–7.

¹⁴ *Ibid.* 43.3.   ¹⁵ *Ibid.* 47.2.

¹⁶ *Ibid.* 40.1: the difference in tense is perhaps significant; the garrisoning of the cities had not
yet taken place.

when they separated.[17] If Sicinius had already crossed with a small ‖ expeditionary force, it is strange that Perseus made no mention of it: hence there is a strong *argumentum ex silentio* that he had in fact not yet crossed.

In connection with this last point, Geyer[18] seizes upon the Polybian reference in Livy to the actual receipt of this letter by Marcius at Corcyra and, without considering the later discussion of its contents in Thessaly, attempts to link it up with Sicinius' force. In this earlier passage[19] the letter is said to enquire 'quae causa Romanis aut in Graeciam traiciendi copias aut urbes occupandi esset'. By implication Geyer suggests that this refers to the occupation of 'Dassaretiorum et Illyriorum castella'[20] by 2,000 of Sicinius' force. Marcius' words at the Peneus conference are enough to show that this is not the meaning, and that the cities to which Perseus refers are very clearly the cities of Greece, where there were strong pro-Macedonian factions,[21] against which he rightly suspects that these Roman soldiers were designed to operate.[22] But even without this confirmation, it cannot for a moment be supposed that the frontier fortresses of Illyria and Dassaretia would be designated *urbes*.

However, there is a further important piece of evidence in support of Kahrstedt's view, which he fails to use. Upon arriving at Corcyra the five *legati* separated, and while Marcius and A. Atilius visited Epirus, Aetolia and Thessaly, and L. Decimius Illyria, the two Lentuli were dispatched to Cephallenia, 'ut in Peloponnesum traicerent oramque maris in occidentem versi ante hiemem circumirent'.[23] Clearly *hiems* in this passage is a translation of the Polybian χειμών; and, as Holleaux has demonstrated,[24] χειμών to Polybius is a season beginning about the time of the autumn equinox. In passages depending on Polybius Livy frequently uses such expressions as *hiems instabat, appetebat*, to signify a period towards the autumn equinox;[25] hence it is likely that *ante hiemem* here means 'before the autumn equinox'. Examination of the context converts the probability into a certainty; for it is specifically a sea-voyage round the dangerous coasts of the Peloponnese that the Lentuli wish to complete *ante hiemem*. It is well known that the autumn equinox normally marked the ‖ conclusion of naval activity for the season[26]; and though voyages were made later (for instance, Sicinius' crossing in November), it was

---

[17] Livy (P) XLII.37.1.
[18] Geyer, *op. cit.* (n. 11) col. 1011.   [19] Livy (P) XLII.37.5.
[20] Livy XLII.36.9.
[21] On the divisions inside the Greek cities at this time, and the importance to Perseus of the pro-Macedonian parties see Niese, *Geschichte der griechischen und makedonischen Staaten* 3 (Gotha, 1903) 102f.
[22] *Cf.* the Roman reply (Livy (P) XLII.37.6): 'cui rescribi non placuit, nuntio ipsius, qui litteras attulerat, dici praesidii causa ipsarum urbium Romanos facere'.
[23] Livy (P) XLII.37.3.
[24] *REA* 25 (1923) 354; *BCH* 56 (1932) 533f.
[25] *E.g.* Livy (P) XXXII.4.7, XXXIII.41.9, XXXVI.45.8. Similarly, in Livy (P) XXXII.32.1, 'hiems iam eo tempore erat' refers to October; *cf.* Walbank, *Philip V of Macedon* (Cambridge, 1940) 320 n. 4.
[26] *Cf.* Livy (P) XXXI.47.1: 'Iam autumnale equinoctium instabat: ... itaque ante hiemales motus evadere inde [*sc.* from the Euboean channel] cupientes Piraeum ... repetunt'; De Sanctis, *op. cit.* (n. 4) 389; Holleaux, *BCH* 56 (1932) 533f.

understandable that the Lentuli should try to complete this part of their journey before the bad season.[27].

If we accept the implications of this passage, Marcius' embassy crossed to Corcyra not later than the middle of September 172; whereas Sicinius' force did not follow until almost two months later. This order of events does no violence to the account in Livy, provided Nissen's attribution of two short passages is rejected.[28] Livy XLII.18.1–5 and 36.8–9 must both be regarded as annalistic in origin; and the phrase 'paucis post diebus' (37.1) is then nothing more than a loose copula,[29] without chronological significance. This view has its advantages. Once the Romans had decided on war with Perseus, their first and most obvious step was to dispatch a propaganda mission to Greece, as they had done in preparation for their wars with Philip and Antiochus:[30] this would most naturally precede the sending of forces, as on both these occasions. Further if, as seems probable, Marcius and his colleagues returned to Rome in January or early February,[31] their mission lasted about four months, and not the one month that De Sanctis gives them: in view of the importance of their activities, the longer period seems in every way the more likely. In dispatching Sicinius and his force two months later, the Senate was following the precedent of 192, when M. Baebius Tamphilus had crossed over to Apollonia in October–November, in order to be ready for action the following spring, before the arrival of the consular forces;[32] and it is in accordance with this chronology ‖ that the first reference in a Polybian section of Livy to the forces of Sicinius is in XLII.47.10, which describes the sending of 2,000 of his men to help in the garrisoning of Larisa, at a time subsequent to Marcius' return to Rome, *i.e.* later than January–February 171.[33]

---

[27] *Cf.* Kahrstedt, *op. cit.* (n. 4) 424: '*Ante hiemem* war Marcius abgereist (Sept./Oktob., das ist nach polybianischer Rechnung schon κατὰ χειμῶνα), die Konferenz mit Perseus mag um den 1. November herum erfolgt sein, damals gab es noch kein Korps des Sicinius.' It is, I think, clear that Kahrstedt has not appreciated the full implications of *ante hiemem* in this passage: hence even he puts Marcius' embassy rather too late.

[28] See above, nn. 5–7. Kahrstedt, *op. cit.* (n. 4) 416, suggests that having already taken his account of Sicinius' movements from an annalist, Livy was obliged to ignore Polybius' record of the same events, when he mentioned them in their proper chronological place.

[29] This possibility is recognised by De Sanctis, *op. cit.* (n. 4) 398: 'Il *paucis post diebus* dunque di 37.1 o è una forma di transizione cronologica introdotta autoschediasticamente ed erroneamente da Livio per collegare due racconti di provenienza diversa i cui rapporti cronologici in realtà Livio non si è studiato di chiarire; ovvero. ...' It cannot, in any case, as De Sanctis clearly shows, refer to the hearing of Perseus' *legati* at Rome, described in the early part of ch. 36 from annalistic sources.

[30] On the embassy of 200 see Walbank, *op. cit.* (n. 25) 128–35, 313–17; on that of 192, *ibid.* 194f. In addition to the latter commission, Cato was sent in the autumn of 192 to Athens, Patrae, Aegium and Corinth (Plut. *Cat. Mai.* 12.4–5). In both years the *legati* were in Greece for some months before any troops crossed the straits.

[31] *Cf.* Kahrstedt, *op. cit.* (n. 4) 428; De Sanctis, *op. cit.* (n. 4) 398.

[32] The position in 200 was a little different. Then the main Roman force crossed over in September, owing to the delay the Senate had experienced in getting the war-vote through the Centuries.

[33] *Cf.* Kahrstedt, *op. cit.* (n. 4) 416.

II

The meeting between Marcius and Perseus, then, which preceded the crossing of Sicinius,[34] was in October 172. As its outcome Perseus was granted a truce[35] for a specified time,[36] to enable him to send envoys to Rome. In this way he was successfully immobilised throughout the winter months, in the vain hope of a peace which the Senate had never the slightest intention of granting. Though condemned by the older members of the Senate as 'nova et nimis callida sapientia', Marcius' efforts were duly sanctioned by the majority as having served the state well.[37] Clearly the Romans were under a disability, if Perseus cared to adopt a vigorous policy of action. It is the exact nature of this disability which I now propose to examine. This is necessary owing to the popular, and now almost orthodox, view that in taking the initiative in this war, and so logically in any war overseas, the Senate was at a disadvantage because of a purely arbitrary and traditional procedure in declaring war. 'The fact that the Senate was taking the initiative,' writes one of the most eminent historians of Rome,[38] 'by the nature of the situation placed the Romans in a position of inferiority during the necessarily considerable time between the presentation of the ultimatum and the vote of the Comitia. This inferiority could be remedied by a piece of sharp practice which would prevent Perseus taking advantage of it.' A few lines earlier he states that 'it was clear that Rome could only dispose of large armies when, after the presentation of the ‖ ultimatum to Perseus and his refusal to satisfy its demands, the vote had been carried by the Comitia'. Nissen,[39] similarly, suggests that the decision in the Comitia 'was perhaps formally taken only after the last negotiations with Perseus (ch. 48)', *i.e.* after an ultimatum had been presented to his envoys at Rome.[40]

---

[34] See preceding section.

[35] T. Frank, *CP* 5 (1910) 358–61, 'The diplomacy of Q. Marcius in 169 B.C.', rejects the whole story of this 'truce' (followed in this by Scullard, *History of the Roman world 753–146* (London, 1935) 292). He argues that a 'truce' six months before hostilities break out has no meaning. However, what Marcius did secure was a postponement of hostilities; and this Polybius terms ἀνοχαί and Livy *indutiae* (Polyb. xxvII.5.8; Livy (P) xLII.43.4). It is difficult to see what other words they could have used. Frank's arguments are rejected by Münzer, *RE* 14.2 (1930) 'Marcius Philippus (79)', col. 1577, and by Otto, *ABAW* 11 (1934) 'Zur Geschichte der Zeit des 6. Ptolemäers', 64 n. 1.

[36] Livy (P) xLII.47.10: 'A. quoque Atilium miserunt ad occupandam Larisam in Thessalia timentes ne, *si indutiarum dies exisset,* ⟨Perseus⟩ praesidio eo misso caput Thessaliae in potestate haberet.' This takes place after the approval of Marcius' proceedings, but just before the hearing of the Macedonian envoys (ch. 48 (P)): hence it follows that the truce was near its expiry when this interview took place. T. Frank, *op. cit.* (n. 35) 359, has no grounds for describing the *indutiae* as 'a month's truce': its length is in fact unknown.

[37] Livy (P) xLII.47.9.   [38] De Sanctis, *op. cit.* (n. 4) 275.

[39] Nissen, *op. cit.* (n. 5) 254.

[40] Apparently this is also the view of Benecke, *CAH* 8.261, who, after describing Marcius' return to Rome and, by implication, the dismissal of Perseus' envoys, begins a new paragraph with the words, 'Rome had at last decided to declare war': the actual war-motion is unfortunately not mentioned, nor is it clear where or when Benecke imagines the *rerum repetitio* or *indictio belli* to have been presented.

Now if it were in fact true that at this period the Senate was hampered by an antiquated fetial law which required a *rerum repetitio* to be presented to a potential enemy and rejected by him before the Centuries were allowed to give the sanction of the Roman people to the war-motion, then the Romans were indeed an exceptionally unadaptable race, little deserving the well-worn claim to be so ready to learn from their enemies.[41] But, in fact, as I have shown elsewhere,[42] fetial procedure had by this time been considerably modified. Since before the time of the Second Punic War it had been customary for Senate and people to sanction a war *conditionally*, so that rejection of the *rerum repetitio* – now in effect the *indictio belli* – implied the immediate commencement of the war. This was indeed no unique change, but part and parcel of a gradual readjustment of fetial practice to meet changing conditions: it was a sequel to the earlier transfer of the duties of the *fetiales* in delivering the *rerum repetitio* to senatorial *legati*,[43] and like that step results in a considerable increase in the Senate's power. Under the original procedure, which placed both the *senatus consultum* and the popular vote subsequent to the presentation and rejection of the *rerum repetitio*,[44] the Centuries were in a position to estimate the exact situation in which they were being asked to approve the war. Now, by their conditional vote, they gave the Senate *carte blanche* to pass judgement upon the adequacy or inadequacy of any reply that might be given to the Roman demands.[45] Furthermore, the phrasing of the decisions taken by the Comitia before the Hannibalic and Second Macedonian Wars, as recorded ‖ in Livy,[46] suggests that the time-honoured formula in which the vote was expressed remained unchanged, even after its effect had become conditional. The result of this was twofold: first, there was a standing temptation for the Senate to slur over the proper procedure either by dispensing with the *rerum repetitio* altogether or at least by making some doubtful substitute serve instead;[47] secondly, it is questionable whether it was always made clear to the voters that they were voting for war conditionally and not absolutely. The annalistic

[41] For this τόπος see the examples quoted by Gelzer, *Hermes* 68 (1933) 139 n. 2.

[42] *Cf.* McDonald and Walbank, *JRS* 27 (1937) 192ff.

[43] On this see McDonald and Walbank, *ibid.* 192–3, and A. Heuss, *Die völkerrechtlichen Grundlagen der römischen Aussenpolitik in republikanischer Zeit* (*Klio*, Beiheft 31, 1933) 22, who, however, has no grounds for assuming that sacral law forbade the *fetiales* to leave Italian soil; Livy (A) xxx.43.9, which he quotes in evidence, states in fact the contrary: 'fetiales cum in Africam ad foedus feriundum ire iuberentur ...'.

[44] *Cf.* Livy 1.32.5, vii.6.7, 32.1, x.45.7: Dion. Hal. *Ant. Rom.* ii.72.6: L. Lange, *Röm. Altertümer* i³ (Berlin, 1862–74) 322f.

[45] This appears clearly in the preliminaries to the Syrian War, Livy (A) xxxvi.1.5: 'si ea rogatio perlata esset, tum si ita videretur consulibus, rem integram ad senatum referrent.' Any subsequent *rerum repetitio* would thus be a matter falling wholly within the Senate's competence.

[46] Livy (A) xxi.17.4: 'latum inde ad populum, vellent iuberent populo Carthaginiensi bellum indici.' Livy (A) xxxi.6.1: '(P. Sulpicius) ... rogationem promulgavit, vellent iuberent Philippo regi Macedonibusque qui sub regno eius essent ob iniurias armaque illata sociis populi Romani bellum indici'; *cf.* 8.1: 'bellum iusserant'.

[47] If, as seems probable, the reply to Perseus' envoys at Rome (Livy (A) xlii.36.1f.) was the *rerum repetitio* and *indictio belli* before the Third Macedonian War (see below, n. 56), it is very doubtful if it conforms to the usual procedure.

account in Livy of events leading up to Rome's major wars in the East is invariably marked by tendencious and inaccurate details of imaginary injuries done to Rome and her allies, insults to embassies which probably never left Italy and claims for restitution which were never submitted.[48] These details are part of a widespread propaganda of Roman justification which in many cases goes back to a contemporary source: an interesting example of this propaganda in the making is furnished by the events of 200, when the war with Philip was being prepared.[49] Thus there seems at least a strong probability that the Senate, faced with the need of securing a ready authorisation of war from the people, may have deliberately manufactured the kind of details which Livy so often gives as the prelude to a war-motion, in order to mislead the voters on the real issue. For it still remained true that a major war could not be declared until it had been authorised by the people.[50] ‖

However, the interesting feature of the preliminaries to the outbreak of war with Perseus is that now, for the first time, in describing the vote of the Comitia

[48] *E.g.* Livy (A) xxxi.3.4–6, 7.2–15, 42.1–10; and the war-motion quoted in n. 46 above (Second Macedonian War); xlii.25.1f. (war with Perseus). The loose claim in the last-mentioned passage that a *rerum repetitio* was delivered to Perseus before the resolution of the Senate and the vote of the Centuries is paralleled by the similar reference (Livy (A) xxxvi.3.10) to the reply of the *fetiales* to the question whether war should be declared on the Aetolians separately: 'amicitiam renuntiatam videri, cum legatis totiens repetentibus res nec reddi nec satisfieri aequum censuissent.'

[49] *Cf.* Livy (A) xxxi.7.2–15, giving the speech of C. Sulpicius: the stress on the threat of an invasion was clearly a propaganda move.

[50] *Cf.* Sallust, *Cat.* 29.3: 'aliter [*i.e.* without the *SCU*] sine populi iussu nullius earum rerum consuli ius est.' For the second century this point is well illustrated by the outcry raised by the political enemies of Cn. Manlius Vulso in 187, to prevent his being given a triumph over the Galatians (Livy (A) xxxviii.44.9f). Manlius had carried out this campaign without authorisation from Rome and is therefore accused of pursuing a 'privatum latrocinium' (45.7) a war 'nullo gentium iure' (45.11), of wanting 'tolli fetialia iura' and reducing the *fetiales* to a cypher (46.12). His enemies ask: 'num senatum quoque de bello consuli non placet? non ad populum ferri, velint iubeantne cum Gallis bellum geri?' And in a passage which is discussed below (n. 61) they contrast the proper procedure and stigmatise Manlius' conduct as 'iactura religionis' and 'deorum oblivio' (46.12). Allowing for the acrimony of political controversy, the discussion makes it quite clear that Manlius' conduct was unprecedented. Not so, however, the situation in which he had taken this step. In fact Flamininus had faced a similar dilemma in winter 196, when he was within an ace of waging on his own initiative what, according to Livy, he termed a just and pious war against the Boeotians (Livy (P) xxxiii.29.1f.). Sooner or later it was inevitable that a situation would arise requiring decisive action on the part of a consul or proconsul without reference to the distant Senate and people; and eventually the Senate had to acquiesce, contenting itself with characterising as *bellum iniustum* such action as it could not subsequently approve (*e.g.* Livy (A) xliii.4.13: compensation of the Abderites in 170 for their ill-treatment at the hands of Hostilius). In 81 Sulla tried to revert to the old position by making it treasonable for a provincial governor to leave his province, march his army beyond its frontiers or start a war on his own initiative, without the authorisation of Senate and people (Cic. *Pis.* 21.50); his failure is apparent from the career of Caesar. On this question see further Heuss, *op. cit.* (n. 43) 22f., who, however, in consequence of his legalistic approach, does not trace the historical situation in which the problem arose, the Senate's attitude of drift towards it, and the important distinction between a major war undertaken *ab initio*, and minor operations carried out by a general already operating on a distant front, which might by a stretch of procedure be regarded as a tail-piece to a war already declared. I have dwelt on this point, as it affords another example of the decay of the rigid *ius fetiale* in second-century conditions – this time to the advantage of the individual commander rather than that of the Senate as a whole.

Livy's annalistic source explicitly refers to its conditional nature. Immediately upon entering office on the Ides of March 171 (*i.e.* probably December 172 (Julian))[51] the new consuls were instructed by the Senate to bring before the people a motion that since Perseus, son of Philip, king of the Macedonians, had committed various specified offences, 'nisi de eis rebus satisfecisset, bellum cum eo iniretur'.[52] This measure went before the people and was carried;[53] and the provinces, including Macedonia, were then allotted, and it was laid down that whichever consul obtained Macedonia by lot was to carry on the war against Perseus and his allies, 'nisi populo Romano satisfecissent'.[54] Now it is clear both from Livy's account and from previous precedents[55] that this war-measure was amongst the earliest business of the new consular year, and so was passed in December 172 (Julian). Yet the final interview with Perseus' *legati*, sent in accordance with the agreement made on the Peneus, did not take place according to the annalists until after the Kalends of June (*c.* March 171 (Julian));[56] and in spite of some ‖ confusion and repetition, Livy's account affords no justification for removing the war-vote from its place in ch. 30, and placing it after the interview with the Macedonian *legati* in ch. 36.[57]

[51] Above, n. 4.   [52] Livy (A) XLII.30.10–11.

[53] Though not specifically mentioned, the passing of the war-motion follows logically from the narrative, and is never in question (*cf.* Kahrstedt, *op. cit.* (n. 4) 421 n. 1).

[54] Livy (A) XLII.31.1.

[55] *E.g.* the war-motion against Philip in 201/0 (Livy (A) XXXI.6.3) or that against Carthage in 218 (Livy (A) XXI.17.1–4).

[56] Above, n. 47. The interview with Perseus' *legati* is described twice in Livy, once in 36.1f., after an annalist (*cf.* Nissen, *op. cit.* (n. 5) 249; *contra*, Soltau, *op. cit.* (n. 7) 45, who makes it Polybian, see Kahrstedt, *op. cit.* (n. 4) 422), and again after Polybius (48.1f.; see Nissen, *op. cit.* (n. 5) 252). The first version is subsequent to the holding of the Latin Games 'Kalendis Iuniis, quo maturius in provincias magistratus proficiscerentur' (35.3), a date which is to be equated with March 171, and there is no reason to question this order of events. It may be observed that this doublet is rejected by Geyer, *op. cit.* (n. 11) col. 1007, who treats 36.1 and 48.1 as referring to quite separate embassies, and apparently by Benecke, *CAH* 8.260, though his account is far from clear (Marcius 'advised the king to send a further embassy to Rome (*i.e.* at the Peneus interview), though his last envoys had received no answer'). The issue is slightly complicated by the fact that there is some evidence for an embassy sent by Perseus to Rome between that of Harpalus (Livy (P) XLII.14.2; App. *Mac.* 11.3; Diod. XIX.34) and the one to which the ultimatum was presented; thus Appian, *Mac.* 11.3, records: ὁ δ' αὖθις ἔπεμπεν ἑτέρους, and Livy (P) XLII.40.9, giving Marcius' speech in Thessaly, has a reference to this embassy in his words: 'certum habeo et scripta tibi omnia ab Roma esse et legatos renuntiasse tuos', which refer to events subsequent to the departure from Rome of Harpalus (*cf.* Nissen, *op. cit.* (n. 5) 250, who is preferable on this point to Kahrstedt, *op. cit.* (n. 4) 430). But this does not involve the identification of this embassy with that in Livy (A) XLII.36.

[57] As Nissen implies; see above, *op. cit.* (n. 4) nn. 39 and 40. *Cf.* also De Sanctis, *op. cit.* (n. 4) 280 n. 116: 'Qui sembra che vada inserito Liv. XLII.30.10.' There is in fact a slight inconsistency in De Sanctis on this point, since elsewhere he appears to regard the meeting between Perseus and Marcius on the Peneus as the real ultimatum; see above, n. 38, and *cf. Enciclopedia italiana* 26 (1935) *s.v.* 'Perseo', 803: 'L'ultimatum romano fu presentato al re da Marcio Filippo che, tuttavia, non essendo ancora votata la guerra dai comizî nè iniziati i preparativi militari, concesse a P. una tregua per trattative ulteriori e così gli legò le mani nel momento in cui un'ardita offensiva in Grecia poteva essere promettente di successo.' On this subject no help is to be expected from Polybius, who was not awake to the significance of the fetial procedure (*cf.* Gelzer, *Hermes* 68 (1933) 165). He records (XXVII.6.3) how the Senate dismissed Perseus' envoys προδιειληφότες ὑπὲρ τοῦ πολεμεῖν. But from Polybius' use of προδιαλαμβάνω (*e.g.* V.29.4, IX.31.2, XI.1.3) it is clear that

The conditional nature of the war-motion passed in December 172, which is so clearly indicated by Livy, is recognised by Kahrstedt alone;[58] and he erroneously regards it as something exceptional. The decision, he argues, had to be conditional because it was necessary to take official cognisance of the still unknown results of Marcius' embassy and his interview with Perseus. This interview Kahrstedt treats as a *rerum repetitio*,[59] ignoring the fact that without a *senatus consultum* and popular authorisation a *legatus* would not at this time have been empowered to present a *rerum repetitio*.[60] The point is that at this period the *rerum repetitio* was something presented subsequent to the passing of the ‖ war-vote by the Centuries.[61] There was no gap such as De Sanctis and

it means nothing more than 'come to a previous decision' and has no technical relevance to the procedure of the war-motion. Appian, *Mac.* 11.5, writes: οἱ δὲ [*sc.* the Senate] οὐδὲν αὐτοῖς ἀποκρινάμενοι, τὸν πόλεμον ἐς τὸ φανερὸν ἐκύρουν. This last phrase (which Schweighaeuser translates 'sed protinus bellum publice decretum') should mean 'the Senate openly *ratified* the war'; and it is noteworthy that in Polybius (*e.g.* 1.11.3, 17.1) κυρόω is usually used of the δῆμος and seems to be the equivalent of *iubeo*. But at this period the only way in which the Senate could ratify a war was by giving effect by means of the *indictio belli* to the people's conditional declaration of war. Hence, if Appian is to be pressed, what he means is 'the Senate openly *proclaimed* that they were at war (*i.e.* to the envoys and the world at large)'. Thus, in so far as fetial procedure was being observed, this passage confirms the view that this interview with Perseus' envoys was regarded in the subsequent tradition as the combined *rerum repetitio* and *indictio belli*.

[58] *Op. cit.* (n. 4) 425.

[59] So too, apparently, De Sanctis: above, n. 57.

[60] I ignore in this connection the account of Livy (A) XLII.25.1ff., which describes an embassy sent to Perseus early in 172 'ad res repetendas … renuntiandamque amicitiam', since it is generally recognised to be a part of the Roman propaganda of justification, and a thoroughly unreliable record; *cf.* Nissen, *op. cit.* (n. 5) 246–7; Heuss, *op. cit.* (n. 43) 50–1. (Pais-Bayet, *op. cit.* (n. 11) 1.556, however, still accepts its authenticity.) On the peculiar case of the ultimatum delivered to Nicanor in 200 (which had at any rate the sanction of a *senatus consultum*) and the difficulties felt later on in connection with it, see McDonald and Walbank, *JRS* 27 (1937) 194–5; Walbank, *op. cit.* (n. 25) 131.

[61] It is unfortunate that in Livy (A) XXXVIII.45.4–5, a passage contrasting the correct procedure adopted in the preliminaries to the wars with Antiochus, Philip and Hannibal with the lack of all formalities in Manlius' attack on the Galatians (above, n. 50), the reading is uncertain. The MS has: 'de omnibus his consultum senatum populum fuisse saepe legatos ante res repetitas postremo qui bellum indicerent missos'; and if the usual emendation ('… populum iussisse, saepe legatos ante missos, res …') be accepted, this gives the four constituents of a correct war-declaration in the order proper to this period, viz. *senatus consultum, populi iussum, rerum repetitio, indictio belli*. Madvig, followed by Weissenborn-Müller (Teubner, ed. 1900) reads: '… iussisse, per legatos ante res repetitas, postremo…', thus referring the *rerum repetitio* to an earlier period; and though the third edition of Weissenborn-Müller's commentary (1909) reverts to the earlier reading, it refers the *ante* to both *legatos … missos* and *res repetitas*. This reading is preferable to Madvig's; but Weissenborn-Müller's interpretation of it *ought* not to be right: *ante* should refer only to the sending of *legati* (a common theme among annalistic exaggerations: above, n. 48), and not to the *rerum repetitio* as well. Unfortunately it cannot be considered certain that Livy necessarily recorded the correct historical situation (for his frequent references to *rerum repetitiones* preceding senatorial and popular decisions prove that he was not personally clear on the exact fetial position during the second century); and moreover the *fifth* item ('saepe legatos ante missos') comes in awkwardly. It is not impossible that the original source of this passage had the four constituents in their correct order, but that some intermediate annalist or even Livy himself sought to 'rectify' and improve the account with references to *legati anti missi*. There is in fact no reason why the four stages of the war-declaration should not have been mentioned in their due chronological order; and I am personally inclined to go behind the present doubtful reading to the *order* which Livy gives, and to treat that as evidence.

Nissen assume between this ceremony and the people's final decision: the precedent of the conditional war-vote had eliminated (as it was intended to eliminate) this gap effectively.

III

Thus the need for a truce with Perseus sprang from something much simpler and more fundamental than a flaw in the fetial procedure: it arose out of the geographical relationship between Rome and Macedon and the exigencies of a calendar governing the entry into office of annual magistrates. The Roman consular year at this time began on the Ides of March, roughly in November–December (Julian); and it was the Senate's well-established practice to have new wars declared immediately upon the entry of new consuls into office, so that the latter might take the responsibility for the campaigns *ab initio*, and enrol their troops before the spring campaigning season.[62] But when the war was to be in the Balkan peninsula, these winter months gave any opponent already established there a chance to steal a march on the Romans; and because the sea was not used for major transport during the real winter months, any counter-measures had to be taken the previous autumn.‖

Gradually, under pressure of circumstances, the Senate developed a technique to meet this difficulty: it comprised the appointment of a preliminary *legatio* and the dispatch of a holding force the previous autumn. In the war with Philip the normal course of events had been interrupted by the Senate's failure to obtain popular sanction for the war; and the senatorial *legati* who were preparing the ground in Greece in 200 were caught in an awkward dilemma. But Philip let the chance slip, and before the summer was over a consular army was in Illyria.[63] In 192 Antiochus, whose position relative to Greece was geographically similar to that of the Romans, took the initiative by crossing over in the autumn, thus winning the winter for intensive work among the Greek states. But the Senate was quick to follow suit, and within a week or two had dispatched Baebius to Epirus to watch the situation until the consul and his army could follow in the spring. Moreover, several diplomats including Flamininus had already been active throughout the summer of 192.[64]

It is these same two instruments of policy which appear in the account of the events leading up to the war with Perseus. The Senate's decision to make war had been taken early in the second half of the consular year 172, following

[62] On the close connection between the change in the year and the war-declaration see Kahrstedt, *Die Annalistik von Livius, B.* xxxi–xlv (Berlin, 1913) 21 n. 1. The relation of the consular year to the campaign is brought out clearly by the events of 153, when, in order that the consul Q. Fulvius Nobilior might proceed without delay to Spain, the day of entry into office was brought forward to 1 January; *cf.* Münzer, *RE* 7.1 (1910) 'Fulvius (95)', col. 268.

[63] For a full treatment of the problems of this embassy see Walbank, *op. cit.* (n. 25) 313–17.

[64] *Ibid.* 198f. Baebius made no move during the winter, but was able to come to an important agreement with Philip, and open the campaign in 191 some time before the consular army crossed over from Italy.

Eumenes' visit to Rome and the 'evidence' against Perseus brought back from Greece by C. Valerius.[65] As we saw,[66] a senatorial *legatio* left Italy towards the end of September to approach in particular those states which were most likely to contain elements sympathetic to Macedon – Epirus, Thessaly, Boeotia, Euboea and Aetolia.[67] The expeditionary force was prepared and sent out as soon as possible under Cn. Sicinius: that it did not sail until the middle of November – well after the good season – is a comment on the backwardness of Roman preparations.[68] Sicinius' force was not, however, equal to an offensive against the powerful resources of ‖ Perseus; and had Perseus possessed his father's spirit, there might have been a real danger of a Macedonian offensive.[69] As it was, he hoped in vain to secure peace and sacrificed his advantage to Marcius' new diplomacy. The envoys spent a busy winter in Boeotia; and when the new campaigning season arrived, Perseus found himself isolated and deceived, and face to face with the conflict he had ruined his chances to avoid.

Thus Marcius' 'truce' was designed specifically to prevent a repetition of the situation of 192/1. And notwithstanding the opposition which it is said to have encountered among the more old-fashioned of the senators,[70] the majority in that body, loyal to that policy of realistic self-interest which was the mainspring of Roman action throughout the whole of this century, not merely approved of Marcius' Machiavellism, but extracted the last ounce of profit from his manoeuvre by postponing the hearing of Perseus' envoys until the latest possible date. As we saw above,[71] Livy places his annalistic account of the audience to this embassy[72] after the holding of the Latin Games on the

---

[65] *Cf.* Livy (P) XLII.15.1–2: 'nondum quidem parantis bellum … Romanos, sed ita infestos, ut facile appareret non dilaturos'; 18.2 (probably annalistic; see above, n. 28): 'belli administratio ad novos consules reiecta est.'

[66] Above, pp. 183ff.

[67] On the significance of the choice of these states, all previous possessions or close allies of Macedon, with the exception of Aetolia, which had moved towards her after the Syrian War (*cf.* Walbank, *op. cit.* (n. 25) 219–20), see W. Theiler, *Die politische Lage in den beiden makedonischen Kriegen* (Diss. Halle, 1914) 67. It should, however, be noted that the Lentuli visited the Peloponnese, though Livy does not give the details of their mission.

[68] This was mainly due to the fact that the Roman decision was prompted by two *external* considerations, Eumenes' visit and allegations, and the convenient isolation of Perseus (*cf.* De Sanctis, *op. cit.* (n. 4) 273). In addition there was the slight disadvantage that the years 173–170 were marked by quite acute factional struggles inside the ruling oligarchy, which had resulted in the election of a series of plebeians to the consulship; *cf.* Livy (A) XLII.10.11ff.: 'patres … utrique pariter consuli infensi'; 18.2 (quoted above, n. 65); see on these struggles F. Münzer, *Römische Adelsparteien und Adelsfamilien* (Stuttgart, 1920) 219f.

[69] Sicinius had 5,000 infantry and 300 cavalry, and of these 2,000 were employed garrisoning the forts of Dassaretia and Illyria in the districts marching with Macedon (Livy (A) XLII.36.8–9). As these fortresses were occupied peacefully, the problem of a winter campaign in these difficult districts, such as had confronted L. Apustius in 200 (Livy (P) XXXI.27.1–8) did not arise. On the wide support for Perseus in Greece at this time, there is the evidence of Cato (Gell. *NA* VI.3.16). See also above, n. 21.

[70] Above, n. 1. But the majority supported Marcius: 'vicit tamen ea pars senatus, cui potior utilis quam honesti cura erat'.   [71] Above, n. 56.

[72] Livy (A) XLII.36.1f.; the Polybian account (Livy XLII.48.1f.) is subsequent to the return of Marcius to Rome, his despatch to Greece once more, and various provisions for the affairs of

Kalends of June, which at this time corresponded to the Julian March. Kahrstedt[73] assumes that this delay was the fault of Perseus who, through indecision or the desire to have Marcius present in Rome when his *legati* were heard, postponed sending them till now. But as the truce was for a definite period,[74] Perseus could not possibly have afforded this delay, which was in any case so clearly in the Senate's interest that it seems natural to assume the responsibility of the latter.[75] For some four months the Macedonians were left to cool their heels on the threshold of the Curia, and by the time they brought the Senate's uncompromising answer back to Pella, it was almost April. A Roman army was on its way to Illyria.[76] The war could begin.

Thessaly, etc.: it is followed immediately by the preparations of the commanders for 171 to leave the city.

[73] *Klio* 11 (1911) 430.   [74] Above, n. 36.

[75] An interesting parallel is provided by the interview given to the Aetolians in 191 (Livy (P) XXXVI.35.5–6.). In this case too the envoys came under a truce, and it was also in the interest of Rome to immobilise the enemy for as long as possible: consequently the envoys do not appear to have been granted a hearing until after the expiry of the truce (*cf.* Walbank, *op. cit.* (n. 25) 212 n. 6). They were then given a sharp interview and told to leave Italy within fifteen days. The difference lies in the fact that the Aetolians were already at war with Rome.

[76] Livy (P) XLII.49.10.

13

VIA ILLA NOSTRA MILITARIS:
SOME THOUGHTS ON THE VIA EGNATIA*

I

The Via Egnatia was one of the most dramatic of Rome's provincial roads. It was also the first to be built east of the Adriatic and it played a fundamental role in the development of Roman expansion in Macedonia and Thrace during the half-century which followed the abolition of the Macedonian monarchy in 168 and the establishment of a Roman province in Macedonia after Andriscus' defeat in 148. For a long time both the date of its construction and its original scope and purpose have been the subject of controversy. Fortunately there is now new evidence concerning its western section in the shape of an inscribed milestone from Macedonia;[1] and in addition a passage from Book VII of Strabo, properly interpreted, confirms the statement made elsewhere in that book concerning the original eastern end of the road, thus throwing light on the location of the provincial frontier.[2] I hope therefore that as a tribute to his many contributions in the fields of both Greek and Roman history Professor Bengtson will find something of interest in the following pages dealing with an area that lies on the fringe of both worlds.

After Caecilius Metellus defeated and captured Andriscus and Macedonia became a province,[3] the Romans very soon realised that they had inherited from earlier governments operating in that area a never-ending struggle against the tribes of Thrace.[4] Fighting the barbarians who lived to the east and north of Macedonia had been a constant preoccupation of all the Antigonids. To pass over his predecessors, Philip V had particular trouble with the Maedi, who inhabited the middle reaches of the Strymon. In 211 he had seized their main town, Iamphorynna,[5] but only four years later they were back again threatening Macedonia.[6] Towards the end of his reign, in 181, he had once again taken the offensive, invaded Maedica and marched his troops ‖

* ⟦*Althistorische Studien: Hermann Bengtson zum 70. Geburtstag dargebracht*
(Wiesbaden, 1983) 131–47⟧

[1] *Cf.* C. Romiopoulou, 'Un nouveau milliaire de la via Egnatia', *BCH* 98 (1974) 813–16; *cf.* P. Collart, 'Les milliaires de la via Egnatia', *ibid.* 100 (1976) 181–3, 187, 197 no. 1.
[2] Strabo VII. fr. 57 (56 Loeb); *cf.* VII.7.4, C 322.
[3] This may not have taken place before the arrival of L. Mummius in 146; see M. G. Morgan, 'Q. Metellus Macedonicus and the province Macedonia', *Historia* 18 (1969) 422–46.
[4] *Cf.* A. H. M. Jones, *The cities of the eastern Roman provinces*[2] (Oxford, 1971) 8ff.
[5] Livy XXVI.25.8, 25.15; *cf.* Polyb. IX.44; F. W. Walbank, *Philip V of Macedon* (Cambridge, 1940) 86.
[6] Polyb. X.41.4; Livy XXVIII.5.7.

to the top of Mt Haemus[7] in the vain belief that from there it was possible to catch a glimpse of the Danube and the seas surrounding the Balkan peninsula. Such a vast panorama would indeed have been a conspicuous aid to his plans for expansion,[8] but as so often happens on mountain tops, all he saw there was mist. The Maedi were implacable enemies of Macedonia and in 172 the Romans welcomed their alliance against Perseus.[9] In the subsequent arrangements for the kingdom they were therefore left outside Macedonia Prima and were later excluded from the Roman province. But old habits died hard and they soon transferred their hostility and raids to the Romans.[10]

The Maedi were not the only Thracian tribe to worry Rome. In the war of 150–148 the pretender Andriscus received assistance from the Thracian chieftains Teres and Barsabas and at one time found a temporary refuge in Thrace.[11] Moreover the Thracians were enemies of the friendly state of Pergamum. In 145 Attalus II overthrew Diegylis, the king of the Caeni, who in alliance with Prusias of Bithynia was harassing such Greek cities of the Chersonese as Lysimacheia.[12] But from 146 onwards Thracian attacks became the special concern of the Roman governors of Macedonia and their responsibilities grew greater after Attalus III's death in 134 or 133[13] and the bequest of his kingdom to Rome. M. Cosconius, the governor of Macedonia from 135 to 134,[14] is known to have fought successfully against the troublesome Scordisci in central Thrace. It has also been supposed[15] that he was involved in suppressing the troubles in the Chersonese described in a long honorific inscription from Sestus,[16] which mentions Thracian attacks on the town 'after the kings had turned into gods', that is, after ‖ Attalus III's death. But the hypothesis that these attacks link with the atrocities committed by Diegylis' son Zibelmius, which are recorded by Diodorus and Valerius Maximus,[17] and

---

[7] Livy XL.21.1–2, 22.1; cf. Polyb. XXIV.4 = Strabo VII.5.1, C 313. Here 'Haemus' is probably Mt Vitosha, the mountain overlooking Sofia; see Walbank, *op. cit.* (n. 5) 249–50 (giving other identifications).

[8] On these see Walbank, *op. cit.* (n. 5) 236ff.   [9] Livy XLII.19.6.

[10] On the boundaries of Macedonia Prima see Livy XLV.29.5–6; Diod. XXXI.8.8. *Cf.* F. Papazoglou, 'Le nom antique de Sveti-Vrač (Sandanski)', *BCH* 87 (1963) 535–44, for the exclusion of Maedica.

[11] Diod. XXXII.15.6–7 (Teres and Barsabas); Zon. IX.28.7; Vell. Pat. I.13.11; Eutrop. IV.13; Livy, *Epit.* 50; Florus I.30.5; Ampel. 16.5; Porphyry, *FGH* 260F3 (§19).

[12] App. *Mith.* 6; Diod. XXXIII.14–15; Strabo XIII.4.2, C 624; for the date see *OGIS* 330. The Pergamene forces were probably commanded by Strato, the general of the Chersonese and Thrace; *cf.* H. Bengtson, *Die Strategie in der hellenistischen Zeit* 2² (Munich, 1964) 228, referring to *OGIS* 339, ll. 13–14. On the Attalid province of the Chersonese see M. Holleaux, *Études d'épigraphie et d'histoire grecques* 2 (Paris, 1938) 86–7.

[13] In favour of 134 see A. N. Sherwin-White, 'Roman involvement in Anatolia, 167–88 B.C.', *JRS* 67 (1977) 68 n. 40.

[14] On M. Cosconius see Livy, *Epit.* 56 (Scordisci); *IGR* 4.134, ll. 1 and 9–11, 4.1537; Th. Ch. Sarikakis, Ῥωμαῖοι ἄρχοντες τῆς ἐπαρχίας Μακεδονίας (Thessalonica, 1971) 44–5; D. Magie, *Roman rule in Asia Minor* 2 (Princeton, 1950) 1038 n. 13.

[15] See for example F. Münzer, *RE* 4.2 (1901) 'Cosconius (8)', col. 1669, following C. Cichorius.

[16] *OGIS* 339 l. 16.   [17] Diod. XXXIV/XXXV.12; Val. Max. IX.2 ext. 4.

that Cosconius was involved in their suppression, is unlikely since he appears to have returned to Rome at the end of 134, well before these events took place. It was while he was governor that a representative of Cyzicus, Machaeon the son of Asclepiades, made a journey to Macedonia to solicit help against an unnamed enemy who was attacking the town.[18] The outcome is not recorded; but presumably either Roman or allied help was sent since the mission is said to have been successful. These events demonstrate that within about a decade of the setting up of the province of Macedonia its governors were deeply involved well to the east of its boundaries.

From 133 onwards there was constant fighting between the governor of Macedonia and the tribes of Thrace. It was marked by great savagery on both sides and it is impossible to assign responsibility for the separate incidents since while punitive expeditions were often provoked by Thracian invasions of Roman territory, it will have been easy even when there was no provocation to represent Roman expeditions as retaliation or a preventive strike. Moreover, when fighting barbarians the Romans were apt to ignore the rules to which they usually conformed in their wars in Italy and against more civilised peoples. War-declarations were dispensed with,[19] and fearing no adverse publicity governors felt themselves free to press ahead in search of plunder and triumphs. But the Thracians gave as much as they got, for their economy was largely geared to plunder, as Herodotus explains[20] in a passage describing the ideals of the Thracian aristocracy of his own time. In the following century Seuthes II sketched a similar way of life to Xenophon.[21]

Where did most of this fighting take place? The question is easier to put than to answer, for much of the evidence for Roman campaigning in Thrace is laconic and gives no indication of the locality. One commonly used route was clearly that along the Bregalnitza into the Axius valley. Tipas, the king of the Maedi, probably came that way in 119 when, along with the Celtic Scordisci, he invaded Macedonia and defeated the praetor Sex. Pompeius 'who happened to die in the battle' – so we are informed on an inscription recording honours voted by the Macedonian town of Lete to the quaestor M. Annius, who later avenged Pompeius' death by defeating Tipas.[22] It is clear that in the penultimate decade of the second century, for whatever reason, ‖ the scale of fighting was growing. For seven years, beginning in 114, Macedonia was

---

[18] *IGR* 4.134, ll. 1 and 9–11.
[19] See J. W. Rich, *Declaring war in the Roman Republic in the period of transmarine expansion* (Coll. Latomus 149, Brussels, 1976) 16.
[20] Hdt. v.6.
[21] Xen. *Anab.* vii.3.33–4; see Chr. M. Danov, *Altthrakien* (Berlin–New York, 1976) 171.
[22] *SIG* 700; the date is not 117 (so Dittenberger and N. G. L. Hammond, *A history of Macedonia* I (Oxford, 1972) 184). Hammond draws attention to the Roman troops stationed in advanced positions which were concentrated by the quaestor, M. Annius; but those stationed on the borders of Macedonia in 167 (Diod. xxxi.8.9) should not be adduced as a parallel, for they are Macedonian (*cf.* Livy xlv.29.14). The Romans left no troops in the independent republics after the fall of the monarchy.

declared a consular province.[23] In 114 C. Porcius Cato attacked the Scordisci, though ineffectively;[24] he was condemned for extortion, but his two successors in 113 and 112, C. Caecilius Metellus and M. Livius Drusus, both triumphed.[25] In 110–106 M. Minucius campaigned against the Triballi on the upper Hebrus – probably following a defensive action in the Axius valley commemorated on an inscription from Europus[26] – and he went on to win victories over the Scordisci, the Daci and the Bessi. He used the substantial plunder which he won from these campaigns to endow the building of the porticus Minucia at Rome.[27]

We hear of further fighting under the praetor T. Didius (101–100) and again under L. Julius Caesar (94),[28] after which C. Sentius was appointed and remained in Macedonia for six years (93–87).[29] By 87 the Thracians were being stirred up by a new champion, Mithridates VI of Pontus, and it was probably in 88 and at his instigation that a Thracian prince called Sothimus had eluded C. Sentius and invaded Greece.[30] By 87 the governor had been expelled from Macedonia and it was only with the savage reprisals of Sulla and his *legatus*, Hortensius, in 85 that the tables were turned.[31] 'Sulla', writes Appian (*Mith.* 55), 'attacked and ravaged the tribes adjacent to Macedonia, who were constantly invading the province, thus giving his army practice and enriching them at the same time.' In these campaigns, which were probably launched by way of the Strymon valley,[32] Sulla defeated the Maedi, the Dardani and the Sinti; but a year later the two former joined the Scordisci to invade Greece and got as far as Delphi, and the Maedi and Dardani only escaped the vengeance of the propraetor, L. Cornelius Scipio Asiagenus, by bribery.[33] It marked the end of over ten years of almost incessant fighting, which may also

[23] See Sarikakis, *op. cit.* (n. 14) 55–63, for the governorships of C. Porcius Cato (119), C. Caecilius Metellus Caprarius (113/12), M. Livius Drusus (112/11) and M. Minucius Rufus (110–106).

[24] Eutrop. iv.24, 'bellum intulit'.

[25] *Fast. tr.* in Degrassi, *Insc. Ital.* 13.1 (Rome, 1947) pp. 85 and 561.

[26] The sources for Minucius' campaigns are listed in Sarikakis, *op. cit.* (n. 14) 60–2; T. R. S. Broughton, *MRR* 1.543 and 554. For the Europus inscription see J. Kougeas, Ἑλληνικά 5 (1932) 5–16; *cf.* J. and L. Robert, *Bull. épig.* (1955) no. 1369.

[27] Vell. Pat. ii.8.3; Cic. *Phil.* ii.84; SHA, *Comm.* 16.5.

[28] See Sarikakis, *op. cit.* (n. 14) 64–6 (T. Didius), 67–9 (L. Julius Caesar); on the former see below, pp. 204f.

[29] *Cf.* Sarikakis, *op. cit.* (n. 14) 69–72.

[30] Oros. v.18.30; H. Gaebler, *ZN* 23 (1902) 170 n. 3, took Sothimus to be a king of the Maedi.

[31] Livy, *Epit.* 83; Plut. *Sulla* 23; Eutrop. v.7.1; on Hortensius see Gran. Lic. 35 (Bonn).

[32] This follows from the point from which he started, somewhere between Macedonia proper and the Hellespont; after ravaging the land of the Maedi πάλιν ἀνέστρεψεν εἰς Μακεδονίαν (Plut. *Sulla* 23).

[33] App. *Ill.* 5, accepting the emendation of τριακοστόν to τριακοσ⟨ιοσ⟩τόν; the Thracian attack on Delphi was 302 years after the Celtic attack on Rome in 387. For discussion see G. Daux, *Delphes au IIe et au Ier siècle av. J.-C.* (Paris, 1936) 392–7; Broughton, *MRR* 2.59 n. 2; Sarikakis, *op. cit.* (n. 14) 74 nn. 1–2. Not all Thracians were hostile to Rome at this time. Sadalas, the king of the Odrysae, remained faithful to the Roman alliance; see the inscription from Chaeronea, honouring Amatocus, son of Teres, whom Sadalas had evidently sent to serve under Sulla (*cf.* Holleaux, *op. cit.* (n. 12) 1.143–60).

have involved Thracian attacks on the mainland ‖ possessions of Thasos.[34] In 77/6 the proconsul Ap. Claudius Pulcher died fighting in Rhodope;[35] but his successor, C. Scribonius Curio, proconsul in Macedonia from 75 to 72, was the first Roman to bring his troops to the Danube.[36]

II

The base for all this campaigning was the province of Macedonia. But of what did it consist? There has been no agreement concerning the boundaries of that province and on the stages by which the Roman frontier was advanced to the east. There has also been disagreement about the development of the Via Egnatia, the main Roman line of communication across the spine of the Balkans from Apollonia (or Epidamnus) to Thessalonica and beyond. It is to this problem that I now want to turn.

The eastern boundary of the province as it was established in 146 will have coincided at least in part with the limits of Macedonia Prima, since it took in the Strymon valley up to a point a little north of modern Sandanski (formerly Sveti-Vrač), including the Sinti but not (as Papazoglou has shown)[37] the Maedi, who lived along the middle reaches of the river.[38] The coastal boundary is more controversial. In his speech against Piso (38) Cicero asserted that 'such vast barbarian tribes lie in its proximity that generals operating in Macedonia have always equated the limits of the province with those imposed by their swords and javelins'. It is not wholly clear whether this piece of rhetoric is concerned with Roman martial spirit (in which Piso had been so deplorably lacking) or with alert preparedness: were the frontiers expandable to match Roman military advances or vulnerable and liable to contraction if the army was not on a constant alert? Perhaps the nuance does not matter greatly. Roman generals, Cicero goes on to say, usually triumphed from Macedonia. It was a nursery of war.

But that does not of course mean that the province had no official coastal boundary. From an early date under the Roman administration this lay at the river Hebrus, the modern Evros or Maritza, or to be more specific at Cypsela, the bridgehead on its left bank. The proof of this is to be found in what Strabo has to say about the Via Egnatia and its extension eastward from Thessalonica. There had of course been a road ‖ through coastal Thrace from the Hellespont and the Chersonese westward at least since the Persian advance into Macedonia and Greece early in the fifth century.[39] According to Herodotus (VII.115) the Thracians revered this road, neither destroying it nor planting

[34] See R. K. Sherk, *Roman documents from the Greek East* (Baltimore, 1969) no. 21 (letter of Dolabella, c. 80–70 B.C.).

[35] Obsequens 59; cf. Eutrop. vi.2.1; Sarikakis, *op. cit.* (n. 14) 79–81.

[36] Eutrop. VI.2.2; Ruf. Fest. *Brev.* 7; Iordanis, *De summa temporum vel origine actibusque gentis Romanorum*, 216 (*Mon. Germ. Hist., auct. ant.* 1.27); Sarikakis, *op. cit.* (n. 14) 82–5.

[37] F. Papazoglou, *art. cit.* (n. 10) 537.

[38] See above, pp. 193f.   [39] See Danov, *op. cit.* (n. 21) 141.

it with crops – which suggests that was what they would normally have done to a road built by others through their territory.[40] It continued to be used and is probably identical with what Livy, following Polybius, calls 'the ancient royal road leading to Paroreia in Thrace' – Paroreia seems to have been the mountainous area included in Macedonia and lying west of the Strymon[41] – 'and nowhere deviating towards the coast'.[42] In 185 Philip V diverted this road southwards to take in some of the land and settlements belonging to the city of Maronea (about 20 km west of Alexandroupolis); and it must have been the same road which Manlius Vulso had followed three years earlier after the disaster in which he lost most of his Galatian plunder between Cypsela and the Hebrus on his way back from Asia Minor.[43] It was no doubt a primitive road by Roman standards and though it could at a pinch be used by the legions, any eastward extension of the Macedonian frontier was likely to require its reconstruction. Conversely, the extension of a Romanised road to the Hebrus must be regarded as *prima facie* evidence that the province now reached as far as that river.

This is the background against which it is appropriate to examine two passages from Strabo, Book VII. The first of these is Strabo VII.7.4, C 322, which tells us that the Via Egnatia runs east from Apollonia and Epidamnus[44] to Macedonia, and that it has been measured and provided with milestones as far as Cypsela and the Hebrus. The distance from either starting-point is 535 *m.p.* and this, converted into stades on the usual 1:8 ratio, comes to 4,280 stades, though if one accepts Polybius' ratio of 1:8⅓ one has to add another 178 stades (it is in fact 178⅓, but Strabo has not unreasonably ignored the ⅓), making in all a total of 4,458 stades. The reason for adjusting the total to match Polybius' method of calculation is, of course, that Polybius reckoned *mille passus* as equivalent to 8 stades 2 plethra, as Strabo here informs us.[45] That is not because Polybius operated with a short stade, still less (as Hammond has suggested[46]) with a long mile, but simply because on the few occasions when it was necessary to convert *milia passuum* into stades[47] he insisted on a greater degree of ‖ accuracy than was implied in the common 1:8 ratio. The whole road, Strabo adds, is called the Via Egnatia, but the first part as far as the frontier between Illyria and Macedonia is called the Candavian Road. The length of the section from the Adriatic to Thessalonica is given by Polybius, he says, as 267 *m.p.*

---

[40] So, rightly, S. Casson, *Macedonia, Thrace and Illyria* (Oxford, 1926) 43. For a similar example from near Cyzicus *cf. OGIS* 18 ll. 4–6 (254/3 B.C.).

[41] *Cf.* Livy XLII.51.5.

[42] Livy XXXIX.27.10.　　　　　　[43] Livy XXXVIII.40.6ff.

[44] The use of the name Epidamnus suggests an early source, since it was superseded by 'Dyrrhachium' in imperial times; *cf.* Collart, *art. cit.* (n. 1) 182, quoting Philippson, *RE* 5.2 (1905) 'Dyrrhachion', col. 1884.

[45] VII.7.4, C 322.　　　　　　[46] *Op. cit.* (n. 22) 55–6.

[47] This was rarely required; *cf.* M. G. Morgan, 'Pliny, *N.H.* III.129, the Roman use of stades and the elogium of C. Sempronius Tuditanus (cos. 129 B.C.)', *Philologus* 117 (1973) 34–5.

When Strabo says that the whole road is called the Via Egnatia (ἡ μὲν οὖν πᾶσα 'Εγνατία καλεῖται), he clearly means the whole road as far as the Hebrus. Of this there could be no doubt but for two passages in the Palatine and Vatican epitomes of Strabo (vii frs. 10 and 13) which suggest or state that Strabo made Thessalonica the terminus of the road. The first of these (fr. 10, epit. Pal.) contains a schematic account of the limits of Macedonia in which the eastern boundary is the meridian passing through Cypsela and the Hebrus mouth, and the southern boundary the Via Egnatia, 'which runs from Dyrrhachium towards the east as far as Thessalonica'. Since east of that city the southern boundary of Macedonia must be the sea (though the epitomator says nothing about this), it is only that part of the road between the Adriatic and Thessalonica which is relevant to the description. The second fragment (13, epit. Vat.) is a discussion of the coastline of Macedonia (meaning the Roman province so called, since the southern section runs down to Sunium), and in it Thessalonica is mentioned as a point of division between the southern section of the coast (from Sunium) and the eastern section as far as the Thracian Chersonese. Almost as an afterthought the epitomator, after describing the southern stretch, goes on to add the observation that Strabo says that the Via Egnatia too (*i.e.* as well as the coastline from Attica), beginning at the Ionian Gulf, terminates at Thessalonica. The fragment ends here, but the original passage in Strabo must have gone on to discuss the coastline running eastward from Thessalonica, which thus forms a kind of pivotal point for the two stretches of coast and the road from the Adriatic. In this context the part of the Via Egnatia east of Thessalonica is as irrelevant as it is in fr. 10, and in view of this it seems methodologically sounder to accept the statement in the complete text of Strabo in preference to what stands in the epitomes. Collart, in a study of the milestones of the Via Egnatia,[48] regards the reference to Thessalonica in the two epitome passages as 'a recollection of the conditions governing the exchange of commodities' between the Aegean and the Adriatic, for which Thessalonica in the east and Apollonia or Epidamnus in the west would be the relevant ports. This does not seem to me very likely.

There is disagreement about when this road to Thessalonica and then on to the Hebrus was built. Radke, in his Pauly-Wissowa article[49] on the 'viae publicae Romanae (via Egnatia)', and Hammond in his article in *JRS*[50] (which in some respects supersedes his account of the Via Egnatia in his *History of Macedonia*)[51] both argue that the Via Egnatia (under that name) dates to after Polybius' death which, though it is not determinable with certainty, probably fell a little after 118. ‖ Hammond indeed argues both in his *History of Macedonia* and in his *JRS* article that the Via Egnatia was not built before the decade 110–100;[52] it was 'designed', he says, 'for armies defending the

---

[48] *Art. cit.* (n. 1) 180.
[49] G. Radke, *RE* Suppl. 13 (1973) 'Viae publicae Romanae: via Egnatia', cols. 1666–7.
[50] N. G. L. Hammond, 'The western part of the Via Egnatia', *JRS* 64 (1974) 192–4.
[51] *Op. cit.* (n. 22) 1.19–58.   [52] *Op. cit.* (n. 22) 1.56 n. 2, *art. cit.* (n. 50) 192.

civilised parts against the barbarians', rather than for advance into Asia, and he associates it with the period of annual expeditions (119–106 and *c.* 100), details of which have already been touched on.[53] This, I would suggest, is to assign far too passive a role to this road. Roman governors of frontier provinces did not restrict their activities to 'defending civilised parts against the barbarians': there were more effective ways of qualifying for triumphs. But, apart from that, we have already seen M. Cosconius active in central Thrace as early as 135/4 and responding to an appeal, perhaps against Thracians, from Machaeon of Cyzicus.[54] No Roman governor can have been ignorant of the Thracian problem since the war with Andriscus – and few Romans fortunate enough to be assigned to such a splendid arena for the acquisition of glory and material plunder would be likely to ignore its opportunities.

Probability would seem therefore to be against so late a date for the building of the road to Roman standards. Granted, it remains possible to argue, with Hammond, that, in view of the fact that the only distance given in *milia passuum* and actually attributed to Polybius is that from the Adriatic coast to Thessalonica, nothing prevents our supposing that the section from Thessalonica to the Hebrus was built after Polybius' death; in that case the 178 stades which have to be added to the 4,280 stades to arrive at the total distance from the Adriatic coast to Cypsela and the Hebrus could have been calculated by Strabo himself, using the Polybian formula of 1 : 8⅓. Fortunately this hypothesis can be eliminated on the basis of a further passage from the same book of Strabo, which has not always been properly understood (VII. fr. 57).[54a] In this Strabo tells us that the distance from the Hebrus and Cypsela to Byzantium 'as far as the Cyanean rocks' – these rocks lie at the Black Sea mouth of the Bosporus and Strabo ignores the 160 stades between them and Byzantium, just as he ignores the shorter distance between the Hebrus and Cypsela – this distance from the Hebrus to Byzantium, he tells us, comes to 3,100 stades on the authority of Artemidorus: and the entire distance from Apollonia to Byzantium is 7,320 stades, 'although', he continues, 'Polybius adds 180 more, since he adds a third of a stade to the eight stades in the mile'. It is not immediately obvious why Polybius should be adding 180 stades to 7,320; and Radke[55] dismisses the figure 180 as 'freilich irrig', since that addition would be valid only for a stretch of 4,320 stades; and 4,320 stades cannot be fitted into Strabo's calculations. Radke's scepticism is, however, unwarranted. The figure of 180 is certainly correct, for added to 7,320 it gives a total of 7,500, which looks like ‖ a rounded-off figure; and a satisfactory explanation is in fact available. We know from the passage of Strabo already looked at (VII.7.4, C 322) that on the 1 : 8 ratio the section of the road from Apollonia to Cypsela

---

[53] Above, pp. 195f.   [54] Above, p. 195.

[54a] J. P. Adams, in the paper mentioned below in n. 112, has proposed a divergent and, in my opinion, overcomplicated interpretation of this passage. His paper was published too late to be taken into account here, but I hope to discuss it in another place [see below, p. 359 no. 272].

[55] *Art. cit.* (n. 49) col. 1666.

measured 4,280 stades, but that to this 178 stades must be added on account of the 1:8⅓ Polybian ratio. In view of this it seems virtually certain that the 180 stades which Strabo proposes to add to the distance Apollonia–Byzantium is the rounded-off version of the 178 stades, which cover only the distance Apollonia–Cypsela. The reason for this limitation will be that Polybius recorded the distance in *milia passuum* only as far as Cypsela, and that the distance from Cypsela to Byzantium (or the Cyanean Rocks), having come from Artemidorus, was in stades to begin with and therefore an adjustment was neither necessary nor possible.

We therefore get the following figures:

4,280 stades (Apollonia–Cypsela on 1:8 ratio)
  180 stades (Polybian adjustment rounded off from 178 – actually 178⅓)
3,100 stades (Cypsela–Byzantium, from Artemidorus)
7,560 stades total, rounded off as 7,500 stades.

Without the Polybian addition, the distance from Apollonia to Byzantium would, on this calculation, have come out as 7,380 – *i.e.* 4,280 + 3,100 – stades, but Strabo has 'adjusted' it to 7,320 stades in order that, having included the 180 stades added by Polybius, he can end up with the round figure of 7,500 stades. Evidently he felt it important to keep the Polybian adjustment as a separate figure, and this is very helpful to us, for it confirms the impression given by the other Strabonian passage that the whole distance from Apollonia to Cypsela was recorded *by Polybius* – not merely by Strabo – in *milia passuum*, since it is only from Cypsela onwards, where the figures are taken from Artemidorus, that no Polybian adjustment is required. It consequently follows that the Via Egnatia was built and provided with milestones as far as Cypsela in Polybius' lifetime.

This conclusion based on the figures in Strabo has been very happily confirmed for the section as far as Thessalonica by the recent discovery of a milestone, inscribed in what appear to be letter-forms of the second half of the second century B.C. at the crossing of the Gallikos, about seven Roman miles west of Thessalonica. This milestone, found approximately *in situ*,[56] gives the name of *Cn. Egnatius C. f. proconsul* and records the figure of 260 in Greek and Latin numerals. This, added to the 7 *m.p.* from that point to Thessalonica, matches exactly the figure of 267 *m.p.* which Strabo tells us Polybius assigned to the section Apollonia–Thessalonica.[57] Consequently, it is now certain that the Via Egnatia was built, with that name, at least as far as Thessalonica shortly after Macedonia became a province, and virtually certain that it did ‖ not stop there but continued to the Hebrus and Cypsela, which constituted the provincial boundary and had certainly been reached before Polybius' death soon after 120.

---

[56] See n. 1.   [57] Strabo VII.7.4, C 322.

That is not the orthodox view. Geyer in his Pauly-Wissowa article on Macedonia[58] tells us that when the province was set up its frontier was the Nestus. That river was certainly the boundary of Macedonia under Philip II and Alexander, as we learn from Strabo;[59] but, as we have seen,[60] Philip V extended his territory to take in Maronea beyond the Nestus and Aenus beyond the Hebrus, and Strabo (vii. fr. 48 (47 Loeb)) records that both after 168, when the Macedonian *merides* were converted into independent republics, and again after Andriscus' defeat, the frontier of Macedonia was the Hebrus.[61] His statement is confirmed for 168 by Livy,[62] who, after declaring that Macedonia Prima was to include the area between the Strymon and the Nestus, adds 'accessurum huic parti trans Nestum ad orientem versus, qua Perseus tenuisset vicos castella oppida praeter Aenum et Maroneam et Abdera'.[63] Diodorus[64] also includes τὰ πρὸς ἀνατολὴν τοῦ Νέστου ἐρύματα in Macedonia in a passage which, like Livy's, seems to derive from Polybius. Finally, as we have already observed,[65] Strabo states categorically that the Via Egnatia is marked out with milestones from Apollonia as far as Cypsela and the river Hebrus, a distance of 535 *m.p.* The overwhelming likelihood is therefore that the road was built from Apollonia (and from Epidamnus–Dyrrhachium) to Cypsela from the outset.

The province of Macedonia extended to the Hebrus (or beyond) at any rate down to the end of the Republic. As A. H. M. Jones has remarked,[66] Pompey got help in 48 from Rhascuporis, a prince of the Sapaei *ex Macedonia* (Caesar, *BCiv.* iii.4.3); and it is ‖ clear from Appian's account of events leading up to the battle of Philippi in 42[67] that Rhascuporis, who now threw in his lot with Brutus, ruled over the Corpili,[68] who occupied the area between the Nestus

---

[58] *RE* 14.1 (1928) 'Makedonia', col. 764.

[59] Strabo vii. frs. 33, 35; *cf.* Collart, *art. cit.* (n. 1) 179 n. 18. The Nestus seems to have been the frontier again later, under the Empire; *cf.* Ptol. iii.13.1–8.

[60] See above, p. 198.

[61] Strabo vii. fr. 48 (47 Loeb), Ἕβρος... τῆς Μακεδονίας φησὶ τοῦτο ὅριον, ἣν ἀφείλοντο Περσέα Ῥωμαῖοι καὶ μετὰ ταῦτα τὸν Ψευδοφίλιππον; fr. 10.

[62] Livy xlv.29.6.

[63] The Livian passage is ambiguous since it is not clear whether the words 'praeter...Abdera' are to be taken with 'accessurum huic parti' or with 'qua Perseus tenuisset vicos castella oppida'; but *praeter* must here mean 'except' rather than 'as well as' (which is what it seems to mean in Livy xxxvii.56.3–5; see my note on Polyb. xxi.46.10 in my *Historical commentary on Polybius* 3 (Oxford, 1979) 173), since we know that Abdera (Livy xliii.4.11–12), Aenus and Maronea (Polyb. xxx.3.3, 3.7) were all declared free. U. Kahrstedt, *Beiträge zur Geschichte der Thrakischen Chersones* (Baden-Baden, 1954) 48, is in error in stating that the three towns were included in Macedonia Prima; see B. Niese, *Geschichte der griechischen und hellenistischen Staaten* 3 (Gotha, 1903) 180.

[64] Diod. xxxi.8.8; the words πλὴν τὰ πρὸς Ἄβδηραν καὶ Μαρώνειαν καὶ Αἶνον πόλεις cannot be used to interpret Livy xlv.29.6 (see previous note) since ἐρύματα πλήν is Wesseling's emendation of the MS ἐρύμην καί.   [65] See above, p. 198.

[66] *Op. cit.* (n. 4) 8; I would no longer hold to the objections which I raised against Jones's view in 'The original extent of the Via Egnatia', *LCM* 2 (1977) 73–4, a note which is in several details superseded by the present paper.

[67] App. *BCiv.* iv.87; see T. Rice Holmes, *The architect of the Roman Empire* 1 (Oxford, 1928) 82–3, and map facing 81 for the situation of the Sapaei and Corpili.

[68] *Cf.* App. *BCiv.* iv.87 (quoted by Jones, *op. cit.* (n. 4) 377 n. 10).

and the Hebrus, as well as the Sapaei to the west of the Nestus. It therefore looks as if Rhascuporis' kingdom was included within the general bounds of the province of Macedonia rather as the later client-kingdoms were in the province of Britain.

The Via Egnatia, we now know, was named after the governor who built it; and his governorship is likely to have occurred soon after the establishment of the province, since the road was essential for communications at the western end and for both defence and aggression in the area east of Thessalonica. There are plenty of empty spaces for Cn. Egnatius' governorship between 146 and 133. On present evidence he may well have been Metellus Macedonicus' immediate successor in 145.[69] He is perhaps to be identified with the Cn. Egnatius C. f. Stell(atina) mentioned in a letter written by the praetor P. Cornelius Blasio to the Corcyreans.[70] Blasio's praetorship is probably to be dated, not in 175–160,[71] but rather, as Mattingly and Crawford have argued,[72] in the late 140s.

III

In 146 the Hebrus represented the eastward limit of Roman territory in Thrace. This was no longer true after 129 when, following on the suppression of Aristonicus, the European territories of Pergamum,[73] the so-called 'Chersonese and the places in Thrace', which had probably been originally organised as an administrative area by Antiochus III and had fallen to the Attalids in 188, were annexed by Rome. It has usually, and I think correctly, been assumed that this territory was placed under the control of the governor of Macedonia.[74] Against that view Kahrstedt argued[75] that down to the time of Augustus and Tiberius the Thracian Chersonese was the ‖ responsibility of the proconsul of Asia, and in support of that thesis he quoted a statement in Strabo (XIII.1.22, C 591) that owing to the proximity of the two towns Sestus was assigned to the same governor as Abydus, 'since at that time governorships had not yet been delimited by continents'. This passage of Strabo will not sustain the interpretation that Kahrstedt lays upon it. It certainly refers to a period earlier than the time when Strabo was writing, and pretty certainly before Augustus' provincial arrangements; but it also suggests a special arrangement for Sestus

---

[69] We know of no named governor of Macedonia between Metellus and Licinius Nerva, whose praetorship is to be dated 143 or 142 (since in it a revolt of a Pseudoperseus was put down by L. Tremellius Scrofa, his quaestor; *cf.* Livy, *Epit.* 53); Broughton, *MRR* 1.472, 476; Sarikakis, *op. cit.* (n. 14) 38–9, 170.

[70] *SEG* 3.451 = Sherk, *op. cit.* (n. 34) no. 4; *cf.* Romiopoulou, *art. cit.* (n. 1) 814.

[71] So Holleaux, *op. cit.* (n. 12) 5.438–46; Broughton, *MRR* 1.438.

[72] H. B. Mattingly, *NC* 9 (1969) 103–4; M. H. Crawford, *Roman Republican coinage* (Cambridge, 1974) 1.239–40 no. 189.

[73] Polyb. XVIII.51.3; *OGIS* 339, ll. 12ff.; *cf.* Bengtson, *op. cit.* (n. 12) 2.227.

[74] See for example Bengtson, *op. cit.* (n. 12) 2.232 n. 2.

[75] *Op. cit.* (n. 63) 51–3. When, however, Cicero refers to Piso's maladministration in the Chersonese (*Pis.* 86), this cannot be pressed as evidence that the Chersonese was part of Piso's province, since he also refers to outrages in Byzantium, which was a free city.

which, it is implied, received different treatment from that of the rest of the Chersonese. At what date and for how long this special arrangement came into operation we are not told.[76] When Rome annexed the peninsula not only Sestus but the other cities of the Chersonese as well retained the nominal status of free cities, though the royal domains of Attalus became *ager publicus*.[77] But, separated as they were from the province of Asia not only by the Hellespont, but also by the territories of the free cities of Cyzicus, Lampsacus and Ilium,[78] it was more natural that they should be placed under the general supervision of the governor of Macedonia, who was far better equipped with troops to deal with their problems. It is tempting to seek support for this assumption in a building inscription[79] found at Bolayır near the site of Lysimacheia, which was set up by the century of M. Caecilius from the tenth cohort of the seventh legion Macedonica (the later seventh Claudia). Ritterling[80] argued that the title Macedonica was granted to the legions stationed in Macedonia, including the seventh, and he associated the activity of this legion with L. Calpurnius Piso's campaigns in Thrace in 13–11 B.C. But, as Syme has pointed out,[81] this explanation of the name is quite hypothetical, since Piso may 'have brought the legion with him from the east, and it may have returned there with C. Caesar in 1 B.C.'. It is safer therefore not to try to use this inscription as evidence confirming the attribution of the Chersonese to the governor of Macedonia.

More conclusive is the new evidence for what took place in this area when fresh circumstances led the Romans to advance the boundaries of Macedonia still further eastward into Thrace. I refer to the newly discovered Cnidus inscription.[82] According ‖ to Iordanis,[83] under T. Didius, praetor in Macedonia in 101 and propraetor in 100,[84] 'the Thracians were subdued and their territory reduced to a province'. This statement, if it stood alone, would merit little credence. But it had already received some confirmation from the so-called

---

[76] *OGIS* 339, the Sestian decree honouring Menas, son of Menes, and dated shortly after Aristonicus' revolt, speaks of Menas' undertaking embassies πρός τε τοὺς στρατηγοὺς τοὺς ἀποστελλομένους ὑπὸ Ῥωμαίων εἰς τὴν Ἀσίαν καὶ τοὺς πεμπομένους πρεσβευτάς (21f.), but this was very natural in the immediate circumstances of the revolt and need not imply that Sestus was attached from the outset to the province of Asia.

[77] Cic. *Leg. Agr.* II.50, 'Attalicos agros in Cherroneso'; later this area, not necessarily just the *agri publici*, passed into Agrippa's hands (Dio LIV.29.5, Χερρόνησος... ἡ πρὸς Ἑλλησπόντῳ, οὐκ οἶδ' ὅπως ἐς τὸν Ἀγρίππαν ἐλθοῦσα); see further Jones, *op. cit.* (n. 4) 16; Kahrstedt, *op. cit.* (n. 63) 52ff.

[78] *Cf.* Sherwin-White, *art. cit.* (n. 13) 69.   [79] *CIL* 3.7386.

[80] *RE* 12.2 (1925) 'legio', col. 1616.

[81] 'Some notes on the legions under Augustus', *JRS* 23 (1933) 23 n. 67. See also L. Robert, *Hellenica* 5 (1948) 53 n. 4.

[82] M. Hassall, M. H. Crawford and J. Reynolds, 'Rome and the eastern powers at the end of the second century B.C.', *JRS* 64 (1974) 195–220.

[83] Iordanis, *De summa temporum vel origine actibusque gentis Romanorum*, 219 (*Mon. Germ. Hist., Auct. ant.* V.1, p. 28), 'ad postremum a Marco (*sic*!) Didio et ipsi (*sc.* Thraces) subacti, et loca eorum in provinciam redacta, iugum excepit Romanum'.

[84] For the evidence see Sarikakis, *op. cit.* (n. 14) 64–6; *cf.* G. V. Sumner, 'The "Piracy Law" from Delphi and the law of the Cnidos inscription', *GRBS* 19 (1978) 218–19.

Piracy Law,[85] discovered at Delphi in the last century, which recorded an extension of the province of Macedonia into Thrace under T. Didius, though owing to a lacuna in the text it was not possible to discover what part of Thrace was being referred to. The new Cnidian inscription, which almost certainly contains a copy of the same law in a variant translation – perhaps the official one[86] – now makes it possible to fill the lacuna in the Delphic text.

The Cnidus inscription has raised many wider issues which are not relevant to this paper. It seems to me, however, that Giovannini and Grzybek have made a strong case[87] for regarding the Piracy Law not, as used to be supposed, as a *popularis* measure designed to gain some advantage for Marius,[88] but as a piece of legislation intended to strengthen the authority of the Senate. But their date of 99 for its promulgation is improbable, since this would imply that the person entrusted with the task of publishing the relevant measures throughout the East (Delphic text B lines 20ff.) was not, as one might expect, the present or even future proconsul of Asia, but instead the man who had held that position the previous year. The most likely date for the law still seems to me to be towards the end of 100, after the downfall of Glaucia and Saturninus, and before the elections for 99 had been completed; and I am happy to find that this view is also that of Sumner.[89]

The part of Thrace conquered and annexed by T. Didius while governor of Macedonia in 101 was an area called the Caeneic Chersonese. This name was not previously known, though the Caeni are of course familiar.[90] Pliny (*NH* IV.40 and 47) mentions a *regio Caenica* containing a town Flaviopolis,[91] the site of which is uncertain – though Robert[92] has argued strongly for locating it on the coast of the Chersonese rather than in Thrace, as Pliny suggests. Rather more can be ascertained from Ptolemy. It is known that the *strategiae* into which the kingdom of Thrace had ‖ been divided continued to exist as administrative divisions of the later Roman province of Thrace. Several appear on imperial inscriptions[93] and Ptolemy lists fourteen such *strategiae*.[94] Of those lying along the north Aegean coast the most easterly is *Caenice* and its eastern limit is indicated by Ptolemy's statement that 'along the sea-coast from the city of Perinthus as far as Apollonia' – that is, Sozopol in Bulgaria – '(lay) the *strategia*

---

[85] *SEG* 3.378B l. 28 (improved text in *JRS* 64 (1974) 28).

[86] See Sumner, *art. cit.* (n. 84) 211–25.

[87] A. Giovannini and E. Grzybek, 'La lex de piratis persequendis', *MH* 35 (1978) 33–47.

[88] This view was already queried by the authors of the publication of the Cnidus inscription.

[89] Sumner, *art. cit.* (n. 84) 223.

[90] *Cf.* W. Tomaschek, *Die alten Thraker*, *SAWW* 128 (1893) 4. Abh., 84 (reprinted in a single volume, Vienna, 1980); *cf.* R. Macaluso, 'Monete a leggenda Kainon', *Miscellanea di studi classici in onore di Eugenio Manni* (Rome, 1980) 4.1365–74.

[91] On this see Jones, *op. cit* (n. 4) 17 (who thinks it is Aphrodisias), and Kahrstedt, *op. cit.* (n. 63) 69–73 (who thinks it is Callipolis); against Jones's view that it was a *colonia* see Robert, *art. cit.* (n. 81) 42 n. 5.

[92] *Art. cit.* (n. 81) 41ff.

[93] *IGR* 1.677; *IGBulg.* 1116, 2338; Ἀρχ. ἐφ. (1953–4) 233–4; see Jones, *op. cit.* (n. 4) 10–11 with n. 14.   [94] Ptol. III.11.6.

of *Astice'*. The Astae were evidently neighbours of the Caeni in the early second century B.C. too, since both tribes took part in the attack on Manlius Vulso in a pass somewhere between Cypsela and the Hebrus, on his return journey from Asia in 188.[95]

Ptolemy indicates that in imperial times the hinterland of Byzantium and the coast from Perinthus to the Black Sea Apollonia belong to the Astae. Consequently, unless a major shift in tribal territories took place between *c.* 100 B.C. and the date at which Pliny's source was writing – and such a shift seems highly unlikely at a time when the whole of this area lay exposed to Roman eyes – the Caeneic Chersonese of the new Cnidian inscription cannot be 'the peninsula running down to the Bosporus', as its editors suppose.[96] It must lie further west and I would suggest that its name indicates an extension inland of the Thracian Chersonese proper – as one might say, the Caeneic end of the Chersonese. A similar extension of the word 'Chersonese' is found in imperial times, when Pliny (*NH* IV.48) records that the Chersonese 'nunc habet ...Resisthon' – which is otherwise known as Raedestus, and stood on the site of modern Tekirdagh, some 80 km north-east of the real neck of the Chersonese. It was the Caeni who had attacked and destroyed Lysimacheia under Diegylis in 145[97] and so long as they remained independent not only the Chersonese proper, together with the other territories inherited by the Romans from Attalus III, but also Roman communications eastward along the coast were under threat.

Inscriptions from Panium (Panadus) honouring Eumenes II and Attalus II[98] show that the lands which Eumenes received at Apamea extended along the coast of the Propontis north-eastward to a point not more than 10 km short of Tekirdagh; these territories are referred to on an inscription as οἱ κατὰ τὴν Θράκην τόποι.[99] But to the west there is no evidence of any such coastal extension in Attalid times and so it seems most likely that the Caeneic Chersonese was the area to the north and west ‖ of the Chersonese proper, centring on the valley of the river Melas,[100] but extending inland to include the range of hills now called Kuru Dagh south of Keşan and Malkara and, probably, the region around the tributaries of the Ergene as far as Cypsela; eastward to Panium the coast was already in Roman hands. By this annexation T. Didius secured the lines of communication between the Hebrus and the Thracian Chersonese and provided greater security for the inhabitants of the latter.

[95] See above, n. 43.
[96] Hassall, Crawford and Reynolds, *art. cit.* (n. 82) 213.
[97] See above, n. 12.
[98] *OGIS* 301, 302–4; see Kahrstedt, *op. cit.* (n. 63) 47–8. On the site of Panium see Johanna Schmidt, *RE* 18.3 (1949) 'Panion (2)', col. 601. Robert (*art. cit.* (n. 81) 55 n. 10) has identified Panium as the site of earlier Bisanthe, which had traditionally been located at Resisthon (*cf.* Tomaschek, *Die alten Thraken*, *SAWW* 131 (1894) 1. Abh., 60; Danoff, *Der Kleine Pauly* 1 (1975) 'Bisanthe', col. 908).
[99] *OGIS* 339, l. 13; see Kahrstedt, *op. cit.* (n. 63) 55.
[100] On this see Kahrstedt, *op. cit.* (n. 63) 70.

IV

We are badly informed about T. Didius' reasons for annexing the Caeneic Chersonese. The Piracy Law, from which our information is derived, contains several clauses affecting the governors of Asia and Macedonia and is concerned generally with the aftermath of M. Antonius' campaigns against the pirates of the eastern Mediterranean in 102–101. But we have no reason to think that the instructions given to present and future governors of Macedonia were directly concerned with the pirate menace. Sumner,[101] it is true, believes those clauses in the law which concern the governor of Macedonia to be directly linked with the general purpose of making the seas safe against the pirates. But there is no evidence at all that the troops which, in consequence of the law, are not to be sent to Macedonia are intended for Cilicia. Furthermore, Sumner's assumption that T. Didius' conquest of the Caeneic Chersonese would help to control the approaches to the Thracian Bosporus from the Black Sea coast only makes sense if one follows the authors of the article publishing the Cnidus inscription in identifying the newly conquered territory as the hinterland of the Bosporus and Byzantium.

The Piracy Law lays down that the governor of Macedonia – he will be T. Didius' successor – is to proceed as soon as possible to the Caeneic Chersonese, which will now form part of his province,[102] and is to remain there for not less than sixty days – a period of time familiar in other Roman measures, such as the *Tabula Heracleensis*[103] – and to take steps to arrange for the collection of the revenues (perhaps through *publicani*),[104] to secure any friends or allies of Rome against eviction, hindrance or injustice, and before leaving to demarcate the new territories. This clause mainly concerns the man acting as governor at the time of the promulgation of the law but the ‖ inclusion of the words 'sixty days in each year' (καθ᾽ ἕκαστον ἐνιαυτόν) shows that subsequent governors were also required to spend the same length of time in the new territories. Another clause[105] cancels the provision already made to send out troops, corn and supplies to the governor of Macedonia. This both the editors of the Cnidus inscription[106] and Lintott[107] regard as a routine countermanding of orders now redundant since T. Didius had completed his work. Giovannini and Grzybek[108] interpret it less convincingly as a senatorial check on future

---

[101] *Art. cit.* (n. 84) 225.

[102] The rather ambiguous language of the Cnidian inscription col. iv, ll. 11–13, might suggest that the Caeneic Chersonese and Macedonia are separate provinces held by the same man; but the same awkwardness of phraseology is also found in relation to Lycaonia and Asia in col. iii, ll. 22–7; see Hassall, Crawford and Reynolds, *art. cit.* (n. 82) 211.

[103] *ILS* 6085 §§ 143, 151.

[104] Hassall, Crawford and Reynolds, *art. cit.* (n. 82) 204–5, 208; Cnidian inscription, col. iv, ll. 11–18. The editors suggest that καρπίζεσθαι may point to the use of *publicani*.

[105] Cnidian inscription, col. ii, ll. 18–22.

[106] *Art. cit.* (n. 82) 40.

[107] A. W. Lintott, 'Notes on the Roman law inscribed at Delphi and Cnidos', *ZPE* 20 (1976) 66–9.   [108] *Art. cit.* (n. 87) 40.

governors who might wish to pursue a policy of aggression, glory and personal aggrandisement; and Sumner, as we have just seen,[109] thought it was designed to divert troops and supplies to Cilicia. These various interpretations are some indication of how far we still are from certainty about the intentions of the Piracy Law. About the situation which led to Didius' annexation we know even less. The literary sources which refer to his governorship,[110] when they go beyond the mere mention of his name, speak of his repelling wandering Scordisci or merely wandering Thracians ('vagos et libera populatione diffusos' (Florus 1.39.5); 'vagantes...sine cultu vel legibus...ingenti destinatione repressit' (Ammianus xxvii.4.10)). But the Scordisci lived far away in central Thrace and can have nothing to do with the area east of the Hebrus. Iordanis' reference to the setting up of a province has already been noted;[111] it tells us nothing of the background of Didius' actions.

V

The purpose of this paper has been to throw some light on the successive stages of Roman expansion eastward from Macedonia in the second half of the second century. Of these stages we can now detect three. First, in setting up the province in 148–146 the Romans occupied the coastal plain of Thrace as far east as Cypsela and the Hebrus. A solid road was built almost immediately following an older track up the Shkumbi valley and north of the Great Lakes into Macedonia proper and from there down to Thessalonica and eastward across the Strymon and the Nestus as far as the Hebrus. Later, in 133, following on Attalus' death and the defeat of Aristonicus, they added the Thracian Chersonese and the former Pergamene possessions to its north-east as far as Bisanthe. But it was not until 101 and the governorship of T. Didius that they consolidated their hold on the hinterland of the Chersonese and so at last acquired a continuous provincial territory extending along the Propontis to a point just short of Perinthus. It is hard to relate this expansion to any clear plan of territorial annexation, ‖ nor can we detect in its various stages a continuous and consistent policy. The war with Aristonicus gave Rome the Chersonese, but thirty years of random campaigning intervened before T. Didius took steps to close the gap in Roman territory between the Hebrus and the Hellespontine crossing; and even then the authorities were quick to suspend the sending of troops and supplies which might possibly have been used to extend the new lands further east.

The explanation of this apparent indecisiveness lies, I suspect, in the comparative lack of interest in this part of the frontiers; and the events I have traced illustrate to what extent in such an area the Romans were often content to allow outside events to control and set the pace of their expansion. What

---

[109] Above, p. 207.
[110] Conveniently assembled in Sarikakis, *op. cit.* (n. 14) 64–6.
[111] Above, n. 83.

remains constant is the military technique and mode of operation: the immediate construction of the main artery from the Adriatic to the Hebrus, the Via Egnatia, facilitating quick movement east and west to the mouth of the particular river valley down which hostile raids had developed or up which in return Roman armies would march to inflict punitive measures in the course of campaigns which provided the legions with plunder and exercise. Though far less wild and bleak than the commonplaces of the Greek literary tradition would lead us to believe, the interior of Thrace hardly justified anything more; and perhaps, despite the concern to cut a good figure in the East which is revealed in the Piracy Law, the Senate and its more ambitious members were not unduly worried by the continued possession of a frontier which both demanded and invited repeated military intervention.[112]

[112] For convenience I append a short bibliography of work on the Via Egnatia published since 1970:

Adams, J. P. 'Polybius, Pliny and the Via Egnatia', in *Philip II, Alexander the Great and the Macedonian heritage*, edd. W. L. Adams and E. N. Borza (Washington, 1982) 269–302.

Ceka, H. 'La branche sud de la voie Egnatia', *Monumentet* 2 (1971) 25–32 (French version, 33–5).

Ceka, N. and Papajani, L. 'La route de la vallée du Shkumbin', *Studia Albanica* 1 (1972) 85–106.

Collart, P. 'Les milliaires de la via Egnatia', *BCH* 100 (1976), 177–200.

Daux, G. 'Le milliaire de la via Egnatia au musée du Louvre', *JS* (1977) 145–63.

Hammond, N. G. L. *A history of Macedonia* 1 (Oxford, 1972) 19–58.

— 'The western part of the Via Egnatia', *JRS* 64 (1974) 185–94.

McKay, P. A. 'The route of the Via Egnatia round Lake Ostrovo', in *Ancient Macedonia* 2 (Thessalonica, 1977) 201–10.

O'Sullivan, F. *The Egnatian way* (Newton Abbot, 1972).

Radke, G. *RE* Suppl. 13 (1973) cols. 1666–7, 'Viae publicae Romanae: via Egnatia'.

Romiopoulou, C. 'Un nouveau milliaire de la via Egnatia', *BCH* 98 (1974) 813–16.

Walbank, F. W. 'The original extent of the Via Egnatia', *LCM* 2 (1977) 73–4.

— *A historical commentary on Polybius* 3 (Oxford, 1979) 622–8 (on Polyb. xxxiv.12.2a–8).

14

ΦΙΛΙΠΠΟΣ ΤΡΑΓΩΙΔΟΥΜΕΝΟΣ:
A POLYBIAN EXPERIMENT*

'The story, which ends with the poisoning and suffocation of Demetrius, has reached us in a form that suggests, as do also certain other features of the later life of Philip and of the reign of Perseus, that some author or authors wrote tragedies or historical novels dealing with the ruin of the Macedonian royal house.' Such is the startling, if cautiously phrased conclusion of a recent historian, discussing the last years of Philip V in a standard work;[1] it is a conclusion which deserves careful consideration, for if it can be substantiated, it will be necessary to revise seriously our usual estimate of Polybius' merits as a historian. And since no discussion of the problem can be fruitful until Polybius' own attitude towards tragedy and its relations to history has been considered, it is from this aspect that Benecke's suggestion must be approached.

I

Aristotle[2] defines the tragic hero as 'a man who is not eminently good and just, yet whose misfortune is brought about not by vice or depravity, but by some error or frailty. He must be one who is highly renowned and prosperous – a personage like Oedipus, Thyestes or other illustrious men of such families.' Now, undoubtedly the character in Polybius' histories most readily answering to such a definition is Philip V of Macedon. Plainly Philip is highly renowned and prosperous; and Polybius repeatedly emphasises his change from 'the darling of Hellas' to a cruel and ruthless tyrant,[3] showing how 'his good qualities were, in my opinion, natural to him, but his defects were acquired as he advanced in age'.[4] And from one passage in particular[5] it is clear that it was to weakness of character played upon by Demetrius of Pharos, rather than to any innate viciousness, that Philip owed his μεταβολή. Furthermore, in Philip's career might be traced the requisites for the best kind of tragic plot; the proper effect of tragedy, explains Aristotle,[6] 'is best produced when the events come on us by surprise; and the effect is heightened when, at the same

* [*JHS* 58 (1938) 55–68]

[1] P. V. M. Benecke, *CAH* 8 (1930) 254.
[2] *Poet.* 13.3, 1453 a 8 (Butcher's translation).
[3] *E.g.* v.10.9, vii.11, 13. [References without the author's name are to Polybius.]
[4] x.26.   [5] v.102, 1.
[6] *Poet.* 9.11–12, 1452 a 1–11.

time, they follow as cause and effect'. To Polybius it was a matter beyond doubt that the disasters which clouded Philip's last years were the just retribution of Tyche for the misdeeds of his youth; and since it is these last years that are in question, it is worth recalling that Aristotle elsewhere[7] lays down as a dictum that the plot of a tragedy need not ‖ necessarily deal with the whole life of the hero, but only with a single set of events forming a unity.

The series of events beginning with the quarrel between Perseus and Demetrius and ending with the death of Philip undoubtedly form such a unity; hence, from the point of view of subject-matter there is nothing inherently unreasonable in Benecke's suggestion.

II

Tragedy in its own sphere is a subject that Polybius never discusses; though his occasional quotations from Euripides[8] would alone be enough to show that he had an average acquaintance with the tragic stage and its literature. On the other hand, he devotes considerable space to the question of the relation between tragedy and history, and in four places[9] he goes out of his way to criticise his predecessors, who confounded the two *genres*, and to explain what history was and what it was not. For our present purpose it is plainly very important to define what Polybius means by 'tragedy' in these four contexts.

The first[10] is short and simple; the historian is describing the geography of the Po valley and, in an aside, explains that the Greek myths concerning the river, the fall of Phaethon, the weeping poplars, the black clothing worn by the inhabitants of the district καὶ πᾶσαν δὴ τὴν τραγικὴν καὶ ταύτῃ προσεοικυῖαν ὕλην will be ignored for the present, since detailed treatment of such things is not appropriate to the plan of his work; but that later he hopes to find a suitable occasion to make proper mention of them, 'particularly as Timaeus has shown much ignorance concerning the district'.[11]

In the second passage[12] Polybius is discussing the historian Phylarchus and criticises him on three scores:

(a) for his inaccuracy (πολλὰ παρ' ὅλην τὴν πραγματείαν εἰκῇ καὶ ὡς ἔτυχεν εἴρηκε, 56.3),

(b) for his sensational exaggeration (τῆς τερατείας χάριν οὐ μόνον ψεῦδος εἰσήνεγκε τὸ ὅλον, ἀλλὰ καὶ τὸ ψεῦδος ἀπίθανον, 58.12; τὰς μὲν Μαντινέων ἡμῖν συμφορὰς μετ' αὐξήσεως καὶ διαθέσεως ἐξηγήσατο, 61.1),

(c) for his lack of any attention to the causes underlying the events he describes (τὰς πλείστας ἡμῖν ἐξηγεῖται τῶν περιπετειῶν, οὐχ ὑποτιθεὶς αἰτίαν καὶ τρόπον τοῖς γινομένοις, 56.13).

---

[7] *Poet.* 8.1–2, 1451 a 15.

[8] 1.35.4 (from the *Antiope*; repeated in a paraphrase VIII.3.3); V.106.4 (origin uncertain); XII.26.5 (from the *Cresphontes*).

[9] II.16.14, II.56.1f., III.48.8, VII.7.2.   [10] II.16.14.

[11] If Polybius did fulfil this promise in Book XII, the passage has not survived.

[12] II.56–60.

The historian, he claims, is not free καθάπερ οἱ τραγῳδιογράφοι (56.10) to thrill his reader by sensational and exaggerated accounts, or to try to imagine all the probable utterances of his characters and add incidental embroidery of detail to make the subject he is treating more palatable. Of this method ‖ of writing he quotes two examples:[13] the description of the sack of Mantinea by the Achaeans and Macedonians (56.6, 57.1f.) and the fate of Aristomachus of Argos (59.1f). In these Phylarchus had worked up emotional descriptions, in one case of the hosts of captives with dishevelled hair, clinging to the altars, in the other of the screams that brought out all the neighbours, as the unhappy tyrant was tortured to death upon the rack. In both cases, too, Polybius stresses Phylarchus' failure to put the incidents in proper relation to their causes; but, he says, this is Phylarchus' constant method – ποιεῖ δὲ τοῦτο παρ' ὅλην τὴν ἱστορίαν, πειρώμενος ἐν ἑκάστοις ἀεὶ πρὸ ὀφθαλμῶν τιθέναι τὰ δεινά.[14]

Our third passage[15] refers to certain unnamed historians, who have used Hannibal's passage of the Alps as a subject for inaccurate and sensational writing; they have exaggerated the difficulties so much that Hannibal appears condemned as incompetent for ever attempting them. And so, finally, they have to introduce gods and heroes to help him out of the situation in which they have placed him. Thus, says Polybius (III.48.9), they fall into a position similar to that of the tragic dramatists (εἰς τὸ παραπλήσιον τοῖς τραγῳδιο-γράφοις), all of whom require a deus ex machina (προσδέονται θεοῦ καὶ μηχανῆς), because the data on which they choose to found their plots are false and contrary to reason and probability.

Finally,[16] there is the criticism of certain λογογράφοι, who, in describing the downfall of Hieronymus, have written at great length and, introducing much that is marvellous (πολλὴν τερατείαν), have described the prodigies that preceded his reign and the misfortunes of the Syracusans; these writers, τραγῳδοῦντες τὴν ὠμότητα τῶν τρόπων καὶ τὴν ἀσέβειαν τῶν πράξεων, and stressing the strange and terrible (παράλογον καὶ δεινόν) features of his death, have made him appear to be a tyrant far worse than Phalaris or Apollodorus.

These four passages have much in common; directed against former historians, they are all written in the tone of polemic. And from the phraseology it is clear that what Polybius was attacking was a particular form of historical writing, to which he chose to apply the term 'tragic'. Analysis of the examples he quotes shows that the characteristics to which he objected were in all cases those which he specially criticised in that of Phylarchus:

(1) Inaccuracy: a basis of facts that were unreasonable and self-contradictory.
(2) Sensationalism: an emotional treatment of the subject-matter, with the intro-duction of rhetorical speeches and incidental embroidery for effect.
(3) Neglect of underlying causes.

---

[13] The cases of Megalopolis (61.1f.) and the figures of the booty taken (62.1f.) are rather criticisms of Phylarchus' factual accuracy; and, of course, like the whole of the passage, they are even more criticisms of his anti-Achaean point of view.
[14] II.56.8.   [15] III.48.8.   [16] VII.7.2.

And of these the last is undoubtedly the worst, since 'in every case the ‖ final criterion of good and evil lies not in what is done, but in the different reasons and different purposes of the doer'.[17]

But in applying the word 'tragedy' to such a form of writing, Polybius is deliberately using it in a loose and vulgar sense; this is borne out by his inaccurate statement, quoted above, that *all* dramatists base their plots on inaccuracies and have to fall back on the *deus ex machina*.[18] This is simply the well-worn device of giving a dog a bad name as a preliminary to hanging him. 'Tragic' is no more than a label selected by Polybius to vilify a school of historians, whose faults were approximately those of our contemporary press. Today we might prefer the term 'sensational' or 'melodramatic': but Polybius has a right to his own terminology, and it would be making a serious mistake to assume either that Polybius had any objection to tragedy in itself, or that his condemnation of the tragic mode of writing history included anything more than we have seen to be covered by his somewhat peculiar use of the word τραγικός.

III

Against this 'tragic' or 'melodramatic' school, Polybius puts up a moralist's view of history; to him history is a store-house of moral examples, a training for life's vicissitudes.[19] Sensationalism obscures the moral issues, inaccuracy of detail puts the later events in their wrong perspective, neglect of cause and effect ruins the whole moral scheme. Polybius was a firm believer in the power of Fortune (Tyche) to bring a man the destiny he had earned;[20] the historian had only to sift the details carefully and patiently – the bald record of what was said and done[21] – bring out the nexus of cause and effect and the moral lesson would emerge, clear for all to see.

The process by which Fortune ensures that a man's misdeeds finally (and often when least expected) meet with their retribution is clearly brought out in Polybius' description of the fate of Regulus.[22] 'He who had but a short time before refused either pity or mercy to those in misfortune was now almost

[17] II.56.16. In general, Polybius' emphasis upon causation is too well known to need stressing; *cf.* III.6, and Bury, *Ancient Greek historians* (London, 1909) 200.

[18] It is also borne out by an examination of Polybius' use of the words τραγικός and τραγῳδία in other contexts: *e.g.* v.26.9, τραγικὴ εἴσοδος, that is, Apelles' entry into Corinth with great pomp; v.48.9, τραγικὴ καὶ παρηλλαγμένη φαντασία, of a river full of drowning men, with all their baggage, horses, mules and armour; *i.e.* it is not the *tragic* (in our modern sense), but the *extraordinary* (παρηλλαγμένη) nature of the sight that is stressed; VI.56.11, ἡ τοιαύτη τραγῳδία used of the pageantry of a religious kind by which the Roman people were kept in a state of awed obedience.

[19] I.1.2.

[20] For the distinction between the incalculable, unforeseeable τύχη of Demetrius of Phalerum (*cf.* XXIX.21) and Polybius' own 'pragmatical' conception of a force which worked through error and retribution, in a way profitable for the historian to study, see R. Laqueur, *Polybios* (Leipzig, 1913) 253–4, 276.

[21] II.56.10, τῶν δὲ πραχθέντων καὶ ῥηθέντων κατ' ἀλήθειαν αὐτῶν μνημονεύειν πάμπαν, κἂν πάνυ μέτρια τυγχάνωσιν ὄντα.   [22] I.35.1f.

immediately led captive himself and forced to implore pity for his own life' (35.3). Furthermore, in his downfall Regulus confirmed the truth of a saying of Euripides, that 'one wise counsel is victor over many hands',[23] since the skill of Xanthippus had been sufficient to ‖ counterbalance the Roman superiority in arms. From this Polybius then proceeds to draw certain moral conclusions on the use of studying history as an aid to practical life. Now, admittedly it may be sheer chance that a quotation from Euripides is introduced at this particular point. On the other hand, the traditional and best-known examples of moral retribution were those contained in Attic tragedy. When Polybius' thoughts were upon the fate of Regulus, it is natural that he should find images from Euripides occurring to him; whenever a Greek thought of moral weakness, folly, pride, infatuation and retribution, it was inevitably to the figures of tragedy, to Agamemnon, Orestes or Pentheus, that he turned for concrete illustration.

Moreover, in his *Persae* Aeschylus had gone further and applied these moral conceptions to an actual historical figure. In so doing he took a dangerous step towards confusing the two forms of writing. Henceforward, there was a distinct risk that a historian with a moral bias might under certain circumstances reverse the process and read such a moral scheme into the life of a real historical personage. Polybius possessed such a moral bias; but for him, generally speaking, this risk would be small. Thus it could hardly occur in his treatment of a Philopoemen or a Flamininus; Polybius knew too much about Achaea and Rome and about the objects and conduct of these individuals personally, to fall into such a trap. But given a figure sufficiently great, of alien race and ambitions, whose actions were on a world scale, whose faults were many and patent and whose end was unhappy, under these conditions such an approach was not impossible; certainly it was not ruled out by anything which Polybius had written about Phylarchus and included under the loosely-applied label τραγικός.

As we have seen, such a figure, corresponding closely to these conditions and excellently suited to moralising,[24] exists in Philip V of Macedon and, in particular, in the last years of his reign. Our next task will therefore be to consider the tradition for our knowledge of those years.

IV

Our tradition for the last years of Philip goes back partly to Polybius and partly to Livy, following Polybius; how far Livy is accurately reproducing his authority will shortly be considered. In the meantime, three problems suggest themselves:

---

[23] Quoted again in paraphrase, VIII.3.3.

[24] *Cf.* VII.12.2 (referring to the μεταβολή in Philip's character), δοκεῖ γάρ μοι τοῖς καὶ κατὰ βραχὺ βουλομένοις τῶν πραγματικῶν ἀνδρῶν περιποιεῖσθαι τὴν ἐκ τῆς ἱστορίας διόρθωσιν ἐναργέστατον εἶναι τοῦτο παράδειγμα.

(a) How much of the 'tragic' tradition of these years can be attributed to Polybius himself?

(b) How far is Polybius guilty of the fault for which he condemns Phylarchus? In short, in so far as his version may be termed tragic, has this word the same connotation as it has when applied by Polybius himself to Phylarchus? ‖

(c) If the tradition goes back to Polybius, what grounds are there for Benecke's suggestion that he used tragedies as his source?

We have already seen that if Benecke's suggestion can be substantiated, it deals a very heavy blow at Polybius' reputation as a conscientious historian; hence the tradition needs careful analysis.

1. Polybius XXIII.10 (§§ 1–15 Exc. Vales., §§ 15–16 Mai).

(a) §§ 1–15. 'In this year (183/2) was the first outbreak of the misfortunes which attacked Philip of Macedon. Fortune sent a host of furies etc. to haunt Philip for his past sins and

(1) These persuaded him to transfer families to Emathia (formerly called Paeonia) from the coast and vice versa, in readiness for his war with Rome. In the consequent scenes of distress men openly cursed Philip.

(2) Secondly he ordered officers to imprison the children of those he had murdered, quoting a line of verse. Owing to their high birth, the misfortune of these children excited the pity of all.

(3) The third tragedy which fortune produced was that concerning his sons.

Who can help thinking that it was the wrath of heaven which had descended on his old age? And this will be clearer still from what follows.'

(b) §§ 15–16. 'Philip, after killing many notable men, *killed* their sons too, quoting a line of verse.... [25] And while his mind was almost maddened by these things (διὰ ταῦτα), the quarrel of his sons burst into flame, as if Tyche were deliberately bringing their misfortunes on the stage at one and the same time.'

2. Livy XL.3–5. 'The Romans were alarmed at the account brought back by Marcius [envoy to Macedon 183, returned 183/2 winter]; plainly Philip was going to rebel and all his words and actions pointed that way. For

(1) First of all he transported people to Emathia (formerly Paeonia) from the coast, and vice versa, in preparation for his war with Rome. Their curses could be heard throughout Macedon.

(2) When he heard these curses, Philip became more fierce, and he ordered the imprisonment of the children of those he had killed. This cruelty was rendered more loathsome by reason of the misfortunes of the house of Herodicus.' (Chapter 4 is a digression on the story of Theoxena and her children.) 'The horror of this deed added as it were a new flame to the hatred of the king, so that both he *and his children* were openly cursed.

(3) These curses, heard by the gods, caused Philip to turn upon his own house. For Perseus...' (Here follows the story of the plot against Demetrius.) ‖

[25] There is undoubtedly a gap in the text at this point; otherwise, what follows makes no sense. See Büttner-Wobst (ed. Polyb.) *ad loc.*

There can be no doubt that Livy is here following Polybius and that, as Nissen first saw,[26] we have Polybius in a very abridged form; for instance, the story of Theoxena, reproduced in Livy, is so relevant to its place and so irrelevant to Livy's own subject, that it cannot have come from any source but Polybius. Further, the Polybian excerptor has reduced a narrative in which a series of tragic events are built up to a climax in a sequence of cause and effect, to a tabulated scheme in which this sequence is obscured. To take a single example, the curses which are heard by Philip and so bridge the gap between his first act and his second, and then those which are heard by the gods and so lead over from act two to act three are so dramatically right and part of the narrative, that they cannot possibly be rhetorical overlay from the hands of Livy. Indeed, it is mainly thanks to the accuracy with which Livy has reproduced an original, the form of which appealed to his dramatic sense, that it is possible to reconstruct this original with some degree of accuracy.[27]

'This year witnessed the outbreak of disaster for Philip and for Macedon, an event worthy of attention and careful record.[28] Fortune, wishing to punish Philip for all his wicked acts, sent against him a host of furies, torments and avenging spirits of his victims; these tortured him up to the day of his death, never leaving him, so that all realised that, as the proverb goes, "Justice has an eye" and men must not scorn her.' (Next come the details of how these furies work – by inspiring infatuation, which leads their victim to commit acts leading to his own downfall.) 'First these furies inspired Philip to carry out exchanges of population between Thrace and the coast towns, in preparation for his war with Rome; and as a result *men's hatred grew greater than their fear* and they cursed Philip openly. *Eventually, his mind rendered fiercer by these curses, Philip came to feel himself in danger unless he imprisoned the children*[29] *of those he had killed.* So he wrote to the officers in the various cities and had this done; he had in mind chiefly the children of Admetus, Pyrrhichus and Samus and the rest he had executed at the same time, but he included all who had been put to death by royal command, quoting the line

νήπιος ὃς πατέρα κτείνας υἱοὺς καταλείπει.[30] ||

---

[26] *Kritische Untersuchungen* (Berlin, 1863) 234. It is the failure to realise the extent to which Livy is here following Polybius that robs Conway's short study of the question ('A Graeco-Roman tragedy', *Rylands Bulletin* 10 (1926) 309–29) of any value. While appreciating the tragic form in which the narrative is cast, the writer attempts to attribute it to Livy and to connect it with the dynastic schemes of Augustus.

[27] The sentences in italics have only the authority of Livy; the rest is either Polybius or both.

[28] Livy connects the passage with the return of Marcius; this is probably to give it an appearance of importance for Roman affairs which much of it does not possess. The fact was, as in the death of Philopoemen (Livy xxxix.49–50), Livy liked the story and was not going to leave it out.

[29] xxiii.10.15 (Mai) states that the children also were killed. But this can be dismissed in view of the agreement between Livy and the Excerptae Valesianae; *cf.* also Suidas: Φίλιππος: τοὺς υἱέας...συμπεριέλαβεν.

[30] Was this verse (from Stasinus, *cf.* Clem. Alex. *Strom.* vi.ii.19.1) actually quoted by Philip, or is it part of the tragic elaboration of the historian? The sentiment was a common one and is to be found, for example, in Herodotus (1.155) and, significantly, in Euripides, *Andromache* 519–21: καὶ γὰρ ἄνοια | μεγάλη λείπειν ἐχθροὺς ἐχθρῶν, | ἐξὸν κτείνειν | καὶ φόβον οἴκων ἀνελέσθαι. We have

The general effect of this was to awaken pity for the children of men of high station; *but a particular incident brought the corresponding loathing for Philip to a climax. This was the death of Theoxena and her sister's children.'* (Here occurred the account of this, as given in Livy.) *'This incident added new flame to the hatred of his people, and they now openly cursed Philip and his sons; and these curses, heard by all the gods, caused Philip to turn his anger against his own blood.* For while his mind was almost maddened on this account (διὰ ταῦτα),[31] the quarrel of his sons burst into flame simultaneously, Fortune as if of set purpose bringing their misfortunes on the stage at one and the same time. The quarrel was referred to Philip and he had to decide which of his two sons he should murder and which he should fear as his own possible murderer for the rest of his life. Who can help thinking that the wrath of heaven was descending on him for his past sins? The details that follow will make this clearer.' (Then come the details of the quarrel between Demetrius and Perseus: Livy XL.5–24; Polyb. XXIII.10.17, 11.)

V

Such, in essentials, must have been Polybius' introduction to the account of Philip's last years. The question arises: how far can Polybius' own criticism of Phylarchus be applied to it? First and foremost, to what extent does it neglect the nexus of cause and effect? A close examination of the passage, from a purely rational point of view, does in fact reveal a clearly defined sequence of cause and effect operating (with one apparent exception) throughout. Philip made the great error (in Polybius' eyes) of planning war on Rome, and to secure the safety of Macedon he carried out exchanges of populations; unfortunately this had the effect of arousing a great deal of popular antagonism, so that Philip, becoming alarmed, was driven to adopt severe measures against certain individuals (the children of men he had already executed) who might prove a focus for disaffection. However, his decree, couched in general terms, embraced more people than was really necessary, thus increasing the popular outcry; the sensational case of Theoxena was seized upon as perhaps the most outrageous injustice and Philip and all his family were openly cursed throughout the land. It so happened that at the very moment that this outcry was at its height the quarrel between Perseus and Demetrius burst out and, naturally, in Macedon men saw in it the answer to the curses.

The main difficulty is to see any real connection between Philip's actions and the quarrel between Perseus and Demetrius; for plainly the answer to a curse is not a satisfactory rational explanation. And if Polybius proves on

---

seen above, p. 214, how a quotation from Euripides crept into the account of Regulus' downfall. If the present quotation is to be placed in a similar category, its appearance in hexameter form may be not unconnected with the less 'quotable' form of Euripides' choral metre. But whether Polybius had, in fact, epic or tragedy in his mind is of course not important; what matters is that the moral emphasis was leading him away from a purely 'historical' approach.

[31] XXIII.10.16, almost certainly referring to the curses.

examination to have accepted this explanation alone, he stands·condemned of abandoning a rational criterion. Apart from the curses, it is Fortune or Tyche who forms the connecting link: Tyche, ὥσπερ ἐπίτηδες, brings the two sets of events on to the stage at the same time. Now it was Tyche who first launched Philip on his path of infatuation, and her method ‖ was to inveigle him into a war on Rome; from this step all else followed. But Polybius was interested in the moral lesson, and if Philip's infatuation was due to Tyche alone, how could he be accounted responsible for the results of his actions? The answer was that from the year 183 onwards Philip was indeed infatuated, caught in a chain of destruction and no longer master of his own actions. But the reason for this fate is to be sought earlier, in his impiety at Thermum,[32] his brutality at Messene,[33] his treachery at Rhodes,[34] his cruelty at Cius,[35] his sacrilege at Pergamum,[36] and, perhaps above all, in the scandalous compact made in 203/2 with Antiochus against the infant Ptolemy Epiphanes.[37] This last outrage, Polybius had already explained, was avenged by Tyche doubly, immediately, in that she raised up the Romans against Philip and Antiochus and forced them both within a short time to pay tribute to her, and then again afterwards, by re-establishing the dynasty of Ptolemy, while those of his enemies sank in ruin.

The revenge of Tyche for the offence against Egypt was to exalt the power of Rome above Philip. Thus clearly Rome was the chosen favourite of Tyche, 'who had guided almost all the affairs of the world in one direction, and had forced them to incline towards one and the same end', that is, towards the world domination of Rome.[38] Hence it is significant that when Tyche is about to accomplish the infatuation and downfall of Philip, her method is to tempt him to plan a war on Rome; and that, just as the wrong done to Epiphanes is righted ultimately in the fate of his oppressors' sons, so Philip's infatuation extends to Perseus, whose hostility to Rome is the main reason for his quarrel with Demetrius, the Roman favourite. Here, then, under all the superstructure of curses and Tyche is the link common to these two sets of events, which are at first sight mere coincidence; it is by a policy of blind hostility to Rome that both Philip and Perseus show their infatuation and take their place in the tragic sequence presented by Polybius.

On the assumption that Tyche plays an active part in directing the lines of history – and that Polybius believed this cannot, I think, be denied – his analysis becomes understandable.[39] To avenge the sins of Philip's youth, Tyche incites him to oppose the power whose rise is inevitable; this policy leads him to a series of actions which bring Macedon to a state of suppressed revolt; then at the proper moment Tyche presses Perseus along the same path in opposition to his brother, so that Philip's life ends amid murder and hatred.

---

[32] v.9f., XI.7.   [33] VII.11, 13; Plut. *Arat.* 49–51.
[34] XIII.3.   [35] XV.22.
[36] XVI.1.   [37] XV.20.
[38] 1.4.1f.
[39] The factual accuracy of this analysis will, on the other hand, be considered below.

VI

So much is understandable. But Polybius did not leave it at that. Instead he built on these 'basic facts' a superstructure of tragedy, in the Aristotelian sense; the steps leading to Philip's death are embellished ‖ with a mass of tragic paraphernalia – furies, torments and avenging spirits of his victims, Justice and her eye, curses answered by the gods. How far do these render him vulnerable to the second criticism against Phylarchus: the use of sensationalism, the introduction of embroidered detail and an emotional treatment of the subject?

The last charge is easily rebutted; Polybius makes no attempt to involve the reader emotionally in the development of the situation, as, for instance, Phylarchus did in his description of the capture of Mantinea. Nor are the curses and furies, the supernatural machinery, sensational in the way that Phylarchus was sensational; they are here, not for an emotional, but for a moral purpose. But even so, how does Polybius intend his readers to regard these supernatural figures? Are we to imagine that Philip was visited by real Furies, that actual gods sitting on Olympus heard and answered the curses against Philip's line? The notion is preposterous; and Polybius himself gives plenty of hints that this machinery is not to be interpreted too literally. His conscious use of theatrical terminology is a cue that the dramatic form of the passage and the rhetorical introduction of supernatural paraphernalia are merely convenient means of emphasising the moral to be drawn. Polybius is casting the account of Philip's last years as a tragedy and, lest any reader should fail to understand what he is about, he introduces such expressions as τῆς τύχης ὥσπερ ἐπίτηδες ἀναβιβαζούσης ἐπὶ σκηνήν,[40] or τρίτον δρᾶμα.[41] And finally, in Philip's speech to his sons (partly, at least, a rhetorical composition, notwithstanding Polybius' strictures on such writing elsewhere),[42] the broadest hint of all is offered in the words δεῖ μὴ μόνον ἀναγινώσκειν τὰς τραγῳδίας καὶ τοὺς μύθους καὶ τὰς ἱστορίας, ἀλλὰ καὶ γινώσκειν καὶ συνεφιστάνειν ἐπὶ τοῦτο τὸ μέρος.

VII

Now, as we saw, the basis of this superstructure, this dramatisation of Philip's last years, the better to bring out the doctrine of sin and retribution, is the

[40] XXIII.10.16. This phrase occurs in two other places in Polybius, once exactly the same as here (XXIX.19.2, on the folly of the Rhodians), and once with the substitution of τὴν ἐξώστραν for σκηνήν (XI.5.8, on the folly of the Aetolians); in both places it comes somewhat oddly, and without the kind of context which here gives it particular significance. Polybius was always ready to repeat a phrase that took his fancy; thus τῆς τύχης ὥσπερ ἐπίτηδες is also to be found at I.86.7, and II.4.3.

[41] XXIII.10.12. Admittedly, this expression may belong to the excerptor rather than to Polybius himself; but if so, it merely shows that he had appreciated the tone of Polybius' writing in this passage.

[42] XII.25b.4. Polybius may, of course, have some information on which the speech is founded; there is no justification for condemning it as pure invention (as is done by C. F. Edson, 'Perseus and Demetrius', HSPh 46 (1935) 196).

assumption that Philip planned an aggressive war on Rome; it was this primary act of folly and infatuation which caused the transfer of populations and the whole sequence which followed it, and it was this alone that formed the rational connection with the quarrel between Perseus and Demetrius. The third accusation against Phylarchus was that of inaccuracy in his basic facts; and it is the accuracy of this theory of Philip's war-policy that must next be considered. The first suggestion in our ‖ sources that Philip was planning a fresh war on Rome comes in Livy,[43] in connection with the schemes of consolidation carried out by Philip between 188 and 185; 'cum Perseo rege et Macedonibus bellum quod imminebat non unde plerique, nec ab ipso Perseo causas cepit: inchoata initia a Philippo sunt; et is ipse, si diutius vixisset, id bellum gessisset.'[44] From this time on the Macedonian war-plans are a constant theme in Livy. Thus, in discussing the consolidation of 188–185, after admitting that the annexation of the Thracian towns of Aenus and Maronea had soothed Philip's anger against the Romans, he adds:[45] 'nunquam tamen remisit animum a colligendis in pace viribus, quibus, quandoque data fortuna esset, ad bellum uteretur.'

There is, however, in Polybius, the report of a conversation which puts these statements in a fresh light. In 184 Appius Claudius was sent out to Macedon to investigate the massacre at Maronea; after he had censured Philip and returned to Rome, the king confidentially informed his friends Apelles and Philocles[46] that war with Rome was in his opinion now inevitable, but that he was not yet prepared for it. Sooner or later, Rome was going to force a war upon him; in the meantime, he would avoid the clash, consolidate his possessions and manoeuvre for position.

What was Polybius' authority for this private conversation? Both Apelles and Philocles may be ruled out. In 179 they were denounced by Philip as being party to Perseus' plot against Demetrius: Philocles was arrested and put to death, Apelles took refuge in Italy, probably in Rome, but was later recalled by Perseus and, rumour claimed, assassinated.[47] It is, however, clear from his vivid and detailed description of the Macedonian army review[48] and the subsequent brawl at Perseus' house,[49] that Polybius had some Macedonian informant for his account of the last years of Philip. As an exile at Rome, from 167 onwards he must have come into contact with most Greeks of any note who were living in the city. Many of these, today unidentifiable, there acted as informants concerning events in which they had taken part: for instance, Nicander of Trichonium, who was exiled to Rome in 170, probably served as

---

[43] XXXIX.23.5.

[44] This passage is taken from XXII.18, which is placed too late in Büttner-Wobst, and should in fact precede XXII.6; cf. De Sanctis, Storia dei Romani 4.1 (Turin, 1923) 250 n. 24.

[45] XXXIX.24.1.

[46] XXII.14.7f., γενόμενος καθ᾽ ἑαυτὸν καὶ συμμεταδοὺς τῶν φίλων ᾿Απελλῇ καὶ Φιλοκλεῖ περὶ τῶν ἐνεστώτων.

[47] Livy (P) XL.55.6–8, XLII.5.4.   [48] Livy (P) XL.6.

[49] Livy (P) XL.7.

an important source for Aetolian affairs.[50] It is thus probable that Polybius' Macedonian informant was a member of the circle of Apelles and Philocles, who had fled to Rome, and, wiser than Apelles, had stayed there. Be that as it may, the confident account of Philip's conversation with Philocles and Apelles suggests that here too Polybius' authority was this same highly-connected Macedonian; and its contradiction of the general pro-Demetrian thesis[51] that Philip was planning a war of aggression entitles the passage to particular consideration. ‖

As here expressed, Philip's policy did not rule out a Macedonian offensive, if the situation should develop favourably to this; but fundamentally it was merely the reply to a Roman policy, designed, in Philip's opinion, first to weaken and ultimately to engulf him. And certainly this reply has nothing in common with the insane aggression which figures in the narrative of Polybius and so, of course, of Livy. Polybius, in fact, normally neglects the implications of this reported conversation; he speaks as if the third Macedonian War were something engineered by Philip and passed on, all ready for the waging, to Perseus.[52] In this view, however, he ignores the fact that this war did not break out until 172, seven years after Philip's death, and then only after a series of fresh incidents and embassies; and that when it did come, the time of it was decided by the Romans who declared it. The line between deliberate aggression and a precautionary offensive is, indeed, not easy to demarcate; Philip's manoeuvres for position and his determination to face the inevitable blow under the most favourable circumstances possible led him to adopt measures that bore very many marks of an aggressive policy. For example, his negotiations with the barbarians on the northern frontiers must have seemed aggressive in Roman eyes.[53] Nevertheless, his fundamental position is quite clear from this conversation, which Polybius repeats.[54] Here, if nowhere else, the truth comes out; the whole policy of Philip's last years, internal and foreign alike, was based on a conviction that Rome was only waiting her time to annihilate him.

[50] W. J. Woodhouse, *Aetolia, its geography, topography and antiquities* (Oxford, 1897) 258 n. 1.

[51] This pro-Demetrian source is probably to be sought in Achaea itself, where there were two opposing traditions for the account of Demetrius' death, cf. Livy (P) XLI.23.10–11 and 24.3–5. Here Callicrates, voicing the view of the anti-Persean, pro-Roman faction, gives what is essentially the account already presented by Polybius, while in reply Archon asserts that 'nec ob quam causam nec quem ad modum perierit Demetrius scimus'. Polybius has followed the general lines of the anti-Persean version, adding details of incident (but not motive) from his Macedonian source. (I am grateful to Mr A. H. McDonald of University College, Nottingham, for drawing my attention to this passage in Livy.)

[52] E.g. XXII.18.10.

[53] Cf. A. J. Reinach, BCH 34 (1910) 249–330. It is, however, probable that the alarm felt at Rome was no more justified than it had been during the periods preceding the second war with Philip and that with Antiochus.

[54] There are other occasions on which Polybius gives an accurate report of some speech or incident without himself seeing its full implications; cf. v.104, the speech of Agelaus of Naupactus in 217 (Walbank, *Aratos of Sicyon* (Cambridge, 1933) 153–4); XVIII.1–12, the conference on the Malian Gulf in November 198 (Holleaux, *REG* 36 (1923) 115–71).

Not everyone in Macedon shared this conviction. When Demetrius returned from Rome in spring 183, he received a warm reception from many who had feared that Philip's policy of resistance might precipitate an immediate war.[55] In the winter of the same year, we read of measures taken against the children of Admetus, Pyrrhichus, Philip's own foster-brother Samus and others put to death at the same time.[56] Evidently their execution had been the sequel to some kind of conspiracy; and it is not unreasonable to connect this with the faction which favoured Demetrius' policy of collaboration with the Senate and had been driven by fear to the desperate scheme of getting rid of Philip. Once before, in his youth, Philip had had to face a similar plot from a party of highly-placed ministers, ‖ who believed his policy to be contrary to the best interests of the state; now as then he had succeeded in crushing the opposition.[57]

These, then, are the ingredients out of which Polybius has built up his tragic version: first, Philip's policy of resistance to the Senate, misinterpreted as an anti-Roman offensive; secondly, the reorganisation of the population in preparation for war; thirdly, the ruthless suppression of the pro-Roman faction and the measures taken against their children; and finally, the assassination of Demetrius, the Roman candidate for the throne. All this Polybius read as the insane policy of a man infatuated by Fortune as a penalty for the many crimes of his past life; misunderstanding the real political situation, he laid every emphasis on the personal tragedy and the moral to be drawn.

VIII

Polybius undoubtedly made a mistake; but it was not the mistake that Benecke would attribute to him. The tragic version in Polybius is of his own construction and does not spring from the uncritical use of tragedies or historical novels (if indeed such a thing as a historical novel existed in the Greek literature of Polybius' time). Polybius' strictures on Phylarchus make it at least extremely unlikely that he could have fallen into such a crude error in a matter of source-selection. Moreover, there is in Polybius adequate material to reconstruct the real motives which influenced Philip throughout these years, a thing most improbable had his sources been mainly of a tragic or fictional nature. Polybius' mistake, either his own, or perhaps one prompted by his Macedonian informant, who may have retailed popular gossip and superstition then current in Macedon, was to interpret Philip's last years as a career of

---

[55] Polyb. xxiii.7.2–4; Livy (P) xxxix.53. Polybius' distinction between οἱ μὲν Μακεδόνες and ὁ δὲ Φίλιππος καὶ Περσεύς is, however, tendenciously over-simplified by the pro-Demetrian tradition.

[56] xxiii.10.9. Niese (*Geschichte der griechischen und makedonischen Staaten* 2 (Gotha, 1899) 570 n. 1) appears to identify these men with the five counsellors executed at the instigation of Heracleides of Tarentum (Diod. xxviii.2) in or about the year 205; in this case, the delay of twenty years before proceeding against their children would be inexplicable.

[57] For the conspiracy of Leontius and Apelles cf. v.25–8.

infatuation induced by Tyche and showing itself in an unreasoned programme of planned aggression against Rome. The moral lesson, here Polybius' supreme concern, comes from regarding this sequence as the direct outcome of a misled and misspent youth.

These conclusions are important for their bearing on Polybius' reliability as a source. He certainly does not suffer the blow that would have come from a substantiation of Benecke's theory. He is not convicted of studied incompetence in his choice of sources, of treating a tragedy or a novel as proper material for history. On the other hand, he does appear to have misunderstood Philip's position and policy, when he had in fact the material available to understand it. Furthermore, his excessive emphasis on the moral issues and his unique and unfortunate use of a tragic scheme and tragic terminology – not in the Phylarchean sense, admittedly, yet none the less tragic in a manner opposed to the requirements of scientific history – these factors make Polybius' account of these last years of Philip one of the least satisfying in his whole work. In the realm of pure fact, in his account of the measures Philip took and the order in which he took them, in so far as they can be gleaned from the fragmentary nature of the text and a careful study of Livy, Polybius is in the ‖ main to be trusted.[58] But in anything connected with motivation, his inordinate stress on the moral issue, his misunderstanding of Philip's real position and, finally, his unhappy experiment in the tragic mode make it necessary to treat his picture of Philip's last years with the utmost suspicion.

[58] An exception to this, however, is the story of the 'revealing' of Perseus' plot against Demetrius by the 'loyal' Antigonus, the torturing of Xychus and the 'proof' that Flamininus' letter was forged. There seems little doubt that Polybius has here accepted a pro-Roman tradition current in Achaea for the facts as well as the motives; cf. n. 51 above, and Edson, *op. cit.* (n. 42) 200–2.

15

HISTORY AND TRAGEDY*

Two centuries divide Xenophon's *floruit* from that of Polybius, and no Greek history of any substance survives from this period. Discussion about the character of Hellenistic history writing depends therefore in the main on fragments preserved in later authors, along with the occasional remarks of critics whose assumptions may be very different from ours. It seems clear that much of the history written at this time aimed at stirring the reader's emotions. Phylarchus, for example, was obviously not unique in his pathetic accounts of captured cities, clinging women, with hair dishevelled and breasts bare, and crowds of children and aged parents weeping and lamenting as they were led off into slavery.[1] This style of writing Polybius calls 'tragic', and it certainly shared many of the characteristics of tragedy, though indeed it contained several other ingredients, for instance the marvellous and the monstrous (τὸ τερατῶδες), which Aristotle specifically excluded from tragedy,[2] as well as the trivial, the meretricious and the sentimental – night scenes, detailed descriptions of clothing, love-interest, and the almost human behaviour of animals.

If there was a Hellenistic theory behind all this it has not survived, and modern attempts to discover one have enjoyed limited success. Perhaps the most popular hypothesis, and one which still holds the field, is that propounded fifty years ago in a series of articles by Ed. Schwartz, and later developed in an important pamphlet by Scheller, which derives tragic history from the Peripatetics as a result of a curious reversal of Aristotle's own teaching.[3] In the *Poetics*,[4] as is well known, Aristotle draws a clear line between poetry and history. But someone within Aristotle's school, it was supposed, blurred this distinction and diverted those features characteristic of poetry, and in particular of tragedy, to the field of history. About fifteen years ago this view was challenged by B. L. Ullman,[5] who tried to establish the origins of tragic history in the school of Isocrates, but not I think with success. Ullman's thesis revived

* [*Historia* 9 (1960) 216–34]

[1] Polyb. 11.56. 7–12.

[2] Arist. *Poet.* 14.2, 1453 b 8.

[3] Ed. Schwartz, *Fünf Vorträge über den griechischen Roman*² (Berlin, 1943) 123–5; *Hermes* 32 (1897) 56off.; 35 (1900) 107ff.; 44 (1909) 491; P. Scheller, *De hellenistica historiae conscribendae arte* (Diss. Leipzig, 1911).

[4] *Poet.* 9.2–9, 1451 b 1–32.

[5] *TAPhA* 73 (1942) 25ff.

interest in the problem and was followed by a good deal of discussion;[6] and ‖ on the whole opinion was tending to the view that 'tragic history' was perhaps being rather too rigidly defined and that its origins were to be sought over a wider area and at an earlier date than had hitherto appeared. However, any further consideration of the matter now has to take account of an extremely stimulating paper read by Professor Kurt von Fritz to a meeting of the Fondation Hardt in August 1956, and recently published in the fourth volume of the *Entretiens sur l'antiquité classique* under the title of 'Die Bedeutung des Aristoteles für die Geschichtsschreibung'.[7] In this paper I propose first of all to consider von Fritz's new arguments in favour of a Peripatetic origin for 'tragic history', and then to give reasons why I still believe that this problem has to be approached in a rather different way.

I

Concerning poetry, Aristotle[8] remarks that it is more philosophical and a higher thing than history; ἡ μὲν γὰρ ποίησις μᾶλλον τὰ καθ' ὅλου, ἡ δ' ἱστορία τὰ καθ' ἕκαστον λέγει – poetry tends to express the universal, history the particular. And by the particular Aristotle means τὰ γενόμενα, by the universal οἷα ἂν γένοιτο, 'what a certain type of person on a certain occasion will do or say according to the law of probability or necessity'. μᾶλλον, as von Fritz rightly insists, goes with both halves of the sentence: poetry is *more* concerned with the universal, history *more* concerned with the particular – for clearly it would be absurd to argue that there is no element of τὰ καθ' ἕκαστον in tragedy, which deals with the fate of individual men, just as it would be absurd to deny to history any concern with τὰ καθ' ὅλου, inasmuch as historical situations can be repeated and the lessons of one apply quite often to another. This is, I think, true and was worth saying; though it is perhaps not so novel as von Fritz suggests, for Butcher's translation, 'poetry *tends* to stress the universal, history the particular', had already accurately rendered the Greek, and given μᾶλλον its force in both clauses.

It is this μᾶλλον which, according to von Fritz, leaves the door open for the supposed Peripatetic theory of tragic history. If history was less philosophical (and so less meritorious) than poetry, this was because poetry dealt with the universal. The conclusion was clear: to raise the status of history, it too must be made more universal, and so more like poetry. Aristotle, von Fritz rightly points out, had not said that history *ought* to be more concerned with the particular, but merely that it *tended* to be so, as compared with poetry; but he

---

[6] *Cf.* M. Laistner, *The greater Roman historians* (Berkeley, 1947) 14ff.; F. Wehrli, *Phyllobolia für Peter von der Mühll zum 60. Geburtstag* (Basel, 1946) 9–34; *Eumusia: Festgabe für Ernst Howald zum 60. Geburtstag* (Zürich, 1947) 54ff.; G. Giovannini, *PhQ* 22 (1943) 308–14; F. W. Walbank, *BICS* 2 (1955) 4ff.

[7] *Histoire et historiens dans l'antiquité* (Vandoeuvres-Geneva, 1958) 85–145 (including discussion).

[8] *Poet* 9.3, 1451 b 5–7.

was, after all, not discussing history, and had only made reference to it incidentally. There was nothing in what he had said to prevent anyone propounding and developing the view that history would be improved by becoming more universal and hence more like poetry. ‖

As an *a priori* argument this is plausible; and von Fritz would appear to be right in claiming that if it was put forward, it is more likely than not to have come from a follower of Aristotle, since obviously the compulsion to take the master's definition into account would be felt by a Peripatetic rather than by someone without his affiliations. Such a Peripatetic, it is suggested, was Duris of Samos, who is known not only as a writer of emotional and sensational scenes,[9] but also as the author of a famous criticism of two eminent historians of Isocrates' school. 'Ephorus and Theopompus', he wrote,[10] 'proved for the most part unequal to the events they described, τῶν γενομένων ἀπελείφθησαν; for in their presentation they made no attempt at dramatic *mimesis* with its associated pleasure in the narrative, and concerned themselves only with the formal aspects of writing: οὔτε γὰρ μιμήσεως μετέλαβον οὐδεμίας οὔτε ἡδονῆς ἐν τῷ φράσαι, αὐτοῦ δὲ τοῦ γράφειν μόνον ἐπεμελήθησαν.' Clearly this implies that Duris believed μίμησις to be an integral part of the historian's task; but before he can link Duris with his hypothetical theorist inside the Peripatos von Fritz has to trace a connection between μίμησις and τὰ καθ' ὅλου, since although Aristotle has a good deal to say about μίμησις in various art-forms it is in terms of τὰ καθ' ὅλου and τὰ καθ' ἕκαστον, the universal and the particular, and not by virtue of the presence or absence of μίμησις, that he distinguishes history from tragedy.

What is μίμησις? Bywater thought it was 'imitation' in the straightforward sense of producing a copy; but Gomme very properly corrected this.[11] μίμησις, he argued in his Sather lectures on poetry and history, is rather to be rendered by 'representation'. Von Fritz quotes Gomme with approval, but in fact he reads very much more than Gomme into μίμησις. μίμησις in tragedy, he argues,[12] μίμησις which inspires fear and pity in the spectator, is to be defined as a 'concentrated representation' of what in real life is much less concentrated; and it is in this 'concentrated representation' that the universality emerges. 'The universality of tragedy', he goes on, 'consists of the fact that it represents what stands as an extreme possibility behind every life and perhaps also in a less extreme form becomes reality in every life.' Now I am not quarrelling with this as a description of what happens in tragedy. But it does seem extremely unlikely that the word μίμησις can be stretched to mean 'concentrated representation' in this sense, and still more unlikely that 'the special tragic

---

[9] *Cf. FGH* 76 T 12, F5, 7, 14, 18, 52.
[10] *FGH* 76 F 1 = Phot. *Bibl.* p. 121 a 41; the passage came from Book I of the *Histories* and almost certainly from the prologue, the traditional place for polemic and the discussion of general principles.
[11] A. W. Gomme, *The Greek attitude to poetry and history* (Berkeley, 1954) 53ff. (quoted as *Poetry and history*).   [12] *Op. cit.* (n. 11) 120ff.

form of concentration [*i.e.* of μίμησις] consists of the presentation of the extreme case'. In the first chapter of the *Poetics* Aristotle in fact discusses ‖ the different forms of μίμησις exhibited by epic, tragedy, comedy, dithyramb and instrumental music.[13] All these, he says, are forms of μίμησις; but they differ from each other in their medium, their subjects, and their mode of representation. What then is the form of μίμησις peculiar to tragedy? Is it 'representation of the extreme case'? Aristotle does not say so. When he seeks to establish the mode in which the μίμησις of tragedy differs from other forms of μίμησις he simply says that the poet may represent by narration, like Homer, or 'he may present all his characters as living and moving before us'. In short, the special tragic form of μίμησις consists of putting people on the stage.

Now if Aristotle had meant to define μίμησις as '*concentrated* representation' with 'concentrated representation of the extreme case' as the specific aspect peculiar to tragedy, here was his opportunity to make that distinction. Since he does not, we are hardly justified in reading such an idea into the word, and then asserting that this concentrated representation of the extreme case is in fact τὰ καθ' ὅλου of tragedy. The reason von Fritz tries to read all this into μίμησις is of course that he has to bridge the gap between Aristotle's distinction between poetry and history in terms of the particular and the universal, and Duris' remark about the need for μίμησις and ἡδόνη in the writing of history. If von Fritz is right, Duris was here demanding that history should depict the extreme case, οἷα ἂν γένοιτο. It seems far more likely that the μίμησις which he desiderates is simply a vivid presentation of events, emotive writing, as we might say; this would certainly fit what is known of his technique, for judging from the extant fragments anything capable of moving and titillating his readers finds a place in his pages – wonder-stories and travel-tales, prodigious births, and scandalous customs, love-intrigue, the robes of Demetrius Poliorcetes, the dolphin that fell in love with a boy – all is grist to his mill. But little of this is tragic in the true sense or can in any way be regarded as depicting the universal; nor does Duris ever define the μίμησις which he requires as specifically tragic.

It is true that Duris was a pupil of Theophrastus; and I have no doubt that he used the word μίμησις in relation to history – for the first time (as far as we know) – because he was familiar with it from the Peripatos. But we are not therefore justified in describing the vivid and melodramatic history which he composed as Peripatetic history. Both Theophrastus and Praxiphanes, another Peripatetic, are known to have written works entitled Περὶ ἱστορίας; and it can be reasonably assumed that these were concerned with the theory of historiography.[14] But *what* they wrote is a question which we are in no position

---

[13] *Poet.* 1.2–3, 1447 a 13–18; *cf.* 3.1, 1448 a 19–23.

[14] It has recently been argued by G. Avenarius (*Lukians Schrift zur Geschichtsschreibung* (Diss. Frankfurt, 1954) 171), that these cannot be treatises on the theory of history because Cicero, *De Or.* II.62, puts into the mouth of M. Antonius the explicit declaration 'neque eam (*sc.* historiam)

‖ to answer. There is however one scrap – and it is only a scrap – of evidence which perhaps militates against the view that Theophrastus' theory was the counterpart to Duris' practice. In a passage in Cicero's *Orator*,[15] Theophrastus praises Thucydides and Herodotus for their rich and ornate diction which, however, avoided the *deliciae vel potius ineptiae* of Gorgias. It is not unreasonable to think that Theophrastus' treatise on history paid some attention to the appropriate style; and if he approved of Thucydides it is on the whole unlikely that he approved of Duris, who, according to Dionysius of Halicarnassus,[16] was one of those whose neglect of stylistic principles ensured that no one ever read their books to the end. Not perhaps a point to press hard; but, for what it is worth, against the view that Theophrastus provided the theoretical blueprint for Duris and Phylarchus.

There is a case for making Duris an important link in the development of sensational historiography, and also for thinking that he had a theory of sorts, to the extent at least that he knew what he wanted to do, and that his aims were something quite other than those of Theopompus and Ephorus. But there is no evidence that his theory is the Peripatetic theory, or that Theophrastus would have endorsed history as he wrote it. Further there is no evidence that his μίμησις has anything at all to do with universality in the Aristotelian sense, or with the presentation of the extreme case as von Fritz argues that it is presented in tragedy. Finally, Schwartz's hypothesis that some successor of Aristotle applied the master's definition of tragedy to history remains just as hypothetical as it was before. Though ingenious and illuminating, von Fritz's thesis fails to make its main point.

Perhaps the whole problem of 'tragic history' has suffered from a concentration on theory, on what Aristotle said, and how far the practice of later historians conformed with it. In the discussion which followed von Fritz's paper several scholars expressed reasonable doubts whether historians are very much moved by writers on the theory of history;[17] and there was widespread agreement that many other factors, political and social, the climate of the time and the example of predecessors, counted far more in shaping a tradition of writing. Among such factors are the presuppositions which a historian will inherit; and in the second half of this paper I want to examine certain factors which taken together were likely to predispose a Hellenistic historian, despite the dicta of Aristotle, and the kind of criticisms familiar to us from Polybius and Lucian, to confuse the categories of history and tragedy. ‖

reperio usquam separatim instructam rhetorum praeceptis'. But this means only that in the rhetorical handbooks history is not given special treatment distinct from the general precepts of the *ars*. See my comments in *Gnomon* 29 (1957) 418–19.

[15] Cic. *Or.* 39.

[16] *FGH* 76 T 10 = Dion. Hal. *Comp.* 4.

[17] *Op. cit.* (n. 7) 131ff.; observations of Latte, Syme, Hanell, de Romilly, Momigliano.

II

A good reason why tragedy and history were from their beginnings regarded as akin was their employment of the same subject-matter. Thucydides, for example, in his review of early Greek history in Book I[18] is dealing up to a point with precisely the same facts as Homer or Euripides. His purpose is of course different; but it does not occur to him, any more than it occurs to them, to question the historicity of Hellen, the son of Deucalion, of Minos and his thalassocracy, of Achilles, Pelops, Tyndareus, Atreus, Agamemnon and the rest. He does of course distinguish between the traditions surrounding these characters and the element which he calls τὸ μυθῶδες and regards as inappropriate to history.[19] τὸ μυθῶδες Gomme[20] took to mean 'the story-telling aspect', 'for example Candaules and Gyges, Croesus and Adrestus, Polycrates and his ring, Xerxes' dream before the sailing of the armada and Hippias' dream before Marathon, Themistocles and the allied admirals before Salamis, *i.e.* historical romance. It has nothing', he goes on, 'to do with belief or disbelief in the main traditions of what we call the "mythical" period of Greek history (the Theban and Trojan wars, the migrations and so forth, which Thucydides accepted).' One might perhaps add to this explanation that τὸ μυθῶδες also includes the 'mythical' or miraculous aspects of the legends. Achilles, Minos and Agamemnon are discussed as ordinary human beings in a world free from miracles, and any supernatural incidents attached by tradition to their names, such as Achilles' descent from a goddess, or Minos' possession of the Minotaur, are simply omitted from the discussion. This element of rational scepticism is not however peculiar to the historian; it can be detected under a flimsy disguise in Euripides, who, Aristophanes alleged,[21] 'by representing the gods, persuaded men that they did not exist'. It constitutes no fundamental distinction between the historian and the tragic writer.

The relationship between the two can be further illustrated from the character of the first Greek historians. Thucydides' treatment of early legend in Book I is of course outstanding in its clarity and in its firm grasp of the nature of historical evidence; but it also follows a tradition going back to Hecataeus, which can be summed up in Jacoby's remark that the main source for the early history of the Greek people was the panhellenic epic.[22]

Both the panhellenic historians of Ionia and such local historians as the Atthidographers who built on their work dealt with legendary times and derived their narrative from a critical analysis of the subject-matter of epic. ‖ Some were more credulous, some less; but it is interesting to find Dionysius

---

[18] Thuc. I.1–23.
[19] *Cf.* Thuc. I.21.1, 22.4; *cf.* Lucian, *Hist. Conscr.* 42.55.
[20] *Commentary on Thucydides* I (Oxford, 1945) 149; *cf. Poetry and history* (n. 11) 117.
[21] *Thesm.* 450–1.
[22] *Atthis* (Oxford, 1949) 202; *cf.* J. F. d'Alton, *Roman literary theory and criticism* (London, 1931) 491–2.

of Halicarnassus[23] using the same kind of language to criticise early Ionian history as Polybius uses concerning Phylarchus. 'It contained', he writes, 'myths which had been believed from time immemorial and many theatrical reversals of fortune which seem very naïve to the modern reader' – ἐν αἷς καὶ μῦθοί τινες ἐνῆσαν ἀπὸ τοῦ πολλοῦ πεπιστευμένοι χρόνου καὶ θεατρικαί τινες περιπέτειαι πολὺ τὸ ἠλίθιον ἔχειν τοῖς νῦν δοκοῦσαι.

It was perhaps this naïveté and theatricality to which Thucydides was objecting when he asserted[24] that his own observations about early Greek history 'will not be disturbed either by the lays of a poet displaying the exaggeration of his craft, or by the compositions of prose-writers whose attraction is gained at the expense of truth, the subjects they treat of being out of the reach of evidence, and time having robbed most of them of historical value by enthroning them in the region of legend'. Similarly Hecataeus of Miletus opened his work with his famous expression of incredulity[25] about the 'stories of the Hellenes' which were 'many and ridiculous'.

It is these same 'stories of the Hellenes' which form the material of Attic tragedy; for, as Jacoby has pointed out,[26] despite the fact that tragedy was a local Athenian product, it took the bulk of its subject-matter from panhellenic myths, only rarely introducing specifically Athenian material. As Aeschylus remarked about his own plays,[27] they were 'slices from the great feast of Homer'. In short, as far as subject-matter went, tragedy and history were both derived from a single source – epic.

The historian had a good deal of work to do on this material before he could reduce it to a form suited to his purpose. Many legends were so interwoven with impossibilities that only a radical process of rationalisation or 'historicising' would make them literally credible. There is plenty of evidence for this, especially among the Atthidographers. Plutarch, for instance,[28] in his *Life of Theseus* contrasts the rationalised versions of the Minotaur story, such as the Cretan one which turns the Minotaur into an arrogant general called Bull (Tauros), with the τραγικώτατος μῦθος of the hybrid monster and the victims in the labyrinth. This kind of treatment was forced on the Atthidographers, who were compelled to use legendary material if they were to write the early history of Athens at all.[29] They had to take their subject-matter where they could find it, and they were in fact as ready to draw on tragedy as on epic – certainly from the fourth century onwards;[30] and indeed Jacoby has suggested ‖ that even in the fifth century Hellanicus may have let his discussion of the founding of the Areopagus be influenced by the version in the *Oresteia*.[31]

---

[23] *Thuc.* 5.   [24] Thuc. 1.21.1.
[25] *FGH* I F I a.   [26] *Atthis* (n. 22) 220.
[27] Athen. VIII.39, p. 347e.   [28] Plut. *Thes.* 15.2.
[29] So, rightly, Jacoby, *Atthis* (n. 22) 136; for the various forms of the Minotaur legend in the various Atthidographers see his comments on Philochorus fr. 17 (*FGH* 328 F 17).
[30] Jacoby, *Atthis* (n. 22) 220, argues that Hellanicus felt an antipathy for Euripides which prevented his use of him as a source.
[31] Commentary on *FGH* 323aF I (Hellanicus).

These facts are not of course new. Most of the details I have mentioned can be found in the well-known handbooks. But it seemed worth while to recall this background before returning to what is probably the most famous ancient statement on the question, Aristotle's discussion of the nature of history and tragedy in the *Poetics*.[32] In that passage, as we saw, Aristotle distinguishes poetry as a more philosophical and higher thing than history, because it tends to express the universal, and history the particular. The universal, τὰ καθ᾽ ὅλου, is how a person of a certain type will on occasion speak or act, according to the law of probability or necessity; and it is this universality at which poetry aims, just adding proper names to the characters.[33] The particular, τὰ καθ᾽ ἕκαστον, is what Alcibiades did or what happened to him. At this point comes a significant statement: ἐπὶ μὲν οὖν τῆς κωμῳδίας ἤδη τοῦτο δῆλον γέγονεν – which I take, with Gomme,[34] to mean 'in the case of comedy this is at once apparent'. For in comedy, Aristotle continues, the plot is invented on lines of probability (διὰ τῶν εἰκότων) and names assigned to the characters; hence it is clearly universal on his definition. Tragic writers on the contrary keep to real names (τῶν γενομένων ὀνομάτων ἀντέχονται). By real names he means of course the names of real people like Agamemnon and Orestes; and what they did has been defined as history. That is why the claim of tragedy to be accounted universal has to be specially argued.

In this chapter Aristotle takes it for granted that his readers will immediately appreciate the distinction between comedy (which is universal) and history (which deals with the particular); but he expects the difference between tragedy and history to need special argumentation. This contrast between the two dramatic forms is widely made, and its echoes appear in both earlier and later critics. In the fourth century the comic writer Antiphanes,[35] for example, asserted that the tragic poet merely reminds his audience of what they all know, whereas the comic poet has to make it all up, πάντα δεῖ εὑρεῖν. This view might appear at first sight to contradict Aristotle's insistence[36] that the tragic poet is the creator of plots rather than verses (μᾶλλον τῶν μύθων ‖ εἶναι δεῖ ποιητὴν ἢ τῶν μέτρων), since he is a poet because he represents (κατὰ τὴν μίμησιν), and what he represents are actions. Certainly this statement of Aristotle implies – as both Gomme[37] and Baldry[38] have recently insisted – that the poet had a considerable freedom of invention in relation to the traditional themes;

---

[32] See above n. 4.

[33] I agree with Gomme (*Poetry and history* (n. 11) 71) that the adding of the proper names is mentioned as something which does not really hinder the universality of tragedy. Butcher translates 'it is this universality at which poetry aims in the names she attaches to the personages'; but though the proper names may constitute no serious obstacle, they can hardly *help* to make tragedy more universal. Bywater agrees with Gomme.

[34] *Poetry and history* (n. 11) 72 n. 6. Alternatively Gudeman's rendering makes good sense: 'It is now agreed by all for comedy, but not for tragedy'; for in the case of comedy it is easily apparent.

[35] *CAF* (ed. Kock) 2.90–1, fr. 191 = Athen. vi.222. a–c; see G. Giovannini, *PhQ* 22 (1943) 308.

[36] *Poet.* 9.9, 1451 b 27–30.	[37] *Poetry and history* (n. 11) 5–6, 54–5.

[38] H. C. Baldry, *CQ* 4 (1954) 156 n. 1.

but the limits of such freedom are indicated in another passage[39] in which Aristotle states that 'the poet may not destroy the framework of the received legends, the fact for instance that Clytemnestra was slain by Orestes and Eriphyle by Alcmaeon', and goes on to show by examples that what he means when he calls the poet a creator of plots is that he ought to show skill in the manipulation of the traditional material (τοῖς παραδεδομένοις χρῆσθαι καλῶς). Hence, despite the difference of nuance between one play on the Orestes legend and another, the main outlines of the story would be preserved, and would confirm the average Athenian theatre-goer in his belief that the tragedies he saw represented the fortunes of real people, just as Elizabethan audiences by and large must have taken *Richard II* to be a representation of what had happened to a real English king.

But if to the fifth- and fourth-century spectator tragedies dealt with traditional stories and real people, to that extent they came very close to history. Consequently when Aristotle goes on to establish the universality of tragedy – its concern with οἷα ἂν γένοιτο rather than with τὰ γενόμενα – this superficial closeness to history causes him some embarrassment. The poet, he argues, is to relate οἷα ἂν γένοιτο, what is possible according to the laws of probability or necessity; and the poet includes the writer of tragedy for these reasons. Tragedians keep to real names, because the use of real names (like Orestes and Clytemnestra) is as it were a guarantee of credibility. We feel a certain natural doubt as to whether something that has not happened could have happened at all; whereas what *has* happened is clearly possible. On the other hand, tragedies may contain some fictitious characters, as well as real ones (one thinks for instance of the watchman in the *Antigone*), or even nothing but fictitious ones, like Agathon's *Antheus*, in which both the incidents and names are alike made up. In any case, he adds, since most of the audience are ignorant of the traditional stories, they are as good as fictitious: τὰ γνώριμα ὀλίγοις γνώριμά ἐστιν ἀλλ' ὅμως εὐφραίνει πάντας – which seems to imply that what is fictitious can make a more immediately obvious claim to universality than what is based on the literally true legends.

This argument might, however, lead to the conclusion that tragedies like the *Antheus* were in fact superior to those based on the traditional panhellenic legends; and this would be paradoxical, since the majority of the tragedies and virtually all the most famous ones fell into the second category. So Aristotle concludes by saying that in any case if a poet happens to take real events as ‖ the subject of his poetry, γενόμενα ποιεῖν – which must mean actual happenings, the received legends as opposed to the fictional events in tragedies like the *Antheus*, and not, as some have believed, specifically historical tragedies like the *Persae* – there is no reason why *some* actual events should not also conform to the law of the probable and the possible, and it is by virtue of that quality in the events that the author is a poet.

---

[39] *Poet.* 14.5, 1453b22-6.

The amount that has been written about this argument clearly indicates its difficulties;[40] and these, I suggest, arise to a large extent from the embarrassment Aristotle experiences in the face of the firmly established belief that the subject-matter of almost all Greek tragedies was also the subject-matter of history. The Greeks, it has been said, had only historical tragedies. This is true for almost the whole range of tragedy, and it means that the only difference between a play like the *Persae* and the *Troades* lies in the fact that one conforms to the custom of going back to the old traditional stories, while the other does not; but both alike are regarded as based on historical material.[41]

III

This view of the matter long continued to be the usual one. As an American scholar, Giovannini,[42] has recently pointed out, it can be well illustrated from the way in which the later grammarians divided up their material for classification. In his second book Quintilian[43] divides the field of *narrationes* (excluding those used in law-court speeches) into three categories, which he calls *fabulae, argumenta* and *historiae*. The Greek equivalents are given in Sextus Empiricus,[44] for *fabula* μῦθος, for *argumentum* πλάσμα, while ἱστορία serves in both languages. The same divisions appear with slightly different names in Asclepiades of Myrleia,[45] in the *ad Herennium*, in Cicero's *De Inventione*, and in the Byzantine *scholia* to Dionysius Thrax.[46] ‖

These three types of *narratio* are sharply distinguished. 'History', says Sextus,[47] 'ἱστορία, is the recording of certain things which are true and have happened, as for example that Alexander died at Babylon through having been poisoned by conspirators [perhaps an unfortunate example!]; fiction (πλάσμα, *argumentum*) is the narrating of things which are not real events but are similar

---

[40] It has even been argued recently, by F. Grayeff (*Phronesis* 1 (1955–6) 110–18), that *Poetics* 9 is a composite production incorporating the arguments of a series of Peripatetic lecturers who have tried, each in turn, to add his comments to a rather abortive discussion without great success. This argument, which takes no account of Baldry's discussion in *CQ* 4 (1954) 151–7, does not convince me.

[41] Isoc. *Euag.* 36 has been adduced (by Gudeman on Arist. *Poet.* 9) in support of this view, but wrongly. Its meaning is that 'of all the poets who have told of returning exiles, both real and of their own imagining (παρ' αὐτῶν καινὰς συντιθέασιν), none has told a story (of anyone) who returned home after enduring such dreadful and fearful dangers (as Euagoras)'. It does not mean that no tragedian ever told a μῦθος, as indeed the previous sentence makes clear. In the context of the *Euagoras*, however, Isocrates is led to stress the differences between the poet and the prose panegyrist (*cf.* §§8–11).

[42] *PhQ* 22 (1943) 308–14.   [43] *Inst.* II.42.

[44] *Math.* 1.263f.

[45] Viz. ἀληθὴς ἱστορία (= ἱστορία), ψευδὴς ἱστορία (= μῦθος, *fabula*), and ὡς ἀληθὴς ἱστορία (= πλάσμα, *argumentum*). On Asclepiades see Reitzenstein, *Hellenistische Wundererzählungen* (Lepizig, 1906) 90ff.; K. Barwick, *Hermes* 63 (1928) 270. The relevant text is from Sext. Emp. *Math.* 1.252, where both Reitzenstein and Barwick are agreed in accepting Kaibel's emendation, so as to include τὴν περὶ πλάσματα under ὡς ἀληθῆ.

[46] See *ad Herenn.* 1.12f.; Cic. *Inv. Rhet.* 1.27; Barwick, *op. cit.* (n. 45) 261ff.

[47] *Math.* 1.263–4.

to real events in the telling, such as the hypothetical situations in comedies and mimes; and legend (μῦθος, *fabula*) is the narrating of events which have never happened and are false, like the story that the species of venomous spiders and snakes were born alive from the blood of the Titans, that Pegasus sprang from the Gorgon's head when her throat was cut, and that Diomedes' companions were changed into sea-birds, Odysseus into a horse and Hecuba into a dog.' Quintilian likewise defines *fabula* as what has neither truth nor verisimilitude.

Asclepiades discusses the subject-matter of tragedy in relation to these categories and differentiates what is ἱστορία and so true from what is μῦθος (or ψευδὴς ἱστορία) and so false. But remarkably little falls into the latter category; indeed he mentions only one heading, τὸ γενεαλογικόν, which probably includes the fabulous origins of living creatures mentioned by Sextus under μῦθος – the spiders springing from the Titans' blood, Pegasus from the Gorgon's head and so on. Indeed it seems[48] as though the ancient grammarians, Greek and Roman, reserved the name μῦθος or *fabula* for what was impossible κατὰ φύσιν, while all the subject-matter of legend, as well as what we should call history, fell under ἱστορία, provided that it was physically possible.

Now it is precisely the residuary 'mythical' element in the early legends which hinders the full identification of this traditional material with history. Thucydides, as we saw, excluded τὸ μυθῶδες from his history; and later Polybius,[49] in his account of Cisalpine Gaul and the course of the river Po, criticises the legends told of this area – of Phaethon and his fall, the transformation of his sisters into weeping poplars, and 'the black clothing of the inhabitants near the river who, they say, still dress thus in mourning for ‖ Phaethon, καὶ πᾶσαν δὴ τὴν τραγικὴν καὶ ταύτῃ προσεοικυῖαν ὕλην – and all similar matter for tragedy'.

These stories are of the kind Sextus quotes to illustrate the nature of μῦθος, and Asclepiades reckons under τὸ γενεαλογικόν, if this can be stretched to include metamorphoses; certainly the transformation of Phaethon's sisters into poplars is exactly parallel to Hecuba's metamorphosis into a dog, or that of Diomedes' companions into sea-birds. Such stories must be excluded from history; but by a careful process of rationalisation the amount sacrificed could be reduced to a minimum. For example, Polybius himself finds it possible by

---

[48] For example, Theon in his *Progymnasmata* reckons the story of Medea's murder of her children as πραγματική, not μυθική (*cf.* Barwick, *Hermes* 68 (1928) 271 n. 1, quoting a point made by Heinze).

[49] Polyb. II.16.13–15. Whom Polybius is attacking is not clear. He says that to take issue with these stories is not suitable at this point in his work (presumably because it is in one of the introductory books), but he promises to do so later, 'especially as Timaeus has shown much ignorance concerning the district'. This sounds as if the object of criticism was Timaeus, and this view, accepted by Müllenhoff, has been recently argued afresh by Ruth Stiehl (*Palaeologia* 4 (1955) 244–9), who thinks Polybius took most of his account of Lombardy from Timaeus. But Polybius attacks Timaeus, not for the myths, but for general ignorance, a very different matter (*cf.* Pédech, *LEC* 24 (1956) 19 n. 58); and if Diod. v.23.5, dealing with the same stories, derives from Timaeus (as seems likely), Timaeus also regarded such myths as out of place in history.

this method to accept almost the whole of Homer against the more sceptical attitude of Eratosthenes, who had remarked that we might perhaps find out where Odysseus travelled when we found the cobbler who sewed up the bag of the winds. Polybius admits that some mythical elements have been added but, he says, 'Homer's main statements about Sicily correspond to those of other writers who treat the local history of Italy and Sicily.'[50] Even the account of Scylla ravening after dolphins, dog-fish, and the like can be directly compared with the methods used by natives of the Straits of Messina in catching sword-fish.[51]

In this way the amount of μῦθος or *fabula* in the epics and tragedies was minimised, and the amount falling under the heading of ἱστορία extended. The third category, fiction (*argumentum* or πλάσμα), hardly concerns us here, since it is proper to mime and comedy. Originally all three categories seem to have applied only to poetry;[52] but by the second century at the latest some critics, such as Asclepiades, were employing them in relation to narratives throughout the whole field of literature. Where they originated is uncertain. Barwick suggests that they arose in the Peripatetic school, but his arguments are not very strong.[53] On the other hand, Asclepiades' version at least seems to ‖ imply a fairly advanced stage of the theory, since he refers the three categories to a field which has been extended from that of poetry to the whole of literature. It therefore looks as though one might safely take the original, limited form of the theory back to an earlier date than Asclepiades, and it *may* derive from the Peripatos.

The grammarians, it is true, like Aristotle are concerned with the relationship between history and legend from the point of view of poetry. They postulate that such parts of tragedy as are not specifically ἀδύνατα shall be accounted *historia* (as well as tragedy based on recent events, like the *Persae*); but they are not interested in the historian's conception of history. On the other hand, although the grammatical categories may originally have referred only to poetry, their influence will obviously have been felt by anyone who came within

---

[50] Polyb. xxxiv.2.9–10.

[51] The same tendency to rationalise Homer also appears in the Stoic Strabo, who in a discussion of the place of the false, mythical, element in the poet explains (1.2.9, C 20) that his work fell within the province of education, τὸ παιδευτικὸν εἶδος, but that he mingled therein a false element to give sanction to the truth, and to win popular favour – adding myth to real events (ταῖς ἀληθέσι περιπετείαις προσετίθει μῦθον) 'as when some skilful man overlays gold on silver', and so aiming at the same purpose as the historian or the person who relates facts. This emphasis on the paedeutic function of myth to control and out-manoeuvre the masses (δημαγωγῶν καὶ στρατηγῶν τὰ πλήθη) links up with Plato; but the distinction between the true legends and the small admixture of the false is not restricted to any one school. Some of the most striking examples of the rationalising of myth are to be found in Palaephatus, a Peripatetic.

[52] *Cf.* Barwick, *Hermes* 63 (1928) 282, who points to their appearance in the scholia to Dionysius Thrax, and notes too that the examples of them quoted by Cicero and in the *ad Herennium* are all taken from poetry.

[53] His argument rests on association of Palaephatus' rationalisation of myth with the tripartite division into history, myth and *argumentum*; but Palaephatus makes no reference to this division, and seems merely concerned to explain away apparent improbabilities in the traditional stories.

the range of rhetorical education, and with the early extension outside the narrow field of poetry they must have affected the historian too. The very use of the word ἱστορία to describe the bulk of the traditional subject-matter of epic and tragedy will have contributed to a blurring of the distinction which Aristotle had tried to draw, and so to a confusion about where precisely the historian was to set up the frontier between his own craft and tragedy.

IV

To this factor making for confusion can be added yet another. Aristotle's definition of tragedy was not universally accepted. The grammarians, and the scholiasts on whom we have often to rely for their views, believed that it was the main function of tragedy to provide examples of virtue and so to point a moral. 'Tragedy', we read in the scholia on Dionysius Thrax,[54] 'is the name given to the poems of the tragic writers, for example those of Euripides, Sophocles and Aeschylus, and similar authors. These men lived in Athenian times (ἐπὶ τῶν χρόνων τῶν ᾿Αθηναίων). Being tragic writers, and wishing to help the people of the city as a body, they took certain ancient stories of heroes, containing certain sufferings, sometimes deaths and lamentations, and exhibited these in the theatre to the eyes and ears of the spectators, demonstrating that they should be on their guard against sin. For if heroes such as these suffered such things, clearly because of the sins they had committed, how much more shall we or our contemporaries suffer if we sin? Therefore...we ought as far as possible to lead lives that are free from sin and devoted to philosophy (ἀναμάρτητον καὶ φιλοσοφώτατον). Hence the poetry of the tragic writers was produced with a view to helping the citizens.'

This is obviously both a narrower and a more naïve view of the function of tragedy than Aristotle's; but it is remarkably similar to the Isocratean ‖ – and Polybian – view of the purpose of history, which regarded it as a store-house of examples calculated to help the reader either morally or practically according to the bent of the particular writer. Moreover, it is not simply a late view of the purpose of tragedy; on the contrary it is recognised as early as Aristotle's own time, for his contemporary, the dramatist Timocles – a practitioner, no mere theoretician – according to Athenaeus[55] attributed the moral benefits of tragedy to the realism with which it displayed events which were clearly to be regarded as historical. 'Man', he says, 'is a creature born to labour, and many are the distresses which his life carries with it. Therefore he has contrived...respites from his cares...Look...at the tragedians and see what benefit they are to everybody. The poor man, for instance, learns that Telephus was more beggarly than himself, and from that time on he bears his poverty more easily...One has lost his son in death: Niobe is a comfort.

---

[54] See Kaibel, *CGF* 1.11. scholia ad Dion. Thrac. p. 746.1.
[55] Athen. vi.223b–d; *cf.* Giovannini, *PhQ* 22 (1943) 314 n. 33.

Another is lame: he sees Philoctetes....Thus he is reminded that all his calamities...have happened to others, and so he bears his own trials more readily.'

As the counterpart to this tragedy and its stories may likewise act as a moral deterrent. 'If', writes Diodorus in his prologue,[56] 'myths about Hades (μυθολογία), containing fictional material, conduce greatly to inspiring men to piety and justice, how much more must we suppose history, the interpreter of truth and the source of all philosophy, capable of shaping men's characters in honourable ways!' Myths about Hades are of course a traditional ingredient of tragedy, as we know from the *Poetics*,[57] where Aristotle refers to 'the spectacular element exemplified by...the *Prometheus* and scenes laid in Hades'; and it seems likely that in this passage Diodorus (or whatever the source from whom he derives the substance of his prologue)[58] is tendentiously selecting one of those features of tragedy which, while being morally efficacious, nevertheless fall traditionally under the heading of μῦθος rather than ἱστορία, in order to demonstrate the superiority of history, the προφῆτις τῆς ἀληθείας, as an instrument of ethical instruction. But the fact that he institutes the comparison at all illustrates yet again how closely the two fields are associated in the popular mind.

V

History and tragedy are thus linked together in their common origin in epic, in their use of comparable and often identical material, and in their moral purpose. It is therefore not very surprising that the treatment proper to ‖ one *genre* should fairly frequently be applied to the other, and that the historian who seeks to play upon his reader's emotions should be attacked as a would-be tragedian. There is, however, yet a further point which is not wholly without relevance to this question. The reaction to any particular dramatic performance will obviously vary greatly according to the character of the audience. 'In our London theatres', writes George Thomson,[59] 'the members of the audience usually keep their emotional reactions (other than laughter) to themselves; but in the cinemas of the west of Ireland, where the spectators are peasants, the atmosphere is far more intense. At the critical moments of the plot almost every face wears a terrified look and continuous sobbing may be heard. In this respect, an Athenian would undoubtedly have felt more at home in the west of Ireland than in the West End of London.' In support of this view Thomson quotes the famous passage from Plato's *Ion* in which the sophist describes his

[56] Diod. 1.2.2.

[57] *Poet.* 18.3, 1456a1–3.

[58] Barber, *The historian Ephorus* (Cambridge, 1935) 103, makes the source Ephorus; but it looks post-Polybian and may be from Poseidonius. M. Kunz, *Zur Beurteilung der Prooemien in Diodors historischer Bibliothek* (Diss. Zürich, 1935) 101, however, claims it for Diodorus himself; *cf.* also A. D. Nock, *JRS* 49 (1959), on Poseidonius; J. Palm, *Über Sprache und Stil des Diodoros von Sizilien* (Lund, 1955) 140n.1.

[59] *Aeschylus and Athens* (London, 1941) 380–1.

own effect upon his audience.[60] 'From the platform I see the audience weeping, and with looks of horror on their face, as they respond emotionally to what I am saying.'

There is, I think, reason to believe that this high degree of Athenian sensibility, this naïveté one might almost say, is perceptible in the Greek reaction to narrative descriptions as well as to dramatic representations. This point can be illustrated if one considers some of the comments by Greek critics on passages in surviving historians and observes their apparent exaggeration. It is of course perfectly true that Thucydides contains some highly dramatic elements. It has often been pointed out[61] that the juxtaposition of the Melian Dialogue and the start of the Sicilian Expedition creates some of the tension of tragedy; and even if the main thesis of *Thucydides Mythistoricus* has to be rejected, the fact that Cornford ever wrote it is in itself a significant comment on the effect the historian can produce. But despite these dramatic elements, the picture which ancient critics draw of Thucydides, and even of Xenophon, is hardly recognisable when set up beside the authors themselves.

'Sometimes', writes Dionysius,[62] 'Thucydides makes the sufferings [*sc.* in conquered cities] so cruel, so terrible, and so deserving of pity, that he leaves nothing worse for either historians or poets to describe.' The examples he quotes are Plataea, Mytilene and Melos; in all three a modern critic would be inclined to regard Thucydides' treatment as vivid, but emotionally restrained. Plutarch, however, shares the views of Dionysius. Xenophon, he tells us,[63] by his moving and lifelike account of the battle of Cunaxa creates in the reader the impression of actually taking part in the events and of sharing in the perils of the battle. Similarly[64] Thucydides constantly strives after a high degree of ‖ vividness (ἐνάργεια) in his passion to convert the listener into a spectator (οἶον θεατὴν ποιῆσαι τὸν ἀκροατὴν...λιχνευόμενος) and to engender in his readers the consternation and emotional disturbance actually experienced by those who saw the events (τὰ γινόμενα περὶ τοὺς ὁρῶντας ἐκπληκτικὰ καὶ ταρακτικὰ πάθη τοῖς ἀναγινώσκουσιν ἐνεργάσασθαι). This recalls a remark of Isocrates,[65] who spoke of tragedians who introduced myths into their plays, ὥστε μὴ μόνον ἀκουστοὺς ἡμῖν ἀλλὰ καὶ θεατοὺς γενέσθαι. In short, Plutarch is criticising Thucydides in precisely the same kind of terms as are elsewhere used of Duris and Phylarchus.

This suggests one of two conclusions. Either later critics such as Plutarch and Dionysius described the effects of Thucydides and Xenophon on their readers in terms that were obviously exaggerated, and could be seen to be exaggerated by anyone who took the trouble to read the account of Cunaxa or the siege of Plataea for himself. Or alternatively the Greeks – I suppose one must say

---

[60] Plato, *Ion* 535 c.
[61] *Cf.* Laistner, *op. cit.* (n. 6) 14. For other dramatic elements in Thucydides see J. R. Finley, *Thucydides* (Harvard, 1942) 321–4.
[62] Dion. Hal. *Thuc.* 15.
[63] Plut. *Artax.* 8.1.
[64] Plut. *De glor. Ath.* 347 a.
[65] Isoc. *In Nicocl.* 49.

of Plutarch's and Dionysius' age, though it would probably be true of ancient Greeks at all times – reacted more directly and emotionally to both the written and spoken word than we normally do. As between the two explanations a choice is not difficult. The history of Greek literature suggests beyond doubt that the Greeks were especially sensitive to the effects of language. The intense interest shown in verbal devices from the time of Gorgias, the wide and persistent influence of Isocrates and his school, the receptivity of the Greek audience to rhapsode and declaimer – all point in the same direction; and this furnishes yet a further reason why the reaction to tragedy should so frequently be confused with the reaction to a historical narrative constructed with all the resources of ἐνάργεια and designed to play upon the emotions of the reader or listener. When finally one bears in mind that history like other compositions would normally be read aloud, often in public gatherings, with the additional attractions with which the skilful declaimer can invest a narrative, it is easy to see why the confusion between tragedy and history should have been of such long standing.

VI

In discussing this question von Fritz made Aristotle's influence his starting-point. But, as he admits, many of the characteristics of so-called tragic history appear in Callisthenes, though Callisthenes' work was written long before the *Poetics*.[66] One need only recall the story of the ravens rounding up Alexander's stragglers by cawing during the famous visit to the oracle of Ammon,[67] that of the *proskynesis* of the sea when Alexander passed the Climax after leaving Phaselis,[68] an anecdote designed, says Plutarch,[69] to provide historians with material ‖ for a bombastic and terrifying description – ὑπόθεσις γραφικὴ πρὸς ἔκπληξιν καὶ ὄγκον, or the sudden reanimation of the oracle of Branchidae, the transition to which from the story of the visit to Ammon is referred to by Strabo[70] with the phrase: προστραγῳδεῖ τούτοις ὁ Καλλισθένης. This does not of course mean that Callisthenes was the originator of this kind of history, any more than Duris. For, long before Callisthenes, Ctesias of Cnidus, writing with an Ionian background,[71] was composing Persian and Indian histories in a sensational and credulous manner which does no credit to his scientific training as a doctor. In later critics at any rate, his work inspired much the same feelings as Phylarchus' histories inspired in Polybius. 'The charm of his history', writes Photius,[72] 'springs above all from his manner of constructing narrative passages which arouse emotion (τὸ παθητικόν), and afford many examples of the unexpected and of various embellishments which bring them close to

[66] *Op. cit.* (n. 7) 130.
[67] Plut. *Alex.* 27 = *FGH* 124 F 14 (b).
[68] *FGH* 124 F 31.   [69] Plut. *Alex.* 17.3.
[70] *FGH* 124 F 14 (a) = Strabo XVII.1.43, C 814.
[71] *Cf.* Wehrli, *Eumusia* (n. 6) 68.
[72] *FGH* 688 T 13 = Phot. *Bibl.* 72 p. 45 a 12ff.

the confines of the mythical.' To Plutarch,[73] who used him in his *Artaxerxes*, his work 'often turns aside from the truth into fable and romance (πρὸς τὸ μυθῶδες καὶ δραματικόν)'; and in his account of the bringing of the news of Cunaxa to the queen-mother Parysatis, he conceals the news of Cyrus' death until the very end of the speech for dramatic effect, as if it were a messenger's speech in a tragedy.[74] In such ways as these, remarks Demetrius in his treatise *On Style*, he aims at pathetic and vivid effects precisely as if he were a poet.

It is tempting to bring Gorgias too into the picture. Gorgias developed a theory and a style which drew no clear distinction between poetry and prose,[75] and probably set up ψυχαγωγία as the common goal of works of art, literature and oratory.[76] But despite his stylistic influence on Thucydides who, as Bury remarked,[77] would occasionally write 'crooked passages which produced upon a Greek ear almost the effect of dithyrambs released from the bonds of metre', there is no evidence to show that Gorgias concerned himself with the writing of history or influenced views concerning its purpose. But even without Gorgias there is no difficulty in reaching the fifth century. Lucian links Herodotus himself with Ctesias[78] as a composer of 'monstrous little fables', τεράστια μυθίδια. To Aristotle he was a μυθόλογος;[79] and Diodorus[80] accuses him of inventing wonder-stories and myths at the expense of truth in order to entertain (τὸ παραδοξολογεῖν καὶ μύθους πλάττειν ψυχαγωγίας ἕνεκα). Here again, significantly, there is no division between the fifth century and later writers: the line of development is continuous. There is then sufficient indication that the main features of 'tragic history' go back well beyond the Hellenistic ‖ period, and Aristotle, who is supposed to have played so vital if involuntary a part in their formulation.

VII

In the discussion which followed von Fritz's paper, and which is printed after it, there was a general and it would seem wholly justified reluctance to accept the Peripatos in the important role to which the speaker had assigned it. It appeared improbable that theory had so decisive a part to play in the shaping of practice. Were there not more likely to be predisposing causes for this form of historiography, it was asked, in the climate of the times, in the demands of the reading public, in the nature of the historical material available, in itself often violent and sensational, and even in the political sympathies of the historians?[81] As factors likely to accentuate a trend towards vivid and sensational historiography these are all possibilities worth bearing in mind. But

---

[73] Plut. *Artax.* 6.9.
[74] *FGH* 688 F 24 = Demetr. *Eloc.* 216.
[75] Arist. *Rhet.* III.1, 1404 a 29.
[76] *Cf.* Avenarius, *op. cit.* (n. 14) 140.
[77] J. B. Bury, *Ancient Greek historians* (London, 1909) 111.
[78] Lucian, *Philops.* 2.   [79] Arist. *Gen. Anim.* 3, 75 b 5.
[80] Diod. 1.69.7.   [81] *Op. cit.* (n. 7) 129–45.

it is perhaps no less important to recognise that the sharp isolation of 'tragic history' as a separate school in need of explanation and of a definite and immediate ancestry is very largely a figment and a distortion. Duris may have borrowed a vogue-word μίμησις from the Peripatos. That is not important. What matters is that the link between tragedy and history, which constituted the main feature of the supposed tragic-historical school and was felt to need special elucidation, is in fact a fundamental affinity going back to the earliest days of both history and tragedy, and insisted upon throughout almost the whole of the classical and later periods down to the Byzantine scholiasts. It was there by virtue of descent and of analogous literary techniques, it was encouraged by a common moral aim and by the sharpness of Greek emotional sensibility, and it was taught in the rhetorical schools to generations of Greek students.

What should have been a patent fact staring us in the face has been obscured through the prestige of Aristotle's name and his analysis of the *difference* between tragedy and history. And because two of his successors, Polybius and Lucian, whose interests lay in history, both to some extent accepted his distinction, it has tended to be regarded as the normal belief of educated Greeks. As a result we have had to invent the expression 'tragic history' in order to reunite what few Greek writers were interested in dividing. To ignore this is not merely to misunderstand Hellenistic history: it is also to underestimate the character of Polybius' protest. For the reasons indicated most of his predecessors and contemporaries aimed at stirring the emotions by the vivid representation of scenes sensational in themselves, and at titillating their readers' palates by serving up the wonder-stories which went back originally to the Ionians including Herodotus, but for which there was a growing taste, stimulated of course by the Alexander-historians, and such ‖ figures as Pytheas of Marseilles. Polybius' criticism is not therefore to be regarded as simply polemic against a single limited school with a specific and clearly defined theory and practice of recent origin. On the contrary, it is to be taken seriously as a demand for new standards and canons in Greek historiography. Perhaps it will make for a more sympathetic understanding both of him and of his opponents, if the term 'tragic history' is discarded from subsequent discussion.[82]

[82] This paper was read at a meeting of the Hellenic Society in London on 24 April 1959.

16

SPEECHES IN GREEK HISTORIANS*

To have been invited to deliver the Myres Memorial Lecture is an honour of which I am deeply sensible but one which I am bound to regard as intended in some large measure for the University of Liverpool.

From 1907 to 1910 Sir John Myres occupied our Gladstone Chair of Greek, relinquishing it only to assume his duties as the first Wykeham Professor. To any member of the Liverpool Senate the affectionate remarks about our City and University printed in the preface to his inaugural lecture at Oxford still make agreeable and flattering reading,[1] though perhaps not all of us would share what he describes as his chief anxiety on Merseyside – that his students might overwork. The subject I have chosen for my lecture this afternoon is not closely related to Myres's central interests; but his mind and pen ranged widely over most fields of Greek activity and his life-long devotion to Herodotus would at any rate, I venture to hope, have made him charitably disposed towards a theme relevant to the aims and purposes of Greek historiography.

I

It would not occur to a modern historian to insert in his work versions of speeches delivered, or reputedly delivered, by historical characters. But this practice is almost universal among ancient historians, who regarded it as an important part of their work;[2] and it persisted throughout antiquity and the middle ages and indeed right down to the time of Clarendon. Conventional Greek theory regarded history as a matter of πράξεις καὶ λόγοι – action and speeches. This is a division made by Thucydides[3] and echoed frequently in later writers, for instance in Plato and Ephorus[4] and in literary critics such as Dionysius and Quintilian.[5] The precise function of the speech within the history varies from writer to writer; but behind the convention, as its logical justification, is the concept that man is a rational being, whose actions are the

* [Third Myres Memorial Lecture: Oxford, 1965]

[1] Cf. J. L. Myres, *Geographical history in Greek lands* (Oxford, 1953) 3.

[2] Exceptions are Cratippus and Trogus Pompeius (cf. *FGH* 64 F 1; Justin xxxviii.3.11, recording Trogus' criticism of Livy and Sallust); cf. P. Pédech, *La méthode historique de Polybe* (Paris, 1964) 254.

[3] Thuc. 1.22.1–2, τὰ λεχθέντα καὶ τὰ πραχθέντα.

[4] Plato, *Tim.* 19c; Ephorus, *FGH* 70F9.

[5] Dion. Hal. *De Imit.* 3.3, *Pomp.* 3.20, *Thuc.* 25.55; Quint. *Inst.* x.1.101.

result of conscious decisions, and that these decisions are the outcome of discourse either in the form of speeches or in that of dialogue. As Polybius remarks, the peculiar function of history is to ‖ discover in the first place the words actually spoken, whatever they were, and next to ascertain the reason why what was done or spoken led to failure or success.[6] Good advice means successful policy and the reader of history can learn from this. Speech is at the roots of all political life.

This is a good reason why historians should pay attention to what was said. But it does not in itself warrant the reproducing of speeches as an integral part of history. It would have been just as easy to summarise policies in the way a modern historian does and as, for instance, Polybius often does when he gives a short précis of what was said in *oratio obliqua*.[7] To let historical characters speak for themselves is, however, a more dramatic method and recalls the long association of historiography from its earliest beginnings with epic and drama.[8] This association derived from a combination of causes. There was an identity of subject-matter in as far as the Greeks regarded the stories of the heroic age as historical. As Jacoby observed,[9] the main source for early Greek history was the panhellenic epic, which furnished the themes of both tragedy and history. There was also the naïve but commonly accepted belief that the true function of both tragedy and history was to serve as a store-house of moral examples and to act as a deterrent from wickedness.[10] In addition, there seems no doubt that the Greeks with their quick response to language reacted to the more vivid passages in the historian, declaimed with the rhetorical resources of the skilful practitioner, in much the same way as they reacted to dramatic performances. Attempts have been made to define 'tragic history' as a special product of the Hellenistic age, when historians like Duris of Samos, it is alleged, adapted the Peripatetic theories of tragedy to the writing of history.[11] The evidence for this is however slight and unconvincing, for the characteristics supposedly peculiar to tragic historians are to be found equally well in earlier writers, in Ctesias of Cnidus, for instance or, as Strasburger has recently observed,[12] in Philistus of Syracuse and Timonides of Leucas in the fourth century – quite apart from

---

[6] Polyb. XII.25b, I.

[7] *E.g.* Polyb. xv.19, XXI.10.

[8] *Cf.* F. W. Walbank, *BICS* 2 (1955) 4–14; *Historia* 9 (1960) 216–34 ⟦above, pp. 224–41⟧ where full references are given.

[9] *Atthis* (Oxford, 1949) 202; *cf.* J. F. D'Alton, *Roman literary theory and practice* (London, 1931) 491–2.

[10] This view left a clear trace in a tradition descending from the fourth-century dramatist and critic Timocles down to the late scholia on Dionysius Thrax; cf. Historia 9 (1960) 228–9.

[11] *Cf.* E. Schwartz, *Fünf Vorträge über den griechischen Roman*[2] (Berlin, 1943) 123–5; *Hermes* 32 (1897) 560, 35 (1900) 107, 44 (1909) 491; P. Scheller, *De hellenistica historiae conscribendae arte* (Leipzig, 1911). For recent discussion, see, besides the articles mentioned in n. 8, K. von Fritz, *Histoire et historiens dans l'antiquité* (Vandoeuvres-Geneva, 1958) 85–145; N. Zegers, *Wesen und Ursprung der tragischen Geschichtsschreibung* (Diss. Cologne, 1959); C. O. Brink, *PCPS* 6 (1960) 14–19; R. Syme, *Sallust* (Berkeley-Los Angeles, 1964) 50–1.

[12] H. Strasburger, *Festgabe für Paul Kirn* (Berlin, 1961) 30; *cf. FGH* 556 F 28, 40, 60; *FGH* 561, and much of Plutarch's *Dion*, which draws on Timonides.

Herodotus, whom later writers certainly regarded as a μυθόλογος[13] and the inventor of wonder-stories.[14] Thus its origins in epic and its close associations with tragedy ensured that speeches were an integral part of historical composition from the start. It is only when we come to Thucydides that we become aware of any problem. ‖

II

It is of course a problem of first-class dimensions, frequently discussed but never yet satisfactorily solved.

As A. H. M. Jones has very justly observed,[15] Thucydides' speeches bear little resemblance in either argumentation or style to the genuine speeches of orators surviving from the fourth century, though indeed they follow fairly closely the rhetorical precepts set out in Aristotle's *Rhetoric* and the *Rhetorica ad Alexandrum*;[16] and other scholars have not hesitated to describe the Melian and Mytilenean Debates as 'dialogues masquerading as history'.[17] Concerning Thucydides' speeches there are clearly three possibilities.[18] They might be entirely subjective, a mere mouthpiece for Thucydides' own views. That this cannot be wholly true, however, follows from the fact that they sometimes adopt conflicting points of view and so must contain an element of characterisation. The second possibility is that they are 'true to the situation', that is, they may represent Thucydides' attempt to say the kind of thing a particular speaker would or might have said at a particular juncture – in short that they avoid anachronism and give objectivity in the dramatist's or novelist's sense. Thirdly, the speeches may set out to give what Thucydides knew or believed to have been actually said. The well-known passage in which he enunciates his programme is 1.22.1, where he remarks: 'my practice has been to make the speakers say what in my opinion was demanded of them by the various occasions – or, what in my opinion they had to say on the various occasions – (περὶ τῶν αἰεὶ παρόντων τὰ δέοντα μάλιστα εἰπεῖν), of course adhering as closely as possible to the general sense (τῆς ξυμπάσης γνώμης) of what was really said'. This sentence could well occupy the rest of this lecture, but I do not propose to let it. Passing over τὰ δέοντα, which may mean either what the various occasions demanded or what the speakers had to say (and so *did* say), the crux of the matter is the meaning of τῆς ξυμπάσης γνώμης, for it is of course self-evident that the style and actual flavour of the argumentation, with their unmistakeable Thucydidean stamp, whoever is speaking, are imposed on the material by the historian. If ἡ ξυμπᾶσα γνώμη is simply 'the general intention'

---

[13] Arist. *Gen. Anim.* III, 75b5.   [14] Diod. 1.69.7.

[15] *Athenian democracy* (Oxford, 1957) 66–7.

[16] See especially P. Moraux, *LEC* 22 (1954) 1–23, for an analysis of the speeches of Cleon and Diodotus in Thuc. III.37–48; *cf.* L. Bodin, *REA* 42 (1940) 36–52.

[17] *Cf.* T. W. Africa, *Phylarchus and the Spartan Revolution* (Berkeley-Los Angeles, 1961) 285ff.

[18] *Cf.* Gomme, *Commentary on Thucydides* (5 vols., Oxford, 1945–81) 1.143–8; *Essays in Greek history and literature* (Oxford, 1937) 156–89.

of the speech, as deduced from Thucydides' knowledge of the political colour
of the speaker and the historical situation in which the speech was delivered
or was supposed to have been delivered,[19] then Thucydides' speeches are in
effect no more than free composition and afford some justification of Collingwood's anguished query:[20] could a just man who had a really historical
mind have permitted himself the use of such a convention? But Thucydides
also used the phrase ‖ τῶν ἀληθῶς λεχθέντων, 'what in truth was said', and
it is surely hard to reconcile these three words with any theory which envisages
that Thucydides simply composed his speeches without reference to the
original words. True, the *ipsissima verba* are qualified, as Adcock points out,
in two ways, by the reference to Thucydides' opinion and by the limitation
implied in ἡ ξυμπᾶσα γνώμη – which will mean 'the overall purport of what
was said'. But they remain the foundations of the speech, if modified by the
historian's opinion of what the situation demanded and by his giving the
general purport rather than the words themselves (which were, as Thucydides
remarks, difficult for either himself or his informants to carry in their heads);
and Adcock has shown that for all his speeches it was feasible for Thucydides
to have obtained some sort of authentic information.[21]

Even so, the difficulty remains. There is a contradiction between the two
ideas of recording what was actually said and recording what the historian
thought the speakers would have said (ὡς... ἂν ἐδόκουν μάλιστ' εἰπεῖν) on the
various occasions. The criterion of the one is quite simply the truth, the
criterion of the other is suitability, τὸ πρέπον,[22] πιθανότης, a concept which
was frequently to arise in connection with the rhetorical theory about speeches
in history. In the ambiguous formulation of 1.22.2 Thucydides calls for truth
and then confuses it with something quite other. Thus his theory contains a
residual contradiction, never fully surmounted and an unfortunate legacy to
his successors. His practice is less easy to assess; but Adcock concedes[23] that
closeness to reality must vary in accordance with Thucydides' sources of
information and he suggests that in composing the speech of a general like
Nicias encouraging his troops before battle he may have felt so reasonably
certain of what must in such a situation have been said that he may conceivably
have taken it for granted in a way which he will scarcely have done in recording
a speech containing advice on policy. Even Gomme, quick to leap to
Thucydides' defence, asserts[24] that such speeches as those at Plataea for which
evidence was exceedingly scanty may give us οἷον ἂν γένοιτο, 'what would

---

[19] So F. Egermann, *DLZ* 58 (1937) 1471f.; *Das neue Bild der Antike* (Leipzig, 1942) 1.285ff. This
view has been widely accepted in Germany, *cf.* G. Avenarius, *Lukians Schrift zur Geschichtsschreibung*
(Diss. Frankfurt, 1954) 156.
[20] *The idea of history* (Oxford, 1946) 30.
[21] F. E. Adcock, *Thucydides and his History* (Cambridge, 1963) 27–42, 120–2.
[22] On the development of the criterion of τὸ πρέπον see M. Pohlenz, *NAWG* (1933) 53ff.;
Antikes Führertum (Leipzig, 1934) 58ff.
[23] *Op. cit.* (n. 21) 29.
[24] *The Greek attitude to poetry and history* (Berkeley-Los Angeles, 1954) 141–2.

be likely to happen' – poetry in Aristotle's sense of the phrase. It is a slippery business; but however long the chain, Thucydides does his best to remain anchored to τὰ ἀληθῶς λεχθέντα.

III

After Thucydides the whole picture changes, concern for τὰ ἀληθῶς λεχθέντα weakens. Ctesias adorned his histories with many of the devices of drama; the messenger who announces Cyrus' death to Parysatis the queen-mother – himself demonstrably a stock-character from tragedy – elaborately conceals the news ‖ until the very end of the speech for dramatic effect.[25] No one will imagine that factual accuracy played any part here. Xenophon of course provides speeches, but to express his own views; and if he takes a speaker's known opinions into account, the speeches remain none the less inventions.[26] Theopompus, Ephorus and Anaximenes are all criticised by Plutarch[27] for their folly in ascribing artificial ῥητορεῖαι καὶ περίοδοι to generals addressing troops as they stand ready for battle; but the fragmentary nature of the surviving passages of these authors makes it difficult to put this accusation to the test. Ephorus at least seems to have attached some importance to having a factual basis for his speeches. In a passage in the general introduction to his *Histories*[28] he observes that when one is dealing with remote periods circumstantial detail in a writer is not necessarily evidence of reliability, since it is unlikely that all the actions or the greater part of the speeches can be recalled so long afterwards – οὔτε τὰς πράξεις ἁπάσας οὔτε τῶν λόγων τοὺς πλείστους εἰκὸς εἶναι μνημονεύεσθαι διὰ τοσούτων. This seems at least to raise a *caveat* against speeches invented without access to any genuine information about what was said; but how far Ephorus followed up its implications is hard to say.

In the fourth century a new criterion emerges and finds expression in a famous statement by Callisthenes of Olynthus, who declared[29] that it was the duty of anyone who set out to write (γράφειν τι πειρώμενον) 'not to fail to hit off the character, but to match his speeches to the person and the situation' (μὴ ἀστοχεῖν τοῦ προσώπου, ἀλλ' οἰκείως αὐτῷ τε καὶ τοῖς πράγμασι τοὺς λόγους θεῖναι). Here, once again, is the criterion of suitability, τὸ πρέπον, but applied now not merely to the situation but also to the individual. Now Aristotle laid emphasis on τὸ πρέπον and Callisthenes was Aristotle's nephew. But it does not therefore follow that he is retaining an Aristotelian or Peripatetic theory about speeches in history.[30] Rather this new interest in the personality

---

[25] Demetr. *Elocut.* 215.

[26] On the speeches Xenophon attributes to Procles of Phleius (*Hell.* vi.5.38, vii.1.2) see H. R. Breitenbach, *Historiographische Anschauungsformen Xenophons* (Freiburg (Switzerland), 1950) 102, 125f.   [27] *Praecept. ger. reip.* 803b.

[28] Harpocration *s.v.* ἀρχαίως and καινῶς = *FGH* 70F9.

[29] *FGH* 124F44.

[30] So, most recently, Pédech, *op. cit.* (n. 2) 255 n. 12.

reflects new preoccupations which are as evident in the Platonic corpus and in the biographies of Isocrates as they are in the *Characters* of Theophrastus.

How far Callisthenes' precept found followers during the next hundred years is not easy to say. The wreckage of the historiography of the fourth and third centuries has left little evidence as to how authors whose works are now lost treated the speeches which they undoubtedly incorporated in their works. Thus not a single one of the eighteen fragments recorded by Jacoby under the name of Hieronymus of Cardia comes from or deals with a speech; and the prologue to Diodorus xx.i, which attacks the excessive introduction of speeches into history as an unnecessary interruption of the narrative, besides being variously ascribed ‖ to Duris[31] and to Ephorus,[32] merely discusses how many speeches are to be introduced, not how they should be composed. Phylarchus, however, whose *Histories* were as important for the fifty years 272–220 as those of Hieronymus were for the previous half-century, evidently included speeches which had little contact with reality, judging by Polybius' criticism; for, after describing the emotional treatment which Phylarchus accords to events, he goes on: 'a historian should not..., like a tragic poet, try to imagine the probable remarks of his characters...but should simply record what really happened and what really was said, however commonplace'.[33] It has been observed that Plutarch's *Lives* of *Agis* and *Cleomenes*, which go back to Phylarchus, contain more direct speeches than do his *Lives* generally, and this may well be due to Phylarchus displaying his affinity with the dialogue and set speeches of tragedy.[34]

Thanks to Polybius we also know something about the methods of one or two other historians of this period. For example Chaereas and Sosylus, who described the Hannibalic War from the Punic side,[35] set down speeches allegedly delivered in the Senate after the Saguntine débâcle supporting and opposing a war policy although, as Polybius points out, they themselves admit that senatorial proceedings were strictly secret; the result, he adds in a famous phrase, is nothing more than 'the gossip of a barber's shop'. He has even stronger criticism for Timaeus,[36] who puts into the mouths of two eminent statesmen, Hermocrates and Timoleon, speeches which sink to the very depths of puerility. Polybius, it is true, had several extraneous and personal reasons for ridiculing and denigrating Timaeus[37] and may have quoted commonplaces out of context; but the details he gives are specific and circumstantial and seem

---

[31] *Cf.* C. Gramann, *Quaestiones Diodoreae* (Diss. Göttingen, 1907) 25ff.; M. Kunz, *Zur Beurteilung der Prooemien in Diodors historischer Bibliothek* (Diss. Zürich, 1935) 91ff. N. Zegers, *op. cit.* (n. 11) 37ff., also argues that Diod. xx.1 (but not xx.2 with its contradictory defence of speeches in history) is from Duris.

[32] *Cf.* Laqueur, *Hermes* 46 (1911) 206; Jacoby, *FGH* 70F111 (commentary); Avenarius, *op. cit.* (n. 19) 152–3.   [33] Polyb. ii.56.10.

[34] *Cf.* Zegers, *op. cit.* (n. 11) 52.

[35] *Cf. FGH* 176 (Sosylus) and 177 (Chaereas) for fragments.

[36] Polyb. xii.25k–26a.

[37] *Cf.* Walbank, *JRS* 52 (1962) 1–12 [below, pp. 262–79].

to represent a fairly honest account of the contents of these speeches.[38] That of Hermocrates has been analysed in some detail by Nestle,[39] who has shown its sophistic origins as revealed in its Gorgianic antitheses, its set passage in praise of peace as κατά φύσιν,[40] its emphasis on the paradox of Heracles as the founder of the Olympic truce, and its Homeric quotations. He has not, I think, proved that the whole composition derives from Gorgias' *Olympikos*, simply because it is impossible to be absolutely certain about a work of which only two short fragments survive;[41] but he has left Timaeus little claim to have his speeches regarded as more than rhetorical fireworks. ‖

IV

This was the general situation when Polybius began to write his account of the rise of Rome to world-empire. Like his predecessors Polybius employed the convention of including speeches. These, he tells us,[42] 'as it were sum up events and hold the whole history together'. About fifty examples survive, but it is clear from the Polybian parts of Livy that many more are lost. In the main they are in *oratio obliqua*, but quite often the more formal ones begin in *oratio obliqua* and after a few lines switch to *oratio recta*.[43] Sometimes *oratio obliqua* and *oratio recta* alternate; and occasionally the whole speech is in *oratio recta*.[44] Gelzer has suggested[45] that where part of a speech is in *oratio recta*, this implies some compression in the part in *oratio obliqua*. But any reported speech in history will contain some compression, whether in direct speech or indirect, and in Polybius *oratio obliqua* seems often to be used as a stylistic device to bridge the transition from narrative to direct speech. It is however true that the most elaborate pair of speeches we possess is in *oratio recta*.

Despite the personal prejudice that lies behind much of his polemics against earlier authors, there seems no doubt that Polybius was deeply and sincerely concerned about standards in historical composition.[46] In particular he sought to disparage and eliminate the romantic approach to history which had always been there but had gained a new lease of life in the epoch after Alexander. He felt such an approach to be an obstacle to the practical and moral didacticism which he held to be the most important part of the historian's task. It is, I would suggest, as part of this campaign of revolt that one must assess his attitude towards the use of speeches in a historical narrative.

[38] *Cf.* Truesdell A. Brown, *Timaeus of Tauromenium* (Berkeley-Los Angeles, 1958) 65–6; Jacoby, *FGH* 3b, 554.
[39] W. Nestle, *Phil. Woch.* 52 (1932) 1357ff.; *Augustin und der Friedensgedanke in der antiken Welt, Philologus* Suppl.-B. 31 (1938) 17–18.   [40] Polyb. XII.26.7.
[41] Diels, *Vorsokr.*⁵ frs. 7–8. Philostratus, *Vit. Gorg.* 2, adds the information that Gorgias στασιάζουσαν τὴν Ἑλλάδα ὁρῶν ὁμονοίας ξύμβουλος αὐτοῖς ἐγένετο.
[42] Polyb. XII.25a.3.
[43] *E.g.* III.108–9, 111, XI.28–9, XV.1.5ff., 6–8, XXI.10.5–11, 18–23, 31.6–15, XXX.31.
[44] *E.g.* IX.28–39, XI.4–6, XVIII.23.3–6.
[45] *Die Arbeitsweise des Polybios* (*SHAW* (1956.3) 24 〚= *Kleine Schriften* 3 (Wiesbaden, 1964) 188–9〛.
[46] *Cf.* Walbank, *Historia* 9 (1960) 216–34 〚above, pp. 224–41〛.

As I have just indicated,[47] he regarded them as an essential part of history, and he expresses views on the subject in several passages. I quoted his comment on Phylarchus: '[the historian] should simply record...what was really said, however commonplace';[48] and this sentiment is repeated elsewhere. In Book xxxvi, for instance, in reference to speeches delivered before the Third Punic War,[49] he remarks that in his opinion 'it is not the proper part of a politician to be ready with argument and exposition on every subject of debate without distinction, but simply to say what the particular situation demands, and likewise it is not the business of a historian to practise his skill and show off his ability to his readers, but rather to devote his whole energy to discovering and recording what was really and truly said, and even of this only the most vital and effective parts' – ⟨τὰ⟩ κατ' ἀλήθειαν ῥηθέντα ⟨καθ'⟩ ὅσον οἷόν τε πολυπραγμονήσαντας διασαφεῖν, καὶ τούτων τὰ καιριώτατα καὶ πραγματικώτατα. ‖

Selection is to be exercised – a subjective operation: not everything said is to be recorded, but only what was most effective. Moreover it is clearly permissible for such select material to be worked over and cast into what may be called a Polybian form; for in Book xxix,[50] in a long criticism of writers of monographs, who elaborate their descriptions of sieges from lack of genuine source material, he remarks: 'The same applies to descriptions of battles, the reports of speeches and the other parts of history. In all these...I may be justly excused if I am found to be using the same style or the same disposition and treatment, or even actually the same words as on a previous occasion.... For in all such matters the large scale of my work is sufficient excuse.' Though the exact words are uncertain, the sense is clear: in reporting a speech a historian must restrict himself to what was actually said, and indeed the most important part of that, but he may cast it in his own words, which may in fact be identical for different occasions. In short, τὰ κατ' ἀλήθειαν ῥηθέντα does not mean 'the actual words spoken'; it means 'the sense of what was said', indeed something very close to Thucydides' ἡ ξύμπασα γνώμη τῶν ἀληθῶς λεχθέντων.

V

The relation between Polybius and Thucydides is not an obvious one. In the whole of the surviving parts of Polybius – perhaps a third of what he wrote – Thucydides is only mentioned once, and then only incidentally to indicate where Theopompus began his history.[51] Throughout the many

---

[47] See n. 42.   [48] See n. 33.
[49] Polyb. xxxvi.1.6–7.
[50] Polyb. xxix.12.10. The text is uncertain; see *JRS* 53 (1963) 9 n. 70 where by a slip it is stated that λήμμασι...τοῖς αὐτοῖς means 'the same words as I have used elsewhere'. It is of course the words τοῖς αὐτοῖς...τοῖς τῆς λέξεως ῥήμασι which bear this meaning; and that they do mean this and not 'the words that were actually pronounced' (so Ziegler) is clear from the fact that Polybius is referring to descriptions of battles etc. as well as speeches. [See above p. 151 n. 70, where the correction has been made.]   [51] Polyb. viii.11.3.

polemical passages directed against previous historians[52] Thucydides is completely omitted. Nevertheless there is some evidence that he affected Polybius' thought more deeply than a superficial reading of the latter's work might suggest.[53] When Polybius remarks that, whereas tragedy charms its audience κατὰ τὸ πάρον, history brings them profit εἰς τὸν πάντα χρόνον,[54] one recalls Thucydides' famous claim that his work is destined to become a κτῆμα ἐς αἰεὶ μᾶλλον ἢ ἀγώνισμα ἐς τὸ παραχρῆμα;[55] and as if to demonstrate that the parallel is not coincidental, a book later Polybius observes[56] that without a proper study of causes what remains ἀγώνισμα μὲν, μάθημα δ' οὐ γίνεται. When he wants to speak of historians who have introduced a marvellous element and tragic colouring into their accounts of the fall of Hieronymus of Syracuse,[57] he employs an unusual word, λογόγραφοι, which, while ‖ colourless in itself, here assumes a critical overtone precisely because Thucydides had used it[58] of his predecessors, whose chronicles were designed to provide exciting reading rather than the truth.

Like Thucydides, Polybius feels the need to distinguish clearly the several links in the chain of causation which leads to any important action such as the outbreak of a war.[59] His use of ἀρχαί, αἰτίαι and προφάσεις cannot fail to recall Thucydides' own distinction between αἰτίαι καὶ διαφοραί and the ἀληθεστάτη πρόφασις of the Peloponnesian War, the grievances and points of difference which constitute the proximate *casus belli* and the ‘truest explanation’. But Polybius tacitly inserts a third term, ἀρχαί, and uses αἰτίαι and προφάσεις in a different sense from Thucydides. To him ἀρχαί are the first actions of the war itself, αἰτίαι are not grievances but those events which lead the individual to conceive a will to war, and the pretext then alleged for going to war – whether genuine or not – is the πρόφασις. For Thucydides the grievances are the form in which the deeper antagonism, which is the real cause, finds expression. Thus Polybius – not unexpectedly – is more mechanical and superficial, and he substitutes a unilateral sequence for mutual antagonism. But there can be little doubt that he is here criticising and, as he believes, correcting Thucydides, though he does not name him. Similarly when, as his reason for venturing an explanation of the intrigues between Perseus and Eumenes,[60] he gives the fact that he himself ‘lived at the time and had been more impressed by all that happened than anyone else’, Ziegler *may* be right[61] – I would not say more – in detecting an echo of that famous opening

---

[52] *Cf.* Walbank, *JRS* 52 (1962) 1–12.
[53] For what follows *cf.* E. Mioni, *Polibio* (Padua, 1949) 127–31; K. Ziegler, *RE* 21.2 (1952) 'Polybios', cols. 1522–4.
[54] Polyb. II.56.11.   [55] Thuc. I.22.4.
[56] Polyb. III.31.12. The same passage may be echoed in XXXVIII.4.8, but hardly (despite Ziegler, *op. cit.* (n. 53) col. 1503) in III.57.8.   [57] Polyb. VII.7.1.
[58] Thuc. I.21.1; *cf.* Gomme, *Commentary* (n. 18) *ad loc.*; Jacoby, *Atthis* (n. 9) 300 n. 28.
[59] *Cf.* Polyb. III.6.3 with the note in my *Historical commentary on Polybius* (3 vols., Oxford, 1957–79) 1.305–6; Thuc. 1.23.6.
[60] Polyb. XXIX.5.3.   [61] *Op. cit.* (n. 53) col. 1513.

sentence in which 'Thucydides, an Athenian, wrote the history of the war between the Peloponnesians and the Athenians, beginning at the moment it broke out, and believing it would be a great war, and more worthy of relation than any that had preceded it'.[62]

Indeed, if one looks beyond individual passages, which are perhaps not of great significance in themselves, it is clear that between the two historians there existed marked similarities of theme, temperament and experience. Each had grown up to play an active political role in his native state and then, suddenly, had been forced into an unwelcome exile which, however, by broadening his horizon, contributed to his development as a historian; and each alike eventually saw his country overwhelmed with disaster. Each wrote contemporary or near contemporary history,[63] each prefaced his main narrative with an introductory period of roughly fifty years[64] – and each was a historian who had first acquired a training in public affairs.[65] Both were men of politics through and through, both were convinced of the importance of constitutions for the welfare of states ‖ and both wrote to inform and instruct statesmen who might choose to seek profit from the perusal of their works.

The parallelism, though in part fortuitous, is striking; and since Polybius betrays his knowledge of Thucydides in several places, his failure to mention him by name demands some explanation. One possibility would be that a fifth-century historian was too remote to exercise his attention; that it was only with the fourth century and the problems associated with the Theban hegemony and the rise of Macedonia that history began to seem 'modern' to a second-century Achaean historian. But this can hardly be the full story, for though Polybius is certainly interested in the century that saw the foundation of Megalopolis,[66] he is quite ready to discuss Gelon's behaviour in the Persian Wars[67] and he singles out for detailed criticism a speech attributed by Timaeus to Hermocrates of Syracuse at the Congress of Gela, which falls right into the very period covered by Thucydides' history.[68] Nor was Thucydides a dead letter at this time. Agatharchides of Cnidus, Polybius' younger contemporary, is said by Photius to have emulated Thucydides in the abundance and elaboration of his speeches, to have been not inferior in the splendour of his style and to have excelled him in clarity.[69] In such circumstances Polybius'

---

[62] Thuc. i.i.i.

[63] *Cf.* Polyb. iv.2.2.

[64] In Polybius' case the years between the 129th and 140th Olympiads, 264/260–220/216; but in fact he goes back a little earlier to include the rise of Hiero (Polyb. 1.7ff.).

[65] On this see Polyb. xii.28.5.

[66] *Cf.* Polyb. viii.11.3; Walbank, *JRS* 52 (1962) 2 [below, pp. 263–4].

[67] Polyb. xii.26b, 1ff.   [68] Polyb. xii.25k, 5ff.

[69] *FGH* 86 т 2 § 6, καὶ ζηλωτὴς μέν ἐστι Θουκυδίδου ἔν τε τῇ τῶν δημηγοριῶν δαψιλείᾳ τε καὶ διασκευῇ, τῷ μεγαλείῳ δὲ μὴ δευτερεύων τοῦ λόγου τῷ σαφεῖ παρελαύνει τὸν ἄνδρα. Pédech, *op. cit.* (n. 2) 300–1 (*cf.* his commentary on xii.25a in his edition of that book, Paris, 1961), translates the last phrase 'il ne lui est pas inférieur pour la magnificence de la pensée et il le dépasse par la précision', but after τῷ μεγαλείῳ it is likely that λόγος is 'diction' or 'style'. Agatharchides' style is as elevated as Thucydides', and he avoids his obscurity.

silence is certainly odd; and it is especially odd in the context of his criticism
of Timaeus' version of Hermocrates' speech, just mentioned, since a Thucydidean version of this speech existed[70] and an elementary argument against
Timaeus would have been that his speech bore no resemblance to that in
Thucydides, and hence one (or both) must be false.[71]

It has recently been suggested[72] that in his emulation of Thucydides
Agatharchides may have been typical of others who at that time copied the
Athenian and that in his attacks on Timaeus Polybius is really aiming at
them – and so by implication at Thucydides himself. However, Timaeus is
criticised by Polybius because οὐ... τὰ ῥηθέντα γέγραφεν, οὐδ' ὡς ἐρρήθη κατ'
ἀλήθειαν – which must mean 'because he has reproduced neither what was
said nor the real sense of what was said', *i.e.* he has given us neither a
transcription (which cannot of course be reasonably required) not yet an
accurate résumé of the original speech.[73] For Polybius this is a fair criticism,
for he himself never wavers in his firm requirement that a speech must give
the essential part of what was actually said and, as we have seen, it is for
neglecting this that he condemned Phylarchus, Chaereas and ‖ Sosylus. It is
true that one chapter in Book XII[74] has been taken to concede the historian's
right to improvise by choosing arguments suitable to the speaker and the
occasion, regardless of what was actually said; but this view rests on a
misunderstanding of Polybius' meaning. It is in fact the statesman, not the
historian, whose task is to select appropriate arguments; here as elsewhere, the
historian is restricted to retailing what was really said and indicating why the
speakers failed or succeeded in their object.[75] Polybius' position then is clear
and uncompromising. Thucydides, on the other hand, was less certain. As we
saw, he left an unresolved antithesis between 'the general purport of what was
actually said' and 'what the situation seemed to me to require each party to
say'.

Nevertheless I do not believe that in attacking Timaeus Polybius was
attacking contemporary emulators of Thucydides, still less Thucydides himself.
His silence concerning his great predecessor seems to me to bear a different
explanation, viz. that on the general matter at issue between Polybius and those
historians he attacks, Polybius and Thucydides stood in the same camp.
Polybius did not not wish to put himself in the false position of seeming to

[70] Thuc. IV.59–65.

[71] As Gomme, *Commentary* (n. 18) 3.523, points out.

[72] By Pédech, commenting on Polyb. XII.25a.

[73] H. Welzhofer, *NJbb* 121 (1880) 541, takes the sense to be 'he has not reproduced the words
spoken nor the actual form in which the speech was given'. But it is clear from XXIV.12.10. (above
n. 50) that Polybius did not require a historian to reproduce either the form of the original oration
or the exact words in which it was delivered.

[74] XII.25i, 4–8; for the view attacked see Gomme, *Commentary* (n. 18) 3.522; C. Wunderer,
Polybios-Forschungen 2 (Leipzig, 1901) 11; Ziegler, *op. cit.* (n. 53) col. 1527; Avenarius, *op. cit.*
(n. 19) 155 n. 135.

[75] See my analysis of this chapter in *Miscellanea di studi alessandrini in memoria di Augusto Rostagni*
(Turin, 1963) 211–13 and in my *Commentary* (n. 59) 2.397–9.

criticise Thucydides. He preferred to concentrate on the main enemy, and in this context that means the writers whose speeches were purely rhetorical compositions quite unsullied by any trace of veracity.

VI

So much for theory: but how far does Polybius maintain those tenets in actual practice? To answer this question it will be necessary to examine several examples together with some of the objections which have been raised against regarding them as authentic. It is not, I think, necessary to make a distinction between the different categories of speech. In Book xii, it is true,[76] Polybius distinguishes between public speeches (δημηγορίαι), harangues, usually to troops (παρακλήσεις) and speeches made by ambassadors (πρεσ-βευτικοὶ λόγοι), and in the main his own speeches fall into these three groups; on the other hand the division is not intended to be an exhaustive one, for he adds the words 'and in short all speeches of this sort'; and unless παρακλήσεις are to be interpreted in the very restricted sense of speeches in the field to soldiers, there are several orations that qualify equally as παρακλήσεις and as δημηγορίαι, or even as πρεσβευτικοὶ λόγοι.[77] However there seems no reason to suppose that Polybius employed different criteria ‖ in composing the different types of speech – though he almost certainly drew on different kinds of source material. In Book iii, for instance, he records two harangues to troops preceding the Ticinus battle, one by Hannibal, the other by P. Scipio.[78] I have deliberately taken these two speeches first since they are among the greatest stumbling blocks to the theory that Polybius is an honest man. The pairing of speeches is of course an old rhetorical device and so perhaps calculated to arouse our suspicions; and these are not lulled when we observe that both harangues are based on commonplaces about the relative strength of forces and the chances of battle. It is true that commonplaces are apt to be uttered on such occasions and their inclusion does not damn a speech as fictitious. But not only are these above all occasions when no one is likely to be taking notes but, as De Sanctis has pointed out,[79] Scipio did not expect a major battle at this juncture. Hence it follows that his speech is unhistorical and evidently serves to balance Hannibal's and to build up Scipio into a worthy opponent of the great Carthaginian. In this context it is perhaps worth noting that of Polybius' Roman speeches (which form a minority of those he includes) by far the greater number are delivered by men connected in some way with the original or adopted family of his friend Scipio Aemilianus – a fact which clearly reflects his personal interest in Scipio rather than the intrinsic importance of

---

[76] xii.25a.3; *cf.* 25i.3; Diod. xx.1.2; Dion. Hal. *Pomp.* 3.20, 5.6; *Ant. Rom.* vii.66.3; Cic. *Orat.* 66.

[77] *E.g.* Critolaus' address to the Achaeans (xxxviii.12–13) or those of Chlaeneas and Lyciscus at Sparta (ix.28–39), which were certainly exhortations as well as ambassadorial speeches.

[78] iii.63–4; see my *Commentary ad loc.*

[79] De Sanctis, *Storia dei Romani* 3.2 (Turin, 1917) 172.

this particular group of nobles.[80] Before Zama there is a similar pair of speeches, first Africanus', then Hannibal's;[81] once again a bundle of *communes loci*, including one very worrying phrase in which Scipio tells his men that they are fighting to win undisputed sovereignty over the rest of the world, which corresponds exactly to Polybius' own estimate of the importance of this battle (expressed over thirty years later) but is somewhat surprising as a contemporary utterance.

Nevertheless, I do not think that we should rush to condemn Polybius' honesty on the basis of these passages. He may, as Adcock suggests in the case of Thucydides,[82] have taken for granted the contents of a παράκλησις on the battlefield in a way which he would, on his own showing, have regarded as illegitimate in a speech concerned with policy. But the simpler and, to me, the more likely explanation is that he found versions of these speeches in the general written source (or one of the sources) from which he drew his account of these battles, and developed them because of his interest in the family of Scipio. This seems at any rate more likely than that he deliberately violated his own strongly felt principles by composing passages of rhetorical fiction. ‖

VII

It has sometimes been urged that repetitions of metaphors, phrases and sentiments between one speech and another, or between a speech and a narrative passage, are an argument against the authenticity of the speeches. There are for instance examples of this kind in the Ticinus and Cannae speeches which we have just seen reason to regard as deriving ultimately, perhaps *via* Fabius or some other source, from artificial compositions. In the former[83] Fortune, *Tyche*, is said by Hannibal to offer to the Punic troops certain prizes (ἆθλα προτεθεικέναι); the same metaphor is used by Scipio in his address to his men before Zama[84] – and only a page before Polybius has used it himself.[85] There is another example in Aemilius' speech before Cannae.[86] After listing all the advantages which made the Roman position so much stronger than it was before Trebia and Trasimene, he continues: 'since then all the conditions are now the reverse of those in the battles I spoke of, we may anticipate that the result of the present battle will likewise be the opposite'. This hazardous conclusion – to be refuted so ironically by events – is very typical of Polybius'

---

[80] *Cf.* H. Ullrich, *Die Reden bei Polybios* (Progr. Zittau, 1905) 8–9. The only exception among the surviving speeches is that of Flamininus before Cynoscephalae (Polyb. xviii.23.3–6); but if one takes account of speeches in Livy which are probably derived from Polybius one must add the names of M'. Acilius Glabrio (Livy xxxvi.17), Q. Marcius Philippus (Livy xlii.40–2) and L. Furius Purpurio, the Roman *legatus* at the Aetolian meeting of 200 (Livy xxxi.31).

[81] xv.10–11; *cf.* Walbank, *JRS* 53 (1963) 10 [above, p. 152]. The speeches of Aemilius and Hannibal before Cannae (iii.108–11) fall into the same category.

[82] Above n. 23.   [83] Polyb. iii.63.2.

[84] Polyb. xv.10.5.   [85] Polyb. xv.9.4.

[86] Polyb. iii.109.3.

own way of thinking. In his description of the battle of the Aegates Islands in Book I[87] he remarks: 'as the condition of each force was just the reverse of what it had been at the battle of Drepana, the result also was naturally (εἰκότως) the reverse for each'. If Aemilius' speech was an artificial product deriving from Polybius' source, was this turn of phrase borrowed from the same source? or was it perhaps a commonplace too and incorporated by Polybius in the organisation of his material?

There are similar repetitions elsewhere. For example, in his speech at Sparta in the late spring of 210 Lyciscus of Acarnania recalls the Aetolian raids in the Peloponnese when the general Timaeus plundered temples at Taenarum and Lusi;[88] but the same point had already been raised by some Spartans in answer to an Aetolian envoy at Sparta in 220.[89] Does this mean, as a recent work argues,[90] that Lyciscus' speech is therefore a rhetorical composition? Surely not. If a point is valid, it may be made twice, and if all fourth-century speeches which mention the services of Athens against the Persians were to be branded as rhetorical forgeries, we should have few pro-Athenian apodeictic speeches left. The debate at Sparta, at which Chlaeneas and Lyciscus spoke, is perhaps the most striking example of Polybius' use of speeches and could well stand as a touchstone for his honesty. I shall return to it shortly. Meanwhile I should like to discuss one or two other passages in which repetition occurs. ‖

At a meeting of the Senate held after the Aetolian War, Leon of Athens delivered a speech[91] which Polybius says made a particular impression through his use of a simile well suited to the occasion. Leon remarked that the Aetolian people should not be considered guilty, since the populace is like the sea, calm when left alone but made terrible by winds blowing upon it; these winds correspond of course to the guilty agitators who stirred up the Aetolians, making them, contrary to their nature, reckless in word and deed. Unfortunately this comparison, which Polybius so much admires, had already been used in very similar circumstances by Scipio when quelling a mutiny in Spain;[92] and I see no reason to think that on either occasion its presence indicates that the speech containing it is not authentic. Leon's speech is certainly genuine, for Polybius would never have invented the statement that the Aetolian people were not by nature reckless in word and deed; this must be what Leon said. As regards Scipio, he was sufficiently well read in Greek literature to quote what was no more than an ancient commonplace going back to Solon[93] –

$$\text{ἐξ ἀνέμων δὲ θάλασσα ταράσσεται· ἢν δέ τις αὐτὴν}$$
$$\text{μὴ κινῇ, πάντων ἐστὶ δικαιοτάτη}$$

---

[87] Polyb. 1.61.2.
[88] Polyb. IX.34–9.   [89] Polyb. IV.34.9.
[90] Pédech, *REG* 71 (1958) 440; but in *Méthode* (n. 2) 265–6, he appears to accept the authenticity of the speeches of Lyciscus and Chlaeneas, explaining the antithetical form as due to the background of pamphleteering on which the two speakers drew.
[91] Polyb. XXI.31.6–15.   [92] Polyb. XI.29.9–10.   [93] Fr. 12.

– to Herodotus, who puts it in Artabanus' speech to Xerxes,[94] and to Demosthenes.[95] The only strange feature in the whole business is Polybius' naïve admiration for what Livy,[96] more experienced in *communes loci*, was later to call a *vulgata similitudo*.

There are, similarly, at least two occasions where speakers appeal to the common fortune of mankind, to that Tyche which is so powerful against all men, as a reason why those who are temporarily at an advantage should not press it too hard. The Roman envoys at Carthage at the end of the Hannibalic War state that this argument had been adduced by the Carthaginians themselves a little time before,[97] and later it was employed by Heracleides of Byzantium, Antiochus' envoy to Scipio.[98] Polybius uses it himself in commenting on the unexpected reversal that befell the Aetolians at Medeon, after they had already passed a decree regulating the disposal of the booty, which still remained to be taken: 'we should never', he says, 'have confident hopes about things that may still turn out quite otherwise'.[99] Like the simile about the sea, this is a commonplace which goes back to Herodotus and Sophocles and appears in Stoic and Peripatetic writers alike.[100] Its use, I suggest, warrants no conclusions either for or against the genuineness of a speech in which it appears. To sum up this part of my argument: repetitions of phrases, similes, commonplaces and historical arguments occur in several of ‖ Polybius' speeches. In part, they are perhaps covered by the statement quoted earlier,[101] in which Polybius asks his reader's pardon if, in retailing speeches, he uses the same style, disposition, treatment and even the same words as on a previous occasion; but mostly they can be explained as having indeed been uttered by the speakers to whom Polybius attributes them.

VIII

A special category of speech is represented by Polybius' account of various gatherings at which a succession of speakers took the floor. Examples are the conference at Naupactus which brought the Social War to a close,[102] the congress at Sparta from which Polybius reports the speeches of Chlaeneas and Lyciscus,[103] the conference in Locris between Philip and Flamininus and his Greek allies[104] and various Achaean meetings, especially towards the end of the work when Polybius was able to draw on personal knowledge or enquiry.

These gatherings are usually described with a wealth of personal detail which

[94] Hdt. vii.16a.   [95] Dem. xix.136.
[96] Livy xxxviii.10.5 [*cf.* Curtius x.7.11].
[97] Polyb. xv.1.8.   [98] Polyb. xxi.14.4.
[99] Polyb. ii.4.5.
[100] See the references in my *Commentary* (n. 59) on ii.4.5.
[101] See above p. 249 and n. 50.
[102] Polyb. v.103.8–104.11.
[103] Polyb. ix.28–39.
[104] Polyb. xviii.1–9.

is in marked contrast to the colourless settings of Thucydides' conferences[105] and Polybius seems to command good sources for them. To identify these in detail is now impossible; but it is not impossible to hazard plausible guesses about some of them.[106] Thus the extremely detailed description of the Locrian congress of 198 and the speeches delivered there probably goes back ultimately to the report of the Achaean representative Xenophon, who subsequently went on to Rome and was therefore able to report as well on the sequel to Flamininus' intrigue.[107] Even for events before 200 Polybius may have had access to official records as well as to oral traditions and contemporary historians like Zeno and Antisthenes of Rhodes. It is clear that he often had at his disposal more detailed and more comprehensive reports of such congresses than he chooses to pass on to his readers. In such cases it is of interest to observe the criteria which lead him to report one speech and omit another, for this may throw some light on the purpose which he attaches to speeches in history. I should like to mention two examples.

From the conference of Naupactus in 217 he reports only one speech, that of Agelaus. 'There was a constant interchange of communications on points of detail;' he writes, 'most of these I shall pass over as they have nothing worthy of mention in them.' The speech he chose to record, that of Agelaus, is remarkable on two scores: first, it emphasised the supposed danger to Greece from whoever ‖ proved victor in the Hannibalic War, underlining the point with the famous metaphor of the cloud in the west, and secondly it was effective in disposing everyone for peace.[108] The belief that Roman aggressive intervention in Greece was to be feared as soon as the Hannibalic War was over, can be shown, I believe, to be illfounded;[109] nevertheless, for reasons which I need not go into here, the Greeks, or some of them, held that belief, and the metaphor of the cloud in the west made a deep impression and was echoed by Lyciscus in 210[110] in his speech against the Aetolians, who had called in the Romans.

Secondly, in his account of the embassies received by the Senate after the war with Antiochus Polybius gives a full version of Eumenes' speech and of that of the Rhodians on the question of liberating the cities of Asia. But between the two speeches he observes that, because one of the Rhodian envoys was delayed, the Senate meanwhile gave an audience to representatives of Smyrna. 'As they had the undisputed approbation of the House,' Polybius remarks, '...I do not think it is necessary to report this speech in detail'; and in fact

---

[105] *Cf.* Pédech, *Méthode* (n. 2) 289ff.

[106] See for further discussion Pédech, *Méthode* (n. 2) 259–76.

[107] Polyb. XVIII.1–12; for discussion see M. Holleaux, *Études d'épigraphie et d'histoire grecques* 5 (Paris, 1957) 29–79; A. Aymard, *Premiers rapports de Rome et la confédération achaienne* (Bordeaux, 1938) 114–27; F. M. Wood, *TAPhA* 65 (1939) 93–103; *AJP* 62 (1941) 277–98 (defending Flamininus); Walbank, *Philip V of Macedon* (Cambridge, 1940) 159–62; H. H. Scullard, *Roman politics* (Oxford, 1951) 101–4; H. E. Stier, *Roms Aufstieg zur Weltmacht* (Cologne-Opladen, 1957) 129–30.

[108] Polyb. V.105.1.

[109] *Cf.* Walbank, *JRS* 53 (1963) 1–13 [above, pp. 138–56].

[110] Polyb. IX.37.10.

he omits it completely but for a bare statement that they referred to their goodwill and services to Rome. In short, the Rhodian and Pergamene speeches are recorded because they bring out a clash in policy and illuminate two contemporary points of view about a matter of vital importance to any Greek, namely what was to happen concerning the freedom of the Greek cities in Asia.

Both these examples are of speeches by Greeks. It is a striking feature of Polybius' *History* that, as I have already mentioned,[111] if we except a few 'pairs' of battle speeches by Hannibal and a series of Roman commanders,[112] a few harangues of Hannibal alone,[113] a speech of Mago to the Carthaginian senate[114] and several addresses by Scipio Africanus (concerning whom Polybius had both a special interest and special sources of information),[115] by far the greater number of the speeches he includes are by Greeks; and this is increasingly true in the later books. Indeed of the five longest speeches singled out in Ziegler's Pauly-Wissowa article four are by Greeks and only one, that of Africanus to the mutineers, by a Roman.

The two most elaborate speeches in the whole *History* are perhaps those delivered at Sparta by the Aetolian Chlaeneas and the Acarnanian Lyciscus.[116] These, I have already argued, are to be regarded as authentic.[117] Admittedly they are 'worked over' in the way I have already discussed; and the fact that the Acarnanian speech is twice as long as the Aetolian certainly reflects the historian's own sympathies. But with this qualification, the two speeches give a remarkable picture of the cleavage of feeling that tore Greece apart during the early years of ‖ Roman intervention. The issue is quite shortly: which constitutes the greater danger to Greece, Rome or Macedonia? It is illuminated, not with the generalisations one would find in Thucydides, but with a wide range of *exempla* taken from the past history of Greece and going back, as always, to the fourth century, when the issue of Macedonian domination was fought out both on the ideological level in pamphlets and on the battlefield. A citizen of Megalopolis, Polybius naturally approved what was done by Philip II, who reduced Sparta and extended the bounds of Arcadia; and elsewhere[118] he has a long attack on Demosthenes and a defence of the Peloponnesian patriots whom Demosthenes had condemned as traitors. It is therefore to be expected that his sympathies will be with Lyciscus, who praises Philip II and the other kings of Macedonia down to Philip V, rather than with Chlaeneas, who defends the Roman alliance and condemns Macedonia as the perennial enemy of Greece. Nevertheless by the second century the issue had changed. Even

[111] Above, n. 80.

[112] Polyb. III.63–4 (Ticinus), 108–9, 111 (Cannae), xv.10–11 (Zama).

[113] Polyb. III.44.10–13, 54.2–3, xv.19.

[114] Polyb. xxxvi.5.1–5.

[115] Polyb. xi.28–9, 31, xv.6–8 (discussion with Hannibal), 17–18, xxi.15.5–11 (really a reply to Antiochus' envoy Heracleides), 17.1–8. On Polybius' special interest in the family of Scipio Aemilianus, *i.e.* the Cornelii Scipiones and the Aemilii Paulli, see above n. 80.

[116] Polyb. ix.28–39.   [117] Above n. 90.

[118] Polyb. xviii.14–15.

earlier Aratus, the great Achaean hero, had built the Confederation in opposition to Macedonia, though he had to call upon Antigonus Doson to save it from Cleomenes of Sparta; and in the Second Macedonian War the Achaeans had gone over to Rome and fought against Philip. Throughout Polybius' childhood the Roman alliance had dominated Achaean policy. When Lyciscus calls the Romans barbarians, he uses words of which we have no reason to think Polybius would have approved; he had come to know them too well to acquiesce in so easy and conventional a snap judgement. Looking back, the issues raised on this occasion at Sparta and later at other conferences where Achaeans as well as Spartans had to make their choice cannot have seemed crystal clear. If, as is likely, Polybius was composing this part of his work at Rome, while still held in detention, he must have been asking such questions as: Had Achaean policy been right throughout? Was alliance with Macedonia right in the first war with Rome and wrong in the second? If so, what were the criteria of wise policy and of political morality?

It is, I believe, because of the far-reaching nature of these issues, raised now in a striking form at Sparta, that Polybius develops the speeches of Chlaeneas and Lyciscus at such length. But there is perhaps another reason. The first book of Thucydides is largely built around the two famous congresses at Sparta. At the first we are confronted with the rival speeches of the Corinthians and the Athenians, urging and deprecating war, followed by those of Archidamus and the ephor Sthenelaidas;[119] at the second the Corinthians again press for war in a speech which has to wait for an answer until that of Pericles which ends the book. These speeches discuss the issues for which the forthcoming war is to be fought. Is it, I wonder, pure fantasy to suggest that Polybius may also have had this in mind when he chose to record in such detail – greater than on any other occasion in the whole surviving part of his work – these two speeches delivered at another Spartan meeting, where representatives of the two sides thrashed out some of the problems that were to dominate the period of Roman intervention in the Greek East and now for the first time found open and public expression? ‖

IX

If I may now pull some strings together, the conclusion to which an examination of Polybius' speeches, long and short, leads is that he cannot be fairly accused of inventing. He is using a long-established convention, and like Thucydides before him he shapes and rephrases his material so that the result takes on a decidedly personal colouring. Sometimes too, especially in addresses to troops before battle, he seems to be drawing on sources which have not scrupled to invent words appropriate to the occasion; therein he shows perhaps less critical judgement than we are entitled to expect. But I can find no passage

119 Thuc. 1.68–71, 73–8, 80–85.2, 86.

where one can say confidently that Polybius has followed the formula to which
even Thucydides in part subscribed when he spoke of recording 'what he
thought the speakers would have said'.[120] The provenance of most of Polybius'
speeches, a majority of them delivered by Greeks, and most of them on
occasions concerning which he will have had authentic sources of information,
reflect the predominantly Greek character of his *History*. It recounts the rise
of Rome to world power, but it is a story told by a Greek writing from the
Greek point of view and always conscious that it was the Greek world that was
being subjected to Roman domination. Polybius' account of Roman policy,
it must be conceded,[121] is schematic, monolithic and faulty; it can be corrected
from his own narrative. The ideological conflict and the clashes that he records
are all Greek; it is significant that he sneers at Chaereas and Sosylus for
suggesting that Roman policy was split on the eve of the Hannibalic War, and
he himself rather ostentatiously refuses to record similar speeches on the eve
of the Third Punic War, remarking that 'they had long made up their minds
to act then, but they were looking for a suitable opportunity and a pretext that
would appeal to foreign nations'.[122] But in speeches made at gatherings in
Greece or before the Senate at Rome Polybius allows us to hear the genuine
voice of leading Greek statesmen of the time and to share in their dilemmas
and clashes of policy. Only in this way could the *History* become that handbook
of political and moral instruction for a Greek public which Polybius intended
it to be.

X

There is no evidence that Polybius' protest had much effect in changing the
current attitude towards writing history. As before, the criterion by which the
literary critics judge speeches in histories continues to be, not their accuracy,
but their appropriateness, not ἀλήθεια but πιθανότης and τὸ πρέπον. Thucydides, Dionysius tells us,[123] maintains a certain sameness of style throughout
his speeches and so is less successful than Herodotus in achieving τὸ πρέπον –
which is πασῶν ‖ ἐν λόγοις ἀρετῶν ἡ κυριωτάτη, the most sovereign virtue
in speeches. True, in some places he is more successful than in others. Some
speeches can be described as 'suited to the characters and in conformity to the
events', τοῖς προσώποις πρέποντας καὶ τοῖς πράγμασιν οἰκείους, but others,
like Pericles' defence or the Melian dialogue, fail on both counts.[124] Cicero,
it may be noted, found Thucydides' speeches obscure or almost incomprehensible and certainly no use as a model for orators.[125] Xenophon and
Philistus, Dionysius remarks elsewhere,[126] are also open to the same criticism.
The criterion here adduced is of course the one we have already seen

[120] See above, pp. 244f.   [121] See above, n. 109.
[122] Polyb. III.20.5, XXXVI.1.1–2.1.   [123] Dion. Hal. *Pomp.* 3.20.
[124] Dion. Hal. *Thuc.* 36.
[125] Cicero, *Brutus* 287f., *Orat.* 30ff.; *Opt. Gen. Orat.* 15f.; *cf.* Syme, *Sallust* (n. 11) 53.
[126] Dion. Hal. *Vett. Cens.* 3.2; *Pomp.* 5.6.

expounded by Callisthenes.[127] It appears again in Lucian, who insists that speeches in history must match the character and the situation, τῷ προσώπῳ καὶ τῷ πράγματι.[128] Naturally the doctrine crops up in the Roman schools. Quintilian, who regards the writing of speeches as useful to both poets and would-be historians,[129] praises Livy as highly successful in his speeches – 'in contionibus supra quam enarrari potest eloquentem: ita quae dicuntur omnia cum rebus, tum personis accommodata sunt'.[130] Indeed the composition of such speeches was a regular part of the training in the rhetorical schools and Theon, who was perhaps a contemporary of Quintilian,[131] reckoned it under 'character-drawing', προσωποποιία. In his *Progymnasmata*[132] he judges success according as a historical character is made to deliver speeches that are 'appropriate to himself and to the underlying situation', οἰκείους ἑαυτῷ τε καὶ τοῖς ὑποκειμένοις πράγμασιν.

Granted, what literary men like Theon and Quintilian say does not necessarily reflect the historian's purpose; perhaps not all speeches in later historians are artificial compositions. But the one example of which chance has preserved the original – Claudius' speech granting citizenship to the Gallic *principes* – does not emerge particularly well from the comparison.[133] It is significant for the general picture that Dionysius, a third of whose history consists of speeches, should be so blind to the question of truth, and that Lucian, whose concern is not with 'how history can help the orator', but specifically with 'how to write history', should follow blindly the old criterion of τὸ πρέπον, 'what is fitting'. It was this doctrine that prevailed; and that is why one should give full credit to Polybius who, if he failed to carry his successors with him, at least in his own practice and expressed principles made a stand for truth as the chief criterion in composing speeches in history.

---

[127] See above p. 246.   [128] Lucian, *Hist. Conscr.* 58.
[129] Quint. III.8.49.   [130] Quint. *Inst.* X.1.101.
[131] Cf. Stegemann, *RE* 5A.2 (1934) 'Theon (5)', col. 2037.
[132] Cf. Spengel, *Rhet.* 2.115; for all this section I am indebted to Avenarius, *op. cit.* (n. 19) 150.
[133] Tac. *Ann.* XI.24; *ILS* 212; *cf.* Syme, *Tacitus* (Oxford, 1958) 1.317ff.

17

POLEMIC IN POLYBIUS*

I

When ancient historians wanted to take cognisance of what their predecessors had written, they seem usually, though not always, to have preferred an anonymous reference to one by name. To this practice the most noteworthy exception is Polybius. In his *Histories* he mentions about a score of previous writers, including philosophers, orators and historians, a large number of whom are the object of quite bitter self-righteous polemic. This harsh trait in Polybius' character appears slightly odd, when one considers his generally sanguine and optimistic view of the world he lived in and of the advantages which he himself enjoyed over his predecessors. This optimism survived the rigours of exile: though, indeed, it might be argued that an exile passed among the amenities of the Scipionic circle presented no particular hardship. Be that as it may, his attitude towards his own age was not unlike that of an eighteenth-century *savant*. 'Thanks to Alexander's empire in Asia,' he writes (III.59.3ff.),[1] 'and that of the Romans in other parts of the world, nearly all regions have become approachable by sea and land, and since Greek men of action are relieved from the ambitions of a military or political career and have therefore ample means for enquiry and study, we ought to be able to arrive at ... something more like the truth about lands which were formerly little known.' Therefore we should not 'find fault with writers for their omissions and mistakes, but should praise and admire them, considering the times they lived in, for having ascertained something on the subject and advanced our knowledge' (III.59.2). This attitude is not limited to matters of geography. 'Nowadays,' Polybius writes elsewhere (IX.2.5), 'the progress made in the arts and sciences (τὰς ἐμπειρίας καὶ τέχνας) has been so rapid, that those who study history are equipped with the means of dealing, one might say, scientifically (μεθοδικῶς) with any emergency that may arise.'

If Polybius really believed this – and I see no reason to think he did not – one might have expected him to show a little more of the charity he preaches towards those less favourably placed, and rather more effort to live up to his own principles. Such charity is, however, conspicuously lacking, and why it is lacking is a question that needs discussing, for two reasons. In the first place, it is in polemical passages directed against his predecessors that a historian most

---

* [*JRS* 52 (1962) 1–12]

[1] Unless otherwise indicated references are to Polybius.

clearly defines his own position in relation to them, so throwing light on the process by which historical knowledge is built up. Secondly, it is in polemic with its emotional overtones that a historian is most likely to give himself away, and reveal motives which usually lie concealed behind a smoke-screen of rational discourse. Both reasons can be exemplified in Polybius.

The greater part of Greek and Roman history writing has a moral tone. This disposes it towards praising or condemning the historical characters under discussion. There was a theory about this, perhaps most conveniently summed up by Lucian in his tract on *How to write history*: 'eulogy and censure', he writes (*Hist. Conscr.* 59), 'should be careful and considered, free from slander, supported by evidence, cursory, and relevant to the occasion, for those involved are not in court; otherwise *you* will be censured just like Theopompus, who made a business of impeaching everyone in a quarrelsome spirit acting as a prosecutor rather than a recorder of events'. This reference to Theopompus is not surprising, for he, more than anyone, had acquired an evil reputation for the unrestrained violence of his language. Polybius speaks most censoriously (VIII.10.5) about his attack on Philip II, the nominal hero of his *Philippika*, and quotes a famous passage (VIII.9.6–13) in which he abused Philip's *hetairoi* as a band of debauchees assembled from all over Greece. This passage was famous in antiquity; full of antitheses directly borrowed from Gorgias,[2] it interested literary critics. It was later to be condemned by Demetrius (*Eloc.* 247) for its artificiality and frigidity, but Polybius' objections are based, not, of course, on its style, but on a feeling of outrage that Theopompus should use such terms about Philip II. 'If one set oneself the task of singing the praises of Philip and his friends,' he observes (VIII.10.5–6), ‖ 'one could scarcely find terms adequate to characterise the bravery, industry and in general the virtue of these men who indisputably by their energy and daring raised Macedonia from the rank of a petty kingdom to that of the greatest and most glorious monarchy in the world'.

Theopompus' abuse is couched in strong terms. But the ancients were less squeamish than we are about such matters, and Dionysius of Halicarnassus later defended Theopompus' attack against Polybius' criticism as a praiseworthy example of παρρησία.[3] One is bound to ask: why is Polybius so sensitive about Theopompus' attack on Philip? Not all such attacks arouse his resentment. Plutarch (*Cleom.* 16.3) tells us that Aratus of Sicyon filled his *Memoirs* with abuse of Antigonus Doson, the very man whom he had summoned into the Peloponnese to save the Achaean League from Sparta; Polybius never mentions this. We may suspect that in the case of both Theopompus and Aratus political attitudes have played an important part in influencing his judgement. In the second century the role of Philip II was still

---

[2] E. Norden, *Antike Kunstprosa*[2] (Leipzig, 1915) 1.122 n., compares Gorgias' *Epitaphios* (Diels, *Vorsokr.*[5] 2.285 B 6).

[3] *De Imit.* III.3 p. 428; *Pomp.* 6.7–10; *cf.* G. Avenarius, *Lukians Schrift zur Geschichtsschreibung* (Diss. Frankfurt, 1954) 161–2.

a subject to raise violent passions among Greeks.[4] To Polybius, a loyal son of Arcadia, he was the benefactor of Greece who had brought freedom to a Peloponnese oppressed by Sparta, and had treated the misguided Athenians with true magnanimity.[5] Consequently Theopompus' vilification of Philip must be condemned in the strongest language. On the other hand, Theopompus was guilty of yet another offence equally culpable in Polybius' eyes; he had abandoned his Ἑλληνικαὶ ἱστορίαι in order to write Φιλιππικά, so producing a history with Philip rather than Greece at its centre. 'Surely,' remarks Polybius (VIII.11.4), 'it would have been much more dignified and more just to include Philip's achievement in the history of Greece than to include the history of Greece in that of Philip.' The 'brilliant period of Greek history' (VIII.11.3) which Theopompus thus omitted to write was that in which Epaminondas founded Megalopolis and established the Arcadian League. No history of Philip was sufficient compensation for that omission. Indeed, it is quite clear that behind his moral strictures on Theopompus we can detect the political sympathies of the historian of Megalopolis, who applauds the achievements of Philip II, but insists that they be judged against the background and criteria of the Peloponnese.

This example illustrates clearly the different levels at which Polybius' polemic operates; it is not always candid, and it is prone to express political antipathy in moral terms. These are characteristics which are exemplified in other polemical passages. But before looking at these, it is perhaps worth while to consider how far such criticisms of earlier historians have their counterpart in those historians themselves; how strong in fact was the general rule of anonymity about one's predecessors and how often was it broken?

II

We are handicapped of course by the fragmentary nature of almost all these earlier historians. Apart from Herodotus, Thucydides and Xenophon we have no more than a random sampling, and often far less than that; and so we have to make do with what happens to survive. Herodotus clearly wrote some parts of his history, especially the geographical sections, with an eye on Hecataeus, just as Hecataeus had written with an eye on those Hellenes whose λόγοι, he said (*FGH* I F I), were varied and ridiculous. Porphyry indeed accuses Herodotus of having plagiarised his account of the phoenix, the hippopotamus and the crocodile from Hecataeus (*FGH* I F 324 a); but whatever his borrowings and whatever we may think about his hinted criticism, Herodotus contains no open polemic.[6] The reference to Hecataeus by name as the authority for one account of how the Pelasgians came to be expelled from Attica (Hdt. VI.137), and the story of how he was snubbed by an Egyptian

[4] *Cf.* IX.28 and 33 for rival views; and see in general P. Treves, *LEC* 9 (1940) 167–8; Walbank, *CQ* 37 (1943) 9.

[5] V.10.1, XVIII.14, XXII.16.   [6] See Jacoby on *FGH* I F 302.

priest for boasting about his genealogy (Hdt. ΙΙ.143), are not fundamentally hostile; and Hecataeus' part in the Ionian revolt is mentioned with sympathy.[7] Thucydides is similarly sparing in his references to his predecessors. There is a good deal of implied criticism of Herodotus, which Jacoby not unfairly characterises as intolerant and ‖ uncompromising;[8] and Thucydides' rejection of dating by archons (Thuc. v.20.2) as 'inaccurate' seems to be directed against Hellanicus, who used archons to date his *Atthis* (*FGH* 323a F 25–6) and in his work on the Priestesses of the temple of Hera at Argos developed a similar method of chronology (*FGH* 4 F 74–84). But Herodotus' name is never quoted and Hellanicus' only once, in a grudging reference (Thuc. 1.97.2) to the latter's account of the Pentecontaetia as having been written βραχέως τε καὶ τοῖς χρόνοις οὐκ ἀκριβῶς, summarily and with a vague chronology – a criticism which, it has been frequently observed, accurately describes Thucydides' own version of the years from 478 to 431.

Hellanicus is a frequent object of criticism among subsequent historians. Ctesias of Cnidus accused both him and Herodotus of falsehood (*FGH* 687a T 2); Theopompus coupled him with Herodotus and Ctesias in a reference to myths (*FGH* 115 F 381); and Ephorus censured him for omitting Lycurgus from his account of the Spartan constitution and attributing his achievements to others (*FGH* 70 F 118). All our references here are indeed second-hand and throw no light on the tone of these criticisms; but they seem to be concerned with charges of inaccuracy. Inaccuracy is also the fault alleged against both Ephorus and Theopompus by Agatharchides of Cnidus (*FGH* 86 F 19) in the second century, in his account of the Nile which Diodorus reproduces (Diod. 1.32–42.9). As a pupil of Isocrates Ephorus was also linked with Theopompus in a famous criticism of the pair by Duris of Samos,[9] who attacked them for failing to do justice to their subject-matter; their narratives, he said, were devoid of the delights that come from dramatic *mimesis*, and were concerned only with the formal aspects of writing. This observation represents a new type of polemic, directed against a particular theory of history and the style of presentation, and it almost certainly occurred in Duris' preface, the traditional place for polemic and discussion of general principles. Both Theopompus (*FGH* 115 F 24) and Anaximenes of Lampsacus (*FGH* 72 F 1) used their prologues in order to attack their predecessors – διαβολὰς καθ' ἑτέρων ... ποιεῖσθαι συγγραφέων, according to Dionysius (*Ant. Rom.* 1.1.1). We are not told specifically that they attacked them by name, but the word διαβολαί suggests that they did. I have already referred to the violence of Theopompus' polemic against Philip II; but apart from this passage in Dionysius we know nothing of his attitude towards former writers.

Indeed it is not until we reach Timaeus that we have evidence for a sustained verbal assault on a wide front against earlier historians. Timaeus seized on

---

[7] Hdt. v.36.2, 125; see against Macan, Jacoby, *RE* 7.2 (1912) 'Hekataios', col. 2669.

[8] *FGH* 3 b, Suppl. 2, p. 16.

[9] *FGH* 70 T 22 = 76 F 1; on this see Walbank, *Historia* 9 (1960) 218ff. [above, pp. 226f.].

factual errors in both Theopompus and Ephorus – though in the case of
Ephorus Polybius (XII.4a.2–6) remarks with justice that he was obviously
misled by a scribe's error; he also took issue with Ephorus on questions of
theory, on the relative training needed for the composition of declamations on
the one hand and history on the other (XII.28.8–10 = *FGH* 566 F 7). He
attacked Aristotle, Callisthenes and Theophrastus from the Peripatetic camp,
and the Athenian democrat Demochares (XII.13.23–8). In the case of Demochares it is indeed not certain whether the polemic was personal or literary,[10]
whether in fact it was as a statesman or as a writer that the Athenian had fallen
foul of Timaeus; but since Polybius couples him with the other writers
(XII.23.8), it seems likely that it was his accuracy rather than his statesmanship
that Timaeus had challenged. Timaeus' bitterness in controversy was of course
well known and probably exceptional; it earned him the nickname Ἐπιτίμαιος
(*FGH* 566 T 1, *cf.* T 16) from the Athenians among whom he lived, for close
on fifty years, unloving and unloved.

These examples are typical rather than comprehensive. Their survival is due
to chance, and we must assume that many other instances equally significant
are lost. Moreover, the presence of the actual words used in this polemic is rare;
we are usually compelled to rely on references which may of course be
inaccurate, and in any case rarely reproduce the tone in which the criticism
was delivered. The only development which can be traced is a growing
readiness to quote the names of those who are being attacked, and perhaps
an increasing tendency to employ vicious and less restrained forms of abuse;
though even this impression may be due to the part which Timaeus plays in
the story, and that rests very largely on the evidence of Polybius. As far as the
fragments allow us to judge, the polemic ‖ used by Greek historians against
their predecessors is never excessive until we come to Timaeus. The anonymity
with which Thucydides cushions his captiousness is on the whole typical. The
main grounds for polemic are charges of inaccuracy; though Duris and
Timaeus are interested in the character of history and attack those whom they
regard as writing it in the wrong way or failing to attribute to it its proper
importance. Unfortunately, we have not a sufficient body of polemic to carry
the analysis further. For that we have to turn to Polybius.

III

As we saw, Polybius attacks a wide variety of previous writers in those parts
of his history which have come down to us. The first thing that strikes one on
looking at this considerable mass of polemical writing is the extent to which
it is directed, not against writers whom Polybius believes to be in error on the
period he is dealing with himself, 220 to 146, but rather against more famous
historians of earlier times. Contemporary writers, by and large, remain

----

[10] See A. Momigliano, *RSI* 71 (1959) 532ff. [= *Terzo contributo*, 26ff.].

anonymous. We are frequently told of authors of monographs – unnamed – whose works lack the merits of his own universal history – for example the historians of Hannibal who make the siege of Saguntum and the crossing of the Ebro the causes of the Second Punic War (III.6.1) – probably Roman senatorial writers, judging by the anti-Hannibalic version which they give. There are also writers of monographs (III.32) – perhaps both Greek and Roman – whose works are far too long, and obscure the relations between cause and effect by artificially isolating one set of events. Others are criticised (III.36.2) for quoting names of countries, rivers and cities which can mean nothing to the reader; the references here may be to Sosylus and Silenus, who accompanied Hannibal. Others again, or perhaps the same ones – who can tell? – indulge in sensational details (III.47.6–48.12); they exaggerate the horrors of the Alpine crossing and even introduce a *deus. ex machina* to get Hannibal out of his imaginary difficulties. Sensationalism of this kind is Polybius' special *bête noire*. There are, for example, he says, writers on Hieronymus (VII.7), the young king of Syracuse, who represent him quite unconvincingly as a monster of depravity; how much better, had they chosen to write about Hiero and Gelo, his grandfather and his father, two sterling characters! The reference may be to Baton of Sinope or Eumachus of Naples: we cannot be sure. Finally, there appear to be writers of monographs on the Hellenistic kings, on Philip and Perseus, who suppress facts calling for censure through fear (VIII.8.3): their names are unknown, but presumably they write from the Macedonian court and temper their criticism accordingly. Here we can perhaps detect traces of an uneasy conscience. A consistent and truthful account, observes Polybius (VIII.8.8–9), commenting upon them, is extremely hard to achieve, 'because there are so many varied conditions and circumstances, yielding to which men are prevented from uttering or writing their real opinions. Bearing this in mind we must pardon these writers, in some cases, but in others we should not.' These somewhat cryptic words remind us that Aratus of Sicyon, an Achaean who enjoyed a very special place in Polybius' regard, 'was compelled in public both to do and to say many things quite contrary to his real intention, so as to keep his design concealed. ... Hence there are some matters that he does not even refer to in his *Memoirs*' (II.47.10). Ziegler would go further. He suggests[11] that Polybius has in mind some compromises of his own, particularly in relation to Rome. This is not impossible, but we can hardly get beyond conjecture.

Amidst this long list of anonymous offenders there are a few exceptions. I have counted eight writers who deal with events between 264 and 146 and whom Polybius criticises by name, and, of these, three are quoted in connection with the introductory period 264 to 220. They are Philinus of Agrigentum and Fabius Pictor, almost certainly his sources for the First Punic War;[12] Phylarchus,

[11] *RE* 21.2 (1952) 'Polybios', col. 1558.
[12] *Cf.* I.14–15, III.26.3–4. The doubts of Pédech, *REA* 54 (1952) 246–66, and Momigliano, *RAL* 15 (1960) 318–19 〚= *Terzo contributo*, 66–7〛 seem to me unfounded.

whose version of Achaean events down to 220 is contrasted unfavourably with
Aratus' *Memoirs* (II.56–63);[13] Chaereas and Sosylus, Greek writers on Hannibal
who 'retail the gossip of the barber's shop' (III.20.5) – a judgement ‖ scarcely
borne out by the fragment of Sosylus surviving on papyrus (*FGH* 176 F 1); Zeno
and Antisthenes who write on Rhodes and whose work displays the showiness
common to monographs (XVI.14ff.);[14] and finally A. Postumius Albinus, who
like Polybius himself tried to write πραγματικὴ ἱστορία but whom Polybius
characterises as loquacious and excessively vain-glorious (XXXIX.1). Cicero,
however, it should be noted, calls Albinus 'doctum sane hominem ut indicat
ipsius historia scripta graece' (*Acad. Pr.* II.137), so there was clearly another
point of view. Indeed, the venom with which Polybius attacks and ridicules
Albinus as a historian might even suggest that he was jealous of a rival; but
that, I think, would be a wrong conclusion. Polybius' hostility to Albinus rests
quite simply on political grounds. Despite his philhellenism Albinus had shown
hostility towards the Achaean exiles. As praetor in 155 (XXX.1.5) he presided
over the Senate when the question of their release was under discussion, and
by his manipulation of the business from the chair he apparently secured the
rejection of the motion. If Polybius accompanied Scipio Aemilianus to Spain
in 151 he may once more have come into contact with Albinus,[15] who was
consul there in that year – though it is perhaps more relevant that Scipio had
volunteered to serve under Lucullus, not Albinus (Val. Max. III.2.6). Finally,
as one, and perhaps the chief, of the *legati* sent out to help L. Mummius organise
Achaea (XXXIX.3–4), Polybius will again have had dealings with him in 146–5;
it was probably not by chance that he never recorded the names of these *legati*,[16]
and merely referred to Postumius' cowardice at Scarpheia and his boasting
afterwards (XXXIX.1.11–12).

These eight are the only authors who figure in polemic for the period of
Polybius' history. Whereas from that prior to 264 he criticises five major
historians – Timaeus, Ephorus, Xenophon, Callisthenes and Theopompus –
together with many other important philosophers, orators and polymaths,
such as Eudoxus of Cnidus, Plato, Demosthenes, Strato, Eratosthenes and
Pytheas of Marseilles; moreover, in bulk the pages devoted to this earlier
group far outweigh the passages on contemporary and near-contemporary
writers.

So marked a disproportion may be due to chance; but this seems highly
unlikely. If it is deliberate, there must be some reason for it. It is, of course,
possible that to mention one's contemporaries by name was not a thing one

---

[13] On Phylarchus see E. Gabba, *Studi su Filarco* (Pavia, 1957) = *Athenaeum* 35 (1957) 3–55,
193–239; T. W. Africa, *Phylarchus and the Spartan Revolution* (Berkeley-Los Angeles, 1961);
H. Strasburger, 'Komik und Satire in der griechischen Geschichtsschreibung', in *Festgabe für
Paul Kirn* (Berlin, 1961) 30–5.

[14] See H. Ullrich *De Polybii fontibus Rhodiis* (Diss. Leipzig, 1898) 1–17.

[15] See Walbank, *Historical commentary on Polybius* I (Oxford, 1957) 382 (on III.48.12).

[16] Cic. *Att.* XIII.30.2, 'Polybius non nominat': *cf.* Münzer, *RE* 22.1 (1953) 'Postumius',
col. 906. [See, however, below, p. 291 n. 56.]

did. There is, in fact, a good deal of evidence in favour of this hypothesis: there is the practice of earlier historians already mentioned above and there is the large number of anonymous references in Polybius himself, scattered throughout his main narrative. One can well see that a historian might not be anxious to direct his public to a rival work, especially if he had made more use of it than his criticisms might suggest (and there is evidence that Polybius had so used Phylarchus,[17] whom he does mention). But this alone would not explain why so many pages of Polybius' polemic are devoted to writers who could not possibly be concerned with his period because they had been dead for decades and even centuries before it opened. In short, much of Polybius' polemic must be prompted by quite different considerations from the normal one of establishing a reliable account of one's chosen period and defending it. Can we ascertain what those considerations were?

IV

We may perhaps begin by considering to what extent Polybius' criticism is fair. It is not always possible to answer this question with any certainty, since we are often restricted to his own version of the point at issue and obviously it is quite likely that in a given instance Polybius will appear to be writing fairly in the light of his own statement of the facts, yet these facts may be considerably mis-stated in order to make the case.

Moreover in controverting statements which he holds to be incorrect, Polybius frequently does not adduce any new facts at all, as a modern historian would: he argues from what is *a priori* probable. For example, in xii.25k–26, he has a long criticism of a speech which Timaeus attributes to Hermocrates of Syracuse at the Conference of Gela in 424; but where a modern historian would have cast suspicions on its genuineness by pointing out ‖ that it bore no resemblance to the same speech in Thucydides (Thuc. iv.59–64) – hence one or the other, or both, must be false – Polybius simply argues that not even a schoolboy, still less Hermocrates, could have used the arguments which Timaeus puts into his mouth. Two chapters further on (xii.26b), he discusses the conversations between the Greek envoys and the elder Gelo when the question of help against Persia was raised; but again he argues entirely from probability, without referring to Herodotus' account of the same events (Hdt. vii.153, 157). I mention this point because it is a failing not confined to Polybius – we find it equally in Timaeus. It springs, I believe, from the Greek tendency to rate 'what is reasonable', τὸν εἰκότα λόγον, far too highly, and so to regard it as a substitute for proof.

Polybius' methods in polemic are well illustrated by the curious argument (xii.5–11) about the origins of Epizephyrian Locri. Aristotle, probably in his *Constitutions*, had asserted that this Italian city was founded by slaves from

---

[17] *Cf.* Walbank, *op. cit.* (n. 15) 1.260 (on ii.56.2 n), 565–7 (on v.35–9 n).

Locris who had cohabited with their mistresses while their masters were away fighting beside their Spartan allies in the Messenian War. Timaeus rejected Aristotle's account on several grounds, which Polybius tries to controvert. Timaeus' first point (XII.6.7–8) is a strong one: it is, that it was not the custom of the Greek Locrians to have domestic slaves in early times. Polybius' reply to this cannot be discovered from our current text of the *Histories*, since the editors for some reason best known to themselves have chosen to curtail the two passages from Athenaeus in which it is recorded. The first of these (Athen. VI.264c) gives Timaeus' full answer to Aristotle: the Greeks did not possess purchased slaves, and neither the Locrians nor the Phocians were allowed by law to acquire domestic slaves until recent times; indeed the first Phocian woman to be attended by two servants was the wife of Philomelus (the Phocian leader during the Sacred War), and it was Aristotle's own friend Mnason who became obnoxious to the Phocians by having 1,000 slaves and so robbing free citizens of their livelihood, since hitherto it had been the custom in Phocis for the younger men to wait on the elder. Now the argument was about Locris, and this emphasis on Phocis certainly looks like a red herring; it is in fact a trick of Timaeus to discredit Aristotle by dragging in his friend Mnason and his 1,000 slaves.

What does Polybius make of it? The answer is also in Athenaeus: 'Timaeus', he says (Athen: VI.272a), 'forgets himself – he is refuted by Polybius – when he (*sc.* Timaeus) says that it was once not the custom for Greeks to possess slaves, for he himself mentioned that Mnason the Phocian had over a thousand.' Did Polybius really argue like this? Truesdell Brown, in his recent book on Timaeus,[18] refuses to believe it; Athenaeus, he says, must have made a mistake. But Timaeus' assertion that the Greek Locrians did not have domestic slaves could only be countered successfully by proving that they did; and I am afraid that it is not easy to acquit Polybius of having obscured the chronology relative to the development of slavery, and twisted Timaeus' reference to Mnason's slaves, who were brought in, nominally at any rate, as evidence for the late introduction of slavery into central Greece, so as to provide a refutation of his general thesis. If this is true, it is of course thoroughly dishonest. But, as we shall see, no holds are barred when the opponent is Timaeus.

Timaeus' next argument against Aristotle (XII.6a.2) was that the people of Italian Locri, like those of Greek Locris, were friendly to Sparta and hostile to Athens; indeed Locri had been ravaged by Laches and the Athenians in 426 (XII.6b.3; *cf.* Thuc. III.103.3). But if its founders had been slaves, it was improbable that they would have taken over the friendships of their former masters. Here Polybius fares a little better, since Timaeus' point is rather a silly one. On the contrary, says Polybius, to take over the friendships of their masters would be a natural step for ex-slaves anxious to represent themselves as their masters' descendants; and as regards the Athenian attack, that was to be

---

[18] *Timaeus of Tauromenium* (Berkeley-Los Angeles, 1958) 49.

explained solely in terms of the strategy of the Peloponnesian War, and had nothing to do with descent.

Next Timaeus argues against the story of Locrian women cohabiting with their slaves (xii.6b.5). This, he says, implies that the Spartans would not let the Locrians return home from Messene to visit their wives; and this is highly improbable in view of the tradition that the Spartans themselves sent their own young men home to beget children. To this ‖ argument from probability Polybius replies in the same coin. The Locrians, he says, were in a different category from the Spartans. First, they did not share the Spartan custom of polyandry with its tendency towards promiscuity, and secondly they were not bound by any oath not to return home until the Messenians were beaten, as the Spartans were. They will, therefore, have returned home, not in a general despatch of young men, like the one which tradition attributed to the Spartans, but on individual leave and at intervals, and in this way they will have allowed their wives to grow intimate with their slaves. Which of these two methods of granting leave would be more likely to result in promiscuity at home, is a question on which I do not feel competent to pronounce. Arguments based on probability are notoriously perilous, and this particular one seems especially futile, both on Timaeus' side and on Polybius'. Perhaps the less said about it the better.

Timaeus now passes to documentary evidence. The normal relationship of mother city to colony was confirmed, he said (xii.9.3), by a treaty, still in existence, between Greek Locris and Italian Locri, which he had himself seen and which began with the words 'as parents to children' (ὡς γονεῦσι πρὸς τέκνα); in addition there were also in existence decrees establishing sympolity between the two states (xii.9.4). Here Polybius' argument is particularly bare-faced. Timaeus, he says, fails to tell us which Locris he saw the treaty in, eastern or western: this is a clear proof that he is deliberately lying. It is, of course, nothing of the sort. It shows that Timaeus was careless, but that does not mean that he had not been shown a document. Whether the document was a forgery is another question and one which Polybius, having denied its existence outright, is not in a position to raise. Presumably he would have countered the reference to sympolity between Locris and Locri in the same way, by an absolute denial; but, unless there is some compression in our text, he simply ignores that argument. So too with Timaeus' final contention, which is that the laws and constitution of Locri belied Aristotle's view of its origins; for the constitution and cultural practices were similar to those of Greek Locris (xii.11.5), and the laws laid down such penalties for adulterers and runaway slaves as one would hardly expect to find in a community derived from such people (xii.9.5).

Although the question would take us much farther than we have time to follow it here, the probability is that on the origins of Locri Aristotle for once was wrong and Timaeus right (notwithstanding the shakiness of some of his arguments, which are based, like those of Polybius, on probability, τὸν εἰκότα λόγον). But the real question with which we are concerned here is not who was right, but why Polybius becomes so emotional about it. It might of course be through affection and respect for Aristotle, but this seems on the whole an inadequate motive. It might be, indeed one would like to think it was, the result of a disinterested passion for the truth; but although Polybius does indeed rate truth highly,[19] this again would hardly account for the tone of this controversy. Finally, he can hardly be motivated by his high regard for Locri (with which he makes great play in a passage (XII.5.1–3) which emphasises his own services to that city, and which is probably reflected in the very favourable remarks about Locri in Livy XXIX), for after all it is Aristotle, not Timaeus, whose version is discreditable to the origins of that state. I conclude that both this long discussion on Locri and indeed the whole of Book XII spring from an intense personal antipathy to Timaeus. After all, the polemic against him, indeed the whole book of it, constitutes a digression; and although Locri was to play a part in the prelude to Scipio's invasion of Africa, it was not, as Reiske supposed, anything to do with Locri, but rather Timaeus' alleged mis-statements about Africa which afforded Polybius an excuse for the sustained and malevolent invective to which Book XII is devoted.

V

Throughout Book XII Polybius is consistently abusive towards Timaeus.[20] There are very few places where he speaks of him in any but the most contemptuous tones. Normally the blackness is unrelieved. Timaeus is casti-gated for his own abusive treatment of former ‖ writers; for his cavilling criticism of Theopompus and Ephorus (XII.4a.2, 28.8–10); for his vilifying, both of Agathocles, the tyrant of Syracuse (XII.15.1–12; *cf.* VIII.10.12, XV.35.2), and of Demochares, the nephew of Demosthenes and spokesman of the Athenian democracy (XII.13–14, 15.4, 23.8); and for his bitter animosity towards Aristotle, against whom he raked up all the old scandal about his having kept a drug-store, which goes back to Epicurus.[21] Timaeus' acceptance of myths he says is wholly reprehensible – for instance his childish explanation (XII.4b.1–4c.1) of the Roman custom of sacrificing the October Horse as being a commemoration of the capture of Troy by means of the Wooden Horse, or his readiness to believe that the Alpheius dives under the sea and comes up again in Syracuse (XII.4d.5–8). His pedantry is to be seen in the purely rhetorical speeches which he puts into the mouths of Hermocrates of Syracuse (XII.25k.5–11) and Timoleon (XII.26a.1–4). Indeed, Polybius adds, he actually makes Timoleon say to his troops (XII.25.7) 'the earth lying under the heavens

[19] *Cf.* Walbank, *op. cit.* (n. 15) 1.10ff.

[20] In VIII.10.12 and XV.35.2 Polybius, though clearly no friend of Timaeus, treats him comparatively gently and even defends his invective against Agathocles. His real hostility only emerges in Book XII, which (as I argue in *Miscellanea di studi alessandrini in memoria di Augusto Rostagni* (Turin, 1963) 203–13) was probably written after Polybius' journeys in the West.

[21] XII.8.1–6; *cf.* Epicurus, fr. 171.235 Usener.

is divided into three parts named Asia, Africa and Europe' – a piece of criticism, the precise point of which, incidentally, is far from clear. Paton thinks that Polybius was objecting to the phrase ὑπὸ τῷ κόσμῳ κειμένης, but this is a normal piece of Greek and is to be found in a precisely similar context in Isocrates' *Panegyricus* 179, τῆς ... γῆς ἁπάσης ὑπὸ τῷ κόσμῳ κειμένης δίχα τετμημένης. On the whole, I think Laqueur[22] is probably right when he suggests that Polybius is objecting to the introduction of such a pedantic piece of geography in a military speech: presumably it was all right in epideictic.

In any case Timaeus' geography was all wrong (XII.4c.2): he said the Rhône had five mouths, whereas Polybius knows that it has only two (XXXIV.10.5);[23] and his battles are artificial (XII.28a.5–10). Instead of reliable information he goes in for sensationalism, τερατεία, the very fault which he himself urged against Callisthenes (XII.12b.1–3). This is because he entirely scamped the task of personal enquiry, which is the most important part of history (XII.4c.2–5); this consists of consulting as many people as possible, believing only those who deserve credit, and being a good judge of reports. This procedure was impossible for Timaeus who had sat in a library in Athens for fifty years (XII.25d.1, 25h.1), and the result was inaccuracy not only about Italy and Sardinia, but even about Sicily, the place where he was born and bred (XII.4d.3–8). He is in fact like a painter who imagines that he can become competent simply by studying the works of old masters (XII.25e.7). This is at first sight an unjust and inaccurate comparison, since the historian of course studies memoirs and the like as *sources*, whereas the painter studies old masters for their *technique*. But Polybius seems in fact to be thinking of library work as an alternative and inferior method of acquiring the historian's craft, not simply as the assembling of material; the study of memoirs is thus a way – an inferior way – of learning to write. Now the truth is that Timaeus differs from Polybius in being mainly concerned with events which took place before his own time or that of anyone he could consult; consequently library work necessarily played a larger part in his research than it did in that of Polybius who was writing contemporary or near-contemporary history. But, by laying stress upon recent history (which only comprises a small part of Timaeus' subject), Polybius manages to make him look ridiculous; and indeed he enhances this effect by putting into Timaeus' mouth the words (XII.25h.1) 'living away from home at Athens for fifty years continuously, and having, as I confess, no experience of active service in war or any personal acquaintance with places'. It is difficult to believe that Timaeus actually said 'I confess' (ὁμο-λογουμένως); and the words 'for fifty years' are inconsistent with another passage (XII.25d.1) where Polybius says 'for *nearly* fifty years'. So these are

[22] *RE* 6A.1 (1936) 'Timaios', col. 1080. This view seems supported by the argument in XII.25a–b and by the criticisms of other speeches in 25k.26, 26a and 26b. Pédech, *Polybe* XII (Paris, 1961) 123, however, prefers Valesius' explanation that Timaeus has used γῆ where he should have said οἰκουμένη; the references in this chapter he argues, are to Timaeus' ignorance, not to his use of rhetoric. The passage I quote from Isocrates is against this.

[23] Artemidorus said there were three (Strabo IV.1.8, C 183; *cf.* Pliny, *NH* III.33).

probably not Timaeus' own words, and it seems in fact more than likely, as Jacoby suggested,[24] that Polybius has twisted a reference by Timaeus to his long exile from his native Sicily into a general admission damaging to his repute as a historian. Indeed we know from Polybius himself that Timaeus visited at any rate one of the states of Locris (XII.9.2), and also that he studied 'inscriptions ‖ on the backs of buildings and lists of *proxeni* on the doorposts of temples' (XII.11.2); Polybius does not say that these were all at Athens, and in view of Timaeus' chronological work which included the Priestesses of Hera[25] it may reasonably be assumed that he at least visited the Argive Heraeum. He will also have consulted the lists of victors at Olympia. What he could not easily do was to visit the West, at any rate Sicily, though he is mentioned as an eye-witness for details at Agrigentum including the famous 'bull of Phalaris' (XII.25.1–5); perhaps he saw this city before his exile. But, as Polybius points out somewhat sneeringly (XII.27.6, *cf.* XXXIV.5.7), to travel one needs money. He himself, as a rich Achaean and as the protégé of the Scipionic family, seems not have lacked the wherewithal for his journeys. Timaeus *should* have had money, for his father was rich (Diod. XVI.7.1 = *FGH* 566 T 3a); but how far the historian was able to get his wealth out of Syracuse we do not know. Whatever the reason, predilection or lack of money, Athens remained his base, and the historian of the West was for most of his life without access to the area with which his work was concerned.

This work had a definite political bias.[26] It was centred on Sicily, hostile to the tyrants, such as Agathocles, and above all it glorified Timoleon, the Corinthian liberator of Syracuse (XII.23.4f.). To Polybius it seems preposterous that Timaeus should attack Callisthenes for seeking to deify Alexander, 'whose soul, as all admit, had something superhuman in it' (XII.23.5), and at the same time make Timoleon 'greater than the most illustrious gods', a man who (he says) in the whole of his life made only one move, the comparatively small move from Corinth to Syracuse (XII.23.6).[27] The implications are clear enough. Timaeus, the arm-chair historian, naturally picks a somewhat sluggish hero! And naturally too, someone whose achievements took place in Sicily, καθάπερ ἐν ὀξυβάφῳ, 'as it were in a saucer' (XII.23.7)! In praising Timoleon Timaeus is obviously trying to enhance his own reputation so that the historian of Italy and Sicily would bear comparison with writers whose works dealt with the whole world and with universal history – in a word, with men like Polybius.

Wherever one looks at Polybius' accusations in detail, they appear to be

---

[24] Commentary on *FGH* 566 F 34.

[25] XII.11.1. The reference is probably to a comprehensive study correlating various chronological systems and designed as a preparation for his general history (*cf. FGH* 566 T 1, Ὀλυμπιονίκας ἤτοι Χρονικὰ Πραξιδικά).

[26] See on this Momigliano, *RSI* 71 (1959) 529ff. [= *Terzo contributo*, 23ff.].

[27] The metaphor is probably from the board-game of Five Lines (ε΄ γραμμαί), similar to backgammon (*cf.* Lamer, *RE* 13.2 (1927) 'lusoria tabula', cols. 1970–3; Pédech, *op. cit.* (n. 22) *ad loc.*).

disproportionate or vicious, or both. Timaeus no doubt had many faults. He may well have been pedantic, excessive in his polemic, sensational, with a preference for research in a library rather than tramping the hills of Greece or sailing the Atlantic, and he may like many other Greek historians have composed rhetorical speeches to put in the mouths of his characters. But all this is not enough to explain Polybius' attack. *Why* does he dislike Timaeus so much, a writer to whom he pays the unconscious compliment of continuing his *History* (1.5.1, xxxix.8.4), and who does not in fact directly cross his own tracks?

VI

Before trying to answer this question there is one point on which it is as well to be quite clear. Polybius takes Timaeus seriously. 'He seems to me', he writes (xii.27a.3) 'to have acquired both practical experience and the habit of industrious study of documents, and indeed generally speaking to have approached the task of writing history in a painstaking spirit, but in some matters we know of *no author of repute* who seems to have been less experienced and less painstaking.' He clearly admits then that Timaeus has a reputation. He feels it necessary to convince those who are disposed to champion him (τοὺς φιλοτιμότερον διακειμένους) (xii.25a.3), and he admits that he 'meets with widespread acceptance and credit from certain people' (xii.25c.1). In an elaborate comparison between the art of medicine and the systematic study of history (xii.25e.2), Polybius remarks that there are quacks in both professions, on the one hand the drug-store men and on the other the popular authors who bring no qualities to their writing except recklessness and irresponsibility, and are only concerned to make money. But Timaeus is not included among these. He is taken seriously and compared to the λογικοί (xii.25e.4), of the school of ‖ Herophilus and Callimachus, the theoreticians who were linked with the Stoics and who concerned themselves with the causes of disease, in contrast to the more sceptical empiricists whom Polybius favoured because of their primary interest in curing patients, though I suspect that their entire disregard for theory may have caused him some embarrassment (*cf.* iii.7.5).

   Timaeus is a serious opponent; and the reason for Polybius' hostility is not, I believe, any of the ones he alleges, but quite simply jealousy of a western Greek who seemed to challenge his own position.[27a] I have already quoted some of the evidence for Polybius' resentment of the importance Timaeus attributes to the West. Elsewhere he is even more explicit. 'Timaeus', he says (xii.26b),

----

[27a] Pédech, *op. cit.* (n. 22) xxxi, argues that this jealousy dates from Polybius' visit to Alexandria, which he dates betwen 144 and 134; it was Timaeus' high reputation there which provoked Polybius' attack. But Book xii is not the only place where Polybius declares his hostility towards Alexandrian scholarship; and in any case his criticism of the Alexandrian λογικοί in this book (25d) is no sharper than his remarks against the New Academy at Athens. It was not merely in Alexandria that Timaeus' reputation still stood high, but also in Greece and Rome. I doubt therefore if Polybius had to wait until his Alexandrian visit for his jealousy to be aroused.

'is so long-winded [in discussing the question whether Gelo should help the Greeks against Persia] and so obviously anxious to make clear that Sicily was more important than all the rest of Greece – the events occurring in Sicily being so much more magnificent and more noble than anywhere else in the world, the sagest of men distinguished for wisdom coming from Sicily and the most capable and wonderful leaders being those from Syracuse – that no boy in a school of rhetoric who is set to write a eulogy of Thersites or a diatribe against Penelope ... could surpass him in paradox.'

First then, as a Peloponnesian Polybius rejected a history which put Sicily and Magna Graecia at the centre of the picture. But Timaeus' history was more than that. According to Dionysius (*Ant. Rom.* 1.6.1) the first writer to sketch the Roman *archaeologia* was Hieronymus; but Hieronymus is unlikely to have done more than touch on the Roman background of the war with Pyrrhus. After him came Timaeus, who included τὰ ἀρχαῖα τῶν ἱστοριῶν in his general history; and whatever importance is to be attached to the work of Lycus of Rhegium, whom Agatharchides (*De mari rubro* 64 = *FGH* 570 T 3) mentioned along with Timaeus – and Lycus seems to have been an ethnographer rather than a historian – it seems clear that it was Timaeus who, both in his general history and in his books on Pyrrhus, was regarded as the first historian of Rome. That is why Gellius (Gell. XI.1.1 = *FGH* 566 T 9c), following Varro, speaks of his *Historiae de rebus populi Romani*, probably with reference to the Pyrrhic books.[28] The full significance of Timaeus' role as the first historian of Rome has recently been discussed by Momigliano,[29] who raises the interesting question whether it was Timaeus or the poet Lycophron who first recognised the true importance of Rome, and investigates their relations with Callimachus; he points out that it was still to Timaeus that the Romans of the age of Varro and Cicero turned for the history of Sicily and the Pyrrhic War. There can then be little doubt that this was Polybius' main reason for attempting to discredit the Sicilian. He resented Timaeus' reputation, and he had to ensure that his work was rejected, if his own *Histories* were to become the definitive account of Rome for the Greek public. 'As an honourable man', writes Jacoby,[30] 'he ought to have recognised Timaeus as his true predecessor for the central fact of the Roman hegemony; but perhaps such objectivity is too much to ask, or else Polybius had not got the decisive facts clear himself.' Polybius sincerely regarded his own work as superior to that of Timaeus and more enlightening and profitable to its readers: but this, I believe, merely confirmed him in his conscious determination for quite personal reasons to diminish Timaeus' repute.

This interpretation gains support from the parallel treatment of Pytheas, whom Polybius attacks with the same ferocity in XXXIV.5ff. Here, quite obviously, he resents the claim of Pytheas, another western Greek, to have

---

[28] *Cf.* Momigliano, *RSI* 71 (1959) 55off. [[= *Terzo contributo*, 44ff.]].   [29] *Ibid.*
[30] *FGH* 566, commentary, p. 527.

explored the northern seas and to have circumnavigated Britain; for this infringes his own reputation as the man who opened up the Atlantic ocean with his 'journeys through Africa, Spain and Gaul, and voyages on the seas that lie on the farther side of these countries' (III.59.7). Polybius' desire to be known as the second Odysseus is betrayed in the well-known passage in which, after quoting Homer on Odysseus' qualities, he claims (XII.28.1)[31] that 'the dignity of history demands ‖ such a man'; and it was perhaps also familiar to those Greeks of Megalopolis who composed the inscription seen there by Pausanias which recorded (Paus. VIII.30.8) how Polybius ἐπὶ γῆν καὶ θάλασσαν πᾶσαν πλανηθείη – had wandered over every land and sea. Polybius included in Book XXXIV[32] a detailed account of his journeys in Spain and Gaul; this involved him not only in polemic against Pytheas but also raised the question of his relationship with Timaeus, for whom Sicily was merely the centre of a geographical and ethnographical account of the whole of the West, including Italy, Gaul, Spain, Britain, Libya, Corsica, Sardinia and the islands of the western Mediterranean.

There is, however, yet a further reason for Polybius' antipathy towards Timaeus. For close on fifty years the Sicilian lived and worked at Athens, where, as Momigliano has shown,[33] he accepted the republican traditions of the Athenian democrats *vis-à-vis* Macedon, but without ever becoming reconciled with Athens as it now was. He attacks the character of Demochares in the vilest terms (XII.13–14) and he declines to include continental Greece in his history. We have two fragments (*FGH* 566 F 135–6) testifying that Timaeus asserted that Thucydides had spent part of his exile in Italy – as he himself, ironically, was spending his in Athens. If that was true, by Polybius' time the wheel had turned full-circle once again, and a Greek historian of the mainland was once more condemned to exile in a western city. But Polybius' exile had turned out very differently from that of Timaeus. No one could accuse Polybius of a lack of adaptability; and it seems clear that Timaeus' provincial rigidity and his rejection of all that mattered vitally to an Achaean, the Hellenistic world with its ideologies and its confederations delicately poised between the monarchs, proved excessively irksome to the Megalopolitan who, far from resisting the atmosphere of Italy, had adjusted himself within a year or two to the predominance of Rome, and without ceasing to be first and foremost an Achaean, was very soon writing the story of Rome's rise to world dominion for the benefit of his fellow-Greeks.

This does not imply that Polybius' polemic against Timaeus was dishonest. Timaeus' emphasis, methods of work and conception of the nature of history were all anathema to Polybius, who cared seriously for history as well as for his own reputation as a historian. But this combination of motives all pulling

[31] See further Walbank, *C et M* 9 (1948) 171–3.
[32] On Book XXXIV see Pédech, *LEC* 24 (1956) 3–24.
[33] *RSI* 71 (1959) 534–49 ⟦= *Terzo contributo*, 28–44⟧.

in the same direction does explain the passion which goes into Polybius' polemic against Timaeus and which we are unlikely to have found there, had his opposition rested solely on theoretical grounds.

VII

Timaeus provides the main object of polemic in Polybius' work. In his case, there is so much material that it is possible to penetrate fairly easily to the personal motives which give the criticism its emotional overtones. But what is true here, is true elsewhere. Nearly always Polybius' motives are mixed; and his attitude towards earlier historians can usually be seen to reflect personal or political considerations no less than those of literary and historical merit. I have argued elsewhere[34] that the sustained attack on Phylarchus in Book II represents an honest demand for new standards and canons in Greek historiography. But at the same time we are bound to note that Phylarchus is identified with the cause of Cleomenes of Sparta, the enemy of the Achaean League and of Aratus of Sicyon, and it is significant that details of Polybius' criticism largely concern issues in which he was emotionally involved – the execution of Aristomachus of Argos (II.59–60), the Achaean punishment of Mantinea (II.56.6ff.), and the behaviour of the people of Megalopolis when their city was taken by Cleomenes (II.61). In XII.17–22 Callisthenes' account of the battle of Issus is subjected to a long and detailed criticism, which, however, when examined proves to be illogical, trivial and careless. This criticism can hardly be divorced from Polybius' expressed opinion (XII.23.3–4) that Callisthenes fully deserved a death under torture for having sought to deify Alexander.[35] Ephorus is attacked for saying that music was designed ‖ for deception and delusion (IV.20.5). The rejection of this view connects with the fact that it would discredit the cultivation of the popular musical education practised in Arcadia (IV.20.6ff., 21.10–11). Finally, we have already seen how Polybius' criticism of Theopompus and Postumius Albinus reflected political loyalties or personal resentment.

Throughout his *Histories*, then, Polybius allows his private sympathies to colour his attitudes towards earlier writers, and indeed one may suspect that it is primarily because of these attitudes that such writers are discussed at all in what are, after all, digressions. Through these digressions and this polemic we recognise more clearly Polybius' strong local patriotism as an Arcadian, an Achaean and a Greek of the mainland. His historical sense is as highly

---

[34] *Historia* 9 (1960) 216–34 [above, pp. 224–41]. On the formal side I would accept Pédech's definition of Polybius XII (*op. cit.* (n. 22) xxvii) as an exposition of his views on historical method in the shape of an ἀντιγραφή; but the polemic in that book must be considered alongside his polemic elsewhere and, as Pédech recognises, formal considerations do not provide answers to the questions considered here.

[35] Polybius may also have resented the fact that, just as Theopompus abandoned *Hellenica* to write on Philip, so Callisthenes abandoned *Hellenica* to compose Ἀλεξάνδρου πράξεις (*cf.* L. Pearson, *The lost historians of Alexander the Great* (Philadelphia, 1960) 33).

developed as – shall we say? – that of a modern Irishman, in the sense that the grievances and loyalties of the previous three hundred years have become an integral part of his thoughts and feelings. The conflict between Athens and Philip II is still vivid, and furnishes overtones to the current tensions between Macedon, Achaea and Rome.[36] Then there is the personal issue, again linked up with historical thinking. If the rise of Rome to world-power is the most important event of the years following 220, nothing must be allowed to obscure the importance of Polybius' world-history. Timaeus must be displaced from his pedestal to make way for the genuine historian of Rome; and at the same time the pretensions of Greeks from Italy and Sicily who claim a special knowledge of the western Mediterranean must be made to take second place to the discoveries of the man who has brought the qualities of Odysseus to the writing of history.

We are apt to think of Polybius as a didactic and even prosy writer. His long passages of polemic, properly read, enable us to correct that picture and to see something of the strong emotional background which coloured his attitudes and probably gave him the impetus to carry through his great enterprise to a successful conclusion.[37]

[36] See above, n. 4.
[37] A paper read at the Oxford Conference of the Greek and Roman Societies on 15 August 1961.

18

POLYBIUS BETWEEN GREECE AND ROME*

In his excellent recent survey of work on Polybius[1] our colleague Dr Musti makes an important point. In a historian like Polybius, he says, it must not be assumed that his analysis of the forms taken by Roman imperialism and the reasons behind it necessarily implies that these had his approval. The exact relationship between analysis and approval must be a subject of investigation. This seems to me to be well said; and it is as a contribution to that investigation that I offer this paper. One of the immediate difficulties is Polybius' caution in making explicit statements about the Romans and their policy. But there are others which I may conveniently begin by considering.

I

The first is the sheer length of time with which we are concerned. Between Polybius' youth in the days of Philopoemen and the Numantine War, at which he may have been present as an old man, there is a gap of about fifty years. It is on the face of it unlikely that his views on Rome remained constant during the whole of this time; and what we need to know is in what ways and at what stages of his life his attitude towards Rome – and his view about the right policy for Greek states to adopt towards Rome – changed. The answer is difficult because the evidence comes from the *Histories*, so that one must first reach conclusions about the dates at which Polybius prepared, wrote, revised ‖ and published his work. I do not, however, wish to become involved in this ancient problem any more than I have to for my immediate purpose.

Polybius' life falls into four main periods. First, there is his youth in Achaea and career as a statesman down to his holding of the hipparchy in 170/69, and his relegation to Rome with the other Achaean detainees in 168/7. Next, his *de facto* exile at Rome, with (apparently) some trips elsewhere, especially in the late fifties, when his friend Scipio Aemilianus was becoming influential. Thirdly, there are the five years following his repatriation, during which he attended Scipio at the destruction of Carthage, made his famous voyage of exploration on the Atlantic, and acted as mediator in Achaea after th catastrophe of 146. Finally, there are the years of which we know least, frc

---

* [*Polybe* (Entretiens Hardt 20: Geneva, 1974) 1–31]

[1] D. Musti, *ANRW* 1.2 (Berlin, 1972) 1114–81, esp. 1136.

280

145 down to his death, which was perhaps as late as 118 (though Professor Pédech would put it earlier).[2]

Of these four periods only the first three are covered in the *Histories*; and only the first, down to 168/7, fell within the original plan for a work going down to the battle of Pydna and its aftermath. It is, I think, generally agreed that Polybius was working on his original draft while he was at Rome between 167 and 150; but there is no unanimity concerning how many books he had written (or actually published) by 150. The decision to extend the *Histories* beyond 167 could have been taken any time after that date; but in the form in which we have it, and as Polybius sketches it in Book III, i.e. to cover the years 167 to 145, the extension must obviously have been planned after 145. Furthermore, we must allow some time after Polybius' arrival in Rome before he conceived his original project, and a longer period after that during which he was working on it. There is therefore quite a strong probability that several of the thirty ‖ books which made up the original *Histories* were still unwritten in 150 and had to be finished after 145 (for it is a fair assumption that the events of 150–145 left little time or opportunity for the actual writing of history). The last ten books covering the years 167 to 145 were both conceived and written after the latter date; and this raises an important question. Do opinions expressed in Books XXXI to XXXIX reflect the views Polybius held at the time about which he is writing, or the conclusions which he had reached at the date of composition?

It is a problem which concerns all writers of contemporary history; but it happens to be especially acute in Polybius' case because of the obvious contrast between his situation immediately after 167 and his situation after 146. As regards the events of the Third Macedonian War, it seems a fair assumption that for some time after their arrival in Rome the Achaean detainees will have been expecting some kind of enquiry; hence, that in preparation for that Polybius will have written up, while it was still fresh in his mind, a memorandum on his hipparchy – no doubt phrased so as to put the most favourable interpretation on his actions. And as regards subsequent events which occurred while he was at Rome, M. Gelzer[3] has shown that an important aspect of Polybius' technique of historical composition was his use of memoranda prepared either by himself or by other interested parties concerning contemporary incidents. A significant example exists in Polybius' account of the escape of Demetrius I from Rome to Syria,[4] with the historian's personal assistance. The reference to Carthage as still existing suggests that his account of the episode was composed shortly after it occurred and was incorporated in the *Histories* virtually as it stood. At that time Polybius was almost certainly still ‖ working on the original plan of his *Histories*; but the

---

[2] *LEC* 29 (1961) 145–56; see my *Polybius* (Berkeley, 1972) 6 n. 26.
[3] M. Gelzer, *Kleine Schriften* 3 (Wiesbaden, 1964) 168.
[4] XXXI.11–15; reference to Carthage: 12.12.

preparation of such memoranda perhaps implies that he was already envisaging at any rate the *possibility* of writing up this later period. Be that as it may, my immediate point is that if such memoranda lie behind Polybius' account of the years following 168, there is a reasonable likelihood that it reflects views on Roman policy and the policies of Greek statesmen which he held at that time.

II

The question of relations with Rome dominated Achaean policy from Polybius' earliest years. In 198 – after a painful debate – the Macedonian alliance had been abandoned in favour of collaboration with Rome. But on what terms? That was a subject that was to be hotly debated throughout the next three decades. Philopoemen died in 182. And, until then, Lycortas, Polybius' father, and (one may fairly assume) Polybius himself, from the age when he was capable of holding political views, supported the policy of the great man. The comparison which Polybius draws (in Book xxiv) between the policies of Philopoemen and Aristaenus ends with the conclusion that both were safe, but whereas that of Aristaenus was εὐσχήμων (plausible), that of Philopoemen was καλή (honourable).[5] Since this comparison does not figure in Plutarch's *Philopoemen*, which is generally taken to be derived from Polybius' biography, K.-E. Petzold has argued[6] that it must have been composed later, at a time when Polybius had come to assign greater importance in history to ethical factors. This I cannot accept, partly ‖ because I do not believe that Polybius became interested in ethical criteria only in his mature years, and partly because I hesitate to base an opinion about Polybius on an *argumentum ex silentio* in Plutarch. In fact I see no good reason why this comparison of Aristaenus and Philopoemen should not represent a fair account of views which Polybius had heard debated in Lycortas' circle during his early years.

Aristaenus was for anticipating and complying with all Roman wishes, whereas Philopoemen was for collaboration only within the strict conditions of the Achaean laws and the Roman alliance. The latter was Lycortas' policy too. But ten years after Philopoemen's death, in 170 just before Polybius entered upon the office of hipparch, we find him opposing Lycortas at an Achaean assembly.[7] Lycortas had proposed that Achaea should remain neutral in the Third Macedonian War: Rome must not grow too powerful. This policy, a direct continuation of Philopoemen's, recalls an earlier comment by Polybius himself, in which he approved the view of Hiero of Syracuse that Carthage should be preserved as a counter-balance to Rome.[8] But now, in 170, we find Polybius advocating, not indeed full collaboration (like Aristaenus), but a cautious policy of being guided by circumstances and giving the pro-Roman party no chance to denounce its opponents. This extremely flexible approach

---

[5] xxiv.11–13.
[6] K.-E. Petzold, *Studien zur Methode des Polybios und zu ihrer historischen Auswertung* (Munich, 1969) 45–6, 49 n. 1. [7] xxviii.6–7. [8] i.83.4.

may mirror the apprehensions of a man about to assume the responsibilities of office at a critical moment; bu⁺ also perhaps it indicates a realisation that the Roman attitude towards Greece was hardening.

This hardening had come largely as a result of advice given to the Senate in winter 180/79 by Callicrates, the leading advocate of completely subordinating Achaea to the will of Rome. On the occasion of his visit to Rome in that ‖ year Callicrates had urged the Senate to give open support throughout Greece to those who, whatever their personal character, put the wishes of the Romans even above their own laws and oaths.[9] It was Polybius' view[10] that Callicrates had thereby done untold harm to the Greeks generally since he had made it impossible for Achaeans to speak to Romans on equal terms – and so prevented them henceforth from securing adjustments in Roman policy by adducing arguments based on justice and *fides*. The Romans were now surrounded by mere flatterers, who neither would nor could advise them honestly. The validity of this judgement has been hotly debated. For many years scholars accepted Polybius' estimate of Callicrates' influence, and some even went further and condemned him as a traitor to Greece and Achaea. More recently E. Badian and R. M. Errington[11] have argued that Callicrates' advice was well conceived and salutary, since it ended the vacillation at Rome which had merely caused tension and uncertainty in Greece. For my own part, I have much sympathy for P. Derow's argument[12] that the Senate was not so much vacillating as divided in its views on Greece and that Callicrates' intervention gave a fillip to such tough-minded men as Q. Marcius Philippus. What was perhaps worse, it had the effect of forcing Greek moderates into the extremist camp, a tendency well exemplified by the melancholy story of Cephalus in Epirus; while the unrestrained and partisan behaviour of those who now had the Roman ear caused even greater tension and ‖ bitterness than before. A verdict in this dispute is not essential to my argument for in any case it is clear that Callicrates' policy led to a polarisation of attitudes in Greece. Men like Cephalus moved to the left and became more actively anti-Roman while others, like Polybius, became more cautious and so in effect moved to the right.

III

This can be seen from Polybius' comments on the anti-Roman groups in the Greek states at the time of the Third Macedonian War.[13] Polybius was writing his account of that war at the earliest in the late fifties and more probably after

---

[9] xxiv.9.   [10] xxiv.10.8–14.

[11] E. Badian, *Foreign clientelae* (Oxford, 1958) 90–3; R. M. Errington, *Philopoemen* (Oxford, 1969) 195–205.

[12] P. Derow, 'Polybios and the embassy of Kallikrates', in *Essays presented to C. M. Bowra* (Oxford, 1970) 12–23, esp. 22–3; since Polybius usually treats the Senate as monolithic in its decisions, such division of opinion would be unlikely to be expressed in his pages.

[13] *Cf.* J. Deininger, *Der politische Widerstand gegen Rom in Griechenland, 217–86 v.Chr.* (Berlin, 1971).

145. By then of course he was a protégé of Scipio Aemilianus, with whom he enjoyed close relations of friendship and – may one say? – *clientela*. He may have resided in his household.[14] This could have helped to colour his views on the pro-Macedonian party. But in any case his own policy during the war with Perseus had been one of cautious collaboration with Rome, even if he did employ some cunning in delaying his offer of Achaean help to Q. Marcius Philippus until it seemed likely to be rejected.[15] Thus Perseus had been Achaea's enemy as well as Rome's, and Polybius describes his conduct in hostile and unsympathetic terms. It is not surprising that some of this hostility rubs off on Perseus' Greek supporters. But these men had not merely backed the anti-Roman side: they had backed the losing side, and the excessively harsh tones in ‖ which Polybius condemns them illustrates, I suggest, the extent to which, in such a situation, he made success or failure a criterion in judging policy.

In Boeotia, for instance, Roman envoys arranged to procure the arrest and suicide of the anti-Roman partisans and dissolve the League. Polybius condemns the Boeotians for 'rashly and thoughtlessly supporting Perseus'.[16] The Rhodian supporters of Macedonia are accused of being motivated by private debt and unscrupulous avarice[17]. No one, Polybius insists, could approve of men like Hippocritus and Diomedon of Cos, or Deinon and Polyaratus of Rhodes, who did all they could to help Perseus yet, after his defeat, could not muster up enough courage to commit suicide. Posterity had therefore not the slightest grounds for pitying or pardoning them[18].

These judgements have to be considered in the light of an Achaean policy for which Polybius, as envoy to Q. Marcius Philippus, carried a considerable responsibility. That policy had failed: of this the summoning of the 1,000 to Rome left no doubt. But it had failed less disastrously than had that of Rhodes, and Polybius' comments on the anti-Roman partisans perhaps contain an element of self-defence. About the Romans themselves he is fairly reticent – with one exception. According to Livy, who is here following Polybius, the sharp diplomacy of Q. Marcius Philippus had been characterised by older senators as *nova sapientia*; that was not how the Romans used to behave. Philippus was no friend of Achaea or of Aemilius Paullus, and Livy (*i.e.* Polybius) records his success thus: 'vicit... ea pars senatus, cui potior utilis quam honesti cura erat'[19]. But the defenders of old-time ‖ morality did not reject the advantages brought by Philippus' policy; and when, by 168, Aemilius Paullus and his friends had gained the ascendancy over the harsh and brutal *novi homines* who had recently made their power felt, their own behaviour

---

[14] Perhaps implied in xxxi.24.9.

[15] *Cf.* xxviii.13; there is no reason to suppose that Polybius was acting on secret instructions from Archon, the general (as assumed by G. De Sanctis, *Storia dei Romani* 4.1 (Turin, 1923) 300, 307; *cf.* P. Meloni, *Perseo* (Rome, 1953) 313 n. 3; P. Pédech, *LEC* 37 (1969) 257).

[16] xxvii.2.10.   [17] xxvii.7.12.

[18] xxx.7.9–8.4.   [19] Livy xlii.47.9.

was by no means free from either treachery or brutality – as Paullus' conduct of affairs in Epirus and elsewhere demonstrates.[20] Polybius may express moral disapproval of a Postumius Albinus or a Marcius Philippus. But by the time he came to write his account of the war with Perseus, he seems to be capable of a fairly detached view of Machiavellian politics, when they were employed against the enemies of Rome (and Achaea) – especially when it was Aemilius Paullus who employed them.

IV

Once settled in Rome Polybius was forced to judge Roman policy from a detached point of view, which was in any case perhaps more congenial to the historian than to the politician. His comments on what was happening during the next fifteen years (166–151) contain an occasional criticism of Roman behaviour towards the Greek world, but in general the cynical aloofness of a man debarred from political action. I will refer briefly to one or two passages. Consider, for example, Polybius' description of the unsuccessful attempt of certain Romans to persuade Attalus to join a plot against his brother, King Eumenes, in 168/7, and the Senate's subsequent failure to hand over Aenus and Maronea to Eumenes, as it had promised,[21] or his account of the rewards which ‖ Prusias derived from his servility,[22] of Eumenes' humiliation at Rome in 167/6,[23] or of the Senate's unprincipled acquiescence in Athens' claim to Haliartus.[24] Occasionally Polybius specifically states that the Senate was moved by self-interest. They refused to restore Demetrius because they preferred to have an inexperienced youth on the Seleucid throne.[25] They sponsored the revision of the agreement between the two Ptolemies in 163/2, because it was in their interest to keep Egypt weak and divided.[26] Very many Roman decisions', Polybius adds, 'are of this kind; profiting by others' mistakes they effectively increase and build up their own power, simultaneously favouring and apparently conferring a benefit on the guilty party (τοὺς ἁμαρτάνοντας).' Does he disapprove? One might assume so. But twice in this very passage he uses the word πραγματικῶς of Roman policy; and in Polybius this usually indicates a praiseworthy quality. In the clashes between Carthage and Masinissa, decisions generally favoured the latter, because that was to the advantage of Rome.[27] The Romans had already decided on the Third Punic War, but postponed its start until they had a pretext that would appeal to foreign opinion – καλῶς φρονοῦντες, Polybius adds.[28] He was of course not always so detached. He scarcely conceals his anger

---

[20] See J. Briscoe, *JRS* 54 (1964) 74–5, who points out that all our sources except Polybius emphasise that Paullus was carrying out the order of a *senatus consultum* in Epirus.

[21] xxx.1–3.   [22] xxx.18.1–7.

[23] xxx.19.1–13.

[24] xxx.20; cf. xxxii.10 for the Senate's refusal to support Priene.

[25] xxxi.2.1–7.   [26] xxxi.10.

[27] xxxi.21.6.   [28] xxxvi.2.

when a Charops or a Callicrates persuades the Senate to refuse the Greek detainees permission to return home.[29] But in general his judgement of Roman policy ‖ during those years – formulated, I am inclined to think, at the time rather than superimposed later when he was composing the last ten books – was aloof and cynical, no doubt reflecting the views of Greeks living at Rome – οἱ ἐπιδημοῦντες, as he calls them – and perhaps of his fellow-detainees in the towns of southern Etruria.

V

The harsh assumption that for the Romans wise statesmanship naturally meant putting Roman interests first is continuous from the Third Macedonian War, when he recorded the *nova sapientia* of Q. Marcius Philippus, down to the later years of his detention. It goes with an impatient rejection of Greeks foolish enough to work against Rome. During the years just before his release Polybius' position perhaps improved. He now had considerable freedom of movement. It is not known when he visited Locri, but his journey to Spain, Gaul and North Africa in 151/50 clearly connects with the growing authority of Scipio Aemilianus, whom he accompanied.

This close identification with Scipio's family continues throughout the rest of the period covered by his extended *Histories*. It may help to account for the increasingly pro-Roman character of the later books, especially those covering the years 150 to 146, when Polybius was himself making history in Scipio's camp at Carthage or as mediator in Achaea. This development in his views is expressed less in positive statements of approval of Roman policy than in the violent and even emotional terms in which he discusses the methods and personalities of the enemies of Rome, his hostile contempt for whom surpasses that which he displayed towards the pro-Macedonian parties at the time of the war with Perseus. It is also expressed in his account of the arguments ‖ which, he says, were propounded by the Greeks in discussing the rights and wrongs of Roman action in the Third Punic War – a passage which has been variously interpreted.

Four views are recorded.[30] Some urged that since Carthage had been a constant menace to Rome, and might be again, her destruction was a wise and statesmanlike action (φρονίμως καὶ πραγματικῶς βουλεύσασθαι) designed to secure Roman rule. Others argued that the Roman treatment of Carthage represented a change of policy – already visible in the destruction of the Macedonian kingdom in 168; Rome was following in the footsteps of Athens and Sparta and was likely to end the same way.[31] A third group, also critical of Rome, alleged that she had committed impiety and treachery (ἀσέβημα καὶ

---

[29] xxx.32, xxxii.3.14–17, xxxiii.1.3–8.3, 14.2.
[30] xxxvi.9; see my *Polybius* (n. 2) 174 n. 112.
[31] He means either that she will become a tyrant or that her empire will be of short duration (*cf.* my *Polybius* (n. 2) 175 n. 114).

παρασπόνδημα) towards Carthage, thus lapsing from standards of honourable warfare, judged against the background of the *iustum bellum*. But this allegation plays straight into the hands of the fourth group, who argued that the Punic *deditio* completely justified the Roman treatment of Carthage, especially as the Carthaginians had broken both the treaty with Masinissa and the obligations incurred in the *deditio* itself. Polybius does not state which (if any) of these views coincides with his own; hence his readers are forced back on speculation. A case can be made for thinking that he accepted the arguments of Rome's critics.[32] In Book x, commenting on the failure of the Carthaginians to exploit the situation in Spain after the death of the two Scipios, he remarks[33] that they had acted on the belief that 'there is one method by which power should be acquired and another by which it should be ‖ maintained. They had not learnt that those who preserve their supremacy best are those who adhere to the same principles by which they originally established it.' The Carthaginians were enemies of Rome (and of the Scipios); but Philip V, an ally of Achaea during the Social War, is condemned in Book v for sacking the Aetolian centre at Thermum, on the moral grounds that 'good men should not make war on wrongdoers with the object of destroying and exterminating them, but with that of correcting and reforming their errors'.[34] This sententious observation should perhaps be seen in the general context of Philip's later 'moral deterioration' when these defects were to prove disadvantageous to Achaea. But the views expressed would certainly be in keeping with those of Rome's critics at the time of the Third Punic War. They were moreover views once propounded by the Romans themselves; for, if we can believe Polybius, Flamininus remarked after his victory at Cynoscephalae that the Romans never exterminated their enemies after a single war (as their treatment of Hannibal after Zama demonstrated), and that brave men ought to be hard on their enemies and angry with them while fighting, if beaten courageous and highminded, and if victorious moderate, gentle and humane.[35] Whether the expression of the same sentiments in Diodorus xxxi.3 is from a version of Cato's speech on the Rhodians and whether in that case it derives from Polybius, I leave open; but a similar passage in Diodorus xxix.31 certainly seems to be Polybian.[36]

These passages, taken together, apparently afford strong support for the view that Polybius took sides with Rome's critics over the Third Punic War. Nevertheless, I believe it to be wrong. Three arguments seem to be decisive ‖ against it. The first is that although Polybius gives no overt expression of opinion about Roman policy, he sets out the various Greek views in such a way as to indicate clearly which he regarded as decisive. The arguments are arranged chiastically, so that those favouring Rome begin and end the

---

[32] *Cf.* K.-E. Petzold, *op. cit.* (n. 6) 62–3.
[33] x.36.2f.   [34] v.11.5.
[35] xviii.37.2, 37.7.
[36] *Cf.* Diod. xxi.9; he seems fond of the *sententia*.

'debate'; and the space allotted to them (in lines of the Teubner text) is, for the first eight lines, for the second fifteen, for the third fifteen but for the fourth and last twenty-eight. This answers the third argument in detail, and I find it hard to believe that it does not represent Polybius' view of the matter.[37] That he gave the other side the last word and twice as much space as he allotted to the view he is supposed to have held himself – this is *prima facie* incredible. The second reason for supposing that Polybius approved the Roman policy towards Carthage is that it had the backing of Scipio Aemilianus, and that Polybius was present throughout at Scipio's headquarters, and shared his experiences when the city fell. Was he all the time condemning the policy to which by his presence he lent not only moral support but also perhaps technical assistance?

Finally Polybius represents the Third Punic War as the most notable event within the period which he regards as one of ταραχή καὶ κίνησις (which perhaps recalls the ἀκρισία καὶ ταραχή which Xenophon[38] saw as supervening upon the battle of Mantinea). The main feature of this period, which includes the Spanish War, Andriscus' revolt in Macedonia, and the Achaean War, is that there is no sense in what happened. Events were unforeseen, παράδοξα; policy (in the states opposing Rome) did not obey the rules of reason. Macedonia presents the unbelievable story of a ‖ pseudo-Philip virtually falling out of the sky (ἀεροπετὴς Φίλιππος) and winning victory after victory. The Macedonians, to whom Rome had brought freedom in place of slavery, rushed to fight for this impostor, who in return exiled, tortured and murdered them in large numbers – an example of heaven-sent insanity (δαιμονοβλάβεια).[39] In Achaea, disaster took the form of a universal catastrophe, disgraceful and lacking in any of those features which in former disasters had inspired appropriate feelings of consolation and pride: 'the whole country was visited by an unparalleled attack of madness, with people flinging themselves into wells and over precipices'.[40] This general madness and demoralisation was such as is scarcely to be met among barbarians, and that Greece did ultimately emerge can only be attributed to the 'successful intervention of some kind of smart and ingenious fortune' – who saved the Greeks only by bringing about this downfall with such speed.[41]

The men involved in these disreputable incidents were such as one might expect. Diaeus and Critolaus 'and all who shared their views' were, one might say, a deliberate selection of the worst men from each city, hateful to the gods and corruptors of the nation;[42] their political naïveté combined with sheer wickedness led the Achaeans to ruin.[43] Similarly at Carthage, Hasdrubal was

---

[37] For a similar example see the speeches of the Aetolian and Acarnanian envoys at Sparta in 211; *cf.* IX.28–39 and my remarks in *Ancient Macedonia* (Salonica, 1970) 295–6.

[38] *Hell.* VII.5.27.

[39] XXXVI.17.12–15.

[40] XXXVIII.16.7.

[41] XXXVIII.18.8–12.

[42] XXXVIII.10.8.

[43] XXXVIII.10.13.

an empty-headed fool without political or military capacity, flaunting purple robes and full armour, but never realising that Carthage was lost.[44] Pot-bellied and apoplectic of countenance, he was like a fatted ox at a festival, and he gave lavish dinners while his ‖ fellow-citizens were daily dying of famine in hordes.[45] I have mentioned the resemblance to Polybius' comments on the Greeks who earlier had made the mistake of supporting Perseus; but the present remarks are much more extreme and emotional. No one surely can doubt where Polybius' sympathies lay, as between Scipio's Rome and these despicable and insane men who were at this time opposing her.

VI

If this is accepted, the possibility arises that Polybius had changed his mind about how conquered peoples should be treated when they repaid benefits with breach of faith, crass ingratitude and revolt. The Roman policy exemplified at Carthage and Corinth was that of eliminating dangerous and intransigent enemies. At Carthage (and later at Numantia) its instrument was Scipio himself. The view has been expressed that Polybius formulated such a policy in a lost part of one of his later books, and that a passage in Diodorus xxxii, to which M. Gelzer first drew attention in a famous essay on Scipio Nasica's opposition to the proposal to destroy Carthage, is derived from Polybius.[46] Diodorus here enunciates a doctrine diametrically opposed to that in which Polybius criticised Carthaginian policy in Spain.[47] 'Those', he says, 'whose object it is to attain hegemony over others use courage and intelligence to gain it, moderation and respect for others to extend it widely, and paralysing terror to secure it against attack.' He then proceeds to illustrate this principle from Macedonian history, with Philip II's destruction of Olynthus and the razing of ‖ Thebes by Alexander, and from Roman history with the destruction of Corinth, the eradication of Perseus and the obliteration of Carthage and Numantia. Gelzer's view has been widely accepted;[48] and K.-E. Petzold[49] has underlined verbal parallels between this passage in Diodorus and Polybian passages which it appears to echo – though, unlike Gelzer, he draws the conclusion that Polybius was indicating that Rome was bent on a φιλαρχία which would lead to her destruction.

Recently, however, J. Touloumakos[50] has emphasised the fact that the two Greek examples quoted to illustrate the theory – Philip's destruction of Olynthus and Alexander's destruction of Thebes – in fact illustrate it rather badly, since the first was followed by Philip's φιλανθρωπία towards Athens

[44] xxxviii.7.1.   [45] xxxviii.8.7.

[46] Diod. xxxii.2 and 4; M. Gelzer, *Kleine Schriften* 2 (Wiesbaden, 1963) 64ff.

[47] x.36.

[48] For references see my *Polybius* (n. 2) 179 n. 130.

[49] K.-E. Petzold, *op. cit.* (n. 6) 63.

[50] J. Touloumakos, *Zum Geschichtsbewusstsein der Griechen in der Zeit der römischen Herrschaft* (Göttingen, 1971) 28–9 n. 28.

and the second by Alexander's φιλανθρωπία towards the Persians. In accepting Gelzer's attribution of the Diodoran passage to Polybius I had already mentioned[51] that 'the three stages – acquisition, extension and securing of empire – are not necessarily envisaged as always following that chronological order'. On this view, Alexander's punishment of Thebes could have been seen within a European context, with the winning over of the Persians as something quite separate. However, on further consideration, I am inclined to think that J. Touloumakos must be right and that the examples quoted from Greece are too inept to be the work of Polybius; and it is on the whole unlikely that Diodorus took over the formulation from Polybius and added the Greek examples himself. Moreover, the mention of Numantia is also an obstacle to the view ‖ that Diodorus' source was Polybius, since the *Histories* ended in 145. True, at the time Diodorus was writing, the fates of Carthage and Numantia were closely associated in people's minds as Scipio's two great military achievements, perpetuated indeed in the titles *Africanus* and *Numantinus*,[52] so that the addition could have come from Diodorus. But taken together with the Greek examples, it seems to weigh against the attribution to Polybius.

However, the elimination of this passage does not greatly affect the issue. For it seems clear that Polybius approved a Roman policy associated with Scipio Aemilianus more than with any other man (unless it was Aemilius Paullus, the destroyer of Macedonia and Epirus); for Scipio, I need hardly say, was a very different man from the fictional Aemilianus drawn in Cicero's *De Republica*.[53] That Polybius did condemn Scipio's policy I find quite improbable as a hypothesis and I would argue that Polybius accepted the events at Carthage, Corinth, and later Numantia, as perhaps inevitable and certainly not blameworthy manifestations of the evolution of imperial power.

How far his support for Roman policy at this time implies a reversal of his earlier approval of the principle of *parcere subiectis* is perhaps a moot point. On the one hand, although expressed in moral terms in reference to Philip V, that principle was basically utilitarian; it was the policy that gave the best results. But that was true only if one had to go on living with the defeated and governing them. If, however, one decided to *destroy* Carthage or Numantia, to make an end of the Macedonian kingdom, to enslave the ‖ Epirotes, that was indeed a more ruthless solution, but one perhaps simpler and safer for a dominant power. For, in fact, since 168 Rome's position was new and unprecedented. Hitherto the Carthaginians in Spain, for example, or the Romans themselves after Cynoscephalae, had operated within something

---

[51] *JRS* 55 (1965) 11 [above, p. 172].

[52] *Cf.* Plut. *Aem.* 22.4, Σκιπίων ὁ Καρχηδόνα καὶ Νομαντίαν κατάσκαψας; Val. Max. IV.3.13, V.3.2, IX.12.3.

[53] See H. Strasburger, *JRS* 55 (1965) 41f., 52f.; *Hermes* 94 (1966) 60–72; J. E. G. Zetzel, *HSPh* 76 (1972) 173–9; *cf.* A. Astin, *Scipio Aemilianus* (Oxford, 1967) 294–306; E. S. Gruen, *Roman politics and the criminal courts* (Cambridge, Mass., 1968) 17–18.

approaching a balance of power: now Rome enjoyed virtual supremacy, and the balance of power was dead (as indeed Polybius wrote his *Histories* to demonstrate).

Roman policy at this time was certainly harsh by our standards. But there is no reason to think that Polybius rejected harshness, when it was a question of punishing intransigence or treachery. Standards of harshness vary; and I would remind you of Polybius' criticism of Phylarchus, who had expressed sympathy for Mantinea, and his remark that 'nothing more serious befell the Mantineans in their hour of calamity than the pillage of their property and the enslavement of their free population',[54] or his assertion that the ex-tyrant Aristomachus of Argos deserved to be led around the whole Peloponnese and tortured to death as a deterrent spectacle, whereas 'despite his abominable character all the harm he suffered was to be drowned in the sea by the officials in command at Cenchreae'.[55] Whether Polybius was conscious of any contradiction between Roman policy in 146 and the views he had expressed earlier is another matter. But in this context it is perhaps worth recalling that in his general comments on Roman policy after the Achaean War – a policy in which he was personally much involved – he stresses the fine impression left behind in Greece by the ten commissioners and by Mummius himself.[56] ‖

VII

I would argue then that from the late years of his detention in Italy and throughout the period down to 146 Polybius grew increasingly sympathetic towards Rome, where Scipio was now a leading figure. But I have still to consider one important fact – his decision sometime after 145 to extend his *Histories* to cover events down to that year, a period of twenty-two years which was to require another ten books and thereby to add an extra third to his original work. Any discussion of Polybius' position relative to Greece and Rome must take this revision of plan into consideration.

The reasons Polybius alleges for thus extending his *Histories* are rather remarkable. He writes,

If from their success alone we could adequately judge how far states and individuals merit praise or blame, I could here [i.e. at 168/7] bring my narrative to a close... in accordance with the plan set out at the beginning of my work.... But since judgements regarding either victors or vanquished based purely on the actual struggle are by no means final...I must append... an account of the subsequent policy of the conquerors and how they exercised their universal rule, as well as of the various opinions...entertained by the rest about their rulers, and finally I must describe what were the prevailing and dominant tendencies and ambitions of the various peoples in their private and public life.... Contemporaries will thus be enabled to see clearly whether

---

[54] II.58.12.   [55] II.60.8.
[56] XXXIX.5.1, 6.2.

Roman rule is acceptable or the reverse, and future generations whether their government should be considered to have been worthy of praise or admiration or rather of blame.[57]

So the extension of the *Histories* down to 145 is to facilitate passing judgement on Rome – both now, when it is a ‖ practical issue, and in the future when it will have become the material of history. K.-E. Petzold[58] has recently argued that the kind of judgements which Polybius expected his readers to pass would resemble the accusations of Roman aggression, and the allegations that the Romans exploited grievances to further their own imperial ends, which are to be found attributed to Greeks in many passages of Polybius (or in Polybian parts of Livy) from the time of the Hannibalic War onwards; and he associates this with an increased sensitiveness in Polybius to moral issues and with the alleged moral deterioration visible at Rome. Concerning this argument I should like to make three points. First, as I have already said, it is certainly true that Polybius admits that from about 171 onwards the Romans exploited Greek quarrels and weaknesses to further their own ends. Their opponents had alleged it earlier: now Polybius admits it. My second point is that there is no reason to suppose that Polybius was more sensitive to moral issues as he grew older than he had been earlier. Book VI, written I would say before 150, lays much stress on ethical factors, and Polybius' criticism of Philip V (of which I quoted an example earlier) and his discussion of the influence of Aratus, Apelles and Demetrius of Pharos on that king show that he was alert to such matters long before he adopted the revised plan of his *Histories*. Moreover, the question of moral decline had been actively discussed at Rome ever since Cato's censorship of 184, and must have been familiar to Polybius from the time of his arrival there in 167. My third point is that Petzold's theory confuses two separate issues; for I see no reason why the moral decline which Polybius describes – perhaps, incidentally, in somewhat exaggerated colours so as to underline the contrasted abstemiousness of the virtuous young Scipio – need have had ‖ anything to do with a growth in Machiavellian policies, nor are there grounds for thinking that Polybius' comments on moral decline imply that he disapproved of the use of ruthless and self-interested politics by Rome.

When he sketches his plan to extend his *Histories* Polybius puts forward an unusual criterion – the acceptability of Roman rule to the subject peoples. The implications of this are far-reaching, for it raises the whole question of the purpose of imperial expansion and how imperial achievement is to be assessed. It was generally assumed that the subjection of other states and the preservation of acquisitions without damage to the imperial power were justification enough in themselves. To judge empire from the point of view of the conquered was a novel concept indeed. As H. Strasburger observed a few years ago in an important paper on Poseidonius, Polybius propounded this concept but never

---

[57] III.4.1f.   [58] *Op. cit.* (n. 6) 59ff.

in fact made any serious attempt to apply it.[59] In Books XXX to XXXIX the matter is slightly complicated by the fact that he divided the twenty-five years between Pydna and the sack of Corinth into two periods – though he did not draw a very clear chronological line of demarcation between them. 'The final end achieved by this work', he wrote, 'will be to learn what was the condition of each people after all had been crushed and brought under Roman domination, down to the disturbed and troubled time (ταραχὴ καὶ κίνησις) that afterwards ensued. About this', he goes on, 'I was induced to write as if beginning a new work, both because of the importance of the actions and unexpected character of the events it contained, and also because I not only witnessed most of these, but also took part in or actually directed others.'[60] ‖

What exactly the time of ταραχὴ καὶ κίνησις included is not wholly clear, since Polybius does not list the events which fall between Pydna and its onset. He does list[61] several events which he associates with the κίνησις; but since these include Ariarathes' expulsion in 158 and the war between Prusias and Attalus in 156–154, one is bound to conclude that he had not sorted out his two periods very clearly. This conclusion is perhaps supported by the fact that a passage which seems most obviously designed to enable his readers to judge the character of Roman imperialism – which is allegedly his purpose in describing the years down to the period of disturbance – is that which records the various Greek views of Roman behaviour in the Third Punic War,[62] and that falls clearly *within* the period of disturbance. Insofar as Polybius envisaged a chronological demarcation, it perhaps came where Book XXXIV interrupts the narrative between Ol. 156 and 157, and so in 152 B.C. Book XXXIV certainly stands immediately before the books covering the years of Polybius' personal involvement in world affairs (especially if we include his journey to Spain and Africa in 151). They contained the Third Punic War, during which he was with Scipio at Carthage, his voyage of exploration in the Atlantic, and his mediation in Greece after the fall of Corinth. But for the reasons I have given this cannot be pressed very hard; and it may well be that Polybius thought of the period after Pydna as gradually merging into the 'time of disturbance' without any very clear line of demarcation.

However, neither the years after Pydna nor the years of disturbance are described and discussed in such a way as to facilitate passing judgement on Rome as an imperial power from the point of view of the defeated. There are, as I have ‖ emphasised, several cynical observations about Roman policy, which is influenced by self-interest; but, especially as one comes down to the years from 152 onwards, the defeated states receive virtually no sympathy. Moreover, if one tries to justify Polybius' claim by reference to his comments on the way the Romans received the many embassies which came to Rome from the various Greek states (and these are often quite mordant) there is much

---

[59] H. Strasburger, *art. cit.* (n. 53) 46 and n. 57.
[60] III.4.12.   [61] III.5.1f.
[62] XXXVI.9.

more about that in the books dealing with the years *before* Pydna, which contain a very full account of internal factions in Greece, than in Books xxx to xxxix, when of course the anti-Roman and even the moderate elements had been mostly eliminated.

It is because of this gap between what Polybius says he is providing in Books xxx to xxxix and what he actually does provide that in my recent Sather lectures I threw out the suggestion[63] that his real reason for extending the *Histories* to 145 was not to facilitate passing judgement on Roman rule (as he claims), but rather to enable him to publish important material which he had assembled since 168. Clearly, while he was at Rome Polybius was collecting information and writing and soliciting memoranda, at the same time that he was composing his *Histories*; and I think it is fair to assume that his attitude to Rome at that time was considerably more cynical than it was later when he came to use the material. From about 151 onwards he was caught up in a series of events about which, in retrospect, he had a personal story of interest and importance to tell. He might have turned *this* into a monograph; but against that solution was the fact that it did not conform to the character of a monograph (as the Numantine War did later). On the contrary, these years covered separate and quite disconnected actions – Andriscus' revolt, the destruction of Carthage, the voyage on the outer Ocean, and the Achaean ‖ War and settlement – episodes linked neither causally nor geographically, but only in time; and the irrational character of many of them made them typical of ταραχὴ καὶ κίνησις. So Polybius decided to add a pendant to his *Histories*; and that had the additional advantage of enabling him to include the material which he had collected while at Rome. The only difficulty lay in providing a *rationale* for the addition of two decades, which would make sense in the light of the original plan. This, I have suggested, is the real function of the programme which Polybius propounds but never actually fulfils. The main body of the *Histories* was written under the stimulus of an idea, the pendant because Polybius had material urgently needing to be published. The new programme – to enable his readers to pass judgement on Rome – was not perhaps very important – a εὐσχήμων πρόφασις, one might say. In fact, the ‘period of judging’ slides away imperceptibly into the ‘period of confusion’, and in the very last chapter of the whole work,[64] when Polybius is summarising the contents and purpose of his *Histories*, the whole business of ‘passing judgement’ has slipped out of sight and he simply repeats his original programme, adding the new terminal date of 145.

VIII

In 145 Polybius stood closer to Rome than ever before. But this did not mean that he was or had been in any sense, politically or ideologically, a ‘quisling’.

---

[63] *Op. cit.* (n. 2) 182–3.   [64] xxxix.8.

He had a hard realistic sense which led him to judge policies in terms of the possible. He had no sympathy for Demosthenes as against Philip II, and he was apt to make success or failure his criterion (though if one had to go down, like the ‖ Abydenes, there was something to be said for going down with one's flag flying). Decisions in politics should be based, not on abstract rules, but on the demands of the immediate situation. That was why Polybius opposed his father in 172. This sense of realism (together with less obvious pressures, such as his growing intimacy with Scipio and Scipio's growing influence exercised on his behalf) led him to see collaboration with Rome as the only realistic policy for Carthage, Macedonia or Achaea in 150–145. For the leaders in those countries to have taken a different view strikes him as sheer insanity. But Polybius would never have given the Senate the sort of advice Callicrates gave. As an active politician in Achaea it had seemed only reasonable to take account of the growing acceleration in Roman control over Greece, which Callicrates' evil counsel had helped to bring about; but he would do nothing to speed it up and so hasten the end of Achaean independence. It was only later, at Rome and as a historian, that he came, in retrospect, to recognise this accelerated control as part of the grand design of Tyche.

In 146 Polybius' influence and mediation brought practical results, and many inscriptions testified to the services he was able to render his country. Of course we have only the official version, and no way of knowing how the many Achaeans who had followed their leaders to defeat in a futile and ill-planned struggle for independence felt about their prosperous and benevolent fellow-countryman who had worked to mitigate their misfortunes – from the victor's camp. One thing worries me a little. Polybius' commitment to the doctrine of 'the possible' is no doubt a praiseworthy quality in a statesman – even though the really 'great' statesman is the man who makes his own definition of the possible. But had this commitment perhaps a slightly corrupting effect on Polybius as a historian? With his increasing sympathy for Rome, the successful super-power, goes a ‖ marked lack of sympathy for those who had resisted her. The arguments defending Roman policy against Carthage in the Third Punic War – which, I have argued, Polybius accepted – coincide with those which must have been bandied about in 'hawkish' circles at Rome; they are harsh and legalistic to a fault, and ignore much – for instance the successive decisions favouring Masinissa (which Polybius else-where admits[65] were motivated by Roman self-interest), the Numidian provo-cation and the trickery which led to Carthage being disarmed before the final ultimatum was presented – that the historian surely ought to take into account. The result is a very one-sided assessment of Punic responsibility which certainly does not show Polybius at his most attractive.

[65] XXXI.21.6.

IX

Despite his commitment to Scipio and to Rome, however, Polybius remained primarily an Achaean. Both in his life and in his writing he never wavered in one criterion – what he regarded as the best policy for Achaea. He rather carefully avoids instituting embarrassing comparisons between Achaea and Rome, and this may be one reason why Achaea does not figure among the highly-rated constitutions discussed in Book VI. (In parenthesis, I am not persuaded by K.-E. Petzold[66] that the chapters on Achaea in Book II were introduced at a late stage in order to contrast a state based on equality and philanthropy – Achaea – and Rome based on power.) Polybius' regard for Achaean advantage colours his judgement at all stages. His early hero is Aratus, campaigning to expel the Macedonians; but when Antigonus Doson is called in to defeat Cleomenes, he becomes a ‖ benefactor receiving undying honour and glory. Philip V is commended so long as he listens to Aratus, but having laid hands on Messene he becomes a veritable werewolf. In the clash between Rome and Macedonia Achaea had to look to her own survival. Aristaenus' policy of neglecting oaths to Macedon and switching to Rome has Polybius' full approval. In the early years of the Roman alliance he favoured Philopoemen's policy – collaboration within strict limits and no giving away of freedom before it became absolutely necessary: but under the burden of political responsibility and the pressures of the war with Perseus he recognised the need to define more clearly the Achaean alignment with Rome. Exiled in Rome between 167 and 150, his relations with Achaea were tenuous and broken: policies there developed without reference to him, and on his return he found himself out of sympathy with those in power. To be away on the Atlantic during the Achaean War must have been a relief from the embarrassment of having to choose between his Roman friends and his fellow-countrymen.

After 145 we know virtually nothing of Polybius. Presumably he lived in Achaea when he was not on some journey; but he must have been several times at Rome to meet Scipio and join him and Panaetius in the discussion mentioned by Cicero (assuming Cicero is not dealing in historical fiction). I suspect the *Histories* were in the main finished before he wrote the *Numantine War*: but we cannot be wholly certain. This monograph was probably based on autopsy. We are nowhere told that Polybius was at Numantia, but when Scipio invited all his friends and clients to join him there, Polybius is likely to have been among them. By now he no doubt moved at ease between the worlds of Rome and Achaea, the victors and the vanquished. But, as I have argued above, the original purpose of his *Histories* remained unchanged – despite additions and pretexts for adding them. It was to explain to the Greek world the causes and

---

[66] *Op. cit.* (n. 6) 25–128; see my comments in *JRS* 60 (1970) 252.

course ‖ of Rome's rise to world power. It was intended, in short, as a contribution to co-existence and to the solving of such problems as co-existence created – and these continued to exist if in a less urgent form, even after 146. Indeed, the Mithridatic War was to show that several decades after Polybius' death the lessons he had tried to inculcate had still to be learnt the hard way.

19

SYNCHRONISMS IN POLYBIUS, BOOKS IV AND V*[1]

I

Polybius devotes Books III to V to Olympiad 140 (220–216 B.C.), and in these he organises his narrative differently from elsewhere in the *Histories*. There, events in the various theatres, viz. Italy, Sicily, Spain, Africa, Greece and Macedonia, Asia, and Egypt,[2] are dealt with year by year, in that order;[3] but, he explains,[4] it was only at the conference of Naupactus (217) that the affairs of Greece, Italy and Africa first came together, and shortly afterwards that those of the Aegean and Asia Minor were involved. Consequently, in Ol. 140, instead of proceeding year by year, and theatre by theatre within each year, Polybius devotes long sections to the Hannibalic War, the Social War, and the Fourth Syrian War, neglecting the separate Olympiad years. To help the reader he introduces eight synchronisms,[5] listing events which allegedly occurred about the same time. In V.31.3–5 he explains why. 'I am confident', he writes, 'that I shall effectively prevent my readers from going astray about dates, if I indicate...at what times in this Olympiad, and contemporaneously with what events in Greece each episode elsewhere began and ended. So that my narrative may be easy to follow and lucid, I think it most essential for this Olympiad not to interweave the histories of the various countries, but to keep them as separate and distinct as possible until, upon reaching the next and subsequent ‖ Olympiads, I can begin to narrate the events of each year which occurred at the same time.'

This is the only passage where Polybius explains why he introduces these eight synchronisms;[6] his frequent discussions of his chronological methods do

---

* [*Polis and imperium: studies in honour of Edward Togo Salmon* (Toronto, 1974) 59–80]

[1] This paper owes a great deal to many friends and colleagues who discussed it with me at a seminar held in the State University of New York at Buffalo in October 1970. They included several from McMaster University, but Togo Salmon could not be among them, as he was directing the *Centro Universitario per Studi Classici* in Rome. It is therefore an especial pleasure to submit the results to him now as a token of a friendship lasting over many years. (References without the author's name are to Polybius.)

[2] See my *Historical commentary on Polybius* (3 vols., Oxford, 1957–79) 2.1.

[3] Exceptions: XIV.12.1–6, XXXII.11.2–4.

[4] V.105.3.

[5] See the appended table, pp. 310–11.

[6] P. Pédech, *La méthode historique de Polybe* (Paris, 1964) 467, argues that there is a reference to the synchronisms in XXXIX.8.6; but this passage describes Polybius' programme for his *Histories* generally, and the arranging of events in different theatres in each Olympiad year, not the synchronisms of Books IV–V.

not mention them at all.[7] Recently, however, it has been argued that they form an important part of Polybius' structural machinery and have a significance not previously discerned. Pédech describes Polybius' procedure as follows:[8] 'He has divided the Olympic year into two equal semesters. It would be tempting to put the points of transition at the equinoxes. But this division would have no raison d'être in a system resting, not on the tropical year, but on a luni-solar calendar. Moreover, it is contrary to the usage of the ancients, who determined the seasons not by tropical signs, but by the signs of the zodiac. Consequently the six-monthly periods instituted by Polybius for Ol. 140 have slightly variable dimensions, of which the appended table[9] indicates the limits.' Pédech asserts that Polybius treats all events occurring within such a six-monthly period as synchronous. It is this hypothesis that I wish to examine.

II

Polybius' first synchronism is at IV.28.1. Philip V's departure from Macedonia – it is convenient to call this the 'primary event' of the synchronism – took place, he says, at the time that Hannibal, having subdued all Spain south of the Ebro, was setting out against Saguntum (ἐποιεῖτο τὴν ὁρμὴν ἐπὶ τὴν Ζακανθαίων πόλιν). The Aetolians had just elected Scopas general (27.1), and the decree passed by the Greek Symmachy was in the first year of Ol. 140; clearly it is late September 220.[10] What is the meaning of ἐποιεῖτο τὴν ὁρμήν? According to III.16.7–17.1 Aemilius Paullus was sent to operate in Illyria ὑπὸ τὴν ὡραίαν, 'just before the campaigning season' of 219, and Hannibal advanced on Saguntum (ποιούμενος τὴν πορείαν ἐπὶ τὴν Ζάκανθαν). Polybius implies (both here and in IV.37.4) that these two events ‖ occurred simultaneously. Hence the siege of Saguntum began in spring 219. The common phrase ποιεῖσθαι τὴν ὁρμήν usually means 'to set out', often against someone. That is the natural meaning here. It would imply, however, that the siege of Saguntum began in autumn 220 and (since it lasted eight months)[11] ended by late spring 219. This is Schnabel's date,[12] and more recently Werner's,[13] who thinks Roman propaganda put the siege later so as to relate it more closely to the Hannibalic War. But the remaining evidence strongly favours putting the siege in 219, and late April/early May[14] seems a likely date; it could be a little later to allow flooded Spanish rivers to subside, but hardly earlier.

Consequently, either Polybius is mistaken in connecting Hannibal's attack on Saguntum with events of autumn 220 (as well as with those of spring

[7] *E.g.* XIV.12, XV.24a, XXVIII.16.10, XXXII.11.2–4.
[8] *Op. cit.* (n. 6) 472.
[9] I have indicated Pédech's divisions in my table on pp. 310–11.
[10] On the date of the Aetolian elections *cf.* IV.37.2; below, p. 300 n. 20.
[11] *Cf.* III.17.9; see G. V. Sumner, *PACA* 9 (1966) 7 n. 15.
[12] P. Schnabel, *Klio* 20 (1926) 113ff.
[13] R. Werner, *Der Beginn der römischen Republik* (Munich, 1963) 54ff.
[14] Sumner, *PACA* 9 (1966) 5.

219) or else ἐποιεῖτο τὴν ὁρμήν (IV.28.1) bears some other meaning. In my *Commentary*[15] I took the former view, suggesting that 'Polybius has been led to make a false synchronism by his desire to insert the didactic observations contained in IV.28.2–6'; more recently, however, Eucken[16] has argued that ὁρμή here means 'Unternehmen, Anschlag', *i.e.* 'undertaking, plan'. This would save Polybius from the charge of careless writing; but in the only other passage which Eucken quotes to support his view (IX.31.2), παρώξυνε... ὁρμήν means 'he aroused their hostility', which clearly furnishes no parallel.

Polybius' reference to Hannibal as master of all Spain south of the Ebro echoes III.14.9,[17] where he explains that after Hannibal's campaign of 220 'none of the peoples within the river Ebro dared lightly to face the Carthaginians, except the Saguntines'. Hannibal held off from Saguntum for reasons of policy, but the Saguntines foreseeing the danger informed the Romans, and Roman envoys sent to Hannibal διεμαρτύροντο Ζακανθαίων ἀπέχεσθαι.[18] Polybius, then, believed Hannibal's hostility towards Saguntum to have become acute by autumn 220, and it is tempting to translate ἐποιεῖτο τὴν ὁρμὴν ἐπὶ τὴν Ζακανθαίων πόλιν (IV.28.1) as 'he directed his hostile intentions against Saguntum'. This ‖ involves an unusual meaning for a common phrase; but it is clearly possible, and avoids assuming that Polybius was careless at a point where chronological clarity was important.

Pédech would save Polybius' credit differently, with the aid of his six-monthly periods. Hannibal, he argues, set out against Saguntum 'at the soonest at the end of winter 220/19', and so in the half Olympiad year running allegedly from 26 July 220 to 13 February 219. Unfortunately the validity of these Julian calendar equivalents is far from being established. The Julian date of the Olympic games cannot be determined within a month. Ancient sources say only that it was in high summer and at full moon.[19] Moreover, even if Olympiad 140 proved to have begun on 26 July 220, an event occurring ὑπὸ τὴν ὡραίαν, *i.e.* at the earliest in April 219, could hardly fall within a half Olympiad year ending 13 February 219. Thus Polybius' first synchronism is not satisfactorily explained by Pédech's theory.

In the second (IV.37.1–7), the 'primary event', to which the rest are related, is the moment when Aratus' year as Achaean general for 220/19 was ending and his son was about to succeed him. Scopas was now half-way through his year of office, since at that time the Aetolian elections were held just after the autumn equinox and the Achaean about the rising of the Pleiades, *i.e.* late May.[20] Since Polybius here draws no distinction between election and entry

---

[15] *Op. cit.* (n. 2) 1.328 (on III.17).

[16] H. C. Eucken, *Probleme der Vorgeschichte des zweiten punischen Krieges* (Diss. Freiburg, 1968) 106.

[17] *Cf.* Sumner, *PACA* 9 (1966) 7.

[18] III.15.5.

[19] See R. Sealey, *CR* 10 (1960) 185–6; the implications for Pédech's theory are underlined by R. M. Errington, *JRS* 57 (1967) 99.

[20] *Cf.* my *Commentary* (n. 2) 1.258 (on II.55.5). I made this 22 May, but Werner, *op. cit.* (n. 13) 47 n. 5 has elaborate calculations pointing to 28 May; *cf.* Sumner, *PACA* 9 (1966) 6.

into office, presumably no substantial period was involved or else he considered the interval negligible for his purpose. In fact he makes the younger Aratus assume office τῆς θερείας ἐνισταμένης, but ends his year at the rising of the Pleiades (v.1.1). The primary event may therefore be dated as late May 219.

At this time (Polybius refers back specifically to III.16.7–17.1) Hannibal was opening the siege of Saguntum (ἐνεχείρει... πολιορκεῖν), the Romans were dispatching Aemilius Paullus to Illyria, Antiochus was about to invade Coele-Syria (after Theodotus' surrender of Ptolemais and Tyre)[21] and Ptolemy was preparing to resist,[22] Lycurgus of ‖ Sparta was besieging the Athenaeum,[23] the Achaeans were collecting mercenaries,[24] and Philip was moving from Macedonia.[25] (The Rhodian war on Byzantium which opened κατὰ... τοὺς αὐτοὺς χρόνους (37.8) seems to be a new episode loosely linked to what precedes, and not part of the synchronism;[26] see below, p. 302.)

Having made the siege of Saguntum begin in the previous half-Olympiad year, ending 13 February, Pédech has to attach a different meaning to ἐνεχείρει... πολιορκεῖν. Polybius often uses πολιορκία and πολιορκεῖν to mean ‘taking by storm’ rather than ‘besieging’.[27] Following Schnabel, Pédech gives πολιορκεῖν this meaning here.[28] But the cross-reference to III.16.7–17.1 shows that Polybius here refers to the siege, not to the final assault. Moreover, there would still be chronological problems. The siege of Saguntum lasted eight months.[29] From III.15.13–16.1 it is clear that when the Romans decided to send Aemilius Paullus to Illyria, they had not yet heard of Hannibal's attack on Saguntum. Aemilius and Hannibal both set out simultaneously (III.16.7–17.1). Pédech, however, having dated the assault on Saguntum before 12 August (when his six-monthly period ends), cannot date its fall later than September; equally he has to make the beginning of the siege coincide with Aemilius' departure for Illyria (which cannot precede his entry upon the consulship for 219). On the assumption that the Roman year coincided with Julian reckoning at this time, and that the consular year began on the Ides of March,[30] he therefore concludes: ‘If Aemilius Paullus set out about 1 March (since he entered office on the Ides of March, he could not set out earlier), Hannibal did not march against Saguntum before February, and he did not capture it before September.’ This seems to confuse the Ides and the Kalends. Aemilius Paullus could not leave before 15 (not 1) March; consequently Hannibal set out against Saguntum in mid-March, not February. Pédech dates the march on Saguntum to February so as to include it within the six-monthly period

---

[21] v.40.1ff.   [22] v.63ff.

[23] IV.60.3.   [24] IV.60.4.

[25] IV.57.1.

[26] *Cf.* IV.56.1 for a similar lead into the war between Mithridates and Sinope.

[27] See my *Commentary* (n. 2) 2.120 (on IX.3.2); K.-E. Petzold, *Studien zur Methode des Polybios und zu ihrer historischen Auswertung* (Munich, 1969) 132 n. 1.

[28] Schnabel, *Klio* 20 (1926) 114; Pédech, *op. cit.* (n. 6) 468.

[29] See above, n. 11.

[30] Pédech, *op. cit.* (n. 6) 469 n. 216

ending on 13 February. This is hardly reconcilable with ‖ Polybius' statement that Hannibal left New Carthage and Aemilius set out for Illyria ὑπὸ τὴν ὡραίαν (III.16.7). Furthermore,[31] it is not certain that the consuls of 219 entered office on 15 March. This was so for 217 and Mommsen[32] put the change from 1 May in 222. But it could have occurred in 218, thus invalidating Pédech's calculations for 219 based on 15 March (or 1 March). Nor is it possible[33] to determine which years at this time were intercalary, nor how closely the Roman and the Julian years coincided. Probability is against the Romans' having sent their forces across the Adriatic in March; still less will Hannibal have left New Carthage in February. The rivers would be swollen and neither month is ὑπὸ τὴν ὡραίαν. But on Pédech's scheme the siege of Saguntum must start at the *beginning* of February and its *fall* occur at the end of September – about six weeks after the assault began. These assumptions seem fragile.

Other events in the synchronism provide problems for Pédech's theory. The Pithom stele[34] dates the agreement made after the battle of Raphia to October 217, two years and two months after the Ptolemaic generals defected. This brings one to August 219, and the warlike preparations mentioned follow that date. Only the tightest reckoning, therefore, can bring them within the six-monthly period ending 12 August 219. Lycurgus' attack on the Athenaeum cannot be independently dated; and, as I have indicated, the Rhodian–Byzantine war is not strictly part of the synchronism. Pédech[35] argues that it is, but that assumption is not without difficulty. According to IV.48.1–3, once Rhodes had declared war, the Byzantines sent envoys to Attalus and Achaeus requesting help. Achaeus had recently (προσφάτως) assumed the royal title; and V.57.5 indicates that this was in summer 220. Since the Rhodians sent ships to Crete before winter 220/19, their war with Byzantium was probably over by then;[36] Schmitt[37] has argued convincingly that the number of events to be fitted in before the winter suggests that Achaeus took the royal title in early summer 220.[38] Consequently, the Rhodian–Byzantine War cannot have broken out within ‖ the period 14 February–12 August 219, as Pédech's theory requires.

---

[31] See R. M. Errington, *Latomus* 29 (1970) 54–5.

[32] T. Mommsen, *Römische Chronologie bis auf Cäsar*[2] (Berlin, 1859) 102; *Römisches Staatsrecht*[3] (3 vols., Leipzig, 1887–8) 1.599.

[33] A. K. Michels, *The calendar of the Roman Republic* (Princeton, 1967) 167f.

[34] See my *Commentary* (n. 2) 1.611–13 (on V.83).

[35] *Op. cit.* (n. 6) 469

[36] IV.53.1; *cf.* B. Niese, *Geschichte der griechischen und makedonischen Staaten* (Gotha, 1893–1903) 3. 383 n. 5.

[37] H. H. Schmitt, *Untersuchungen zur Geschichte Antiochos des Grossen und seiner Zeit* (Wiesbaden, 1964) 114.

[38] Not in autumn (as in my *Commentary* (n. 2) 1.502 (on IV.48.12)).

III

The 'primary event' of Polybius' third synchronism (IV.66.7–67.1) is Philip's dispatch of Macedonian troops home for the fruit-harvest (ὀπώρα), hence August/September 219.[39] Philip spent the rest of the summer in Thessaly.[40] Three other events followed: (a) Aemilius Paullus' return from Illyria and triumph; (b) Hannibal's dismissal of his army to winter quarters after taking Saguntum; (c) the Roman dispatch of envoys to Carthage to demand the surrender of Hannibal, following the news of the fall of Saguntum, and Roman war-preparations after the consular elections for 218. Immediately afterwards Polybius states that the first year of Olympiad 140 was drawing to a close and Dorimachus was elected general in Aetolia. This remark is an embarrassment if one supposes the synchronism to be closely related to the first half of Ol. 140.2; Pédech therefore argues[41] that it is not part of the synchronism, but serves only 'to take up the thread of Greek history which Polybius was anticipating'. This seems unlikely.[42] If the synchronisms are to help the reader, Dorimachus' election is an obvious point of orientation, like that of Scopas (autumn 220),[43] of the younger Aratus (spring 219),[44] and of Eperatus (spring 218).[45] To exclude it from the synchronism of IV.66.8–10 seems arbitrary, especially as it is one of the few events here mentioned with a close chronological relationship to the return home of the Macedonian troops.

The date of neither Aemilius' return from Illyria nor his triumph is known for certain; III.19.12, ληγούσης ἤδη τῆς θερείας, furnishes a *terminus post quem*[46] but the triumph may have been later. It is not recorded in the *Fasti*, but even after the beginning of the consular year changed from 1 May to 15 March, February, the intercalary month, and early March remained the favourite months for triumphing. Aemilius' triumph was probably not celebrated before December 219.[47] In view of ληγούσης...θερείας Pédech puts it in ‖ October;[48] and Werner,[49] closely equating it with the ὀπώρας συγκομιδή in Macedonia (which he takes to be the corn harvest), puts it in August. The latter certainly, the former probably, is too early.

Pédech assumes that the synchronism of IV.66.7–67.1 mentions events occurring between 13 August 219 and 7 February 218. He argues[50] that the Ides of March 217 fell shortly after the eclipse mentioned by Livy (XXII.1.4–9), and identifiable with that of 11 February; hence if 218 was intercalary, the

---

[39] *Cf.* Pédech, *op. cit.* (n. 6) 458 n. 154.

[40] IV.66.7, τὸ λοιπὸν μέρος τοῦ θέρους (hardly a technical term, as Pédech, *loc. cit.*, asserts).

[41] *Op. cit.* (n. 6) 469.

[42] *Cf.* Eucken, *op. cit.* (n. 16) 105 n. 3.

[43] IV.28.1.   [44] IV.37.1.

[45] V.1.1.

[46] See my *Commentary* (n. 2) 1.331–2 (on III.20.1), rejecting Schnabel's view, *Klio* 20 (1926) 114, that this passage implies that Aemilius triumphed after news of the fall of Saguntum reached Rome.

[47] *Cf.* Sumner, *PACA* 9 (1966) 9–10.   [48] *Op. cit.* (n. 6) 469.

[49] *Op. cit.* (n. 13) 52.   [50] *Op. cit.* (n. 6) 469.

Ides of March 218 may have fallen a little after 1 February (Julian), and so in time for the consuls of 218 to assume office within the six-monthly period ending 7 February 218. Unfortunately, as mentioned above,[51] it cannot be determined which years were intercalary at this time.

The fall of Saguntum creates no problems; this and Hannibal's winter quarters, eight months after the first attack (III.17.9), fall in late December 219 or early January 218. But the date of the Roman embassy to Carthage is controversial. If the names of the envoys in Livy are genuine, and M. Livius and L. Aemilius are, as seems likely, the consuls of 219,[52] they cannot have left Rome before 15 March 218 (if the consular year began then).[53] Summing up, it is difficult to accommodate all the events of this synchronism within the period 13 August 219 to 7 February 218. Read without preconceptions, IV.66.7–67.1 gives the impression of being at the end of the campaigning season of 219 and of the first year of the Olympiad (which Polybius usually interprets as running on to the end of the campaigning period);[54] but Polybius then goes on to mention other later events only loosely connected and occurring in later months – the fall of Saguntum, news of this at Rome, Hannibal's winter quarters, and the Roman elections and embassy to Carthage. Pédech rightly underlines the long period covered by these events, which form no strict synchronism at all: but whether his own explanation is valid is another matter. ‖

IV

Book v opens with a 'primary event', the end of the younger Aratus' *strategia* and Eperatus' succession; Dorimachus was still Aetolian general (his election having been mentioned in the previous synchronism).[55] The date is the rising of the Pleiades, hence towards the end of May 218.[56] Three other events are contemporaneous (v.1.1–4). Hannibal, ἀρχομένης τῆς θερείας, having set out from New Carthage and crossed the Ebro, was beginning his journey to Italy; the Romans were sending the consuls to Africa and Spain; and Antiochus and Ptolemy were beginning to make war on each other. The first of these fits Pédech's scheme. The words ἀρχομένης τῆς θερείας clearly refers to the date when Hannibal set off northwards after crossing the Ebro.[57] In my *Commentary*,[58]

---

[51] See above, n. 33.

[52] Livy XXI.18.1; M. Gelzer, *Kleine Schriften* 3 (Wiesbaden, 1964) 211, thinks the names untrustworthy, and Sumner, *PACA* 9 (1966) 24 n. 63, questions the presence of the consuls of 219 on this embassy.

[53] See above, n. 31. Sumner, *PACA* 9 (1966) 11, argues that news of the fall of Saguntum reached Rome in January or February and that the embassy was not sent until the new consuls had taken office – on 3/4 March (Julian) on his calculations; leaving on 5 March (Julian) it would deliver the ultimatum *c.* 15 March (Julian). This is feasible, but hypothetical; *cf.* Errington, *Latomus* 29 (1970) 54ff.

[54] See my *Commentary* (n. 2) 1.36–7.   [55] IV.67.1.

[56] See above, n. 20.

[57] According to III.34.6 Hannibal left winter quarters ὑπὸ τὴν ἐαρινὴν ὥραν.

[58] *Commentary* (n. 2) 1.365 (on III.34.6).

assuming that he could not be on the Alpine pass after the third week in September, I calculated that he left New Carthage about the end of April, implying an Ebro crossing in May. This could be described as 'the beginning of summer', for in IV.37.3 the same time of the year is ἤδη τῆς θερείας ἐνισταμένης. But Proctor, in the most recent study of Hannibal's march,[59] makes Hannibal leave Emporiae in mid-September, to reach the Rhône at the end of September and the Po valley in mid-November. These dates fit Polybius' statement[60] that Hannibal was on the pass at the setting of the Pleiades (early November). Whether a crossing so late in the year was feasible is problematical. Either date, however, allows the Ebro crossing to fall within the six months ending on 2 August 218.

According to III.41.2 the consuls were sent to Spain and Sicily ἐπὶ τὴν ὡραίαν,[61] presumably 'in the campaigning season', a vague phrase. Scipio coincided with Hannibal at the Rhône crossing, and if Hannibal reached the Po valley at the end of September, he must have crossed the Rhône towards the end of August: hence Scipio left Rome a little before mid-August.[62] Whether his colleague left earlier is unknown; Polybius suggests that they left simultaneously. This hardly fits into Pédech's six-monthly period ending ‖ 2 August 218; and if Proctor's dates are right, the coincidence at the Rhône was at the end of September, creating an even greater discrepancy. Pédech's explanation of his scheme at this point is unsatisfactory. 'If Hannibal arrived in Italy towards the setting of the Pleiades (end of October),' he writes,[63] 'he set out at the end of April.' The consuls were sent to their provinces later, since the passage of the Ebro was then already known at Rome; and Pédech uses Asconius' dating for the foundation of Placentia as *pridie kal. Iun.*[64] to date the consuls' departure about that time. But this will not do, for it rests on an unusual Julian equivalent (Oct. 20/24) for the morning setting of the Pleiades, normally dated to early November,[65] and it treats this as the date of Hannibal's arrival in the Po valley, although according to Polybius this is when Hannibal was on the pass, a week earlier. Pédech also makes the fifteen days spent crossing the Alps additional to the five months Polybius allows for the journey from New Carthage to the Po valley, though clearly they are included. Finally, if Hannibal, setting out at the end of April, reached the Po valley at the end of October, his journey took not five, but six months. Given the usual dating for the setting of the Pleiades, however, Hannibal must have started out, not at the end of April, but at the end of May or even in early June, with

---

[59] Sir Dennis Proctor, *Hannibal's march in history* (Oxford, 1971) 13–75.

[60] III.54.1.

[61] ὑπό edd., until Büttner-Wobst restored the MSS reading.

[62] See the calculations in my *Commentary* (n. 2) 1.377 (on III.41.2).

[63] *Op. cit.* (n. 6) 470.

[64] Asc. *Pis.* 3; this passage is suspect evidence, however, since *Iun.* is Madvig's emendation of the MS *Ian.*

[65] 10 Nov. (Euctemon and Callippus), 11 Nov. (Hipparchus), 14 Nov. (Eudoxus), 20–24 Oct. (Aelius, Clodius Tuscus and Columella); *cf.* Pédech, *op. cit.* (n. 6) 450 and 470 n. 219.

obvious repercussions on the date of Scipio's arrival at the Rhône and so on that of his departure from Rome.

The consuls then seem to have left Rome well into summer 218, and after 2 August, when Pédech's six-monthly period terminates. In III.41.2 Polybius is not apparently conscious of Scipio's late departure, and in v.1.1–4 there is no difficulty if he is merely indicating the parallel actions of Hannibal and the Romans in the campaigning season of 218. But on Pédech's hypothesis the dates established create serious problems. In v.68.1 Polybius confirms that the preparations of Aetolia and Ptolemy were in spring (συνῆπτε . . . τὰ τῆς ἐαρινῆς ὥρας);[66] this causes no difficulties. ‖

V

The synchronism at the end of summer 218 (v.29.5–8) is quickly dealt with. The 'primary event' is Philip's dismissal of his troops and their dispatch through Thessaly; simultaneously Hannibal was encamped opposite the Romans in the Po valley. Antiochus having seized most of Coele-Syria went into winter quarters, and Lycurgus of Sparta escaped to Aetolia. Hannibal's presence in the Po valley has already been discussed.[67] Antiochus' winter quarters cannot be dated more closely than the end of the campaigning season;[68] and Lycurgus' flight is not mentioned elsewhere. Polybius here omits to mention the Aetolian elections; but in the next chapter he refers to the Achaean demoralisation which ended with Aratus' election as general the following year (30.7, τῆς θερείας ἐναρχομένης). Thus he keeps the readers in touch with the chronology of the confederations; the slight irregularity in the form of reference matters less if the synchronisms are not held to constitute a highly formal system.

The next synchronism also shows some irregularity since the date proper (at v.105.3) is anticipated with a subsidiary synchronism (v.101.3), in which Philip's siege of Phthiotic Thebes coincides with the battle of Trasimene. The reason is clear. It was the news of Trasimene that led Philip to summon the conference to Naupactus, at which the events of Greece, Italy and Africa first began to be intertwined. Polybius is therefore concerned to establish the relative chronology, even if this involves introducing a subsidiary synchronism. In v.105.3 he says that 'all these events – Trasimene, Raphia, and the treaty of the Achaeans and Philip with the Aetolians – took place in the third year of Ol. 140'. From then on – and precisely from the conference at Naupactus – events of the *oecumene* began to be interconnected. This conference thus constitutes the 'primary event' (it is in fact the only Greek event mentioned) and the purpose of the synchronisms was to indicate 'at what times in this Olympiad and contemporaneously with ‖ what events in Greece each episode elsewhere began and ended'.[69]

---

[66] On this phrase see Pédech, *op. cit.* (n. 6) 464.

[68] v.71.12.

[67] Above, pp. 304ff.

[69] v.31.3; see above, p. 298.

Trasimene was probably fought in June 217: Ovid (*Fasti* vi.767–8) dates it 21 June and Philip heard of it at Argos at the Nemean games in July. Uncertainty about the Julian equivalents would however permit a few weeks' error either way.[70] The Pithom stele[71] shows Ptolemy setting out for Coele-Syria on 13 June (1 Pachons), and Polybius[72] confirms the statement there that Raphia was fought ten days later, on 22 June (10 Pachons). The conference of Naupactus must have been round about August, and the 'lateness' of this synchronism is due to the importance of that conference in Polybius' scheme.

VI

The autumn synchronism of 217 follows shortly afterwards (v.108.9–10). Its 'primary event' is typical: Philip, after campaigning in Dassaretia, sent his troops into winter quarters. Hannibal was going into winter quarters at Gerunium; and the Romans appointed Varro and Aemilius Paullus consuls (two events also closely linked at III.105.11–106.1). The final synchronism (v.109.4–6) has for its 'primary event' Philip's setting out round Malea with his fleet, ἀρχομένης τῆς θερείας. His arrival near Cephallenia and Leucas coincided with Antiochus' crossing of Taurus;[73] and Pédech argues[74] reasonably that the reference to the Roman fleet off Lilybaeum and (at v.110.10) to the imminence of Cannae provides a correlation with Italian events, while Prusias' crushing of the Gauls κατὰ τούτους τοὺς χρόνους (v.111.1–7) fills out the synchronism with a reference to Asia. Antiochus' crossing of Taurus cannot be dated more closely than spring 216,[75] and Philip will have sailed as soon as the weather allowed. The fleet at Lilybaeum creates a problem. According to III.106.7, the consuls of 216 were to effect the recall τοῦ παραχειμάζοντος ἐν τῷ Λιλυβαίῳ στόλου. Pédech[76] would apply παραχειμάζειν to the whole period of naval seasonal inactivity, observing that 'the fleet ‖ could still worry Philip in May'; but Thiel has argued[77] from Livy that Otacilius had 50 ships at Lilybaeum independent of Servilius' squadron and if that were so, it could have been these that alarmed Philip in 216.

VII

It remains to consider how far Pédech's theory explains the synchronisms and how far it is consonant with their function in the *Histories*. The following considerations seem to me to weigh against it:

(i) Polybius nowhere suggests that his synchronisms are closely linked with

[70] See Errington, *Latomus* 29 (1970) 55.
[71] See above, n. 34.
[72] v.80.3, πεμπταῖος; 82.1, πένθ' ἡμέρας.
[73] *Cf.* v.107.4.
[74] *Op. cit.* (n. 6) 471–2.
[75] O. Leuze, *Hermes* 58 (1923) 188 n. 1.
[76] *Op. cit.* (n. 6) 472 n. 229.
[77] J. H. Thiel, *Studies on the history of Roman sea-power in Republican times* (Amsterdam, 1946) 57–8, *cf.* 46ff.

Olympiad years, still less half years. In the whole of Books III to V only twelve passages mention Olympiads or Olympiad years. Of these, five (III.1.11, III.118.10, IV.1.3, V.30.8, V.111.9) simply refer to Ol. 140; one (IV.14.9)[78] mentions the point in Greek events at which that Olympiad began; two (III.16.7, IV.26.1) date Aemilius' expedition to Illyria and the symmachic decree launching the Social War in the first year of Ol. 140; one (IV.67.1) mentions that that year was drawing to a close; two (IV.28.5, V.105.3) stress the συμπλοκή of the various theatres in the third year of the Olympiad; finally V.31.3–5 is the discussion already mentioned of the special use of synchronisms for this Olympiad. Nowhere is there any reference to half Olympiad years.

(ii) To render his system plausible Pédech must demonstrate that every date in every synchronism fits his half-year periods. Many do, some are dubious, and two do not. These are Hannibal's ὁρμή on Saguntum which, if taken literally, cannot be before 13 February 219, and Scipio's departure for Spain, which cannot be before 2 August 218.

(iii) Polybius indicates (IV.28.2ff.) that the synchronisms are intended to orientate the reader on the chronological relationship of events occurring in theatres not yet organically connected. But a system treating as simultaneous events which can be as much as six months apart, simply because they fall within an arbitrarily defined 'half Olympiad year' – a wholly artificial concept – could only confuse a reader. ‖

(iv) Not only are such 'half Olympiad years' unhelpful to the reader (who is never even told of their existence), but one can hardly conceive how Polybius could determine their beginning and end or assign events to them. An Olympiad was the period between two celebrations of the games; but how could anyone determine at what point in the intermediate summers year one became year two, etc.? Pédech claims[79] that Polybius used a luni-solar *octaeteris* – an eight-year cycle covering two Olympiads – and divided up the Olympiad years by lunar months; it is on this basis that he assigns Julian dates to his sixth-month periods. The *octaeteris* is known from Geminus and elsewhere; but it is highly unlikely that any Greek state actually used it,[80] and there is no evidence suggesting that Polybius took any account of it. For how could events, perhaps dated to a Roman month (which might or might not be part of an intercalated year) be equated with anything so elusive as a 'half Olympiad year'? Faced with a narrative based, for example, on summer campaigns and winter quarters, how could any historian divide it up into such sub-divisions of the Olympiad? As I hope to have shown, the Julian equivalents are quite uncertain in view of the unknown variables.

Pédech has done well to draw attention to these synchronisms, and to the

---

[78] Unless this strange sentence is a gloss inserted in the text; see my *Commentary* (n. 2) 1.462 (on IV.14.9).

[79] *Op. cit.* (n. 6) 456–61.

[80] E. J. Bickerman, *Chronology of the ancient world* (London, 1968) 29; M. P. Nilsson, *RE* 18.2 (1937) 'Oktaeteris', cols. 2387–92.

fact that there are two for each year. But that, I suggest, is not because Olympiad years have been neatly bisected, but because Polybius is describing campaigns on various unconnected fronts which usually began in spring, or thereabouts, and ended in autumn, or thereabouts. Hence, as he says,[81] he tries to provide a clear chronology for this Olympiad by indicating the beginning and end of various actions and putting them into relation with what was happening in Greece at the same time. Of the eight 'primary events', five refer to Philip V entering or leaving winter quarters,[82] two are the entry of Achaean generals into office,[83] and one is the Peace of Naupactus;[84] other synchronised events include four references to the election of Aetolian generals.[85] This suggests that Polybius has used a simple method of relating events elsewhere to ‖ those most familiar to his primarily Greek (and even Achaean) readers. The basic narrative is the Social War in mainland Greece. The important thing is clarity – knowing which year one is in – since events are not being described theatre by theatre within each Olympiad year, as they would be later. There is nothing esoteric about it: the mechanism largely exploits a convenient coincidence – that at this time Achaean generals took office in spring and Aetolian in autumn.

VIII

One difficulty remains: undoubtedly many of the events mentioned are only approximately contemporary. But that is perhaps not serious. If the purpose of the synchronisms is in general[86] to mark the beginning and end of campaigning seasons and to ensure that the reader is in the right year, it does not matter overmuch if, for instance, Antiochus' invasion of Coele-Syria after August 219 is correlated with Hannibal's siege of Saguntum in April–May of that year, or if Hannibal's entry into winter quarters after the fall of Saguntum, probably in January 218, was related to the return home of Macedonian troops the previous August–September. The point is that that synchronism marks the end of operations for the year we call 219. In fact, as far as we can tell, serious discrepancies are rare. I have already discussed the problem of Hannibal's ὁρμή against Saguntum. There is the stretching of the events of late 219 to include Hannibal's winter quarters, the election of next year's consuls and the sending of Roman envoys to declare war on Carthage; there is the dispatch of the consuls of 218 to their provinces as late as August. And that is all. None of these is likely to confuse the reader, especially in view of the many other chronological indications interspersed in the narrative.

---

[81] v.31.3–5; see above, p. 298.
[82] IV.27.9–10, 66.7, v.29.5, 108.9, 109.4.
[83] IV.37.1, v.1.1.   [84] v.105.3.
[85] IV.27.1, 37.2, 67.1, v.1.2.
[86] The synchronism with the Peace of Naupactus performs a slightly different function; for this marked the beginning of the συμπλοκή of events in different parts of the *oecumene*. See above, n. 4.

Synchronisms in Polybius IV and V

Synchron- isms	References	Events: 'primary events' italicised	Dates	Pédech's 'six-month' periods
I	iv.27.1–28.1	1. Scopas' election in Aetolia	late Sept. 220	(Ol. 140.1 (I)) 26 July 220–13 Feb. 219
		2. *Philip's return to Macedon*	autumn 220	
		3. *Hannibal ἐποιεῖτο τὴν ὁρμὴν on Saguntum*	April/May 219(?) [error?] more probably autumn 220	
II	iv.37.1–7	1. *Aratus Jr succeeds his father as Achaean general*	late May 219	(Ol. 140.1 (II)) 14 Feb.–12 Aug. 219
		2. Scopas half way through his year of office	do.	
		3. Hannibal ἐνεχείρει...πολιορκεῖν Saguntum	April/May 219 (?)	
		4. L. Aemilius sent to Illyria	April/May 219 (?)	
		5. Antiochus about to invade Coele-Syria and Ptolemy to resist him	after Aug. 219	
		6. Lycurgus besieging Athenaeum	?	
		7. Achaeans gathering mercenaries	? (May?)	
		8. Philip moving from Macedonia	spring 219	
		9. Rhodian war on Byzantium	summer 220]	
III	[iv.37.8 iv.66.7–67.1	1. *Philip sends his troops home for fruit-harvest and goes to spend the rest of the summer at Larisa*	Aug./Sept. 219	(Ol. 140.2 (I)) 13 Aug. 219–7 Feb. 218
		2. Aemilius Paullus returns from Illyria and triumphs	end of summer 219?	
		3. Hannibal, after fall of Saguntum, goes into winter quarters	? Dec. 219/Jan. 218	
		4. Romans send envoys to Carthage	? after 15 March 218	

general

IV	v.1.1-4			
		1. *Eperatus succeeds Aratus as Achaean general*	late May 218	(Ol. 140.2 (II)) 8 Feb.–2 Aug. 218
		2. Dorimachus still Aetolian general	late May 218	
		3. Hannibal begins his journey to Italy	May 218 (?) (or later)	
		4. Consuls setting off for Africa and Spain	mid-Aug. 218 (?) or later	
		5. Antiochus and Ptolemy beginning their war	spring 218	
V	v.29.5-8			
		1. *Philip sends his troops home for the winter*	autumn 218 (?)	(Ol. 140.3 (I)) 3 Aug. 218–11 Feb. 217
		2. Hannibal and Romans encamped in Po Valley	Oct. (or Nov.) 218	
		3. Antiochus' winter quarters	autumn 218 (?)	
		4. Lycurgus escaped to Aetolia	?	
VI	[v.101.3]	Philip's siege of Phthiotic Thebes contemporary with Trasimene	June 217 (?)]	(Ol. 140.3 (II)) 12 Feb.–20 Aug. 217
	v.105.3	1. *Peace of Naupactus*	Aug. 217	
		2. Trasimene	June 217?	
		3. Raphia	22 June 217	
VII	v.108.9-10	1. *Philip sends his troops into winter quarters*	end of campaigning season 217	(Ol. 140.4 (I)) 21 Aug. 217–14 Feb. 216
		2. Hannibal winters at Gerunium	do.	
		3. Romans appoint Varro and Aemilius coss. for 216	?	
VIII	v.109.4-6	1. *Philip sails round Malea to Cephallenia* ἀρχομένης τῆς θερείας	'early summer' 216	(Ol. 140.4 (II)) 15 Feb.–10 Aug. 216
		2. Antiochus crosses Taurus against Achaeus	do.	
		3. Roman fleet at Lilybaeum	do.	
	[v.111.1]	4. Prusias destroys the Galatians	?]	

Partly because his public was primarily Greek and partly of course because the events of the Illyrian War and the Hannibalic War down to Cannae had already been described in Book III, the synchronisms had to be pegged to Greek events. For mainland Greeks the movement of Macedonian ‖ troops and the familiar electoral arrangements of the two confederacies provided the basis for a very simple, rough and ready, pragmatic device for orientating Polybius' readers in this exceptional Olympiad.

20

SYMPLOKE: ITS ROLE IN POLYBIUS' HISTORIES*

Polybius was not the first historian who claimed to write 'universal' history, as he admits;[1] but the only one of his predecessors whose claim he concedes is Ephorus, and Ephorus in fact did not produce a history of the whole world, but merely combined a number of separate accounts of the Greek states in a single work.[2] Polybius' *Histories* were universal in a different sense, for they dealt with a period in which (he tells us) events themselves had begun to interlock; and in his discussion of that process a great part is played by the concept of συμπλοκή. It is this concept and its relevance to Polybius' idea of universal history that I want to examine here. I do so in the hope that the subject may seem not inappropriate as a tribute to Adam Parry, whose keen interest in problems of literary composition was well known, and who had recently turned his attention to the field of Greek history.

I

Clearly Polybius attached great importance to the idea of συμπλοκή. 'It is only from the interconnection of all the events one with another and from their comparison (συμπλοκῆς καὶ παραθέσεως), and from their resemblances and differences, that a man can obtain his object and, thanks to a clear view of these matters, can derive both profit and pleasure from history.'[3] This συμπλοκή, this linking together of events throughout the inhabited world, is not something available to all historians at will. On the contrary, it is characteristic only of a particular period, that with which Polybius is himself concerned. Previously the doings of the ‖ world had been, as it were, scattered;[4] but from the 140th Olympiad onwards the affairs of Italy and Africa were

* [*YClS* 24 (1975) 197–212]

[1] *Cf.* v.33.2: several other writers have boasted that they have written τὰ καθόλου, and on a vaster scale than anyone else.

[2] See on this E. Mioni, *Polibio* (Padua, 1949) 23.

[3] 1.4.11; as Schweighaeuser points out, κατοπτεύσας, 'getting a clear view', is probably to be taken with the 'resemblances and differences'.

[4] 1.3.3: this passage is unfortunately marred by a lacuna, which has, however, been convincingly restored by J. M. Moore, who reads (*CQ* 16 (1966) 245–7), διὰ δὲ ⟨τοῦ⟩το καὶ τὰς ἐπιβολὰς ‖ ⟨αὐτῶν ἔτι⟩ δὲ συντελείας ‖ αὐτ⟨οτελεῖς εἶναι,⟩ καὶ κα|τὰ το⟨ῦτο δὴ διαφέρ⟩ειν ἕ|καστα ⟨τῶν πεπραγμ⟩ένων. This indicates that prior to the 140th Olympiad events throughout the *oecumene*, being scattered, were linked together neither in their beginnings nor in their outcome.

313

joined together (συμπλέκεσθαι) with those of Greece and Asia, all leading to a single end (πρὸς ἓν γίνεσθαι τέλος τὴν ἀναφορὰν ἁπάντων).[5] The First Illyrian War (229/8) might seem to have been an anticipation of this; but no, that was only an ἐπιπλοκή, a contact, not a genuine involvement.[6] But from the 140th Olympiad (220/216) history had become a unified whole (σωματοειδής).[7]

At first sight the metaphors contained in the words συμπλοκή and σωματοειδής may seem incompatible; but I doubt if this is really so. It has been argued by Pédech that Polybius uses the word συμπλοκή because of its 'philosophical implications'.[8] As he points out, it forms part of the vocabulary of Leucippus and Democritus, who use it to describe the conjunction of the first elements.[9] But this is a secondary, derived meaning of a word which in its primary sense means 'a weaving or plaiting together'; and it is probably this meaning, frequently to be found in Plato in a metaphorical sense,[10] that Polybius intends here. The συμπλοκή of events is thought of as being like the weaving of a fabric; and inasmuch as the historian in his narrative produces a 'universal history' which copies the macrocosm of real events,[11] it is perhaps not too imaginative to detect a resemblance between the movement of the shuttle as it passes backwards and forwards across the warp and ‖ the historian's pen as he passes from area to area, describing the events of one year after another, and so composing the fabric of his written history.[12] Alternatively the stress of the metaphor may be not so much on the process of weaving as on the finished fabric. Or is it perhaps concerned with both? For it is after all the process of narration which produces the finished *Histories*. Whatever the exact nuance, this interpretation of συμπλοκή as referring to the interweaving of threads finds some support in a passage of Book III,[13] in which Polybius speaks of his finished work in forty books as easy to acquire and read, since they are 'as it were woven together in an unbroken series'.[14]

σωματοειδής, on the other hand, though it can indicate what is corporeal

---

[5] I.3.4.   [6] II.12.7.

[7] See F. W. Walbank, *Polybius* (Berkeley-Los Angeles, 1972) 67-8. K. Lorenz. *Untersuchungen zum Geschichtswerk des Polybios* (Stuttgart, 1931) 17-18, compares the terminology in which Polybius describes the conditions of early human society, in which scattered individuals combine to form social units (XI.5); the comparison seems to me forced and unconvincing.

[8] P. Pédech, *La méthode historique de Polybe* (Paris, 1964) 507.

[9] *Cf.* H. Diels, *Vorsokr.*[7], II.70 n. (Simplicius, *in Phys.* p. 446, Diels); 74 (Hippol. *Haer.* I.12); 75 (Arist. *Cael.* III.4, 303 a 7); see Pédech, *op. cit.* (n. 8) 507 n. 66.

[10] See for instance *Polit.* 281 a, 306, etc.

[11] The weaver is presumably Tyche.

[12] Clearly to press the resemblances too far would be absurd. One obvious difference is that the shuttle goes *boustrophedon*, whereas the historian's path is a cyclical one, completing all the theatres of activity for one Olympiad year, and then starting afresh with Italy in the next.

[13] III.32.2; this passage implies that forty books were planned, but not necessarily that they had already been published; see the note in my *Historical commentary on Polybius* (3 vols., Oxford, 1957-79) on III.1-5.

[14] κατὰ μίτον means 'thread by thread, in due order, continuously', and the sense here is that Polybius' forty books lie side by side, like the threads of a warp, which are woven (ἐξυφασμένας) into a single fabric by means of the weft. See my note *ad loc.* in my *Commentary*.

as opposed to what is unsubstantial – for example, an epiphany of Apollo[15] – is clearly used by Polybius as a technical term taken from Hellenistic literary theory and derived ultimately from the Platonic and Aristotelian concept of the unity of a literary work;[16] it means 'forming a unified whole', and since, as I have just pointed out, a literary work can be envisaged by Polybius as (metaphorically) woven,[17] there is no inconsistency between σωματοειδής and συμπλοκή.

II

The precise point of time at which the συμπλοκή began to show ‖ itself in the history of Rome is indicated in an important chapter in Book IV,[18] where Polybius explains that Ol. 140 opened with separate events in Italy, Greece and Asia, and with wars breaking out in those areas quite independently of each other, but that towards the end of the Olympiad these wars had conclusions 'common to all' (τὰς συντελείας κοινάς), and at that point events became interconnected (συνεπλάκησαν) and began to tend towards a single end (πρὸς ἕν τέλος ἤρξαντο τὴν ἀναφορὰν ἔχειν).[19] This development in historical events finds its appropriate reflection in Polybius' procedure as a historian; for by giving a separate account of the various wars down to the moment of combination he is able (so he says) to make the beginnings clearer and the συμπλοκή itself plain, and so to show 'when and how and for what reasons it came about'. That done, and the point of interconnection having been reached, he will proceed to compose a common history about all three areas,[20] in which he will deal with events all together 'following their chronology.[21] But up to that point (which is defined more precisely as occurring in the third year of the 140th Olympiad, *i.e.* 217 B.C.)[22] he proposes to treat each theatre separately, merely using synchronisms with the events of the Hannibalic War (which he has already related in Book III).[23] This will render his narrative easy to follow and more likely to create an impression on

[15] *Cf.* Ephorus, *FGH* 70 F 31 (b); for a similar meaning on a *tabula defixionis* from Egypt see P. Collart, *RPh* 56 (1930) 250 (quoted in LSJ *s.v.* σωματοειδής).

[16] See Lorenz, *op. cit.* (n. 7) 87 n. 92, 99 n. 227, and my *Commentary* (n. 13) on I.3.4. Paton in the Loeb edition mistranslates σωματοειδής as 'lifelike' both in I.3.4 and in XIV.12.5; in both passages it means 'a unified whole'.

[17] See above, n. 14.

[18] IV.28.3–4; *cf.* V.31.4–5.

[19] *Cf.* I.3.4 (quoted above, pp. 313f.).

[20] IV.28.4, κοινὴν ποιήσασθαι περὶ πάντων τὴν ἱστορίαν; Paton translates περὶ πάντων 'about all three wars', *i.e.* the Social War, the Hannibalic War and the Fourth Syrian War. But this is nonsense, since the συμπλοκή came in 217 at a time when two of these wars came to an end. περὶ πάντων means 'about all the events in Italy, Greece and Asia'.

[21] IV.28.5, τοῖς καιροῖς ἀκολουθοῦντες. Polybius means that he will treat events year by year, and within each year area by area; see below, pp. 317f. and v.31.5.

[22] IV.28.5.

[23] I have discussed these synchronisms in *Polis and imperium: studies in honour of Edward Togo Salmon* (Toronto, 1974) 59–80 [above, pp. 298–312].

his readers (εὐπαρακολούθητος... καὶ καταπληκτική).[24] Polybius' concern to stimulate his readers' interest is a subject to which I shall revert below.[25]

Polybius is not content to date the beginning of the universal ‖ συμπλοκή to the year 217; in a passage in the fifth book[26] he tells us that it was at the conference called to Naupactus by Philip V to bring to an end the war between the Aetolian League and the Hellenic Alliance that the affairs of Greece, Italy and Africa were first linked together (τὰς... πράξεις... τοῦτο τὸ διαβούλιον συνέπλεξε πρῶτον). Attributing such ecumenical importance to this somewhat parochial peace conference involves Polybius in some slight difficulty; for previously (in 1.3.4 and IV.28.4)[27] he has defined the συμπλοκή as linking the affairs of Italy and Africa with those of Greece and Asia, but it is rather hard to find any connection with Asia in the Peace of Naupactus. However, he continues with the assertion that speedily (ταχέως) the same thing happened to the islanders and the people of Asia;[28] 'for those with grievances against Philip and some of Attalus' adversaries no longer turned to the south and east, to Antiochus and Ptolemy, but henceforth looked to the west, some sending embassies to Carthage and others to Rome'.

As we shall see,[29] this emphasis on the sending of embassies is important; but in its general terms Polybius' statement here is much exaggerated.[30] There is no evidence for any appeal to Rome by the islanders or the Greeks of Asia Minor for many years after 217. During the First Macedonian War neutral embassies were sent from Egypt, Rhodes, Chios, Mytilene and Byzantium, to endeavour to persuade the belligerents to make peace – but they did not visit Rome or the Roman forces. We have no knowledge of any islanders or Asian Greeks opposed to Attalus sending an embassy to Carthage;[31] and the earliest Roman embassy to cross the Aegean was dispatched in 200.

There were, it is true, good reasons why the eastern Greeks might no longer have felt able to appeal to Ptolemy or Antiochus. Despite his victory over Antiochus at Raphia, the effect of this battle (which was probably fought about the same time as ‖ Trasimene)[32] was to weaken Ptolemy IV, since in the course of his preparations he had armed the Egyptian μάχιμοι, and this step led to the national revolt which went on into the reign of his successor.[33] As for

---

[24] Cf. v.31.4–5, εὐπαρακολούθητον καὶ σαφῆ; cf. v.31.7 for his stress on clarity.
[25] See below, n. 47.
[26] v.105.4.   [27] See above, nn. 5 and 20.
[28] v.105.6–7.   [29] See below, pp. 320f.
[30] On this see my *Commentary* (n. 13) *ad loc.* and *Polybius* (n. 7) 68–70.
[31] Pédech, *op. cit.* (n. 8) 506, interprets v.105.4–10 to mean that Philip's enemies sent envoys to Rome and the enemies of Attalus approached Carthage; though not specifically stated, this seems likely.
[32] The news of Trasimene led Philip to seek a peace with Aetolia (v.101.6–8). The evidence of the Pithom stele suggests that Raphia was fought on 22 June, while Ovid, *Fasti* 6.767–8, dates Trasimene to 21 June; but uncertainty about intercalation in the Roman calendar means that the Julian equivalent of the latter date could very well be two or three weeks different either way (cf. R. M. Errington, *Latomus* 29 (1970) 55).
[33] Cf. v.107.1–3.

Antiochus III, he was soon involved in a campaign against the pretender Achaeus,[34] which lasted until Achaeus' capture and death at Sardes in 213,[35] and after that undertook his eastern *anabasis*, which was to occupy him from 212 until 205.[36] However, the fact that both kings were to some extent out of the picture is not by itself evidence that anyone in the Aegean area or in Asia Minor saw the Romans as an alternative.

It has been argued by Pédech,[37] following Siegfried,[38] that although there were still no contacts with Asia, Naupactus in fact marks a historical turning point, since what matter to Polybius are not so much actual military and diplomatic contacts as men's thoughts; and from now on by his plan against Rome Philip precipitated the συμπλοκή. This may well be a fair account of how Polybius saw the situation; but it does not really explain how the Greeks of Asia came to be involved in the συμπλοκή from 217 onward, for the acceptance of Siegfried's assertion that for Polybius thoughts as well as actions count as πράξεις[39] does not dispose of the historian's palpably false statement that embassies now began to go backward and forward between Asia Minor and Rome or Carthage.[40] Nor can Polybius' remark be taken as a reference to ‖ exchanges which began from the end of the century, since by that time Antiochus was back in the west and fully active in both war and diplomacy.

III

Thus Polybius' picture of a process of universal συμπλοκή beginning in 217 is not without difficulties when measured against the historical facts known to us. But I want to consider now the structural framework which Polybius set up so as to convey the nature of this συμπλοκή to his readers. Events had to be arranged according to both time and place, when they happened and where they happened, and, as I have already mentioned,[41] this was done by dividing up the continuous process of history into Olympiad years (a device borrowed from Timaeus),[42] and within each year treating the happenings in the various regions in a fixed sequence which was only rarely broken: this sequence[43] related the events of Italy, Sicily, Spain, Africa, Greece and Macedonia, Asia and Egypt in that order.[44] Now any such system is to some extent a compromise

---

[34] v.107.4.

[35] VII.15–18, VIII.15.21.

[36] VIII.23, X.27.1–31.15, X.48.1–49.15, XI.34, XIII.9.

[37] *Op. cit.* (n. 8) 507.

[38] W. Siegfried, *Studien zur geschichtlichen Anschauung des Polybios* (Berlin, 1928) 46.

[39] *Cf.* v.105.4 for πράξεις.

[40] Pédech, *op. cit.* (n. 8) 507, further asserts that Polybius' formulation, which makes 217 the decisive year for the συμπλοκή, is based on a Greek point of view 'which considers the fate of Greece and takes no account of the concept of Roman expansion, which imposes itself upon us today'. This is hard to believe, if one considers the fact that Roman expansion is the main subject of Polybius' *Histories*.

[41] See above, n. 21.   [42] See Walbank, *op. cit.* (n. 7) 101.

[43] XXXII.11.2, τὴν εἰθισμένην τάξιν, ᾗ χρώμεθα παρ' ὅλην τὴν πραγματείαν; *cf.* xv.25.19.

[44] See Walbank, *op. cit.* (n. 7) 103–4, for discussion of this device.

for, as Diodorus (probably echoing Duris of Samos)[45] points out, in reality (ἀλήθεια) events occur simultaneously in different places, whereas history (ἱστορία) is forced to divide them up unnaturally and relate them one after another; it is this, in Duris' opinion, that renders written history an inadequate μίμησις of the real events and causes it to fall short of them in πάθος.[46]

Now this difficulty is one inherent in any process of setting down an account of historical events in narrative form, and the combination of Olympiad years and 'theatres of action' goes some way towards overcoming it. But Polybius' problem (after Ol. 140) was ‖ not merely one of narrating in succession events which in reality occurred simultaneously, but also of bringing out the relationship between separate sets of events which, by definition, were becoming causally more and more integrated, as the συμπλοκή grew. This had to be done, moreover, in such a manner as not only to reflect the true character of the συμπλοκή, but also to rivet his readers' attention – for, as we saw, history should ideally be both easy to follow and arresting (εὐπαρακολούθητος...καὶ καταπληκτική).[47] To achieve this aim was not entirely simple, and not every historian accepted Polybius' solution. Appian, for example, who elected to write a continuous history of each area separately, was to complain that those historians of Rome who included material from all over the world in a single narrative 'frequently took me from Carthage to Spain, and from Spain to Sicily or Macedonia, or to some embassies sent to other peoples or alliances made with them; and they brought me back again to Carthage or Sicily as if I were wandering in exile, then they took me off again without finishing the matter'.[48] This is a serious criticism and one to which Polybius is obviously open; his discussion of it and his attempt to answer it will be our next concern.

IV

Polybius' reply to this charge (which had clearly been made by others before Appian) comes in two chapters in Book xxxviii,[49] which have recently been the subject of a study by Klaus Meister.[50] In these chapters Polybius defends his method of dividing up his material so as to treat the events of the various areas under each year, against the charge that this makes his narrative incomplete and disconnected;[51] his method, he claims, follows the example of Nature herself, by providing a proper variety, which is lacking in a treatment

[45] Diod. xx.43.7; cf. H. Strasburger, 'Die Wesensbestimmung der Geschichte durch die antiken Geschichtsschreiber', *SBFrankfurt* 5(3) (1966) 47 n. 4.

[46] For Duris' emphasis on μίμησις in history see *FGH* 76 F 1 = Photius, *Bibliotheca*, p. 121a41.

[47] In iv.28.6 these criteria are applied to his account of events of Ol. 140 *before* the συμπλοκή began; see above, n. 24.

[48] Appian, *Hist.* praef. 12.   [49] xxxviii.5–6.

[50] 'Die synchronistische Darstellung des Polybios im Gegensatz zur Disposition des Ephoros und Theopompos', *Hermes* 99 (1971) 506–8.

[51] xxxviii.5.1, ἀτελῆ καὶ διερριμμένην (the last word is uncertain in the defective MS).

κατὰ γένος. Moreover it is preferable to that of 'the wisest among the ancient writers' – almost certainly he is referring ‖ to Theopompus[52] – who set out to achieve this end in an unorganised way (ἀτάκτως) by the insertion of a series of mythological and anecdotal digressions in their narratives; whereas he himself by his regular switch from theatre to theatre (τεταγμένως) ensures that the necessary variety is as it were built into his history. Now this disagreement with Theopompus over the best method of attaining variety is a comparatively small matter. A much more fundamental quarrel is that with the advocates of a treatment κατὰ γένος in contrast to one based on a year-by-year system. The arguments which he is here attacking are clearly part of the stock-in-trade of Hellenistic literary controversy. I have already quoted Appian's comments;[53] and Dionysius has a similar criticism of Thucydides:[54] 'since in the same summer or the same winter many events occur, in all likelihood, in a variety of places, he [i.e. Thucydides] leaves his first subject incomplete and goes on to the next' – a procedure which, Dionysius claims, makes him 'obscure and hard to follow'.[55] But it has for some time been suspected,[56] and Meister has now confirmed,[57] that Polybius' polemic in xxxviii.5 is directed against Ephorus, who employed the κατὰ γένος method of composition. Incidentally, although Polybius rejects Ephorus' views on this matter, there is reason to believe that he felt them to possess some force, for in one or two places he abandons the Olympiad arrangement in order to achieve clarity and importance for his material. For example, Book xiv contained a single unified account, now lost, of the reign of Ptolemy IV from Raphia onwards;[58] and in Book xxxii[59] he included the whole story of the ‖ relations between Oropus and Athens, 'partly reverting to the past (he says) and partly anticipating the future, so that the separate details being in themselves insignificant, I may not by relating them under different dates produce a narrative that is both trivial and obscure'.

Meister has pointed out a curious omission from Polybius' defence of his literary method against Ephorus and Theopompus: he says nothing about its suitability for securing a proper representation of the συμπλοκή of events throughout the *oecumene*, although, as I have indicated, this was one of the main reasons for adopting it.[60] This omission may suggest that it was not on these grounds that his method had been challenged, and that whereas his critics

[52] *Cf.* Ed. Meyer, *Theopomps Hellenika* (Halle, 1909) 137; Jacoby on *FGH* 115 F 28; K. Ziegler, *RE* 21.2 (1952) 'Polybios', col. 1546; G. Avenarius, *Lukians Schrift zur Geschichtsschreibung* (Diss. Frankfurt/Main, 1954) 126 n. 55. On digressions see also A. E. Wardman, *Historia* 9 (1960) 406.

[53] See above, n. 48.

[54] Dion. Hal. *Pomp.* ii.237.10ff.; *cf.* Thuc. 9.

[55] ἀσαφὴς καὶ δυσπαρακολούθητος.

[56] *Cf.* Avenarius, *op. cit.* (n. 52) 126, 'dürfen wir annehmen, dass er hier sinngemäss wiederholt, was schon Ephoros selbst gegen das synchronistische Prinzip vorgetragen hat'.

[57] *Hermes* 99 (1971) 507–8, comparing Ephorus' views as expressed in Diod v.1.4 (= *FGH* 70 T 11) and xvi.1.1–2.

[58] xiv.12.1–5; according to a note in the manuscript it occupied forty-eight sheets.

[59] xxxii.11.1–6.   [60] See above, pp. 315ff.

charged him with being incomplete, disconnected, trivial and obscure, they did not argue that his procedure failed to do justice to the growing interconnection of political events throughout the Mediterranean area. The point may, of course, have been simply ignored. On the other hand, an examination of the organisation of the *Histories* in relation to the question of συμπλοκή furnishes some support for the claims which Polybius makes on behalf of the method which he adopted.

V

The first and most obvious advantage of that method – that is, the treatment of the separate theatres in a fixed order, Olympiad year by Olympiad year – is that it allows him, so to speak, to keep several balls in the air at once. But, more particularly, the *order* in which he chose to arrange the various theatres was especially well adapted to dealing with the events which he had to describe. The effect of the συμπλοκή was to intensify the links between Rome and the rest of the Mediterranean world;[61] and these links took the form both of peaceful contacts, which expressed themselves (as Polybius says)[62] in the exchange of embassies between the various states and Rome, and of warlike activities involving the dispatch ‖ on various occasions of Roman armies to Africa, Greece, the Balkan peninsula and Asia Minor. I leave aside Roman campaigns in other areas such as northern Italy and Spain because, if the surviving fragments of his *Histories* are anything to go by, Polybius was less interested in these; no doubt they seemed less relevant to his main theme.

The normal procedure at Rome was to hear foreign embassies at the beginning of the new consul-year;[63] even important missions usually had to await the entry into office of the new consuls. Similarly, Roman embassies to foreign states were normally dispatched about the same time. Now Polybius nominally divided up his history into Olympiad years; but in practice these were usually extended to include events up to the end of the current campaigning season.[64] Consequently the dispatch of envoys from the East at any time down to late autumn of any Julian year would be recorded among events occurring in the appropriate geographical area – Greece, Macedonia, Asia, etc. – during the Olympiad year which nominally ended in the August of that year; and since Italy came first in the list of such geographical areas in Polybius' scheme, the hearing of such envoys at Rome would be described at the beginning of the next Olympiad year, not too many pages after the account of their dispatch. Likewise the sending of Roman *legati* would normally

---

[61] v.105.4, discussed above, pp. 316f.

[62] *Ibid.* Polybius' readers are hardly likely to ignore the importance of these embassies in view of the fact that (thanks partly to the chances of manuscript survival) so many of our fragments of Polybius from the Constantinian excerpts are concerned with these.

[63] On this see G. De Sanctis, *Storia dei Romani* 4.1 (Turin, 1923) 387, giving examples of delays in the hearing of foreign embassies.

[64] See my *Commentary* (n. 13) 1.35–6.

be recorded early in a given Olympiad year under *res Italiae*, and their arrival at their destination would be described when Polybius reached the *res Graeciae*, or wherever it might be, of the same Olympiad year.

Of course, events did not always occur in this convenient way. In the late winter or early spring of 170/69 the Rhodians sent envoys to Rome to defend the city against charges arising out of their policy during the Third Macedonian War, and the Senate, contrary to its usual practice, gave these envoys a special hearing when they arrived in Rome late in the summer of 169.[65] Thus both the sending of the envoys and their reception at Rome took place in the same Olympiad year, Ol. 152.3 = 170/69, and in describing their dispatch under the affairs of Rhodes in xxviii.16, Polybius, ‖ after observing that their kindly reception by the Senate has already been related in xxviii.2, continues:

as regards this, it is useful to remind my readers frequently, as indeed I try to do, that I am often obliged to report the hearing and proceedings of embassies before describing their appointment and dispatch; for, since in narrating in their proper order the events of each year I try to bring together in a single section the events that happened in each country in that year, it is clear that this must sometimes happen in my work.[66]

Such occasional dislocations were more likely to occur, however, in the account of embassies moving not between Rome and the East but between two eastern theatres. For example, the negotiations between Ptolemy the son of Sosibius and Philip V of Macedon in 203/2 had to be related before the account of Ptolemy's dispatch from Alexandria, because Macedonia came before Egypt in Polybius' list of theatres of action;[67] and there must have been many other similar cases since Polybius speaks of having to mention the problem frequently (πλεονάκις).[68] Evidently he felt that to tamper with the order in which he had elected to deal with the various countries would be liable to create more difficulties than it solved; and certainly it would have made it more difficult to find one's way around in the *Histories*. In support of this rigid treatment is the fact that, as I have pointed out, both generally and as a device for describing the relations between Rome and the Hellenistic states, the order he had adopted was the one best suited to his purpose. However, he was, very occasionally, prepared to modify his strict scheme. His use in one or two places of Ephorus' division κατὰ γένος has already been mentioned;[69] but in addition we also find him in one place changing the conventional order in which the various regions were treated. After recounting the ‖ restoration of Ariarathes of Cappadocia under the Olympiad year 155.3 = 158/7, he remarks:[70]

---

[65] xxviii.2.1, ἤδη τῆς θερείας ληγούσης.

[66] For similar comments see xv.24a, 25.19; the first of these two passages should stand after the second (see Walbank, *Commentary* (n. 13) 2.23 (discussing the points made by P. Maas, *AIPhO* (1949) 443–6) and *op. cit.* (n. 7) 111 n. 75 (defending Maas against the criticisms of K. Abel, *Hermes* 95 (1967) 81–4)).

[67] xv.25.19; see the previous note.

[68] xxviii.16.10.

[69] See above, p. 319.   [70] xxxii.11.2–3.

Having given a brief account of Ariarathes' restoration, I shall resume the regular course of my narrative, which I follow throughout the whole of this work. For in the present instance, passing over the affairs of Greece, I took out of their turn (προελάβομεν) those matters in Asia relating to Cappadocia, because I could find no justifiable means of separating the departure of Ariarathes from Italy from his return to power. I will therefore now go back to the events that happened in Greece at the same date.[71]

In this year then some at least of the res Asiae preceded res Graeciae.

As Polybius approached the period which in his original plan marked the culmination of the συμπλοκή and the unification of the oecumene under Rome, that is the period dominated by the Third Macedonian War, it looks as if he became increasingly conscious of the hampering effect of his geographical divisions. At any rate, for the years 172/168, dealt with in Books XVII–XXIX, he may have adopted the war with Perseus as a single sub-division into which events from both Europe and Asia might be introduced. For example, the order of events in Livy XLII.43–6, based directly on Polybius, shows that the visit of Roman envoys to Rhodes (in 171), which Polybius records in XXVII.3.1–5, is unlikely to have formed part of his res Asiae for 172/1, since in Livy the narrative reverts immediately afterwards to events occurring the same year in Greece.[72] Similarly in Book XXIX, the passage 19.1–11 (corresponding to Livy XLV.3.3–8), though describing the reception of Rhodian envoys at Rome, must form part of the account of the war with Perseus during Ol. 152.4 = 169/8, since in the excerpts De Leg. Gent., from which it is taken, it is preceded by passages dealing with events at Rhodes (XXIX.10.1–7 and 11.1–6) and followed by the arrival of an Egyptian embassy in Achaea, all from the same ‖ Olympiad year. In the same way Polybius may have adopted a single geographical theatre of action to embrace all the events of the war between Antiochus and Egypt in Books XXVIII and XXIX (Ol. 152.3–4 = 170/69 and 169/8) – though this is less certain.[73] Thus the concept of a single war extending into several geographical areas was in some degree permitted to supersede the rigid division into separate theatres, and thus to become a further expression of the growing συμπλοκή of events. But this extension was limited in scope and rigidly controlled, and in general the regional treatment was maintained down to the end of the Histories.

As we have seen, it generally suited the account of diplomatic exchanges; but it also suited the description of military campaigning, since there again,

[71] The Greek events to which he refers are those of Oropus, on which see above, n. 59; thus Book XXXII contained a double breach of his normal procedure at this point – an inversion of the order of theatres of action and a modification of the principle of recounting events under their appropriate Olympiad year.

[72] Cf. Livy XLII.43–4 (= Polyb. XXXVII.1.1–2. 12: events of Boeotia), XLV.1–8 (= Polyb. XXXVII.3.1–5: Roman envoys in Asia), XLVI.1 ff. (affairs in Greece).

[73] Two fragments dealing with the Egyptian appeal to Achaea in 169/8, XXIX.23.1–24. 16 and 25.1–7, may form part of the res Graeciae of that year, in which case they will have to be transposed to stand between 21.1–9 and 22.1–5; but it is equally possible that they should go after 22.1–5 (where Büttner-Wobst puts them) to form part of a composite section bellum Antiochi et Ptolomaei, embracing both Egypt and Asia.

in the major wars with which Polybius was primarily concerned, the war decision usually followed the entry of the new consuls into office,[74] and could therefore be recorded in the *res Italiae* of any Olympiad year, to be followed in due course by a description of the arrival of the general and his legions in the war-area later in the *res Graeciae* or *res Asiae* etc. of the same year.

VI

Thus Polybius' arrangement of his material under separate theatres within the successive Olympiad years served him very well as a means of describing the growing συμπλοκή of events throughout the civilised world. Of this συμπλοκή Pédech sees an important expression in the way in which one major historical event leads to another.[75] In a passage in Book III Polybius notes ‖ how 'the war with Antiochus derived its origins from that with Philip, the latter from that with Hannibal and the Hannibalic War from that about Sicily [*i.e.* the First Punic War]'.[76] It is true that this nexus of cause and effect is one of the features contributing to the συμπλοκή, if only because as a process it was not confined to one area, but spread its influence over the three continents. But I doubt if Polybius had it prominently in mind in this context, since it is not something peculiar to the period 217–167, as the reference to the First Punic War makes clear. I suspect that he is thinking rather of the kind of thing that happened in 168, when the Roman victory over Perseus at Pydna permitted the sending of Popillius to Egypt, and so settled the conflict between Ptolemy and Antiochus at a stroke.[77] This, rather than the causal nexus between one war and the next, perhaps better illustrates what Polybius meant by συμπλοκή.

Polybius nowhere states clearly whether he believes the συμπλοκή to continue to operate once Rome has become mistress of the world in 168/7. In a passage in Book III he claims a unity for the whole of his *Histories*,[78] which, he says, are easy to acquire and read, since they consist of forty books, 'all, as it were, woven together in an unbroken series'; thus readers can clearly follow events in Italy, Sicily and Africa from the time of Pyrrhus down to the capture of Carthage and those in the rest of the world from the flight of Cleomenes of Sparta down to the battle of the Romans and the Achaeans at the Isthmus. However, this passage, though it employs the metaphor of

---

[74] This point is not easy to illustrate from the extant fragments where the only major war-decision within the period 216/146 to be recorded is that against Carthage in XXXVI.3.9 (150/49). Livy's records of the war-decisions against Philip in 200, Antiochus and Perseus all occur in annalistic passages (Livy XXXI.5–8, XXXVI.1.1–6, XLII.30.8–11). But the sending out of armies at the beginning of a campaigning season (200 is an exception) imposes some such timetable.

[75] Pédech, *op. cit.* (n. 8) 508.

[76] III.32.7; the process is worked out in detail by Pédech, *op. cit.* (n. 8) 507–8, who adds that in the same way the war with Perseus is seen as growing out of the war with Antiochus, since it was Philip's discontent at his inadequate rewards after that war that led to his conceiving the plan for the Third Macedonian War – which Perseus fought; *cf.* Livy XXXIX.23.5–13.

[77] XXIX.27.11–13 for the close connection.

[78] III.32.2–3; see above, p. 314.

weaving, is not concerned only with the period of συμπλοκή. It occurs in a context in which the author is pleading the cause of universal history against the special monograph, and the reference to the time of Pyrrhus as well as to the events of 146 shows that he is not thinking only of the fifty-three years from 220 to 168/7.

Since in fact the συμπλοκή began at a specific moment – the Conference of Naupactus in 217[79] – it would seem reasonable to ‖ assume that with the completion of Roman control over the *oecumene*, the συμπλοκή, as the process which brought that about, was also complete; and Pédech has argued plausibly for this view.[80] After 167 Rome was mistress of the world; henceforth the *oecumene* was under her control and events responded more than ever to her decisions. From that point of view the συμπλοκή was now something in the past. Moreover, the Celtiberian War, the Third Punic War, the rivalries of Asian dynasts, the revolt of Andriscus and that of the Achaean League are not described as events in any way linked together; they were separate in their origins, like the wars of the Olympiad period 220/216, and many were the outcome of decisions (on the part of the opponents of Rome) which seemed to Polybius to show evidence of crazy infatuation. Because this was a time of disjointed and to some extent irrational events, Polybius characterises it as ταραχή καὶ κίνησις and in relating its history feels himself to be virtually starting on a new work.[81] I have argued elsewhere[82] that Polybius added this later period to his *Histories* primarily because it covered events from about 152 onwards in which he had himself played a striking part, and that this decision carried with it the corollary that he must also relate the events of the years between 167 and 152, concerning which in any case he had assembled a mass of useful material during his enforced stay at Rome.

This material, covering more than twenty years, took up another ten books; and Polybius continued to use the same organisation under theatres of action and Olympiad years as he had used for the earlier parts. He had indeed no good reason to stop doing so. But the whole character of this later section (167–146), both in its conception and in its alleged purpose inside the *Histories*,[83] is such that it is no longer concerned with the συμπλοκή which had been so essential an ingredient of the period down to Pydna.

---

[79] See above, n. 26.

[80] *Op. cit.* (n. 8) 508.

[81] III.4.13, οἷον ἀρχὴν ποιησάμενος ἄλλην γράφειν. See on this Walbank, *op. cit.* (n. 7) 182–3; Pédech, *op. cit.* (n. 8) 16.

[82] Walbank, *op. cit.* (n. 7) 182–3.

[83] On Polybius' alleged reason for his extension, viz. to enable readers to pass judgement on Rome, see III.4.1–13 with Walbank, *Commentary* (n. 13) *ad loc.* and *op. cit.* (n. 7) 181–3.

21

POLYBIUS' LAST TEN BOOKS*

At the very beginning of his *Histories*, and repeatedly afterwards, Polybius sets out his purpose: it is to explain 'by what means and thanks to what kind of constitution the Romans in less than fifty-three years had subjected nearly the whole inhabited world to their sole government'.[1] That implied a narrative covering the years from 220 B.C. down to the fall of the Macedonian monarchy and the ensuing settlement in 168/7. In the *Histories* as we know them, Pydna is in Book XXIX; so, too, is the dramatic confrontation between Antiochus IV and C. Popillius which ended that king's invasion of Egypt and served as a landmark in the decline of the Seleucid monarchy. But the *Histories* we possess are a revised edition ending not in 167 but in 145. We cannot be sure that Pydna was intended to go into Book XXIX of the original *Histories*; for one thing it is not certain that that version contained the present Book XII, with its long critique of Timaeus and other historians. But if it did not, and if in consequence Pydna stood originally in Book XXVIII and the settlement of Macedonia in Book XXIX, then perhaps there would have been a Book XXX containing the kind of chronological résumé which in the final version stood in Book XL. For certainly everything favours the view that the *Histories* were planned in the first instance to occupy thirty, not twenty-nine books (an unlikely figure). So we can speak with confidence of an extension of ten books – whether we regard these as XXX–XXXIX or XXXI–XL – which at some later date Polybius added, to carry his story down to the fall of Carthage and Corinth in 146.

It is with that extension that I am concerned here. As I hope to show, we do not know whether a thirty-book edition was ever finished, still less published, in that form. If it was published, it was soon to be ‖ superseded by the forty-book edition, in which Book XXXIV was devoted to geographical matters and Book XL to the chronological résumé. This longer edition also added either the whole or the greater part of Book XII, along with one or two supplements to the earlier books.[2] My discussion of the extension falls into five parts: (I) the dates at which Polybius planned, wrote and published his last

* [*Historiographia antiqua: commentationes Lovanienses in honorem W. Peremans septuagenarii editae* (Leuven, 1977) 139–62]

[1] 1.1.5–6, 2.7, 4.1, III.1.4, 1.9, 2.6, 3.9, 4.2, 118.9, VI.2.3, VIII.2.3, XXXIX.8.7.
[2] See F. W. Walbank, *Polybius* (Berkeley–Los Angeles–London, 1973) 23–5, for the passages, and for Book XII.

ten books; (II) the purpose of the extension, as set out in Book III; (III) the contents of the extension in the light of its alleged purpose; (IV) Polybius' attitude towards Rome, as it emerges from these books; (V) the question of whether in fact the alleged purpose provides a convincing and adequate explanation of what Polybius has written.

I THE DATE OF COMPOSITION

It is clear from a passage in Book XXXIX, which mentions honours paid to Polybius both while he was alive and after his death, καὶ ζῶντα καὶ μεταλλάξαντα,[3] that there was a posthumous edition of the *Histories*; and though in Book III[4] Polybius speaks of the convenience of being able to buy and read a universal history in forty books rather than a series of monographs, this is not in itself proof that such a forty-book edition had actually appeared during Polybius' lifetime.[5] That he finished composing the *Histories* seems clear, however, from XXXIX.8, an epilogue which briefly reviews the general plan of the work, the period covered by it down to 146, and its purpose; but that again is not evidence of publication. Moreover, I must pause a little over this epilogue, since Lehmann has recently argued[6] that it was the posthumous editor and not Polybius himself who wrote it, and therefore that it affords no proof that the work was finished – indeed rather proof of the opposite.

In favour of this hypothesis he adduces two arguments. First there is the fact[7] that this chapter gives it as the purpose of the *Histories* to ‖ explain how the Romans reached universal dominion, but makes no reference to their secondary purpose – on which I shall say more shortly – of judging how Rome used her power in the years following 168; yet the concluding date is here given not as 168, but as 146. Secondly, the account in this chapter[8] of the contents of the *Histories* makes the starting-point for the West – Italy, Sicily and Africa – 264 where Timaeus left off,[9] but for the East the accession of Philip V and the expulsion of Cleomenes from Sparta towards 220.[10] This ignores the Achaean events recounted in Book II, although in II.71.1f. Polybius had emphasised the importance of the Cleomenean War and the earlier history of the Achaean Confederation for his general theme. Lehmann therefore concludes[11] that such a blundering résumé could only have been the work of an editor who had not even read the introductory books. But before attributing the epilogue to a writer as ignorant and deceitful as that, we should perhaps consider whether some alternative explanation is not more likely.

To Lehmann's first point, that the secondary purpose of the *Histories* is here

---

[3] XXXIX.5.4–6.   [4] III.32.2–3.

[5] *Cf.* G. A. Lehmann, *Polybe* (*Entretiens Hardt* 20; Vandoeuvres–Geneva, 1974) 193. Perhaps some groups of books had appeared and been criticised before this passage was written.

[6] *Op. cit.* (n. 5) 186–96, especially 193f.

[7] XXXIX.8.7.   [8] XXXIX.8.4–5.

[9] *Cf.* 1.5.1, συνεχής...τοῖς ἀφ' ὧν Τίμαιος ἀπέλιπε; III.32.2.

[10] III.32.3.   [11] *Op. cit.* (n. 5) 193f.

ignored, I shall return shortly, for it raises some general questions about the historian's aims. But the second point cannot be considered without taking into account the passage in Book III.32.2–3 to which I have already alluded.[12] There Polybius asserts that in a work of forty books the reader can 'follow clearly events in Italy, Sicily and Africa from the time of Pyrrhus to the capture of Carthage and in the rest of the world from the flight of Cleomenes until the battle of the Romans and Achaeans at the Isthmus'. Clearly this passage is echoed in the epilogue in Book XXXIX; and Gelzer[13] explained both as having been included at a stage in the composition of the *Histories* when the account of the rise of Achaea and of the Cleomenean War had not yet been incorporated in Book II. Later he qualified his view,[14] admitting[15] that these Achaean chapters must have been ‖ written before 168 – since in II.37.8 the Achaean League is said to be still flourishing[16] – though it was only much later that they were included in the *Histories*. Gelzer's hypothesis seems to me now[17] to offer the most satisfactory explanation of these two passages, both of which ignore the presence of the Greek events in the προκατασκευή. It implies that Polybius had already completed the extension and that the forty-book edition was virtually ready for publication before he decided to insert the Achaean chapters in Book II.[18] This seems more plausible than Lehmann's theory of a pious but stupid editor, who had not even bothered to read the author whose work he was presenting to the public, especially since that theory takes no account of III.32.3.

If, then, the epilogue is proof that before he died Polybius had already completed his *Histories*, one must next ask when he did this. Lehmann[19] has argued that the extension was not yet written, still less published, when Polybius composed his monograph on the Numantine War, which ended in

---

[12] See n. 4.

[13] M. Gelzer, *Kleine Schriften* 3 (Wiesbaden, 1964) 111f.

[14] *Ibid.* 178.

[15] Following K. Ziegler, *RE* 21.2 (1952) 'Polybios (1)', col. 1476, and F. W. Walbank, *Historical commentary on Polybius* 1 (Oxford, 1957) 215, commenting on II.37–70. My note there pointed out the difficulty for Gelzer's hypothesis presented by II.37.8ff., which assumes the continued existence of the Achaean Confederacy (which was dissolved in 146), yet seems to be an integral part of the introductory chapters. This difficulty disappears, however, if we suppose that Polybius included in the chapters on Achaea incorporated in the *Histories* a sentence about the growth of the Confederation which stood in the original composition. Such a reference to the expansion and unity of Achaea would be less of an anachronism after 129 than it would have been in 146, for by then the Confederacy had been restored, though in a reduced form. For the likelihood that *SEG* 15.234, a dedication on behalf of Damon of Patrae, gives the full extent of the Confederation in 122 see T. Schwertfeger, *Der achäische Bund von 146 bis 27 v.Chr.* (Munich, 1974) 27ff., and my review in *CR* 26 (1976) 238–9.

[16] M. Gelzer, *op. cit.* (n. 13) 116, argued that this passage referred to the past; but that cannot be said of III.37.10–11.

[17] For earlier doubts see n. 15.

[18] See F. W. Walbank, *op. cit.* (n. 2) 14 n.70. A possible way round that conclusion would be to assume that 'forty books' in III.32.3 was a late emendation of the phrase 'thirty books' which could have stood in the original edition, and that the epilogue was taken over from that edition and placed in its present position in Book XXXIX. But this is arbitrary and hypothetical.

[19] *Op. cit.* (n. 5) 192 n. 3; so too K. Svoboda, *Philologus* 72 (1913) 482.

133.[20] As he rightly points out,[21] there are several passages in Books xxx to xxxix which must be of late composition. A reference to the accession of Attalus III in xxx.2.5f., the first book of the extension, must have been written after 138;[22] ‖ and two remarks in the long discussion of Scipio Aemilianus' character and training in Book xxxi (28.13 and 31.30) imply that they were written after his death, and make it at least possible that all this section (23–30) was composed after 129. The first passage tells us that Scipio's reputation for temperance cost him nothing, but by his early austerity he gained a health and vigour which lasted throughout his life (παρ' ὅλον τὸν βίον). The second suggests by its tone and phraseology that Scipio was dead; and that is true also of xxxviii.21.3, which records Scipio's comments on seeing Carthage burning, along with Polybius' remark that Scipio's behaviour was that of a man who was μεγάλου καὶ τελείου καὶ συλλήβδην ἀξίου μνήμης, a great and perfect man, one in short worthy to be remembered.[23]

These passages point to composition after 129. They could, of course, be later additions to a narrative already written earlier. But their position in the general economy of the last books may be thought to be against that assumption. The substantial digression on Scipio's training at Polybius' hands,[24] introduced in the context of Aemilius Paullus' death,[25] outlines a rather extraordinary programme which Polybius sketched for Scipio, and which he carried out over a period of several years with great thoroughness. It involved concentration by the young man on winning a reputation – it is this rather than the virtues themselves that Polybius stresses[26] – for moral abstemiousness, financial generosity and courage, one after the other; and in describing each aspect Polybius points out how little it cost Scipio and how by abstention from immediate pleasures he was able to acquire great advantages in the future. This rational and calculating educational programme has all the marks of Polybius' mind and it is clearly ‖ central to his picture of Scipio. Thus when he comes

[20] In *Polybius* (n. 2) 22, I assumed that as an old man of over 70 Polybius would hardly have turned aside to write his monograph on the Numantine War if he had not yet finished his main work. But clearly this argument does not hold good if the decision to extend the main work was not taken until after 129, as may be the case.

[21] G. A. Lehmann, *op. cit.* (n. 5) 193.

[22] See also xviii.4.10, which must be a late insertion.

[23] G. A. Lehmann, *op. cit.* (n. 5) 153 n. 2, argues that the section of Book xii (5–12a) dealing with Locri must be of late composition, because Polybius mentions the assistance he rendered to that city and was only in a position to do this in the 130s, when he had influence with the Senate. It is quite possible that Book xii is of late composition (see above, p. 325); but Polybius' intervention at Locri can well have been in the 150s, when he could already exploit his friendship with the young Scipio Aemilianus (see my *Commentary* 2 (Oxford, 1967) 331–2 on xii.5.2). Lehmann here follows O. Cuntz, *Polybius und sein Werk* (Leipzig, 1902) 46–9, in making the Dalmatian War mentioned by Polybius refer to the campaigns against the Vardaei (Ardiaei) and Scordisci of 135; but neither people was Dalmatian.

[24] xxxi.23–30. On this passage see now E. Eyben and A. Wouters, *Lampas* 10 (1977) 90–117.

[25] xxxi.22: it is foreshadowed in xviii.36.1.

[26] xxxi.25.2, τὴν ἐπὶ σωφροσύνῃ δόξαν; 25.9, ὥρμησεν ἐπὶ τὸ περὶ τὰ χρήματα μεγαλοψυχίᾳ καὶ καθαρότητι διενεγκεῖν τῶν ἄλλων (for both *cf.* xxxi.28.10); 29.1, λοιποῦ δ' ὄντος τοῦ ἀνδρείαν ⟨μέρους⟩.

to describe[27] the reluctance of young men to enlist for the Spanish war and Scipio's gesture in volunteering for service on that front, he remarks that 'having already attained a reputation for generosity and temperance' he now wished to gain a similar name for courage.[28] Here once more are the three phases of Polybius' educational programme; the Spanish war, and the famous duel with the Spanish chieftain,[29] enable Scipio to complete his reputation for courage, for which his activity as a huntsman had been an ἄσκησις[30] and a beginning.[31] Polybius' picture of Aemilianus' character, as developed under the régime outlined by himself, provides a central theme in these later books; and if we had a fuller Polybian version of the events of the Third Punic War, we should undoubtedly find that Scipio played a major role in it, as he does in Appian. This emphasis lends support to the view that the account of Scipio's training in Book XXXI is not simply a late addition, but an integral part of the extension, which on that hypothesis would, as Lehmann contends, have been composed ‖ after 129. But the case is not irrefutable;[32] and the possibility remains that Polybius started on the extension soon after carrying his narrative down to 168/7. How long after 145 that would take we cannot of course know.

In any case, even assuming that the extension was begun after 129, we need not also assume that work on the last ten books began *ab initio* from that date. The account of Demetrius I's escape from Rome,[33] with Polybius' help, in 162, was clearly written up at the time and later incorporated in the *Histories*, since it contains a reference to Carthage in the present tense.[34] Moreover, as I hope to show, Polybius' account of Roman policy in Books XXX–XXXIII plainly reflects the views he held at the time the events were taking place. It is likely

---

[27] XXXV.4.   [28] XXXV.4.8–9.   [29] XXXV.5.

[30] So XXXI.29.1; in XXXI.29.11, however, Scipio is said by his hunting exploits to have gained a universal reputation for courage. The slight discrepancy is not serious.

[31] The very calculated way in which Polybius represents his educational programme for Scipio recalls his interpretation of Scipio Africanus as ἀγχίνους καὶ νήπτης καὶ τῇ διανοίᾳ περὶ τὸ προτεθὲν ἐντεταμένος (x.3.1). Thus he was able to exploit the reputation for courage which he won by rescuing his father at the battle of the Ticinus in order to refrain from exposing himself to unreasonable risks hereafter, when hopes of success rested on him as commander – caution which Polybius applauds (x.3.3–7, based on Laelius). In x.3.7 I accept the emendation σπανίως (Dindorf and, independently, Paton) for the manuscript reading πάντως. K. Meister, *Historische Kritik bei Polybios* (Wiesbaden, 1975) 163 n. 4, defends πάντως. In reply to my remark that a general should not take unnecessary risks he observes that there is no question of unnecessary risks, ὅτ' εἰς αὐτὸν ἀναρτηθεῖεν ὑπὸ τῆς πατρίδος αἱ τῶν ὅλων ἐλπίδες. But surely then above all times the survival of the general is indispensable. For Polybius' stress on the safety of the general see x.23.3; *cf.* x.33.4, ἀκεραίου μὲν γὰρ καὶ σωζομένου τοῦ προεστῶτος, κἄν ποτε πέσῃ τὰ ὅλα, πολλὰς ἀφορμὰς ἡ τύχη δίδωσι πρὸς τὸ πάλιν ἀνακτήσασθαι τὰς ἐκ τῶν περιπετειῶν ἐλαττώσεις. x.32.9, quoted by Meister to show that in a major engagement a general should take risks, hardly does that. There Polybius is condemning Marcellus for risking (and losing) his life in a small side-show; in such a situation a general should be prepared to sacrifice much 'gun-fodder' before allowing himself to be endangered. But this is far from implying that in a major encounter the general should neglect his own safety. In XI.2.9–11, Hasdrubal is praised for protecting himself so long as there was the slightest hope and only perishing bravely when Fortune had removed his last hope (quite a different situation from any in which Scipio was to find himself). In x.3.7 this point is lost if one reads πάντως.

[32] See for instance the hypothesis suggested in n. 18.

[33] XXXI.11–15.   [34] XXXI.12.12.

therefore that while he was at Rome and busy writing the first part of his
Histories, he was also making notes on what was going on about him. This would
be very natural for a historian who believed that he should not shut himself
away in a study like Timaeus,[35] but should, as far as possible, actively concern
himself with the political life around him[36] – as actively of course as his
situation at Rome would allow. Consequently, when he decided, perhaps
though not certainly after Scipio's death in 129, to write an extension to his
Histories, he already had a large body of material at hand. Much of it would
necessarily reflect his views at the time he wrote it down; and it is not surprising
that it continues to reflect those views in the version that has come down to
us. But before pursuing this matter further, I want to say something about the
reasons which Polybius gives for writing an extension to his original *Histories*.

II THE ALLEGED PURPOSE OF THE EXTENSION TO 145

Polybius' main narrative begins in Book III; and in chapters 1–3 of that book
he prefaces it with a summary of the contents of the *Histories* down to 167. There
follow two chapters (4–5) in which he explains why it has proved necessary
to extend the work to 145.[37] ‖ These must now be examined, since their
argument is not wholly straightforward and their implications are elusive.

It had been Polybius' original intention, κατὰ τὴν ἐξ ἀρχῆς πρόθεσιν,[38] to
end his work at 168/7 since in that year the process of world-conquest was
complete. Indeed, had it been possible to judge how far individuals and states,
ἀνδρῶν καὶ πολιτευμάτων, merit praise and blame simply on the basis of
success or failure in the struggle, that is where he would have stopped. But
judgements on either victors or vanquished based on the actual conflict are
necessarily inconclusive, for two reasons:[39] first, if not properly used, success
may turn to disaster, and secondly, the most terrible catastrophes can turn out
to the advantage of those who bear them courageously.[40] In short, what
matters is how one reacts to success or disaster. Now this claim would seem
to imply that Polybius added his account of the years following 168 to illustrate
its truth, in short that the decision of 168 had not proved final, but that the
Roman victory had somehow been reversed and the defeated powers –
Macedon and perhaps, by implication, Syria – had turned their setback into
success by their firm reaction to it. But that is manifestly untrue, for of course
nothing of the sort happened between 168 and 146. On the contrary, 148
brought further ruin to the Macedonians, who chose to support Andriscus,[41]
and in 146 they were joined in catastrophe by Carthage and Achaea;[42] and

---

[35] XII.25d.1, 25h.1; see Walbank, *op. cit.* (n. 2) 51 n. 111.

[36] *Cf.* XII.25g.1–2, 28.3–5; see my *Commentary* (n. 15) 1.10.

[37] III.4–5.					[38] III.4.1.

[39] III.4.4.					[40] III.4.5.

[41] *Cf.* XXXVI.10; see Walbank, *op. cit.* (n. 2) 176.

[42] On the Achaean War see XXXVI.17.12–15; Walbank, *op. cit.* (n. 2) 176 n. 122. On Carthage
see XXXVIII.19–22.

Syria too was still further weakened, as a result of the struggle between Demetrius I and Alexander Balas.[43] Thus the events of 168–146 in no way illustrate or justify the thesis that misuse of power can turn success into failure or that courageous endurance can turn failure into success. Polybius' two reasons for regarding judgements based on the struggle itself as inconclusive have no obvious place in the period he is writing about in Books xxx–xxxix.

In fact Polybius does not press the point; for he goes on to say[44] that in view of the new criterion he has invoked he must append to his account of the years 220–168/7 a description of the nature of ‖ Roman rule and an account of the opinions and assessment (ἀποδοχαὶ καὶ διαλήψεις) of their rulers entertained by the rest – not merely by the conquered.[45] It is not immediately apparent what such an account has to do with illustrating the reversal of failure and success, unless indeed the views held by the other states concerning Rome can be shown to have helped those peoples to show courage and endurance; for it is *prima facie* unlikely that they would have a substantial effect[46] on the way the Romans themselves exercised their hegemony. Books xxx–xxxiii, covering the years 168–152, do in fact contain several observations on Roman attitudes and behaviour; but there is no evidence at all that the views there expressed (though they are frequently attributed to the Greeks) had any effect on anyone's policy or morale. They are usually reported in a detached and cynical manner, and they not infrequently seem to reflect the attitudes of the Greek community in Rome, whose company Polybius must constantly have frequented during his detention.[47] It was a group doomed by its character to political impotence. Here then is another *non sequitur*. The events and opinions described in Books xxx and following have no connection with the problem of political success and failure or the reversal of these.

Polybius makes a further point. In addition, he says,[48] he must describe the tendencies and ambitions, τὰς ὁρμὰς καὶ τοὺς ζήλους, of the various peoples, παρ' ἑκάστοις, in their public and private life – presumably in order to throw light on the moral atmosphere and on the state of morale, which he firmly believed were directly relevant to political success (as we can see from several passages in Book vi).[49] One obvious example of this is the description of the ‖ ὁρμὴ καὶ ζῆλος τῶν καλῶν exhibited by Scipio Aemilianus himself,[50] so

---

[43] *Cf.* xxxiii.19–22.   [44] iii.4.6.

[45] K.-E. Petzold, *Studien zur Methode des Polybios und zu ihrer historischen Auswertung* (Munich, 1969) 59, thinks that xxx.6.3–4, on different classes of Greek statesmen, illustrates this point. But although that passage may offer an example of 'how far states and individuals deserve blame or praise' (iii.4.1), it has no bearing on iii.4.6, which is concerned with the views the subjected peoples entertained about Rome, not with the characteristics of their statesmen.

[46] Admittedly, Polybius insists (xxiv.10.11–12) that the Romans are ready to accept an appeal to justice for those who have a claim on them (*cf.* xxiv.8.4–5, where Lycortas says the same); but such influence could operate only marginally.

[47] *Cf.* xxx.4.10; on this group see Walbank, *op. cit.* (n. 2) 74–5; Gelzer, *op. cit.* (n. 13) 173. They did not include the detainees, who with the exception of Polybius, were lodged in towns of southern Etruria (xxxi.23.5; Paus. vii.10.11).

[48] iii.4.6.

[49] *E.g.* vi.3.3, 52–3.   [50] xxx.25.1.

clearly the phrase παρ' ἑκάστοις included Rome; but the criticisms of the Achaean and Carthaginian leaders recorded in Book xxxviii[51] and of the reluctance of many Greeks to assume the responsibilities of marriage and parenthood mentioned in a digression in Book xxxvi[52] also come under this category. These examples from Greece and Carthage can be set alongside the criticisms of the Roman youth who were so different in their pursuits from Scipio.[53] But they do nothing, except perhaps in a negative sense, to illustrate how morale can transform defeat into eventual success.

What then is the purpose of this analysis of the social climate? It is, Polybius tells us,[54] to enable contemporaries to see whether Roman rule is acceptable or the reverse (φευκτὴν ἢ τοὐναντίον αἱρετήν), and future generations whether the Roman empire (ἀρχή) should be praised and admired or condemned. In the context of Roman power after 146 it is difficult to see how the words φευκτὴν ἢ αἱρετήν can mean anything else but that the various peoples had a choice between accepting Roman rule willingly and trying to stave it off; in short this is intended as a guide to political action (as the *Histories* in general are meant to be) – though the implications of 'staving off Roman rule' at this time (after 146) would be so serious that one would certainly hesitate to cast Polybius in the role of its advocate. But for posterity the issue is a different one. Here it is the moral historian who speaks: *they* are to pass judgement in retrospect on the Roman empire.

This aim provides a reason for extending the *Histories* down to 146 (which the generalisation about success turning into disaster and disaster into success[55] does not). But it leaves uncertain and undefined from what point of view the future reader is to judge Roman rule. Is her empire to be assessed from the standpoint of Rome herself, or from that of the rest of the world? The latter may seem to be implied; but it is not specifically stated. For Polybius goes on to say[56] that it is in providing the material for this judgement of Roman ‖ rule – not simply in explaining the Roman rise to world empire – that the chief usefulness of his work will lie; and the final end[57] (τελεσιούργημα) achieved by his history will be – one expects to read 'the passing of judgement on the Roman empire': but what Polybius in fact says is 'to learn the condition of each people after the Roman hegemony was complete'. That end could, of course, have been achieved simply by a factual description of the conditions of the various states making up the Roman ἀρχή; but in its context it probably implies an account of the well-being (or the opposite) of the subject peoples, regarded as a criterion for judging Roman rule. However, the period during which this judgement is to be exercised is unexpectedly curtailed, since Polybius goes on to say 'down to the period of disturbance and trouble (ταραχὴ καὶ κίνησις) which afterwards ensued'.[58]

---

[51] *Cf.* xxxviii.7–8, 20 (Hasdrubal), 10.8–9, 12–13, 18 (Diaeus and Critolaus).
[52] xxxvi.20.17.   [53] xxxi.25.3–7.
[54] iii.4.7.   [55] iii.4.5.
[56] iii.4.8.   [57] iii.4.12.   [58] *Ibid.*

This ταραχή καὶ κίνησις is thus apparently distinct from the period which provides the material for judging Rome; and Polybius says that he was led to embark upon the account of it 'as if he were making a new start' (οἷον ἀρχὴν ποιησάμενος ἄλλην), that is, as if he were beginning a new work.[59] That is because of the importance of the events and their unexpected character, and above all because he had been a witness (αὐτόπτης) of most of them, and had shared in some (σύνεργος) and directed others (χειριστής). Chapter 5, which follows, is an account of some of the events comprised in this period of disturbance; but unfortunately this catalogue produces yet further problems. The recovery of the kingdom of Cappadocia by Ariarathes, who had been expelled from it by Orophernes some time earlier,[60] took place in 158/7, and the war between Attalus II and Prusias II lasted from 156 to 154.[61] The Celtiberian War and the Carthaginian War against Masinissa, both of which Polybius mentions first,[62] did not begin, however, until 153 and 151/50 respectively; and the death of Demetrius I of Syria and the restoration of the Greek detainees[63] both belong to 150. Finally Polybius mentions the Third Punic War, the Macedonian War and the Achaean War.[64] These bring the period ‖ of ταραχή to an end; but the date at which it is supposed to begin is not at all clear, particularly since Polybius has no corresponding list of the events which he intends to describe (and does describe) between 168/7 and the onset of the period of disturbance. It could be argued, in view of the dates of some of the events I have just mentioned, that the ταραχή began about 158. But it would be quite false to say that Polybius launched into his account of events from that date onwards 'as if making a new start'. Indeed, bearing that remark in mind, if a firm date is to be assigned to the onset of ταραχή, a more likely one is 151, for it was only from then onwards that Polybius could fairly claim to have been involved in important events as an eyewitness, a collaborator and a director. It is moreover at that point in his narrative that Polybius inserts Book xxxiv, which deals with geographical matters, mainly of the western Mediterranean, and divides off the contents of Books xxxv– xxxix from what went before.[65] There is logic in such a division, for it was in the years 152/1 down to 146/5 that Polybius accompanied Scipio Aemilianus to Spain and Africa, assisted him in the siege and destruction of Carthage, and afterwards returned home to play a major role in the post-war settlement of Achaea.

But if 152/1 was the dividing line, Polybius has expressed himself carelessly: the onset of ταραχή is nowhere clearly indicated in his catalogue. Admittedly, the chapters we are considering[66] are an insertion in the original text, and, as

---

[59] III.4.13.   [60] III.5.2.
[61] III.5.1.   [62] *Ibid.*
[63] III.5.3–4.   [64] III.5.5–6.
[65] In the same way Book vi stands between the first Olympiad of the *Histories* proper (220–216) and the following period, during which the affairs of the whole Mediterranean came together; *cf.* iv.28.1–6, v.105.4–10; and in general F. W. Walbank, *YClS* 24 (1975) 197–212 [above, pp. 313–24].   [66] III.4–5.

we all know, it is precisely in such circumstances that confusion creeps in. Even so, we are left asking questions. Why, for instance, is the period 152–146 attached to the *Histories* 'as if it were a new work'? Why did Polybius not publish it as a separate work since he does not try to relate the events in it to the main programme, and hardly to the subsidiary programme of the *Histories*? These are questions to which I shall return. Meanwhile, I hope that I have shown that Polybius has failed not only to define clearly the period of ταραχὴ καὶ κίνησις, but also to explain unambiguously why he extended his *Histories* to Book XL. With these problems in mind we may now take a closer look at the contents of the last ten books. ‖

III THE CONTENTS OF THE EXTENSION

I have already touched on this a little.[67] But there is something to be learnt from the scale on which the events of 168/7 to 145 are treated, and the way Books XXX to XXXIX are related to those twenty-two years. Apart from Book XXXIV, the geographical excursus, there are nine books, of which the first four, XXX–XXXIII, cover sixteen of the twenty-two years, each containing the events of a single Olympiad. We may call this minimal treatment, since within the main part of the *Histories* one book is the shortest section allotted to an Olympiad; it allows only a quarter of a book for each year. This leaves Polybius with five books, XXXV to XXXIX, in which to cover the seven years from 152/1 to 146/5 inclusive. As we have seen, these years seem to coincide with the period of ταραχὴ καὶ κίνησις, during which the historian had himself occupied a central position as observer or participant. We may, I think, conclude that out of the twenty-two years it is these seven that contain most action and interest him the most. Such a conclusion may help to explain why the 'contents list' in Book III does not clearly distinguish between the two periods but deals primarily with what happened in the later years, neglecting anything prior to 158.

As we saw, in his extension Polybius undertook to discuss Roman rule and the opinions entertained about it by other peoples; and that promise is fulfilled mainly in Books XXX to XXXIII. The comments recorded are almost uniformly cynical and aloof, and critical of Roman conduct. I have analysed Polybius' treatment of the subject elsewhere,[68] and need not do so again here. Let me merely remind you of his description of the attempt made by certain Romans to seduce Attalus from his allegiance to his brother, King Eumenes, in 168/7 and, after that had failed, of the Senate's refusal to fulfil its promise to hand over Aenus and Maronea to Pergamum;[69] or of the advantages which Prusias derived from his servility,[70] of Eumenes' humiliation at Rome in 167/6,[71] and of the Senate's unprincipled acquiescence in Athens' claim to

---

[67] Pp. 327f.
[68] *Op. cit.* (n. 2) 168–72; *Polybe* (n. 5) 11–13 [above, pp. 285f.].
[69] XXX.1–3.   [70] XXX.18.1–7.   [71] XXX.19.1–17.

Haliartus,[72] and its refusal to support ‖ Priene in a just cause.[73] Demetrius was kept a hostage at Rome (until he escaped) because the Senate preferred to see an inexperienced youth on the Seleucid throne.[74] They sponsored a revision of the agreement between the Ptolemy brothers in 163/2 in order to keep Egypt weak and divided;[75] and they generally favoured Masinissa against Carthage, because that was to the advantage of Rome.[76]

Such decisions were prompted by self-interest; and they can hardly have been to Polybius' liking. Certainly when the Senate let Callicrates persuade them to debar the Greek detainees from returning home, he cannot contain his anger.[77] But in the main he controls his own feelings and comments as objectively as he can on Roman policy as he sees it. 'Very many Roman decisions', he says, commenting on the Senate's policy in Egypt, 'are of this kind; profiting by others' mistakes they effectively increase and build up their own power, at the same time favouring and it would seem benefiting the guilty party.'[78] But twice, in describing this policy, he says that the Romans acted πραγματικῶς;[79] and to act πραγματικῶς is normally something praiseworthy in Polybius. In situations where the Romans were not pursuing self-interest, they generally showed no real interest at all, and so let themselves be tricked – for instance by Ariarathes' enemies Diogenes and Miltiades,[80] or by the Seleucid envoy Heracleides[81] in 153/2. The same thing had happened to Ti. Sempronius Gracchus when he was sent out in 167/6 to investigate the affairs of Syria.[82]

Such views as these probably reflect those current among the Greeks resident in Rome, and probably too among Polybius' fellow-detainees, who had been lodged in the towns of southern Etruria,[83] within easy reach, since he was apparently free to move over a wide area.[84] As I have indicated,[85] there seems little doubt that Polybius formulated ‖ them at the time of the events, and that although occupied while at Rome in planning the first draft of his *Histories* and composing perhaps the first fifteen books,[86] he was also making detailed memoranda on what was happening about him. Proof of this exists in his detailed description of the escape – to which he contributed – of Demetrius I from Rome in 162; the reference to Carthage as still in existence[87] indicates a date of composition before 146, and no doubt many other passages in Books xxx–xxxiii incorporate similar memoranda.[88]

[72] xxx.20.   [73] xxxii.10.
[74] xxxi.2.1–7.   [75] xxxi.10.
[76] xxxi.21.6.
[77] xxx.32, xxxii.3.14–17, xxxiii.1.3–8.3, 14.2.
[78] xxxi.10.   [79] xxxi.10.6, 10.7.
[80] xxxii.10.   [81] xxxiii.18.10.
[82] xxx.27, 30.7–8.   [83] See n. 47.
[84] For hunting expeditions into southern Latium see xxxi.14.3; also my *Commentary* (n. 15) 1.4.
[85] Above, pp. 329f.
[86] *Op. cit.* (n. 2) 16ff. (modified in some details in the present paper).
[87] xxxi.11–15; see above, nn. 33–4.
[88] Gelzer, *op. cit.* (n. 13) 161ff.

In recording contemporary views of these events Polybius fulfils his promise to retail the opinions and assessment of the ruling power expressed by the rest, as exemplified by his fellow-Greeks; and we have seen how his digression on the character and training of Scipio Aemilianus gave him the chance to comment on the behaviour of the Romans in their private life.[89] However, Books xxx to xxxiii, though they cover the greater part of the period from 168 to 145, represent less than half of the extension. For Books xxxv to xxxix are all devoted to the three wars which occupy the years 152/1 to 146 and round off the *Histories* – the wars against Carthage, against Andriscus in Macedonia, and against Achaea. Unfortunately the scanty fragments of those books do not adequately represent Polybius' narrative. That is especially true of the Third Punic War, and both Diodorus and Appian may be legitimately used to supplement the fragments. For Polybius was the source for this part of Diodorus,[90] and though the relationship between Polybius and Appian is less clear,[91] the prominence accorded by the latter to Scipio's exploits must derive ultimately from Polybius. Taken together the three authors leave no doubt that Polybius' account of the years from 152 to 146 was largely dominated by the figure of Scipio; but the period was also one in which Polybius himself, as he says, played an ever increasing role.

Why then does he describe it as a time of ταραχή καὶ κίνησις? And what do these words signify in this context? In the Egyptian papyri ‖ ταραχή is used of internal conflict,[92] and Polybius' usage is often similar.[93] For example, he uses both words (or cognates such as κινεῖν and κίνημα) of the Carthaginian mercenary rising and the events leading up to it,[94] and also of a sedition among Macedonian troops stationed at Corinth.[95] A rising at Sparta is a κίνησις[96] and κινεῖν is used of a Gallic *tumultus*.[97] The Latin equivalent of the two words appears to be *motus* and *tumultus*, and in general their sense is that of a military movement or rising within a community which does not come under the heading of regular warfare – though Polybius' usage is not rigid, for the Carthaginian Mercenary War can also be called a πόλεμος.[98] However, the wars fought by the Romans between 152 and 146 do not fit obviously into this category. From the point of view of Macedon, Achaea and Carthage they

---

[89] As he undertakes to do in iii.4.6.

[90] *Cf.* E. Schwartz, *RE* 5.1 (1903) 'Diodorus (38)', cols. 689–90.

[91] It is clear that Appian's account of the Third Punic War derives partly from Polybius, but indirectly; see U. Kahrstedt, *Geschichte der Karthager* (Berlin, 1913) 620, 628; E. Schwartz, *RE* 2 (1896) 'Appianus (2)', cols. 219–21.

[92] See *UPZ* 2.225 recto, line 14 (= U. Wilcken, *Chrestomathie* 167): L. Mooren, *Anc Soc* 5 (1974) 138ff.; W. Peremans, *Le monde grecque: hommages à Claire Préaux* (Brussels, 1975) 396–7.

[93] For the meaning of the words in Thucydides, Xenophon and Demosthenes see Walbank, *Commentary* (n. 15) 1.302, on Polyb. iii.4.13.

[94] *Cf.* 1.69.6 (of Matho), κεκινηκὼς κατὰ τὰς...ταραχάς; iii.9.8–9, κίνημα...ταῖς ἐμφυλίοις ταραχαῖς; 10.1, ταραχήν.

[95] v.25.4, ἐν θορύβῳ καὶ ταραχῇ; 25.7, τῆς κινήσεως.

[96] iv.34.3, οἱ κινήσαντες...τὰ πράγματα; 35.1, τῆς κινήσεως.

[97] ii.21.3. [98] *E.g.* 1.65.5.

certainly are not mutinies or internal risings, since in each case the state was committed to the struggle and with some unanimity. From the point of view of Rome the wars described were fought – if often hard-fought[99] – in the normal fashion. Magistrates were sent out, quite regularly, to take command, and the wars were all brought to a satisfactory conclusion and were followed by duly authorised settlements. There was, it is true, some internal tribunician agitation at Rome over the levy for the Macedonian and Spanish Wars,[100] but this was insufficient to justify the use of such words as ταραχὴ καὶ κίνησις in relation tc Rome; indeed Polybius emphasises the good effect of Scipio's example as a volunteer in checking the opposition to Spanish enlistment.[101] Hence it is not easy to see immediately why Polybius should have used the phrase ταραχὴ καὶ κίνησις of those years, and one can only assume that it was because he regarded the wars fought then as in ‖ effect meaningless risings against what since 168 had been the dominant power of Rome. They were in fact a disturbance of the order set up by the beneficent machinations of Tyche in that year, and their character was evident from the fact that there was no sense in the way they arose. Events were unpredictable,[102] παράδοξα; policy in the enemy states did not conform to reason. Macedonia provided the unbelievable story of a pseudo-Philip virtually falling out of the skies (ἀεροπετὴς Φίλιππος) and winning victory after victory. The Macedonians, to whom Rome had brought freedom, nevertheless rushed to fight for this impostor, who exiled, tortured and murdered them in large numbers – an example of heaven-sent insanity (δαιμονοβλάβεια).[103] In Achaea, the disaster could furnish no consolation, so replete was it with shameful catastrophe; 'the whole country was visited by an unparalleled attack of madness, with people throwing themselves into wells and over precipices'.[104] The Achaeans had brought this fate upon themselves by listening to wicked men, such as Diaeus and Critolaus.[105] Carthage too was in the hands of the vaniloquent and extravagant Hasdrubal, gross in appearance and utterly callous.[106] It is evidently because power was exercised and abused by irresponsible and crazy leaders in so many countries at once that Polybius regarded the period as one of ταραχὴ καὶ κίνησις.

These characteristics divorce the years 152/1 to 146 from what has gone before, and that is why Polybius feels that he must write about them as if making a new start – especially since they provided a new start in his own career as well. But their very confusion and disconnected character meant that he could not deal with them in a separate monograph. Polybius had no objection in principle to writing a monograph, for he wrote one on the Numantine War,

---

[99] This is certainly true of the wars against the Spaniards and against Carthage; and in the Macedonian War, Rome began by suffering serious setbacks.

[100] See L. R. Taylor, *JRS* 52 (1962) 21ff.

[101] *Cf.* xxxv.4.1–14; above nn. 27–8.

[102] III.4.13.

[103] xxxvi.17.12–15.

[104] xxxviii.16.7.

[105] xxxviii.10.8–13.

[106] xxxviii.7.1–8.15.

separate *a perpetuis suis historiis*, as we know from Cicero's letter to Lucceius.[107] A monograph, however, must have a single defined subject.[108] A universal history could become σωματοειδής[109] through the grand unity of its ‖ theme; but six years of disconnected and irrationally motivated wars were no subject for a book. If Polybius ever envisaged treating 152–146 as a monograph, he must quickly have abandoned the idea.

There was therefore a good reason why he chose to attach his account of those years to his main *Histories*. But one feature of that account deserves attention. In contrast to the mainly cool and cynical record of the period from 168 to 152, Polybius' treatment of the last seven years from 152/1 to 146/5 is not only more detailed, but also far more passionate and committed. In the earlier period, 168–152, Roman policy is subjected to unsympathetic scrutiny: in the later period it is defended,[110] while the behaviour of Rome's enemies is castigated in highly prejudiced and emotional language. This contrast requires an explanation. But before attempting to provide this, we should perhaps pause to examine Polybius' attitude to Rome in more detail.

IV POLYBIUS' ATTITUDE TOWARDS ROME

Polybius' views on Roman policy and behaviour during the period of ταραχή καὶ κίνησις are not easily ascertained because they are not straightforwardly expressed. A good example is the passage in Book xxxvi,[111] in which he describes various Greek views about Rome's treatment of Carthage in the Third Punic War. Four views are recorded. There were those who urged that for the Romans to rid themselves of a long-standing menace was a wise and statesmanlike action. A second group retorted that in destroying Carthage the Romans were demonstrating a change in policy already foreshadowed in the destruction of the Macedonian monarchy; Rome was following in the footsteps of Athens and Sparta and would probably end the same way. Others reinforced that criticism by characterising the Romans' action as impious and treacherous, and a lapse from the principles of the *iustum bellum*. But a fourth group replied that it was the Carthaginians who had broken the treaty with Masinissa and in any case by their subsequent *deditio* had empowered the Romans quite legitimately to impose whatever fate on them that they wished.

Polybius does not tell us which, if any, of these views coincided with his own; and many scholars have thought that he sided with ‖ the critics of Rome, merely disguising his sympathies under a veil of objectivity.[112] In favour of that opinion is a passage in Book x,[113] where, commenting on the failure of the Carthaginians

---

[107] Cic. *Fam.* v.12.2.

[108] *Ibid.* v.12.4, defining an appropriate theme for *modicum quoddam corpus*. See further on this subject G. Avenarius, *Lukians Schrift zur Geschichtsschreibung* (Diss. Frankfurt, 1954) 107ff.

[109] 1.3.4.; *cf.* iii.1.4–5, xiv.12.5.

[110] See above nn. 103–6.

[111] xxxvi.9; Walbank, *op. cit.* (n. 2) 174 n. 112.

[112] *Cf.* Petzold, *op. cit.* (n. 45) 62–3.   [113] x.36.2f.

to exploit the situation in Spain after the deaths of P. and Cn. Scipio, Polybius says that they had acted on the belief that 'there is one method by which power should be acquired and another by which it should be maintained. They had not learnt that those preserve their supremacy best who adhere to the same principles by which they originally established it.' Similarly, in Book v[114] Philip V is condemned for sacking Thermum because 'good men should not make war on wrongdoers with the object of destroying and exterminating them, but with that of correcting and reforming their errors'. Such views as these had been enunciated by the Romans themselves; for after Cynoscephalae Flamininus stated that the Romans never destroyed their enemies after a single war, and that brave men ought to press hard on their enemies while fighting, but afterwards show themselves courageous and highminded in defeat, or moderate and humane if victorious.[115]

Together, these passages might suggest that Polybius aligned himself with Rome's critics. But, as I have shown elsewhere,[116] there are three cogent reasons against that view. First there is the structure of the passage, in which the arguments are arranged chiastically, so that those favouring Rome begin and end the pseudo-debate; and the space allotted to the four views is (in lines of the Teubner text); pro-Roman (9.3–4): 8 lines; anti-Roman (9.5–8): 15 lines; anti-Roman (9.9–11): 15 lines; pro-Roman (9.12–17): 28 lines – a clear weighting in favour of Rome. Secondly, Polybius was with Aemilianus at Carthage giving him moral and, as we know,[117] technical support; it is unlikely that he condemned the policy he helped Scipio to carry out. Thirdly, as we have seen,[118] his general account of the events of 152 to 146 in Macedonia, Carthage and Achaea is exceedingly hostile towards the men controlling policy in those states. In Achaea, Diaeus and Critolaus 'and all who shared their views' were a selection of the worst men from each city, hateful to the gods and corruptors of the nation, ‖ politically inept and wicked too.[119] At Carthage Hasdrubal was empty-headed and pompous, flaunting his riches and grandeur, but callous to the suffering of his people.[120] While in Macedonia Andriscus exiled, tortured and murdered those who were so insane as to follow him.[121] In all three cases there can be little doubt where Polybius' sympathies lay. Indeed, even when he asserts that the behaviour of the Achaeans was far worse than that of Carthage, the best he can find to say of the Carthaginians is that 'they left to posterity some ground, however small, τόπον ἔσχατον ἀπολογίας, to speak in their defence'.[122]

---

[114] v.1.5.

[115] xviii.37.2, 37.7; *cf*. Diod. xxix.31. It is indeed a commonplace; *cf*. Walbank, *op. cit.* (n. 5) 15 n. 3 [above, p. 287 n. 36].

[116] *JRS* 55 (1965) 8–11 [above, pp. 168–73]; *op. cit.* (n. 2) 178–81; *op. cit.* (n. 5) 13–18 [above, pp. 286ff.].

[117] *Cf*. xxxviii.19 = Plut. *Apophth*. p. 200. See below, p. 341.

[118] Above, p. 337.   [119] See n. 105.

[120] See n. 106.   [121] See n. 103.

[122] xxxviii.1.5.

Momigliano has argued[123] that by the exceptional character of this long 'debate' between the Greeks Polybius has given some indication of his own mental reservations; and elsewhere[124] he makes the point that there is an inconsistency between the statement that Rome was on sound legal grounds in destroying Carthage – the fourth view propounded in the 'debate'[125] – and Polybius' previous declaration[126] that the Romans had long ago decided to act against Carthage but were waiting for a suitable pretext. This is perhaps not a very valid argument for, as H. H. Schmitt has pointed out,[127] in speaking of the Roman need for a plausible pretext Polybius was concerned only with the advantage, τὸ σύμφερον, of this in relation to opinion abroad.[128] The Romans almost did not go to war for want of such a πρόφασις; and once they had obtained an uncontrovertible pretext both for declaring war and for destroying Carthage, there was no reason why Polybius should condemn them for making full use of it in order to do what they clearly believed to be in their interest.

It therefore seems to me certain that Polybius agreed with those of the Greeks – we do not know who they were or where this subject was being hotly debated – who defended, in legalistic terms, the Roman case for destroying Carthage. He was equally hostile to the ‖ Macedonian and Achaean leaders who were responsible for the wars against Rome during 150 to 146. If that is so, then admittedly he had changed his mind on how conquered peoples ought to be treated when they followed foolish advisers, broke their faith and let themselves be drawn into war. But, as I have observed elsewhere,[129] both his earlier and his later views rested basically on expediency; and since the imperial situation had changed, the behaviour appropriate to the ruling power might also change. Hitherto, the Romans had felt the need to moderate their relations with the Hellenistic powers and the Greek cities within a context in which they were still open to challenge. But with Rome mistress of the *oecumene* that was no longer so. If she now took the ruthless decision to obliterate Carthage, Corinth and later Numantia, that could be the simplest solution. Whatever Flamininus might say, the Romans had never hesitated to inflict savage punitive measures whenever they thought fit. We have certainly no reason to think that the Roman general who proudly took the titles of Africanus and Numantinus felt any scruples about this, nor need we suppose that his friend Polybius felt any either. We may now return to the purpose of Polybius' extension.

---

[123] *Atti Acc. Torino* 107 (1972–3) 698 = *Actes du IXe congrès de l'Association Guillaume Budé, Rome, 13–18 avril 1973* (Paris, 1975) 187–8. See below, n. 148.

[124] *Polybe* (n. 5) 35.   [125] xxxvi.9.16–17.

[126] xxxvi.2.1.–4.   [127] *Polybe* (n. 5) 35.

[128] xxxvi.2.4.   [129] *Op. cit.* (n. 5) 21 [above, pp. 290–1].

V THE REAL PURPOSE OF THE EXTENSION TO 146/5

We have already seen[130] that in the singularly confused chapters of Book III in which he gives his reasons for extending his *Histories* to 146/5 Polybius says that he wants his readers to pass judgement on Rome, yet he never clearly indicates from what point of view they are to do this, and indeed leaves them quite uncertain what conclusions they are expected to arrive at. A careful analysis of the surviving fragments of Books XXX–XXXIII contributes little to the clarification of this problem, since these show a change in Polybius' attitude towards Rome between his account of the years 167–152 and that of the years 151–146/5. Nor can our difficulties be ascribed to the fragmentary nature of the text since the problems spring out of what is there, not out of what is missing.

In view of this one is bound to wonder whether the reason Polybius alleges for his extension is the real, or at any rate the whole, reason. To answer that question we should perhaps recall Polybius' position at ‖ the date when he decided to add Books XXXI–XL to his *Histories*. He had by then, we may assume, completed but not necessarily published his thirty-book edition down to Pydna. We cannot be sure whether he had already written his *Numantine War*.[131] As we saw, he had in his possession extensive memoranda covering the years 167 to 152/1, when he was in Rome, and perhaps equally extensive notes or narratives covering the important events in which he was involved between 151 and 146. During those years he had accompanied Scipio to Spain and Africa, and had crossed the Alps on his way back to Italy.[132] After being repatriated in 150, he had set out to join Scipio in Africa, only to find his instructions countermanded, when he reached Corcyra.[133] He had subsequently gone out again and been close to Scipio throughout the land campaigns in Africa down to the destruction of Carthage. We hear from Ammianus[134] of his share in an attempt to penetrate the city, which some scholars have associated with Scipio's attack on the Megara district of Carthage in 147,[135] but which is perhaps more likely to be an incident in the final assault of 146; and Plutarch tells us of advice which he gave to Scipio to prevent the mole he had built being attacked from the landward side – advice which Scipio disastrously neglected.[136] Once Carthage had fallen Polybius made his famous voyage of exploration through the Straits of Gibraltar and down the coast of Africa;[137] he returned later in the year to Achaea, where he arrived shortly after the

---

[130] See above, pp. 330–4.

[131] This depends on when the extension was written (see above, pp. 327–30). Polybius' presence at Numantia is not attested; but on Scipio's ἴλη φίλων see App. *Hisp.* 84, *cf.* 89; Walbank, *op. cit.* (n. 2) 12 n. 59. On Polybius' monograph on the war see above, n. 107.

[132] See my *Commentary* (n. 15) 4 for references.

[133] XXXVI.11.1.

[134] Amm. Marc. XXIV.2.14–17 = Polyb. XXXVIII.19a.

[135] *Cf.* S. Gsell, *Histoire ancienne de l'Afrique du nord* 3 (Paris, 1918) 376 n. 1.

[136] See above, n. 117.

[137] *Cf.* Pliny, *NH* v.9 = Polyb. XXXIV.15.7.

destruction of Corinth by senatorial decree.[138] He spent the rest of 146 and part of 145 mediating between the Roman authorities and his defeated countrymen and was able to secure concessions;[139] the Commissioners left to him the task of solving many of the problems which concerned the laws of the various cities.[140] This work was recognised ‖ in many honorary decrees set up by those in Achaea who appreciated what he had done. He also made another trip to Rome in furtherance of this object.[141]

We can safely assume that Polybius had full records of all this. The stimulus to write it up *may* have come from Scipio's death and the desire to perpetuate his friend's memory; or it may have come earlier from motives which we can no longer ascertain. I have already given the reasons which seem to favour the later date;[142] but we cannot be sure. I have also explained[143] why Polybius could not incorporate the years 152–146 into a monograph; there was no unity of theme, but merely a succession of chaotic movements and irrational risings. In view of this Polybius seems to have decided to extend his *Histories* down to 146/5, in this way killing two birds with one stone. For he was thus able to use both the material collected at Rome and his records of the more exciting later events in which he had been successively αὐτόπτης, συνεργός and χειριστής.[144] This plan enabled him to make some additions to his original text, to do justice to the geographical interests which had increasingly occupied him since his voyages and journeys in the West,[145] and, at a very late stage in the composition, to incorporate in Book II a study, which he had written much earlier, of the Achaean Confederation and the Cleomenean War, to balance his account of affairs in the West; hitherto his readers had had to rely for this on Aratus' *Memoirs*.[146]

Having decided on this plan to extend his *Histories* to 146 by adding a further ten books, Polybius had to justify this; and the ‖ reason he gave was to enable his readers to judge how Rome had exercised her power. It contained of course an element of truth, for the first four books, XXX–XXXIII, were full of comments

---

[138] XXXIX.2.2.   [139] *Cf.* XXXIX.3.1–11.

[140] XXXIX.5.2–6; on the settlement of Achaea see Schwertfeger, *op. cit.* (n. 15). His argument that the Achaean Confederation was never dissolved *de iure* in 146, despite Paus. VII.16.9, does not convince me.

[141] XXXIX.8.1; the date is probably autumn 145 or even winter 145/4.

[142] See above, pp. 327ff.

[143] See above pp. 337–8.

[144] *Cf.* III.4.13. As Professor Peremans pointed out in the course of the discussion following this paper, Polybius here gives it as his main reason (τὸ...μέγιστον) for describing the period of ταραχὴ καὶ κίνησις that he had himself played a prominent part in its events.

[145] See P. Pédech, *LEC* (1956) 3–24; *La méthode historique de Polybe* (Paris, 1964) 515–97.

[146] *Cf.* I.3.2. This implies that the original version of Book II lacked what are now chapters 37–40, and that would make it disproportionately short. However, the original distribution of events between Books I and II was not necessarily the present one. That gives Book I 118 and Book II 88 Teubner pages. But if Book I originally contained only the First Punic War and Book II events in the West from 241 to 220, including the Carthaginian Mercenary War, the length of Book I would have been approximately 86 and Book II approximately 78 Teubner pages, each thus being slightly shorter than the present Book II. This is of course only surmise, but it shows that the late inclusion of the Achaean chapters in Book II need not necessarily involve structural problems.

on Roman rule reflecting the cynical views of the Greek detainees and those Greeks at Rome. But from 151 onward the perspective has changed. Events are now viewed from the Roman camp, whence they seemed irrational, and wholly to be condemned, a study in ταραχὴ καὶ κίνησις. As Pédech rightly observes,[147] Polybius' views in these ten books represent a compromise, or perhaps an unresolved contradiction; that is because they reflect Polybius' two quite different situations.[148] It is, I would suggest, this unresolved conflict in Polybius' own views throughout these last books which prevents him from clarifying the criteria by which the Romans might have been judged, whether in terms of their own interest or in terms of the interests of the subject peoples. Eventually he may have come to feel that his new purpose, clumsily and obscurely set out and difficult to fulfil, was something of an embarrassment. This could be why we hear nothing of it in the epilogue with which he wound up Book xxxix.[149]

The last five books of the *Histories*, xxxv–xxxix, were very largely concerned with Scipio and Polybius – a personal story, one might say, and one which throws a good deal of light on the historian as well as on his patron. But it was also a story of direct relevance to Rome, not for any moral or political judgements it might authorise, but as a significant chapter in the growing symbiosis of two cultures, which was in the long run to prove as important for the future history of Rome as her conquest of the Mediterranean *oecumene*.[150]

[147] *Cf.* Pédech, *Polybe* (n. 5) 33–4.

[148] Momigliano suggests that they also betray his uncertainty and hidden guilt: *cf. art. cit.* (n. 123) 699, 'arrivato a raccontare gli avvenimenti del 146 Polibio sentì il bisogno di guardarsi intorno, e ciò che vide non era bello'. This view rests on the assumption that Polybius' report of the 'debate' on Roman policy in relation to Carthage reflects his doubts about the justice of the Roman case (see above, n. 123), and I am not persuaded by it.

[149] For Lehmann's theory that the epilogue was not written by Polybius see above, pp. 326ff.

[150] A version of this paper was read in the *Seminarie voor Geschiedenis van de Oudheid* in the Catholic University of Leuven on 24 March 1976, and I should like to express my grateful thanks to the colleagues who took part in the discussion which followed for their comments and suggestions.

PUBLICATIONS OF F. W. WALBANK, 1933–1984

Papers marked with an asterisk are included in the present selection.

1933

1. *Aratos of Sicyon* (Thirwall Prize Essay, 1933). Cambridge: University Press, 1933

1936

2. 'Aratos' attack on Cynaetha', *JHS* 56 (1936) 64–71
*3. 'The accession of Ptolemy Epiphanes', *JEA* 22 (1936) 20–34
4. Review of G. L. Barber, *The historian Ephorus* (Cambridge: University Press, 1935), *JHS* 56 (1936) 103–4
5. Review of W. W. Tarn, *Alexander the Great and the unity of mankind* (London: Milford, 1933), *JEA* 22 (1936) 109

1937

6. (In collaboration with A. H. McDonald) 'The origins of the Second Macedonian War', *JRS* 27 (1937) 180–207
7. Review of E. Kornemann, *Die Alexandergeschichte des Königs Ptolemaios I. von Aegypten: Versuch einer Rekonstruktion* (Leipzig-Berlin: Teubner, 1935), *JHS* 57 (1937) 98–9
8. Review of G. Daux, *Delphes au IIe et au Ier siècle depuis l'abaissement de l'Étolie jusqu'à la paix romaine* (Paris: de Boccard, 1936), *JHS* 57 (1937) 99–100
9. Review of W. P. Theunissen, *Ploutarchos' Leven van Aratos met historisch-topographisch commentaar* (Nijmegen: Berkhout, 1935), *JHS* 57 (1937) 100–1
10. Review of R. Flacelière, *Les Aitoliens à Delphes: Contribution à l'histoire de la Grèce centrale au III siècle av. J.-C.* (Paris: de Boccard, 1937), *JHS* 57 (1937) 271–2
11. Review of W. H. Porter, *Plutarch's Life of Aratus with introduction, notes and appendix* (Cork and Dublin: Cork University Press, 1937), and A. J. Koster, *Plutarchi vita Arati* (Leiden: Brill, 1937), *CR* 51 (1937) 223–5

1938

*12. Φίλιππος τραγῳδούμενος: a Polybian experiment', *JHS* 58 (1938) 55–68
13. Review of R. J. Bonner and Gertrude Smith, *The administration of justice from Homer to Aristotle* (Chicago: University Press, 1938), *G and R* 8 (1938/9) 61

14. Review of J. G. C. Anderson, *Cornelii Taciti de origine et situ Germanorum* (Oxford: Clarendon Press, 1938), *G and R* 8 (1938/9) 126

1939

15. Review of *The Cambridge ancient history* 12, ed. S. A. Cook and others (Cambridge: University Press, 1939), *G and R* 9 (1939/40) 54–5
16. Review of A. Aymard, *Les assemblées de la confédération achaienne: étude critique d'institutions et d'histoire* (Bordeaux: Feret et fils, 1938) and *Les premiers rapports de Rome et de la confédération achaienne (198–189 av. J.-C.)* (Bordeaux: Feret et fils, 1938), *CR* 53 (1939) 139–40

1940

17. *Philip V of Macedon* (Hare Prize Essay, 1939). Cambridge: University Press, 1940
18. 'Licia telae addere (Virgil, *Georg.* 1.284–6)', *CQ* 34 (1940) 93–104

1941

*19. 'A note on the embassy of Q. Marcius Philippus, 172 B.C.', *JRS* 31 (1941) 82–93

1942

20. 'Olympichus of Alinda and the Carian expedition of Antigonus Doson', *JHS* 62 (1942) 8–13
21. 'Alcaeus of Messene, Philip V and Rome, Part I', *CQ* 36 (1942) 134–45
22. Review of Carl A. Roebuck, *A history of Messenia from 369 to 146 B.C.* (Chicago: University Libraries, 1941), *CR* 56 (1942) 39–40
23. Review of Karl Barwick, *Caesar's Commentarii und das Corpus Caesarianum* (*Philologus* Suppl.-Band 31 no. 2) (Leipzig: Dieterich, 1938), *CR* 56 (1942) 80–1
24. Review of M. Rostovtzeff, *The social and economic history of the Hellenistic world* (3 vols., Oxford: Clarendon Press, 1941), *CR* 56 (1942) 81–4
25. Review of J. Göhler, *Rom und Italien: die römische Bundesgenossenpolitik von den Anfängen bis zum Bundesgenossenkrieg* (Breslauer historische Forschungen 13) (Breslau: Priebatsch, 1939), *CR* 56 (1942) 86–8
26. Review of Coleman H. Benedict, *A history of Narbo* (Princeton, N.J.: privately printed, 1941), *CR* 56 (1942) 88–9

1943

27. 'Alcaeus of Messene, Philip V and Rome, Part II', *CQ* 37 (1943) 1–13
28. 'Polybius on the Roman constitution', *CQ* 37 (1943) 73–89
29. Review of John Day, *An economic history of Athens under Roman domination* (New York: Columbia University Press, 1942), *G and R* 12 (1943) 91–2

1944

30. 'Alcaeus of Messene, Philip V and Rome: a footnote', *CQ* 38 (1944) 87–8
31. 'The causes of Greek decline', *JHS* 64 (1944) 10–20; résumé in *PCA* 41 (1944) 11–12
32. Review of R. S. Rogers, *Studies in the reign of Tiberius: some imperial virtues of Tiberius and Drusus Julius Caesar* (Baltimore: Johns Hopkins, 1943), *G and R* 13 (1944) 29–30
33. Review of F. E. Adcock, *The Roman art of war* (Martin Classical Lectures 8) (Cambridge, Mass.: Harvard University Press, 1940), *G and R* 13 (1944) 30–1

1945

*34. 'Polybius, Philinus and the First Punic War', *CQ* 39 (1945) 1–18
35. 'Men and donkeys', *CQ* 39 (1945) 122
36. 'Phalaris' bull in Timaeus (Diod. Sic. XIII.90.4–7)', *CR* 59 (1945) 39–42
37. Review of G. M. Calhoun, *Introduction to Greek legal science* (Oxford: Clarendon Press, 1944), *G and R* 14 (1945) 30
38. Review of R. Taubenschlag, *The law of Greco-Roman Egypt in the light of papyri, 332 B.C.–640 A.D.* (New York: Herald Square Press, 1944), *G and R* 14 (1945) 93

1946

39. *The decline of the Roman Empire in the West*. London: Cobbett Press, 1946
40. (In collaboration with I. F. Brash) 'Classical studies in Great Britain during the war', with an appendix on publications 1940–1945, *BAGB* n.s.1 (1946) 73–105
41. 'Polybius and the growth of Rome', résumé in *PCA* 43 (1946) 11–12
42. Review of J. L. Myres, *Mediterranean culture* (Frazer Lecture, 1943) (Cambridge: University Press, 1943), *G and R* 15 (1946) 31
43. Review of M. Feyel, *Polybe et l'histoire de Béotie au IIIe siècle avant notre ère* (Paris: de Boccard, 1942), *CR* 60 (1946) 41–2

1947

44. Review of J. Vallejo, *Tito Livio, libro xxi: edición, estudio preliminar y comentario* (Madrid: Instituto 'Antonio de Nebrija', 1946), *CR* 61 (1947) 107–9
45. Review of S. Accame, *Il dominio romano in Grecia dalla guerra acaica ad Augusto* (Rome: Signorelli, 1946), *JRS* 37 (1947) 205–7
46. Review of J. H. Thiel, *Studies on the history of Roman sea-power in Republican times* (Amsterdam: North Holland Publishing Co., 1946), *Erasmus* 1 (1947) 655–8

1948

47. 'The geography of Polybius', *C et M* 9 (1948) 155–82
48. Review of W. Kendrick Pritchett, *The five Attic tribes after Kleisthenes* (Baltimore: privately printed, 1943), *Liverpool Annals of Archaeology* 28 (1948) 88–9
49. Review of K. Hanell, *Das altrömische eponyme Amt* (Lund: Gleerup, 1946), *CR* 62 (1948) 83–4

50. Review of Esther V. Hansen, *The Attalids of Pergamon* (Cornell studies in classical philology 29) (Ithaca, N.Y.: Cornell University Press, 1947), *CR* 62 (1948) 149–50
51. Review of A. R. Burn, *Alexander the Great and the Hellenistic empire* (London: Hodder and Stoughton, 1947), *JHS* 68 (1948) 159–60
52. Review of H. E. Stier, *Grundlagen und Sinn der griechischen Geschichte* (Stuttgart: Cotta, 1945), *JHS* 68 (1948) 160–1

1949

53. *Oxford classical dictionary*, ed. M. Cary and others (Oxford: Clarendon Press, 1949). Articles on: Agis IV, Alexander son of Craterus, Alexander Polyhistor, Antigonus II, Antigonus III, Antigonus of Carystus, Aratus of Sicyon, Areus, Biography (Greek), Chamaeleon, Chremonides, Cleomenes III, Cleonymus, Craterus governor of Corinth, Demetrius of Phalerum, Demetrius II, Demetrius of Pharos, Demiourgoi, Demochares, Demophanes and Ecdelus, Duris, Hermippus of Smyrna, Idomeneus of Lampsacus, Lachares, Lydiades, Marcellinus, Olympiodorus, Philip V, Plutarch, Satyrus, Sosicrates, Stesimbrotus, Stratocles
*54. 'Roman declaration of war in the third and second centuries', *CP* 44 (1949) 15–19
55. Review of G. B. Cardona, *Polibio di Megalopoli: Storie interpretate in lingua italiana* 1: *Libri 1 e 2* (Naples: Edizioni scientifiche italiane, 1948), *CR* 63 (1949) 139
56. Review of J. O. Thomson, *History of ancient geography* (Cambridge: University Press, 1948), *EHR* 64 (1949) 360–1
57. Review of M. Cary, *The geographic background of Greek and Roman history* (Oxford: Clarendon Press, 1949), *JHS* 69 (1949) 101

1950

58. *Chambers's encyclopaedia* (Oxford: Pergamum Press, 1950). Articles on: Achaea (history), Aetolia, Alexander, Arcadia, Byzantium, Macedonia (ancient history), Thrace (history)
*59. 'Naval *triarii* (Polyb. 1.26.6)', *CR* 64 (1950) 10–11
60. 'Greek history, 1945–1947', *YWCS* 34 (1950) 43–59
61. 'The classics in England: some problems of the last decade', in *Atti del congresso della Sodalitas Erasmiana* 1 (Naples: Pironti, 1950) 112–17
62. 'Social problems of antiquity', in *IXe congrès international des sciences historiques* 1: *Rapports* (Paris: Arman Colin, 1950) 261–79
63. Review of E. Mioni, *Polibio* (Problemi d'oggi, serie letteraria 3) (Padua: Cedam, 1949), *Erasmus* 3 (1950) 273–6
64. Review of A. J. B. Wace, *Mycenae, an archaeological history and guide* (Princeton, N.J.: University Press, 1949), *Erasmus* 3 (1950) 490–2
65. Review of H. Goldman and others, *Excavations of Gözlü Kule, Tarsus* 1: *The Hellenistic and Roman periods* (Princeton, N.J.: University Press, 1950), *Erasmus* 3 (1950) 759–62
66. Review of H. Bengtson, *Einführung in die alte Geschichte* (Munich: Biederstein, 1949), *JHS* 70 (1950) 79
67. Review of H. U. Instinsky, *Alexander der Grosse am Hellespont* (Godesberg: Küpper, 1949), *JHS* 70 (1950) 79–81

68. Review of R. Paribeni, *La Macedonia sino ad Alessandro Magno* (Milan: Vita e Pensiero, 1947), *JHS* 70 (1950) 81
69. Review of E. Kornemann, *Weltgeschichte des Mittelmeerraumes von Philipp II. von Makedonien bis Muhammed* (2 vols., Munich: Biederstein, 1948–9), *JRS* 40 (1950) 129–32
70. Review of F. Schachermeyr, *Alexander der Grosse: Ingenium und Macht* (Graz-Salzburg-Vienna: Anton Pustel, 1949), *Gnomon* 22 (1950) 188

1951

71. 'Polybius on the Pontus and the Bosphorus (IV.39–42)', in *Studies presented to D. M. Robinson on his seventieth birthday* 1, ed. G. E. Mylonas (St Louis, Mo.: Washington University, 1951) 469–79
*72. 'The problem of Greek nationality', *Phoenix* 5 (1951) 41–60; résumé in *PCA* 48 (1951) 23–4
73. Review of M. Cary, *The geographic background of Greek and Roman history* (Oxford: Clarendon Press, 1949), *History* 36 (1951) 250
74. Review of T. Sinko, *De Lycophronis tragici carmine Sibyllino* (extract from *Eos* 43 (1948/9) 3–39), *CP* 46 (1951) 124–6
75. Review of K. M. T. Chrimes, *Ancient Sparta, a re-examination of the evidence* (Manchester: University Press, 1949), *CR* n.s. 1 (1951) 98–100
76. Review of R. Del Re, *Plutarco, Vita di Bruto, revisione del testo, introduzione e note²* (Florence: Le Monnier, 1948), *CR* n.s. 1 (1951) 115
77. Review of H. H. Scullard, *Roman politics, 220–150 B.C.* (Oxford: Clarendon Press, 1951), *EHR* 66 (1951) 566–8

1952

78. 'Trade and industry under the later Roman Empire in the West', in *Cambridge economic history of Europe* 2, ed. M. M. Postan and E. E. Rich (Cambridge: University Press, 1952) 33–85.
79. Review of H. L. Lorimer, *Homer and the monuments* (London: Macmillan, 1950), *Journal of Aesthetics and Art Criticism* 10 (1951/2) 183–4
80. Review of E. Demougeot, *De l'unité à la division de l'empire romain: essai sur le gouvernement impérial* (Paris: Adrien-Maisonneuve, 1951), *CR* 2 (1952) 212–14

1953

81. *The decline of the Roman Empire in the West.* New York: Henry Schumann, 1953 (*cf.* no. 39)
82. 'The Roman occupation', in *A scientific survey of Merseyside*, ed. W. Smith (British Association Handbook) (Liverpool: University Press, 1953) 214–20
83. Review of E. Mireaux, *La reine Bérénice* (Paris: Albin Michel, 1951), *CR* 3 (1953) 12
84. Review of W. Hartke, *Römische Kinderkaiser: eine Strukturanalyse römischen Denkens und Daseins* (Berlin: Akademie-Verlag, 1951), *CR* 3 (1953) 47–9
85. Review of T. R. S. Broughton, *The magistrates of the Roman Republic* 1: *509–100 B.C.* (New York: American Philological Association, 1951), *CR* 3 (1953) 111–13

86. Review of G. Lopuszanski, *La date de la capture de Valérien et la chronologie des empereurs gaulois* (Cahiers de l'Institut d'études polonaises en Belgique 9) (Brussels: Institut d'études polonaises, 1951), *CR* 3 (1953) 126–7
87. Review of S. Davis, *Race-relations in ancient Egypt: Greek, Egyptian, Hebrew, Roman* (London: Methuen, 1951), *JHS* 73 (1953) 174
88. Review of J. L. Myres, *Geographical history in Greek lands* (Oxford: Clarendon Press, 1953), *EHR* 68 (1953) 629–30
89. Review of V. Ehrenberg, *The people of Aristophanes: a sociology of old Attic comedy*[2] (Oxford: Blackwell, 1951), *Journal of Aesthetics and Art Criticism* 11 (1952/3) 85–6

1954

90. (In collaboration with C. O. Brink) 'The construction of the sixth book of Polybius', *CQ* n.s. 4 (1954) 97–122
91. Review of W. H. Porter, *Plutarch's Life of Dion, with introduction and notes* (Dublin: Hodges, Figgis, 1952), *CR* 4 (1954) 18–20
92. Review of T. R. S. Broughton, *The magistrates of the Roman Republic* 2: *99–31 B.C.* (New York: American Philological Association, 1952), *CR* 4 (1954) 282–3
93. Review of S. Gerevini, *Plutarco, Vita di Flaminino: introduzione, testo, traduzione e commento* (Milan: Marzorati, 1952), *CR* 4 (1954) 298
94. Review of Paul-Marie Duval, *La vie quotidienne en Gaule pendant la paix romaine (Ier-IIIe siècles après J.-C.)* (Paris: Hachette, 1952), *Erasmus* 7 (1954) 49–51
95. Review of Maurice Holleaux, *Études d'épigraphie et d'histoire grecques* 4: *Rome, la Macédoine et l'orient grec, première partie*, ed. L. Robert (Paris: Adrien-Maisonneuve, 1952), *Erasmus* 7 (1954) 51–4
96. Review of J. Béranger, *Recherches sur l'aspect idéologique du principat* (Schweizerische Beiträge zur Altertumswissenschaft 6) (Basel: Friedrich Reinhardt, 1953), *Erasmus* 7 (1954) 624–7
97. Review of M. Grant, *Ancient history* (London: Methuen, 1952), *History* 39 (1954) 102
98. Review of P. Grimal, *La vie à Rome dans l'antiquité* (Que sais-je?) (Paris: Presses universitaires de France, 1953), *History* 39 (1954) 293
99. Review of *Pauly's Realencyclopädie der classischen Altertumswissenschaft* 21.2 (Polemon-Pontanene), ed. K. Ziegler (Stuttgart: Druckenmüller, 1952), *JHS* 74 (1954) 185–6
100. Review of H. H. Scullard, *A history of the Roman world, 753 to 146 B.C.*[2] (London: Methuen, 1951), *JRS* 44 (1954) 122–3

1955

101. 'Tragic history: a reconsideration', *BICS* 2 (1955) 4–14
102. Review-discussion of K. von Fritz. *The theory of the mixed constitution in antiquity: a critical analysis of Polybius' political ideas* (New York: Columbia University Press, 1954), *JRS* 45 (1955) 150–5
103. Review of Piero Meloni, *Perseo e la fine della monarchia macedone* (Rome: 'L'Erma' di Bretschneider, 1953), *JHS* 75 (1955) 194–5
104. Review of A. Aymard and J. Auboyer, *L'orient et la Grèce* (Histoire générale des civilisations 1) (Paris: Presses universitaires de France, 1953), *History* 40 (1955) 116–17

105. Review of A. Aymard and J. Auboyer, *Rome et son empire* (Histoire générale des civilisations 2) (Paris: Presses universitaires de France, 1954), *History* 40 (1955) 326–7

106. Review of Maria Teresa Piraino, *Antigono Dosone re di Macedonia* (Estratto dagli Atti dell'Accademia di Scienze Lettere e Arti di Palermo, serie 4, vol. 13, 1952–3) (Palermo: Accademia, 1954), *Gnomon* 27 (1955) 300

107. Review of Maurice Holleaux, *Études d'épigraphie et d'histoire grecques* 4: *Rome, la Macédoine et l'orient grec, première partie*, ed. L. Robert (Paris: Adrien-Maisonneuve, 1952), *CR* 5 (1955) 220

108. Review of S. I. Oost, *Roman policy in Epirus and Acarnania in the age of the Roman conquest of Greece* (Arnold Foundation Studies n.s. 4) (Dallas: Southern Methodist University Press, 1954), *CR* 5 (1955) 303–4

1956

*109. 'Some reflections on Hannibal's pass', *JRS* 46 (1956) 37–45

110. Review of H. Hubert, *Les Germains* (Évolution de l'humanité) (Paris: Albin Michel, 1952), *Erasmus* 9 (1956) 484–7

111. Review of Denis van Berchem, *L'armée de Dioclétien et la réforme constantinienne* (Institut français d'archéologie de Beyrouth, Bibliothèque archéologique et historique 56) (Paris: Geuthner, 1952), *Erasmus* 9 (1956) 601–5

112. Review of S. Katz, *The decline of Rome and the rise of mediaeval Europe* (Ithaca, N.Y.: Cornell University Press, 1955), *CR* 6 (1956) 291–3

113. Review of J. A. O. Larsen, *Representative government in Greek and Roman history* (Sather Classical Lectures 28) (Berkeley-Los Angeles: University of California Press, 1965), *Gnomon* 28 (1956) 383–5

114. Review of F. J. Wiseman, *Roman Spain* (London: Bell, 1956), *Bulletin of Hispanic Studies* 33 (1956) 234

1957

115. *A historical commentary on Polybius* 1: *Books 1–6*. Oxford: Clarendon Press, 1957

116. Review of P. R. Franke, *Alt-Epirus und das Königtum der Molosser* (Kallmünz-Opf.: Lassleben, 1955), *CR* 7 (1957) 59–60

117. Review of Piero Meloni, *Il valore storico e le fonti del libro macedonico di Appiano* (Annali delle Facoltà di Lettere, Filosofia e Magistero dell'Università di Cagliari 23) (Rome: 'L'Erma' di Bretschneider, 1955), *CR* 7 (1957) 70–2

118. Review of G. Avenarius, *Lukians Schrift zur Geschichtsschreibung* (Diss. Frankfurt a/M, 1954) (Meisenheim am Glan: Anton Hain, 1956), *Gnomon* 29 (1957) 416–19

1958

119. Review of A. K. Narain, *The Indo-Greeks* (Oxford: Clarendon Press, 1957), *History* 43 (1958) 125–6

120. Review of Paul Cloché, *Un fondateur d'empire: Philippe II, roi de Macédoine (383/2–336/5)* (St Etienne: Dumas, 1955), *CR* 8 (1958) 156–8

121. Review of H. Berve, *Dion* (Akademie der Wissenschaften und der Literatur in Mainz: Abhandlungen der geistes- und sozialwissenschaftlichen Klasse, 1956 no. 10) (Wiesbaden: Steiner, 1957), *CR* 8 (1958) 269–71
122. Review of M. Grant, *Roman history from coins* (Cambridge: University Press, 1958), and K. D. White, *Historical Roman coins illustrating the period 44 B.C. to A.D. 55* (Grahamstown: Rhodes University, 1958), *JRS* 48 (1958) 228–9

1959

123. Review of P. Lévèque, *Pyrrhos* (Bibliothèque des écoles françaises d'Athènes et de Rome 185) (Paris: de Boccard, 1957), *EHR* 74 (1959) 93–4
124. Review of T. S. Brown, *Timaeus of Tauromenium* (University of California Studies in History 55) (Berkeley-Los Angeles: University of California Press, 1958), *EHR* 74 (1959) 333–4
125. Review of K. Latte and others, *Histoire et historiens dans l'antiquité* (Entretiens sur l'antiquité classique 4) (Vandoeuvres-Geneva: Fondation Hardt, 1958), *JRS* 49 (1959) 194–6
126. Review of R. Syme, *Colonial élites: Rome, Spain and the Americas* (The Whidden Lectures, 1954) (Oxford: University Press, 1958), *JRS* 49 (1959) 217
127. Review of *Acta congressus Madvigiani: Proceedings of the second international congress of classical studies, Copenhagen, 1954*, ed. C. Høeg and others (5 vols., Copenhagen: Munksgaard (1–14), Nordisk Sprag- og Kulturforlag (5), 1957–8), *JRS* 49 (1959) 218
128. Review of A. J. Toynbee, *Hellenism: the history of a civilisation* (Home University Library) (London: Oxford University Press, 1959), *History* 44 (1959) 244–5

1960

*129. 'History and tragedy', *Historia* 9 (1960) 216–34
130. Review of N. G. L. Hammond, *A history of Greece to 322 B.C.* (Oxford: Clarendon Press, 1959), *History* 45 (1960) 131–3

1961

131. Review of T. R. S. Broughton, *The magistrates of the Roman Republic: Supplement* (New York: American Philological Asociation, 1960), *CR* 11 (1961) 168–9
132. Review of J. Carcopino, *Les étapes de l'impérialisme romain* (Paris: Hachette, 1961), *JRS* 51 (1961) 228–9
133. Review of G. Susini, *Ricerche sulla battaglia del Trasimeno* (Estratto dall'Annuario dell'Accademia etrusca di Cortona 11, 1956–60) (Cortona: Accademia etrusca, 1960), *JRS* 51 (1961) 232–4
134. Review of M. I. Finley (ed.), *Slavery in classical antiquity: views and controversies* (Cambridge: Heffer, 1960), and Dev Raj Chanana, *Slavery in ancient India* (New Delhi: People's Publishing House, 1960), *Economic history review* 14 (1961) 384–5

1962

135. Introduction to reprint of E. S. Shuckburgh, *The histories of Polybius* (Bloomington, Ind.: Indiana University Press, 1962), vii–xxv
*136. 'Polemic in Polybius', *JRS* 52 (1962) 1–12
137. 'Surety in Alexander's letter to the Chians', *Phoenix* 16 (1962) 178–80
138. Review of E. Manni, *Fasti ellenistici e romani (323–31 a.C.)* (Supplementi a *Kokalos* 1) (Palermo: Banca di Sicilia, 1961), *CR* 12 (1952) 272–3
139. Review of B. Ferro, *Le origini della II guerra macedonica* (Estratto dagli Atti dell'Accademia di Scienze, Lettere e Arti di Palermo, serie 4, vol. 19, 1958–9), *CR* 12 (1962) 273–4
140. Review of T. W. Africa, *Phylarchus and the Spartan revolution* (University of California Publications in History 68) (Berkeley–Los Angeles: University of California Press, 1961), *CR* 12 (1962) 315–16

1963

141. *The decline of the Roman Empire in the West.* Revised edition in Japanese, trans. T. Yoshimura. Tokyo: Iwanami Shoten, 1963 (*cf.* no. 39)
142. 'Le istituzioni politiche', in *Tutto su Roma antica*, ed. G. Giannelli and U. E. Paoli (Florence: Bemporad-Marzocco, 1963) 193–211
*143. 'Polybius and Rome's eastern policy', *JRS* 53 (1963) 1–13
144. 'Three notes on Polybius xii', in *Miscellanea di studi alessandrini in memoria di Augusto Rostagni* (Turin: Bottega d'Erasmo, 1963) 203–13
145. Review of W. Hoffmann, *Hannibal* (Göttingen: Vandenhoek and Ruprecht, 1962), *JRS* 53 (1963) 249–50
146. Review of of P. Pédech, *Polybe, Histoires, Livre xii, texte établi traduit et commenté* (Collection Budé) (Paris: Les Belles Lettres, 1961), *CR* 13 (1963) 58–60
147. Review of Claude Mossé, *La fin de la démocratie athénienne* (Paris: Presses universitaires de France, 1962), *CR* 13 (1963) 317–19

1964

148. 'Polybius and the Roman state', *GRBS* 5 (1964) 239–60
149. Review of F. E. Adcock, *Thucydides and his History* (Cambridge: University Press, 1963), *History* 49 (1964) 48
150. Review of C. Hignett, *Xerxes' invasion of Greece* (Oxford: Clarendon Press, 1963), *History* 49 (1964) 48–9
151. Review of A. W. Gomme, *More essays in Greek history and literature*, ed. D. A. Campbell (Oxford: Blackwell, 1962), *JHS* 84 (1964) 201–2
152. Review of E. J. Bickerman, *La cronologia nel mondo antico* (Florence: La Nuova Italia, 1963), *CR* 14 (1964) 186–7
153. Review of L. Moretti, *Ricerche sulle leghe greche (Peloponnesiaca-Beotica-Licia)* (Problemi e ricerche di storia antica 2) (Rome: 'L'Erma' di Bretschneider, 1962), *Erasmus* 16 (1964) 482–3

1965

*154. 'Political morality and the friends of Scipio', *JRS* 55 (1965) 1–16
*155. *Speeches in Greek historians* (Third Myres Memorial Lecture, 1965). Oxford: Blackwell, 1965
156. Review of R. Syme, *Sallust* (Sather Classical Lectures 33) (Berkeley-Los Angeles: University of California Press; Cambridge: University Press, 1964), *History* 50 (1965) 341–2
157. Review of H. H. Schmitt, *Untersuchungen zur Geschichte Antiochos' des Grossen und seiner Zeit* (*Historia* Einzelschriften 6) (Wiesbaden: Steiner, 1964), *JRS* 55 (1965) 262–4
158. Review of *Studi annibalici: Atti del convegno svoltosi a Cortona – Tuoro sul Trasimeno – Perugia, ottobre 1961* (Estratto dall' Annuario dell'Accademia etrusca di Cortona 12, 1961–4) (Cortona: Accademia etrusca, 1964), *JRS* 55 (1965) 309

1966

159. 'The Spartan ancestral constitution in Polybius', in *Ancient society and institutions: studies presented to Victor Ehrenberg*, ed. E. Badian (Oxford: Blackwell, 1966) 303–12
160. Review of P. Pédech, *La méthode historique de Polybe* (Paris: Les Belles Lettres, 1964), *CR* 16 (1966) 37–40
161. Review of M. Fortina, *Cassandro, re di Macedonia* (Turin, etc.: Società editrice internazionale, 1965), *CR* 16 (1966) 243–4
162. Review of A. J. Toynbee, *Hannibal's legacy: the Hannibalic War's effects on Roman life* (2 vols., London: Oxford University Press, 1965), *CR* 16 (1966) 384–8
163. Review of L. Pareti and others (ed.), *The ancient world, 1200 B.C. to A.D. 500*, parts 1 and 2 (History of Mankind: cultural and scientific development 2) (London: Allen and Unwin, 1965), *History* 51 (1966) 197–8

1967

164. *A historical commentary on Polybius* 2: *Books 7–18.* Oxford: Clarendon Press, 1967
165. *Philip V of Macedon*, reprint with corrections. Hamden, Conn.: Archon Books, 1967 (*cf.* no. 17)
*166. 'The Scipionic legend', *PCPS* 13 (1967) 54–69
167. 'Political institutions', in *The world of Ancient Rome*, ed. G. Giannelli and U. E. Paoli (London: Macdonald, 1967), 193–211 (*cf.* no. 142)
168. Review of K. F. Eisen, *Polybiosinterpretationen: Beobachtungen zu Prinzipien griechischer und römischer Historiographie bei Polybios* (Heidelberg: Winter, Universitätsverlag, 1966), *CR* 17 (1967) 35–6
169. Review of J. M. Moore, *The manuscript tradition of Polybius* (Cambridge Classical Studies) (Cambridge: University Press, 1965), *CR* 17 (1967) 151–3
170. Review of A. H. McDonald, *Republican Rome* (Ancient peoples and places 50) (London: Thames and Hudson, 1966), *CR* 17 (1967) 190–2
171. Review of P. Lambrechts, *De geestelijke weerstand van de westelijke provincies tegen Rome* (Med. van de k.Vlaamse Acad. van Belgie, klasse der letteren, 28.1) (Brussels: k.Vlaamse Academie, 1966), *JRS* 57 (1967) 251–2

172. Review of R. H. Barrow, *Plutarch and his times* (London: Chatto and Windus, 1967), *The Listener* (1967) 692–3
173. Review of H. Homeyer, *Lukian, Wie man Geschichte schreiben soll, herausgegeben, übersetzt und erläutert* (Munich: Fink, 1965), *Gnomon* 39 (1967) 833–5

1968

174. Review of V. La Bua, *Filino-Polibio Sileno-Diodoro: il problema delle fonti dalla morte di Agatocle alla guerra mercenaria in Africa* (Σικελικά 3) (Palermo: Flaccovio, 1966), *CR* 18 (1968) 299–302
175. Review of J. A. O. Larsen, *Greek federal states, their institutions and history* (Oxford: Clarendon Press, 1968), *CR* 18 (1968) 190–2
176. Review of D. Earl, *The moral and political tradition of Rome* (Aspects of Greek and Roman life) (London: Thames and Hudson, 1967), *CR* 18 (1968) 332–4
177. Review of E. J. Bickerman, *Chronology of the ancient world* (Aspects of Greek and Roman life) (London: Thames and Hudson, 1968), *JRS* 58 (1968) 251
178. Review of G. A. Lehmann, *Untersuchungen zur historischen Glaubwürdigkeit des Polybios* (Fontes et commentationes 5) (Münster: Aschendorff, 1967), *JRS* 58 (1968) 253–5

1969

179. *The awful revolution: the decline of the Roman Empire in the West.* Liverpool: University Press; Toronto: University Press, 1969
180. 'The historians of Greek Sicily', *Kokalos* 14–15 (1968–9) 476–98
181. (In collaboration with A. H. McDonald) 'The treaty of Apamea (188 B.C.): the naval clauses', *JRS* 59 (1969) 30–9
182. 'M. Gelzer's Theorie über die Ursprünge der römischen Historiographie', in *Römische Geschichtsschreibung*, ed. V. Pöschl (Darmstadt: Wissenschaftliche Buchgesellschaft, 1969) 272–9 (translated from appendix of no. 34 above)
183. Review of G. J. D. Aalders, *Die Theorie der gemischten Verfassung im Altertum* (Amsterdam: Hakkert, 1968), *CR* 19 (1969) 314–17
184. Review of P. Grimal and others, *Hellenism and the rise of Rome* (London: Weidenfeld and Nicholson, 1968), *CR* 19 (1969) 317–19
185. Review of Ioannes A. Vartsos, Ο ΠΥΡΡΟΣ ΕΝ ΙΤΑΛΙΑΙ, ΣΚΟΠΟΙ ΚΑΙ ΔΡΑΣΙΣ ΑΥΤΟΥ (Athens: Pechlivanides, 1967), *CR* 19 (1969) 332–4
186. Review of J. Touloumakos, *Der Einfluss Roms auf die Staatsform der griechischen Stadtstaaten des Festlandes und der Inseln im ersten und zweiten Jhdt. v.Chr.* (Göttingen: privately printed, 1967), *JHS* 89 (1969) 179–80

1970

187. *A historical commentary on Polybius* 1: *Books 1–6*, corrected reprint. Oxford: Clarendon Press, 1970
188. *Oxford classical dictionary*[2], ed. N. G. L. Hammond and H. H. Scullard (Oxford: Clarendon Press, 1970). Additional articles on: Anticleides, Polybius, Silenus
189. 'Pyrrhus', in *Hommes d'état célèbres* 1, ed. J. Pirenne (Paris: Éditions d'art Lucien Mazenod, 1970) 284–7

190. 'Polybius and Macedonia', in *Ancient Macedonia: First International Symposium*, ed. B. Laourdas and Ch. Makaronas (Thessalonica: Institute for Balkan Studies, 1970) 291–307

191. 'The Achaean assemblies again', *MH* 27 (1970) 129–43

192. 'An experiment in Greek union' (Classical Association Presidential Address, 1970), *PCA* 67 (1970) 13–27

193. *Encyclopaedia Britannica* (Chicago: Encyclopaedia Britannica, 1970). Articles on: Achaean League, Aetolia, Aetolian League, Alexander III (the Great), Aratus of Sicyon, Archelaus king of Macedon, Demetrius II, Epirus, kingdom of Macedonia, Paeonia, Perseus, Philip II, Philip V, Philopoemen, Plutarch, Polybius, Pyrrhus, Timaeus

194. Review of K.-E. Petzold, *Studien zur Methode des Polybios und zu ihrer historischen Auswertung* (Vestigia, Beiträge zur alten Geschichte 9) (Munich: Beck, 1969), *JRS* 60 (1970) 252–4

1971

195. 'Livy's fourth and fifth decades', in *Livy*, ed. T. A. Dorey (London: Routledge and Kegan Paul; Toronto: University Press, 1971) 47–72

196. Review of H. H. Schmitt, *Die Staatsverträge des Altertums 3: Die Verträge der griechisch-römischen Welt von 338 bis 200 v.Chr.* (Munich: Beck, 1969), *JHS* 91 (1971) 195

197. Review of P. Pédech, *Polybe, Histoires, Livre I, texte établi et traduit* (Collection Budé) (Paris: Les Belles Lettres, 1969), *CR* 21 (1971) 186–8

1972

198. *Polybius* (Sather Classical Lectures 42). Berkeley-Los Angeles-London, 1972

*199. '*Nationality as a factor in Roman history*', *HSPh* 76 (1972) 145–68

200. *Grote Nederlandse Larousse Encyclopedie* (Hasselt, Belgium: Heideland-Orbis, 1972). Article on: the treaty of Apamea

201. Review of T. A. Dorey and D. R. Dudley, *Rome against Carthage* (London: Secker and Warburg, 1971), *JRS* 62 (1972) 181–2

202. Review of J. de Foucault, *Polybe, Histoires, Livre III, texte établi et traduit* (Collection Budé) (Paris: Les Belles Lettres, 1971), *JHS* 92 (1972) 205–6

1973

203. *Det västromerska rikets fall: ekonomiska, politiska och sociala orsaker*. Stockholm: Wahlström and Widstrand, 1973 (*cf.* no. 179)

204. 'Iliria e jugut ne shekujt e trete dhe te dyte para eres se re', *Studime historike* (Tirana) 27 (1973) 137–47

205. '*Symploke*: son rôle dans les *Histoires* de Polybe', in *Association Guillaume Budé: Actes du IXe congrès, Rome, 13–18 avril 1973* (Paris: Les Belles Lettres, 1973) 1.28–38

206. Review of P. Pédech, *Polybe, Histoires, Livre II, texte établi et traduit* (Collection Budé) (Paris: Les Belles Lettres, 1970), *CR* 23 (1973) 30–2

207. Review-discussion of Arnaldo Momigliano, *The development of Greek biography* (Cambridge, Mass.: Harvard University Press, 1971), *History and Theory* 12 (1973) 230–40

1974

*208. 'Synchronisms in Polybius, Books 4 and 5', in *Polis and imperium: studies in honour of Edward Togo Salmon*, ed. J. A. S. Evans (Toronto: Hakkert, 1974) 59–80

*209. 'Polybius between Greece and Rome', in *Polybe*, ed. E. Gabba (Entretiens sur l'antiquité classique 20) (Vandoeuvres-Geneva: Fondation Hardt, 1974) 1–31

210. 'Polybius and the Sicilian straits', *Kokalos* 20 (1974) 5–17

211. *Encyclopaedia Britannica*[15] (Chicago: Encyclopaedia Britannica, 1974). Articles in the 'Macropaedia' on: Alexander the Great (1.468–73), The Hellenistic age (8.376–92), Plutarch (14.578–80), Polybius (14.762–4)

212. Review of W. V. Harris, *Rome in Etruria and Umbria* (Oxford: Clarendon Press, 1971), *CR* 24 (1974) 92–5

213. Review of G. E. M. de Ste Croix, *The origins of the Peloponnesian War* (London: Duckworth, 1972), *History* 59 (1974) 446

1975

*214. '*Symploke*: its role in Polybius' *Histories*', *YClS* 24 (1975) 197–212 (*cf.* no. 205)

215. Review of J.-A. de Foucault, *Recherches sur la langue et le style de Polybe* (Paris: Les Belles Lettres, 1972), *CR* 25 (1975) 28–30

216. Review of F. P. Rizzo, *La Sicilia e le potenze ellenistiche al tempo delle guerre puniche: i rapporti con Cos, l'Egitto e l'Etolia* (Supplementi a *Kokalos* 3) (Palermo: Banco di Sicilia, 1973), *CR* 25 (1975) 268–9

217. Review of W. den Boer, *Some minor Roman historians* (Leiden: Brill, 1972), *CR* 25 (1975) 275–6

1976

218. 'Southern Illyria in the third and second centuries B.C.', *Iliria* 4.1 (1976) 265–72 (*cf.* no. 204)

219. Foreword to *Illustrated encyclopaedia of the classical world*, ed. M. Avi-Yonah and I. Shatzman (Maidenhead: Sampson Low, 1976) 6–7

220. Review of Pierre Briant, *Antigone le Borgne: les débuts de sa carrière et les problèmes de l'assemblée macédonienne* (Centre de recherches d'histoire ancienne de l'Université de Besançon 10) (Paris: Les Belles Lettres, 1973), *CR* 26 (1976) 93–5

221. Review of B. Shimron, *Late Sparta: the Spartan revolution 243–146 B.C.* (Arethusa Monographs 3) (Buffalo, N.Y.: Dept. of Classics, State University of New York at Buffalo, 1972), *CR* 26 (1976) 140–1

222. Review of T. Schwertfeger, *Der achaiische Bund von 146 bis 27 v.Chr.* (Vestigia, Beiträge zur alten Geschichte 19) (Munich: Beck, 1974), *CR* 26 (1976) 238–9

1977

*223. 'Were there Greek federal states?', *SCI* 3 (1976/7) 27–51

*224. 'Polybius' last ten books', in *Historiographia antiqua: commentationes Lovanienses in honorem W. Peremans septuagenarii editae* (Leuven: University Press, 1977) 139–62

225. 'The original extent of the via Egnatia', *LCM* 2 (1977) 73–4

226. 'The causes of the Third Macedonian War: recent views', *Ancient Macedonia* 2: Papers read at the Second International Symposium held in Thessaloniki, 19–24 August 1973 (Thessalonica: Institute for Balkan Studies, 1977) 81–94

227. Review of H. J. Mason, *Greek terms for Roman institutions: a lexicon and analysis* (American Studies in Papyrology 13) (Toronto: Hakkert, 1974), *CR* 27 (1977) 136

228. Review of R. J. A. Talbert, *Timoleon and the revival of Greek Sicily 344–317 B.C.* (Cambridge Classical Studies) (Cambridge: University Press, 1974), *CR* 27 (1977) 217–18

229. Review of Klaus Meister, *Historische Kritik bei Polybios* (Palingenesia 1) (Wiesbaden: Steiner, 1975), *JHS* 97 (1977) 186–7

230. Review of R. Étienne and D. Knoepler, *Hyettos de Béotie et la chronologie des archontes fédéraux entre 250 et 171 av. J.-C.* (*BCH* Supplément 3) (Athens: École française d'Athènes, 1976), *JHS* 97 (1977) 209

231. Review of J. von Ungern-Sternberg, *Capua im zweiten punischen Krieg: Untersuchungen zur römischen Annalistik* (Vestigia, Beiträge zur alten Geschichte 23) (Munich: Beck, 1975), *Gnomon* 49 (1977) 630–2

232. Review of A. Tovar and J. M. Blázquez, *Historia de la Hispania romana: la peninsula Ibérica desde 218 a.C. hasta el siglo V* (Madrid: Alianza Editorial, 1975), *Bulletin of Hispanic Studies* 54 (1977) 84

233. Review of Ch. M. Danov, *Altthrakien* (Berlin and New York: de Gruyter, 1976), *LCM* 2 (1977) 215–16

1978

234. *La pavorosa revolución: la decadencia del imperio romano en occidente*, trans. Doris Rolfe. Madrid: Alianza Universidad, 1978 (*cf.* no. 179)

1979

235. *A historical commentary on Polybius* 3: *Books 19–40*. Oxford: Clarendon Press, 1979

236. Introduction to *Polybius: the rise of the Roman empire*, trans. Ian Scott-Kilvert (Harmondsworth: Penguin Books, 1979) 9–40

237. 'Egypt in Polybius', in *Glimpses of Ancient Egypt: studies in honour of H. W. Fairman*, ed. J. Ruffle, G. A. Gaballa and K. Kitchen (Warminster: Aris and Phillips, 1979) 180–9

238. 'Storiografia tragica e storiografia pragmatica: la scelta di Polibio', in *La storiografia greca: guida storica e critica*, ed. D. Musti (Bari-Rome: Laterza, 1979) 32–40 (trans. Mario di Nonno, from *Polybius:* above, no. 198)

1980

239. 'The idea of decline in Polybius', in *Niedergang: Studien zu einem geschichtlichen Thema*, ed. R. Koselleck and P. Widmer (Stuttgart: Klett-Cotta, 1980) 81–94

240. 'The surrender of the Egyptian rebels in the Nile delta (Polyb. xxii.16.1–4)', in Φιλίας χάριν: *miscellanea di studi classici in onore di Eugenio Manni* (6 vols., Rome: Giorgio Bretschneider, 1980) 6.2187–97

241. Review of P. Brulé, *La piraterie crétoise hellénistique* (Centre de recherches d'histoire ancienne de l'Université de Besançon 27) (Paris: Les Belles Lettres, 1978), *CR* 30 (1980) 82–3

242. Review of R. Urban, *Wachstum und Krise des achäischen Bundes: Quellenstudien zur Entwicklung des Bundes von 280 bis 222 v.Chr.* (*Historia* Enzelschriften 35) (Wiesbaden: Steiner, 1979), *JRS* 70 (1980) 199–200

1981

243. 'The Hellenistic kingdoms in the third century', Map 11b (drawn by David Cox) in *Atlas of the Greek and Roman world in antiquity*, ed. N. G. L. Hammond (Park Ridge, N.J.: Noyes Press, 1981)

244. *The Hellenistic world* (Fontana history of the ancient world). London: Fontana-Collins (paperback); Brighton: Harvester Press and New Jersey: Humanities Press (hardback), 1981

245. Contribution to *Seminario di ricerca: Polib. i.11.1ff.*, ed. S. Calderone (estratto dagli *Quaderni Urbinati di cultura classica* 36 (1981) 7–78) 43–6.

246. 'Il giudizio di Polibio su Roma', *Atti dell'Istituto Veneto di Scienze, Lettere ed Arti: Classe di scienze morali, lettere ed arti* 140 (1981–2) 1–20

247. Review of P. A. Stadter, *Arrian of Nicomedia* (Chapel Hill, N.C.: University of North Carolina Press, 1980), *History* 66 (1981) 112

248. Review of Olivier Picard, *Chalcis et la confédération eubéenne: étude de numismatique et d'histoire (IVe-Ier siècle)* (Bibliothèque des écoles françaises d'Athènes et de Rome 234) (Athens: École française d'Athènes; Paris: de Boccard, 1979), *JHS* 101 (1981) 202

1982

249. *The Hellenistic world.* Cambridge, Mass.: Harvard University Press, 1982 (paperback: corrected edition of no. 244)

250. Articles in German translation in *Polybios*, ed. K. Stiewe and N. Holzberg (Darmstadt: Wissenschaftliche Buchgesellschaft, 1982): 'Philippos tragodoumenos' (*cf.* no. 12) 1–23; 'Polybios über die römische Verfassung' (*cf.* no. 28) 79–113; 'Der Aufbau des sechsten Buches des Polybios' (*cf.* no. 90: with C. O. Brink) 211–58; 'Polemik bei Polybios' (*cf.* no. 136) 377–404; 'Drei Anmerkungen zu Polybios Buch xii' (*cf.* no. 144) 415–28

251. 'Sea-power and the Antigonids', in *Philip II, Alexander the Great and the Macedonian heritage*, ed. W. L. Adams and E. N. Borza (Washington, D.C.: University Press of America, 1982) 213–36

252. Review of N. G. L. Hammond, *Alexander the Great: king, commander and statesman* (London: Chatto and Windus, 1981), and D. W. Engels, *Alexander the Great and the logistics of the Macedonian army* (Berkeley-Los Angeles-London: University of California Press, 1978), *History* 67 (1982) 300–1

1983

253. *Il mondo ellenistico.* Bologna: Universale Paperbacks il Mulino, 1983 (*cf.* no. 244)

254. *Die hellenistische Welt.* Munich: dtv, 1983 (*cf.* no. 244)

*255. '*Via illa nostra militaris*: some thoughts on the Via Egnatia', in *Althistorische Studien: Hermann Bengtson zum 70. Geburtstag dargebracht von Kollegen und Schülern*, ed.

H. Heinen, K. Stroheker and G. Walser (*Historia* Einzelschriften 40) (Wiesbaden: Steiner, 1983) 131–47

256. 'Polibio nel giudizio di Gaetano De Sanctis', *RFIC* 111 (1983) 465–77
257. 'Polybius and the *aitiai* of the Second Punic War', *LCM* 8 (1983) 62–3
258. 'What made a Hellenistic king?', résumé in *PCA* 80 (1983) 19–20
259. 'Macedonia from 323 to 168 B.C.: political history, political social and economic institutions, intellectual life', in *Macedonia: 4000 years of Greek history and civilization*, ed. M. B. Sakellariou (Athens: Ekdotike Athenon, 1983) 133–69 (also published in Greek)
260. Review of G. W. Trompf, *The idea of historical recurrence in western thought: from antiquity to the reformation* (Berkeley-Los Angeles-London: University of California Press, 1979), *CP* 78 (1983) 84–6
261. Review of G. E. M. de Ste Croix, *The class struggle in the ancient Greek world from the archaic age to the Arab conquests* (London: Duckworth, 1981), *JHS* 103 (1983) 199–200
262. Review of Simon Hornblower, *Mausolus* (Oxford: Clarendon Press, 1982), *Antiquaries Journal* 63 (1983) 160–2
263. Review of Jane Hornblower, *Hieronymus of Cardia* (Oxford Classical and Philosophical Monographs) (Oxford: University Press, 1981), *Antiquaries Journal* 63 (1983) 162–3

1984

264. *Cambridge ancient history* 7.1²: *The Hellenistic world*, ed. F. W. Walbank, A. E. Astin, M. W. Frederiksen and R. M. Ogilvie (Cambridge: University Press, 1984). Chapters on 'Sources for the period' (1–22); 'Monarchies and monarchic ideas' (62–100); 'Macedonia and Greece' (221–56); 'Macedonia and the Greek leagues' (446–81)
265. 'Howard Hayes Scullard, 1903–1983', *Gnomon* 56 (1984) 189–91
266. 'Howard Hayes Scullard, 1903–1983', *Proc. Brit. Ac.* 89 (1983) 111–26 (London: Oxford University Press for the British Academy, 1984)
267. Review of E. E. Rice, *The grand procession of Ptolemy Philadelphus* (Oxford Classical and Philosophical Monographs) (Oxford: University Press, 1983), *LCM* 9 (1984) 52–4
268. Review of P. Roesch, *Études béotiennes* (Centre de recherches archéologiques, Institut Fernand-Courby, units recherches archéologiques 15) (Paris: de Boccard, 1982), *JHS* 104 (1984) 243–4

Forthcoming:

269. 'Trade and industry under the later Roman Empire in the West', revision of chapter in *Cambridge economic history of Europe* 2² (*cf.* no. 78)
270. 'Polybius, Mr Dryden and the Glorious Revolution', in *Festschrift* for Wilhelmina Jashemski
271. 'The Via Egnatia: some outstanding problems', in *Ancient Macedonia* 4 (Proceedings of the Fourth International Symposium held in Thessaloniki and Khalkidiki, 20–26 September, 1983)
272. 'The Via Egnatia: its original scope and date', in *Festschrift* for Christo M. Danov

273. 'Two misplaced Polybian passages from the Suda (XVI.29.1 and XVI.38)', in *Festschrift* for Piero Treves

274. Japanese edition of *The Hellenistic world* (*cf.* no. 244)

275. Review of C. W. Fornara, *The nature of history in ancient Greece and Rome* (Berkeley: University of California, 1983), *JHS*

276. Review of A. N. Sherwin-White, *Roman foreign policy in the East 167 B.C.–A.D. 1* (London: Duckworth, 1984), *JRS*

277. Review of K. Buraselis, *Das hellenistische Makedonien und die Ägäis: Forschungen zur Politik des Kassandros und der drei ersten Antigoniden im Ägäischen Meer und in Westkleinasien* (Münchener Beiträge zur Papyrusforschung und antiken Rechtsgeschichte 73) (Munich: Beck, 1982), *JHS*

278. (In collaboration with N. G. L. Hammond) *A history of Macedonia 3: 336–168 B.C.* Oxford: Clarendon Press

INDEXES

I. GENERAL

Abydus: Roman *legati* visit (200), 102–3; destruction by inhabitants, 173

Acarnania, treaty with Anactorium, 28, 34

Achaea, Achaean League, 15; powers of cities in, 31; variety of constitutions in cities of, 31–2; method of voting in, 30–1, 30 n. 60 (possible difference in this respect between *synkletoi* and *synodoi*); honours Phocian and Boeotian hostages, 34; treaty with Orchomenus, 37; detainees at Rome, 163, 281; ruin by demagogues, 337

Achaean War, Greeks' allegedly irrational behaviour in, 162

Achaeus, capture and death (213), 317

Aegeira, treaty with Stymphalus, 32

Aegosthena, dispute with Pagae, 32

Aelius, Q., Tubero, 158

Aemilius, M., Lepidus (cos. 187), 103 n. 14

Aemilius Sura, on successive world empires, 147

Aenus, denied to Philip V, 163, 334

Aetolian League, honoured by Chios, 34

Agatharchides of Cnidus: emulates Thucydides, 251; criticises Ephorus and Theopompus, 265

Agathocles of Alexandria, 44, 46, 49, 51, 54

Agathocles of Syracuse, treatment at hands of Tyche, 84

Agelaus of Naupactus, 150, 153, 257

Agrigentum, popular party pro-Carthaginian, 93–4

Agrinium, dispute with Stratus, 32

Alexander the Great, multi-racial monarchies arise after his death, 60

Alexon, Achaean mercenary, 90

Allobroges, 108, 111, 116

Amphictyonic oath, 12–13, 59

Amyzon, letter from Antiochus, 48

Anactorium, treaty with Acarnania, 28, 34

Anaximenes: speeches in, 246; attacks predecessors, 265

Andriscus: ruins Macedonia, 330; helped by Thracians, 194

annales, meaning of, 94–8

annalistic tradition for Republican history, 142–3, 156

Annius, M. (quaest. 119), honoured by Lete, 195

Antiochus III: campaign against Achaeus, 317; eastern *anabasis*, 317; return, 48; compact with Philip to plunder Egypt, 44, 52, 218; letter to Amyzon, 48

Antisthenes, Rhodian historian, 268

Apelles, friend of Philip V, 220

Arar, R., identification of, 115–16

Aratus of Sicyon, 15; policy towards Macedon, 259; abuses Antigonus Doson, 263; conceals some facts in his *Memoirs*, 267

Araxa, and Lycian League, 27, 32–3

Arcadia: as federal state in Aristotle, 23–4; musical education in, 278

Ariarathes V: expelled from Cappadocia, 161; recovers it, 333; discredited at Rome, 163

Aristaenus, policy towards Rome, 282

Aristonicus, defeat of, 208

Aristophanes, and panhellenism, 9

Aristotle: on difference between *polis* and *ethnos*, 23–4; on slavery, 176; distinction between history and tragedy discussed, 231–3; on origins of Locri, 269–72

Arsinoe, wife of Ptolemy IV, 49, 50, 51; priestess-ship instituted, 53

Asclepiades, on subject-matter of tragedy, 234

Astae, location of, 206

Athens, given Delos, Lemnos and Haliartus by Senate, 163, 285, 334–5

Atilius, M., Regulus (cos. 267, 256): tradition on, 81–5; example of retribution in Polybius, 213–14

Attalus II: Roman attempts to set him against Eumenes, 163, 285, 334; honoured at Panium (Panadus), 206; war with Prusias II, 333; overthrows Diegylis (145), 194

Attalus III: accession, 328; bequeaths kingdom to Rome, 194, 208

Attica, synoecism in, 14

Aygues, R., various forms of name, 115–16

Baebius, M., Tamphilus (cos. 181), crosses to Apollonia (Oct.–Nov. 192), 184

II. AUTHORS AND PASSAGES

III. INSCRIPTIONS AND PAPYRI

IV. GREEK WORDS